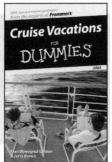

Mexico's Beach Resorts

FOR

DUMMIES®

3RD EDITION

by David Baird and Lynne Bairstow

WILEY

Wiley Publishing, Inc.

Mexico's Beach Resorts For Dummies, 3rd Edition
Published by
Wiley Publishing, Inc.
111 River St.
Hoboken, NJ 07030-5774
www.wiley.com

WILEY

About the Authors

Lynne Bairstow now considers Mexico to be more her home than her native United States. After living in Puerto Vallarta and exploring Mexico for most of the past 17 years, she's developed not only an appreciation but also a true love for the country and its complex, colorful culture. Her travel articles on Mexico have been published in the *New York Times, San Francisco Chronicle, Los Angeles Times, Luxury Living, Frommer's Budget Travel* magazine, and *Alaska Airlines Magazine.* In 2000, the Mexican government awarded Lynne the Pluma de Plata, a top honor granted to foreign writers, for her work in the Frommer's guidebooks to Mexico.

David Baird is a writer, editor, and translator who feels uncomfortable writing about himself in the third person (too much like writing your own obituary). Now based in Austin, Texas, he has spent years living in various parts of Mexico, Brazil, Peru, and Puerto Rico. But whenever possible, he manages to get back to the Yucatán's turquoise-blue waters because he thinks he looks good in that color and because he's excessively fond of the local cooking.

Dedication

This book is dedicated to my many friends in Mexico who, through sharing their insights, anecdotes, knowledge, and explorations of Mexico, have shared their love of this country. In particular, Silver, Ricardo, Santiago, and Carlos have shared with me and have shown me what a magical place Mexico is and how much more I have to discover and enjoy.

— Lynne Bairstow

To my brother John, whose sheer willpower overcame my objections and forced me to take the vacation many, many years ago that first brought me to the Caribbean shores of Mexico.

— David Baird

Authors' Acknowledgments

Many thanks to all the many people who helped me gather the information, tips, and treasures that have made their way into this book. I am especially grateful for the assistance of Cecilia Mendicuti, her valuable ideas and contributions, and her tireless work in ensuring that the information in this book is correct.

— Lynne Bairstow

I would like to acknowledge my indebtedness to the irrepressible Desiré Sanromán, a Cozumeleña who knows her island and who befriended me for reasons that aren't quite clear. (Sympathy? Pity? Concern for all the readers I may mislead?) I also thank that most capable of guides, Claudia Hurtado Valenzuela, who opened the doors of the Riviera Maya to me, and whose views on all matters touristic were well worth hearing.

— David Baird

Publisher's Acknowledgments

We're proud of this book; please send us your comments through our Dummies online registration form located at www.dummies.com/register/.

Some of the people who helped bring this book to market include the following:

Editorial

Editors: Suzanna R. Thompson, Production Editor; Marc Nadeau, Development Editor

Copy Editor: Doreen Russo

Cartographer: Guy Ruggiero

Senior Photo Editor: Richard Fox

Cover Photos
Front: Cancún, Quintana Roo (© Michael Melford/Getty Images)

Back: Chichén Itzá, Yucatán Peninsula (© Panoramic Images/ Getty Images)

Cartoons: Rich Tennant, www.the5thwave.com

Composition Services

Project Coordinator: Michael Kruzil

Layout and Graphics:
Carl Byers, Joyce Haughey, Stephanie D. Jumper, Lynsey Osborn, Heather Ryan, Julie Trippetti

Proofreaders: Leeann Harney, Jessica Kramer, Christine Pingleton, Techbooks

Indexer: Techbooks

Publishing and Editorial for Consumer Dummies

Diane Graves Steele, Vice President and Publisher, Consumer Dummies

Joyce Pepple, Acquisitions Director, Consumer Dummies

Kristin A. Cocks, Product Development Director, Consumer Dummies

Michael Spring, Vice President and Publisher, Travel

Kelly Regan, Editorial Director, Travel

Publishing for Technology Dummies

Andy Cummings, Vice President and Publisher, Dummies Technology/General User

Composition Services

Gerry Fahey, Vice President of Production Services

Debbie Stailey, Director of Composition Services

Contents at a Glance

Introduction 1

Part 1: Mexico's Beach Resorts 9
Chapter 1: Discovering the Best of Mexico's Beach Resorts 11
Chapter 2: Digging Deeper into Mexico 22
Chapter 3: Choosing Where to Go in
Mexico's Beach Resorts 35
Chapter 4: Deciding When to Go 48

Part II: Planning Your Trip to Mexico's Beach Resorts 53
Chapter 5: Managing Your Money 55
Chapter 6: Getting to Mexico's Beach Resorts 66
Chapter 7: Booking Your Accommodations 74
Chapter 8: Tips for Travelers with Special Needs
or Interests 80
Chapter 9: Taking Care of the Remaining Details 89

Part III: Cancún 107
Chapter 10: The Lowdown on Cancún's Hotel Scene 109
Chapter 11: Settling into Cancún 124
Chapter 12: Dining in Cancún 132
Chapter 13: Having Fun on and off the Beach in Cancún 143

Part IV: Cozumel and the Riviera Maya 169
Chapter 14: Cozumel 171
Chapter 15: Playa del Carmen and the Riviera Maya 192

Part V: Puerto Vallarta and the Central Pacific Coast 211
Chapter 16: The Lowdown on Puerto Vallarta's
Hotel Scene 213
Chapter 17: Settling into Puerto Vallarta 228
Chapter 18: Dining in Puerto Vallarta 236
Chapter 19: Having Fun on and off the Beach in
Puerto Vallarta 250

Part VI: Ixtapa and Zihuatanejo 281
Chapter 20: The Lowdown on the Ixtapa and
Zihuatanejo Hotel Scenes 283
Chapter 21: Settling into Ixtapa and Zihuatanejo 294

Chapter 22: Dining in Ixtapa and Zihuatanejo 300
Chapter 23: Having Fun on and off the Beach in Ixtapa and
    Zihuatanejo 306

Part VII: Acapulco 317
Chapter 24: The Lowdown on Acapulco's Hotel Scene 319
Chapter 25: Settling into Acapulco..330
Chapter 26: Dining in Acapulco 336
Chapter 27: Having Fun on and off the Beach in Acapulco......344

Part VIII: Huatulco and the Southern Pacific Coast 363
Chapter 28: Bahías de Huatulco 365
Chapter 29: Puerto Escondido 379

Part IX: Los Cabos and Southern Baja 397
Chapter 30: The Lowdown on the Hotel Scene
    in Los Cabos 399
Chapter 31: Settling into Los Cabos...413
Chapter 32: Dining in Los Cabos 421
Chapter 33: Having Fun on and off the Beach
    in Los Cabos 432

Part X: The Part of Tens 455
Chapter 34: Ten Top Mexican Moments 457
Chapter 35: Ten Myths and Misconceptions about Mexico 460
Chapter 36: Ten Most Deliciously Mexican Dishes 464

Part XI: Appendixes 467
Appendix A: Quick Concierge 469
Appendix B: Glossary of Spanish Words and Phrases..............482
Appendix C: Authentic Mexican Cuisine 488

Index 494

Maps at a Glance

Mexico 12
Accommodations in Isla Cancún (Hotel Zone) 113
Accommodations in Ciudad Cancún 115
Isla Cancún Dining 135
Ciudad Cancún Dining 137
Cancún & Environs 145
Isla Mujeres (The Island of Women)...152
Tulum Ruins 155
Chichén Itzá Ruins 157
Cancún Area 163
Cozumel Island 173
San Miguel de Cozumel 175
Playa del Carmen 197
The Riviera Maya 201
Puerto Vallarta Hotel Zone Accommodations 219
Downtown Puerto Vallarta Accommodations.................................221
Marina Vallarta Dining 239
Downtown Puerto Vallarta Dining 241
Puerto Vallarta Area 251
Zihuatanejo and Ixtapa Area Accommodations 287
Zihuatanejo and Ixtapa Area Dining..303
Ixtapa and Zihuatanejo Area 307
Acapulco Bay Area Accommodations 322
Acapulco Bay Area Dining 338
Acapulco Bay Area 346
Bahías de Huatulco..367
Puerto Escondido 381
San José del Cabo Accommodations 403
Cabo San Lucas Accommodations 405
The Corridor Accommodations 407
San José del Cabo Dining...423
Cabo San Lucas Dining...425
The Corridor Dining 427
Los Cabos 433

Table of Contents

Introduction *1*

   About This Book...2

   Conventions Used in This Book 2

   Foolish Assumptions 3

   How This Book Is Organized...................................4

      Part I: Mexico's Beach Resorts.....................4

      Part II: Planning Your Trip to Mexico's

        Beach Resorts..4

      Part III: Cancún..5

      Part IV: Cozumel and the Riviera Maya.......5

      Part V: Puerto Vallarta and the Central

        Pacific Coast 5

      Part VI: Ixtapa and Zihuatanejo...................5

      Part VII: Acapulco 5

      Part VIII: Huatulco and the Southern

        Pacific Coast 6

      Part IX: Los Cabos and Southern Baja.........6

      Part X: The Part of Tens 6

      Part XI: Appendixes 6

   Icons Used in This Book..6

   Where to Go from Here..7

Part 1: Mexico's Beach Resorts *9*

  Chapter 1: Discovering the Best of Mexico's
  Beach Resorts..11

   The Best Beach Vacations.....................................11

   The Best Luxury Resorts 15

   The Best Good-Value Accommodations.................16

   The Most Unique Places to Get Away from It All 17

   The Best Active Vacations 17

   The Best Dining Experiences.................................19

   The Best Shopping 20

   The Best Nightlife..21

  Chapter 2: Digging Deeper into Mexico.....................22

   Introducing Mexico 22

   History 101: The Main Events................................23

      Pre-Hispanic Civilizations 23

      The Conquest 26

      The Colonial Period................................27

Independence 27
The Porfiriato and the Revolution 27
Modern Mexico 28
Building Blocks: Local Architecture 29
Pre-Hispanic Forms 29
Spanish Influence 30
Religion, Myth, and Folklore 30
Taste of the Yucatán: Local Cuisine 31
Background Check: Recommended Books and Movies 33
Books 33
Movies 34

**Chapter 3: Choosing Where to Go in
Mexico's Beach Resorts 35**

Understanding the Lay of the Land 36
Picking the Right Beach Resort 36
Choosing Cancún 36
Diving into Cozumel 38
Exploring the Riviera Maya 39
Playing in Puerto Vallarta 40
Introducing Ixtapa and Zihuatanejo 41
Getting acquainted with Acapulco 42
Hanging out in Huatulco 43
Kicking back in Puerto Escondido 44
Lazing in Los Cabos 45

Chapter 4: Deciding When to Go 48

Forecasting the Weather 48
Considering Mexico's Travel Seasons 49
Mexico's Calendar of Events 49
January/February/March 50
April/May/June 51
July/August/September 51
October/November/December 51

**Part II: Planning Your Trip to Mexico's
Beach Resorts 53**

Chapter 5: Managing Your Money 55

Planning Your Budget 55
Calculating your hotel cost 56
Totaling transportation costs 56
Estimating dining dollars 57
Tipping tips 58
Sightseeing 58

Shopping 59
Nightlife..59
Cutting Costs — But Not the Fun 59
Making Sense of the Peso................................61
Choosing Traveler's Checks, Credit Cards, or Cash 62
ATMs and cash 62
Credit cards 63
Traveler's checks 63
Taxing Matters...64
Dealing with a Lost or Stolen Wallet.................64

Chapter 6: Getting to Mexico's Beach Resorts 66

Flying to Mexico's Beach Resorts 66
Researching and Booking Your Trip Online....................69
Understanding Escorted and Package Tours 70

Chapter 7: Booking Your Accommodations.................74

Getting to Know Your Options 74
Finding the Best Room at the Best Rate............76
Surfing the Web for hotel deals....................77
Reserving the best room.............................79

Chapter 8: Tips for Travelers with Special Needs or Interests 80

Traveling with the Brood: Advice for Families................80
Making Age Work for You: Tips for Seniors 82
Accessing Mexico's Beaches: Advice for Travelers
with Disabilities 83
Following the Rainbow: Resources for Gay
and Lesbian Travelers 85
Traveling Solo...86
Planning a Wedding in Mexico...........................87

Chapter 9: Taking Care of the Remaining Details.......89

Arriving In and Departing From Mexico...........................89
Getting a Passport..90
Applying for a U.S. passport.........................91
Applying for other passports 91
Clearing U.S. Customs 92
Playing It Safe with Travel and Medical Insurance 93
Staying Healthy When You Travel....................94
Keeping the kids healthy 96
Staying Safe..97
Renting a Car 97
Finding the best car-rental deal 98
Remembering safety comes first 99

Staying Connected by Cellphone or E-mail......................100
Accessing the Internet Away from Home........................101
Keeping Up with Airline Security Measures 103
Packing for Mexico's Beaches 104

Part III: Cancún *107*

Chapter 10: The Lowdown on Cancún's Hotel Scene **109**
Choosing a Location 110
Cancún's Best Accommodations.....................................111

Chapter 11: Settling into Cancún **124**
Arriving in Cancún 124
   Navigating passport control and Customs 124
   Getting to your hotel 125
   Hiring a taxi 125
   Renting a car..126
Getting Around Cancún 127
   Taking a taxi 128
   Catching a bus...128
   Zipping around on a moped 129
Fast Facts: Cancún 129

Chapter 12: Dining in Cancún **132**
Cancún's Best Restaurants 133

Chapter 13: Having Fun on and off the Beach in Cancún **143**
Finding Water Fun for Everyone......................................144
   Basking on a Cancún beach.....................................144
   Skiing and surfing..146
   Exploring the deep blue..147
   Reeling in the big one...148
   Swimming with dolphins..149
Enjoying Land Sports..149
   Teeing off..150
   Making time for tennis 150
   Galloping along 150
   Trailing away 151
Traveling to the Island of Women 151
Touring Ruins or an Eco-Theme Park..............................154
   Seeing the archaeological sites...............................154
   Exploring an eco-theme park 157

Sightseeing in Cancún 161
Shopping in Cancún...162
Discovering Cancún after Dark..................................165
    Partying at a club...165
    Hanging out after dinner 167
    Enjoying a cultural event 167

Part 1V: Cozumel and the Riviera Maya...........*169*

Chapter 14: Cozumel...171

Choosing a Location 172
Evaluating the Top Accommodations 172
Settling into Cozumel...178
    Knowing your way around town 179
    Getting around town.......................................180
Fast Facts: Cozumel 181
Dining in Cozumel 182
Having Fun on and off the Island.............................185
    Combing the beaches 185
    Exploring the depths 186
    Sailing away 188
    Catching a big one 188
    Hitting the links 188
    Seeing the sights 188
    Taking in the shops...190
    Enjoying the nightlife 191

Chapter 15: Playa del Carmen and the Riviera Maya 192

Deciding Where to Stay 193
Evaluating the Top Accommodations 195
Settling into the Riviera Maya 200
    Knowing where to go......................................202
    Getting around the area 203
Fast Facts: Riviera Maya and Playa del Carmen.............204
Dining along the Riviera Maya.................................205
Having Fun on and off the Beach 207
    Scuba and snorkeling 207
    Swimming with dolphins................................208
    Gone fishing...209
    Getting in touch with nature 209
    Teeing off and playing tennis 209
    Going shopping..210
    Enjoying the nightlife 210

Part V: Puerto Vallarta and the Central Pacific Coast 211

Chapter 16: The Lowdown on Puerto Vallarta's Hotel Scene 213

Choosing a Location 213
 Nuevo Vallarta and the northern coast 214
 Marina Vallarta 214
 Hotel Zone 215
 El Centro Vallarta 215
 The southern shore 216
Puerto Vallarta's Best Accommodations 217

Chapter 17: Settling into Puerto Vallarta 228

Arriving in Puerto Vallarta 228
 Navigating passport control and Customs 228
 Getting to your hotel 229
Getting Around Puerto Vallarta 229
 Taking a taxi 230
 Catching a bus 231
 Renting a car 231
 Cruising around 231
Fast Facts: Puerto Vallarta 232

Chapter 18: Dining in Puerto Vallarta 236

Puerto Vallarta's Best Restaurants 237

Chapter 19: Having Fun on and off the Beach in Puerto Vallarta 250

Hitting the Beaches 250
 Northern beaches 252
 Central and town beaches 253
 South-shore beaches 254
Finding Water Fun for Everyone 255
 Cruising Puerto Vallarta 255
 Skiing and surfing 257
 Exploring the deep blue 257
 Sailing away 257
 Reeling in the big one 258
 Swimming with dolphins 258
Enjoying Land Sports 259
 Teeing off 260
 Taking time for tennis 261
 Trailing away 261
 Saddling up 261
 Enjoying an ecotour 262

Sightseeing in Puerto Vallarta 263
Shopping Puerto Vallarta 265
    Clothing 268
    Contemporary art 268
    Crafts and gifts 269
    Decorative and folk art 270
    Jewelry and accessories 270
    Tequila and cigars 271
Embarking on a Side Trip 271
    Mining historic San Sebastián 272
    Relaxing in Yelapa 273
Discovering Puerto Vallarta after Dark 274
    Taking in a cultural event 275
    Celebrating a fiesta 275
    Enjoying the club and music scene 276

Part VI: Ixtapa and Zihuatanejo 281

Chapter 20: The Lowdown on the Ixtapa and Zihuatanejo Hotel Scenes 283

Choosing Your Location 284
Ixtapa's and Zihuatanejo's Best Accommodations 285

Chapter 21: Settling into Ixtapa and Zihuatanejo 294

Arriving in Ixtapa and Zihuatanejo 294
    Navigating passport control and Customs 295
    Getting to your hotel 295
Getting Around Ixtapa and Zihuatanejo 296
Fast Facts: Ixtapa and Zihuatanejo 297

Chapter 22: Dining in Ixtapa and Zihuatanejo 300

Finding Fast and Cheap Eats 300
Ixtapa and Zihuatanejo's Best Restaurants 301

Chapter 23: Having Fun on and off the Beach in Ixtapa and Zihuatanejo 306

Hitting the Beaches 306
Finding Water Fun for Everyone 310
    Skiing and surfing 310
    Exploring the deep blue 310
    Reeling in the big one 311
    Cruising Ixtapa and Zihuatanejo 311
Enjoying Land Sports 312
    Teeing off 312
    Taking time for tennis 312
    Galloping along 313

Sightseeing in Ixtapa and Zihuatanejo..................313
Shopping in Ixtapa and Zihuatanejo...................313
Taking a Side Trip.........................314
Discovering Ixtapa and Zihuatanejo after Dark.............315

Part VII: Acapulco *317*

Chapter 24: The Lowdown on Acapulco's Hotel Scene......................319
Choosing a Location 319
Acapulco's Best Accommodations 321

Chapter 25: Settling into Acapulco 330
Arriving in Acapulco.........................330
Navigating passport control and Customs............330
Getting to your hotel 331
Getting Around Acapulco......................331
Taking a taxi..........................332
Catching a bus.........................332
Renting a car........................333
Fast Facts: Acapulco 333

Chapter 26: Dining in Acapulco 336
Acapulco's Best Restaurants 337

Chapter 27: Having Fun on and off the Beach in Acapulco 344
Hitting the Beaches.........................344
Finding Water Fun for Everyone...................349
Skiing and surfing.........................349
Exploring the deep blue 350
Reeling in the big one.....................350
Finding family fun 350
Cruising Acapulco's shores 351
Enjoying Land Sports.........................351
Teeing off............................351
Taking time for tennis...................352
Galloping along 352
Experiencing Acapulco's Front Row Attractions 352
Sightseeing in Acapulco 353
Shopping in Acapulco.........................354
Taking a Side Trip to Taxco...................355
Getting to Taxco.........................356
Exploring Taxco 356
Staying a night........................357

Dining in Taxco..358
Discovering Taxco after dark 359
Discovering Acapulco after Dark 359

Part VIII: Huatulco and the Southern Pacific Coast 363

Chapter 28: Bahías de Huatulco 365

Choosing a Location 366
Evaluating the Top Accommodations 366
Settling into Huatulco......................................370
Arriving in Huatulco by air 370
Getting from the airport to your hotel...............371
Knowing your way around town..........................371
Fast Facts: Huatulco.......................................372
Dining in Huatulco 374
Having Fun on and off the Beach 376
Hitting Huatulco's best beaches 376
Cruising Huatulco 376
Taking time for tennis or golf 377
Sightseeing and shopping...............................377
Enjoying the nightlife 378

Chapter 29: Puerto Escondido 379

Evaluating the Top Accommodations 379
Settling into Puerto Escondido 384
Knowing your way around town..........................384
Getting around Puerto Escondido 385
Fast Facts: Puerto Escondido 385
Dining in Puerto Escondido 387
Having Fun on and off the Beach 390
An unusual spa experience.............................391
Embarking on an excursion.............................391
Planning a side trip to Puerto Angel and Playa
Zipolite 392
Shopping in Puerto Escondido..........................394
Enjoying the nightlife 395

Part IX: Los Cabos and Southern Baja 397

Chapter 30: The Lowdown on the Hotel Scene in Los Cabos 399

Choosing a Location 400
Best Accommodations in Los Cabos 401

Chapter 31: Settling into Los Cabos 413

Arriving in Los Cabos by Air..413
   Navigating passport control and Customs............413
   Getting to your hotel 414
   Renting a car..415
   Hiring transportation 415
Getting Around Los Cabos 416
   Touring around town...417
   Taking a taxi...417
   Considering a car rental...417
Fast Facts: Los Cabos 417

Chapter 32: Dining in Los Cabos 421

The Best Restaurants in Los Cabos 422

Chapter 33: Having Fun on and off the Beach
in Los Cabos 432

Hitting the Beaches...432
   Cabo's northern beaches...434
   Corridor beaches 434
   Cabo's southern beaches...435
Finding Water Fun for Everyone.......................................435
   Cruising Los Cabos 436
   Preferring a paddleboat 437
   Catching a wave...437
   Exploring the deep blue 438
   Reeling in the big one..438
Enjoying Land Sports...440
   Teeing off...440
   Making time for tennis 441
Taking Adventure and Nature Tours.................................444
   Driving Tours..444
Sightseeing in Los Cabos..445
Shopping in Los Cabos 445
   Clothing...446
   Contemporary art 446
   Crafts, gifts, and jewelry 447
   Decorative and folk art...447
   Other stores..447
Embarking on a Side Trip..448
Discovering Los Cabos after Dark....................................450
   Enjoying a theme night 450
   Watching a sunset..451
   Hanging out and happy hours...................................451

Going dancing..452
Mens' clubs..453

Part X: The Part of Tens 455

Chapter 34: Ten Top Mexican Moments 457

Enjoying a Mexican Fiesta...............................457
Setting Sail at Sunset.....................................457
Mixing It Up with Mariachi Music 458
Sipping on Margaritas at Sunset.....................458
Strolling the Malecón......................................458
Feasting on Fresh Fish under a Palapa............458
Looking for Whales in Baja or Puerto Vallarta.....458
Watching Cliff Divers in Acapulco...................458
Visiting Tulum..459
Shopping — While Sunbathing.........................459

Chapter 35: Ten Myths and Misconceptions about Mexico......................................460

Mexico Is a Desert, and It's Hot Everywhere.....460
Mexico Is the Land of Sombreros and Siestas.....461
Mexico Has No Drinking or Drug Laws............461
If in Trouble, Pay a Mordida 461
All Mexican Food Is Spicy 461
Don't Drink the Water.....................................462
Tequila Is Best with a Pinch of Salt and Lime.....462
A Jeep Rental Is Really $10 a Day....................462
Going Anywhere in Just Your Swimsuit Is Okay.....462
Mexicans Who Don't Speak English Are Hard
   of Hearing..462

Chapter 36: Ten Most Deliciously Mexican Dishes 464

Café de Olla..464
Ceviche..464
Chilaquiles 465
Licuados 465
Mole 465
Pescadillas 465
Pescado Sarandeado or Pescado en Talla 465
Pozole..466
Tacos al Pastor 466
Tamales 466

Part XI: Appendixes *467*

Appendix A: Quick Concierge.......................**469**

Fast Facts 469

Toll-Free Numbers and Web Sites 475

Major car-rental agencies 476

Major and select local hotel and motel chains 477

Where to Get More Information 478

**Appendix B: Glossary of Spanish
Words and Phrases**......................................**482**

Appendix C: Authentic Mexican Cuisine..................**488**

Knowing the Basic Dishes...............................488

Dishes made with tortillas 488

All about beans 489

Getting to know tamales 489

Understanding the chile pepper 490

Eating Out: Restaurants, Taquerías, and Tipping 490

Drinking in Mexico 491

Glossary of Spanish Menu Terms.....................491

Index *494*

Introduction

Mexico not only offers travelers some of the world's best beaches, but it also presents a rich, 1,000-year-old culture and amazing natural wonders to explore. Whether it's the desert caves of Los Cabos or the Caribbean reefs off Cancún and Cozumel, Mexico's largely untouched coastline is a virtual playground for travelers. In addition to the many natural attractions, Mexico's beach resorts have added golf, tennis, diving, and abundant watersports to their lures. But can the rest of your knowledge about this vast country fit inside a mango seed? For many people, Mexico is both familiar and a mystery, and some opinions of this land are influenced by inaccurate or outdated stereotypes. If you're a traveler who's more attuned to the culture, you may have visited one or two Mexican beach resorts, but you're probably curious about some of the others.

How do you sift through the destination choices — and then all the hotel options — without throwing in the beach towel in a daze of confusion? How do you plan a vacation that's perfect for you — not one that simply follows the recommendations of a friend or travel agent? You've come to the right place. This guide rescues you from both information overload and detail deficit — those annoying syndromes that afflict far too many would-be travelers. We give you enough specifics to plan the type of trip you want and steer clear of the type of trip you don't want.

Sure, plenty of other guidebooks are available that cover Mexico and its beach destinations, but many of them may as well be encyclopedias: They include practically everything you can possibly see and do. When the time comes to decide upon accommodations, attractions, activities, and meals, you probably have a tough time finding the best options because they're buried in with the rest of the mediocre to not-so-hot suggestions.

Mexico's Beach Resorts For Dummies, 3rd Edition, is a whole new enchilada. In this book, we streamline the options, focusing on each vacation spot's high points (and warning you about the low points). We leave out the less-visited, harder-to-reach beach resorts so that we can concentrate on the most popular (and most exciting) destinations. With the straightforward tips that we offer — how to get there, what to expect when you arrive, where to stay, where to eat, and where to have big fun — arranging your dream vacation can't be easier.

About This Book

You can use this book in three ways:

- ✔ **As a trip planner:** Whether you think you know where you want to go in Mexico, or you don't have a clue, this book helps you zero in on the ideal beach resort for you. It guides you through all the necessary steps of making your travel arrangements, from finding the cheapest airfare and considering travel insurance to figuring out a budget and packing like a pro. Chapters are self-contained, so you don't have to read them in order. Find the chapters you want in the table of contents, and just flip to them as you need them.

- ✔ **As a beach-resort guide:** Pack this book along with your sunscreen — it comes in just as handy while you're away, though not to prevent sunburn. Turn to the appropriate destination chapters whenever you need to find the best beaches, a good place to eat, a worthwhile boat cruise, a challenging golf course, the lowdown on a hot nightspot, or tips on any other diversions.

- ✔ **For an enjoyable overview:** If you want a feel for Mexico's most popular beach resorts, read this book from start to finish to get a taste of all the highlights.

Travel information is subject to change at any time — call ahead for confirmation when making your travel plans. Your safety is important to us (and to the publisher), so we encourage you to stay alert and be aware of your surroundings. Keep a close eye on cameras, purses, and wallets — all favorite targets of thieves and pickpockets.

Conventions Used in This Book

In this book, we include reviews of our favorite hotels and restaurants, as well as information about the best attractions at each of Mexico's top beach resorts. In these reviews, we use abbreviations for commonly accepted credit cards. Here's what those abbreviations stand for:

AE: American Express

DC: Diners Club

MC: MasterCard

V: Visa

We also include some general pricing information to help you as you decide where to unpack your bags or where to dine on the local cuisine. We use a system of dollar signs to show a range of costs (in U.S. dollars) so that you can make quick comparisons.

Unless stated otherwise, the lodging rates that we give are for two people spending one night in a standard double room. Prices are provided for both high season — the most popular travel time that runs roughly from Christmas to Easter — and the generally lower-priced summer season (or low season). Note that the following dollar sign pricing system indicates only the high-season rates for lodging, and applies to main courses only for restaurants.

Some hotel rates are much higher than others no matter what time of year it is. Don't be too quick to skip an accommodation that seems out of your price range, though. Some rates include breakfast, both breakfast and dinner, or even three meals per day. Other resorts are *all-inclusive,* which means that after you pay for your room, you never have to dip into your pocket again for meals, beverages, tips, taxes, most activities, or transportation to and from the airport. So, although a price tag may seem sky-high at first, you may actually find it affordable upon second glance.

Check out the following table to decipher the dollar signs:

Cost	Hotel	Restaurant
$	Less than $75	Less than $15
$$	$76–$125	$16–$30
$$$	$126–$175	$31–$50
$$$$	$176–$250	$51 and up
$$$$$	More than $251	

Foolish Assumptions

As we wrote this book, we made some assumptions about you and what your needs may be as a traveler. Here's what we assumed about you:

- ✔ You may be an inexperienced traveler looking for guidance when determining whether to take a trip to a Mexican beach resort and how to plan for it.

- ✔ You may be an experienced traveler who hasn't had much time to explore Mexico or its beaches and wants expert advice when you finally do get a chance to enjoy some fun in the sun.

- ✔ You're not looking for a book that provides all the information available about Mexico or that lists every hotel, restaurant, or attraction available to you. Instead, you're looking for a book that focuses on the places that offer the best or most unique experiences in these beach resorts.

How This Book Is Organized

We divide this book into 11 parts. The chapters within each part cover specific subjects in detail. Skip around as much as you like; you don't have to read this book in any particular order. In fact, think of these pages as a buffet. You can consume whatever you want — and no one cares if you eat the flan for dessert before you have the enchiladas.

For each beach resort, we include a section called "Fast Facts." These sections give you handy information that you may need when traveling in Mexico, including phone numbers and addresses to use in an emergency, area hospitals and pharmacies, names of local newspapers and magazines, locations for maps, and more.

Part 1: Mexico's Beach Resorts

Let's cut to the chase: Where are the best beaches, most romantic places to stay, best bets for families, and hottest nightlife? We cover all of this and more in this section — think of it as your personal tip sheet of the very best of Mexico's Beach Resorts.

Your vacation will be much more enjoyable if you take the time to learn a bit about the wealth of this magical land. Sure, Mexico is a close neighbor, but the nuances of its culture are fascinating. Here, we give you a brief overview of local history, architecture, customs, cuisines, and fiestas and celebrations. We also give you a list of some popular movies and books to make exploring these topics even more enjoyable.

Also in this section, we compare and contrast Mexico's most popular beach resorts so that you can decide which place best suits your tastes and needs. Sure, they all have gorgeous beaches, but that's where the similarities end. To help you plan a vacation that's tailored to your preferences, this part guides you through the process of figuring out which resort or resorts are best for you.

We take you through the best — and worst — times of year to travel, and we explain the differences between high season and low season. We also tell you about special holidays that may help you decide when to visit Mexico.

Part 11: Planning Your Trip to Mexico's Beach Resorts

This section is where we lay out everything you need to know about making all the arrangements for your trip. We help you decide whether to use a travel agent, a packager, or the Internet. We offer advice on finding the best airfare — and airline — for your destination. Likewise, we explain how to estimate the total cost of your vacation and how to stay within your budget.

We also offer up some special trip-planning advice for families, singles, gay and lesbian travelers, seniors, and travelers who are physically challenged. Finally, we take you through all the ins and outs of other vacation essentials, from getting a passport and considering travel insurance, to staying connected, staying safe, and packing like a pro.

Part III: Cancún

For years, this has been Mexico's most popular beach resort, however it took a wallop of a hit by hurricane Wilma in October 2005. We'll help guide you to the places that have recovered, to ensure you won't be disappointed by those places that haven't. Popular with first-time travelers to Mexico, this area has all the comforts of home: familiar restaurant and hotel chains along with great shopping, easy access to diverse cultural and geographical activities and excursions to the ancient ruins of Tulum, world-class scuba diving, and plenty of Mexican fiestas. We provide all the details for getting to, eating at, staying in, and playing at all of Cancún's hot spots.

Part IV: Cozumel and the Riviera Maya

Staying on a tropical island is a dream for many, and Cozumel offers a distinctive island destination for a laid-back vacation with a myriad of water activities, many centered around the famous reef that outlines the southwest coast. Back on the mainland, the Riviera Maya provides a stunning stretch of pristine beaches, unique towns, and mega-resorts from Cancún to Tulum. Check out the ultra-trendy town of Playa del Carmen or visit one of the eco-parks. This area also suffered extensive damage from October 2005's hurricane Wilma, so we'll let you know of any areas that haven't fully recovered. In this part, we cover all the information you need to travel to and around these two beach resorts.

Part V: Puerto Vallarta and the Central Pacific Coast

Turn to this part for the inside scoop (Lynne, one of the authors of this book, is a long-time resident!) on visiting the picturesque city of Puerto Vallarta. From viewing historic landmarks to dining in world-class restaurants to finding the perfect beach along the 81km (50 miles) of coastline surrounding Banderas Bay, a trip to this part of Mexico is sure to please even the most discriminating vacationer.

Part VI: Ixtapa and Zihuatanejo

Who says you can't get it all in one destination? Traveling to the towns of Ixtapa and Zihuatanejo provides the best of two worlds: Ixtapa gives you high-class hotels along a beautiful strip of sand, and nearby Zihuatanejo wraps you in the warmth of its small-town charms. This part offers advice on staying and dining in both of these great vacation spots.

Part VII: Acapulco

The grande dame of Mexico's west coast, Acapulco draws many visitors to its glittering bay and glamorous nightlife. Enjoy the excitement of a bustling city combined with the amenities of a beachfront resort. This part gives you the lowdown on vacationing in Mexico's first beach resort.

Part VIII: Huatulco and the Southern Pacific Coast

For details on a vacation that centers on the natural beauty of the land and the sea, turn to Part VIII. This part offers a close-up look at two towns along the southern Pacific coast: Huatulco and Puerto Escondido.

Part IX: Los Cabos and Southern Baja

Want to take time out for a great golf vacation? Ready to reel in a big one? Want to relax in one of Mexico's most deluxe resorts? Or, just need to let your hair down and enjoy some super-charged nightlife? Then turn to Part IX for all the details on vacationing in Los Cabos and on the Baja Peninsula.

Part X: The Part of Tens

Every *For Dummies* book has a Part of Tens. In this section, you can find out about ten marvelous Mexico moments, ten common myths about Mexico, and ten delicious Mexican dishes to try.

Part XI: Appendixes

Do you want to locate a quick phone number or Web site, touch up on a few common Spanish words and phrases, or get your hunger pangs going for some authentic Mexican cuisine? Check out this part for all that information and more.

Icons Used in This Book

Throughout this book, helpful icons highlight particularly useful information. Here's a look at what each symbol means:

Keep an eye out for the Bargain Alert icon as you look for money-saving tips and great deals.

Watch for the Heads Up icon to identify annoying or potentially dangerous situations such as tourist traps, unsafe neighborhoods, budgetary rip-offs, and other things to avoid.

Look to the Kid Friendly icon for attractions, hotels, restaurants, and activities that are particularly hospitable to children or people traveling with kids.

The Romance icon signals the most romantic restaurants, hotels, and attractions that Mexico's beach resorts have to offer.

The Tip icon alerts you to practical advice and hints to make your trip run more smoothly.

 Note the ¡Viva Mexico! icon for food, places, or experiences that offer a true taste of Mexico.

Where to Go from Here

There's nothing like a beach vacation — whether you spend it lazing in the sun or pursuing active, water-bound activities — and it's even better when planned with the right advice and insider tips. Whether you're a veteran traveler or new to the game, *Mexico's Beach Resorts For Dummies*, 3rd Edition, helps you put together just the kind of trip you have in mind. So, start turning these pages, and before you know it, you'll feel those balmy beach breezes on your face!

Part I
Mexico's Beach Resorts

The 5th Wave   By Rich Tennant

The Mexican Experience

Your glass of water...

In this part . . .

Planning a trip can be daunting — so we're here to help give you a sense of the place you're considering visiting. Mexico is a vast and varied country with a bevy of unique beach resorts. We introduce you to the highlights of the most popular ones, so you can pick the destination that best matches your idea of the perfect seaside getaway.

In Part I, we cover the basics: Each of Mexico's beach resorts has a charm all its own, so deciding which one best suits your preferences is the first step in planning your ideal vacation. We delve the fascinating details of Mexico's past and introduce you to some of the delicacies of Mexican dining. Most importantly, we discuss the details — such as when to go and which type of hotel is best for you.

Chapter 1

Discovering the Best of Mexico's Beach Resorts

· ·

In This Chapter

▶ Scoping out Mexico's stellar beaches

▶ Discovering the top places to stay

▶ Exploring Mexico's most unforgettable places and experiences

▶ Uncovering the best restaurants and nightlife

· ·

*M*exico should be the beach vacation of your dreams. All those glossy images of long stretches of pure, powdery, white-sand beaches and dramatic coastlines do exist — and they're found along the entire shoreline of Mexico.

Between the two of us, we've logged thousands of miles crisscrossing the peninsula, and these are our personal favorites — the best places to go, the best restaurants, the best hotels, and must-see, one-of-a-kind experiences.

This chapter gives you a sneak preview of the absolute best that Mexico's beach resorts have to offer — the cream of the crop. Each of these places and experiences is discussed in detail later in this book; for now, you can skim them all at a glance and whet your appetite.

The Best Beach Vacations

Mexico has a multitude of stunning beaches — in a variety of forms — any of which will make for a great vacation. The following are our favorite beach getaways:

> ✔ **Puerto Vallarta:** Puerto Vallarta is Mexico's only beach resort where authentic colonial ambience mixes with true resort amenities. Spectacularly wide Banderas Bay offers 42km (26 miles) of beaches. Some, like Playa Los Muertos — the popular public beach in town — abound with *palapa* (thatched roof) restaurants, beach volleyball,

Mexico

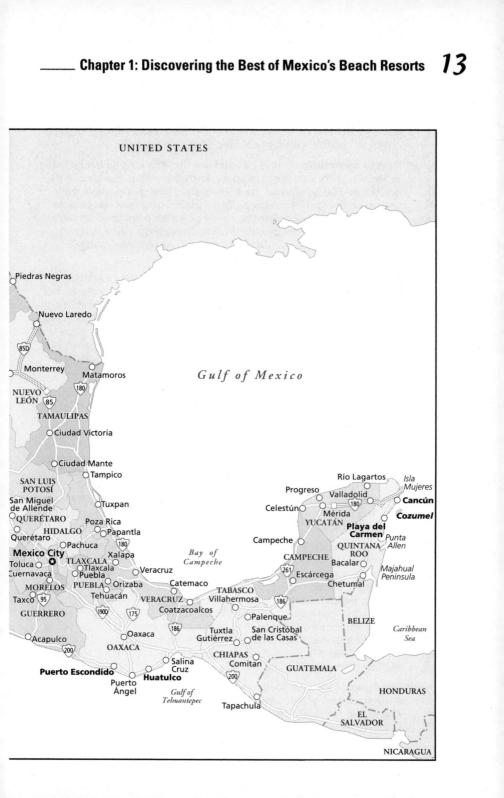

and parasailing. The beaches of Punta Mita, the exclusive development north of Vallarta, are of the white-sand variety, with crystalline waters and coral reefs just offshore. Others around the bay nestle in coves, accessible only by boat. See Chapters 16 to 19.

✔ **Puerto Escondido:** This is our pick for the best overall beach value in Mexico. Although it's principally known for its world-class surfing beach, Playa Zicatela, the surrounding beaches all have their own appeal; colorful fishing *pangas* (small boats) dot the central town beach, parked under the shade of palms leaning so far over they almost touch the ground. Puerto Escondido offers unique accommodations at excellent prices, with exceptional budget dining and nightlife. See Chapter 29.

✔ **Ixtapa/Zihuatanejo:** These side-by-side resorts offer beachgoers the best of both worlds: serene simplicity and resort comforts. For those in search of a back-to-basics beach, the best and most beautiful is Playa La Ropa, close to Zihuatanejo. The wide beach at Playa Las Gatas, with its restaurants and snorkeling sites, is also a great place to play. The luxury hotels in Ixtapa, on the next bay over from Zihuatanejo, front Playa Palmar, a fine, wide swath of beach. See Chapters 20 to 23.

✔ **Cancún:** Despite the well-documented damage from 2005's Hurricane Wilma, Cancún is rapidly recovering, and is known as Mexico's most popular beach playground. Essentially one long ribbon of white sand bordering aquamarine water, Cancún has one of Mexico's most beautifully situated beaches. If you want tropical drinks brought to you while you lounge in the sand, this is the vacation for you. In addition to being a bustling, modern mega-resort, it's also a great place for exploring Caribbean reefs, tranquil lagoons, and the surrounding jungle. The most tranquil waters and beaches on Cancún Island are those at the northern tip, facing the Bahía de Mujeres. See Chapters 10 to 13.

✔ **Playa del Carmen:** This is one of our absolute favorite Mexican beach vacations. Stylish and hip, Playa del Carmen offers a beautiful beach and an eclectic assortment of small hotels, inns, and *cabañas* (cabins). The social scene is focused on the beach by day and the pedestrian-only Quinta Avenida (Fifth Avenue) by night, with its fun assortment of restaurants, clubs, sidewalk cafes, and shops. You're also close to the coast's major attractions, including nature parks, ruins, and, *cenotes* (sinkholes or natural wells). Cozumel Island is just a quick ferry trip away. Enjoy it while it's a manageable size. See Chapter 15.

✔ **Los Cabos:** Dramatic rock formations and crashing waves mix with wide stretches of soft sand and a rolling break. Start at Pueblo la Playa, just north of San José del Cabo, and work your way down the Cabo Corridor to the famed Playa de Amor at Land's End. Some beaches are more appropriate for contemplation than for swimming, which isn't all bad. See Chapters 30 to 33.

The Best Luxury Resorts

If money is no object, Mexico's beach resorts have no shortage of places to park yourself in style. As an extra-added bonus, most of Mexico's resorts have recently added brand-new spas that raise the art of relaxation and pampering to a new level. What could be better than a massage on the beach? (Maybe a massage on the beach *with* a margarita, too?)

The following are a few of our favorite luxury resorts:

- ✔ **Four Seasons Resort Punta Mita** (north of Puerto Vallarta): This luxury resort has soared in popularity since opening in 1999. It offers an unrivaled location (on a remote, pristine stretch of beach) and the stellar service characteristic of the Four Seasons chain. Also on-site are an expansive spa and a private Jack Nicklaus Signature golf course. See Chapter 16.

- ✔ **Las Ventanas al Paraíso** (Los Cabos): Stunning in its relaxed elegance, Las Ventanas comes complete with a deluxe European spa, excellent gourmet restaurant, and elegantly appointed rooms and suites. From fireplaces and telescopes to private pools and rooftop terraces, each suite is a private slice of heaven. See Chapter 30.

- ✔ **One&Only Palmilla** (Los Cabos): Currently the most popular Mexican resort with the Hollywood crowd, the recently renovated Palmilla has earned its spot as the most deluxe hotel in this seaside playground known for sumptuous accommodations and great golf. The exceptional spa, fitness center, and yoga garden, as well as a restaurant by renowned chef Charlie Trotter are added bonuses. See Chapter 30.

- ✔ **Villa del Sol** (Zihuatanejo): Few hotels meet the demanding standards of luxury and attention to detail required to be a member of the French Relais & Châteaux, but this small beachfront inn does. It's also a member of the Small Luxury Hotels of the World. See Chapter 20.

- ✔ **Le Méridien Cancún Resort & Spa** (Cancún): Although there are grander hotels in Cancún, we prefer this resort, as it's the most intimate of the luxury hotels, with an understated sense of highly personalized service. Especially notable is its 1,394-sq.-m (15,000-sq.-ft.) Spa del Mar. See Chapter 10.

- ✔ **Fiesta Americana Grand Aqua** (Cancún): This resort was undergoing repairs from Hurricane Wilma damage at press time, but is expected to return to its previous splendor by fall 2006. Its exquisite design and detailed amenities set a new standard for Cancún chic when it opened in early 2005. It offers luxury that indulges the senses without overwhelming them. Clean design and a color scheme that mirrors the aquamarine and white beach landscape are inherently relaxing. Add a superb spa, dazzling selection of restaurants, and a chill-music scene in the evenings around the pool, and the mood is set for a more modern take on luxury. See Chapter 10.

✔ **Maroma** (Riviera Maya): You cannot ask for a better setting for a resort than this beautiful stretch of Caribbean coast with palm trees and manicured gardens. You begin to relax before you even take the first sip of your welcome cocktail. Service is very attentive, and the rooms are large and luxurious. See Chapter 15.

The Best Good-Value Accommodations

Being on a budget in Mexico doesn't mean you'll have to sacrifice style — or the perfect beach vacation. There are plenty of well-priced options, and here are our favorites:

✔ **Paraíso Escondido** (Puerto Escondido): This eclectic inn is a great bargain, especially for the originality of the décor, and the excellent service. It's a short walk to both the beach and the action along Puerto's main street. See Chapter 29.

✔ **Misión de los Arcos** (Huatulco): Just 1 block from the central plaza, this hotel has a similar style to the elegant Quinta Real, at a fraction of the cost. An all-white facade and intriguing decorative touches give it an inviting feel, plus there's also a cute cafe, stocked gym, and Wi-Fi everywhere. A shuttle service takes you to Huatulco's beaches. See Chapter 28.

✔ **Hotel Los Flamingos** (Acapulco): Take a break and step back in time, to the Hollywood heyday of Old Acapulco, when you stay here. Set on a dramatic cliff, away from the bustle of Acapulco's beach zone, this hotel was once the private retreat of movie greats including John Wayne, Cary Grant, and Johnny "Tarzan" Weissmuller. Its funky charm still captivates. See Chapter 24.

✔ **Cabo Inn** (Cabo San Lucas): This former bordello is the best budget inn in the area. Rooms are small but extra-clean and invitingly decorated, amenities are generous, and the owner-managers are friendly and helpful. Ideally located, close to town and near the marina, the inn caters to sportfishers. See Chapter 30.

✔ **Rey del Caribe Hotel:** Not only will you find exceptional value here, but you'll also support a true ecological hotel, which uses environmentally sensitive practices like collecting rainwater and composting. Sunny rooms are surrounded by lush jungle landscaping — and all in the heart of downtown Cancún! See Chapter 10.

✔ **Treetops** (Playa del Carmen): An economical, quiet hotel steps from both the beach and Avenida 5, Treetops could easily get by on its location alone. But the owners have gone out of their way to create distinctive lodging with plenty of amenities. The hotel has its very own *cenote* and piece of shady jungle, making it a lovely place to relax after a trying day of strolling the beach and wandering the village streets. See Chapter 15.

The Most Unique Places to Get Away from It All

Mexico offers a multitude of unique places to escape the world and relax in seaside splendor. While some of the specific hotels below offer more activity than others, all are what we consider to be the most unique places in Mexico to transport you to a truly "away" state of mind:

- ✔ **Verana** (Yelapa, south of Puerto Vallarta): The stylish Verana adds a dash of sophistication to funky Yelapa — a remote village accessible only by boat, about 45 minutes from Puerto Vallarta. Each of the six handcrafted casas has a unique architectural style that complements the expanse of vistas to the surrounding jungle and ocean. It's a perfect blend of style, romance, and nature. See Chapter 16.

- ✔ **Quinta María Cortez** (Puerto Vallarta): This is one of Mexico's most original places to stay; it's an eclectic B&B uniquely decorated with antiques, curios, and original art. It sits on a beautiful cove on Conchas Chinas beach. See Chapter 16.

- ✔ **La Casa Que Canta** (Zihuatanejo): This architecturally dramatic hotel incorporates wonderful Mexican adobe and folk art in grandly scaled rooms. It's a delightful place to unwind, read on the terrace overlooking the bay, and order room service. See Chapter 20.

- ✔ **Casa Natalia** (San José del Cabo): This renovated historic home, now a charming inn, is an oasis of palms, waterfalls, and flowers against the desert landscape. Each room and suite is an artful combination of modern architecture and traditional Mexican touches. The restaurant is the hottest in town. See Chapter 30.

- ✔ **Hotel Jungla Caribe** (Playa del Carmen): In a town filled with exceptional inns, this one's a standout. The eclectic décor combines neoclassical details with a decidedly tropical touch. The rooms and suites surround a stylish courtyard, restaurant, and pool. You couldn't be better located — a block from the beach, with an entrance on happening Avenida 5. See Chapter 15.

The Best Active Vacations

With the ocean as tempting as it is off of Mexico's miles of coastline, you're certain to find multiple ways to enjoy it above and below the surface. There's also plenty to do on land as well. Here are our favorite things to do:

- ✔ **Golf in Los Cabos and Puerto Vallarta:** Puerto Vallarta, with its seven championship courses, is *the* new destination for golfers to keep their eyes on. See Chapter 19. The Corridor between San José del Cabo and Cabo San Lucas is one of the world's premier golf destinations, with five championship courses open and a total of 207 holes slated for the area. See Chapter 33.

✔ *Cenote* **Diving on the Yucatán Mainland:** Dive into the clear depths of the Yucatán's *cenotes* for an interesting twist on underwater exploration. The Maya considered the *cenotes* sacred — and their vivid colors indeed seem otherworldly. Most are located between Playa del Carmen and Tulum, and dive shops in these areas regularly run trips for experienced divers. For recommended dive shops, see Chapter 15.

✔ **Scuba Diving in Cozumel and along the Yucatán's Caribbean Coast:** The coral reefs off the island, Mexico's premier diving destination, are among the top five dive spots in the world, though damage from 2005's Hurricane Wilma has affected some areas. The Yucatán's coastal reef, part of the second-largest reef system in the world, affords excellent diving all along the coast. Especially beautiful is the Chinchorro Reef, lying 32km (20 miles) offshore from Majahual or Xcalak. Diving from Isla Mujeres is also quite spectacular. See Chapters 14 and 15.

✔ **Surfing Zicatela Beach in Puerto Escondido:** This world-class break is a lure for surfers from around the globe. It challenges the best in the sport each September and October, when the waves peak and the annual surf competitions take place. See Chapter 29. Other noted surf breaks in Mexico include Sayulita and Las Islitas Beach near **San Blas** (both north of Puerto Vallarta), and Playa Costa Azul, on the outskirts of **San José del Cabo.** See Chapter 33.

✔ **Sportfishing in Cabo San Lucas:** Billfishing for magnificent marlin and sailfish is a popular sport throughout southern Baja, and it's what originally put Cabo San Lucas on the map. See Chapter 33. Fishing is also excellent in Puerto Vallarta, and Zihuatanejo. See Chapters 19 and 23.

✔ **Sea Kayaking in the Sea of Cortez:** From Cabo San Lucas to La Paz, and continuing north, the Sea of Cortez is a sea kayaker's dream. It has dozens of tiny coves and impressive inlets to pull into and explore, under the watchful gaze of sea lions and dolphins. Professional outfitters provide gear, guides, and instruction for novices. See Chapter 33.

✔ **Exploring the Bays of Huatulco:** Whether you travel by party boat or in a small skiff to a pristine cove, the nine Bays of Huatulco offer beach lovers a treasure-trove of sand and sea pleasures. See Chapter 28.

✔ **Whale-Watching in Puerto Vallarta's Banderas Bay:** From December to May each year, the magnificent humpback whales make their annual migration to these waters to breed and bear calfs. Watching these mammoth yet highly social sea mammals entertain an audience is a truly life-enhancing experience. See Chapter 19. Whale-watching is also a popular pastime in mid-Baja's Magdalena Bay, with trips available from Cabo San Lucas. See Chapter 33.

The Best Dining Experiences

Best doesn't necessarily mean most luxurious. Although some of the restaurants listed here are fancy affairs, others are simple places to get fine, authentic Mexican cuisine:

- ✔ **Arrayán, for Tacos Like You've Never Before Tasted** (Puerto Vallarta): The colorful atmosphere may be casual, funky, and fun, but the food is seriously and authentically Mexican. Prime beef filet tacos are just one specialty — others include Mexican duck confit, shrimp *pozole* (broth with hominy and shrimp), and homemade ice creams from indigenous fruits. See Chapter 18.

- ✔ **El Mirador, for Margaritas** (Acapulco, in the Hotel Plaza Las Glorias): You can enjoy a great margarita at many places in Mexico, but this is the only one that serves them with a view of the spectacular La Quebrada cliff divers. See Chapter 24.

- ✔ **Labná:** A showcase of authentic Yucatecan cuisine and music, in downtown Cancún, this is the place to sample regional specialties such as pork *pibil* (pit-baked pork) and *poc chuc* (slices of pork with onion, marinated in a tangy orange sauce). See Chapter 12.

- ✔ ***Pozole* in Acapulco:** If it's Thursday, there will always be *pozole* in Acapulco. Sample this locally popular meal comprised of hominy and meat in a broth garnished with savory seasonings. Our favorite place to indulge is at the cliffside restaurant at the Los Flamigos Hotel. See Chapter 24.

- ✔ **El Cafecito, for Mango Eclairs and Coffee** (Puerto Escondido): Worthy of the trip to Puerto Escondido itself are El Cafecito's mango éclairs, accompanied by a steaming mug of coffee and served beachside on Playa Zicatela. Also noteworthy are the ample "surfer's special" breakfasts at numerous other cafes along the beachfront. See Chapter 29.

- ✔ **Cabaña del Pescador (Lobster House; Cozumel):** If you want an ideally seasoned, succulent lobster dinner, Cabaña del Pescador (Lobster House) is the place. If you want anything else, you're out of luck — lobster dinner, expertly prepared, is all it serves. When you've achieved perfection, why bother with anything else? See Chapter 14.

- ✔ **Media Luna** (Playa del Carmen): The inviting atmosphere of this sidewalk cafe on Avenida 5 is enough to lure you in. The expertly executed and innovative menu, together with great prices, makes it one of the top choices on the Caribbean coast. See Chapter 15.

The Best Shopping

Beyond the ubiquitous T-shirts and glass pyramids, you'll find captivating treasures to take home from your trip to Mexico's beach resorts. Here are our favorite shopping experiences:

- **Huichol Art in Puerto Vallarta:** One of the last indigenous cultures to remain faithful to their customs, language, and traditions, the Huichol Indians come down from the Sierra Madre to sell their unusual art to Puerto Vallarta galleries. Inspired by visions received during spiritual ceremonies, the Huichol create their art with colorful yarn or beads pressed into wax. See Chapter 19.

- **Oaxacan Textiles in Huatulco:** The valley of Oaxaca produces the best weavings and naturally dyed textiles in Mexico; it's also famous for its pottery (especially the black pottery), and colorful, imaginative woodcarvings. Both can be found in shops in Huatulco, on Oaxaca's coast. See Chapter 28.

- **Taxco Silver:** Mexico's silver capital, Taxco, has hundreds of stores featuring fine jewelry and decorative objects. See Chapter 27.

- **Resort Wear in Cancún:** Resort clothing — especially if you can find a sale — can be a bargain here. And the selection may be wider than what's available at home. Almost every mall on the island contains trendy boutiques that specialize in locally designed and imported clothing. See Chapter 13.

- **Duty Free in Cancún or Los Cabos:** If you're looking for European perfume, fine watches, or other imported goods, you'll find the prices in the duty-free shops in both Cancún (at the major malls on the island and in downtown Cancún) and in Los Cabos hard to beat. See Chapters 13 and 33.

- **Precious Gemstones in Isla Mujeres:** Isla Mujeres, also a duty-free zone, offers an impressive selection of both precious stones and superb craftsmen who can make jewelry designs to order. See Chapter 13.

- **Quinta Avenida, Playa del Carmen:** This pedestrian-only street offers leisurely shopping at its best. No cars, no hassle, simply stroll down the street and let your eye pick out objects of interest. Expect a good bit of merchandise popular with counterculture types, such as batik clothing and fabric, Guatemalan textiles, and inventive jewelry and artwork. But you'll also find quality Mexican handicrafts, premium tequilas, and Cuban cigars. See Chapter 15.

The Best Nightlife

Rivaling the midday sun on the beach, most of Mexico's coastal resorts have a simmering hot nightlife. Here are the liveliest places for nocturnal diversion among Mexico's Beach Resorts:

- ✔ **Puerto Vallarta:** Of all the beach destinations, Puerto Vallarta enjoys the most sophisticated and varied nightlife. An excellent selection of small clubs features live jazz, blues, salsa, and good old rock 'n' roll. You'll also find mariachi, pre-Columbian, and traditional Mexican ballads. Heating up the scene are a new group of contemporary clubs and lounges — including the international set at Nikki Beach — with DJs spinning house, trance, and chill. See Chapter 19.

- ✔ **Acapulco Discos:** Nightlife can't possibly get more lavish, extravagant, or flashy than it is in Acapulco, Mexico's hands-down diva. This city's main cultural attractions are the clubs that jam until sunrise, several of which have walls of windows overlooking the bay. See Chapter 27.

- ✔ **Cancún's Clubs in Malls:** Cancún's wide-ranging hot spots include most of the name-brand nightlife destinations, concentrated in entertainment malls and festival shopping centers, as well as hotel-lobby bars with live music, and sophisticated discos. Popular nightlife tours allow you to bypass lines and sample various clubs in a single night. The clubs here can accommodate up to 3,000, and there are plenty of options for staying out until the sun comes up. See Chapter 13.

- ✔ **Cabo San Lucas Beach Bars:** In the nightlife capital of Baja California, after-dark fun centers on the casual bars and restaurants that line the main drag, as well as those on the town's public Medano Beach. The place retains a rowdy, outlaw feel, despite the influx of tony hotels nearby. A new lounge scene is, thankfully, updating this lively town's nightlife. See Chapter 33.

- ✔ **Quinta Avenida, Playa del Carmen:** Stroll along the lively, pedestrian-only Fifth Avenue to find the bar that's right for you. With live music venues, tequila bars, sports bars, and cafes, you're sure to find something to fit your mood. See Chapter 15.

Chapter 2

Digging Deeper into Mexico

In This Chapter
▶ Uncovering Mexico's fascinating past
▶ Discovering the delicacies of Mexican dining
▶ Mastering a few key words and phrases in Spanish

*T*he resorts of Mexico are known for a dazzling array of every type of beach — from glorious white-sand beaches bordering tranquil, translucent waters, to dramatic cliffs alongside crashing waves. It would be easy to let that be the sole draw to this destination, but there's so much more here to enjoy. Mexico's rich history has left mysteries still to be discovered, and ruins that make for popular explorations. So, what's the story behind them?

In this chapter, we'll relay a brief history of Mexico and its cultural highpoints. We'll sample the unusual and memorable culinary specialties of the region, and we'll even provide some tips to the local lingo, as well as some recommended reading and films that will help you enjoy this place much more than you would if you limit your perspective to a beach blanket in the sand.

Introducing Mexico

Mexico stretches nearly 3,220km (2,000 miles) from east to west and more than 1,600km (1,000 miles) north to south. Only one-fifth the size of the United States, its territory includes trackless deserts in the north, dense jungles in the south, thousands of miles of lush seacoast and beaches along the Pacific and Caribbean, and the central highlands, crisscrossed by mountain ranges. Mexico has close to 100 million inhabitants, and 22 million of them live in the capital, Mexico City. By most measurements, the disparity between rich and poor has increased in the last 30 to 40 years. Cycles of boom and bust weigh heavier on the poor than on the rich. But in the face of all of this, Mexican society shows great resilience, due in part to the values Mexicans live by. For them, family and friends, social gatherings, and living in the present remain eminently important. In Mexico, there is always time to meet relatives or friends for a drink, a cup of coffee, or a special occasion.

Mexico's mysterious ancient inhabitants, the **Aztecs** and the **Maya,** are another fascinating part of this land. The ancients left behind elegant and mysterious ruins that, despite all that we now know, seem to defy interpretation. Almost every year, archaeological excavation leads to the discovery of more ruins, adding to a growing picture of an urban civilization that thrived in an area where only scantily populated jungle now exists. What can we make of such a civilization? What value do we accord the Maya among the other lost civilizations of the ancient world? Even this is unclear, but the art and architecture they left behind are stunning expressions of a rich and complex cosmological view.

Then there was the arrival of the Spaniards, in the early 1500s — an event that in hindsight seems almost apocalyptic. Military conquest and old-world diseases decimated the native population. A new social order predicated on a starkly different religion rose in place of the old one. Through all of this, the Maya held on to their language but lost most of the living memory of their pre-Hispanic ways. What they retained they cloaked in the language of myth and legend that was worked into a rough synthesis of old and new. They selectively appropriated elements of the new religion that could help make sense of the world, and this process continues today in the many Maya communities that have native churches.

For these reasons and more, Mexico is a curious place; it may beckon you with its enticing beaches and tropical climate, but what will ultimately hold your attention is the unique character of the land and its people. There is no other place like it.

History 101: The Main Events

Mexico's history extends much longer than that of her neighbor to the north. Once the center of civilization in the Western Hemisphere, Mexico's ancient civilizations were sophisticated and cultured. While the Aztecs settled in central Mexico — at the site of present-day Mexico City, the Yucatán was home to the Maya, and remnants of their advanced, mysterious civilization are still being found, unlocking clues to this fascinating culture. Modern-day Mexicans are proud of their deep, rich history, and you will find integrated within many aspects of daily life a bow to the mysticism and sacred traditions of ancient times.

Pre-Hispanic Civilizations

The earliest "Mexicans" were perhaps Stone Age hunter-gatherers coming from the north, descendants of a race that had crossed the

Bering Strait and reached North America around 12,000 B.C. This is the prevailing theory, but there is a growing body of evidence that points to an earlier crossing of peoples from Asia to the New World. What we know for certain is that Mexico was populated by 10,000 B.C. Sometime between 5200 and 1500 B.C. they began practicing agriculture and domesticating animals.

The Pre-Classic Period (1500 B.C.–A.D. 300)

Eventually, agriculture improved to the point that it could provide enough food to support large communities and enough surplus to free some of the population from agricultural work. A civilization emerged that we call the **Olmec** — an enigmatic people who settled the lower Gulf Coast in what is now Tabasco and Veracruz. Anthropologists regard them as the mother culture of Mesoamerica because they established a pattern for later civilizations in a wide area stretching from northern Mexico into Central America. The Olmec developed the basic calendar used throughout the region, established principles of urban layout and architecture, and originated the cult of the jaguar and the sacredness of jade. They may also have bequeathed the sacred ritual of "the ball game" — a universal element of Mesoamerican culture.

The Maya civilization began developing in the pre-Classic period, around 500 B.C. Our understanding of this period is only sketchy, but Olmec influences are apparent everywhere. The Maya perfected the Olmec calendar and, somewhere along the way, developed their ornate system of hieroglyphic writing and their early architecture. Two other civilizations also began their rise to prominence around this time: the people of Teotihuacán, just north of present-day Mexico City, and the Zapotec of Monte Albán, in the valley of Oaxaca.

The Classic Period (A.D. 300–900)

The flourishing of these three civilizations marks the boundaries of this period — the heyday of pre-Columbian Mesoamerican artistic and cultural achievements. These include the pyramids and palaces in Teotihuacán; the ceremonial center of Monte Albán; and the stelae and temples of Palenque, Bonampak, and the Tikal site in Guatemala. Beyond their achievements in art and architecture, the Maya made significant discoveries in science, including the use of zero in mathematics and a complex calendar with which the priests could predict eclipses and the movements of the stars for centuries to come.

The inhabitants of **Teotihuacán** (100 B.C.–A.D. 700, near present-day Mexico City) built a city that, at its zenith, is thought to have had 100,000 or more inhabitants covering 14 sq. km (5½ sq. miles). It was a well-organized city, built on a grid with streams channeled to follow the city's plan. Different social classes, such as artisans and merchants, were assigned to specific neighborhoods. Teotihuacán exerted tremendous influence as far away as Guatemala and the Yucatán Peninsula. Its feathered serpent god, later known as **Quetzalcoatl,** became part of the pantheon of many succeeding cultures, including the Toltecs, who brought the cult to the Yucatán where the god became known as Kukulkán. The ruling classes were industrious, literate, and cosmopolitan. The beautiful sculpture and ceramics of Teotihuacán display a highly stylized and refined aesthetic whose influences can be seen clearly in objects of Maya and Zapotec origin. Around the seventh century, the city was abandoned for unknown reasons. Who these people were and where they went remains a mystery.

Farther south, the **Zapotec,** influenced by the Olmec, raised an impressive civilization in the region of Oaxaca. Their two principal cities were **Monte Albán,** inhabited by an elite class of merchants and artisans, and **Mitla,** reserved for the high priests.

The Post-Classic Period (A.D. 900–1521)

Warfare became a more conspicuous activity of the civilizations that flourished in this period. Social development was impressive but not as cosmopolitan as the Maya, Teotihuacán, and Zapotec societies. In central Mexico, a people known as the **Toltec** established their capital at Tula in the 10th century. They were originally one of the barbarous hordes of Indians that periodically migrated from the north. At some stage in their development, the Toltec were influenced by remnants of Teotihuacán culture and adopted the feathered serpent Quetzalcoatl as their god. They also revered a god known as **Tezcatlipoca,** or "smoking mirror," who later became a god of the Aztecs. By the 13th century, however, the Toltec had exhausted themselves, probably in civil wars and in battles with the invaders from the north.

Of those northern invaders, the **Aztecs** were the most warlike. At first they served as mercenaries for established cities in the valley of Mexico — one of which allotted them an unwanted, marshy piece of land in the middle of Lake Texcoco for their settlement. It eventually grew into the island city of Tenochtitlán. Through aggressive diplomacy and military action, the Aztec soon conquered central Mexico and extended their rule east to the Gulf Coast and south to the valley of Oaxaca.

During this period, the Maya built beautiful cities near the Yucatán's Puuc hills. The regional architecture, called **Puuc style,** is characterized by elaborate exterior stonework appearing above door frames and extending to the roofline. Examples of this architecture, such as the Codz Poop at Kabah and the palaces at Uxmal, Sayil, and Labná, are beautiful and quite impressive.

The precise nature of this Toltec influence is a subject of debate. But there is an intriguing myth in central Mexico that tells how Quetzalcoatl quarrels with Tezcatlipoca and through trickery is shamed by his rival into leaving Tula, the capital of the Toltec empire. He leaves heading eastward towards the morning star, vowing someday to return. In the language of myth, this could be a shorthand telling of an actual civil war between two factions in Tula, each led by the priesthood of a particular god. Could the losing faction have migrated to the Yucatán and formed the ruling class of Chichén Itzá? Perhaps. What we do know for certain is that this myth of the eventual return of Quetzalcoatl became, in the hands of the Spanish, a powerful weapon of conquest.

The Conquest

In 1517, the first Spaniards arrived in Mexico and skirmished with Maya Indians off the coast of the Yucatán Peninsula. One of the fledgling expeditions ended in a shipwreck, leaving several Spaniards stranded as prisoners of the Maya. The Spanish sent out another expedition, under the command of **Hernán Cortez,** which landed on Cozumel in February 1519. Cortez inquired about the gold and riches of the interior, and the coastal Maya were happy to describe the wealth and splendor of the Aztec empire in central Mexico. Cortez promptly disobeyed all orders from his superior, the governor of Cuba, and sailed to the mainland.

He and his army arrived when the Aztec empire was at the height of its wealth and power. **Moctezuma II** ruled over the central and southern highlands and extracted tribute from lowland peoples. His greatest temples were literally plated with gold and encrusted with the blood of sacrificial captives. Moctezuma was a fool, a mystic, and something of a coward. Despite his wealth and military power, he dithered in his capital at Tenochtitlán, sending messengers with gifts and suggestions that Cortez leave. Meanwhile, Cortez negotiated his way into the highlands, always cloaking his real intentions. Moctezuma, terrified, convinced himself that Cortez was in fact the god Quetzalcoatl making his long-awaited return. By the time the Spaniards arrived in the Aztec capital, Cortez had gained some ascendancy over the lesser Indian states that were resentful tributaries to the Aztec. In November 1519, Cortez confronted Moctezuma and took him hostage in an effort to leverage control of the empire.

In the middle of Cortez's dangerous game of manipulation, another Spanish expedition arrived with orders to end Cortez's authority over the mission. Cortez hastened to meet the rival's force and persuade them to join his own. In the meantime, the Aztec chased the garrison out of Tenochtitlán, and either they or the Spaniards killed Moctezuma. For the next year and a half, Cortez laid siege to Tenochtitlán, with the help of rival Indians and a decimating epidemic of smallpox, to which the Indians had no resistance. In the end, the Aztec capital fell, and, when it did, all of central Mexico lay at the feet of the conquistadors.

Having begun as a pirate expedition by Cortez and his men without the authority of the Spanish crown or its governor in Cuba, the conquest of Mexico resulted in a vast expansion of the Spanish empire. The king legitimized Cortez following his victory over the Aztec and ordered the forced conversion to Christianity of this new colony, to be called **New Spain.** In the two centuries that followed, Franciscan and Augustinian friars converted millions of Indians to Christianity, and the Spanish lords built huge feudal estates on which the Indian farmers were little more than serfs. The silver and gold that Cortez looted made Spain the richest country in Europe.

The Colonial Period

Hernán Cortez set about building a new city upon the ruins of the old Aztec capital. Over the three centuries of the colonial period, Spain became rich from New World gold and silver, chiseled out by Indian labor. A new class system developed. Those born in Spain considered themselves superior to the *criollos* (Spaniards born in Mexico). Those of other races and the *castas* (mixtures of Spanish and Indian, Spanish and African, or Indian and African) occupied the bottom rungs of society. It took great cunning to stay a step ahead of the avaricious Crown, which demanded increasing taxes and contributions from its fabled foreign conquests. Still, wealthy colonists prospered enough to develop an extravagant society.

However, discontent with the mother country simmered for years. In 1808, Napoleon invaded Spain and crowned his brother Joseph king in place of Charles IV. To many in Mexico, allegiance to France was out of the question; discontent reached the level of revolt.

Independence

The rebellion began in 1810, when **Father Miguel Hidalgo** gave the *grito,* a cry for independence, from his church in the town of Dolores, Guanajuato. The uprising soon became a full-fledged revolution, as Hidalgo and Ignacio Allende gathered an "army" of citizens and threatened Mexico City. Although Hidalgo ultimately failed and was executed, he is honored as "the Father of Mexican Independence." Independence from Spain was finally achieved on September 28, 1821.

Political instability engulfed the young republic, which ran through a dizzying succession of presidents and dictators as struggles between federalists and centralists, and conservatives and liberals, divided the country. Moreover, Mexico waged a disastrous war with the United States, which resulted in the loss of half its territory.

Political instability persisted, and included a brief period where the control of the country was assumed by Archduke Maximilian of Austria, who accepted the position of Mexican emperor with the support of French troops, until he was captured and executed by a firing squad in 1867. His adversary and successor (as president of Mexico) was **Benito Juárez,** a Zapotec Indian lawyer and one of the great heroes of Mexican history. Juárez did his best to unify and strengthen his country before dying of a heart attack in 1872; his impact on Mexico's future was profound, and his plans and visions bore fruit for decades.

The Porfiriato and the Revolution

A few years after Juárez's death, one of his generals, **Porfirio Díaz,** assumed power in a coup. He ruled Mexico from 1877 to 1911, a period now called the "Porfiriato." He stayed in power through repressive measures and by courting the favor of powerful nations. With foreign investment came the concentration of great wealth in few hands, and social conditions worsened.

In 1910, Francisco Madero called for an armed rebellion that became the **Mexican Revolution** ("La Revolución" in Mexico; the revolution against Spain is the "La Guerra de Independencia"). Díaz was sent into exile. Madero became president, but was promptly betrayed and executed. For the next few years, the revolutionaries fought among themselves, until **Lázaro Cárdenas** was elected in 1934, instituting reforms that solidified the outcome of the Revolution. He implemented massive redistribution of land, nationalized the oil industry, and gave shape to the ruling political party (now the **Partido Revolucionario Institucional,** or **PRI**) by bringing a broad representation of Mexican society under its banner and establishing mechanisms for consensus building. Most Mexicans practically canonize Cárdenas.

Modern Mexico

The presidents who followed were noted more for graft than for leadership. The party's base narrowed as many of the reform-minded elements were marginalized. Economic progress, a lot of it in the form of large development projects, became the PRI's main basis for legitimacy. Though the PRI maintained its grip on power, it lost all semblance of being a progressive party.

In the years that followed, opposition political parties grew in power and legitimacy. Facing pressure and scrutiny from national and international organizations, and widespread public discontent, the PRI had to concede defeat in state and congressional elections throughout the '90s. Elements of the PRI pushed for, and achieved, reforms from within and greater political openness. This led to deep divisions between party activists, rancorous campaigns for party leadership, and even political assassination. The party began choosing its candidates through primaries instead of by appointment.

But in the presidential elections of 2000, Vicente Fox of the opposition party PAN won by a landslide. In hindsight, there was no way that the PRI could have won in a fair election. For most Mexicans, a government under the PRI was all that they had ever known. Many voted for Fox just to see whether the PRI would let go of power. It did, and the transition ran smoothly thanks in large part to the outgoing president, Ernesto Zedillo, who was one of the PRI's reformers.

Since then Mexico has sailed into the uncharted waters of coalition politics, with three main parties, PRI, PAN, and PRD. To the credit of the parties, the sailing has been much smoother than many observers predicted. But the real test will be weathering the economic slowdown that accompanied the downturn in the U.S. economy, and in carrying out the next presidential elections in 2006.

Building Blocks: Local Architecture

Mexico's artistic and architectural legacy reaches back more than 3,000 years. Until the conquest of Mexico in A.D. 1521, art, architecture, politics, and religion were intertwined. Although the European conquest influenced the style and subject of Mexican art, this continuity remained throughout the colonial period.

Pre-Hispanic Forms

Mexico's **pyramids** were truncated platforms crowned with a temple. Many sites have circular buildings, such as El Caracol at **Chichén Itzá,** usually called the observatory and dedicated to the god of the wind. El Castillo at Chichén Itzá has 365 steps — one for every day of the year. The Temple of the Magicians at **Uxmal** has beautifully rounded and sloping sides. Evidence of building one pyramidal structure on top of another, a widely accepted practice, has been found throughout Mesoamerica.

Architects of many Toltec, Aztec, and Teotihuacán edifices alternated sloping panels *(talud)* with vertical panels *(tablero)*. Elements of this style occasionally show up in the Yucatán. **Dzibanché,** a newly excavated site near Lago Bacalar, in southern Quintana Roo state, has at least one temple with this characteristic. The true arch was unknown in Mesoamerica, but the Maya made use of the corbelled arch — a method of stacking stones that allows each successive stone to be cantilevered out a little farther than the one below it, until the two sides meet at the top, forming an inverted V.

Throughout Mexico, carved stone and mural art on pyramids served a religious and historic function rather than an ornamental one. **Hieroglyphs,** picture symbols etched on stone or painted on walls or pottery, functioned as the written language of the ancient peoples, particularly the Maya. By deciphering the glyphs, scholars allow the ancients to speak again, providing us with specific names to attach to rulers and their families, and demystifying the great dynastic histories of the Maya. For more on this, read *A Forest of Kings* (1990), by Linda Schele and David Freidel, and *Blood of Kings* (1986), by Linda Schele and Mary Ellen Miller.

Carving important historic figures on freestanding stone slabs, or **stelae,** was a common Maya commemorative device. Several are in place at Cobá; Calakmul has the most, and good examples are on display in the Museum of Anthropology in Mexico City and the archaeology museum in Villahermosa. **Pottery** played an important role, and different indigenous groups are distinguished by their different use of color and style. The Maya painted pottery with scenes from daily and historic life.

Pre-Hispanic cultures left a number of fantastic painted **murals,** some of which are remarkably preserved, such as those at Bonampak and Cacaxtla. Amazing stone murals or mosaics, using thousands of pieces of fitted stone to form figures of warriors, snakes, or geometric designs, decorate the pyramid facades at Uxmal and Chichén Itzá.

Spanish Influence

With the arrival of the Spaniards, new forms of architecture came to Mexico. Many sites that were occupied by indigenous groups at the time of the conquest were razed, and in their place appeared Catholic churches, public buildings, and palaces for conquerors and the king's bureaucrats. In the Yucatán, churches at Izamal, Tecoh, Santa Elena, and Muná rest atop former pyramidal structures. Indian artisans, who formerly worked on pyramidal structures, were recruited to build the new buildings, often guided by drawings of European buildings. Frequently left on their own, the indigenous artisans implanted traditional symbolism in the new buildings: a plaster angel swaddled in feathers, reminiscent of the god Quetzalcoatl, and the face of an ancient god surrounded by corn leaves. They used pre-Hispanic calendar counts — the 13 steps to heaven or the nine levels of the underworld — to determine how many florets to carve around the church doorway.

To convert the native populations, New World Spanish priests and architects altered their normal ways of teaching and building. Often before the church was built, an open-air atrium was constructed to accommodate large numbers of parishioners for services. *Posas* (shelters) at the four corners of churchyards were another architectural technique unique to Mexico, again to accommodate crowds. Because of the language barrier between the Spanish and the natives, church adornment became more explicit. Biblical tales came to life in frescoes splashed across church walls. Christian symbolism in stone supplanted that of pre-Hispanic ideas as the natives tried to make sense of it all. Baroque became even more baroque in Mexico and was dubbed **Churrigueresque** or **ultrabaroque.** Exuberant and complicated, it combines Gothic, baroque, and Plateresque elements.

Almost every village in Mexico has the remains of **missions, monasteries, convents,** and **parish churches.** Many were built in the 16th century following the early arrival of Franciscan friars. Examples include the Mission of San Bernardino de Sisal in Valladolid; the fine altarpiece at Teabo; the folk-art *retablo* (altarpiece) at Tecoh; the large church and convent at Mani with its *retablos* and limestone crucifix; the facade, altar, and central *retablo* of the church at Oxkutzcab; the 16-bell belfry at Ytholin; the baroque facade and altarpiece at Maxcanu; the cathedral at Mérida; the vast atrium and church at Izamal; and the baroque *retablo* and murals at Tabi.

Religion, Myth, and Folklore

Mexico is predominantly Roman Catholic, a religion introduced by the Spaniards during the Conquest of Mexico. Despite its preponderance, the Catholic faith in many places in Mexico has pre-Hispanic undercurrents. You need only visit the *curandero* section of a Mexican market (where you can purchase copal, an incense agreeable to the gods; rustic beeswax candles, a traditional offering; the native species of tobacco used to ward off evil; and so on), or attend a village festivity featuring pre-Hispanic dancers, to understand that supernatural beliefs often run parallel with Christian ones.

Mexico's complicated mythological heritage from pre-Hispanic religion is full of images derived from nature — the wind, jaguars, eagles, snakes, flowers, and more — all intertwined with elaborate mythological stories to explain the universe, climate, seasons, and geography. Most groups believed in an underworld (not a hell), usually containing nine levels, and a heaven of 13 levels — which is why the numbers 9 and 13 are so mythologically significant. The solar calendar count of 365 days and the ceremonial calendar of 260 days are significant as well. How one died determined one's resting place after death: in the underworld (*Xibalba* to the Maya), in heaven, or at one of the four cardinal points. For example, men who died in battle or women who died in childbirth went straight to the sun. Everyone else first had to make a journey through the underworld.

Taste of the Yucatán: Local Cuisine

Authentic Mexican food differs dramatically from what is frequently served in the United States under that name. For many, Mexico will be new and exciting culinary territory.

Despite regional differences, some generalizations can be made. Mexican food usually isn't pepper-hot when it arrives at the table (though many dishes must have a certain amount of piquancy, and some home cooking can be very spicy, depending on a family's or chef's tastes). Chiles and sauces add piquant flavor after the food is served; you'll never see a table in Mexico without one or both of these condiments. Mexicans don't drown their cooking in cheese and sour cream, a la Tex-Mex, and they use a great variety of ingredients. But the basis of Mexican food is simple — tortillas, beans, chiles, and tomatoes — the same as it was centuries ago, before the Europeans arrived.

Throughout Mexico, you'll frequently encounter these basic foods. Traditional **tortillas** are of the corn variety — they are actually made from a paste of ground corn, water, and lime, called *masa.* This grainy dough is patted and pressed into flat round cakes, tortillas, or take on a variety of other shapes that hold meat or other fillings.

A **taco** is anything folded or rolled into a tortilla, and sometimes a double tortilla. The tortilla can be served either soft or fried. *Flautas* and *quesadillas* are species of tacos. For Mexicans, the taco is the quintessential fast food, and the taco stand *(taquería)* — a ubiquitous sight — is a great place to get a filling meal.

Chiles are also a staple in Mexico. Many kinds of chile peppers exist, and Mexicans call each of them by one name when they're fresh and another when they're dried. Some are blazing hot with only a mild flavor; some are mild but have a rich, complex flavor. They can be pickled, smoked, stuffed, stewed, chopped, and used in an endless variety of dishes.

As distinctive as the food itself is the meal system in Mexico. The morning meal, known as *el desayuno,* can be something light, such as coffee and sweet bread, or something more substantial: eggs, beans, tortillas, bread, fruit, and juice. It can be eaten early or late and is always a sure bet in Mexico. The variety and sweetness of the fruits is remarkable, and you can't go wrong with Mexican egg dishes.

In Mexico, the main meal of the day, known as *la comida* (or *el almuerzo*), is eaten between 2 and 4 p.m. Stores and businesses close, and most people go home to eat and perhaps take a short afternoon siesta before going about their business. The first course is the *sopa,* which can be either soup *(caldo)* or rice *(sopa de arroz)* or both; then comes the main course, which ideally is a meat or fish dish prepared in some kind of sauce and served with beans, followed by dessert.

Gods and Goddesses

Each of the ancient cultures had its gods and goddesses, and while the names might not have crossed cultures, their characteristics or purposes often did. Chaac, the hook-nosed rain god of the Maya, was Tlaloc, the squat rain god of the Aztecs; Quetzalcoatl, the plumed-serpent god/man of the Toltecs, became Kukulkán of the Maya. The tales of the powers and creation of these deities make up Mexico's rich mythology. Sorting out the pre-Hispanic pantheon and beliefs in ancient Mexico can become an all-consuming study (the Maya alone had 166 deities), so here's a list of some of the most important gods:

Chaac   Maya rain god.

Ehécatl   Wind god whose temple is usually round; another aspect of Quetzalcoatl.

Itzamná   Maya god above all, who invented corn, cacao, and writing and reading.

Ixchel   Maya goddess of water, weaving, and childbirth.

Kinich Ahau   Maya sun god.

Kukulkán   Quetzalcoatl's name in the Yucatán.

Ometeotl   God/goddess, all-powerful creator of the universe, and ruler of heaven, earth, and the underworld.

Quetzalcoatl   A mortal who took on legendary characteristics as a god (or vice versa). When he left Tula in shame after a night of succumbing to temptations, he promised to return. He reappeared in the Yucatán. He is also symbolized as Venus, the moving star, and Ehécatl, the wind god. Quetzalcoatl is credited with giving the Maya cacao (chocolate) and teaching them how to grow it, harvest it, roast it, and turn it into a drink with ceremonial and magical properties.

Tlaloc   Aztec rain god.

Between 8 and 10 p.m., most Mexicans have a light meal called *la cena*. If eaten at home, it is something like a sandwich, bread and jam, or perhaps a couple of tacos made from some of the day's leftovers. At restaurants, the most common thing to eat is *antojitos* (literally, "little cravings"), a general label for light fare. *Antojitos* include tostadas, tamales, tacos, and simple enchiladas, and are big hits with travelers. Large restaurants offer complete meals as well.

There are also some unique attributes to beverages in Mexico. All over the country you'll find shops selling *jugos* (juices) and *licuados* (smoothies) made from several kinds of tropical fruit. They're excellent and refreshing; while traveling, we take full advantage of them. You'll also come across *aguas frescas* — water flavored with hibiscus, melon, tamarind, or lime. Soft drinks come in more flavors than in any other country we know. Pepsi and Coca-Cola taste the way they did in the United States years ago, before the makers started adding corn syrup. The coffee is generally good, and **hot chocolate** is a traditional drink, as is *atole* — a hot, corn-based beverage that can be sweet or bitter.

Of course, Mexico has a proud and lucrative **beer**-brewing tradition. **Mezcal** and **tequila** come from the agave plant, which is not a type of cactus, but is actually a distant cousin of the lily. Tequila is a variety of mezcal produced from the *A. tequilana* species of agave in and around the area of Tequila, in the state of Jalisco. Mezcal comes from various parts of Mexico and from different varieties of agave. The distilling process is usually much less sophisticated than that of tequila, and, with its stronger smell and taste, mezcal is much more easily detected on the drinker's breath. In some places, it comes with a worm in the bottle; you are supposed to eat the worm after polishing off the mezcal. *¡Salud!*

Background Check: Recommended Books and Movies

Studying up on Mexico can be one of the most fun bits of "research" you'll ever do. If you'd like to learn a bit more about this fascinating country before you go — which we encourage — these books and movies are an enjoyable way to do it.

Books

For an overview of pre-Hispanic cultures, pick up a copy of Michael D. Coe's *Mexico: From the Olmecs to the Aztecs* (Thames & Hudson) or Nigel Davies's *Ancient Kingdoms of Mexico* (Penguin). For the Maya, Michael Coe's *The Maya* (Thames & Hudson) is probably the best general account. For a survey of Mexican history through modern times, *A Short History of Mexico* by J. Patrick McHenry (Doubleday) provides a complete, yet concise account.

John L. Stephens's *Incidents of Travel in the Yucatan, Vol. I and II* (Dover Publications) are considered among the great books of archaeological discovery, as well as being travel classics. The two volumes chart the course of Stephens's discoveries of the Yucatán, beginning in 1841. Before his expeditions, little was known of the region, and the Mayan culture had not been discovered. During his travels, Stephens found and described 44 Mayan sites, and his account of these remains the most authoritative in existence.

For contemporary culture, start with Octavio Paz's classic, *The Labyrinth of Solitude* (Grove Press), which still generates controversy among Mexicans. Lesley Byrd Simpson's *Many Mexicos* (University of California Press) provides a comprehensive account of Mexican history within a cultural context. A classic on understanding the culture of this country is *Distant Neighbors,* by Alan Riding (Vintage).

Maya Art and Architecture, by Mary Ellen Miller (Thames & Hudson), showcases the best of the artistic expression of this culture, with inter-pretations into its meanings.

For a wonderful read on the food of Mexico, pick up *Mexico, One Plate at a Time,* by celebrity chef and Mexico aficionado Rick Bayless (Scribner).

Movies

Mexico has served as a backdrop for countless movies. Here are just a few of our favorites, all available on DVD.

The 2003 blockbuster *Frida* starring Salma Hayek and Alfred Molina is not only an entertaining way to learn about two of Mexico's most famous personalities, but also of its history. The exquisite cinematography perfectly captures Mexico's inherent spirit of Magic Realism.

Que Viva México is a little-known masterpiece by Russian filmmaker Sergei Eisenstein, who created a documentary of Mexican history, politics, and culture, out of a series of short novellas, which ultimately tie together. Although Eisenstein's budget ran out before he could complete the project, in 1979 this film was completed by Grigory Alexandrov, the film's original producer. It's an absolute must for anyone interested in Mexico or Mexican cinema.

Like Water for Chocolate is the 1993 film based on the book of the same name by Laura Esquivel, filmed by the author's husband, acclaimed contemporary Mexican director Alfonso Arau. Expect to be very hungry after watching this lushly visual film, which tells the story of a young woman who suppresses her passions under the watchful eye of a stern mother, and channels them into her cooking. In the process, we learn of the traditional norms of Mexican culture, and a great deal of the country's culinary treasures.

Chapter 3

Choosing Where to Go in Mexico's Beach Resorts

In This Chapter
▶ Introducing Mexico's beach resorts
▶ Deciding which area to visit
▶ Examining the pros and cons of each destination

Mexico has a lot going for it in terms of attracting travelers: warm weather, miles and miles of coastline, and a location so close to the United States that sometimes it almost seems like a part of it. Although the official language is Spanish, the use of English is almost as common as Spanish in resort areas. A visit to Mexico can offer the experience of visiting a foreign country accompanied by many of the familiarities of home.

Mexico's beaches are generally spectacular. But they're also as varied as the country itself. Deciding which one is right for you depends a lot on what you're looking for in a vacation. As you read this chapter, think about what you really want in a destination. Romance? Family fun? Lively singles scene? And consider how you want to travel. Budget? Luxury? Somewhere in between? These considerations can help narrow down your planning. One thing's for certain — no matter what you're seeking, you can find at least one Mexican beach resort that fits the bill.

Because of Mexico's sheer size, covering more than one of its beach resorts in a single trip isn't practical, with the exception of the Riviera Maya, found south of Cancún. In this chapter, we help you decide which resort best matches your wish list. Although Mexico has many more beaches than you could possibly dream of exploring in one trip, in this book, we only include those with the easiest air access and the best services and facilities for tourism.

If you don't know where to begin in choosing between Acapulco and Cancún, or Los Cabos and Puerto Vallarta, don't worry. In this book, we tell you what you need to know to help you decide which destination is right for you. In this chapter, we give you a rundown of the highlights and drawbacks of each of Mexico's most popular beach resorts. Because the type of accommodations you want may determine where you go — or don't go — we also explain the different lodging options available at each destination.

Understanding the Lay of the Land

Mexico is a country known for both its geographical and cultural diversity. And, as a country with more than 13,000km (8,000 miles) of shoreline, you can choose between a quiet stretch of sand, a pounding surf break, or a dynamic beach resort with nonstop nightlife.

Mexico's beach resorts are located in one of three main regions of the country: the Caribbean coast, along the eastern seaboard; the Pacific coastline; or on Mexico's Baja Peninsula, an extension of California that is almost completely separated from mainland Mexico.

The eastern destinations are known for their crystalline waters, which border the coral reefs of the Caribbean, and flat, scrubby landscapes. This area was the land of the ancient Maya, and their impressive remains are close enough to the popular beach destinations to explore. The Pacific beach resorts tend to have mountainous backdrops and dramatic tropical jungles bordering cobalt blue waters. Baja's beach resorts combine a stunning desert landscape with oceans teeming with sea life.

Picking the Right Beach Resort

Although Acapulco was Mexico's first beach to attract international travelers, the white-sand beaches and nearby ruins have made Cancún the most popular choice in recent years. When hurricane Wilma hit Cancún in October 2005, travelers opened their minds to exploring other parts of Mexico, and the Pacific coast resorts experienced a surge in popularity, while Cancún recovered. Puerto Vallarta and Huatulco offer a strong dose of natural charm and ecotourism, and Los Cabos has become Mexico's mecca for golfers and fishermen. Ixtapa and Zihuatanejo, Cozumel, and Puerto Escondido offer a laid-back retreat beneath palm fronds and sunny skies, and the rapidly growing Riviera Maya region draws adventurers and relaxation-seekers alike. In a nutshell, each resort has its own look, character, and special something. The following sections are snapshots to help you focus on the resort that's right for you.

Also see "Mexico's Beach Resorts: The Scorecard," at the end of this chapter, for a concise rating of each aspect of the resort areas that we cover in this book. After you decide which amenities are the highest priorities, you can use the table to find the resort that most meets your particular wishes.

Choosing Cancún

Despite the severe hit it took from hurricane Wilma in October 2005, Cancún is Mexico's most popular beach resort, and the reason most people travel to Mexico. It perfectly showcases both the country's breathtaking natural beauty and the depth of its 1,000-year-old history. Cancún is also especially comforting for first-time visitors to Mexico because it offers a taste of life back home that makes foreigners feel instantly at ease in this beach resort.

Cancún offers an unrivaled combination of high-quality accommodations, dreamy beaches, and diverse shopping, dining, and nightlife. While the hurricane washed away the white sands in the resort's northern hotel zone, it broadened the beaches in the isle's southern region. An ambitious restoration program should pump enough sand back to the northern shores to restore its original beauty by late 2006.

The added lure of ancient culture is also evident in all directions. And the best part? Cancún is also a modern mega-resort. Even if you're a bit apprehensive about visiting foreign soil, you'll feel completely at home and at ease in Cancún. Many people speak English, vendors and stores accept dollars, the roads are well paved, and most lawns are manicured. Malls are the places for shopping and dining, and you quickly spot recognizable names for dining, shopping, nightclubbing, and sleeping.

Two principal parts comprise Cancún: **Isla Cancún (Cancún Island),** with a 23km-long (14-mile) strip of beachfront hotels reminiscent of Miami Beach, and **Ciudad Cancún (Cancún City),** on the mainland, with hotels to accompany the functional elements of any community.

Cancún, located on the Yucatán Peninsula, is also the departure point for wonderful day trips to the nearby islands of Cozumel and Isla Mujeres (Island of Women), where you can enjoy first-class diving, as well as the remains of ancient cultures.

If you're looking for an incredible introduction to Mexico's beaches and a Mexican-lite vacation while enjoying world-class shopping in a pampered environment, Cancún is your beach. (Check out the chapters in Part III for more detailed information on this resort.)

Top aspects of a vacation in Cancún include

- ✔ Great beaches of powdery, white sand and turquoise-blue water

- ✔ First-class facilities, modern accommodations, and tons of shopping and dining options

- ✔ Numerous outdoor activities including jungle tours, visits to Mayan ruins, and eco-oriented theme parks

- ✔ No need to worry about communication at this English language–friendly destination

But also consider the following:

- ✔ Cancún is so visitor-friendly that you may forget you're in Mexico and miss the Mexican experience altogether.

✔ Built for tourism, the prices in Cancún are higher than in most other Mexican beach resorts.

✔ The impact of Hurricane Wilma affected many hotels and attractions, so be sure to check on the status of openings prior to traveling through early 2007 to be sure your expectations for attractions and services will be met.

Diving into Cozumel

If underwater beauty is your most important criterion for choosing a beach, then Cozumel is a perfect pick. Considered by many to be one of the world's top-ten diving spots, few places can top the aquatic life of the waters surrounding this island. Hurricane Wilma hit Cozumel directly in October 2005, and among the damage done was breakage of the island's coral reefs. Still, there remains enough sub-sea beauty to dazzle you, but it will take several years to restore the aquatic environment to its previous splendor.

And when you come up for air, or if you're a nondiver, Cozumel has several inland attractions, a variety of watersports, a new golf course, and ample choices for dining and libations. As Mexico's most important port of call for cruise ships, Cozumel also has the best duty-free shopping and one of the largest selections of fine jewelry shops in the country. The island's one town, San Miguel, has a charming old-Mexico feel to it.

Cozumel has more budget-friendly accommodations and places to dine than newer, nearby Cancún. However, even though the island is really active during the day, it's generally a quiet place at night.

Just a 45-minute ferry ride away from mainland Mexico, Cozumel makes for a great jumping-off point for explorations along the Yucatán's coastline. Just across the channel from Cozumel is captivating Playa del Carmen, quickly growing in popularity due to its central location and funky-sophisticated charms.

In addition to being a diver's dream destination, staying in Cozumel can be like enjoying multiple beach resorts in one vacation! (Take a look at Chapter 14 for more on Cozumel.)

Top aspects of a vacation in Cozumel include

✔ World-class diving

✔ Secluded beaches to get away from it all

✔ Relaxed island atmosphere

✔ A short ferry trip away from the mainland's cultural and historical attractions

But also consider the following:

- ✔ The nightlife is almost nonexistent.

- ✔ Cozumel is super-casual; you won't find a dress-up place on the island.

- ✔ Stores tend to be more expensive than elsewhere because they cater to cruise-ship visitors.

- ✔ When the cruise ships arrive, Cozumel is very crowded.

Exploring the Riviera Maya

Cancún's popularity has given rise to a growing curiosity and desire to explore other parts of the pristine coastline to the south. New venues started popping up along the shoreline heading south to Tulum. Now officially dubbed the Riviera Maya, this stretch of peaceful places to stay is ideal for either more adventurous travelers or those who simply want to stay put in an all-inclusive enclave.

The hottest spot along the Riviera Maya is Playa del Carmen, which lies more than 64km (40 miles) south of Cancún. Playa — as locals refer to it — is a small town that's both funky and sophisticated. In the early '80s, Playa del Carmen was nothing more than the ferry landing for Cozumel, but it has since developed into an engaging resort town of its own merit, with powdery-sand beaches and an eclectic collection of lodging, dining, and shopping.

Playa seems to attract younger visitors who are looking for a combination of simplicity and variety. Recently, though, Playa has also attracted developers. As they rapidly change the beachscape to the north and south with the addition of mega-resorts, they're also changing Playa's previously playful vibe. But Playa still has enough of its original flavor to make it different from any other resort in the area.

South of Playa del Carmen lie a succession of commercial nature parks, planned resort communities, and a few rustic beach hideaways including Xcaret, Puerto Aventuras, Xpu-Ha, Akumal, Xel-Ha, and Tulum. This stretch of coast is also sprinkled with newly developed, all-inclusive resorts, and is seeing the most dynamic growth in tourism development in all Mexico.

If you love getting away from it all, the Riviera Maya is a natural choice for exploration and relaxation. (See Chapter 15 for more details.)

Top aspects of a vacation in the Riviera Maya include

- ✔ Beautiful beaches and an array of eco-parks ideal for nature lovers

- ✔ Favored by more adventurous travelers, some of whom have settled here to offer eclectic accommodations, shopping, and dining options

- ✔ Smaller crowds and lower prices

- ✔ All-inclusive haven with great savings if traveling with children

But also consider the following:

- ✔ Limited shopping and dining exist outside of Playa del Carmen.
- ✔ Nightlife? What nightlife? Unless you consider stargazing an aspect of nightlife.
- ✔ Without a rental car, you're stuck where you stay.

Playing in Puerto Vallarta

Puerto Vallarta is the place to go if you're looking to experience a beach resort with authentic Mexican flavor. Unlike other resorts, such as Cancún, Ixtapa, and Huatulco, Puerto Vallarta grew up around an original beach community. To this day, it has a seductively simple pace of life that's reflected in the warmth of its people and the spirit of the place itself.

Puerto Vallarta, with its traditional Mexican architecture and gold-sand beaches bordered by jungle-covered mountains, is currently the second most visited resort in Mexico (trailing only Cancún). Vallarta, as locals prefer to call it, maintains its small-town charm despite being home to sophisticated hotels, great restaurants, a thriving arts community, an active nightlife, and a growing variety of ecotourism attractions that range from mountain biking in the Sierra foothills to whale-watching.

Natural beauty and modern infrastructure aside, Puerto Vallarta is remarkable for the number of options it offers for different types of tourists. Whether you're a couple looking for a romantic getaway, a family trying to find a great value, or senior travelers in search of new shores to explore, Vallarta has something to fit everyone. This resort is also known for being very gay-friendly, and it has a selection of hotels, excursions, and nightlife options that cater specifically to same-sex couples.

If you're an avid golfer with family members who don't share your passion for the links, you can take advantage of the six championship-quality courses that are now available for play, making Vallarta an up-and-coming golf resort. And the resort provides ample activities for the non-golfers in your group.

With an ideal mix of modern services and traditional charms, Puerto Vallarta is both a great first-time introduction to Mexico and a wonderful place for those looking to explore more of this country's natural and cultural riches. (Look at the chapters in Part V for more on this area.)

Top aspects of a vacation in Puerto Vallarta include

- ✔ Considered Mexico's friendliest beach resort
- ✔ An authentic sense of community
- ✔ Ideal combination of natural beauty and modern infrastructure
- ✔ An epicurean's delight with more than 250 restaurants, as well as varied nightlife and great shopping

✔ Wide variety of lodging options to fit all tastes and pocketbooks

✔ Countless activities, including mountain biking, hiking, bird-watching, jungle trekking in ATVs, diving, snorkeling, ocean kayaking, and surfing

✔ Excellent and uncrowded golf courses

But also consider the following:

✔ The beaches, at least those in central Puerto Vallarta, aren't the best in Mexico. They feature a golden sand that's darker than most. However, the northern and southern shores offer exquisite options, and they're only a short distance away.

✔ The presence of numerous beach vendors and timeshare salespeople means that you'll have plenty of practice saying, "No, *gracias!*"

✔ The town is jam-packed during the major Mexican holidays — Easter, September 16, November 20, and Christmas — which means higher prices, fewer lodging opportunities, and tangled traffic.

Introducing Ixtapa and Zihuatanejo

If you can't decide between a modern beach resort and a typical Mexican seaside village, then consider Ixtapa and Zihuatanejo, located north of Acapulco on Mexico's Pacific coast. These side-by-side destinations offer the best of both worlds less than 7km (4 miles) from one another. Although they share common geography, they couldn't be more different in character. Ixtapa is a model of modern infrastructure, services, and luxury hotels, while Zihuatanejo — or Zihua, to the locals — is the quintessential Mexican beach village.

If you favor luxury over charm, opt for Ixtapa and take advantage of the well-appointed rooms in this pristine setting of great natural beauty. You can easily and quickly make the 7km (4-mile) trip into Zihuatanejo for a sampling of the simple life in this seaside *pueblo* (small town). However, if you prefer a more rustic retreat with real personality, settle in Zihuatanejo.

Although this dual destination is a good choice for the traveler looking for a little of everything, from resort-style indulgence to unpretentious simplicity, keep in mind that these two resorts are more welcoming to couples and adults than families with small children. A number of places are off-limits to children under the age of 16 — something of a rarity in Mexico.

Ixtapa and Zihuatanejo offer active days and relaxed evenings. During the day, you can choose between scuba diving, deep-sea fishing, bay cruises to remote beaches, and golfing. The nightlife in both towns borders on the subdued, but Ixtapa is the livelier of the two. The favored evening activity here tends to be a late dinner on the beach.

Enjoy a sense of two-for-one in this dual destination that's truly an optimal combo of the best of Mexican beach resorts. (See the chapters in Part VI for more on these two destinations.)

Top aspects of a vacation in Zihuatanejo include

- Beautiful beaches within a bay that ensures calm waters with ample stretches of sand for sun worshipers
- Traditional Mexican beach-town atmosphere
- Smaller, more unique accommodations in a variety of price ranges
- A casual, relaxed atmosphere
- One of the best-priced destinations in Mexico

But also consider the following:

- The nightlife is very quiet.
- Going to the beach sums up the daytime activity; however, you can take short trips to find horseback riding, bird-watching, and other, more active endeavors.
- It's among the least kid-friendly destinations in Mexico.
- The summers are extremely hot, and air-conditioning isn't prevalent.

Top aspects of a vacation in Ixtapa include

- Modern infrastructure and expansive beaches
- Larger chain hotels and nicely appointed accommodations
- Two good golf courses with some of the lowest greens fees in Mexico
- Enough variety in the nightlife, especially fun for the 20- and 30-year-old crowd

But also consider the following:

- It lacks the true "feeling" of being in Mexico.
- Mexican tourists can make the Easter and Christmas holidays crowded.
- Summers are very hot.

Getting acquainted with Acapulco

Acapulco is known for its sultry beaches for tanning during the day and its glitzy discos for partying at night. To this day, Acapulco has a non-stop, 24-hour-a-day energy, which clearly demonstrates why it was the largest and most renowned Mexican resort from the 1940s to the 1970s, when movie stars made it their playground. Although golf and tennis are played here with intensity, the real participant sport is the nightlife, which has made this city famous for decades.

Despite the seemingly decadent, nocturnal attractions, Acapulco is also a charmingly ideal place for a fun-filled family vacation. Many activities and destinations cater to children, including water parks, zoos, and exciting tours down a nearby river. Accommodations fit every budget, and, in the true spirit of Mexican family hospitality, children are welcome almost everywhere in town.

In addition to the broadest range of late-night entertainment in Mexico, this beach resort also has excellent airline connections, outstanding dining, and a wide array of daytime activities. You can stay at luxurious hillside villas, resort hotels, or modest inns on the beach and in the old center of Acapulco. It's got something for everyone.

Although the view of the bay is stunning, the bay's cleanliness is still somewhat in question, despite valiant efforts by city officials. The water's cleanliness is an important consideration if your ideal beach getaway includes tons of time in the ocean. If you plan on spending your afternoons in the sea, you may want to choose a different resort or, at least, a place located south of town in one of the areas fronting the Pacific Ocean rather than Acapulco Bay.

Acapulco is for you if you want to dine at midnight, dance until dawn, and sleep all day on a sun-soaked beach. (For more information, check out the chapters in Part VII.)

Top aspects of a vacation in Acapulco include

- ✔ Nightlife so hot it rivals the sunshine
- ✔ Unforgettable views of the breathtakingly beautiful bay
- ✔ An average of 360 days of sunshine per year
- ✔ Wide variety of lodging options
- ✔ Excellent air-travel connections

But also consider the following:

- ✔ The cleanliness of the bay remains questionable.
- ✔ The most popular resort with residents of Mexico City, it tends to fill up with city dwellers on weekends and major holidays.
- ✔ Acapulco has a somewhat outdated feel to it, and as a big city, it can seem less clean than other Mexican beach resorts.

Hanging out in Huatulco

The resort found farthest south along Mexico's Pacific coastline, Huatulco is the perfect place for those travelers who want to enjoy pristine beaches and jungle landscapes but would rather view them from a luxury-hotel balcony. If you want to enjoy nature's beauty during the day and then retreat to well-appointed comfort by night, Huatulco is for you.

The area offers undeveloped stretches of pure, white sands. Isolated coves lie in wait for the promised growth of Huatulco, which luckily, isn't occurring as rapidly as Cancún's expansion. Huatulco is a FONATUR development project that aims to cover 20,800 hectares (52,000 acres) of land. Of that area, more than 16,000 hectares (40,000 acres) are to remain as ecological preserves. (FONATUR is a government agency that develops strategic plans and assists in arranging financing for tourism development projects. It's the agency responsible for the site selection and planning of Cancún; Ixtapa and Los Cabos are other FONATUR destinations.)

Huatulco has developed a name because of its ecotourism attractions: river rafting, rappelling, and jungle hiking, to name a few. However, the shopping, the nightlife, and even the dining options outside the hotels are scarce, and what is available is high priced for the quality.

If you're especially drawn to snorkeling, diving, boat cruises to virgin bays, and simple relaxation, Huatulco fits the bill. (See Chapter 28 for more information.)

Top aspects of a vacation in Huatulco include

- ✔ Magnificent, unspoiled beaches where you can get away from it all
- ✔ Beautifully appointed accommodations
- ✔ Slow-paced, small-town atmosphere with modern infrastructure
- ✔ Plenty of eco-oriented activities such as river rafting, rappelling, and jungle hiking
- ✔ Water-lovers paradise with plenty of snorkeling, diving, and boating
- ✔ Superb service and friendliness from the locals

But also consider the following:

- ✔ The nightlife is almost nonexistent.
- ✔ The dining and shopping options are limited.
- ✔ Reaching Huatulco is more difficult than many resorts, and a limited number of direct flights service the area.
- ✔ It's slightly more expensive than other beach resorts in Mexico.

Kicking back in Puerto Escondido

Puerto Escondido — usually referred to as Puerto — is known for its great surf, breathtaking beaches, friendly locals, and inexpensive prices. Located just north along the Pacific coastline from Huatulco, Puerto Escondido is another "real" place — not a planned development — which gives it a unique and authentic character. And it almost seems as though the locals would rather keep the place small.

In addition to its legendary surf break, Puerto is increasingly gaining a reputation with travelers seeking both spiritual and physical renewal. Abundant massage and body-work services, yoga classes, and exceptional and varied vegetarian dining options — not to mention seaside tranquillity — are hallmarks of this resort. We consider it the single best beach value in all Mexico.

European travelers make up a significant number of the visitors, and hearing a variety of languages on the beach and in the bars is common. Puerto is also a place that younger travelers favor — and one of the few resorts that offers welcoming options for the backpack- and hammock-type of traveler.

Puerto is definitely the place for surf lovers, but it's also great for those who are looking for a funky, relaxed beach attitude infused with a cosmopolitan appreciation for espresso drinks and world music. (See Chapter 29 for details on Puerto Escondido.)

Top aspects of a vacation in Puerto Escondido include

- ✔ The best surfing beaches in Mexico

- ✔ The best overall value

- ✔ Vibrant nightlife with plenty of live music

- ✔ Simple atmosphere with no pretensions of being a grand place

- ✔ Plenty of healthful and healing-oriented services

But also consider the following:

- ✔ Accommodations are generally in independent inns that feature fewer services.

- ✔ Puerto Escondido isn't a resort that caters to children. That aspect, combined with a concern about the powerful ocean surf, makes this a destination that we don't recommend for family travelers.

- ✔ Challenging air access is the rule. It usually involves complicated connections through Mexico City and/or Oaxaca, which makes travel time lengthy.

Lazing in Los Cabos

What was once considered an offbeat outpost for only the most rugged of sportsmen and vagrants has somehow evolved into Mexico's most posh beach resort. Los Cabos, located on the Baja Peninsula just south of California, actually refers to three areas: the quaint town of **San José del Cabo,** the high-energy tourist enclave of **Cabo San Lucas,** and the 29km-long (18-mile) stretch of highway connecting the two, known as **the Corridor,** which is lined with luxury resorts.

Each town has its own distinct personality: San José is a gentrified version of a small Mexican town, and Cabo San Lucas is a party place that attracts the most visitors. Alternately known as "the end of the line" and "the last resort," Cabo San Lucas boasts a let-loose nightlife that frequently goes until breakfast the next morning. Cabo San Lucas, in particular, is so American-friendly that you may find you rarely get the chance to practice your Spanish, and dollars are accepted as readily as pesos. In fact, many visitors find that it feels more like an extension of Southern California than Mexico.

Although sportfishing originally took credit for putting Los Cabos on the map, golf is now the stronger attraction. The Corridor that connects the two "Cabos" has an impressive collection of championship golf courses interspersed at respectable distances among the gorgeous resorts dotting the coastline. Accommodations in the two bookend towns range from smaller inns to larger chain hotels.

The beaches are breathtaking — cobalt-blue ocean meeting terra-cotta desertscapes speckled with cacti. Surfing is challenging here, and the numerous inlets seem custom-made for sea kayaking. Favored landbound activities beyond golf include ATV tours and horseback riding.

 In terms of everything from taxis to dining out, Los Cabos is much more expensive than other Mexican beach resorts. One contributing factor is its remote location; other than the abundant seafood caught offshore, almost everything else needs to be trucked down the long peninsula. (The chapters in Part IX go into detail about Los Cabos.)

Top aspects of a vacation in Los Cabos include

- ✔ The sheer beauty of the combination of desert and seascapes
- ✔ Outstanding sporting opportunities, from the legendary sportfishing to premier golf, plus exceptional spas to take out the kinks
- ✔ No need to worry about speaking Spanish at this English language–and U.S. dollar–friendly destination

But also consider the following:

- ✔ It's indisputably Mexico's most expensive beach resort.
- ✔ If you plan on doing any exploring, you may need to consider renting a car because the distance from one "Cabo" to another is significant.
- ✔ You may feel more like you're in Southern California than Mexico; Los Cabos has become very Americanized.
- ✔ Despite the level of sophistication of the hotels (especially along the Corridor), the region's dining and nightlife options are lacking, and they're likely to appeal to a college-age crowd at best.

Table 3-1   Mexico's Beach Resorts: The Scorecard (3 points indicate the highest rating)

Points for:	Cancún	Cozumel	Riviera Maya	Puerto Vallarta	Ixtapa	Zihuatanejo	Acapulco	Huatulco	Puerto Escondido	Los Cabos
Luxury	3	1	1	2	3	2	2	2	1	3
Nightlife	3	1	1	3	1	1	3	1	2	3
Great food	2	1	1	3	2	1	3	1	2	2
Beaches	3	1	3	1	1	2	2	3	1	2
Bargain rates	1	2	2	3	1	3	2	1	3	1
Local color	1	2	1	3	1	3	3	1	3	1
Mexican culture	2	1	2	3	1	2	3	1	1	0
Golf	1	1	1	3	1	0	1	1	0	3
Senior appeal	2	1	1	3	1	1	1	1	0	3
Hiking	1	1	1	3	1	1	2	1	3	3
Natural beauty	2	3	3	3	1	2	1	3	3	3
Sightseeing	3	1	3	2	1	1	3	3	2	3
Diving/snorkeling	3	3	3	1	1	1	1	3	1	3
Watersports	3	2	2	3	3	3	2	3	3	3
Peace and quiet	1	2	3	1	2	3	1	3	3	2
Family friendly	3	1	3	3	3	2	3	2	1	3
Easy access	3	1	1	3	2	2	2	1	1	3

Chapter 4

Deciding When to Go

● ●

In This Chapter

▶ Understanding Mexico's weather
▶ Knowing the high and low travel seasons
▶ Planning your trip around festivals and special events

● ●

*M*exico's beach resorts enjoy sun-drenched and moderate winters, and they logically attract the most visitors when the weather at home is cold and dreary. However, almost any time of the year has its pros and cons for travel. In this chapter, we review what you can expect from the weather during different months of the year. We also highlight some of Mexico's most festive celebrations that you may want to plan your trip around.

Forecasting the Weather

Mexico has two main climatic seasons: a **rainy season** (May to mid-Oct) and a **dry season** (mid-Oct to Apr). The rainy season can be of little consequence in the country's dry, northern region, but the southern regions typically receive tropical showers, which begin around 4 or 5 p.m. and last a few hours. Though these rains can come on suddenly and be quite strong, they usually end just as quickly as they begin, and they cool the air for the evening. We favor the rainy season because that's when the landscape is at its most lush and tropical flowers are everywhere. The lightning flashes offshore also make for a spectacular show.

 Hurricane season — June through October — particularly affects the Yucatán Peninsula and the southern Pacific coast.

June, July, and August are very hot and humid on the Yucatán Peninsula, with temperatures rising into the mid-80s and 90s Fahrenheit (low 30s Celsius). Most of coastal Mexico experiences temperatures in the 80s in the hottest months. Very high summer temperatures are reserved for Mexico's northern states that border the United States. During winter months, temperatures average 70°F to 75°F (21°C–24°C) during the day and about 55°F to 65°F (13°C–18°C) in the evening, in most of the resorts in this book. Los Cabos is often cooler (50°F/10°C) during winter-month evenings.

Considering Mexico's Travel Seasons

Mexico has two principal travel seasons: high and low. The **high season** begins around December 20 and continues to Easter, although in some places the high season can begin as early as mid-November. The **low season** begins the day after Easter and continues to mid-December; during the low season, prices may drop between 20 percent and 50 percent. At beach destinations popular with Mexican travelers, such as Acapulco, the prices revert back to high-season levels during July and August, the traditional, national summer vacation period. Prices at inland cities seldom fluctuate from high to low season, but they may rise dramatically during the weeks of **Easter** and **Christmas.** In Isla Mujeres and Playa del Carmen, both on the Yucatán coast, the high season starts in mid-November as well, but they also have a "second" high season, in August, when many European visitors arrive. We mention all these exceptions in the relevant chapters that follow.

We find **November** to be the best month to travel to Mexico. The scenery is still green from the recently ended rainy season, and temperatures are just beginning to turn a bit cooler, which can produce crystal-clear skies. This is especially true in Los Cabos, when even the desert is in bloom. Crowds are also at a minimum, and you're likely to find some good deals.

One time you may want to avoid is **spring break.** You find the highest concentration of high-octane party crowds in Cancún, but Puerto Vallarta also gets its fair share of craziness. Frankly, why travel to see American youth behaving badly? Other times you may want to avoid are the weeks of Christmas and Easter. During these traditional Mexican holiday periods, both crowds and prices are at their highest, but the crowds consist more of families and couples than young and rowdy revelers.

Mexico's Calendar of Events

Mexicans are known for throwing a great party — *¡fiesta!* — and their love of fireworks is legendary. You may choose to plan your visit around a colorful national or religious celebration. Watersports enthusiasts may consider visiting during one of the numerous regattas and sportfishing festivals held at many of the resorts. Remember that during national holidays, Mexican banks and government offices — including immigration — are closed.

Mexicans celebrate Christmas and Easter similarly to the way they're celebrated in the United States, but Christmas is much more religiously oriented, and they place less emphasis on Santa and gift exchanges.

January/February/March

Día de Reyes (Three Kings Day) commemorates the three kings bringing gifts to the Christ child. On this day, children receive gifts, much like the traditional exchange of gifts that accompanies Christmas in the United States. Friends and families gather to share the *Rosca de Reyes*, a special cake. A small doll representing the Christ child is placed within the cake; whoever receives the doll in his or her piece must host a *tamales*-and-*atole* (meat or sweet filling wrapped in a corn husk and a hot drink) party the next month. January 6.

Music, dances, processions, food, and other festivities are features of **Día de la Candelaria (Candlemas)** and lead up to a blessing of seed and candles in a celebration that mixes pre-Hispanic and European traditions marking the end of winter. All those who attended the Día de Reyes celebration reunite to share *atole* and *tamales* at a party hosted by the recipient of the doll found in the *rosca*. February 2.

Día de la Constitución (Constitution Day) is a celebration in honor of the current Mexican constitution that was signed in 1917 following the Mexican Revolution of 1910. If you're in Mexico on this day, you find a parade wherever you are. February 5.

Carnaval (Carnival) is the last celebration before Lent, and it's celebrated with special gusto in Cozumel and in Mazatlán, north of Puerto Vallarta. Here, the celebration resembles New Orleans's Mardi Gras with a festive atmosphere and parades. Transportation and hotels are packed, so try to make reservations six months in advance and arrive a couple of days before the beginning of celebrations. Three days preceding Ash Wednesday and the beginning of Lent.

Benito Juárez was a reformist leader and a Mexican president who became a national hero. The national holiday honoring **Benito Juárez's birthday** is the same date as the **spring equinox,** an important celebration of the ancient Mexicans. In Chichén Itzá (chee-*chehn* eet-*zah*), the ancient Maya city located 179km (112 miles) from Cancún, the celebration of the first day of spring is particularly impressive. The Temple of Kukulcán — Chichén Itzá's main pyramid — aligns with the sun, and the shadow of the body of its plumed serpent moves slowly from the top of the building downward. When the shadow reaches the bottom, the body joins the carved-stone snake's head at the base of the pyramid. According to ancient legend, at the moment that the serpent is whole, the earth is fertilized to assure a bountiful growing season. Visitors come from around the world to marvel at this sight, so advance arrangements are advisable. Elsewhere, festivals and celebrations to welcome spring mark the equinox. In the custom of the ancient Mexicans, people perform dances and say prayers to the elements and the four cardinal points (north, south, east, west) in order to renew their energy for the upcoming year. Wearing white with a red ribbon is customary. March 21. (You can see the serpent's shadow at Chichén Itzá Mar 19–23.)

April/May/June

Semana Santa (Holy Week) celebrates the last week in the life of Christ from Palm Sunday through Easter Sunday with somber religious processions, spoofs of Judas, and reenactments of specific biblical events, plus food and craft fairs. Businesses close during this traditional week of Mexican national vacations. If you plan on traveling to or around Mexico during Holy Week, make your reservations early. Airline seats on flights into and out of the country are reserved months in advance. Buses to almost anywhere in Mexico are always full, so try arriving on the Wednesday or Thursday prior to the start of Holy Week. Easter Sunday is quiet. The week following is a vacation period. Week before Easter.

Labor Day is a national holiday celebrating workers. It features country-wide parades and fiestas. May 1.

Cinco de Mayo is a national holiday that celebrates the defeat of the French at the Battle of Puebla in 1862. May 5.

July/August/September

Mexico begins **Día de Independencia (Independence Day)** — the holiday that marks Mexico's independence from Spain — at 11 p.m. on September 15, with the president of Mexico's famous independence *grito* (shout) from the National Palace in Mexico City. The rest of the country watches the event on TV or participates in local celebrations, which mirror the festivities at the national level. September 16 is the actual Independence Day and is celebrated with parades, picnics, and family reunions throughout the country. September 15 and 16.

During the **fall equinox,** Chichén Itzá once again takes center stage as the same serpent shadow play that occurs during the spring equinox repeats itself for the fall equinox, representing the fall harvest. September 21 and 22.

October/November/December

What's commonly called the **Día de los Muertos (Day of the Dead)** is actually two days: All Saints Day, honoring saints and deceased children, and All Souls Day, honoring deceased adults. Relatives gather at cemeteries countrywide, carrying candles and food, and often spend the night beside the graves of loved ones. Weeks before, bakers begin producing bread formed in the shape of mummies and round loaves decorated with bread "bones." Decorated sugar skulls emblazoned with glittery names are sold everywhere. Many days ahead, homes and churches erect special altars laden with bread, fruit, flowers, candles, photographs of saints and of the deceased, and favorite foods and photographs of the deceased. On these two nights, children walk through the streets dressed in costumes and masks, often carrying mock coffins and pumpkin lanterns, into which they expect money to be dropped. November 1 and 2.

Día de Revolución (Revolution Day) is a national holiday commemorating the start of the Mexican Revolution in 1910 with parades, speeches, rodeos, and patriotic events. November 20.

During the **Día de Nuestra Señora de Guadalupe (Feast of the Virgin of Guadalupe),** people throughout the country honor Mexico's patroness with religious processions, street fairs, dancing, fireworks, and Masses. It's one of Mexico's most moving and beautiful displays of traditional culture. In December 1531, the Virgin of Guadalupe appeared to a young man, Juan Diego, on a hill near Mexico City. He convinced the bishop that he had seen the apparition by revealing his cloak, upon which the Virgin was emblazoned. In Puerto Vallarta, the celebration begins on December 1 and extends through December 12, with traditional processions to the church for a brief Mass and blessing. In the final days, the processions and festivities take place around the clock. A major fireworks exhibition takes place on December 12 at 11 p.m. December 1 to 12.

Christmas Posadas celebrates the Holy Family's trek to Bethlehem. On each of the nine nights before Christmas, people customarily reenact the Holy Family's search for an inn with door-to-door candlelit processions in cities and villages nationwide. December 15 to 24.

Part II

Planning Your Trip to Mexico's Beach Resorts

The 5th Wave   By Rich Tennant

"Do you mind <u>NOT</u> practicing your 'Olés!' while I'm vacuuming?"

In this part . . .

Ready to travel to Mexico? Well then, it's probably time
to do a little planning. In the next five chapters, we help
you with the basics you need to consider when booking your
ideal trip to one of Mexico's beach destinations. We give tips
and tricks for accurately planning your vacation budget.
Nothing can take away the pleasure of lazy days faster than
worries about spending too much money, so spend some
time here to ward away those stressful thoughts. We help you
decide whether to use a travel agent or to take care of the
arrangements on your own, cover the pros and cons of package deals, and point you in the direction of the best places to
find the information you need to accurately plan and budget
your trip. We also offer some tips for travelers with special
needs in order to help ensure that you choose exactly the
right place that fulfills both your personal requirements and
your expectations. Finally, we cover the nitty-gritty details —
from getting your passport to packing your bags — you need
to know so that you can enjoy a hassle-free vacation.

Chapter 5

Managing Your Money

In This Chapter

▶ Figuring out the expenses of your trip
▶ Discovering budget-saving tips
▶ Understanding Mexican currency
▶ Dealing with a stolen wallet

*T*he brochures are in front of you, and visions of lazy, sunny days fill your thoughts — so who wants to think about money? Trust me — take a few minutes to figure out your expected expenses now, so you can enjoy a worry-free vacation later.

Your budget is greatly affected by your choice of beach resort. An all-inclusive resort on the Riviera Maya costs more than a modest beach-side hotel in Acapulco. Within Cancún itself, a room on the beach of Isla Cancún is considerably more expensive than one in Cancún City (Ciudad Cancún), and ditto for all the other expenses down the line. After you decide where you want to go, and you have your hotel and airfare down, it's a good idea to calculate the other estimated costs associated with your trip to plan a proper budget.

Most people save all year to be able to enjoy a wonderful vacation, so in this chapter, we share with you the finer points of stretching your dollars into pesos. We tell you about the nuances of changing currency to get more for your money and present the pros and cons of traveler's checks, credit cards, and cash. Finally, we tell you how to regroup if your wallet is lost or stolen.

Planning Your Budget

To make certain that you don't forget any expenses, try taking a mental stroll through your entire trip. Start with the costs of transportation from your home to the airport, your airline tickets, and transfers to your hotel. Add your daily hotel rate (don't forget taxes!), meals, activities, entertainment, taxis, tips, your return to the airport, and finally, your return trip home from the airport and any parking fees you may have incurred. Just to be safe, add an extra 15 percent to 20 percent for extra, unexpected costs that may pop up.

You can use the notes page at the back of this book to jot down antici-pated costs so that you can easily see whether you need to trim any of your expenses. Or even better, you may discover that you can afford to slip into that oceanfront room or plan that sunset sail you've been dreaming of.

Calculating your hotel cost

The biggest part of your vacation budget will go toward your hotel and airfare, so we suggest getting those expenses down to as low as possi-ble. In the various destination chapters, we use dollar signs ($–$$$$$) to indicate the price category of each hotel. (Check out Chapter 7 of this book for a rundown on the price categories and their corresponding dollar signs.) You can get a room for $30 a night, or you can get a room for $700 a night!

Keep in mind that some room rates include breakfast — or all meals, beverages, and entertainment — so be sure to compare mangoes with mangoes. Also, when finalizing your reservations, be sure to check whether the total cost includes taxes and tips. Even within a resort, the price of rooms can vary widely.

Room location — oceanfront versus a view of a dumpster — is one dif-ferential. Ask yourself how much your room location matters. Do you view your room as simply a place to sleep, shower, and dress? Or will you not feel officially "on vacation" unless you can fall asleep to the sound of the surf? If so, a pricier room may well be worth it. However, remember that many "gardenview" rooms in our recommendations are only steps away from the beach and possibly even more tranquil than their oceanfront counterparts.

Feeling romantic? Special packages for **honeymooners** are really popular in Mexican beach resorts. Even if you've been hitched for a while, it could be a second honeymoon, right? If you ask, you may end up with a complimentary bottle of champagne and flower petals on your bed.

Mexico couldn't be more accommodating to travelers with children. Many of the larger chains don't charge extra for children staying in the same room as their parents, and some offer special meal programs and other amenities for younger travelers. While rollaway beds are common, you may have a challenge finding a crib. Ask about this contingency when making your reservation.

Totaling transportation costs

After taking care of your airfare (for tips on keeping airfare costs down see Chapter 6), your transportation costs vary depending upon your choice of Mexican beach resorts. While some areas — like Cancún — offer economical shuttles and great public transportation options, others, such as in Los Cabos, are more expensive to get to and have little in the way of local transportation once you've arrived at your resort, making a rental car desirable if you're the type of traveler who likes to explore. These extra charges, however, can make getting around cost even more than getting there.

One advantage of a **package** tour (when you make one payment that covers airfare, hotel, round-trip transportation to and from your accommodations, and occasionally meals or tours) is that the round-trip ground transportation between the airport and your hotel is usually included. If you're not sure whether your package covers ground transportation, ask. Note that the taxi union inside Mexico is strong, so you're unlikely to find any shuttle transportation provided by your hotel.

Generally, renting a car doesn't make sense, unless you're planning to explore on your own (the one exception for us is Los Cabos, due to the high taxi costs there). Renting a small car runs about $70 a day on average, including insurance, so you may want to squeeze your car-dependent explorations into a day or two at the most. You should also try to time your rental-car excursions to coincide with your arrival or departure so that you can use your wheels for either leg of your airport-hotel transportation needs.

As a rule, taxis tend to be the most economical and efficient transportation for getting around Mexico's beach resorts. In each of the chapters detailing these resorts, we provide taxi rates for getting around town.

Estimating dining dollars

In each resort's dining section, we describe our favorite restaurants, all of which include dollar signs ($–$$$$$) to give you an idea of the prices you can expect to pay. Refer to the Introduction of this book for a detailed explanation of these price categories.

The prices quoted refer to main courses at dinner, unless otherwise specified. we eliminated the most expensive shrimp and lobster dishes from our estimates to avoid pre-trip sticker shock. In most cases, you can find additional entrees above and below the quoted price range. To estimate your total dining expenses, add in estimated costs for beverages, appetizers, desserts, and tips as well.

Hotels increasingly are offering dining plans. To help you wade through the terminology, here's a review of the basics:

- ✔ **Continental plan (CP):** Includes a light breakfast — usually juices, fruits, pastries or breads, and coffee.

- ✔ **Breakfast plan (BP):** Includes a full, traditional American-style breakfast of eggs, bacon, French toast, hash browns, and so on.

- ✔ **Modified American plan (MAP):** Includes breakfast (usually a full one) and dinner.

- ✔ **Full American plan (FAP):** Includes three meals a day.

✔ **All-inclusive:** Includes three all-you-can-eat meals a day, plus
    snacks, soft drinks, alcoholic beverages, and entertainment, includ-
    ing special theme parties. Sometimes, additional charges apply for
    premium liquors or wines.

✔ **European Plan (EP):** No meals are included.

Mexican beach-resort hotels are known for their expansive breakfast
buffets. But the buffets can also be expensive, averaging about $20, even
for small children. If breakfast is your main meal or only meal of the day,
these all-you-can-eat extravaganzas may be worthwhile; otherwise,
you're probably better off sleeping in or finding breakfast elsewhere.

Be sure to explore restaurants away from your hotel. You're likely to get
a much better dining value, and you can truly savor the diverse flavors
of Mexico. For eateries that best represent the flavorful (and we don't
mean spicy) cuisine of Mexico, look for the Viva Mexico icon that accompanies some of the restaurant reviews throughout this book.

While you're in Mexico, be sure to try the local beers. Corona is the best-
known brew, but other excellent choices are Bohemia, Modelo Especial,
Pacífico, Indio, and Dos Equis Negro. Beer in Mexico is often cheaper
than soft drinks! Your vacation is looking better and better, isn't it?

Tipping tips

Many travelers skimp on tips in Mexico, but please don't. Most of the
employees in this country's hospitality industry receive the majority of
their income from tips. For bellmen or porters, the equivalent of $1 per
bag is appropriate. For hotel housekeeping, tip between $1 and $2 per
night, depending upon the type of hotel you're staying in. For restaurant
service, 15 percent is standard, but consider 20 percent if the service is
particularly noteworthy. Oddly enough, the one area you don't need to
consider tips for is taxis — it's not customary to tip taxi drivers here
unless they help with baggage, or you've hired them on an hourly basis
and they double as a tour guide.

You'll no doubt run into all sorts of enterprising young boys looking for
a tip to point you in the direction of your restaurant, help you into a
parking spot, or do some other sort of unnecessary favor. In cases like
these, tip as you see fit, or as the spirit moves you.

Sightseeing

You're going to a beach resort, so regardless of your budget, you always
have the option of simply soaking up the tropical sun during the day and
then taking in the moonlit nights. It's the most economical plan and a
relaxing and enjoyable option for many. Still, with so much to do and
see, you're likely to want to spend some time and money getting out and
enjoying the many treasures of Mexico.

Pricing for **sightseeing tours** varies by the destination, the length of time of the excursion, whether a meal and beverages are included, and other extras. However, we can give you some pretty typical ranges that you can use as a guideline. A city tour generally runs from $12 to $20; half-day boat cruises that include lunch can cost between $40 and $60; and full-day excursions to neighboring ruins run between $60 and $150.

If you plan to take part in any **sports-related activities** like golf, diving, or sportfishing, you may find the prices to be higher than back home. Dives range from around $50 to $70 for a two-tank dive, but here, you tend to really get what you pay for in terms of quality of equipment and dive guides, so it's best to pay up. Cozumel has the greatest selection of expert dive shops, and the competition makes Cozumel's prices the most reasonable for the quality of experience. Going fishing? You have to decide variables beyond your point of departure, including size of boat, charter options, and type of gear and refreshments, but count on between $50 and $75 per person for a half-day charter.

Shopping

If **shopping** is your call, you can plan to spend or save here. Besides silver jewelry and other souvenirs, the best excuse for shopping in Mexico are the great prices on duty-free perfumes, watches, and other goods in Cancún and in Los Cabos. We discuss shopping specialties in greater detail within the respective destination chapters.

Nightlife

As for **nightlife,** the cost depends more on your personal tastes. The "hot" nightlife spots among Mexico's beach resorts include Cancún, Puerto Vallarta, Acapulco, and Los Cabos, so if that's important to you, these are "the" spots in Mexico for you. When you're out on the town, beer is the best bargain and costs about $1 to $3 per beer. National-branded drinks can run you around $3 to $5 each. Ladies can easily find bargains like "two-for-one" or "all-you-can-drink" specials.

Cutting Costs — But Not the Fun

While planning your trip, you need to keep in mind certain things that may help you save some money. Before you leave for vacation, don't forget to consider the incidentals that can really add up — hotel taxes, tips, and telephone surcharges.

Here are a few other suggestions to help keep a lid on expenses so that they don't run amuck and blow your vacation budget:

 ✔ **Travel in the off season.** If you can travel at nonpeak times (Sept–Nov, for example), you can usually find better hotel bargains.

 ✔ **Travel on off days of the week.** If you can travel on a Tuesday, Wednesday, or Thursday, you may find cheaper flights to your destination. When you inquire about airfares, ask whether flying on a different day is cheaper.

✔ **Try a package tour.** With one call to a travel agent or packager, you can book airfare, hotel, ground transportation, and even some sightseeing for many of these destinations for a lot less than if you tried to put the trip together yourself. (See Chapter 6 for specific suggestions of package tour companies to contact.)

✔ **Always ask for discount rates.** Membership in AAA, frequent-flier plans, AARP, or other groups may qualify you for a discount on plane tickets and hotel rooms if you book them in the United States. In Mexico, you can generally get a discount based on how full the hotel is at the time you show up; however, you're also taking a chance on a vacancy not being available.

✔ **Get a room off the beach.** Accommodations within walking distance of the shore can be much cheaper than those that are right on the beach. Beaches in Mexico are public, so you don't need to stay in a hotel that's on the sand to spend most of your vacation at the beach.

✔ **Share your room with your kids.** In Mexico, this setup is usually the norm rather than the exception, so book a room with two double beds. Most hotels won't charge extra for up to two children staying in their parents' room.

✔ **Use public transportation whenever practical.** Not only will you save taxi fare, but simply getting to where you're going can be like a mini-excursion as you enjoy the local scene. For example, in Cancún, you're apt to run into mostly tourists on the clean, public buses of the hotel zone.

✔ **Cut down on the souvenirs.** We don't expect you to return home without any local treasures, but think hard about whether that oversized sombrero will be as charming back home. Your photographs and memories are likely to be your best mementos.

✔ **Use public phones and prepaid phone cards to call home.** Avoid using the phone in your hotel room to call outside the hotel. Charges can be astronomical, even for local calls. Rather than placing the call yourself, ask the concierge to make a reservation for you — they do it as a service.

You'll even be charged a surcharge for using your own calling card and its 800 number. Remember: Most 800 numbers are not toll-free when dialed from Mexico.

Also avoid using the public phones that urge you, in English, to call home using their 800 number. This ploy is the absolute most expensive way to call home, and the service charges the call to your home phone. The best option? Buy a Ladatel (brand name for Mexico's public phones) phone card, available at most pharmacies, and dial direct using the instructions in Appendix A of this book.

✔ **Drink local.** Imported labels can be twice the price of the locally popular brands, which often are also imported but just different brands from the ones you may be accustomed to seeing. At least ask what's being served as the house brand — you may be pleasantly surprised.

✔ **Follow Mexican custom and have lunch as your main meal.** If the restaurant of your dreams is open only for dinner, save that one for your one "splurge" evening and try out the others for your midday meal. Lunch tabs are usually a fraction of their dinner counterparts, and they frequently feature many of the same specialties.

✔ **Skimp on shrimp and lobster.** Sure, we know — you're sitting seaside and dreaming of that tasty lobster. Just understand that they're the priciest items on the menu, and the less expensive, local, fresh fish is often just as good or better.

✔ **Buy Mexican bottled water.** Forget the water labels that you know — Mexico's bottled waters are just as good as the imports and about half the price. Look for such brands as Santa María, Ciel, and Bonafont.

Making Sense of the Peso

The currency in Mexico is the **Mexican peso,** and in recent years, economists have been talking about its amazing recovery and resiliency against the U.S. dollar. At this book's time of print, each peso is worth close to 11 U.S. cents, which means that an item costing 11 pesos would be equivalent to US$1.20. Like most things in Mexico, the paper currency is colorful, and it comes in denominations of 20 (blue), 50 (pink), 100 (red), 200 (green), and 500 (burgundy) pesos. Coins come in denominations of 1, 2, 5, 10, and 20 pesos and 50 **centavos** (100 centavos equal 1 peso).

New 50- and 500-peso bills look very similar, but 50-peso bills have a slightly pinkish hue and are smaller in size. However, always double-check how much you're paying and your change to avoid unpleasant surprises. The same applies to 10- and 20-peso coins. Twenty-peso coins are slightly larger than the 10-peso coins, but they look very similar.

Getting change continues to be a problem in Mexico. Small-denomination bills and coins are hard to come by, so start collecting them early in your trip and continue as you travel. Shopkeepers — and especially taxi drivers — always seem to be out of change and small bills; that's doubly true in a market. In other words, don't try to pay with a 500-peso bill when buying a 20-peso trinket.

Before you leave your hotel, it's a good idea to get a hundred pesos — about US$9 — in change so that you're sure to have change for cab and bus fares.

In this book, we use the universal currency sign ($) to indicate U.S. dollars. When you're in Mexico, you'll notice the common use of the currency symbol ($), generally indicating the price in pesos. Go ahead and ask if you're not sure because some higher-end places do tend to price their goods in U.S. dollars. Often, if a price is quoted in U.S. dollars, the letters "USD" follow the price.

The rate of exchange fluctuates a tiny bit daily, so you're probably better off not exchanging too much currency at once. Don't forget, however, to have enough pesos to carry you over a weekend or Mexican holiday, when banks are closed. In general, avoid carrying the U.S. $100 bill, the bill most commonly counterfeited in Mexico, and therefore, the most difficult to exchange, especially in smaller towns. Because small bills and coins in pesos are hard to come by in Mexico, the U.S. $1 bill is useful for tipping. A tip of U.S. coins is of no value to the service provider because they can't be exchanged into Mexican currency.

 To make your dollars go further, remember that ATMs offer the best exchange rate; however, you need to consider any service fees. Mexican banks offer the next-best fare, and they don't charge commission, unless you're cashing traveler's checks, in which case they usually charge a small commission. After banks, *casas de cambio* (houses of exchange) are your next best option, and they usually charge a commission. You can almost always get a lower exchange rate when you exchange your money at a hotel front desk.

Choosing Traveler's Checks, Credit Cards, or Cash

You need to think about *what kind* of money you're going to spend on your vacation before you leave home.

ATMs and cash

These days, all the Mexico beach resorts detailed in this book have 24-hour ATMs linked to a national network that almost always includes your bank at home. **Cirrus** (☎ **800-424-7787;** www.mastercard.com/cardholderservices/atm) and **Plus** (☎ **800-843-7587;** www.visa.com/atms) are the two most popular networks; check the back of your ATM card to see which network your bank belongs to. The toll-free numbers and Web sites will give you specific locations of ATMs where you can withdraw money while on vacation. Using ATMs permits you to withdraw only as much cash as you need for a few days, which eliminates the insecurity (and the pickpocketing threat) of carrying around a wad of cash. Note, however, that a daily maximum of about US$1,000 is common, though this amount does depend on your particular bank and type of account.

As in many places worldwide, ATMs in Mexico are often targets for criminals looking to capture your bankcard information for fraudulent card-copying purposes. To be on the safe side, only use bank-sponsored ATMs, and even then, check the ATM carefully before using for any small cameras or other recording devices that could be used to copy your card. Shield the touchpad when entering your PIN for further protection against fraud.

Credit cards

Credit cards are invaluable when traveling. They're a safe way to carry "money," and they provide a convenient record of all your travel expenses when you arrive home.

Travel with at least two different credit cards if you can. Depending on where you go, you may find MasterCard accepted more frequently than Visa (or vice versa), American Express honored or refused, and so on.

You can get **cash advances** from your credit card at any bank, and you don't even need to go to a teller — you can get a cash advance at the ATM if you know your **PIN.** If you've forgotten your PIN or didn't even know you had one, call the phone number on the back of your credit card and ask the bank to send it to you. It usually takes five to seven business days, though some banks will do it over the phone if you tell them your mother's maiden name or some other security clearance.

Remember the hidden expense to contend with when borrowing cash from a credit card: Interest rates for cash advances are often significantly higher than rates for credit-card purchases. More importantly, you start paying interest on the advance *the moment you receive the cash.* On an airline-affiliated credit card, a cash advance does not earn frequent-flier miles.

Traveler's checks

Traveler's checks are something of an anachronism from the days when people wrote personal checks instead of going to an ATM. Because you could replace traveler's checks if lost or stolen, they were a sound alternative to filling your wallet with cash at the beginning of a trip.

Still, if you prefer the security of traveler's checks, you can get them at almost any bank. **American Express** offers checks in denominations of $20, $50, $100, $500, and $1,000. You pay a service charge ranging from 1 percent to 4 percent, though AAA members can obtain checks without a fee at most AAA offices. You can also get American Express traveler's checks over the phone by calling ☎ **800-221-7282.**

Visa (☎ **800-227-6811**) also offers traveler's checks, available at Citibank locations across the country and at several other banks. The service charge ranges between 1.5 percent and 2 percent; checks come in denominations of $50, $100, $500, and $1,000. **MasterCard** also offers traveler's checks; call ☎ **800-223-9920** for a location near you.

Although traveler's checks are very safe, you should consider that:

- ✔ You usually get charged a commission to cash your traveler's checks, and when you add that to the exchange-rate loss, you end up getting fewer pesos for your money.

- ✔ Many smaller shops don't take traveler's checks, so if you plan to shop, cash the traveler's checks before you embark on your shopping expedition.

Taxing Matters

There's a 15 percent **value-added tax (IVA)** on goods and services in most of Mexico, and it's supposed to be included in the posted price. This tax is 10 percent in Cancún, Cozumel, and Los Cabos. Unlike other countries (Canada and Spain, for example), Mexico doesn't refund this tax when visitors leave the country, so you don't need to hang on to those receipts for tax purposes.

All published prices you encounter in your travels around Mexico's beaches are likely to include all applicable taxes, except for hotel rates, which are usually published without the 15 percent IVA and the 2 percent lodging tax.

An **exit tax** of approximately $18 is imposed on every foreigner leaving Mexico. This tax is usually — but not always — included in the price of airline tickets. Be sure to reserve at least this amount in cash for your departure day if you're not certain that it's included in your ticket price.

Dealing with a Lost or Stolen Wallet

Odds are that if your wallet is gone, you've seen the last of it, and the police aren't likely to recover it for you. However, after you realize it's gone and you cancel your credit cards, you need to inform the police. You may need the police-report number for credit-card or insurance purposes later. After you've covered all the formalities and before you head to the nearest bar to drown your sorrows, retrace your steps — you may be surprised at how many honest people are in Mexico, and you're likely to discover someone trying to find you to return your wallet.

Be sure to contact all of your credit-card companies the minute you discover your wallet has been lost or stolen and file a report at the nearest police precinct. Your credit-card company or insurer may require a police report number or record of the loss. Most credit-card companies have an emergency toll-free number to call if your card is lost or stolen; they may be able to wire you a cash advance immediately or deliver an emergency credit card in a day or two. Call the following emergency numbers in the United States:

- ✔ **American Express** ☎ **800-221-7282** (for cardholders and traveler's check holders)
- ✔ **MasterCard** ☎ **800-307-7309** or 636-722-7111
- ✔ **Visa** ☎ **800-847-2911** or 410-581-9994

For other credit cards, call the toll-free number directory at ☎ **800-555-1212.**

To dial a U.S. toll-free number from inside Mexico, you must dial 001-880 and then the last seven digits of the toll-free number.

If you opt to carry **traveler's checks,** be sure to keep a record of their serial numbers so that you can handle this type of emergency.

If you need emergency cash over the weekend when all banks and American Express offices are closed, you can have money wired to you via **Western Union** (☎ **800-325-6000;** www.westernunion.com).

Identity theft or fraud are potential complications of losing your wallet, especially if you've lost your driver's license along with your cash and credit cards. Notify the major credit-reporting bureaus immediately; placing a fraud alert on your records may protect you against liability for criminal activity. The three major U.S. credit-reporting agencies are **Equifax** (☎ **800-766-0008;** www.equifax.com), **Experian** (☎ **888-397-3742;** www.experian.com), and **TransUnion** (☎ **800-680-7289;** www.transunion.com). Finally, if you've lost all forms of photo ID call your airline and explain the situation; they might allow you to board the plane if you have a copy of your passport or birth certificate and a copy of the police report you've filed.

Chapter 6

Getting to Mexico's Beach Resorts

In This Chapter

▶ Taking a look at airlines and airfares

▶ Understanding package tours

*T*he obvious first step in enjoying your Mexican beach vacation is getting there. It's easy to do, but the options available can make a big
difference in the price you'll pay. To help minimize both the cost and the
time it will take to arrive, in this chapter, we point you in the direction of
available planning tools—including the Internet—and explain the benefits and limitations of traveling on a package tour. We offer tips on getting the best airfares and choosing the best airline to whisk you away to
your dreamy beach in Mexico.

Flying to Mexico's Beach Resorts

The first step for the independent travel planner is finding the airlines
that fly to the Mexico beach resort of your choice. Mexico is becoming
more easily accessible by plane, buoyed by its popularity as a nearby,
safe, and attractive place to travel. Many new regional carriers offer
scheduled service to areas previously not served. In addition to regularly scheduled service, direct charter services from U.S. cities to
Mexico's most popular destinations are making it possible to fly direct
from the largest airports in the United States. However, if you find that
no direct flights are available, you can always reach your destination
through an almost painless connection in Mexico City.

If you're booked on a flight through Mexico City, make sure your luggage
is checked through to your final destination. This arrangement is possible if you're flying with affiliated or code-share airlines — separate airlines that work closely together to help travelers reach final destinations
via connecting flights. This way, you don't have to lug your bags through
the Mexico City airport, and it saves a lot of time during the connecting
process.

For information about saving money on airfares using the Internet, see "Researching and Booking Your Trip Online," later in this chapter.

The main airlines operating direct or nonstop flights to points in Mexico include

- ✔ **Aeroméxico** (☎ **800-237-6639**; www.aeromexico.com). Flights to Cancún, Puerto Vallarta, Ixtapa/Zihuatanejo, Acapulco, Los Cabos, Huatulco.

- ✔ **Air Canada** (☎ **888-247-2262**; www.aircanada.ca). Flights to Cancún, Cozumel, Huatulco, Puerto Vallarta, Los Cabos, Ixtapa/Zijuatanejo, Mazatlán.

- ✔ **Alaska Airlines** (☎ **800-252-7522**; www.alaskaair.com). Flights to Cancún, Ixtapa, Puerto Vallarta, Los Cabos, Mazatlán, Manzanillo.

- ✔ **American Airlines** (☎ **800-223-5436**; www.aa.com). Flights to Cancún/Cozumel, Huatulco, Ixtapa/Zihuatanejo, PuertoVallarta, Acapulco, Los Cabos, Mazatlán.

- ✔ **America West** (☎ **800-327-7810**; www.americawest.com). Flights to Cancún, Cozumel, Ixtapa, Puerto Vallarta, Acapulco, Los Cabos, Mazatlán, Manzanillo.

- ✔ **ATA Airlines** (☎ **800-I-FLY-ATA**; www.ata.com). Flights to Cancún.

- ✔ **British Airways** (☎ **800-247-9297**, or 0345-222-111 or 0870-85-098-50 in Britain; www.britishairways.com). Flights to Cancún (from London).

- ✔ **Continental Airlines** (☎ **800-537-9222**; www.continental.com). Flights to Cancún/Cozumel, Puerto Vallarta, Acapulco, Huatulco, Ixtapa/Zijuatanejo, Los Cabos, Mazatlán, Manzanillo.

- ✔ **Delta** (☎ **800-221-1212**; www.delta.com). Flights to Cancún/Cozumel (serviced by Aeroméxico), Puerto Vallarta, Acapulco, Los Cabos, Ixtapa/Zihuatanejo.

- ✔ **Frontier Airlines** (☎ **800-432-1359**; www.frontierairlines.com). Flights to Los Cabos, Cancún, Cozumel, Puerto Vallarta, Ixtapa/Zihuatanejo, Mazatlán.

- ✔ **Mexicana** (☎ **800-531-7921**; www.mexicana.com). Flights to Cancún, Cozumel, Puerto Vallarta, Ixtapa/Zihuatanejo, Acapulco, Huatulco, Los Cabos, Mazatlán, Manzanillo.

- ✔ **Northwest Airlines** (☎ **800-225-2525**; www.nwa.com). Seasonal flights to Cancún/Cozumel, Puerto Vallarta, Los Cabos.

- ✔ **US Airways** (☎ **800-428-4322**; www.usairways.com). Flights to Cancún/Cozumel.

Competition among the major U.S. airlines is unlike that of any other industry. A coach seat is virtually the same from one carrier to another, yet the difference in price may run as high as $1,000 for a product with the same intrinsic value.

Business travelers, who need flexibility to purchase their tickets at the last minute, change their itinerary at a moment's notice, or want to get home before the weekend, pay the premium rate, known as the *full fare.* Passengers who can book their ticket long in advance, who don't mind staying over Saturday night, or who are willing to travel on a Tuesday, Wednesday, or Thursday pay the least — usually a fraction of the full fare. On most flights, even the shortest hops, the full fare is close to $1,000 or more, but a 7- or 14-day advance purchase ticket is closer to $200 to $300. Obviously, it pays to plan.

The airlines also periodically hold sales, in which they lower the prices on their most popular routes. These fares have advance purchase requirements and date-of-travel restrictions, but you can't beat the price: usually no more than $400 for a cross-country flight. Keep your eyes open for these sales as you're planning your vacation. The sales tend to take place in seasons of low travel volume. You almost never see a sale around the peak Thanksgiving or Christmas periods, when people have to fly, regardless of what the fare is.

Consolidators, also known as bucket shops, are great sources for international tickets, although they usually can't beat the Internet on fares within North America. Start by looking in Sunday newspaper travel sections; U.S. travelers should focus on the *New York Times, Los Angeles Times,* and *Miami Herald.* For less-developed destinations, small travel agents who cater to immigrant communities in large cities often have the best deals.

Bucket shop tickets are usually nonrefundable or rigged with stiff cancellation penalties, often as high as 50 percent to 75 percent of the ticket price, and some put you on charter airlines with questionable safety records.

Several reliable consolidators are worldwide and available on the Net. **STA Travel** (☎ 800-781-4040; www.statravel.com), the world's leader in student travel, offers good fares for travelers of all ages. **Flights.com** (☎ 800-TRAV-800; www.flights.com) has excellent fares worldwide and "local" Web sites in 12 countries. **FlyCheap** (☎ 800-FLY-CHEAP; www.1800flycheap.com) is owned by package-holiday megalith MyTravel and so has especially good access to fares for sunny destinations. **Air Tickets Direct** (☎ 800-778-3447; www.airticketsdirect.com) is based in Montreal and leverages the currently weak Canadian dollar for low fares; it'll also book trips to places that U.S. travel agents won't touch, such as Cuba.

Here are some travel tips — tested and true — for getting the lowest possible fare:

✔ **Timing is everything.** If you can, avoid peak travel times. In Mexico, the weeks surrounding the Christmas/New Year holidays and Easter are so jam-packed that we find it unenjoyable to be at a beach resort anyway. Airfares are relatively expensive anytime between January and May, with September through mid-November offering the best deals. Specials pop up throughout the year, however, based on current demand, and last-minute specials on package tours are an increasingly popular way to travel.

✔ **Book in advance for great deals.** Forgetting what we said in the previous sentence, you can also save big by booking early — with excellent fares available for 30-, 60-, or even 90-day advance bookings. Note that if you need to change your schedule, a penalty charge of $75 to $150 is common.

✔ **Choose an off-peak travel day.** Traveling on a Tuesday, Wednesday, or even Thursday can also save you money. Even if you can't travel both ways on these lower-fare days, you can still save by flying off-peak at least one way.

✔ **The midnight hour.** In the middle of the week, just after midnight, many airlines download cancelled low-priced airfares into their computers, so shortly after midnight is a great time to buy newly discounted seats. Midnight is the cutoff time for holding reservations. You may benefit by snagging cheap tickets that were just released by those who reserved — but never purchased — their tickets.

Researching and Booking Your Trip Online

The "big three" online travel agencies, **Expedia** (www.expedia.com), **Travelocity** (www.travelocity.com), and **Orbitz** (www.orbitz.com) sell most of the air tickets bought on the Internet. (Canadian travelers should try www.expedia.ca and www.travelocity.ca; U.K. residents can go for expedia.co.uk and opodo.co.uk.) Each has different business deals with the airlines and may offer different fares on the same flights, so shopping around is wise. Expedia and Travelocity will also send you an **e-mail notification** when a cheap fare becomes available to your favorite destination. Of the smaller travel agency Web sites, **SideStep** (www.sidestep.com) receives good reviews from users. It's a browser add-on that purports to "search 140 sites at once," but in reality only beats competitors' fares as often as other sites do.

Great **last-minute deals** are available through free weekly e-mail services provided directly by the airlines. Most of these deals are announced on Tuesday or Wednesday and must be purchased online. Most are only valid for travel that weekend, but some (such as Southwest's) can be booked weeks or months in advance. Sign up for weekly e-mail alerts at airline Web sites or check mega-sites that compile comprehensive lists of last-minute specials, such as **Smarter Travel** (www.smartertravel.com).

For last-minute trips, www.site59.com in the U.S. and www.last minute.com in Europe often have better deals than the major-label sites.

If you're willing to give up some control over your flight details, use an *opaque fare service* like **Priceline** (www.priceline.com) or **Hotwire** (www.hotwire.com). Both offer rock-bottom prices in exchange for travel on a "mystery airline" at a mysterious time of day, often with a mysterious change of planes en route. The mystery airlines are all major, well-known carriers — and the possibility of being sent from Philadelphia to Chicago via Tampa is remote. But your chances of getting a 6 a.m. or 11 p.m. flight are pretty high. Hotwire tells you flight prices before you buy; Priceline usually has better deals than Hotwire, but you have to play their "name our price" game. *Note:* In 2004 Priceline added non-opaque service to its roster. You now have the option to pick exact flights, times, and airlines from a list of offers — or opt to bid on opaque fares as before.

Great last-minute deals are also available directly from the airlines themselves through a free e-mail service called *E-savers*. Each week, the airline sends you a list of discounted flights, usually leaving the upcoming Friday or Saturday and returning the following Monday or Tuesday. You can sign up for all the major airlines at one time by logging on to **Smarter Travel** (www.smartertravel.com), or you can go to each individual airline's Web site. Airline sites also offer schedules, flight booking, and information on late-breaking bargains.

The good news is that you don't even have to book your trip online to reap the research benefits of the Web. The Internet can be a valuable tool for comparison shopping, for approaching a travel agent with a base of knowledge, and even for chatting with other travelers to truly rate the quality of the buffets at that all-inclusive you may be considering.

Understanding Escorted and Package Tours

First, bear in mind that there's a big difference between an escorted tour and a package tour. With an *escorted tour,* the tour company takes care of all the details and tells you what to expect at each attraction. You know your costs up front, and an escorted tour can take you to the maximum number of sights in the minimum amount of time with the least amount of hassle. However, escorted tours are extremely rare in Mexico's beach resorts; most travelers, once they arrive at their destination, simply book tours and excursions with local travel agents.

Package tours generally consist of round-trip airfare, ground transportation to and from your hotel, and your hotel room price, including taxes. Some packages also include all food and beverages and most entertainment and sports, when booked at an all-inclusive resort. You may find that a package tour can save you big bucks and is an ideal vacation option.

For popular destinations like Cancún and Puerto Vallarta, package tours are the smart way to go. In many cases, a package that includes airfare, hotel, and transportation to and from the airport costs less than just the hotel alone if you booked it yourself. That's because packages are sold in bulk to tour operators who resell them to the public. It's kind of like buying your vacation at one of those large, members-only warehouse clubs — except the tour operator is the one who buys the 1,000-count box of garbage bags and resells them 10 at a time at a cost that undercuts what you'd pay at your average, neighborhood supermarket.

Package tours can vary as much as those garbage bags, too. Some offer a better class of hotels than others. Some offer the same hotels for lower prices. Some offer flights on scheduled airlines; others book charter planes (which are known for having miniscule amounts of legroom). In some packages, your choice of accommodations and travel days may be limited. Some tours let you choose between escorted vacations and independent vacations; others allow you to add on just a few excursions or escorted day trips (also at discounted prices) without booking an entirely escorted tour.

Each destination usually has one or two packagers that are better than the rest because they buy in even bigger bulk. The time you spend shopping around will be well rewarded.

To find package tours, check out the travel section of your local Sunday newspaper or the ads in the back of national travel magazines such as *Travel & Leisure, National Geographic Traveler,* and *Condé Nast Traveler.* **Liberty Travel** (call ☎ **888-271-1584** to find the store nearest you; www.libertytravel.com) is one of the biggest packagers in the Northeast, and usually boasts a full-page ad in Sunday papers.

Other good sources of package deals are the airlines themselves. Most major airlines offer air/land packages, including **Aeroméxico Vacations** (☎ 800-245-8585; www.aeromexico.com), **Alaska Airlines Vacations** (☎ 800-468-2248; www.alaskaair.com), **American Airlines Vacations** (☎ 800-321-2121; www.aavacations.com), **America West Vacations** (☎ 800-2-FLY-AWV; www.americawestvacations.com), **Delta Vacations** (☎ 800-221-6666; www.deltavacations.com), **Continental Airlines Vacations** (☎ 800-301-3800; www.covacations.com), **Mexicana Vacations** (☎ 800-531-7921; www.mexicana.com), and **United Vacations** (☎ 888-854-3899; www.unitedvacations.com). Several big **online travel agencies** — Expedia, Travelocity, Orbitz, Site59, and Lastminute.com — also do a brisk business in packages. If you're unsure about the pedigree of a smaller packager, check with the Better Business Bureau in the city where the company is based, or go online at www.bbb.org. If a packager won't tell you where it's based, don't fly with them.

You can even shop for these packages online — try these sites for a start:

- ✔ One specialist in Mexico vacation packages is www.mexico travelnet.com, an agency that offers most of the well-known travel packages to Mexico beach resorts, plus offers last-minute specials.

- ✔ Check out www.2travel.com and find a page with links to a number of the big-name Mexico packagers, including several of the ones listed in this chapter.

- ✔ For last-minute, air-only packages or package bargains, check out **Vacation Hot Line** at www.vacationhotline.net. After you find your "deal," you need to call them to make final booking arrangements, but they offer packages from both the popular Apple and Funjet vacation wholesalers.

Several companies specialize in packages to Mexico's beaches; they usually fly in their own, chartered airplanes, so they can offer greatly discounted rates. Here are some of the packagers we prefer:

- ✔ **Apple Vacations** (☎ 800-365-2775; www.applevacations.com) offers inclusive packages to all the beach resorts and has the largest choice of hotels in Acapulco, Cancún, Cozumel, Huatulco, Ixtapa/Zihuatanejo, Los Cabos, Puerto Vallarta, and the Riviera Maya. Their packages are available only through travel agents. Apple perks include baggage handling and the services of an Apple representative at the major hotels. Note that Apple vacations must be booked through a travel agent, but both their Web site and toll-free number will easily connect you with one nearby you.

- ✔ **Classic Custom Vacations** (☎ 800-635-1333; www.classiccustom vacations.com) specializes in package vacations to Mexico's finest luxury resorts. It combines discounted first-class and economy airfare on American, Continental, Mexicana, Alaska, America West, and Delta with stays at the most exclusive hotels in Mexico's beach resorts. In many cases, packages also include meals, airport transfers, and upgrades. The prices are not for bargain hunters but for those who seek luxury, nicely packaged.

- ✔ **Funjet Vacations** (bookable through any travel agent, with general information available on its Web site at www.funjet.com) is one of the largest vacation packagers in the United States. Funjet has packages to Acapulco, Cancún, Cozumel, the Riviera Maya, Huatulco, Los Cabos, Ixtapa/Zihuatanejo, and Puerto Vallarta.

- ✔ **GOGO Worldwide Vacations** (☎ 888-636-3942; www.gogowwv.com) has trips to all the major beach destinations, including Acapulco, Cancún, Puerto Vallarta, and Los Cabos, offering several exclusive deals from higher-end hotels. These trips are bookable through any travel agent.

✔ **Pleasant Mexico Holidays** (☎ 800-448-3333; `www.pleasant holidays.com`) is another of the largest vacation packagers in the United States with hotels in Acapulco, Cancún, Cozumel, Ixtapa/ Zihuatanejo, Los Cabos, and Puerto Vallarta.

The biggest hotel chains and resorts also offer packages. If you already know where you want to stay, call the hotel or resort and ask whether it offers land/air packages.

Chapter 7

Booking Your Accommodations

● ●

In This Chapter

▶ Choosing a room that's right for you

▶ Surfing for hotel rooms

▶ Getting the best room at the best rate

● ●

*W*hether you've chosen a package deal or you're planning your trip on your own, getting a room is a crucial part of your vacation planning. In this chapter, we help you decipher the various rates and provide some tips on how to get the best one, including searching the Internet for your ideal place to stay. We also compare the pros and cons of different types of places to stay.

Getting to Know Your Options

From small inns to large all-inclusives, Mexico's beach resorts offer every type of vacation accommodation. And the prices can vary even more! Recommendations for specific places to stay are in the chapters devoted to the individual beach towns. We try to provide the widest range of options — both in types of hotels as well as budgets — but we always keep comfort in mind. What you find in this book is what we believe to be the best value for the money. Here are the major types of accommodations:

✔ **Resorts:** These accommodations tend to be the most popular option — especially with package tours — because they offer the most modern amenities, including cable TV, hair dryers, in-room safes, and generally, a selection of places to dine or have a drink. Large by definition, they may also boast various types of sporting facilities, spa services, shopping arcades, and tour-desk services. These places also tend to be the most expensive type of accommodation, but they can be heavily discounted if your timing is right.

✔ **Hotels:** These quarters tend to be smaller than resorts, with fewer facilities. In terms of style, look for anything from hacienda-style villas to all-suite hotels or sleek, modern structures. Most hotels at Mexican beach resorts have at least a small swimming pool, and if they're not located directly on a beach, hotels frequently offer shuttle service to a beach club or an affiliate beachfront hotel.

✔ **All-inclusives:** In Mexico, all-inclusives are gaining rapidly in popularity, and they seem to be getting larger and larger in size. As the name implies, all-inclusives tie everything together in one price — your room, meals, libations, entertainment, sports activities, and sometimes, off-site excursions. The advantage that many travelers find with this option is an expected fixed price for their vacation — helpful if you need to stay within a strict budget. Many all-inclusives have their own nightclubs or, at least, offer evening shows and entertainment, such as theme nights, talent contests, or costume parties. As for the food, you may never go hungry, but you're unlikely to go gourmet either. Food quality can be an important variable, about which it helps to have talked to someone who's recently been to the particular all-inclusive, or check online message boards for up-to-date commentaries on the buffets.

✔ **Condos, apartments, and villas:** These accommodations can be good options, especially if you're considering a stay longer than a week, and the reach of the Internet has made these lodging options extremely viable. Many condos, apartments, and villas come with housekeepers or even cooks. It's hard to know exactly what you're getting — and often it's futile to complain after you arrive — so again, word of mouth can be helpful here. At the very least, ask for references or search on the Internet to see whether anyone can offer an experience. In addition to the Internet, select options are always advertised in the major metropolitan newspapers, such as the *Los Angeles Times, Chicago Tribune,* and the *New York Times.* My recommendation? Save this option for your second visit when you have a better idea about the various parts of town and the area in general.

In Mexico, where smoking is still the norm, expect that your room will be smoker-friendly. However having said that, an increasing number of hotels — especially the larger resorts — now offer non-smoking rooms. And, many of the holistic-oriented retreats along the Riviera Maya are smoke-free. Be sure to ask when booking a room to ensure you get your preference.

Mexico's system of rating hotels and resorts is rather generous on its handing out of "stars." Here, the top-of-the-line resorts are known as "Grand Turismo," and from there, it ranges from five stars down. So, booking a four-star resort will generally result in much more modest accommodations than the equivalent ranking in the U.S.

Below, Table 7-1 shows you how we've categorized hotel prices in each of the remaining chapters. Our rankings consider prices for a room based on double occupancy for one night during high season.

Table 7-1	Key to Hotel Dollar Signs	
Dollar Sign(s)	**Price Range**	**What to Expect**
$	Less than $75	These accommodations are simple and simply inexpensive. Rooms will likely be small, and televisions are not necessarily provided. Parking is not provided but rather catch-as-you-can on the street. These may include basic rooms with hammocks for sleeping in.
$$	$75–$125	A bit classier, these mid-range accommodations offer more room, more extras (such as irons, hair dryers, or a microwave), and a more convenient location than the preceding category.
$$$	$126–$175	Rooms in this category are generally beachfront, and with plenty of extras to make your stay comfortable — such as restaurants, a large pool, and tour services, but may not be as modern as other choices. Or, in some of the more remote parts of Mexico, this category could be the top of the line.
$$$$	$176–$250	Higher-class still, these accommodations are plush, and with ocean views and direct beach access. Think chocolates on your pillow, a classy restaurant, underground parking garages, and often on-site spas. Many all-inclusives fall into this category, so your meals and drinks will also be part of the price you pay for the room.
$$$$$	$251 and up	These top-rated accommodations come with luxury amenities such as valet parking, on-premise spas, and in-room hot tubs, plasma-screen TVs, and CD players — but you pay for 'em.

Finding the Best Room at the Best Rate

When it comes to rates, the most common term is **rack rate.** The rack rate is the maximum rate that a resort or hotel charges for a room. It's the rate you get if you walk in off the street and ask for a room on a night that the place is close to being full.

The rack rate is the first rate a hotel offers, but you usually don't have to pay it. Always ask whether a lower rate or special package is available — it can't hurt, and you may at least end up with a free breakfast or spa service.

In this book, we use rack rates as a guidepost, not expecting that you'll have to pay them. Minimum night stays, special promotions, and seasonal discounts can all go a long way in bringing the rack rate down. Also, be sure to mention your frequent-flier or corporate-rewards programs if you book with one of the larger hotel chains. Please note that rates change very often, so the prices quoted in this book may be different from the prices you're quoted when you make your reservation.

Room rates also rise and fall with occupancy rates. If your choice of hotels is close to empty, it pays to negotiate. Resorts tend to be much more crowded during weekends. If you're traveling off season (see Chapter 4 for peak and low occupancy times) you can almost certainly negotiate a bargain.

My experience is you'll get the best rate by booking your hotel as part of an air-hotel package (see Chapter 6), but in lieu of that, try contacting the local number for your best chance of negotiating the best rate. Just note — it may help if you speak Spanish.

Surfing the Web for hotel deals

Shopping online for hotels is generally done one of two ways: by booking through the hotel's own Web site or through an independent booking agency (or a fare-service agency like Priceline). These Internet hotel agencies have multiplied in mind-boggling numbers of late, competing for the business of millions of consumers surfing for accommodations around the world. This competitiveness can be a boon to consumers who have the patience and time to shop and compare the online sites for good deals — but shop they must, for prices can vary considerably from site to site. And keep in mind that hotels at the top of a site's listing may be there for no other reason than that they paid money to get the placement.

Of the "big three" sites, **Expedia** offers a long list of special deals and "virtual tours" or photos of available rooms so you can see what you're paying for (a feature that helps counter the claims that the best rooms are often held back from bargain booking Web sites). **Travelocity** posts unvarnished customer reviews and ranks its properties according to the AAA rating system. Also reliable are **Hotels.com** and **Quikbook.com**. An excellent free program, **TravelAxe** (www.travelaxe.net), can help you search multiple hotel sites at once, even ones you may never have heard of — and conveniently lists the total price of the room, including the taxes and service charges. Another booking site, **Travelweb** (www.travelweb.com), is partly owned by the hotels it represents (including the Hilton, Hyatt, and Starwood chains) and is therefore plugged directly into the hotels' reservations systems — unlike independent online agencies, which have to fax or e-mail reservation requests to the hotel, a good portion of which get misplaced in the shuffle. More than once, travelers have arrived at the hotel, only to be told that they have no reservation. To be fair, many of the major sites are undergoing improvements in service and ease of use, and Expedia will soon be able to plug directly into the reservations systems of many hotel chains — none of which can be bad news for consumers. In the meantime, it's a good idea to **get a confirmation number** and **make a printout** of any online booking transaction.

In the opaque Web site category, **Priceline** and **Hotwire** are even better for hotels than for airfares; with both, you're allowed to pick the neighborhood and quality level of your hotel before offering up your money. Priceline's hotel product even covers Europe and Asia, though it's much better at getting five-star lodging for three-star prices than at finding anything at the bottom of the scale. On the down side, many hotels stick Priceline guests in their least desirable rooms. Be sure to go to the BiddingforTravel Web site (www.biddingfortravel.com) before bidding on a hotel room on Priceline; it features a fairly up-to-date list of hotels that Priceline uses in major cities. For both Priceline and Hotwire, you pay upfront, and the fee is nonrefundable. _Note:_ Some hotels do not provide loyalty program credits or points or other frequent-stay amenities when you book a room through opaque online services. Following are some of our favorite resources for booking vacation accommodations:

- ✔ Although the name **All Hotels on the Web** (www.all-hotels.com) is something of a misnomer, the site _does_ have tens of thousands of listings throughout the world. Bear in mind that each hotel has paid a small fee ($25 and up) to be listed, so it's less of an objective list and more like a book of online brochures.

- ✔ **hoteldiscount!com** (www.180096hotel.com) lists bargain room rates at hotels in more than 50 U.S. and international cities. The cool thing is that hoteldiscount!com prebooks blocks of rooms in advance, so sometimes it has rooms — at discount rates — at hotels that are "sold out." Select a city and input your dates, and you get a list of the best prices for a selection of hotels. This site is notable for delivering deep discounts in cities where hotel rooms are expensive. The toll-free number is printed all over this site (☎ 800-96-HOTEL); call it if you want more options than are listed online.

- ✔ **InnSite** (www.innsite.com) has B&B listings in all 50 U.S. states and more than 50 countries around the globe. Find an inn at your destination, see pictures of the rooms, and check prices and availability. This extensive directory of bed-and-breakfasts only includes listings if the proprietor submitted one. (It's free to get an inn listed.) Innkeepers write the descriptions, and many listings link to the inns' own Web sites. Also check out the **Bed and Breakfast Channel** (www.bedandbreakfast.com).

- ✔ **Places to Stay** (www.placestostay.com) lists one-of-a-kind places, with a focus on resort accommodations, in the United States and abroad that you may not find in other directories. Again, listing is selective: This directory isn't comprehensive, but it can give you a sense of what's available at different destinations.

✔ **TravelWeb** (`www.travelweb.com`) lists more than 26,000 hotels in 170 countries, focusing on chains such as Hyatt and Hilton, and you can book almost 90 percent of these listings online. The site's Click-It Weekends, updated each Monday, offers weekend deals at many leading hotel chains.

✔ Specific to Mexico, **Mexico Boutique Hotels** (`http://mexico boutiquehotels.com`) has listings of small, unique properties that are unlikely to show up on the radar screens of most travel agents or large Web travel sites. In addition to complete descriptions, the site also offers an online booking service.

✔ Another site specializing in Mexico accommodations is `www.mexicohotels.com`.

✔ Check the Web sites of Mexico's top hotel chains for special deals. These include `www.caminoreal.com`, `www.hyatt.com`, `www.starwoodhotels.com`, and `www.fiestaamericana.com`.

Reserving the best room

After you make your reservation, asking one or two more pointed questions can go a long way toward making sure you get the best room in the house. Always ask for a corner room. They're usually larger, quieter, and have more windows and light than standard rooms, and they don't always cost more. Also ask if the hotel is renovating; if it is, request a room away from the renovation work — this is especially true in Cancún, where construction following the damage from Hurricane Wilma made the entire beachfront a construction zone. Inquire, too, about the location of the restaurants, bars, and discos in the hotel — all sources of annoying noise. And if you aren't happy with your room when you arrive, talk to the front desk. If they have another room, they should be happy to accommodate you, within reason.

Mention that you are honeymooners, and ask for the best available room — Mexico's beach resorts are especially accommodating to newlyweds.

Most beachfront hotels offer either ground-floor rooms with terraces, or upper-level rooms with balconies. If you have a preference, be sure to request it at the time of booking.

Chapter 8

Tips for Travelers with Special Needs or Interests

....

In This Chapter

▶ Bringing the kids along
▶ Looking at senior citizens' needs
▶ Considering tips for travelers with a disability
▶ Stepping out: Gay and lesbian travel info
▶ Taking a jaunt by yourself
▶ Getting hitched in Mexico

....

*M*ost people consider themselves unique with special needs, but some types of travelers really do warrant a little extra advice. In this chapter, we cover information that's helpful to know if you're traveling with children, if you're a senior traveler, if you have special needs because of a disability, if you're gay or lesbian, if you're traveling solo, or if you're planning on tying the knot in Mexico. Throughout the chapter, we clue you in on what to expect, offer some useful tips, and whenever possible, steer you to experts concerning your particular circumstances.

Traveling with the Brood: Advice for Families

Children are considered the national treasure of Mexico, and Mexicans warmly welcome and cater to your kids. Although many parents were reluctant to bring young children to Mexico in the past, primarily due to health concerns, we can't think of a better place to introduce children to the exciting adventure of exploring a different culture. Some of the best destinations for children include Puerto Vallarta, Cancún, and Acapulco. Hotels can often arrange for a baby sitter. Some hotels in the moderate-to-luxury range have small playgrounds and pools for children and hire caretakers who offer special-activity programs during the day, but few budget hotels offer these amenities. All-inclusive resorts make great options for family travel because, as a rule, they offer exhaustive activities programs. They also make mealtime easy by offering buffet-style meal services almost around the clock.

Before leaving for your trip, check with your pediatrician or family doctor to get advice on medications to take along. Diapers cost about the same in Mexico as they do in the United States, but the quality is poorer. You can get brand-name diapers identical to the ones sold in the United States, but you'll pay a higher price. Many stores sell familiar, brand-name baby foods. Dry cereals, powdered formulas, baby bottles, and purified water are all easily available in midsize and large cities or resorts.

Cribs, however, may present a problem; only the largest and most luxurious hotels provide them. However, rollaway beds to accommodate children staying in a room with their parents are often available. Child seats or highchairs at restaurants are common, and most restaurants go out of their way to accommodate the comfort of your children. You may want to consider bringing your own car seat along because they're not readily available to rent in Mexico.

We recommend that you take coloring books, puzzles, and small games with you to keep your children entertained during the flight or whenever you're traveling from one destination to the next. Another good idea is to take a blank notebook, in which your children can paste little souvenirs from the trip, such as the label from the beer Daddy drank on the beach or small shells and flowers that they collect. And don't forget to carry small scissors (pack the scissors during the flight due to security reasons) and a glue stick with you, or the blank notebook may remain blank.

You can find good family-oriented vacation advice on the Internet from sites like the (www.familytravelforum.com), a comprehensive site that offers customized trip planning; **Family Travel Network** (www.familytravelnetwork.com), an award-winning site that offers travel features, deals, and tips; **Traveling Internationally with Your Kids** (www.travelwithyourkids.com), a comprehensive site that offers customized trip planning; and **Family Travel Files** (www.thefamily travelfiles.com), which offers an online magazine and a directory of off-the-beaten-path tours and tour operators for families.

Throughout this book you'll notice the Kid Friendly icon, which will alert you to those hotels, restaurants, and activities that are especially suitable for family travelers.

For children under 18 traveling without parents or with only one parent, they must travel with a notarized letter from the absent parent or parents authorizing the travel. We go over this in detail in Chapter 9, in the discussion on entry requirements into Mexico. Don't arrive at the airport without it, or your trip to those powdery white beaches will be delayed!

Making Age Work for You: Tips for Seniors

Mexico is a popular country for retirees and for senior travelers. For decades, North Americans have been living indefinitely in Mexico by returning to the border and re-crossing with a new tourist permit every six months. Mexican immigration officials have caught on, and they now limit the maximum time you can spend in the country to six months in any given year. This measure is meant to encourage even partial residents to comply with the proper documentation procedures. The following can provide some information for seniors thinking of retiring in Mexico:

- ✔ *AIM* (*Adventures in Mexico*) is a well-written, candid, and informative newsletter for prospective retirees. Recent issues evaluated retirement in Puerto Vallarta, Puerto Angel, Puerto Escondido, and Huatulco. For subscriptions, which are $18 to the United States and $25 to Canada, write to Apdo. Postal 31–70, 45050 Guadalajara, Jalisco, Mexico. Back issues are three for $5.

- ✔ **Sanborn Tours** (2015 South 10th St., McAllen, TX, 78503; ☎ 800-395-8482; www.sanborns.com) offers a "Retire in Mexico" orientation tour.

- ✔ Puerto Vallarta resident and author Polly Vicars's *Tales of Retirement in Paradise* offers an entertaining account of the pleasures of "retired" life in this seaside town — a very popular beach resort with senior travelers. All proceeds from the book go to the America-Mexico Foundation (www.pvnet.com.mx/amf), which provides scholarships to needy and deserving Mexican students. You can buy the $14 book online through Amazon.com (www.amazon.com) or purchase it directly from the author via e-mail at phvicars@pvnet.com.mx. The book is also available for sale in Puerto Vallarta at bookstores and various shops.

People over the age of 60 are traveling more than ever before. And why not? Being a senior citizen entitles you to some terrific travel bargains. Mention the fact that you're a senior citizen when you make your travel reservations. Although all of the major U.S. airlines except America West have cancelled their senior discount and coupon book programs, many hotels still offer discounts for seniors. In most cities, people over the age of 60 qualify for reduced admission to theaters, museums, and other attractions, as well as discounted fares on public transportation.

Members of **AARP** (formerly known as the American Association of Retired Persons), 601 E St. NW, Washington, DC 20049 (☎ **888-687-2277** or 202-434-2277; www.aarp.org), get discounts on hotels, airfares, and car rentals. AARP offers members a wide range of benefits, including *AARP: The Magazine* and a monthly newsletter. Anyone over 50 can join.

Many reliable agencies and organizations target the 50-plus market. **Elderhostel** (☎ **877-426-8056**; www.elderhostel.org) arranges study programs for those 55 and over (and a spouse or companion of any age) in the United States and in more than 80 countries around the world. Most courses last five to seven days in the United States (two to four weeks abroad), and many include airfare, accommodations in university dormitories or modest inns, meals, and tuition. **ElderTreks** (☎ 800-741-7956; www.eldertreks.com) offers small-group tours to off-the-beaten-path or adventure-travel locations, restricted to travelers 50 and older. **INTRAV** (☎ 800-456-8100; www.intrav.com) is a high-end tour operator that caters to the mature, discerning traveler, not specifically seniors, with trips around the world that include guided safaris, polar expeditions, private-jet adventures, and small-boat cruises down jungle rivers.

Recommended publications offering travel resources and discounts for seniors include: the quarterly magazine ***Travel 50 & Beyond*** (www.travel50andbeyond.com); ***Travel Unlimited: Uncommon Adventures for the Mature Traveler*** (Avalon); ***101 Tips for Mature Travelers,*** available from Grand Circle Travel (☎ 800-221-2610 or 617-350-7500; www.gct.com); ***The 50+ Traveler's Guidebook*** (St. Martin's Press); and ***Unbelievably Good Deals and Great Adventures That You Absolutely Can't Get Unless You're Over 50*** (McGraw-Hill), by Joann Rattner Heilman.

Mature Outlook (☎ 800-267-3277) is a similar organization, sponsored by Sears, which offers discounts on car rentals and hotel stays. The $19.95 annual membership fee also gets you $200 in Sears coupons and a bimonthly magazine, *New Outlook,* plus access to its online version, at www.newoutlook.ca. Membership is open to all Sears customers 18 and over, but the organization's primary focus is on the 50-and-over market.

Accessing Mexico's Beaches: Advice for Travelers with Disabilities

A disability needn't stop anybody from traveling. More options and resources are available than ever before.

Many travel agencies offer customized tours and itineraries for travelers with disabilities. **Flying Wheels Travel** (☎ 507-451-5005; www.flyingwheelstravel.com) offers escorted tours and cruises that emphasize sports and private tours in minivans with lifts. **Access-Able Travel Source** (☎ 303-232-2979; www.access-able.com) offers extensive access information and advice for traveling around the world with disabilities. **Accessible Journeys** (☎ 800-846-4537 or 610-521-0339) caters to wheelchair travelers and their families and friends.

Organizations that offer assistance to disabled travelers include the **MossRehab** (www.mossresourcenet.org), which provides a library of accessible-travel resources online; **SATH** (Society for Accessible Travel and Hospitality; ☎ 212-447-7284; www.sath.org; annual membership fees: $45 adults, $30 seniors and students), which offers a wealth of travel resources for all types of disabilities and informed recommendations on destinations, access guides, travel agents, tour operators, vehicle rentals, and companion services; and the **American Foundation for the Blind** (AFB; ☎ 800-232-5463; www.afb.org), a referral resource for the blind or visually impaired that includes information on traveling with Seeing Eye dogs.

For more information specifically targeted to travelers with disabilities, check out the quarterly magazine *Emerging Horizons* ($14.95 per year, $19.95 outside the U.S.; www.emerginghorizons.com), and *Open World Magazine,* published by SATH (subscription: $13 per year, $21 outside the U.S.).

A World of Options, a 658-page book of resources for travelers with disabilities, covers everything from biking trips to scuba outfitters. It costs $35 and is available from **Mobility International USA** (P.O. Box 10767, Eugene, OR 97440; ☎ 541-343-1284 voice and TTY; www.miusa.org).

However, we need to honestly say that Mexico does fall far behind other countries when it comes to accessible travel. In fact, you may feel like you're maneuvering one giant obstacle course. At airports, you may encounter steep stairs before finding a well-hidden elevator or escalator — if one exists. Airlines often arrange wheelchair assistance for passengers to the baggage area. Porters are generally available to help with luggage at airports and large bus stations after you clear baggage claim.

Escalators (and there aren't many in the beach resorts) are often non-operational. Stairs without handrails abound. Few restrooms are equipped for travelers with disabilities, and when one is available, access to it may be via a narrow passage that doesn't accommodate a wheelchair or a person on crutches. Many deluxe hotels (the most expensive) now have rooms with baths for people with disabilities. Budget travelers may be best off looking for single-story motels, although accessing showers and bathrooms may still pose a problem outside of specially equipped deluxe hotels. Generally speaking, no matter where you are, someone will lend a hand, although you may have to ask for it.

Although Mexico's international airports are become increasingly modernized in recent years, there are still some parts of Mexico that don't regularly offer the luxury of boarding an airplane from the waiting room. You either descend stairs to a bus that ferries you to a waiting plane that you board by climbing stairs, or you walk across the airport tarmac to your plane and climb up the stairs. Deplaning presents the same problems in reverse.

In our opinion, the wide, modern streets and sidewalks of Cancún make it among the most "accessible" resort destinations. In addition to the superior public facilities, you can find numerous accommodation options for travelers with disabilities.

In addition to Cancún, over the past several years, the downtown area of Puerto Vallarta has become almost fully "accessible" for those with disabilities, adding ramps to all sidewalks, the central plaza, and along the seaside *malecón* (boardwalk), thanks to the efforts of a local activist. These enhancements also make Puerto Vallarta especially appealing for those with strollers, or others in search of friendlier curbs and walking areas.

Following the Rainbow: Resources for Gay and Lesbian Travelers

Mexico is a conservative country with deeply rooted Catholic religious traditions. Public displays of same-sex affection are rare, especially outside the major resort areas. Women in Mexico frequently walk hand in hand, but anything more crosses the boundary of acceptability. However, gay and lesbian travelers are generally treated with respect and shouldn't experience any harassment, assuming the appropriate regard is given to local culture and customs. Puerto Vallarta, with its selection of accommodations and entertainment oriented especially toward gay and lesbian travelers, is perhaps the most welcoming and accepting destination in Mexico. Susan Weisman's travel service, **Bayside Properties** (☎ 322-223-4424; www.baysidepuertovallarta.com), rents gay-friendly condos, villas, and hotels for individuals and large groups. Her services are customized to individual needs, and she can offer airport pickups and in-villa cooks.

The International Gay and Lesbian Travel Association (IGLTA; ☎ 800-448-8550 or 954-776-2626; www.iglta.org) is the trade association for the gay and lesbian travel industry, and offers an online directory of gay- and lesbian-friendly travel businesses; go to their Web site and click on "Members."

Many agencies offer tours and travel itineraries specifically for gay and lesbian travelers. **Above and Beyond Tours** (☎ 800-397-2681; www.abovebeyondtours.com) is the exclusive gay and lesbian tour operator for United Airlines. **Now, Voyager** (☎ 800-255-6951; www.nowvoyager.com) is a well-known San Francisco–based gay-owned and -operated travel service. **Olivia Cruises & Resorts** (☎ 800-631-6277 or 510-655-0364; www.olivia.com) charters entire resorts and ships for exclusive lesbian vacations and offers smaller group experiences for both gay and lesbian travelers.

The following travel guides are available at most travel bookstores and gay and lesbian bookstores, or you can order them from **Giovanni's Room** bookstore, 1145 Pine St., Philadelphia, PA 19107 (☎ 215-923-2960; www.giovannisroom.com): *Frommer's Gay & Lesbian Europe,* an excellent travel resource (www.frommers.com); *Out and About* (☎ 800-929-2268 or 415-644-8044; www.outandabout.com), which offers guidebooks and a newsletter ($20 per year; 10 issues) packed with solid information on the global gay and lesbian scene; *Spartacus International Gay Guide* (Bruno Gmünder Verlag; www.spartacusworld.com/gayguide) and *Odysseus,* both good, annual English-language guidebooks focused on gay men; the *Damron* guides (www.damron.com), with separate, annual books for gay men and lesbians; and *Gay Travel A to Z: The World of Gay & Lesbian Travel Options at Your Fingertips* by Marianne Ferrari (Ferrari International; Box 35575, Phoenix, AZ 85069), a very good gay and lesbian guidebook series.

Arco Iris is a gay-owned, full-service travel agency and tour operator specializing in Mexico packages and special group travel. Contact the agency by phone (☎ **800-765-4370** or 619-297-0897; Fax: 619-297-6419) or through its Web site at www.arcoiristours.com. They also publish the Cancún Pink Pages guide, which is free with the booking of any package tour, or can be ordered for $5 online on its Web site.

Traveling Solo

Mexico is a great place to travel on your own without really being or feeling alone. Although identical room rates for single and double occupancy are slowly becoming a trend in Mexico, many of the hotels in this book still offer single rooms at lower rates.

Mexicans are very friendly, and meeting other foreigners is easy. But if you don't like the idea of traveling alone, try **Travel Companion Exchange** (**TCE;** P.O. Box 833, Amityville, NY 11701; ☎ **631-454-0880;** Fax: 631-454-0170; www.travelcompanions.com), which brings prospective travelers together. Members complete a profile and then place an anonymous listing of their travel interests in the newsletter. Prospective traveling companions then make contact through the exchange. Membership costs $99 for six months or $159 for a year. TCE also offers an excellent booklet, for $4.95, on avoiding theft and scams while traveling abroad.

As a female traveling alone, Lynne can tell you firsthand that she generally feels safer traveling in Mexico than in the United States. But she uses the same common-sense precautions she uses when traveling anywhere else in the world, and she stays alert to what's going on around her.

Mexicans, in general, and men, in particular, are nosy about single travelers, especially women. If taxi drivers or anyone else with whom you don't want to become friendly asks about your marital status, family, and so on, my advice is to make up a set of answers (regardless of the truth): "I'm married, traveling with friends, and I have three children."

Saying you're single and traveling alone may send out the wrong message about availability. Face it — whether you like it or not, Mexico is still a macho country with the double standards that a macho attitude implies. Movies and television shows exported from the United States have created an image of sexually aggressive North American women. If someone bothers you, don't try to be polite — just leave or head into a public place.

You may even consider wearing a ring that resembles a wedding band. Most Mexican men stay away at the sight of a ring, and it also deters many uncomfortable questions.

For specific tips and travel packages for single women traveling to Mexico, check out the following online resources:

- ✔ **Gutsy Women Travel:** www.gutsywomentravel.com
- ✔ **Women's Travel Club:** www.womenstravelclub.com

For a directory of travel clubs for women, including solo women travelers, visit Transitions Abroad, at www.transitionsabroad.com/listings/travel/women/websiteswomenclubs.shtml.

Planning a Wedding in Mexico

Mexico's beaches may be old favorites for romantic honeymoons, but have you ever considered taking the plunge in Mexico? A destination wedding saves money and can be less hassle compared with marrying back home. Many hotels and attractions offer wedding packages, which can include everything from booking the officiant to hiring the videographer. Pick the plan you want and, presto, your wedding decisions are done! Several properties also provide the services of a wedding coordinator (either for free or at a reasonable cost) who not only scouts out sweetheart pink roses but also can handle marriage licenses and other formalities. A destination wedding can be as informal or as traditional as you like. After returning from their honeymoon, many couples hold a reception for people back home who couldn't join them. At these parties, couples sometimes continue the theme of their wedding locale (decorate with piñatas or hire a mariachi band, for example) and show a video of their ceremony so that everyone can share in their happiness.

If you invite guests to your destination wedding, find out about group rates for hotels and airfare, which can save 20 percent or more off regular prices. Plan as far ahead as possible so that people can arrange their schedules and join you.

Under a treaty between the United States and Mexico, Mexican civil marriages are automatically valid in the United States. You need certified copies of birth certificates, driver's licenses, or passports; certified proof of divorce or the death certificate of any former spouses (if applicable); tourist cards (provided when you enter Mexico); and results of blood tests performed in Mexico within 15 days before the ceremony.

Check with a local, on-site wedding planner through your hotel to verify all the necessary requirements and obtain an application well in advance of your desired wedding date. Contact the **Mexican Tourism Board** (☎ **800-446-3942;** www.visitmexico.com) for information.

For more information, see _Honeymoon Vacations For Dummies_ (Wiley Publishing, Inc.).

Chapter 9

Taking Care of the Remaining Details

In This Chapter

▶ Getting your entry and departure documents in order

▶ Considering travel and medical insurance

▶ Ensuring a safe vacation

▶ Deciding whether to rent a car

▶ Packing wisely

*A*re you ready? Really ready? Before you can string that hammock between the palms, you need to take care of a few more details to get to your personal paradise.

In this chapter, we cover the essentials and the requirements of getting into Mexico — and then back home again. We also review the ins and outs of dealing with travel insurance, discuss what you need to know to ensure a safe trip, help you decide whether you need to rent a car, and offer tips to make sure you pack everything you need for your Mexican beach vacation.

Arriving In and Departing From Mexico

All travelers to Mexico are required to present **proof of citizenship,** such as a valid passport (the preferred documentation — see the next section), an original birth certificate with a raised seal, or naturalization papers. If you're using a birth certificate, bring a current form of photo identification, such as a driver's license or an official ID card. If your last name on the birth certificate is different from your current name (women using a married name, for example), you also need to bring a photo ID card *and* legal proof of the name change, such as the *original* marriage license or certificate.

When reentering the United States, you must prove both your citizen-ship *and* your identification, so always carry a picture ID such as a driver's license or valid passport.

Birth certificates enable you to enter Mexico, but alone, don't enable you to reenter the United States. And although you can enter Mexico using a driver's license as identification, this document alone isn't acceptable identification for reentering the United States. While in Mexico, you must also obtain a **Mexican tourist permit (FMT),** which is issued free of charge by Mexican border officials after proof of citizen-ship is accepted. Airlines generally provide these forms aboard your flight into Mexico.

The tourist permit (FMT) is more important than a passport in Mexico, so guard it carefully. If you lose your FMT, you may not be permitted to leave the country until you can replace it — a bureaucratic hassle that can take anywhere from a few hours to a week. (If you do lose your tourist permit, get a police report from local authorities indicating that your documents were stolen; having one *may* lessen the hassle of exiting the country without all your identification.) You should also contact the nearest consular office to report the stolen papers so that the consulate can issue a reentry document.

Note that children under the age of 18 traveling without parents or with only one parent must have a notarized letter from the absent parent or parents authorizing the travel. The letter must include the duration of the visit, destination, names of accompanying adults, parents' home addresses, telephone numbers, and so forth. A picture of the child must also be attached to this letter. When applicable, provide divorce, death certificate, or guardianship papers.

Getting a Passport

Although you can enter Mexico without a passport, the only legal form of identification recognized around the world is a valid passport. For that reason alone, having your passport whenever you travel abroad is a good idea. In the United States, you're used to your driver's license being the all-purpose ID card. Abroad, it only proves that some American state lets you drive. Getting a passport is easy, but it takes some time to complete the process.

The U.S. State Department's Bureau of Consular Affairs maintains an excellent Web site (www.travel.state.gov) with good information about passports, including downloadable applications and locations of passport offices; just follow the link to "Passport Information." In addi-tion, the Web site provides extensive information about foreign coun-tries, including travel warnings about health and terrorism. You can also call the National Passport Information Center at ☎ 877-487-2778 ($4.95 per call).

If you're a resident of Canada, the United Kingdom, Ireland, Australia, or New Zealand, you can find passport information for your home country in the upcoming section, "Applying for other passports."

Applying for a U.S. passport

 If you're applying for a first-time passport, follow these steps:

1. Complete a **passport application** in person at a U.S. passport office; a federal, state, or probate court; or a major post office. To find your regional passport office, either check the **U.S. State Department** Web site, http://travel.state.gov, or call the **National Passport Information Center** (☎ 877-487-2778) for automated information.

2. Present a **certified birth certificate** as proof of citizenship. (Bringing along your driver's license, state or military ID, or social security card is also a good idea.)

3. Submit **two identical passport-sized photos,** measuring 2-x-2-inches in size. You often find businesses that take these photos near a passport office. *Note:* You can't use a strip from a photo-vending machine because the pictures aren't identical.

4. Pay a **fee.** For people 16 and over, a passport is valid for ten years and costs $85. For those 15 and under, a passport is valid for five years and costs $70.

 Allow plenty of time before your trip to apply for a passport; processing normally takes three weeks but can take longer during busy periods (especially spring).

If you have a passport in your current name that was issued within the past 15 years (and you were over 16 when it was issued), you can renew the passport by mail for $55. Whether you're applying in person or by mail, you can download passport applications from the U.S. State Department Web site at http://travel.state.gov. For general information, call the **National Passport Agency** (☎ 202-647-0518). To find your regional passport office, either check the U.S. State Department Web site or call the **National Passport Information Center** toll-free number (☎ 877-487-2778) for automated information.

Applying for other passports

The following list offers more information for citizens of Australia, Canada, New Zealand, and the United Kingdom:

- ✔ **Australians** can visit a local post office or passport office, call the **Australia Passport Information Service** (☎ 131-232 toll-free from Australia), or log on to www.passports.gov.au for details on how and where to apply.

✔ **Canadians** can pick up applications at passport offices throughout Canada, post offices, or from the central **Passport Office,
Department of Foreign Affairs and International Trade,** Ottawa,
ON K1A 0G3 (☎ **800-567-6868;** www.ppt.gc.ca). Applications
must be accompanied by two identical passport-sized photographs
and proof of Canadian citizenship. Processing takes five to ten days
if you apply in person, or about three weeks by mail.

✔ **New Zealanders** can pick up a passport application at any New
Zealand Passports Office or download it from their Web site. For
information, contact the **Passports Office** or download it from their
Web site. Contact the **Passports Office** at ☎ **0800-225-050** in New
Zealand or 04-474-8100, or log on to www.passports.govt.nz.

✔ **United Kingdom** residents can pick up applications for a standard
10-year passport (5-year passport for children under 16) at passport offices, major post offices, or a travel agency. For information,
contact the **United Kingdom Passport Service** (☎ **0870-521-0410;**
www.ukpa.gov.uk).

Clearing U.S. Customs

You *can* take it with you — up to a point. Technically, no limits exist on
how much loot U.S. citizens can bring back into the United States from a
trip abroad, but the Customs authority *does* put limits on how much you
can bring in for free. (This limit is mainly for taxation purposes, to separate tourists with souvenirs from importers.)

As a U.S. citizen, you may bring home $800 worth of goods duty-free, as
long as you've been out of the country at least 48 hours and haven't
used the exemption in the past 30 days. This amount includes one liter
of an alcoholic beverage (you must, of course, be older than 21), 200 cigarettes, and 100 cigars. Anything you mail home from abroad is exempt
from the $800 limit. You may mail up to $200 worth of goods to yourself
(marked "for personal use") and up to $100 to others (marked "unso-
licited gift") once each day, so long as the package doesn't include alcohol or tobacco products. You have to pay an import duty on anything
over these limits.

Note that buying items at a **duty-free shop** before flying home doesn't
exempt them from counting toward U.S. Customs limits (monetary or
otherwise). The "duty" that you're avoiding in those shops is the local
tax on the item (such as state sales tax in the United States), not any
import duty that may be assessed by the U.S. Customs office.

If you have further questions, or for a list of specific items you can't
bring into the United States, look in your phone book (under U.S.
Government, Department of Homeland Security, U.S. Customs & Border
Protection) to find the nearest Customs office. Or check out the Customs
& Border Protection Web site at www.cbp.gov.

Playing It Safe with Travel and Medical Insurance

Three kinds of travel insurance are available: trip-cancellation insurance, medical insurance, and lost luggage insurance. The cost of travel insurance varies widely, depending on the cost and length of your trip, your age and health, and the type of trip you're taking, but expect to pay between 5 percent and 8 percent of the vacation itself. Here is our advice on all three:

✔ **Trip-cancellation insurance** helps you get your money back if you have to back out of a trip, if you have to go home early, or if your travel supplier goes bankrupt. Allowed reasons for cancellation can range from sickness to natural disasters to the State Department declaring your destination unsafe for travel. (Insurers usually won't cover vague fears, though, as many travelers discovered who tried to cancel their trips in Oct 2001 because they were wary of flying.)

A good resource is **"Travel Guard Alerts,"** a list of companies considered high-risk by Travel Guard International (`www.travel insured.com`). Protect yourself further by paying for the insurance with a credit card — by law, consumers can get their money back on goods and services not received if they report the loss within 60 days after the charge is listed on their credit-card statement.

Note: Many tour operators, particularly those offering trips to remote or high-risk areas, include insurance in the cost of the trip or can arrange insurance policies through a partnering provider, a convenient and often cost-effective way for the traveler to obtain insurance. Make sure the tour company is a reputable one, however: Some experts suggest you avoid buying insurance from the tour or cruise company you're traveling with, saying it's better to buy from a "third party" insurer than to put all your money in one place.

✔ For domestic travel, buying **medical insurance** for your trip doesn't make sense for most travelers. Most existing health policies cover you if you get sick away from home — but check before you go, particularly if you're insured by an HMO.

For travel overseas, most health plans (including Medicare and Medicaid) do not provide coverage, and the ones that do often require you to pay for services upfront and reimburse you only after you return home. Even if your plan does cover overseas treatment, most out-of-country hospitals make you pay your bills upfront, and send you a refund only after you've returned home and filed the necessary paperwork with your insurance company. As a safety net, you may want to buy travel medical insurance, particularly if you're traveling to a remote or high-risk area where emergency evacuation is a possible scenario. If you require additional medical insurance, try **MEDEX Assistance** (☎ **410-453-6300;** `www.medexassist.com`)

or **Travel Assistance International** (☎ 800-821-2828; www.travel assistance.com; for general information on services, call the company's Worldwide Assistance Services, Inc., at ☎ 800-777-8710).

✔ **Lost luggage insurance** is not necessary for most travelers. On domestic flights, checked baggage is covered up to $2,500 per ticketed passenger. On international flights (including U.S. portions of international trips), baggage coverage is limited to approximately $9.07 per pound, up to approximately $635 per checked bag. If you plan to check items more valuable than the standard liability, see if your valuables are covered by your homeowner's policy, get baggage insurance as part of your comprehensive travel-insurance package, or buy Travel Guard's "BagTrak" product. Don't buy insurance at the airport, as it's usually overpriced. Be sure to take any valuables or irreplaceable items with you in your carry-on luggage, as many valuables (including books, money, and electronics) aren't covered by airline policies.

If your luggage is lost, immediately file a lost-luggage claim at the airport, detailing the luggage contents. For most airlines, you must report delayed, damaged, or lost baggage within four hours of arrival. The airlines are required to deliver luggage, once found, directly to your house or destination free of charge.

For more information, contact one of the following recommended insurers: **Access America** (☎ 866-807-3982; www.accessamerica. com); **Travel Guard International** (☎ 800-826-4919; www.travel guard.com); **Travel Insured International** (☎ 800-243-3174; www. travelinsured.com); and **Travelex Insurance Services** (☎ 888-457-4602; www.travelex-insurance.com).

Staying Healthy When You Travel

Apart from how getting sick can ruin your vacation, it also can present the problem of finding a doctor you trust when you're away from home. Bring all your medications with you, as well as a prescription for more — you may run out. Bring an extra pair of contact lenses in case you lose one. And don't forget the Pepto-Bismol for common travelers' ailments like upset stomach or diarrhea.

If you have health insurance, check with your provider to find out the extent of your coverage outside of your home area. Be sure to carry your identification card in your wallet. And if you worry that your existing policy isn't sufficient, purchase medical insurance for more comprehensive coverage. (See "Playing It Safe with Travel and Medical Insurance," earlier in this chapter.)

Talk to your doctor before leaving on a trip if you have a serious and/ or chronic illness. For conditions such as epilepsy, diabetes, or heart problems, wear a **MedicAlert identification tag** (☎ 888-633-4298;

www.medicalert.org), which immediately alerts doctors to your condition and gives them access to your records through Medic Alert's 24-hour hot line. Contact the **International Association for Medical Assistance to Travelers (IAMAT; ☎ 716-754-4883** or, in Canada, 416-652-0137; www.iamat.org) for tips on travel and health concerns in the countries you're visiting, and lists of local, English-speaking doctors. The United States **Centers for Disease Control and Prevention (☎ 800-311-3435;** www.cdc.gov) provides up-to-date information on health hazards by region or country and offers tips on food safety.

If you do get sick, ask the concierge at your hotel to recommend a local doctor — even his or her own doctor, if necessary. Another good option is to call the closest consular office and ask for a referral to a doctor. Most consulates have a listing of reputable English-speaking doctors. Most beach destinations in Mexico have at least one modern facility staffed by doctors used to treating the most common ailments of tourists.

In the case of a real emergency, a service from the United States can fly people to American hospitals: **Air-Evac (☎ 888-554-9729;** www.airevac.com) is a 24-hour air ambulance. You can also contact the service in Guadalajara (**☎ 01-800-305-9400,** 3-616-9616, or 3-615-2471). Several companies offer air-evacuation service; for a list, refer to the U.S. State Department Web site at http://travel.state.gov.

From our 12 years' experience of living in and traveling throughout Mexico, we can honestly say that most health problems that foreign tourists to Mexico encounter are self-induced. If you take in too much sun, too many margaritas, and too many street tacos within hours of your arrival, don't blame the water if you get sick. You'd be surprised how many people try to make up for all the fun they've missed in the past year on their first day of vacation in Mexico.

Avoiding *turista!*

It's called "travelers' diarrhea" or *turista,* the Spanish word for "tourist." I'm talking about the persistent diarrhea, often accompanied by fever, nausea, and vomiting, that used to attack many travelers to Mexico. Some folks in the United States call this affliction "Montezuma's revenge," but you won't hear it referred to this way in Mexico. Widespread improvements in infrastructure, sanitation, and education have practically eliminated this ailment, especially in well-developed resort areas. Most travelers make a habit of drinking only bottled water, which also helps to protect against unfamiliar bacteria. In resort areas, and generally throughout Mexico, only purified ice is used. Doctors say this ailment isn't caused by just one "bug," but by a combination of consuming different foods and water, upsetting your schedule, being overtired, and experiencing the stresses of travel. A good high-potency (or "therapeutic")

(continued)

(continued)

vitamin supplement and extra vitamin C can help. And yogurt is good for healthy diges-
tion. If you do happen to come down with this ailment, nothing beats Pepto-Bismol,
readily available in Mexico.

Preventing *turista*: The U.S. Public Health Service recommends the following measures for preventing travelers' diarrhea:

✔ Get enough sleep.

✔ Don't overdo the sun.

✔ Drink only purified water, which means tea, coffee, and other beverages made
  with boiled water; canned or bottled carbonated beverages and water; or beer
  and wine. Most restaurants with a large tourist clientele use only purified water
  and ice.

✔ Choose food carefully. In general, avoid salads, uncooked vegetables, and unpas-
  teurized milk or milk products (including cheese). However, salads in a first-class
  restaurant, or in a restaurant that serves a lot of tourists, are generally safe to eat.
  Choose food that's freshly cooked and still hot. Peelable fruit is ideal. Don't eat
  undercooked meat, fish, or shellfish.

✔ In addition, something as simple as washing hands frequently can prevent the
  spread of germs and go a long way toward keeping *turista* at bay.

Because **dehydration** can quickly become life-threatening, be especially careful to
replace fluids and electrolytes (potassium, sodium, and the like) during a bout of diarrhea. Rehydrate by drinking Pedialyte, a rehydration solution available at most
Mexican pharmacies, sports drinks, or glasses of natural fruit juice (high in potassium)
with a pinch of salt added. Or try a glass of boiled, pure water with a quarter teaspoon
of sodium bicarbonate (baking soda) and a bit of lime juice added.

Keeping the kids healthy

If you're traveling with **infants and/or children** in Mexico, be extra careful to avoid anything that's not bottled. You can readily purchase infant
formulas, baby foods, canned milk, and other baby supplies from grocery stores. Your best bet is to carry extra baby eats when you go out.
Most Mexican restaurants cheerfully warm bottles and packaged goods
for your child.

Be especially careful of sun exposure because **sunburn** can be extremely
dangerous. Protect the little ones with special SPF bathing suits and
cover-ups and regularly apply a strong sunscreen. (While you're at it,
don't forget a fairly strong sunscreen for yourself.)

Dehydration can also make your child seriously ill. Make sure your child
drinks plenty of water and juices throughout the day. Especially when

they're in the pool or at the beach having fun, they may not remember that they're thirsty, so reminding them is your job. Sunburn also contributes to and complicates dehydration.

Staying Safe

If you find yourself getting friendly with the locals — and we mean friendly to the point of a fling — don't be embarrassed to carry or insist on stopping for condoms — then use them! Too many vacationing men and women are filled with morning-after regrets because they didn't protect themselves. Don't allow your fear of being judged make you unprepared. Also know that Mexico's teen-to-20-something population has a rapidly escalating **HIV/AIDS** rate — especially in resort areas — due to the transient nature of the population and poor overall education about this disease.

And when it comes to **drugs,** many outsiders have the impression that the easy-going nature of these tropical towns means an equally laid-back attitude exists toward drug use. Not so. Marijuana, cocaine, Ecstasy, crystal methamphetamine, and other mood-altering drugs are illegal in Mexico. In some resorts, such as Puerto Vallarta, police randomly search people — including obvious tourists — who are walking the streets at night. However, unless you seek drugs out, whatever behind-the-scenes action there is won't likely affect you.

If you do choose to indulge, don't expect any special treatment if you're caught. In fact, everything bad you've ever heard about a Mexican jail is considered to be close to the truth — if not a rose-colored version of it. Mexico employs the Napoleonic Code of law, meaning that you're guilty until proven innocent. Simply stated, using drugs isn't worth the potential high. That's what tequila's for!

Renting a Car

First, know that car-rental costs are high in Mexico because cars are more expensive here. However, the condition of rental cars has improved greatly over the years, and clean, comfortable, new cars are the norm. At press time, the basic cost for a one-day rental of a Volkswagen (VW) Beetle, with unlimited mileage (but before the 15 percent tax and $15–$25 daily charge for insurance), was $48 in Cancún, $44 in Puerto Vallarta, and $40 in Acapulco. Renting by the week gives you a lower daily rate. Avis was offering a basic seven-day weekly rate for a VW Beetle (before tax or insurance) of $220 in Cancún and Puerto Vallarta and $200 in Acapulco. Prices may be considerably higher if you rent in these same cities around a major holiday.

Car-rental companies usually write up a credit-card charge in U.S. dollars.

Be careful of deductibles, which vary greatly in Mexico. Some deductibles are as high as $2,500, which immediately comes out of your pocket in case of car damage. Hertz has a $1,000 deductible on a VW Beetle; the deductible at Avis is $500 for the same car.

Always get the insurance; any coverage provided by your credit card or your own insurance policy isn't valid in Mexico. Insurance is offered in two parts. Collision and damage insurance covers your car and others if the accident is your fault, and personal accident insurance covers you and anyone in your car. Read the fine print on the back of your rental agreement and note that insurance may be invalid if you have an accident while driving on an unpaved road.

Personally, we think that Los Cabos is the only destination that is really enjoyed best if you have a car to get around. For all other beach destinations, we prefer to use taxis, which are reasonably priced except in Los Cabos.

Finding the best car-rental deal

Car-rental rates vary even more than airline fares. The price depends on the size of the car, the length of time you keep it, where and when you pick it up and drop it off, where you take it, and a host of other factors.

Asking a few key questions can save you hundreds of dollars. For example, weekend rates may be lower than weekday rates. Ask whether the rate is the same for pickup Friday morning as it is for Thursday night. If you're keeping the car five or more days, a weekly rate may be cheaper than the daily rate. Some companies may assess a drop-off charge if you don't return the car to the same renting location; others, notably National, don't. Ask whether the rate is cheaper if you pick up the car at the airport or a location in town. Don't forget to mention membership in AAA, AARP, frequent-flier programs, and trade unions. These memberships usually entitle you to discounts ranging from 5 percent to 30 percent. Ask your travel agent to check any and all these rates. And most car rentals are worth at least 500 miles on your frequent-flier account!

As with other aspects of planning your trip, using the Internet can make comparison-shopping for a car rental much easier. All the major booking Web sites — **Travelocity** (www.travelocity.com), **Expedia** (www.expedia.com), **Yahoo Travel** (www.travel.yahoo.com), and **Cheap Tickets** (www.cheaptickets.com), for example — have search engines that can dig up discounted car-rental rates. Just enter the size of the car you want, the pickup and return dates, and the city where you want to rent, and the server returns a price. You can even make the reservation through these sites.

In addition to the standard coverage, car-rental companies also offer additional liability insurance (if you harm others in an accident), personal accident insurance (if you harm yourself or your passengers), and personal effects insurance (if your luggage is stolen from your car). If you have insurance on your car at home, you're probably covered for most of these unlikelihoods. If your own insurance doesn't cover you for rentals or if you don't have auto insurance, you should consider the additional coverage. But weigh the likelihood of getting into an accident or losing your luggage against the cost of these insurance options (as much as $20 per day combined), which can significantly add to the price of your rental.

Some companies offer refueling packages, in which you pay for an entire tank of gas upfront. The price is usually fairly competitive with local gas prices, but you don't get credit for any gas remaining in the tank. If you reject this option, you pay only for the gas you use, but you have to return the car with a full tank or face charges of $3 to $4 a gallon for any shortfall. If a stop at a gas station on the way to the airport will make you miss your plane, by all means take advantage of the fuel purchase option. Otherwise, skip it.

Remembering safety comes first

If you decide to rent a car and drive in Mexico, you need to keep a few things in mind:

- ✔ Most Mexican roads are not up to U.S. standards of smoothness, hardness, width of curve, grade of hill, or safety markings. The roads in and around Cancún are a notable exception, but elsewhere in the Yucatán, this observation generally holds true.

- ✔ Driving at night is dangerous — the roads aren't good, and they're rarely lit; trucks, carts, pedestrians, and bicycles usually have no lights; and you can hit potholes, animals, rocks, dead ends, or uncrossable bridges without warning.

- ✔ Never turn left by stopping in the middle of a highway with your left signal on. Instead, pull off the highway onto the right shoulder, wait for traffic to clear, and then proceed across the road.

- ✔ Credit cards are generally not accepted for gas purchases.

- ✔ Places called *vulcanizadora* or *llantera* repair flat tires. Such places are commonly open 24 hours a day on the most-traveled highways. Even if the place looks empty, chances are you'll find someone who can help you fix a flat.

- ✔ When possible, many Mexicans drive away from minor accidents, or try to make an immediate settlement, to avoid involving the police.

- ✔ If the police arrive while the involved persons are still at the scene, everyone may be locked up until responsibility is determined and damages are settled. If you were in a rental car, notify the rental company immediately and ask how to contact the nearest adjuster. (You did buy insurance with the rental, right?)

Staying Connected by Cellphone or E-mail

The three letters that define much of the world's **wireless capabilities** are GSM (Global System for Mobiles), a big, seamless network that makes for easy cross-border cellphone use throughout Europe and dozens of other countries worldwide. In the U.S., T-Mobile, AT&T Wireless, and Cingular use this quasi-universal system; in Mexico, USACell and Telcel are the predominant mobile carriers, and both use GSM.

If your cellphone is on a GSM system, and you have a world-capable multiband phone such as many Sony Ericsson, Motorola, or Samsung models, you can make and receive calls across civilized areas on much of the globe, from Andorra to Uganda. Just call your wireless operator and ask for "international roaming" to be activated on your account. Unfortunately, per-minute charges can be high — usually $1 to $1.50.

That's why it's important to buy an "unlocked" world phone from the get-go. Many cellphone operators sell "locked" phones that restrict you from using any other removable computer memory phone chip card (called a **SIM card**) other than the ones they supply. Having an unlocked phone allows you to install a cheap, prepaid SIM card (found at a local retailer) in your destination country. (Show your phone to the salesperson; not all phones work on all networks.) You'll get a local phone number — and much, much lower calling rates. Getting an already locked phone unlocked can be a complicated process, but it can be done; just call your cellular operator and say you'll be going abroad for several months and want to use the phone with a local provider.

For many, **renting** a phone is a good idea. (Even world phone owners will have to rent new phones if they're traveling to non-GSM regions, such as Japan or Korea.) While you can rent a phone from any number of overseas sites, including kiosks at airports and at car-rental agencies, we suggest renting the phone before you leave home. That way you can give loved ones and business associates your new number, make sure the phone works, and take the phone wherever you go — especially helpful for overseas trips through several countries, where local phone-rental agencies often bill in local currency and may not let you take the phone to another country.

Phone rental isn't cheap. You'll usually pay $40 to $50 per week, plus air-time fees of at least a dollar a minute. The bottom line: Shop around.

Phone rentals in Mexico are still rare, so it's best to rent before your arrival. One option is to purchase an inexpensive phone that takes pre-paid cards, which you can purchase at any Telcel service provider in Mexico, for just the amount of service you feel you'll need during your trip.

Two good wireless rental companies are **InTouch USA** (☎ **800-872-7626**; www.intouchglobal.com) and **RoadPost** (☎ **888-290-1606** or 905-272-5665; www.roadpost.com). Give them your itinerary, and they'll tell you what wireless products you need. InTouch will also, for free, advise you on whether your existing phone will work overseas; simply call ☎ **703-222-7161** between 9 a.m. and 4 p.m. EST, or go to http://intouchglobal. com/travel.htm.

Accessing the Internet Away from Home

Travelers have any number of ways to check their e-mail and access the Internet on the road. Of course, using your own laptop — or even a PDA (personal digital assistant) or electronic organizer with a modem — gives you the most flexibility. But even if you don't have a computer, you can still access your e-mail and even your office computer from cybercafes.

It's hard nowadays to find a city that *doesn't* have a few cybercafes. Although there's no definitive directory for cybercafes — these are independent businesses, after all — two places to start looking are at www. cybercaptive.com and www.cybercafe.com.

Within Mexico's popular tourism destinations, cybercafes are very common, catering to traveler's increasing need — or desire — to stay connected while away. In each of the different locations in *Mexico's Beach Resorts For Dummies,* we list several recommended cybercafes, along with rates and hours.

Most major airports now have **Internet kiosks** scattered throughout their gates, as well as wireless Internet access, provided through the Telcel/Prodigy system. These kiosks, which you'll also see in shopping malls, hotel lobbies, and tourist information offices around the world, give you basic Web access for a per-minute fee that's usually higher than cybercafe prices. The kiosks' clunkiness and high price mean they should be avoided whenever possible.

To retrieve your e-mail, ask your **Internet Service Provider (ISP)** if it has a Web-based interface tied to your existing e-mail account. If your ISP doesn't have such an interface, you can use the free **mail2web** service (www.mail2web.com) to view and reply to your home e-mail. For more flexibility, you may want to open a free, Web-based e-mail account with **Yahoo! Mail** (http://mail.yahoo.com). (Microsoft's Hotmail is another popular option, but Hotmail has severe spam problems.) Your home ISP may be able to forward your e-mail to the Web-based account automatically.

If you need to access files on your office computer, look into a service called **GoToMyPC** (www.gotomypc.com). The service provides a Web-based interface for you to access and manipulate a distant PC from anywhere — even a cybercafe — provided your "target" PC is on and has an always-on connection to the Internet (such as with Road Runner cable). The service offers top-quality security, but if you're worried about hackers, use your own laptop rather than a cybercafe computer to access the GoToMyPC system.

If you are bringing your own computer, the buzzword in computer access to familiarize yourself with is **Wi-Fi** (wireless fidelity), and more and more hotels, cafes, and retailers are signing on as wireless "hot spots" from where you can get high-speed connection without cable wires, networking hardware, or a phone line. You can get Wi-Fi connection one of several ways. Many laptops sold in the last year have built-in Wi-Fi capability (an 802.11b wireless Ethernet connection). Mac owners have their own networking technology, Apple AirPort. For those with older computers, an 802.11b/**Wi-Fi card** (around $50) can be plugged into your laptop. You sign up for wireless access service much as you do cellphone service, through a plan offered by one of several commercial companies that have made wireless service available in airports, hotel lobbies, and coffee shops, primarily in the U.S. (followed by the U.K. and Japan). **T-Mobile Hotspot** (www.t-mobile.com/hotspot) serves up wireless connections at more than 1,000 Starbucks coffee shops nationwide. **Boingo** (www.boingo.com) and **Wayport** (www.wayport.com) have set up networks in airports and high-class hotel lobbies. **iPass** providers also give you access to a few hundred wireless hotel lobby setups. Best of all, you don't need to be staying at the Four Seasons to use the hotel's network; just set yourself up on a nice couch in the lobby. The companies' pricing policies can be Byzantine, with a variety of monthly, per-connection, and per-minute plans, but in general you pay around $30 a month for limited access — and as more and more companies jump on the wireless bandwagon, prices are likely to get even more competitive.

There are also places that provide **free wireless networks** in cities around the world. To locate these free hot spots, go to www.personaltelco.net/index.cgi/WirelessCommunities.

If Wi-Fi is not available at your destination, most business-class hotels throughout the world offer dataports for laptop modems, and a few thousand hotels in the U.S. and Europe now offer free high-speed Internet access using an Ethernet network cable. You can bring your own cables, but most hotels rent them for around $10. **Call your hotel in advance** to see what your options are.

In addition, major Internet Service Providers (ISP) have **local access numbers** around the world, allowing you to go online by simply placing a local call. Check your ISP's Web site or call its toll-free number and ask how you can use your current account away from home, and how much it will cost. If you're traveling outside the reach of your ISP, the iPass network has dial-up numbers in most of the world's countries. You'll have to sign up with an iPass provider, who will then tell you how to set up your computer for your destination(s). For a list of iPass providers, go to www.ipass.com. One solid provider is **i2roam** (☎ **866-811-6209** or 920-235-0475; www.i2roam.com).

Wherever you go, bring a **connection kit** of the right power and phone adapters, a spare phone cord, and a spare Ethernet network cable — or find out whether your hotel supplies them to guests. As Mexico shares the same electric current as the U.S., you'll find you won't need any special adaptors or equipment other than what you'd be using at home.

Keeping Up with Airline Security Measures

With the federalization of airport security, security procedures at U.S. airports are more stable and consistent than ever. Generally, you'll be fine if you arrive at the airport **one hour** before a domestic flight and **two hours** before an international flight; if you show up late, tell an airline employee and she'll probably whisk you to the front of the line.

Bring a **current, government-issued photo ID** such as a driver's license or passport. Keep your ID at the ready to show at check-in, the security checkpoint, and sometimes even the gate. (Children under 18 do not need government-issued photo IDs for domestic flights, but they do for international flights to most countries.)

In 2003, the TSA phased out **gate check-in** at all U.S. airports. And **E-tickets** have made paper tickets nearly obsolete. Passengers with E-tickets can beat the ticket-counter lines by using airport **electronic kiosks** or even **online check-in** from your home computer. Online check-in involves logging on to your airlines' Web site, accessing your reservation, and printing out your boarding pass — and the airline may even offer you bonus miles to do so! If you're using a kiosk at the airport, bring the credit card you used to book the ticket or your frequent-flier card. Print out your boarding pass from the kiosk and simply proceed to the security checkpoint with your pass and a photo ID. If you're checking bags or looking to snag an exit-row seat, you will be able to do so using most airline kiosks. Even the smaller airlines are employing the kiosk system, but always call your airline to make sure these alternatives are available. **Curbside check-in** is also a good way to avoid lines, although a few airlines still ban curbside check-in; call before you go.

Security checkpoint lines are getting shorter than they were during 2001 and 2002, but some doozies remain. If you have trouble standing for long periods of time, tell an airline employee; the airline will provide a wheelchair. Speed up security by **not wearing metal objects** such as big belt buckles. If you've got metallic body parts, a note from your doctor can prevent a long chat with the security screeners. Keep in mind that only **ticketed passengers** are allowed past security, except for folks escorting disabled passengers or children.

Federalization has stabilized **what you can carry on** and **what you can't.** The general rule is that sharp things are out, nail clippers are okay, and food and beverages must be passed through the X-ray machine — but that security screeners can't make you drink from your coffee cup. Bring food in your carry-on rather than checking it, as explosive-detection machines used on checked luggage have been known to mistake food (especially chocolate, for some reason) for bombs. Travelers in the U.S. are allowed one carry-on bag, plus a "personal item" such as a purse, briefcase, or laptop bag. Carry-on hoarders can stuff all sorts of things into a laptop bag; as long as it has a laptop in it, it's still considered a personal item. The Transportation Security Administration (TSA) has issued a list of restricted items; check its Web site (www.tsa.gov/public/index.jsp) for details.

Airport screeners may decide that your checked luggage needs to be searched by hand. You can now purchase luggage locks that allow screeners to open and re-lock a checked bag if hand-searching is necessary. Look for Travel Sentry certified locks at luggage or travel shops and Brookstone stores (you can buy them online at www.brookstone.com). These locks, approved by the TSA, can be opened by luggage inspectors with a special code or key. For more information on the locks, visit www.travelsentry.org. If you use something other than TSA-approved locks, your lock will be cut off your suitcase if a TSA agent needs to hand-search your luggage.

Packing for Mexico's Beaches

Start packing by taking out everything you think you need and laying it out on the bed. Then get rid of half of it.

It's not that the airlines won't let you take it all — they will, with some limits — but why would you want to get a hernia from lugging half your house around with you? Suitcase straps can be particularly painful with sunburned shoulders.

Unless you're attending a board meeting, a funeral, or one of the city's finest restaurants, you probably don't need a suit or a fancy dress in Mexico. Even the nicest restaurants tend to be casual when it comes to dress, especially for men. Women, on the other hand, tend to enjoy those sexy resort dresses, and they're definitely appropriate in any of the resorts covered in this book. But when it comes to essentials, you get more use out of a pair of jeans or khakis and a comfortable sweater.

Electricity runs on the same current in Mexico as in the United States and Canada, so feel free to bring a hair dryer, personal stereo, or whatever else you'd like to plug in. Don't bother to bring a travel iron — most hotels offer irons and ironing boards, or they offer the service at a very reasonable rate.

When choosing your suitcase, think about the kind of traveling you're doing. If you'll be walking with your luggage on hard floors, a bag with wheels makes sense. If you'll be carrying your luggage over uneven roads or up and down stairs, wheels don't help much. A fold-over garment bag helps keep dressy clothes wrinkle-free, but it can be a nuisance if you'll be packing and unpacking a lot. Hard-sided luggage protects breakable items better, but it weighs more than soft-sided bags.

Tips on what to wear to church

Whenever you visit a church in Mexico, no matter how casual the town is or how close the church is to the ocean, you should never enter wearing just a swimsuit or a pareo. Women should wear something other than short shorts and halter tops. Men should always wear some sort of shirt, even if it's just a tank top.

When packing, start with the biggest, hardest items (usually shoes) and then fit smaller items in and around them. Pack breakable items in between several layers of clothes or keep them in your carry-on bag. Put things that could leak, like shampoos or suntan lotions, in resealable plastic bags. Lock your suitcase with a TSA-approved lock (available at most luggage stores if your bag doesn't already have one) and put a distinctive identification tag on the outside so that your bag is easy to spot on the carousel.

Stricter security measures now dictate that each passenger is only allowed to bring one carry-on bag and one personal item (a purse, backpack, or briefcase) on the plane, and the items you do bring onboard are subject to strict size limitations. Both must fit in the overhead compartment or under the seat in front of you.

Among the items you might consider carrying on are a book; any breakable items you don't want to put in your suitcase; a personal stereo with headphones; a snack (in the likely event you don't like the airline food); a bottle of water; any vital documents you don't want to lose in your luggage (your return ticket, passport, wallet, and so on); and some empty space for the sweater or jacket that you won't be wearing while you're waiting for your luggage in an overheated terminal. You should also carry aboard any prescription medications, your glasses or spare contact lenses, and your camera. We always carry a change of clothes (shorts, T-shirt, and swimsuit) — just in case our checked baggage is lost. If the airline loses your luggage, you're likely to have it again within 24 hours, but having these essentials allows you to jump right into vacation fun anyway.

Here's a quick checklist of items you don't want to forget:

- ✔ At least two swimsuits
- ✔ Sunglasses
- ✔ Comfortable walking shoes
- ✔ Sandals
- ✔ Hat or cap
- ✔ Sunscreen

- ✔ Driver's license (if you plan to rent a car)
- ✔ Scuba certification (if you plan to dive)
- ✔ Casual slacks other than jeans (for men, especially if you plan on hitting the trendiest discos, some of which don't allow shorts or jeans)
- ✔ A pareo (sarong) that can double as a long or short skirt, or a wrap (for women)

Part III
Cancún

"I know it's a popular American expression, but you just don't say 'Hasta la vista, baby' to a nun."

In this part . . .

The most popular of Mexico's beach resorts, Cancún perfectly showcases the country's breathtaking natural beauty and the depth of its thousand-year-old history. Cancún is both the peak of Caribbean splendor and a modern mega-resort. It boasts translucent turquoise waters, powdery white-sand beaches, and a wide array of nearby shopping, dining, and nightlife choices, in addition to a ton of other activities. Most accommodations are offered at exceptional value, and Cancún is easily accessible by air.

Many travelers who feel apprehensive about visiting foreign soil feel completely at home and at ease here: Most people speak English, most stores and vendors accept U.S. dollars, roads are well paved, and lawns are manicured. A lot of the shopping and dining takes place in malls, and you'll swear that some hotels seem larger than a small town. Simply stated, Cancún is the reason why most people travel to Mexico. The following chapters introduce you to this Caribbean-coast jewel and include plenty of tips for making the most of your stay on this nonstop island.

Chapter 10

The Lowdown on Cancún's Hotel Scene

by Lynne Bairstow

- -

In This Chapter

▶ Sizing up the hotel locations
▶ Evaluating Cancún's top hotel choices

- -

*I*n 1974, a team of Mexican-government computer analysts selected Cancún as an area for tourism development because of its ideal combination of features to attract travelers — and they were right on the money. Cancún is actually an island: a 23km-long (14-mile) sliver of land shaped roughly like the number 7. Two bridges, spanning the expansive Nichupté Lagoon, connect Cancún to the mainland. (Cancún means "golden snake" in the Mayan language.)

With more than 28,000 hotel rooms in the area to choose from, Cancún has something for every taste and every budget. In this chapter, I review the two main areas — **Isla Cancún (Cancún Island)** and **Ciudad Cancún (Cancún City),** located inland, to the west of the island.

On October 21, 2005, Hurricane Wilma roared ashore with winds reaching 150mph, and then stalled over Cancún for nearly 40 hours. It toppled trees, demolished homes, and damaged the resort's hotels, restaurants, and attractions. However, relief came quickly, as Mexico's government understands the importance of Cancún as the country's most popular playground. The majority of damaged hotels took the opportunity to upgrade their facilities and redecorate their rooms, which should ultimately lead to a new and improved Cancún. However, at press time, many of these were still under construction, so personal reviews of all accommodations were not possible, and details of renovations were not available in complete detail. There have been some reportings of selected rooms retaining a strong smell of mildew, so please, let us know of your experiences or any comments you may have. Also, the noise of construction and piles of debris were omnipresent as this book went to press, but should be but a memory by the fall of 2006.

Cancún is definitely the destination to try out an air-hotel package. Although the rack rates at Cancún's hotels are among the highest in Mexico, the package deals are among the best because of the large number of charter companies operating here. (See Chapter 6 for more information on package deals, as well as some recommendations.) I should also point out that if you do arrive without a hotel reservation — I don't recommend it during peak weeks surrounding the Christmas and Easter holidays — you're likely to be able to bargain your way into a great rate.

Choosing a Location

Island hotels are stacked along the beach like dominoes; almost all offer clean, modern facilities, and most having undergone extensive renovations post–Hurricane Wilma. Extravagance reigns in the more recently built hotels, many of which are awash in a sea of marble and glass. However, some hotels, although they're exclusive, display a more relaxed attitude.

Following Hurricane Wilma's devastation, the news item that received the most coverage was the destruction of Cancún's famed white-sand beaches, certainly key to selecting a hotel location for many. Immediately following the storm, literally all of the sand was washed away from the northern border of Isla Cancún, and Punta Cancún. However, thanks in part to Mother Nature, and in part to a more than $20-million effort by Mexico's government to pump the dislocated sand back to the beach, by fall 2006 this should no longer be an issue. At press time (June 2006) a large beach had already developed along Punta Cancún, in front of the Forum Plaza, with sufficient sand in place along the north shore. The southern beaches of Isla Cancún actually benefited from the storm, and those areas enjoyed especially wide beachfronts.

The water is placid on the island's upper end facing Bahía de Mujeres, while beaches lining the long side of the island facing the Caribbean are subject to choppier water and crashing waves on windy days. Be aware that the farther south you go on the island, the longer it takes (20–30 min. in traffic) to get back to the "action spots," which are primarily located between the Plaza Flamingo and Punta Cancún on the island — close to the point that connects the two parts of the 7 — and along Avenida Tulum on the mainland.

Almost all major hotel chains are represented along **Isla Cancún,** also known as the **Hotel Zone,** so my selections can be viewed as a representative summary, with a select number of notable places to stay. The reality is that Cancún is so popular as a package destination from the United States that prices and special deals are often the deciding factor for vacationers traveling here.

Living *la vida* local

For condo, home, and villa rentals as an alternative to hotel stays, check with **Cancún Hideaways** (☎ **817-468-0564**; Fax: 817-557-3483), a company specializing in luxury properties, downtown apartments, and condos — many offered at prices much lower than comparable hotel accommodations. Owner Maggie Rodriguez, a former resident of Cancún, has made this niche market her specialty. You can preview her offerings at www.cancun-hideaways.com.

 Ciudad Cancún is the more authentic Mexican town of the two locations, where the hotels' employees live and where people not on vacation conduct their day-to-day business. The area offers independently owned, smaller, and much less expensive stays — the difference in prices between these accommodations and their island counterparts is truly remarkable. And many hotels in Ciudad Cancún offer a shuttle service to sister properties in Isla Cancún, meaning you can still access the beach, for a fraction of the price, in return for a little extra travel time. Many of the best restaurants are located here, especially if you're looking for a meal in a type of restaurant that differs from those you can find back home. You can also get the best value for your meal budget in Ciudad Cancún.

Cancún's Best Accommodations

Each hotel listing includes specific rack rates for two people spending one night in a standard room, double occupancy during high season (Christmas to Easter), unless otherwise indicated. *Rack rates* simply mean published rates and tend to be the highest rate paid — you can do better, especially if you're purchasing a package that includes airfare (see Chapter 7 for tips on avoiding paying rack rates). The rack rate prices quoted here include the 12 percent room tax — note that this is 5 percent lower than in most other resorts in Mexico, where the standard tax is 17 percent. Please refer to the Introduction of this book for an explanation of the price categories.

 Hotels often double the normal rates during Christmas and Easter weeks, but low-season rates can be anywhere from 20 percent to 60 percent below high-season rates. Some rates may seem much higher than others, but many of these higher rates are *all-inclusive* — meaning that your meals and beverages are included in the price of your stay. All tips, taxes, and most activities and entertainment are also included in all-inclusive rates.

All hotels listed here have air-conditioning, unless otherwise indicated.

Antillano
$ Ciudad Cancún

A quiet and very clean choice, the Antillano is close to the Ciudad Cancún bus terminal. Rooms overlook the main downtown street (Av. Tulum), the side streets, or the interior lawn and pool. The latter choice is the most desirable because these rooms are the quietest. Each room has coordinated furnishings, one or two double beds, a sink area separate from the bathroom, and red-tile floors. A bonus: This inexpensive hotel provides guests the use of its beach club on the island. To find Antillano from Avenida Tulum, walk west on Claveles a half block; it's opposite the restaurant Rosa Mexicano. Parking is on the street.

Av. Claveles 1 (corner of Av. Tulum). ☎ *998-884-1132. Fax: 998-884-1878.* www.hotel antillano.com. *48 units. Rack rates: High season $75 double; low season $65 double, breakfast included. AE, MC, V.*

Blue Bay Getaway & Spa Cancún
$$$$$ Isla Cancún

Blue Bay is a spirited yet relaxing all-inclusive resort for adults only — no kids under 16 are allowed — that's favored by young adults in particular. One of its best features is its prime location — right at the northern end of the Hotel Zone, close to the major shopping plazas, restaurants, and nightlife, with a beach with calm waters for swimming. Surrounded by acres of tropical gardens, the comfortable, clean, and modern guest rooms are located in two sections: the central building, where rooms are decorated in rustic wood, and the remaining nine buildings, which feature rooms in a colorful Mexican décor. The main lobby, administrative offices, restaurants, and the Las Margaritas bar are all located in the central building, meaning you're close to all the action — and more noise — if your room is in this section. Included are all your meals, served at any of the four restaurants, and libations, which you can find in the five bars. During the evenings, guests may enjoy a variety of theme-night dinners, nightly shows, and live entertainment in an outdoor theater with capacity for 150 guests. Activities and facilities include three swimming pools (with seven outdoor whirlpools), a tennis court, an exercise room, windsurfing, kayaks, catamarans, boogie boards, complimentary snorkeling and scuba lessons, and a marina. Safes are available for an extra charge, as are dry-cleaning and laundry service. Note that clothing is optional on the beaches of this Blue Bay resort.

Paseo Kukulkán Km 3.5. ☎ *800-BLUE-BAY in the U.S., or 998-848-7900. Fax: 998-848-7994.* www.bluebayresorts.com. *216 units. Free parking. Rack rates: High season $325 double; low season $225 double; rates are all-inclusive (room, food, beverages, and activities). AE, MC, V.*

CasaMagna Marriott
$$$$ Isla Cancún

This property is quintessential Marriott. Travelers who are familiar with the chain's standards feel at home here and appreciate the hotel's attention to

Accommodations in Isla Cancún (Hotel Zone)

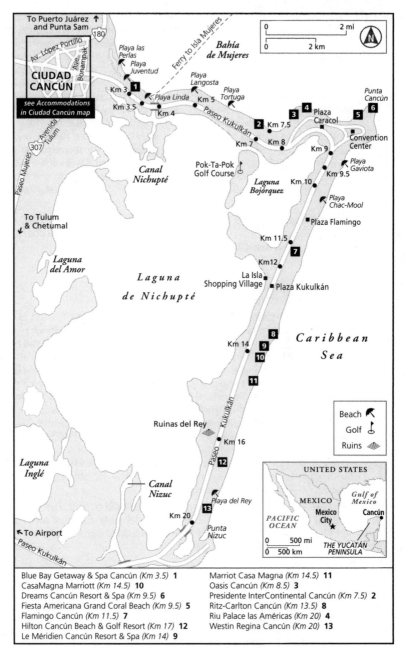

Blue Bay Getaway & Spa Cancún *(Km 3.5)* **1**
CasaMagna Marriott *(Km 14.5)* **10**
Dreams Cancún Resort & Spa *(Km 9.5)* **6**
Fiesta Americana Grand Coral Beach *(Km 9.5)* **5**
Flamingo Cancún *(Km 11.5)* **7**
Hilton Cancún Beach & Golf Resort *(Km 17)* **12**
Le Méridien Cancún Resort & Spa *(Km 14)* **9**

Marriot Casa Magna *(Km 14.5)* **11**
Oasis Cancún *(Km 8.5)* **3**
Presidente InterContinental Cancún *(Km 7.5)* **2**
Ritz-Carlton Cancún *(Km 13.5)* **8**
Riu Palace las Américas *(Km 20)* **4**
Westin Regina Cancún *(Km 20)* **13**

detailed service. In fact, if you're on your first trip to Mexico, and you're looking for a little familiarity of home, this is a great choice because it feels like a slice of the United States transported to a stunning stretch of Caribbean beach. Guest rooms have contemporary furnishings, tiled floors, and ceiling fans; most have balconies. All suites occupy corners and have enormous terraces, ocean views, and TVs in both the living room and the bedroom. The CasaMagna Marriott offers five on-site restaurants, plus a lobby bar with live music. Alongside the meandering oceanfront pool are two lighted tennis courts. The hotel caters to family travelers with specially priced packages (up to two children can stay free with parents) and the Club Amigos supervised children's program. Note that the hotel was undergoing extensive renovations, post-Wilma, at press time, so some of the above details could be subject to change. A more deluxe offering from Marriott, the 450-room luxury **JW Marriott Cancún** (Bulevar Kukulcán Km 14.5; ☎ 998-848-9600; www.marriot.com) is located on the beach next to the CasaMagna. Its hallmark is an 1,858-sq.-m (20,000-sq.-ft.) spa and fitness center.

Paseo Kukulkán Km 14.5. ☎ *800-228-9290 in the U.S., or 998-881-2000. Fax: 998-881-2085.* www.marriott.com. *452 units. Rack rates: $149–$219 double, $309–$339 suite; ask about available packages. AE, MC, V.*

Dreams Cancún Resort & Spa
$$$$$ **Isla Cancún**

Formerly the Camino Real, the all-inclusive Dreams Resort is among the island's most appealing places to stay, located on 1.6 hectares (4 acres) right at the tip of Punta Cancún. The setting is sophisticated, but the hotel is very welcoming to children. The hotel's architecture is contemporary and sleek, with bright colors and strategic angles. Rooms in the newer 18-story Club section have extra services and amenities. The lower-priced rooms have lagoon views. In addition to the oceanfront pool, there's a private saltwater lagoon with sea turtles and tropical fish. Dreams all-inclusive concept is more oriented to quality experiences than unlimited buffets — your room price here includes gourmet meals, 24-hour room service, premium brand drinks, as well as the use of all resort amenities, which include three lighted tennis courts, a fitness center, beach volleyball, a sailing pier, and a watersports center. The hotel's three restaurants — including the popular Paloma Bonita (see Chapter 12) are all on-site.

Av. Kukulkán Km 9.5, Punta Cancún. ☎ *800-722-6466 in the U.S., or 998-848-7000. Fax: 998-848-7001.* www.dreamscancun.com. *379 units. Guarded parking adjacent to hotel. Rack rates: High season $500 double, $560 Club double; low season $370 double, $430 Club double. AE, DC, MC, V.*

Fiesta Americana Grand Aqua
$$$$$ **Isla Cancún**

Stunning, stylish, and sensual, Aqua quickly emerged as Cancún's most coveted place to stay following its 2005 opening — only to be severely damaged by Hurricane Wilma. Extensive repairs rebuilt this mainly glass

Accommodations in Ciudad Cancún

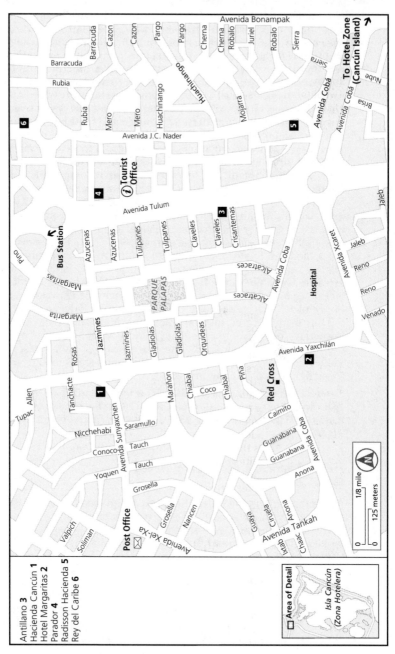

Antillano 3
Hacienda Cancún 1
Hotel Margaritas 2
Parador 4
Radisson Hacienda 5
Rey del Caribe 6

structure, slated to open by late fall 2006. A member of the Fiesta Americana chain, the entire hotel seems to mirror the predominant colors of Cancún — turquoise and white — in a sublimely chic manner. This hotel was built for sophisticated travelers who appreciate hip style and look for the cutting edge in places to stay. Aqua aims to stimulate your five senses, and upon arrival — under a crystal cube fountain—you're offered a fusion tea, and a blend of relaxing and stimulating aromatherapy. The oasis of eight oceanfront pools is surrounded by chaises, queen-size recliners, and private cabanas, as well as a beachfront watersports center. All rooms and common areas emphasize the views to the pool and ocean beyond. Rooms are generous in size, and all face the ocean and have balconies, plus amenities that include plasma TVs, minibars, and high-speed Internet access. Very large bathrooms feature a soaking tub and organic bath products, plus hair dryers. Guests can tailor their turndown service by selecting from a pillow menu and choice of aromatherapy oils and candles. Miniature Zen gardens or a fishbowl add unique touches to room décor. Suites offer extras like Bose surround-sound systems. Twenty-nine rooms are "Grand Club," which include continental breakfast and a club room with butler service, snacks, bar service, and private check-in. The spa is among the hotel's most notable attractions, with 12 treatment rooms offering a blend of Eastern, pre-Hispanic, and Western treatments. Outdoor Pilates, tai chi, and yoga classes are offered daily, and massage cabanas are also available on the beach. Another hallmark of this hotel is its collection of four restaurants, chief among them **SIETE,** under the direction of premier Mexican chef and cookbook author Patricia Quintana, featuring her sophisticated take on traditional Mexican cuisine. Chef Michelle Bernstein, formerly a rising culinary star in Miami, presides over **MB,** serving healthful comfort food. There are also an Italian restaurant, deli, lounge, and room service. After dark, the hotel shifts moods, with fire pits, torch lights, and ambient music.

Paseo Kukulkán Km 12.5. ☎ *800-343-7821 in the U.S., or 998-881-7600. Fax: 998-881-7601.* www.fiestaamericana.com.mx. *371 units. Rack rates: Year-round $254–$379 double, $435 Grand Club double, $580–$1,110 suite. Fiesta Break packages available. AE, MC, V.*

Fiesta Americana Grand Coral Beach
$$$$$ Isla Cancún

A spectacularly grand hotel, the Fiesta Americana has one of the best locations in Cancún with its 300m (1,000 ft.) of prime beachfront and proximity to the main shopping and entertainment centers — perfect for the traveler looking to be at the heart of all that Cancún has to offer. The great Punta Cancún location (opposite the Cancún Center) has the advantage of facing the beach to the north, meaning that the surf is calm and perfect for swimming. When it comes to the hotel itself, the operative word is *big* — everything at the Fiesta Americana seems oversize, from the lobby to the rooms. Service is gracious, if cool, as the hotel aims for a more sophisticated ambience. The finishings of elegant dark-green granite and an abundance of marble extend from the lobby to the large guest rooms, all of which have balconies facing the ocean. Two swimming pools border the beach, including a 198m-long (660-ft.) free-form swimming pool with swim-up bars and a casual poolside snack bar, plus a full watersports equipment rental service on the beach. Two additional restaurants, plus five bars, are inside the hotel, along with a mini-shopping center. If tennis is your game, this hotel has the best facilities in Cancún; three indoor tennis courts with stadium seating are part of an extensive fitness center and spa.

Paseo Kukulkán Km 9.5. ☎ *800-343-7821 in the U.S., or 998-881-3200. Fax: 998-881-3273.* www.fiestaamericana.com.mx. *602 units. Rack rates: High season $442–$465 double, $570–$838 Club Floors double; low season $279–$301 double, $407–$674 Club Floors double. AE, MC, V.*

Flamingo Cancún
$$$–$$$$ Isla Cancún

The Flamingo seems to have been inspired by the dramatic, slope-sided architecture of the Dreams Cancún, but the Flamingo is considerably smaller and less expensive. And with two pools, it's a friendly, accommodating choice for families. The clean, comfortable, and modern guest rooms — all with balconies — border a courtyard facing the interior swimming pool and *palapa* pool bar. A second pool with a sun deck overlooks the ocean. You can choose an all-inclusive plan, which includes meals. The Flamingo is in the heart of the island hotel district, opposite the Flamingo Shopping Center and close to other hotels, shopping centers, and restaurants.

Bulevar Kukulcán Km 11.5. ☎ *998-848-8870. Fax: 998-883-1029.* www.flamingo cancun.com. *221 units. Free, unguarded parking across the street in the Plaza Flamingo. Rack rates: High season $170 double, low season $120 double; all-inclusive plan is $260 double high season, $220 double low season. AE, MC, V.*

Hacienda Cancún
$ Ciudad Cancún

An extremely pleasing little hotel — and a great value — Hacienda Cancún is perfect for travelers on a budget. The facade has been remodeled to look like a hacienda, and rooms continue the theme, with their rustic-style Mexican furnishings. Guest rooms are clean and very comfortable; all have two double beds and windows (but no views). There's a nice, small pool and cafe under a shaded *palapa* in the back. To find it from Avenida Yaxchilán, turn west on Sunyaxchen; it's on your right. Parking is on the street.

Sunyaxchen 39–40. ☎ *998-884-3672. Fax: 998-884-1208.* hhda@Cancun.com.mx. *35 units. Rack rates: High season $60 double; low season $48 double. MC, V.*

Hilton Cancún Beach & Golf Resort
$$$$$ Isla Cancún

The Hilton in Cancún is especially perfect for anyone whose motto is "the bigger the better." Grand, expansive, and fully equipped, this is a true resort in every sense of the word. The Hilton Cancún (formerly the 1994-vintage Caesar Park Resort) is situated on 100 hectares (250 acres) of prime Cancún beachfront property with its own 18-hole, par-72 golf course across the street and a location that gives every room an ocean view (some have both ocean and lagoon views). Like the sprawling resort, rooms are grandly spacious and immaculately decorated. Marble floors and bathrooms throughout are softened with area rugs and pale furnishings. The more elegant Villa rooms are set off from the main hotel in two- and three-story buildings (no elevators) and have their own check-in and concierge service, plus nightly complimentary cocktails. The hotel is especially appealing to golfers because it's one of only two hotels in Cancún with an on-site course. (The other is the Meliá, which has an 18-hole executive course.) The seven interconnected pools with a swim-up bar, two lighted tennis courts, a large, fully equipped gym, and a beachfront watersports center make the Hilton Cancún a good choice for those looking for an action-packed stay. Their Kids Club program is one of the best on the island, making it great for families. Post–Hurricane Wilma, all rooms received an update, and common areas were renovated.

Paseo Kukulkán Km 17, Retorno Lacandones. ☎ *800-774-1500 in the U.S., or 998-881-8000. Fax: 998-881-8080.* www.hiltoncancun.com. *426 units. Rack rates: High season $375–$380 double, $440 Villa Front, $430 Villa Garden; low season $259–$300 double, $419 Villa Front, $399 Villa Garden. AE, DC, MC, V.*

Hotel Margaritas
$$ Ciudad Cancún

Located in downtown Cancún, this four-story hotel (with elevator) is comfortable and unpretentious, offering one of the best values in Cancún. Rooms have white-tile floors and a small balcony, and they're exceptionally clean and bright and pleasantly decorated. The attractive pool is surrounded by lounge chairs and has a wading section for children. The hotel offers complimentary safes at the front desk and more services than most budget hotels, including babysitting.

Av. Yaxchilán 41. ☎ *998-884-9333. Fax: 998-884-1324.* www.margaritascancun.com. *100 units. Rack rates: High season $90 double; low season $78 double. AE, MC, V.*

Le Méridien Cancún Resort & Spa
$$$$$ Isla Cancún

Of all the luxury properties in Cancún, Le Méridien is the most inviting, with a polished yet welcoming sense of personal service. Although other hotels tend to overdo a sense of formality in striving to justify their prices, Le Méridien has an elegantly casual style that makes you comfortable enough to relax thoroughly. From the intimate lobby and reception area to the most outstanding concierge service in Cancún, guests feel immediately pampered upon arrival. The hotel itself is smaller than others and feels more like an upscale boutique hotel than an immense resort — a welcome relief to those overstressed by activity at home. The décor throughout the rooms and common areas is one of understated good taste — both classy and comforting, not overdone. Rooms are generous in size, and most have small balconies overlooking the pool with an ocean view. There's a very large marble bathroom with a separate tub and a glassed-in shower. The hotel attracts many Europeans and younger, sophisticated travelers, and is ideal for a second honeymoon or romantic break. Certainly, a highlight of — or even a reason for — staying here is time spent at the **Spa del Mar,** one of Mexico's finest and most complete European spa facilities, featuring two levels and more than 1,394 sq. m (15,000 sq. ft.) of services dedicated to your body and soul. A complete fitness center with extensive cardio and weight machines is on the upper level. The spa is located below and is comprised of a healthy snack bar, a full-service salon, and 14 treatment rooms, as well as separate men's and women's steam rooms, saunas, whirlpools, cold plunge pools, inhalation rooms, tranquillity rooms, lockers, and changing areas.

The health club may become a necessity if you fully enjoy the gourmet restaurant, **Aioli,** with its specialties based on Mediterranean and Provençal cuisines (check out Chapter 12 for a detailed review of this restaurant). The menu is simply delicious — not pretentious. Adjoining the spa is a large swimming pool that cascades down three levels. Above the spa is a tennis center with two championship tennis courts with lights. Watersports equipment is available for rent on the beach. There's also a supervised children's program with its own Penguin Clubhouse, play equipment, and a wading pool.

Retorno del Rey Km 14. ☎ *800-543-4300 in the U.S., or 998-881-2200. Fax: 998-881-2201.* www.meridiencancun.com.mx. *213 units. Free parking. Rack rates: High season $560 double, $780 suite; low season $280 double, $420 suite; ask about special spa packages. Small pets accepted with advance reservation. AE, DC, MC, V.*

Oasis Cancún
$$$–$$$$ Isla Cancún

From the street, the Oasis may not be much to look at, but the location is ideal because it's set on Cancún's best beach for safe swimming. And it's close to all the shops and restaurants clustered near Punta Cancún and the convention center. The ocean side has a small but pretty patio garden and pool. You can choose between rooms with either a lagoon or ocean view. The rooms are large and undistinguished in décor, but they're comfortable. They feature marble floors and either two double beds or a king-size bed. Several studios with kitchenettes are also available upon request. In addition to a restaurant and three bars, you also can use two lighted tennis courts, watersports equipment rental, and a small marina with its own fishing fleet.

Paseo Kukulkán Km 8.5, next to the Playa Linda dock. ☎ *998-883-0800. Fax: 998-883-2087. 216 units. Free parking. Rack rates: High season $155–$210 double; low season $155–$185 double. AE, MC, V.*

Parador
$ Ciudad Cancún

The convenient location and rock-bottom prices make this otherwise non-descript hotel among the most popular downtown hotels. Guest rooms, located on one of three floors, are arranged around two long, narrow garden courtyards leading back to a small pool (with an even smaller, separate children's pool) and grassy sunning area. The rooms are contemporary and basic, each with two double beds and a shower. The hotel is next to Pop's restaurant, almost at the corner of Uxmal. Street parking is limited.

Av. Tulum 26. ☎ *998-884-1043 or 884-1310. Fax: 998-884-9712.* www.hotelparador cancun.com. *66 units. Rack rates: High season $65 double; low season $50 double; ask about promotional rates. MC, V.*

Presidente InterContinental Cancún
$$$$$ Isla Cancún

On the island's best beach facing the placid Bahía de Mujeres, the Presidente's location is reason enough to stay here, and it's just a two-minute walk to Cancún's public Pok-Ta-Pok Golf Club. Cool and spacious, the Presidente sports a postmodern design with lavish marble and wicker accents and a strong use of color. Guests have a choice of two double beds or one king-size bed. All rooms have tastefully simple white cedar accents, minibars, and complimentary Internet access. The expansive pool area has a pyramid-shaped waterfall and is surrounded by cushioned lounge chairs and five Jacuzzis. In addition to lighted tennis courts and a small fitness center, the marina has watersports equipment rentals. Coming from Ciudad Cancún, the Presidente is on the left side of the street before you get to Punta Cancún. With its ambience, the Presidente is an ideal choice for a romantic getaway or for couples who enjoy indulging in golf, tennis, or even shopping. Extensive renovations and room upgrades occurred post–Hurricane Wilma.

Av. Kukulkán Km 7.5. ☎ *800-327-0200 or 904-4400 in the U.S., or 998-848-8700. Fax: 998-883-2515.* www.interconti.com. *299 units. Rack rates: High season $220–$300 double; low season $150–$350 double; ask about special promotional packages. AE, MC, V.*

Radisson Hacienda
$$$ Ciudad Cancún

The nicest hotel in downtown Cancún, the Radisson Hacienda is also one of the area's best values. It offers all the expected comforts of a known hotel chain, yet in an atmosphere of Mexican hospitality. Resembling a Mexican hacienda, rooms are set off from a large rotunda-style lobby, lush gardens, and a pleasant pool area. All rooms have brightly colored fabric accents; a small sitting area and balcony; and views of the garden, the pool, or the street. Bathrooms have a combination tub and shower. For the price, the extra in-room amenities of a coffeemaker, hair dryer, and iron are nice pluses. In addition to two restaurants, there's also a generally lively lobby bar, as well as tennis courts and a small gym. Guests of the Radisson Hacienda enjoy a complimentary shuttle service to the beach on Isla Cancún or to the Pok-Ta-Pok Golf Course. The hotel is located right behind the state government building and within walking distance of downtown Cancún dining and shopping.

Av. Nader 1. ☎ *800-333-3333 in the U.S., or 998-881-6500. Fax: 998-884-7954.* www. radissoncancun.com. *248 units. Rack rates: $140 double, $168 Jr. Suite. AE, MC, V.*

Refugio del Pirata Morgan
$ Ciudad Cancún

Although not actually in the town of Cancún, but on the highway leading north from Cancún to Punta Sam, this is the place for those who want a true encounter with nature. Located on a wide, virgin stretch of beach (which expanded even more post-Wilma), away from the crowd of hotels and nightlife, this "refuge" is exactly that: no phones, no television, just blissful peace and quiet. There are 10 simple cabañas, with both beds and hammocks, each named for the predominant color of the décor. A small restaurant offers a basic selection of dining choices featuring fresh fish — otherwise, the nearest restaurant is 2km (1¼ miles) away.

Carretera Punta Sam, Isla Blanca Km 9. ☎ *998-860-3386 (within Mexico dial 044 first, as this is a cellphone). 10 units. Rack rates: $40 room; $5 hammock. No credit cards.*

Rey del Caribe Hotel
$–$$ Ciudad Cancún

This hotel, located in the center of downtown, is a unique oasis — a 100 percent ecological hotel, where every detail has been thought out to achieve the goal of living in an organic and environmentally friendly manner. The whole atmosphere of the place is one of warmth, which derives from the on-site owners, who, caring as much as they do for Mother Earth, extend this sentiment to guests as well. You easily forget you're in the midst of downtown Cancún in the tropical jungle setting, with blooming orchids and other flowering plants. Surrounding gardens and the pool and hot tub area are populated with statues of Maya deities — it's a lovely, tranquil setting. There's a daily-changing schedule of yoga, tai chi, and meditation sessions, as well as special classes on astrology, tarot, and other subjects. Rooms are large and sunny, with your choice of one king or two full-size beds, a kitchenette, and terrace. The detail of ecological sensitivity is truly impressive, ranging from the use of collected rainwater to waste composting. Recycling is encouraged and solar power used wherever possible.

Av. Uxmal, corner with Nadar, SM 2A. ☎ *998-884-2028. Fax: 988-884-9857.* www.rey caribe.com. *24 units. Rack rates: High season $63–$100 double; low season $40–$80 double. Rates include breakfast. MC, V.*

Ritz-Carlton Cancún (scheduled to reopen Sept 5, 2006)
$$$$$ Isla Cancún

The grand-scale Ritz-Carlton is a fountain of formality in this casual beach resort, perfect for someone who wants a Palm Beach–style experience in Mexico. The décor — in both public areas as well as guest rooms — is sumptuous and formal with thick carpets, elaborate chandeliers, and fresh flowers throughout. The hotel fronts a 360m (1,200-ft.) white-sand beach, and all rooms overlook the ocean, pool (heated during winter months), and tropical gardens. In all rooms, marble bathrooms have telephones, separate tubs and showers, and lighted makeup mirrors. Ritz-Carlton Club floors offer guests five mini-meals a day, private butler service, and Hermès bath products. **The Club Grill,** a fashionable English pub, is one of the best restaurants in the city, and the **Lobby Lounge** is the original home of proper tequila tastings, featuring one of the world's most extensive menus of fine tequilas, as well as Cuban cigars. I love their white-draped cabañas for two on the beach! There's a very good fitness center and the luxury Kayantá Spa offers an excellent selection of Maya and Mexican-inspired treatments and massages. There are also three lighted tennis courts. The Ritz Kids program has supervised activities for children, and babysitting services are also available. The hotel has won countless recognitions and accolades for service. Special packages for golfing, spa, and weekend getaways are worth exploring. The hotel took the opportunity to make extensive renovations post–Hurricane Wilma.

Retorno del Rey 36, off Paseo Kukulkán Km 13.5. ☎ *800-241-3333 in the U.S. and Canada, or 998-881-0808. Fax: 998-881-0815.* www.ritzcarlton.com. *365 units. Free guarded parking. Rack rates: $299–$439 double, $439–$569 Club floors. AE, MC, V.*

Riu Palace Las Americas
$$$$$ Isla Cancún

The all-inclusive Riu Palace is part of a family of Riu resorts in Cancún known for their grand, opulent style. This one is the smallest of the three in Cancún, and the most elegant, steeped in pearl-white Greco style, and my choice for a high-end all-inclusive vacation in Cancún. The location is prime—near the central shopping, dining, and nightlife centers, just five minutes walking to the Cancún Center. All rooms are spacious junior suites with ocean or lagoon views, a separate seating area, and a balcony or terrace, and come with premium extras such as bathrobes and hair dryers. Eight also feature a Jacuzzi. Two central pools overlook the ocean and a wide stretch of beach, with one heated during winter months. The hotel offers guests virtually 24 hours of all-inclusive snacks, meals, and beverages, as well as six restaurants and five bars. A nicely equipped health club and tennis court complement the resort's ample activities program. And, if that's not enough, guests have exchange privileges at the Riu Cancún, next door.

Paseo Kukulkán, Lote 4. ☎ *888-666-8816 in the U.S., or 998-891-4300.* www.riu.com. *368 suites. Rack rates: High season $413–$627 double, all-inclusive; low season $287–$464 double, all-inclusive. AE, MC, V.*

Westin Resort & Spa Cancún
$$$$$ Isla Cancún

A stunning hotel, the Westin Resort & Spa is great for anyone wanting the beauty of Cancún's beaches and a little distance between them and the more boisterous, flashy parts of Cancún's hotel strip. The strikingly austere but grand architecture of the Westin Regina is the stamp of leading Latin American architect Ricardo Legorreta. A series of five swimming pools front the beach, and the Westin offers two lighted tennis courts and a small fitness center with limited spa services. The hotel is divided into two sections: the main building and the more exclusive six-story, hot-pink tower section. Standard rooms are unusually large and beautifully furnished with cool, contemporary furniture. The rooms on the sixth floor have balconies, and first-floor rooms have terraces. Rooms in the tower all have ocean or lagoon views and extensive use of marble, furniture with Olinalá lacquer accents, Berber-carpet area rugs, oak tables and chairs, and terraces with lounge chairs. It's important to note that this hotel is a 15- to 20-minute ride from the lively strip that lies between the Plaza Flamingo and Punta Cancún, so it's a better choice for those who want to relish a little more seclusion than Cancún typically offers. However, you can easily join the action when you're so inclined — buses stop in front and taxis are readily available. The hotel took the opportunity of Hurricane Wilma damage for a complete renovation.

Paseo Kukulkán Km 20. ☎ *800-228-3000 in the U.S., or 998-848-7400. Fax: 998-885-0666.* www.westin.com. *379 units. Rack rates: High season $319–$499 double; low season $139–$299 double. AE, DC, MC, V.*

Chapter 11

Settling into Cancún

by Lynne Bairstow

In This Chapter

▶ Knowing what to expect when you arrive
▶ Finding your way around
▶ Discovering helpful information and resources

*Y*es, you need a passport or other appropriate credentials (see Chapter 9) to enter Cancún, but after that, you couldn't be in a more American-friendly foreign destination if you tried. If this is your first trip to Mexico — or to a foreign country — you'll probably find that the ensuing culture shock is practically nonexistent. But there are still a few details that you'll be more comfortable knowing before you arrive. In this chapter, I take you from the plane, through the airport, and to your hotel, helping you quickly get your bearings in this easy-to-navigate resort.

Arriving in Cancún

Cancún has one of Mexico's most modern and busiest airports — and one that is being renovated once again, in the wake of 2005's Hurricane Wilma — which will further improve and expand its services. Still, navigating Cancún's airport is easy — both international and national flights are under the same roof. After checking in with immigration, collecting your bags, and passing through the Customs checkpoint, you're ready to enjoy your holiday!

Navigating passport control and Customs

Immigration check-in can be a lengthy wait, depending on the number of planes arriving at the same time, but is a generally easy and unremarkable process in which officials ask you to show your passport and complete a tourist card, known as the **FMT** (check out Chapter 9 for more information).

 Your FMT is an important document, so take good care of it. You're supposed to keep the FMT with you at all times because you may be required to show it if you run into any sort of trouble. You also need to turn the FMT back in upon departure, or you may be unable to leave without replacing it.

Next up is the baggage claim area. Here, porters stand by to help with your bags, and they're well worth the price of the tip — about a dollar a bag. After you collect your luggage, you pass through another checkpoint. Something that looks like a traffic light awaits you here. You press a button, and if the light turns green, you're free to go. If it turns red, you need to open each of your bags for a quick search. It's Mexico's random search procedure for Customs. If you have an unusually large bag, or an excessive amount of luggage, you may be searched regardless of the traffic-light outcome.

Just past the traffic light, you exit to the street, where you can find transportation to your hotel. Choose between a *colectivo* (shared minivan) and a private taxi. If three or more of you are traveling together, you're better off with the private cab service. With so many hotels for the collective van to stop at, it can easily take an hour to get to your room, and believe me, the drivers wait until the vans are packed before departing! Check out the "Accommodations in Isla Cancún" map in Chapter 10 to find out where your hotel is relative to the airport.

If you do choose the *colectivo* service, which consists of air-conditioned vans, buy your ticket at the booth that's located to the far right as you exit baggage claim. You can purchase tickets for private cab service at a booth inside the airport terminal. Tickets for both the *colectivo* vans and the private taxis are based on a fixed rate depending on the distance to your destination. A taxi ticket is good for up to four passengers.

Getting to your hotel

The airport is on the mainland, close to the southern end of the Cancún area. It's about 14km (9 miles) to downtown **Ciudad Cancún (Cancún City),** which is located on the mainland. The start of the **Zona Hotelera (Hotel Zone),** located on **Isla Cancún (Cancún Island),** is 10km (6½ miles) from the airport — about a 20-minute drive east from the airport along wide, well-paved roads.

Hiring a taxi

Rates for a **private taxi** from the airport are around $25 to downtown Cancún or $28 to $45 to the Hotel Zone, depending on your destination. The *colectivos* run from Cancún's international airport into town and the Hotel Zone and cost about $9 per person. There's minibus transportation (for $9.50) from the airport to the Puerto Juárez passenger ferry that takes you to Isla Mujeres. You can also hire a private taxi for this trip for about $40.

No *colectivo* service returns to the airport from Ciudad Cancún or the Hotel Zone, so you must hire a taxi, but the rate should be much less than the trip from the airport. The reason? Only federally chartered taxis

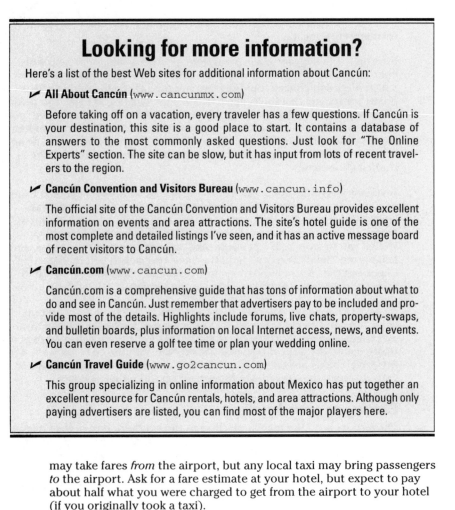

Looking for more information?

Here's a list of the best Web sites for additional information about Cancún:

✔ **All About Cancún** (www.cancunmx.com)

Before taking off on a vacation, every traveler has a few questions. If Cancún is your destination, this site is a good place to start. It contains a database of answers to the most commonly asked questions. Just look for "The Online Experts" section. The site can be slow, but it has input from lots of recent travelers to the region.

✔ **Cancún Convention and Visitors Bureau** (www.cancun.info)

The official site of the Cancún Convention and Visitors Bureau provides excellent information on events and area attractions. The site's hotel guide is one of the most complete and detailed listings I've seen, and it has an active message board of recent visitors to Cancún.

✔ **Cancún.com** (www.cancun.com)

Cancún.com is a comprehensive guide that has tons of information about what to do and see in Cancún. Just remember that advertisers pay to be included and provide most of the details. Highlights include forums, live chats, property-swaps, and bulletin boards, plus information on local Internet access, news, and events. You can even reserve a golf tee time or plan your wedding online.

✔ **Cancún Travel Guide** (www.go2cancun.com)

This group specializing in online information about Mexico has put together an excellent resource for Cancún rentals, hotels, and area attractions. Although only paying advertisers are listed, you can find most of the major players here.

may take fares *from* the airport, but any local taxi may bring passengers *to* the airport. Ask for a fare estimate at your hotel, but expect to pay about half what you were charged to get from the airport to your hotel (if you originally took a taxi).

Renting a car

Most major car-rental firms have outlets at the airport, so if you're renting a car, consider picking it up and dropping it off at the airport to save on airport-transportation costs. Another way to save money is to arrange for the rental before you leave home. If you wait until you arrive, the daily cost of a rental car may be around $65 to $75 for a Volkswagen Beetle. Major car-rental services include:

✔ **Avis** (☎ **800-331-1212** in the U.S., or 998-886-0221; www.avis.com)

✔ **Budget** (☎ **800-527-0700** in the U.S., or 998-884-6955 downtown office; www.budget.com)

✔ **Dollar** (☎ **800-800-3665** in the U.S., or 998-886-2300; www.dollar.com)

✔ **Hertz** (☎ **800-654-3131** in the U.S. and Canada, or 998-884-1326; www.hertz.com)

✔ **National** (☎ **800-CAR-RENT** in the U.S., or 998-886-0153; www.nationalcar.com)

 Although you certainly don't have to rent a car in Cancún — taxis and buses are plentiful — this is one destination where having a car may make sense for a day or two. It can be a convenience, although it's not likely to save you bundles on transportation costs, based on the relatively high prices of car rentals in Cancún. The roads in and around Cancún are excellent, and parking is readily available in most of the shopping/ entertainment malls. The main reason for renting a car, however, is the flexibility that it provides in exploring the surrounding areas — a day trip down the coast or to nearby sights is definitely recommended. But if you're not comfortable driving, you can easily cover this ground on one of the many sightseeing tours available.

 If you do rent a car, keep any valuables out of plain sight. Although Cancún's crime rate is very low, the only real problem tends to be rental-car break-ins.

Getting Around Cancún

As I discuss a bit in the "Getting to your hotel" section earlier in this chapter, there are really two Cancúns: **Isla Cancún (Cancún Island)** and **Ciudad Cancún (Cancún City).** The latter, on the mainland, has restaurants, shops, and less-expensive hotels, as well as all the other establishments that make local life function — pharmacies, dentists, automotive shops, banks, travel and airline agencies, car-rental firms, and so on — which are all located within an approximately nine-square-block area. The city's main thoroughfare is **Avenida Tulum.** Heading south, Avenida Tulum becomes the highway to the airport, Playa del Carmen, and Tulum. (It actually runs all the way down to Belize.) Heading north, Avenida Tulum intersects the highway to Mérida and the road to Puerto Juárez and the Isla Mujeres ferries.

The famed **Zona Hotelera** (Hotel Zone, also called the **Zona Turística,** or Tourist Zone) stretches out along Isla Cancún, which is a sandy strip of land 23km (14 miles) long and shaped like a 7. The Playa Linda Bridge, at the north end of the island, and the Punta Nizuc Bridge, at the southern end, connect Isla Cancún to the mainland. Between these two bridges lies **Laguna Nichupté.** Avenida Cobá from Cancún City becomes Paseo Kukulkán, the island's main traffic artery — actually, the only main road on the island, so getting lost here really takes some effort! To get the hang of pronouncing it quickly enough, say "koo-cool-*can*," as in, "Cancún is sooo cool!" Cancún's international airport is located just inland from the south end of the island.

Ciudad Cancún's street-numbering system is a holdover from its early days. Addresses in the city are still expressed by the number of the building lot and the *manzana* (block) or *supermanzana* (group of city blocks). The city is still relatively compact, and you can easily cover the downtown commercial section on foot. Streets are named after famous Maya cities. Chichén Itzá, Tulum, and Uxmal are the names of the boulevards in downtown Cancún, as well as nearby archaeological sites.

On the island, addresses are given by their kilometer (Km) numbers on Paseo Kukulkán or by reference to some well-known location. The point on the island closest to Ciudad Cancún is Km 1; Km 20 is found at the very bottom of the 7 at Punta Nizuc, where the Club Med is located.

Taking a taxi

Taxi prices in Cancún are clearly set by zone, although keeping track of what's in which zone can take some work. Taxi rates within the Hotel Zone are a minimum fare of $6 per ride, making it one of the most expensive taxi areas in Mexico.

Taxis operating in the Hotel Zone feel perfectly justified in having a discriminatory pricing structure: Local residents pay about half of what tourists pay, and guests at higher-priced hotels pay about twice the fare that guests in budget hotels are charged. You can thank the taxi union for this bit of fun — they establish the rate schedule. Rates should be posted outside your hotel; however, if you have a question, all taxi drivers are required to have an official rate card in their taxi, although it's generally in Spanish.

Within downtown, the cost is about $1.50 per cab ride (not per person); within any other zone, it's $5. Traveling between two zones also costs $5. If you cross two zones, the cost is $7.50; crossing three zones runs about $11. Settle on a price in advance, or check at your hotel, where destinations and prices are generally posted. Trips to the airport from most zones cost $15. Taxis also have a rate of $18 per hour for travel around the city and Hotel Zone, but you can generally negotiate this rate down to $10 to $12. If you want to hire a taxi to take you to Chichén Itzá or along the Riviera Maya, expect to pay about $30 per hour — many taxi drivers feel that they're also providing guide services.

Catching a bus

Bus travel within Cancún continues to improve and is increasingly the most popular way of getting around for both residents and tourists. Air-conditioned and rarely crowded, the Hotel Zone buses run 24 hours a day. You can easily spot the bus stops; look for roadside signs that have a bus on them. Bus stops are in front of most of the main hotels and shopping centers. In town, almost everything is within walking distance. Ruta 1 and Ruta 2 *(Hoteles)* city buses travel frequently from the mainland to the beaches along Avenida Tulum (the main street) and all the way to Punta Nizuc at the far end of the Hotel Zone on Isla Cancún.

Ruta 8 buses go to Puerto Juárez/Punta Sam, where you can catch ferries to Isla Mujeres. The buses stop on the east side of Avenida Tulum. These buses operate between 6 a.m. and 10 p.m. daily. Beware of private buses along the same route; they charge far more than the public ones. The public buses have the fare amount painted on the front; at the time of publication, the fare was 6.50 pesos (60¢).

Zipping around on a moped

Mopeds are a convenient and popular way to cruise around the congested traffic, but they can be dangerous. Rentals start at $25 for a day, and the shops require a credit-card voucher as security for the moped.

When you rent a moped, make sure you receive a crash helmet (it's the law) and instructions on how to lock the wheels when you park. Read the fine print on the back of the rental agreement regarding liability for repairs or replacement in case of accident, theft, or vandalism.

Fast Facts: Cancún

American Express

The local office is located in Ciudad Cancún at Av. Tulum 208 and Agua (☎ 998-881-4000 or 881-4055), a block past the Plaza México. The office is open Monday to Friday 9 a.m. to 6 p.m. and Saturday 9 a.m. to 1 p.m.

Area Code

The telephone area code is **988.**

Baby Sitters

Most of the larger hotels can easily arrange for baby sitters, but many sitters speak limited English. Rates range from $4 to $10 per hour.

Banks, ATMs, and Currency Exchange

Most banks are downtown along Avenida Tulum and are usually open Monday to Friday 9 a.m. to 4 p.m., and many now have ATMs for after-hours cash withdrawals. In the Hotel Zone, you can find banks in the Plaza Kukulkán and next to the convention center. There are also many *casas de cambio* (exchange houses) in the Hotel Zone, in the plazas, and near the convention center. Avoid changing money at the

airport as you arrive, especially at the first exchange booth you see — its rates are less favorable than any in town or others farther inside the airport concourse. In general, you can find the best exchange rates at ATMs, *casas de cambio,* and hotels.

Business Hours

Most downtown offices maintain traditional Mexican hours of operation (9 a.m.–2 p.m. and 4–8 p.m., daily), but shops remain open throughout the day from 10 a.m. to 9 p.m. Offices tend to close on Saturday and Sunday, but shops are open on Saturday, at least, and increasingly offer limited hours of operation on Sunday. Malls are generally open from 10 a.m. to 10 p.m. or later.

Climate

It's hot but not overwhelmingly humid. The rainy season is May through October. August through October is the hurricane season, which brings erratic weather. November through February is generally sunny but can also be cloudy, windy, somewhat rainy, and even cool, so a sweater and rain protection is handy.

Consular Agents

The U.S. consular agent is located in the Plaza Caracol 2, third level, rooms 320–323, Paseo Kukulkán Km 8.5 (☎ 998-883-0272). The office is open Monday to Friday 9 a.m. to 1 p.m. The Canadian consulate is located in the Plaza Caracol, third level, room 330, Paseo Kukulkán Km 8.5 (☎ 998-883-3360). The office is open from Monday to Friday 9 a.m. to 5 p.m.

Emergencies and Hospitals

To report an emergency, dial ☎ 060, which is supposed to be similar to 911 emergency service in the United States. For first aid, the **Cruz Roja (Red Cross; ☎ 065** or 998-884-1616; Fax: 998-884-7466) is open 24 hours a day on Avenida Yaxchilán between avenidas Xcaret and Labná, next to the Telmex building. **Total Assist,** a small, nine-room emergency hospital with English-speaking doctors (Claveles 5, SM 22, at Av. Tulum; ☎ 998-884-1058 or 884-1092; htotal@prodigy.net.mx), is also open 24 hours. American Express, MasterCard, and Visa are accepted. Desk staff may have limited command of English. An **air ambulance service** is also available by calling ☎ 800-305-9400 (toll free within Mexico). *Urgencias* means "emergencies."

Information

The State Tourism Office, Cancún Center, Bulevar Kukulcán Km 9, first floor, Zona Hotelera (☎ 998-881-9000), is centrally located in the Convention Center. The office is open Monday to Friday from 9 a.m. to 5 p.m., and it has maps, brochures, and information on the area's popular sights, including Tulum, Xcaret, Isla Mujeres, and Playa del Carmen. A second tourist information office, the Cancún Municipal Tourism Office (☎ 998-884-6531 or 884-3438), is also located in the Cancún Center, Bulevar Kukulcán Km 9, first floor (☎ 866-891-7773 in the U.S. or 998-881-2745; Fax: 998-881-0402); it's open Monday to Friday

9 a.m. to 7 p.m. Hotels and their rates are listed at each office, as are ferry schedules. For information prior to your arrival in Cancún, visit the Convention Bureau's Web site at www.cancun.info.

Pick up copies of the free monthly *Cancún Tips* or the *Cancún Tips* booklet, which is published four times a year. Both contain lots of useful information and great maps.

Internet Access

C@ncunet (☎ 998-885-0055 or 840-6099), located in a kiosk on the second floor of Plaza Kukulkán (Paseo Kukulkán Km 13), offers Internet access for $4 per 15 minutes or $7 per hour from 10 a.m. to 10 p.m.

Maps

One of the best around is the free American Express map, usually found at the tourist information offices and the local American Express office. The publication *Cancún Tips* (see "Information") also has excellent maps and is generally available through your hotel concierge.

Newspapers and Magazines

Most hotel gift shops and newsstands carry English-language magazines and English-language Mexican newspapers.

Pharmacy

Next to the Hotel Caribe Internacional, Farmacia Canto (Av. Yaxchilán 36, at Sunyaxchen; ☎ 998-884-9330) is open from 8am to midnight. MasterCard, and Visa are accepted. The major shopping malls have plenty of drugstores, open until 10 p.m., in the Hotel Zone. You can stock up on Retin-A, Viagra, and many other prescription drugs without a prescription.

Police

To reach the **police** *(seguridad pública),* dial ☎ 998-884-1913 or 884-2342.

Post Office

The main post office (☎ 998/884-1418) is downtown at the intersection of avenidas Sunyaxchen and Xel-Ha. It's open Monday to Friday 9 a.m. to 4 p.m. Saturdays, from 9 a.m. to noon, it's open just for the purchase of stamps.

Safety

There is very little crime in Cancún. People are generally safe late at night in tourist areas; just use ordinary, common sense. As at any other beach resort, don't take money or valuables to the beach.

Swimming on the Caribbean side presents a danger from undertow. Pay attention to the posted flag warnings on the beaches.

Car break-ins are about the only crimes here, although they do happen frequently, especially around the shopping centers in the Hotel Zone. VW Beetles and Golfs are frequent targets.

Taxes

There's a 10 percent value-added tax (IVA) on goods and services, and it's generally included in the posted price. Cancún's IVA is 5 percent lower than most of Mexico due to a special exemption that dates back to its origins as a duty-free port.

Taxis

Taxi prices in Cancún are set by zone, and keeping track of what's in which zone can take some work. Taxi rates within the Hotel Zone are a minimum fare of $6 per ride, making it one of the most expensive taxi areas in Mexico. Rates within the downtown area are between $1.50 and $2. You can also hire taxis by the hour or day for longer trips, when you'd prefer to leave the driving to someone else. Rates run between $15 and $20 per hour with discounts available for full-day rates, but an extra charge applies when the driver doubles as a tour guide. Always settle on a price in advance, or check at your hotel, where destinations and prices are generally posted.

Telephone

Avoid the phone booths that have signs in English advising you to call home using a special 800 number — these are absolute rip-offs and can cost as much as $20 per minute. The least expensive way to call is by using a Mexican prepaid phone card called Telmex (LADATEL), available at most pharmacies and mini-supermarkets, using the official public phones, Telmex (Lada). Remember, in Mexico, you need to dial 001 prior to a number to reach the United States, and you need to preface long-distance calls within Mexico by dialing 01.

Time Zone

Cancún operates on central standard time, but Mexico's observance of daylight saving time varies somewhat from that in the United States.

Chapter 12

Dining in Cancún

by Lynne Bairstow

In This Chapter

▶ Discovering Cancún's best restaurants
▶ Finding a restaurant with true Mexican ambience

U.S.-based franchise chains, which really need no introduction, populate a large part of Cancún's restaurant scene. These chains include Hard Rock Cafe, Planet Hollywood, Rainforest Cafe, Tony Roma's, Ruth's Chris Steak House, and the gamut of fast-food burger places. Contrary to common travelers' wisdom, many of Cancún's best restaurants are located either in hotels or shopping malls.

The majority of restaurants are located in the Hotel Zone in Isla Cancún, which is logical because that's where most of the tourists who come to dine out are located. However, don't dismiss the charms of dining in Ciudad Cancún. You're likely to find a great meal — at a fraction of the price of an Isla Cancún eatery — accompanied by a dose of local color.

As in many of Mexico's beach resorts, even the finest restaurants in town can be comfortably casual when it comes to dress. Men rarely wear jackets, although you may frequently see women in dressy resort wear — basically, anything goes.

For those traveling with kids, Cancún has no shortage of options. From Johnny Rockets to McDonald's, this destination has plenty of kid-friendly — and kid-familiar — places.

Prices in Cancún can cover an extended range, boosted by shrimp and lobster dishes, which can top $20 for an entree. If you're watching your budget, even the higher-priced places generally have less-expensive options — just avoid the premium seafood dishes. Remember that tips generally run about 15 percent, and most restaurant and bar staff really depend on tips for their income, so be generous if the service warrants.

Cancún's Best Restaurants

The restaurants in this chapter are either locally owned, one-of-a-kind restaurants, or exceptional selections at area hotels. Many feature live music as an accompaniment to the dining experience. I arrange the restaurants alphabetically and note their location, as well as their general price category and cuisine. Please refer to the Introduction of this book for an explanation of the price categories.

Please see Appendix C for more information on Mexican cuisine.

Aioli
$–$$$ Isla Cancún   FRENCH

In the Le Méridien Hotel, the Provençal — but definitely not provincial — Aioli offers simply exquisite French and Mediterranean gourmet specialties served in a warm and cozy country French setting. Though it has perhaps the best breakfast buffet in Cancún (for $15), most visitors outside the hotel enjoy Aioli only for dinner, when low lighting and superb service make the restaurant a top choice for a romantic dinner. Starters include the traditional pâtés and a delightful escargot served in the shell with a white wine and herb butter sauce. A specialty is duck breast in honey and lavender sauce. Equally scrumptious is the rack of lamb, prepared in a Moroccan style and served with couscous. Desserts are decadent in true French style, including the signature "Fifth Element," a sinfully delicious temptation rich with chocolate. For the quality and the originality of the cuisine, coupled with the excellence in service, Aioli gets my top pick for Cancún's best value in fine dining.

Le Méridien Hotel, Retorno del Rey Km 14. ☎ *998-881-2200.* www.meridiencancun.com.mx. *Free parking. Reservations required. Main courses: $15–$40. AE, MC, V. Open: Mon–Sun 6:30 a.m.–11 p.m.*

Captain's Cove (reopening, date to be announced)
$$ Isla Cancún   INTERNATIONAL/SEAFOOD

Recognized for its consistent value — think heaping servings, friendly service, and great sunset views from the upper deck — Captain's Cove regularly packs customers into its several dining levels. Diners face big, open windows overlooking the lagoon and Royal Yacht Club Marina. For breakfast, try the extremely popular all-you-can-eat buffet that beats the price and quality of most hotel buffets. Main courses of USDA Angus steak and seafood are the norm at lunch and dinner, and a menu catering especially to children is available. Dessert standouts include flaming coffees, crepes, and Key lime pie. Captain's Cove sits almost at the end of Paseo Kukulkán, on the lagoon side opposite the Omni Hotel.

Paseo Kukulkán Km 16.5. ☎ *998-885-0016. Reservations recommended. Main courses: $12–$30; breakfast buffet $8.95. MC, V. Open: Daily 7 a.m.–11 p.m.*

Casa de las Margaritas
$$ Isla Cancún MEXICAN

La Casa de las Margaritas is a celebration of the flavors and *¡fiesta!* spirit of Mexico. With a décor as vibrant as a piñata, and a soundtrack of background music that ranges from mariachi to marimba, the experience here is a crash-course in the festive spirit of this colorful country. On the menu, best bets include the Margarita shrimp, sauteed in a garlic, crème, and chipotle chile sauce; chicken breast served with three flavorful mole sauces; or their platter of chicken enchiladas topped with a tomato and sun-dried pepper sauce. They also serve a spectacular Sunday brunch.

Paseo Kukulkán Km 12.5, La Isla Shopping Mall, Local E-17. ☎ *998-883-3222 or 883-3054.* www.lacasadelasmargaritas.com. *Reservations recommended. Main courses: $8–$16. Street parking. Open: Mon–Sat 11 a.m.–midnight; Sun brunch noon–5 p.m.*

Club Grill (Ritz-Carlton Hotel will reopen September 5, 2006)
$–$$$ Isla Cancún INTERNATIONAL

Cancún's most elegant and stylish restaurant, located in the Ritz-Carlton hotel, is also among its most delicious. The gracious service and old-world charm begin the moment you enter the anteroom with its comfortable couches and chairs and selection of fine tequilas and Cuban cigars. The scene continues into a candlelit dining room with padded side chairs and tables shimmering with silver and crystal. Elegant plates of peppered scallops, truffles, and potatoes in tequila sauce; grilled lamb; or mixed grill arrive at a leisurely pace after the appetizer. The restaurant has both smoking and nonsmoking sections. After dinner, take a turn on the dance floor, as a band plays romantic music beginning at 8 p.m. Club Grill is the place for a truly special night out. A dress code is enforced: No sandals or tennis shoes, and gentlemen must wear long pants.

Ritz-Carlton Cancún, Retorno del Rey 36, Paseo Kukulkán Km 13.5. ☎ *998-881-0808. Reservations required. Main courses: $11–$40. AE, DC, MC, V. Open: Tues–Sun 7–11 p.m.*

Glazz
$$–$$$ Isla Cancún ASIAN/FUSION

Glazz combines a sexy lounge and sophisticated dining, right in the heart of Cancun's hotel zone. For dinner, Glazz features a menu of sophisticated and artfully presented Asian entrees and sushi. Specialties include Thai lettuce wraps or green papaya salad for starters. Entrees include wok-cooked Glazz spicy chicken; Mandarin Salmon, wrapped in bok choy and served with mango and asparagus; Panang curry; and the vegetarian Buddah's Feast of seasonal vegetables stir-fried in oyster-flavored sauce with tofu tempura. Specialty sakes, martinis, and creative "sakitinis" round out the drink menu.

Paseo Kukulkán Km 12.5, La Isla Shopping Mall. ☎ *998-883-1881.* www.glazz.com.mx. *Main courses: $9–$14. AE, MC, V. Open: Daily 6 p.m.–12:30 a.m., sushi served until 1:30 a.m.; lounge stays open until 2:30 a.m.*

Isla Cancún Dining

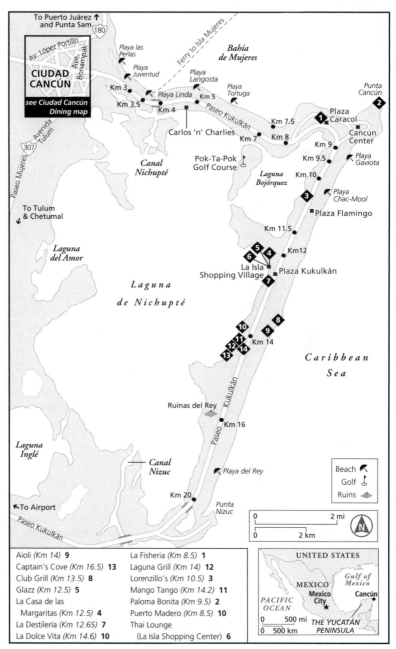

Aioli *(Km 14)* 9
Captain's Cove *(Km 16.5)* 13
Club Grill *(Km 13.5)* 8
Glazz *(Km 12.5)* 5
La Casa de las
  Margaritas *(Km 12.5)* 4
La Destilería *(Km 12.65)* 7
La Dolce Vita *(Km 14.6)* 10

La Fisheria *(Km 8.5)* 1
Laguna Grill *(Km 14)* 12
Lorenzillo's *(Km 10.5)* 3
Mango Tango *(Km 14.2)* 11
Paloma Bonita *(Km 9.5)* 2
Puerto Madero *(Km 8.5)* 10
Thai Lounge
  (La Isla Shopping Center) 6

Labná
$–$$ Ciudad Cancún   YUCATECAN

To steep yourself in Yucatecan cuisine and music, head directly to this showcase of Maya moods and regional foods. Specialties served here include a sublime lime soup, *poc chuc* (marinated, barbecue-style pork), chicken or pork *pibil* (sweet and spicy barbecue sauce served over shredded meat), and appetizers such as *papadzules* (tortillas stuffed with boiled eggs in a green pumpkin sauce). The Labná Special is a sampler of four typically Yucatecan main courses, including *poc chuc,* while another specialty of the house is baked suckling pig, served with guacamole. The refreshing Yucatecan beverage, *agua de chaya* — a blend of sweetened water and the leaf of the chaya plant, abundant in the area, to which D'aristi liquor can be added for an extra kick — is also served here. The large, informal dining room is decorated with fascinating black and white photographs of the region, dating from the 1900s.

Margaritas 29, next to City Hall. ☎ *998-892-3056. Main courses: $5–$18. AE, MC, V. Open: Daily noon–10 p.m.*

La Destilería
$–$$ Isla Cancún   MEXICAN

If you want to experience tequila in its native habitat, don't miss this place — even though it's across the country from the region that produces the beverage. La Destilería is more than a tequila-inspired restaurant; it's a mini-museum honoring the "spirit" of Mexico. It serves more than 150 brands of tequila, including some treasures that never find their way across the country's northern border, so be adventurous! The margaritas are among the best on the island. When you decide to have some food with your tequila, the menu is refined Mexican, with everything from quesadillas with squash blossom flowers to shrimp in a delicate tequila-lime sauce.

Paseo Kukulkán Km 12.65, across from Plaza Kukulkán. ☎ *998-885-1086 or 885-1087. Reservations recommended during high season. Main courses: $8–$30. AE, MC, V. Daily 1 p.m.–midnight.*

La Dolce Vita
$–$$$ Isla Cancún   ITALIAN/SEAFOOD

The casually elegant La Dolce Vita is known as Cancún's favorite Italian restaurant. Appetizers include pâté of quail liver and carpaccio in vinaigrette or mushrooms Provençal. The chef specializes in homemade pastas combined with fresh seafood. You can order green tagliolini with lobster medallions, linguine with clams or seafood, or rigatoni Mexican-style (with chorizo, mushrooms, and chives) as a main course, or as an appetizer for half price. You can dine in air-conditioned comfort or on an open-air terrace with a lagoon view. Dinner is accompanied by live jazz from 7 to 11 p.m., Monday through Saturday. They also have a location downtown, at Av. Cobá 83 (corner with Av. Nader; ☎ 998-884-3393).

Ciudad Cancún Dining

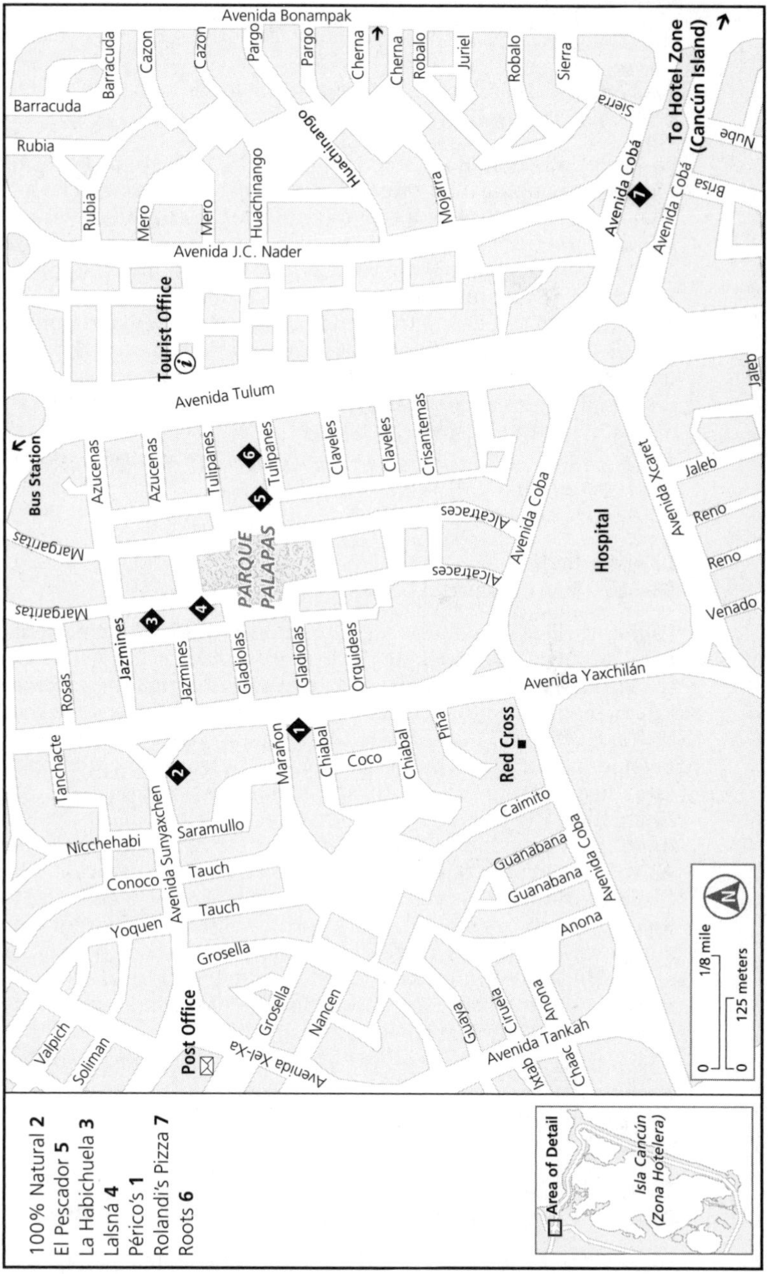

Map labels (streets and landmarks):

Avenida Bonampak

Barracuda, Cazon, Cazon, Pargo, Pargo, Cherna, Cherna, Robalo, Juriel, Robalo, Sierra

Barracuda

Rubia

Huachinango

To Hotel Zone (Cancún Island)

Avenida Cobá, Avenida Cobá, Brisa, Nube, Sierra, Mojarra

Rubia, Mero, Mero, Huachinango

Avenida J.C. Nader

Tourist Office (i)

Avenida Tulum

Jaleb

Bus Station

Azucenas, Azucenas, Tulipanes, 6, Tulipanes, Claveles, Claveles, Crisantemas

Margaritas

Margaritas

Jazmines, 3, Jazmines, Gladiolas, Gladiolas, Orquídeas

Rosas

PARQUE PALAPAS

4

5

Alcatraces, Alcatraces, Avenida Coba

Jaleb, Reno, Reno, Venado

Avenida Xcaret

Hospital

Avenida Yaxchilán

Tanchacte, Nicchehabi, Saramullo, Conoco, Tauch, Tauch, Yoquen, Grosella

Avenida Sunyaxchen

2

Marañon, 1, Chiabal, Coco, Chiabal, Piña

Red Cross

Caimito

Guanabana, Guanabana, Anona

Avenida Coba

Post Office

Grosella, Nancen

Avenida Xel-ha

Valpich, Soliman

Guaya, Ciruela, Ixtab, Anona

Avenida Tankah

Chaac

1/8 mile

125 meters

Area of Detail

Isla Cancún (Zona Hotelera)

100% Natural **2**
El Pescador **5**
La Habichuela **3**
Lalsná **4**
Périco's **1**
Rolandi's Pizza **7**
Roots **6**

Paseo Kukulkán Km 14.6, on the lagoon, opposite the Marriott Casamagna. ☎ *998-885-0150 or 885-0161.* www.dolcevitacancun.com. *Reservations required for dinner. Main courses: $9–$37. AE, MC, V. Open: Daily noon–midnight.*

La Fisheria
$–$$ Isla Cancún SEAFOOD

La Fisheria is one of the exceptions to the rule about never finding good food in a shopping mall eatery. The expansive menu at La Fisheria includes shark fingers with a jalapeño dip, grouper filet stuffed with seafood in a lobster sauce, Acapulco-style ceviche (in a tomato sauce), New England clam chowder, steamed mussels, grilled red snapper with pasta — you get the idea. The menu changes daily, but there's always *tikin xik,* that great Yucatecan grilled fish marinated in *achiote* sauce (made from *achiote* chile paste). And for those diners not inclined toward seafood, a wood-burning, oven-made pizza may do, or perhaps one of the grilled chicken or beef dishes. If you're at the mall shopping, La Fisheria is your best bet — and a reason to stop by if you're not.

Plaza Caracol, Shopping Center second floor. ☎ *998-883-1395. Main courses: $6.50–$21. AE, MC, V. Open: Daily 11 a.m.–11 p.m.*

Laguna Grill
$$–$$$ Isla Cancún FUSION

Laguna Grill offers diners a contemporary culinary experience in a lush, tropical setting overlooking the lagoon. A tropical garden welcomes you at the entrance, while a small creek traverses through the restaurant set with tables made from the trunks of regional, tropical trees. As magical as the décor is, the real star here is the kitchen, with its offering of Pacific-rim cuisine fused with regional flavors. Starters include martini *gyoza* (steamed dumplings) and shrimp tempura served on a mango mint salad, or ahi tuna and shrimp ceviche in a spicy Oriental sauce. Fish and seafood dominate the menu of entrees, in a variety of preparations that combine Asian and Mexican flavors such as ginger, cilantro, garlic, and hoisin sauce. Grilled shrimp are served over a cilantro and *guajillo* chile risotto. For beef-lovers, the rib-eye served over a garlic, spinach, and sweet potato mash is sublime. Desserts are as creative as the main dishes; the pineapple-papaya strudel in Malibu rum sauce is a standout. If you're an early diner, request a table on the outside deck for a spectacular sunset view. An impressive selection of wines is available.

Paseo Kukulkán Km 16.5. ☎ *998-885-0267.* www.lagunagrill.com.mx. *Reservations recommended. Main courses: $15–$45. AE, MC, V. Open: Daily 2 p.m.–midnight.*

La Habichuela
$$–$$$ Ciudad Cancún GOURMET SEAFOOD/CARIBBEAN/MEXICAN

Dine alfresco in a garden setting and enjoy some of downtown Cancún's finest food. Romantic in its setting on a vine-draped patio, La Habichuela

Dining at sea

One unique way to combine dinner with sightseeing is to board the **Lobster Dinner Cruise** (☎ 998-849-4748). Cruising around the tranquil, turquoise waters of the lagoon, passengers feast on lobster dinners accompanied by wine. The cost is $79 per person, and the cruise departs two times daily from the Royal Mayan Marina. A sunset dinner cruise leaves at 4 p.m. during winter months and 5 p.m. during the summer. A moonlight cruise leaves at 7:30 p.m. during the winter and 8:30 p.m. during the summer.

boasts tables that are covered in pink-and-white linens, and soft music playing in the background. For an all-out culinary adventure, try *habichuela* (string bean) soup; shrimp in any number of sauces, including Jamaican tamarind, tequila, and a ginger-and-mushroom combination; and the Maya coffee with *xtabentun* (a strong, sweet, anise-based liquor). The grilled seafood and steaks are excellent as well, but La Habichuela is a good place to try a Mexican specialty such as chicken mole or *tampiqueña*-style beef (thinly sliced, marinated, and grilled). For something totally divine, try the *Cocobichuela,* which is lobster and shrimp in a curry sauce served in a coconut shell and topped with fruit.

Margaritas 25. ☎ *998-884-3158.* www.lahabichuela.com. *Free parking. Reservations recommended in high season. Main courses: $15–$39. AE, MC, V. Open: Daily noon–midnight.*

Lorenzillo's
$–$$$ Isla Cancún   SEAFOOD

Live lobster is the overwhelming favorite here, and part of the appeal is selecting your dinner out of the giant lobster tank. A dock leads down to the main dining area, overlooking the lagoon and is topped by a giant *palapa.* When the place is packed (which is often), a wharf-side bar handles the overflow. In addition to the lobster — it comes grilled, steamed, or stuffed — good bets are the shrimp stuffed with cheese and wrapped in bacon, the admiral's filet coated in toasted almonds and a light mustard sauce, or the seafood-stuffed squid. Desserts include the tempting "Martinique": Belgian chocolate with hazelnuts, almonds, and pecans, served with vanilla ice cream. A sunset pier offers a lighter menu of cold seafood, sandwiches, and salads. A festive, friendly atmosphere dominates, and children are very welcome — after all, most of the patrons are wearing bibs!

Paseo Kukulkán Km 10.5. ☎ *998-883-1254.* www.lorenzillos.com.mx. *Free parking in lot across the street, plus valet parking. Reservations recommended. Main courses: $8–$50. AE, MC, V. Open: Daily noon–midnight.*

Mango Tango
$–$$$ Isla Cancún   INTERNATIONAL

The beauty of dining here is that you can stay and enjoy a hot nightspot — Mango Tango has made a name for itself with sizzling floor shows (featuring salsa, tango, and other Latin dancing) and live reggae music — but its kitchen deserves attention as well. Try the peel-your-own shrimp, Argentine-style grilled meat with *chimichurri* sauce, and other grilled specialties. Mango Tango salad is shrimp, chicken, avocado, red onion, tomato, and mushrooms served on mango slices. Entrees include rice with seafood and fried bananas. Creole gumbo comes with lobster, shrimp, and squid, and coconut-and-mango cake is a suitable finish to the meal.

Paseo Kukulkán Km 14.2, opposite the Ritz-Carlton Cancún. ☎ *998-885-0303.* www. mangotango.com.mx. *Reservations recommended. Main courses: $12–$45; dinner show $49. AE, MC, V. Open: Daily 2 p.m.–2 a.m.*

100% Natural
$ Ciudad Cancún   VEGETARIAN/MEXICAN

If you want a healthy reprieve from an overindulgent night — or just like your meals as fresh and natural as possible — this is your oasis. No matter what your dining preference, you owe it to yourself to try a Mexican tradition: the fresh-fruit *licuado.* The blended drink combines fresh fruit, ice, and either water or milk. More creative combinations may mix in yogurt, granola, or other goodies. And 100% Natural serves more than just meal-quality drinks — there's a bountiful selection of basic Mexican fare and terrific sandwiches served on whole-grain bread, both with options for vegetarians. Breakfast is a delight as well as a good value. The space abounds with plants and cheery colors. Prior to Hurricane Wilma, there were several locations in town, most of which closed due to storm damage. Other branches are located at Playa Chac-Mool, across from Sr. Frogs, and downtown.

Ave. Sunyaxchen #63. ☎ *998-884-0102. Main courses $2.80–$13. MC, V. Daily 8 a.m.–11 p.m.*

Paloma Bonita
$$–$$$ Isla Cancún   REGIONAL/MEXICAN/NOUVELLE MEXICAN

Possibly the most "Mexican" of Isla Cancún's dining options, María Bonita combines the music, food, and atmosphere of Mexico's various regions — it's almost like taking a condensed food tour of this vast country! Being that Paloma Bonita is located in a hotel (the Dreams Cancún), prices are higher and the flavors are more institutionalized than the traditional Mexican restaurants found in Ciudad Cancún, but the restaurant is still a good choice for diners wanting more of Mexico's flavors — without leaving the Hotel Zone. The restaurant overlooks the water, and the interior is divided by cuisine type. For example, one favorite is *La Cantina Jalisco,* which features an open, colorful Mexican kitchen (with pots and pans on the wall) and tequila bar (with more than 100 different tequilas). For the less adventurous in your party, a few international dishes are thrown in for variety. Trios, marimba, and *jarocho* music, as well as the ever-enchanting mariachis, serenade diners. Check out the front of the menu for explanations on the different peppers used. The kitchen marks each dish for its heat quotient (from zero to two chiles). The restaurant is to the left of the hotel entrance, and you can enter from the street.

In the Dreams Hotel, Punta Cancún. ☎ *998-848-7000, ext. 7960. Reservations recommended. Main courses: $25–$31. AE, DC, MC, V. Open: Daily 6:30 p.m.–11:30 p.m.*

Périco's
$–$$$ Ciudad Cancún MEXICAN/SEAFOOD/STEAKS

With colorful murals that almost dance off the walls, a bar area overhung with baskets (and with saddles for bar stools), inviting leather tables and chairs, and waiters dressed like Pancho Villa, it's no wonder that Périco's is always booming and festive. It's arguably the most tourist-friendly spot in Ciudad Cancún. The extensive menu offers well-prepared steak, seafood, and traditional Mexican dishes for moderate rates (except for the lobster), but the food here is less the point than the fun. Périco's is a place not only to eat and drink, but also to let loose and join in the fun. Don't be surprised if other diners drop their forks, don huge Mexican sombreros, and snake around the dining room in a conga dance. You can still have fun whether or not you join in, but Périco's is definitely not the place for that romantic evening alone. There's marimba music from 7:30 to 9:30 p.m. and mariachis from 9:30 p.m. to midnight. Expect a crowd.

Yaxchilán 61. ☎ *998-884-3152. Reservations recommended. Main courses: $14–$39. AE, MC, V. Open: Daily 1 p.m.–1 a.m.*

Puerto Madero
$$–$$$$ Isla Cancún ARGENTINIAN/STEAKS/SEAFOOD

As a tribute to the famed Puerto Madero of Buenos Aires, this restaurant has quickly earned a reputation for its authentic Argentinian cuisine and ambience. Overlooking the Nichupté Lagoon, the décor re-creates a 20th-century dock warehouse, with elegant touches of modern architecture. Puerto Madero offers an extensive selection of prime quality beef cuts, whole wheat pastas, fish, and shellfish, meticulously prepared with the Buenos Aires *gusto*. In addition to the classic carpaccio, their tuna tartar and halibut steak are favorites, but the real standout here is the grilled steak, served in ample portions. It's also a top choice for a splurge on lobster. Enjoy a glass of wine, from their extensive selection, or a cocktail, while viewing the sunset from their lagoon-side deck. Service is excellent.

Marina Barracuda, Bulevar Kukulcán Km 14. ☎ *998-883-2829 or 883-2830.* www. puertomaderocancun.com. *Valet parking. Reservations recommended. Main courses $12–$60. AE, MC, V. Open: Daily 1 p.m.–1 a.m.*

Rolandi's Pizza
$–$$ Ciudad Cancún ITALIAN

Surprised to find great pizza in Cancún? Don't be. Rolandi's Pizza is an institution in Cancún, and the Rolandi name is synonymous with dining in both Cancún and neighboring Isla Mujeres. At this shaded outdoor sidewalk cafe, you can choose from almost two dozen different wood-oven pizzas and a full selection of spaghetti, calzones, Italian-style chicken and beef, and desserts. There's a full bar list as well. Another Rolandi's Pizza is located in Isla Mujeres at Av. Hidalgo 110 (☎ **998-877-0430;** Open: Mon–Sun, 11 a.m.–11 p.m.) and has the same food and prices. Both locations have become standards for dependably good casual fare in Cancún. For a more formal, Italian-dining affair, try the elegant **Casa Rolandi** in Plaza Caracol, Isla Cancún (☎ **998-883-1817**).

Cobá 12. ☎ ***998-884-4047.*** www.rolandi.com. *Main courses and pizza: $6–$15; pasta $8–$18. AE, MC, V. Open: Daily 1 p.m.–midnight.*

Roots
$–$$ Ciudad Cancún INTERNATIONAL

This popular hangout for local residents is also a great spot for visitors to Cancún. Located in the heart of downtown, this restaurant and jazz club offers a unique cosmopolitan ambience. The Caribbean-themed menu offers a range of casual dining choices, including salads, pastas, and even fresh squid. It's all accompanied by the best of Cancún musicians, performing live on their intimate stage. Original works of art by local painters deck the walls.

Tulipanes 26, SM 22. ☎ ***998-884-2437.*** roots@cancun.com. *Main courses: $6–$17. MC, V. Open: Daily 6 p.m.–1 a.m.*

Thai Lounge
$–$$ Isla Cancún THAI

With a backdrop that includes three dolphins cavorting in an enormous aquarium, the Thai Lounge offers a unique and calming setting with individual pagodas for cozy dining, low lights, and soft, chill music. Classic Thai specialties such as spicy chicken soup, Thai salad, chicken satay, and chicken and shrimp curries are served in an atmosphere that takes you to the other side of the world. The service is prompt and attentive.

La Isla Shopping Center, Local B-4. ☎ ***998-883-1401.*** *Reservations recommended during high season. Main courses: $6–$18. AE, MC, V. Open: Daily 6 p.m.–1 a.m.*

Chapter 13

Having Fun on and off the Beach in Cancún

by Lynne Bairstow

In This Chapter

▶ Enjoying Cancún's best activities — on land and at sea
▶ Spending a day on nearby Isla Mujeres
▶ Exploring Maya ruins and environmental "theme parks"
▶ Seeing Cancún's best sights
▶ Experiencing great shopping
▶ Living it up at night in Cancún

*Y*ou're likely to run out of vacation days before you run out of things to do in Cancún. Snorkeling, Jet Skiing, jungle tours, and visits to ancient Maya ruins or modern ecological theme parks are among the most popular diversions in this resort that has a little of everything. Beyond Cancún's renowned beaches are more than a dozen malls with name-brand retailers and duty-free shops (featuring European goods with better prices than you can find in the United States), plus a seemingly endless supply of nightclubs to revel in.

In addition to Cancún's own attractions, the resort is a convenient distance from the more Mexican-feeling beach towns in **Isla Mujeres, Playa del Carmen,** and **Cozumel.** The **Maya ruins** at Tulum and Chichén Itzá, are also close by. All these diversions are within driving distance for a spectacular day trip.

So what's worth your time? To help you decide, I devote this chapter to giving you an overview of the best beaches in this mecca of white sand and crystalline waters. I also give you the rundown on the area's popular day trips and diversions.

Finding Water Fun for Everyone

If you're in Cancún, you probably decided to come here based on the vision of powdery, white-sand beaches and translucent, turquoise waters. If you're in search of a beautiful beach, Cancún may be your nirvana. And with the added bonus of the Nichupté Lagoon on the other side of the island, Cancún is packed with ways to make the most of your time in the water. Although much was made in the news about the loss of Cancún's famed beaches post 2005's Hurricane Wilma, thanks to a beach recuperation project priced at over $20 million, the white sands are quickly coming back, and should be well in place by fall 2006.

Basking on a Cancún beach

The big hotels dominate the best stretches of beaches, so you likely have a fine patch of sand at your hotel. Mexico's beaches are public property, so technically you can use the beach of any hotel by accessing it directly from the sand. *Technically* is the key word here. Although this is the law, the reality is that hotel security guards regularly ask non-guests to relocate. You choose if you want to suffer the potential embarrassment of being asked to leave or, if asked, standing your ground — or beach, as it were.

If you're intent on swimming, be careful on beaches fronting the open Caribbean, where the undertow can be quite strong. By contrast, the waters of **Bahía de Mujeres** at the north end of the island are usually calm and ideal for swimming. Get to know Cancún's water-safety pennant system and make sure you check the flag at any beach or hotel before entering the water.

Here's what each flag means:

White: Excellent

Green: Normal conditions (safe)

Yellow: Changeable, uncertain (use caution)

Black or **red:** Unsafe (use the swimming pool instead)

In the Caribbean, storms can arrive quickly, and conditions can change from safe to unsafe in a matter of minutes, so be alert. If you see dark clouds heading your way, head to shore and wait until the storm passes.

The public beaches located along the stretch of Isla Cancún on the calm, Bahía de Mujeres side include

- **Playa Linda:** Playa Linda (located at Km 4 on Paseo Kukulkán) has a shuttle service to Isla Mujeres, as well as a few dive shops and snack bars.

- **Playa Langosta:** Playa Langosta (Km 5) is a protected cove near the Hotel Casa Maya that features a tour-boat pier and a watersports concession, plus some shops and restaurants.

Cancún & Environs

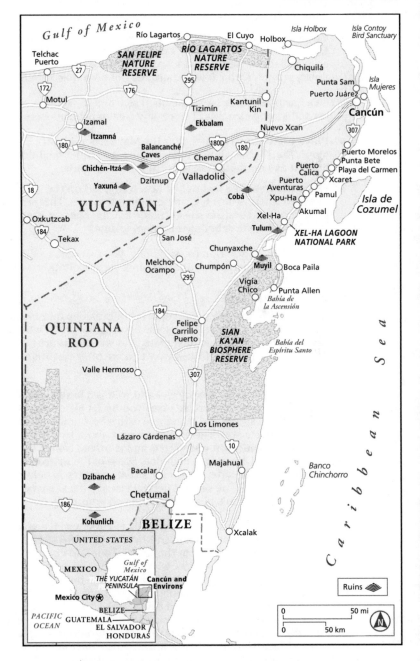

✔ **Playa Tortuga:** At Km 7.5, Playa Tortuga is a popular public beach with changing rooms, public restrooms, and restaurants. On weekends, families frequently overrun this bit of sand.

✔ **Playa Caracol:** The last beach before the island curves toward the Caribbean is Playa Caracol (Km 8), which stretches for about a mile and passes the Fiesta Americana and Camino Real hotels — a lovely stretch with a few restaurants but no public facilities.

Cancún's Caribbean side faces the open sea, and it's subject to frequent riptides and strong currents. The regally named beaches here include

✔ **Playa Chac-Mool** (named after the Maya deity of rain): Playa Chac-Mool (Km 13) has showers, restrooms, and other facilities that make it as popular as Playa Tortuga on weekends.

✔ **Playa del Rey:** The last public beach (Km 20) on the island before Punta Nizac, this beach is an unspoiled treasure. This remarkable stretch of sand ends at the entrance to Club Med (at press time, closed, without a scheduled reopening date).

At most beaches, in addition to swimming, you can rent a sailboard and take lessons, ride a parasail, or partake in a variety of other watersports.

Skiing and surfing

Many beachside hotels offer watersports concessions that include the rental of rubber rafts, kayaks, and snorkeling equipment. Outlets for renting **sailboats, Jet Skis, windsurfers,** and **water skis** are located on the calm Nichupté Lagoon. Prices vary and are often negotiable, so check around.

A very popular option for getting wet and wild is a **jungle cruise,** offered by several companies. The cruise takes you by Jet Ski or WaveRunner through Cancún's lagoon and mangrove estuaries out into the Caribbean Sea and by a shallow reef. The excursion runs about two and a half hours (you drive your own watercraft) and is priced from $35 to $55, with snorkeling and beverages included. Some of the motorized mini-boats seat you side by side; other crafts seat one person behind the other. The difference? The second person can see the scenery or the back of their companion's head, depending on your choice.

The operators and names of boats offering excursions change often. The popular **Aquaworld** (Paseo Kukulkán Km 15.2; ☎ **998-848-8327;** www. aquaworld.com.mx) calls its trip the Jungle Tour and charges $55 for the two-and-a-half-hour excursion, which includes 45 minutes of snorkeling time. Aquaworld even gives you a free snorkel, but its watercrafts have the less-desirable seating configuration of one behind the other. Departures are every hour between 8 a.m. and 3 p.m. daily. To find out what's available when you're here, check with a local travel agent or hotel tour desk; you can find a wide range of options. You can also go to the Playa Linda pier either a day ahead or the day of your intended outing and buy your own tickets for this excursion or for Aquaworld's trips to Isla Mujeres. If you go on the day of your trip for the tour to Isla Mujeres, arrive at the pier around 8:45 a.m.; most boats leave by 9 or 9:30 a.m.

Exploring the deep blue

Known for its shallow reefs, dazzling colors, and diversity of life, Cancún is one of the best places in the world for beginning **scuba diving**. Punta Nizuc is the northern tip of the **Gran Arrecife Maya (Great Mesoamerican Reef)**, the largest reef in the Western Hemisphere and one of the world's largest. In addition to the sea life present along this reef system, several sunken boats add a variety of dive options. Note that 2005's Hurricane Wilma did damage the offshore reef system, so ask your operator about the conditions of the area, in order to ensure you won't have a disappointing dive. Inland, a series of caverns and well-springs, known as *cenotes,* are fascinating venues for the more experienced diver. Drift diving is the norm here, with popular dives going to the reefs at **El Garrafón** and the **Cave of the Sleeping Sharks** — although be aware that the famed "sleeping sharks" have departed, driven off by too many people watching them snooze. For those unfamiliar with the term, drift diving occurs when divers drift with the strong currents in the waters and end up at a point different from where they started. The dive boat follows them. In traditional dives, the divers resurface where they began.

Resort courses that teach the basics of diving — enough to make shallow dives and slowly ease your way into this underwater world of unimaginable beauty — are offered in a variety of hotels. Scuba trips run around $60 for two-tank dives at nearby reefs and $100 and up for locations farther out. One recommended operator is **Scuba Cancún** (Paseo Kukulkán Km 5; ☎ **998-849-7508;** www.scubacancun.com.mx), located on the lagoon side. In addition to calling or visiting, you can make reservations from 7:30 to 10:30 p.m. using the fax line: 998-849-4736. Their full certification course takes three and a half days and costs $410. Scuba Cancún is open from 8:30 a.m. to 8 p.m. and accepts major credit cards.

Scuba Cancún also offers diving trips to 20 nearby reefs and *cenotes.* Dives in these underwater caves are at 9m (30 ft.), and the open ocean at 9m to 18m (30–60 ft.; offered in good weather only). The average dive is around 11m (35 ft.). Two-tank dives cost $140. Discounts apply if you bring your own equipment. Dives usually start around 9 a.m. and return by 2:15 p.m. Snorkeling trips cost $27 and leave every afternoon at 2 p.m. and 4:30 p.m. for shallow reefs located about a 20-minute boat ride away.

The largest dive operator is **Aquaworld** (see contact information in the "Skiing and surfing" section, earlier in this chapter). Aquaworld offers resort courses and diving from a man-made, anchored dive platform, Paradise Island. The price is $99, and includes a basic scuba introductory course in the pool, as well as a general theory class on diving. Aquaworld also has the **Subsee Explorer,** a submarine-style boat with picture windows that hang beneath the surface. The boat doesn't actually submerge — it's more like an updated version of the glass-bottom boat concept — but it does provide non-divers with a look at life beneath the sea. This outfit is open 24 hours a day and accepts all major credit cards.

Most of the beaches in Isla Mujeres are either too rocky or offer no snorkeling opportunities, so Garrafón or a trip to Isla Contoy are the only real options here. There are few beachfront hotels on Isla Mujeres, but those that exist aren't located in good snorkeling areas except Casa de los Suenos, which is adjacent to Garrafón. In addition to **snorkeling** at **Garrafón National Park** (see the "Traveling to the Island of Women" section, later in this chapter), travel agencies offer an all-day excursion to the natural wildlife habitat of **Isla Contoy** that usually includes time for snorkeling. The island, located an hour and a half past Isla Mujeres, is a major nesting area for birds and a treat for true nature lovers. Only two boats hold permits for excursions to the island. They depart at 9 a.m. and return by 5 p.m. The price of $60 includes drinks and snorkeling equipment.

The Great Mesoamerican Reef also offers exceptional snorkeling opportunities. In Puerto Morelos, 37km (23 miles) south of Cancún, this reef hugs the coastline for 14km (9 miles). The reef is so close to the shore (about 455m/1,492 ft.) that it forms a natural barrier for the village and keeps the waters calm on the inside of the reef. The water here is shallow, from 1.5 to 9m (5–30 ft.), resulting in ideal conditions for snorkeling. Stringent environmental regulations implemented by the local community have kept the reef here unspoiled.

Only a select few companies offer snorkel trips, and they must adhere to guidelines that ensure the reef's preservation. **Cancún Mermaid** (☎ **998-843-6517** or cellphone [044] 998-155-1946; www.cancun mermaid.com) is considered the best — it's a family-run ecotour company that has operated in the area since the 1970s and is known for highly personalized service. The tour typically takes snorkelers to two sections of the reef, spending about an hour in each area. When conditions allow, the boat drops off snorkelers and then follows them along with the current — an activity known as *drift snorkeling*, which enables snorkelers to see as much of the reef as possible. The trip costs $50 for adults, $35 for children, which includes boat, snorkeling gear, life jackets, a light lunch, bottled water, sodas, and beer, plus round-trip transportation to and from Puerto Morelos from Cancún hotels. Departures are Monday through Saturday at 9 a.m. or noon; a minimum of four snorkelers is required for a trip, and reservations are required.

Reeling in the big one

You can arrange a day of **deep-sea fishing** at one of the numerous piers or travel agencies for around $220 to $360 for four hours, $420 for six hours, and $520 for eight hours for up to four people. For up to eight people, prices are $420 for four hours, $550 for six hours, or $680 for eight hours. Marinas sometimes assist in putting together a group. Charters include a captain, a first mate, bait, gear, and beverages. Rates are lower if you depart from Isla Mujeres or from Cozumel Island, and frankly, the fishing is better closer to these departure points.

Swimming with dolphins

In Cancún, **Wet n'Wild** (☎ 998-193-2000) marine park offers guests a chance to swim with dolphins (for $115) and view these wonderful creatures in their dolphin aquarium, Atlántido. It's a fun place for a family to spend the day, with its numerous pools, water slides, and rides. Visitors can also snorkel with manta rays, tropical fish, and tame sharks. Admission is $25 for adults, $19 for children 3 to 11, and it's open 10 a.m. to 5:30 p.m. from November to April, and 10 a.m. to 6 p.m. from May to October. American Express, MasterCard, and Visa are accepted. The park is located on the southern end of Cancún (Paseo Kukulkán Km 25), between the airport and the Hotel Zone.

La Isla Shopping Village, Paseo Kukulkán Km 12.5, also has an **Interactive Aquarium** (☎ 998-883-0413, 883-0436, or 883-0411; www.aquarium cancun.com) with dolphin swims and the chance to feed a shark for $110. Interactive encounters and swims start at $50.

The best option for doing dolphin swims is on Isla Mujeres, where you can swim with dolphins at **Dolphin Discovery** (☎ 998-849-4757; Fax: 998-849-4758 or 849-4751; www.dolphindiscovery.com). Each session lasts an hour, with an educational introduction followed by 30 minutes of swim time. The price is $129, and transportation to Isla Mujeres is an additional $15. Advance reservations are required because capacity is limited each day. Assigned swimming times are 9 a.m., 11 a.m., 1 p.m., and 3 p.m., and you must arrive an hour before your scheduled swim time.

Swimming with dolphins has its critics and supporters. You may want to visit the Whale and Dolphins Conservation Society's Web site at www.wdcs.org. For more information about responsible travel in general, check out these Web sites: Tread Lightly (www.treadlightly.org) and the International Ecotourism Society (www.ecotourism.org).

Enjoying Land Sports

Even by land, Cancún has its share of winning ways to spend the day. Although golf is a latent developer here, more courses are popping up along the coast south of Cancún. Tennis, however, is tops as a hotel amenity, and you can find courts throughout Cancún. Horseback riding and all-terrain vehicle (ATV) tours are also great choices for land adventures.

Teeing off

Although the golf options are limited, the most well-known — and well-used — facility is the 18-hole **Club de Golf Cancún** (☎ 998-883-1230 or 883-1277; www.cancungolfclub.com), also known as the Pok-Ta-Pok Club. Designed by Robert Trent Jones Sr., it's located on the northern leg of the island. Greens fees are $140 per 18 holes. Clubs rent for $40, shoes run $18, and caddies charge $35 per bag. The club is open daily; American Express, MasterCard, and Visa are accepted. The club also has tennis courts.

The **Gran Meliá Cancún** (☎ 998-881-1100, ext. 193) offers a nine-hole executive course; greens fee is $43, and the club is open daily from 7 a.m. to 4:30 p.m. American Express, MasterCard, and Visa are accepted.

A more interesting option is at the **Hilton Cancún Beach & Golf Resort** (☎ 998-881-8000; Fax: 998-881-8093). Its championship 18-hole, par-72 course was designed around the Ruinas del Rey (Ruins of the King) archaeological site. Greens fees for the public are $175 for 18 holes and $125 for nine holes, and Hilton Cancún guests pay $125 for 18 holes and $90 for nine holes; all greens fees include a golf cart. Golf clubs and shoes are available for rent, and the club is open daily 6 a.m. to 6 p.m.

The first Jack Nicklaus Signature golf course in the Cancún area is located at the **Moon Palace Golf Resort,** along the Riviera Maya (www.palaceresorts.com). Two additional PGA courses are planned for the area just north of Cancún, Puerto Cancún, scheduled to be completed in 2007 and 2008.

Making time for tennis

Many hotels in Cancún offer excellent **tennis** facilities, and many of the courts are lit for night play. Among the best are the facilities at Le Méridien and the Fiesta Americana Coral Beach hotels. The hotel reviews in Chapter 10 include a number of hotels that have tennis courts on-site.

Galloping along

Rancho Loma Bonita (☎ 998-887-5465 or 887-5423; www.lomabonita mex.com) is Cancún's most popular option for **horseback riding.** Five-hour packages are available for $54 (adults and children 6–12). The packages include two hours of riding to caves, *cenotes* (spring-fed, underground caves), lagoons, and Maya ruins, and also along the Caribbean coast. A donkey polo game (yes, you get to play!) and some time for relaxing on the beach are also included. The ranch also offers a four-wheeler ride on the same route as the horseback tour for $55 double, or $72 if you want to drive solo. Rancho Loma Bonita is located about 30 minutes south of Cancún. The prices include transportation to the ranch, riding, soft drinks, and lunch, plus a guide and insurance. Visa is accepted, but cash is preferred.

Trailing away

Cancún Mermaid (☎ 998-843-6517; www.cancunmermaid.com), in Cancún, offers ATV jungle tours for $49 per person and $66 for two. The ATV tours travel through the jungles of Cancún and emerge on the beaches of the Riviera Maya. The two-and-a-half-hour tour includes equipment, instruction, a tour guide, and bottled water; it departs daily at 8 a.m. and 1:30 p.m. The company picks you up at your hotel. Another ATV option is Rancho Loma Bonita; see "Galloping along," on page 150.

Traveling to the Island of Women

One of the most popular — and in my mind, best — ways to spend the day is to check out a real Mexican beach town across the narrow channel from Cancún. **Isla Mujeres (Island of Women),** located just 10 miles offshore, is one of the most pleasant day trips from Cancún. At one end of the island is **El Garrafón National Underwater Park,** which, although damaged from Hurricane Wilma, still remains a good choice for snorkeling and diving. At the other end is a captivating village with small shops, restaurants, and hotels, along with **Playa Norte,** the island's best beach. Note that while the hurricane stripped sand from Cancún, much of it was swept across the channel to Isla Mujeres, meaning the beaches here have never been wider or lovelier.

To get to Isla Mujeres, you have four options:

- ✔ The **public ferries** from Puerto Juárez take between 15 and 45 minutes and make frequent trips.

- ✔ Traveling by **shuttle boat** from Playa Linda or Playa Tortuga is an hour-long ride. The boats offer irregular service.

- ✔ The **water taxi** is a more expensive but faster option than the public ferry or a shuttle boat. It's located next to the Xcaret terminal.

- ✔ Daylong **pleasure-boat trips** to the island leave from the Playa Linda pier.

Pleasure-boat cruises to Isla Mujeres include practically every conceivable type of vessel: Modern motor yachts, catamarans, trimarans, and even old-time sloops — more than 25 boats a day — take swimmers, sun lovers, snorkelers, and shoppers out into the translucent waters. Some tours include a snorkeling stop at Garrafón, lunch on the beach, and a short time for shopping in downtown Isla Mujeres. Most cruises leave at 9:30 or 10 a.m., last about five or six hours, and include continental breakfast, lunch, and snorkel gear rental. Others, particularly the sunset and night cruises, go to beaches away from town for pseudo-pirate shows and include a lobster dinner or Mexican buffet. If you want to actually see Isla Mujeres, go on a morning cruise or go on your own

Isla Mujeres (The Island of Women)

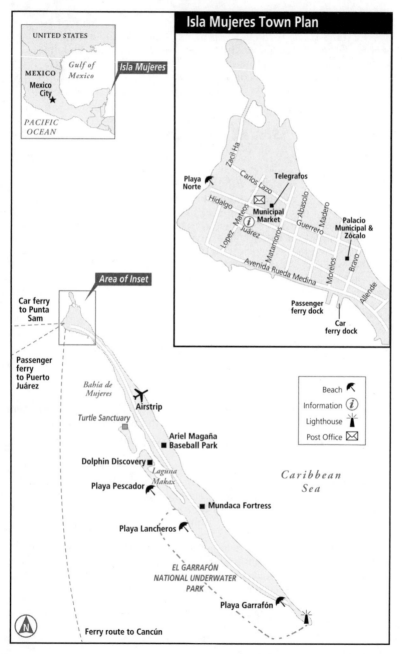

Isla Mujeres Town Plan

UNITED STATES

Gulf of Mexico

MEXICO

Mexico City ★

Isla Mujeres

PACIFIC OCEAN

Zacil Ha

Playa Norte

Carlos Lazo

Telegrafos

Hidalgo

Municipal Market

Abasolo

Madero

Palacio Municipal & Zócalo

Lopez

Mateos

Juárez

Guerrero

Matamoros

Avenida Rueda Medina

Morelos

Bravo

Allende

Passenger ferry dock

Car ferry dock

Area of Inset

Car ferry to Punta Sam

Passenger ferry to Puerto Juárez

Bahía de Mujeres

Airstrip

Turtle Sanctuary

Ariel Magaña Baseball Park

Dolphin Discovery

Laguna Makax

Playa Pescador

Mundaca Fortress

Caribbean Sea

Beach

Information

Lighthouse

Post Office

Playa Lancheros

EL GARRAFÓN NATIONAL UNDERWATER PARK

Playa Garrafón

N

Ferry route to Cancún

using the public ferry at Puerto Juárez. Prices for the day cruises run around $45 per person.

The inexpensive Puerto Juárez **public ferries** are just a few miles from downtown Cancún, and they give you greater flexibility in planning your day. From Isla Cancún or Ciudad Cancún, take a taxi or the Ruta 8 bus (from Av. Tulum) to Puerto Juárez. Choose the fast ferry (a 15-min. ride) that costs $4.50 per person compared to the slower one (a 45-min. ride) that costs $3.50. Departures are every half-hour from 6 a.m. to 8:30 a.m. and then every 15 minutes until 8:30 p.m. Upon arrival, the ferry docks in downtown Isla Mujeres near all the shops, restaurants, hotels, and Playa Norte. Take a taxi or rent a golf cart to get to Garrafón Park at the other end of the island. You can stay on the island as long as you like (even overnight) and return by ferry, but be sure to check the time of the last returning ferry — the hours are clearly posted.

The group that runs Xcaret (see the "Xcaret" section, later in this chapter) now manages **Garrafón** (☎ 998-877-1101; www.garrafon.com), so it has taken on more of a full-service theme-park atmosphere. A basic entrance fee of $20 for adults and $10 for children entitles you to access the reef, nature trails, and a museum, and to use kayaks, inner tubes, life vests, the pool, hammocks, and public facilities and showers. You can rent snorkel gear and lockers for an extra charge. Several restaurants are on-site; an additional $20 (or $17 for kids) to the entrance fee gives you access to the buffet and open bar. An all-inclusive option is available for $44 for adults and $22 for children, which adds dining at any of the restaurants, plus unlimited domestic drinks and use of snorkel gear, lockers, and towels. Garrafón also has full dive facilities and gear rentals, plus an expansive gift shop.

Other excursions from Isla Mujeres go to **Garrafón Reefs** underwater, so you can have a near-scuba-diving experience and see many colorful fish. However, the reefs are some distance from the shore, and they're impossible to reach on windy days with choppy seas. Also keep in mind that the reefs have suffered from the storm, as well as over-visitation, and their condition is far from pristine.

The **Atlantis Submarine** (☎ 987-872-5671; www.atlantisadventures. com) provides a front-row seat to the underwater action. Departures vary, depending on weather conditions. Atlantis Submarine departs Monday to Saturday every hour from 9 a.m. until 1 p.m.; tours last an hour and 45 minutes and cost $79 for adults and $45 per child. You need to take a ferry to Cozumel to catch the submarine. Still other boat excursions visit **Isla Contoy,** a **national bird sanctuary** that's well worth the time. You can call any travel agent or see any hotel tour desk to get a wide selection of tours to Isla Contoy. Prices range from $44 to $65, depending on the length of the trip. If you plan to spend time in Isla Mujeres, the Contoy trip is easier and more pleasurable to take from there.

Touring Ruins or an Eco-Theme Park

One of the best ways to spend a vacation day is by exploring the nearby archaeological ruins or one of the new ecological theme parks near Cancún. Historical and natural treasures unlike any you may have encountered before are within easy driving distance. Cancún is a perfect base for day trips to these places that provide a great introduction to Mexico's rich historical past and diverse natural attractions.

Make the Maya ruins to the south of Cancún at **Tulum** your first goal. Then, perhaps, you can check out the *caleta* (cove) of **Xel-Ha** or take the day trip to **Xcaret.**

Organized day trips are popular and easy to book through any travel agent in town, or you can plan a journey on your own via bus or rental car.

Seeing the archaeological sites

You can choose from three great archaeological sites within proximity to Cancún:

- ✔ **Tulum:** Summer hours: daily from 8 a.m. to 5 p.m.; winter hours: daily from 7 a.m. until 6 p.m. Admission $4.

- ✔ **Ruinas del Rey:** Daily 8 a.m. until 5 p.m. Admission $4.50.

- ✔ **Chichén Itzá:** Daily 8 a.m. to 5 p.m. Admission $8.50.

For all sites, admission for children under 13 and seniors over 60 is free, and admission is free on Sundays and Mexican national holidays for Mexican citizens. Video camera permits cost $4, and parking is additional, varying with the site.

Tulum

Poised on a rocky hill overlooking the transparent, turquoise Caribbean Sea, ancient **Tulum** is a stunning site — and my personal favorite of all the ruins. It's not the largest or most important of the Maya ruins in this area, but it's the only one by the sea, which makes it the most visually impressive in my opinion. Intriguing carvings and reliefs decorate the well-preserved structures, which date back to between the 12th and 16th centuries in the post-Classic period.

The site is surrounded by a wall on three sides, which explains its name — *tulum* means fence, trench, or wall. Its ancient name is believed to have been *Záma,* a derivative of the Maya word for "morning" or "dawn," and the sunrise at Tulum is certainly dramatic. The wall is believed to have been constructed after the original buildings to protect the interior religious altars from a growing number of invaders. Although Tulum is considered to have been principally a place of worship, members of the upper classes later took up residence here to take advantage

Tulum Ruins

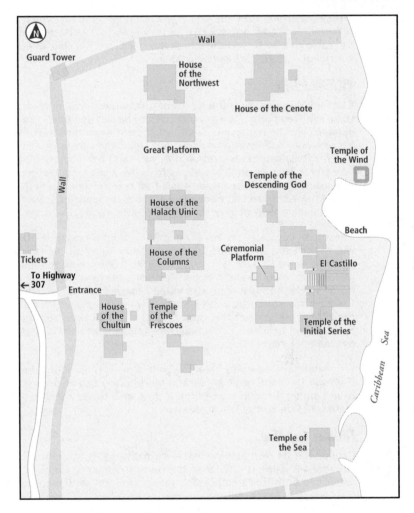

of the protective wall. Between the two most dramatic structures — the castle and the Temple of the Wind — lies Tulum Cove, where you can swim and spend time relaxing on this absolutely magical beach. The cove is a small inlet with a beach of fine, white sand, and it was a point of departure for Maya trading vessels in ancient times. Entrance to the site without a tour is $4; use of a video camera requires a $4 permit. A popular day excursion combines a visit to the ruins at Tulum with the ecological water park Xel-Ha (see the "Xel-Ha" section, later in this chapter).

Tulum is located 130km (81 miles) south of Cancún, along Highway 307. The ruins' entrance is to your left, before you pass through the town of Tulum. After you turn left, you come to the parking lot, which also offers restroom facilities, a snack bar, and some shops. A shuttle train ($1) is available to take to you the site of the ruins, but it's also an easy walk of a little more than a kilometer (½ mile).

Chichén Itzá

The fabled pyramids and temples of Chichén Itzá (no, it doesn't rhyme with "chicken pizza"; the accents are on the last syllables: chee-*chehn* eet-*zah*) are the region's best-known ancient monuments. Walking among these stone platforms, pyramids, and ball courts gives you an appreciation for this ancient civilization that you can't get from reading books. The city is built on such a scale as to evoke a sense of wonder: To fill the plaza during one of the mass rituals that occurred here a millennium ago would have required an enormous number of celebrants. Even today, with the mass flow of tourists through these plazas, the ruins feel empty.

The site occupies 10 sq. km (4 sq. miles) and it takes most of the day to see all the ruins, which are open daily 8 a.m. to 5 p.m. Service areas are open 8 a.m. to 10 p.m. Admission is $8.50, free for children under age 13 and seniors over 60 and free for Mexican citizens on Sundays and holidays. A permit to use your own video camera costs an additional $4. Chichén Itzá's sound and light show is worth seeing and is included in the cost of admission. The show is held at 8 p.m. every night and is in Spanish, but headsets providing translations in several languages are available for rent ($3).

Chichén Itzá is located 179km (112 miles) west of Cancún, along Highway 180, between Cancún and Merida. You can arrange day trips from Cancún through your hotel or through a travel agent in the United States (before you go) or in Mexico.

Ruinas del Rey

Cancún has its own Maya ruins — **Ruinas del Rey** (no phone) — a small site that's less impressive than the ruins at Tulum or Chichén Itzá. Maya fishermen built this small ceremonial center and settlement very early in the history of Maya culture and then abandoned it. The site was resettled again near the end of the post-Classic period, not long before the conquistadors arrived. You can see the platforms of numerous small temples amid the banana plants, papayas, and wildflowers. The Hilton Cancún golf course has been built around the ruins, but the ruins have a separate entrance for sightseers. The ruins are located at Paseo Kukulkán Km 17, about 21km (13 miles) from town, at the southern reaches of the Hotel Zone, close to Punta Nizuc. Look for the Hilton hotel on the left (east) and then the ruins on the right (west). Admission to the site without a tour is $4.50, free for Mexican citizens on Sundays. It's open daily from 8 a.m. to 5 p.m.

Chichén Itzá Ruins

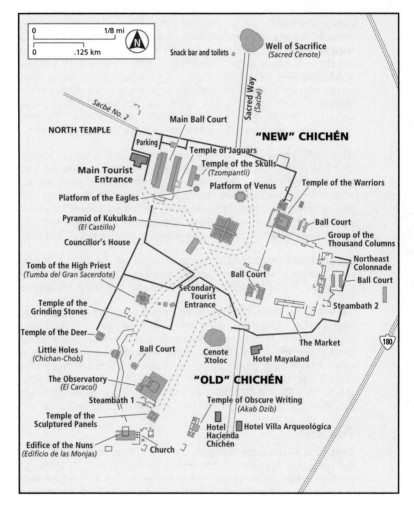

0 — 1/8 mi
0 — .125 km

Snack bar and toilets

Well of Sacrifice
(Sacred Cenote)

Sacbé No. 2

Main Ball Court

Sacred Way
(Sacbé)

NORTH TEMPLE

Parking

Main Tourist
Entrance

Platform of the Eagles

Temple of Jaguars

Temple of the Skulls
(Tzompantli)

Platform of Venus

"NEW" CHICHÉN

Temple of the Warriors

Pyramid of Kukulkán
(El Castillo)

Councillor's House

Ball Court

Group of the
Thousand Columns

Tomb of the High Priest
(Tumba del Gran Sacerdote)

Temple of the
Grinding Stones

Temple of the Deer

Little Holes
(Chichan-Chob)

The Observatory
(El Caracol)

Steambath 1

Temple of the
Sculptured Panels

Edifice of the Nuns
(Edificio de las Monjas)

Secondary
Tourist
Entrance

Ball Court

Ball Court

Cenote
Xtoloc

Church

Northeast
Colonnade

Ball Court

Steambath 2

The Market

180

Hotel Mayaland

"OLD" CHICHÉN

Temple of Obscure Writing
(Akab Dzib)

Hotel
Hacienda
Chichén

Hotel Villa Arqueológica

Exploring an eco-theme park

The popularity of the Xcaret and Xel-Ha eco-parks has inspired a growing number of entrepreneurs to ride the wave of interest in ecological and adventure theme parks. Be aware that "theme park" more than "ecological" is the operative part of the phrase. The newer parks of Aktun Chen and Tres Ríos are — so far — less commercial and more focused on nature than their counterparts.

Aktun Chen

This park, consisting of a spectacular 5,000-year-old grotto and an abundance of wildlife, marks the first time that above-the-ground cave systems in the Yucatán have been open to the public. The name Aktun Chen means "cave with an underground river inside." The main cave containing three rivers is more than 500m (1,640 ft.) long with a magnificent vault. Discreet illumination and easy walking paths make visiting the caves more comfortable, without appearing to alter the caves too much from their natural state. The caves contain thousands of stalactites, stalagmites, and sculpted rock formations, along with a 12m-deep (40-ft.) *cenote* (an underground, spring-fed cave) with clear blue water.

Aktun Chen was once underwater itself, and you notice fossilized shells and fish embedded in the limestone as you walk along the paths. Caves are an integral part of this region's geography and geology, and knowledgeable guides lead you through the site while providing explanations and offering mini-history lessons on the Maya's association with these caves. Tours have no set times — guides are available to take you when you arrive — and groups are kept to a maximum of 20 people.

Nature trails surround the caves throughout the 395-hectare (988-acre) park, where spotting deer, spider monkeys, iguanas, and wild turkeys is common. A small, informal restaurant and gift shop are also on-site.

Traveling to Aktun Chen on your own is easy. From Cancún, go south on Highway 307 (the road to Tulum). Just past the turnoff for Akumal, a sign on the right side of the highway indicates the turnoff for Aktun Chen; from there, it's a 3km (2-mile) drive west along a smooth but unpaved road. Travel time from Cancún is about an hour, and the park is open from 9 a.m. until dark. The entry fee of $18 includes the services of a guide. Call ☎ **998-892-0662** or 984-877-8550 for more information, or you can visit the park via the Internet at www.aktunchen.com.

Tres Ríos

Tres Ríos — meaning three rivers — is the most "natural" of the area's nature parks. Located on more than 60 hectares (150 acres) of land, this park is a true nature reserve that offers guests a beautiful area for kayaking, canoeing, snorkeling, horseback riding, or biking along jungle trails. Essentially, the park is just one big natural spot for participating in these activities. It's definitely less commercial than the other eco-theme parks. Tres Rios closed following the October 2005 hurricane, and took the opportunity to make some improvements to its facilities. At press time it was scheduled to reopen during the summer, 2006.

The park is located just 25 minutes south of Cancún. The entrance fee is $22 for adults and $19 for children, which includes canoe trips; the use of bikes, kayaks, and snorkeling equipment; and the use of hammocks and beach chairs after you tire yourself out. Extra charges apply for scuba diving, horseback riding, and extended guided tours through the

preserve and its estuary. Tres Ríos also has bathroom facilities, showers, and a convenience store; however, the facilities are much less
sophisticated than the area's other, more developed eco-theme parks.

Most Cancún travel agencies sell a half-day "kayak express" tour to
Tres Ríos. Priced at $48, the trip includes admission to the park and its
activities, round-trip transportation, lunch, and two nonalcoholic drinks.
Call ☎ 998-887-8077 in Cancún or visit the park's Web site at www.
tres-rios.com for details and reservations.

Xcaret

Xcaret (*ish*-cah-reht), located 80km (50 miles) south of Cancún (☎ 998-
883-0470 or 984-871-5200; www.xcaretcancun.com), is a specially built
ecological and archaeological theme park and one of the area's most popular tourist attractions. Xcaret has become almost a reason in itself to
visit Cancún. With a ton of attractions — most of them participatory — in
one location, it's the closest thing to Disneyland in Mexico. In Cancún,
signs advertising Xcaret and folks handing out Xcaret leaflets are everywhere. The park has its own bus terminal in Cancún where buses pick up
tourists at regular intervals. Plan to spend a full day here. Children love
it, and the jungle setting and palm-lined beaches are beautiful. Past the
entrance booths (built to resemble small Maya temples) are pathways
that meander around bathing coves, the snorkeling lagoon, and the
remains of a group of real Maya temples.

Xcaret may celebrate Mother Nature, but its builders rearranged quite
a bit of her handiwork in completing it. If you're looking for a place to
escape the commercialism of Cancún, this may not be it. The park is relatively expensive and may be very crowded, thus diminishing the advertised "natural" experience.

Entrance gains you access to swimming beaches, limestone tunnels to
snorkel through, marked palm-lined pathways, a wild-bird breeding
aviary, horseback riding, scuba diving, a botanical garden and nursery, a
sea turtle nursery, a butterfly pavilion, and a tropical aquarium, where
visitors can touch underwater creatures such as manta rays, starfish,
and octopuses. Extra charges apply for some of these activities. One
of the park's most popular attractions is the excellent "Dolphinarium,"
where visitors (on a first-come, first-served basis) can swim with the
dolphins for an extra charge of $115.

Oh, but there's more. Xcaret features a replica of the ancient Maya game,
pok-ta-pok. In this game, six "warriors" bounce around a 9-pound ball
with their hips. The Seawalker, a type of watersport designed for non-
swimmers, is another attraction. By donning a special suit and helmet
with a connected air pump, you can walk on the ocean floor or examine
a coral reef in a small bay.

The visitor center has lockers, first-aid assistance, and a gift shop. Visitors
aren't allowed to bring in food or drinks, so you're limited to the rather

high-priced restaurants on-site. No personal radios are allowed, and you must remove all suntan lotion if you swim in the lagoon to avoid poisoning the lagoon habitat.

The admission price of $59 for adults, $41 for children ages 5 to 12, entitles you to use the facilities, boats, life jackets, snorkeling equipment for the underwater tunnel and lagoon, and lounge chairs. Other attractions, such as snorkeling at $34, horseback riding at $51, scuba diving at $55 for certified divers ($75 for a resort course), and the dolphin swim at $115, cost extra. There may be more visitors than equipment (in the case of beach chairs, for example), so bring a beach towel and your own snorkeling gear to be on the safe side.

Travel agencies in Cancún offer day trips to Xcaret that depart at 8 a.m. and return at 6 p.m. The cost is $89 for adults and $60 for children, which includes transportation, admission, and a guide. You can also buy a ticket to the park at the **Xcaret bus terminal** (☎ **998-881-2401,** 883-3143), located next to the Fiesta Americana Coral Beach hotel on Isla Cancún. The "Xcaret Day and Night" trip includes round-trip transportation from Cancún, a *charreada* festival (where horse-riding and roping skills are showcased), lighted pathways to Maya ruins, dinner, and a folkloric show. The cost is $89 for adults and $45 for children age 6 to 11 (free for kids 5 and under). Buses leave the terminal at 9 and 10 a.m. daily, with the "Day and Night" tour returning at 9:30 p.m. The park itself is open Monday to Saturday 8:30 a.m. to 8:30 p.m., Sunday 8:30 a.m. to 5:30 p.m.

Xel-Ha

The sea has carved the Caribbean coast of the Yucatán into hundreds of small *caletas,* or coves, that form the perfect habitat for tropical marine life, both flora and fauna. Many caletas along the coast remain undiscovered and pristine, but Xel-Ha (shell-*hah*), located near Tulum, plays host daily to throngs of snorkelers and scuba divers who come to luxuriate in its warm waters and swim among its brilliant fish. Xel-Ha is a swimmers' paradise with no threat of undertow or pollution. It's a beautiful, completely calm cove that's a perfect place to bring kids for their first snorkeling experience. Experienced snorkelers may be disappointed because the crowds seem to have driven out the living coral and many of the fish here.

Xel-Ha (☎ **998-884-9422** or 883-3293; www.xelha.com.mx) is 117km (73 miles) south of Cancún along Highway 307. The entrance is a half-mile from the highway. Admission is $33 per adult and $23 for children age 5 to 11 (free for children under 5) and includes use of inner tubes, life vests, and shuttle trains to the river. You can also choose an all-inclusive option for admission, equipment, food, and beverages that runs $59 for adults and $41 for children. The park is open daily 8:30 a.m. to 5 p.m., offers free parking with admission, and accepts American Express, MasterCard, and Visa. After you arrive at the 4-hectare (10-acre) park, you can rent snorkeling equipment and an underwater camera, but you may also bring your own. Food and beverage service, changing rooms, showers, and other facilities are available. Platforms have been constructed that allow decent sea-life viewing for non-snorkelers.

In addition, the resort offers "snuba," a clever invention that combines snorkeling and scuba. Snuba is a shallow-water diving system that places conventional scuba tanks on secure rafts that float at surface level; the "snuba-diver" breathes normally through a mouthpiece, which is connected to a long air hose attached to the tank above. This setup enables a swimmer to go as deep as 6m (20 ft.) below the surface and stay down for as long as an hour or more. It's a great transition to scuba, and many divers may even enjoy it more because snuba leaves you remarkably unencumbered by equipment.

When you swim, be careful to observe the "swim here" and "no swimming" signs. You can see the greatest variety of fish right near the ropes that divide the swimming areas from the non-swimming areas and near any groups of rocks. An interactive dolphin attraction has been added — a one-hour swim costs $115, and an educational 15-minute program runs $15. Make your reservations at least 24 hours in advance for one of the four daily sessions: 9:30 a.m., 12:30 p.m., 2 p.m., and 3:15 p.m.

If you're driving, just south of Xel-Ha turn off on the west side of the highway so you don't miss the ruins of **ancient Xel-Ha.** You're likely to be the only one there as you walk over limestone rocks and through the tangle of trees, vines, and palms. There's a huge, deep, dark *cenote* to one side, a temple palace with tumbled-down columns, a jaguar group, and a conserved temple group. A covered *palapa* on one pyramid guards a partially preserved mural. Admission is $3.50.

Xel-Ha is close to the ruins at **Tulum** (check out "Seeing the archaeological sites," earlier in this chapter) and makes a good place for a dip after you finish climbing the Maya ruins. You can even make the short 13km (8-mile) hop north from Tulum to Xel-Ha by public bus. When you get off at the junction for Tulum, ask the restaurant owner when the next buses come by; otherwise, you may have to wait as long as two hours on the highway.

Sightseeing in Cancún

To the right side of the entrance to the Cancún Convention Center is the small **Museo Arqueológico de Cancún** (☎ 998-883-0305), a small but interesting museum with relics from archaeological sites around the state. Admission is $2. The museum is open Tuesday to Sunday from 9 a.m. to 8 p.m.

During the winter tourist season, **bullfights** are held every Wednesday at 3:30 p.m. in Cancún's small bullring (☎ 998-884-8372), which is located near the northern end of Paseo Kukulkán (avs. Bonampak and Sayil). A sport introduced to Mexico by the Spanish viceroys, bullfighting is now as much a part of Mexican culture as tequila. The bullfights usually include four bulls, and the spectacle begins with a folkloric dance exhibition, followed by a performance by the *charros* (Mexico's sombrero-wearing cowboys). You're not likely to see Mexico's best bullfights in Cancún — the real stars are in Mexico City.

Keep in mind that if you go to a bullfight, *you're going to see a bullfight,* so stay away if you're an animal lover or you can't bear the sight of blood. Travel agencies in Cancún sell tickets: $35 for adults, with children admitted free of charge. Seating is by general admission. American Express, MasterCard, and Visa are accepted.

La Torre Cancún, a rotating tower at the El Embarcadero park and entertainment complex, once offered the best possible view of Cancún and should do so again soon, although its reopening date was uncertain at press time. It's located at Paseo Kukulkán Km 4 (☎ **998-849-7777**). Former prices were $9 for one ride; and $14 for a day and night pass.

Shopping in Cancún

Despite the surrounding natural splendor, shopping has become a favored activity in Cancún, and the place is known throughout Mexico for its diverse array of shops and festive malls catering to large numbers of international tourists. Tourists arriving from the United States may find apparel more expensive in Cancún, but the selection here is much broader than in other Mexican resorts.

Numerous duty-free shops offer excellent value on European goods. The largest shop is **UltraFemme** (☎ **998-884-1402** or 887-4559), specializing in imported cosmetics, perfumes, and fine jewelry and watches. Its Ciudad Cancún location on Avenida Tulum, Supermanzana (intersection) 25, offers lower prices than the locations at Plaza Caracol, Kukulkán Plaza, Maya Fair Plaza, and Plaza Flamingo or at the store at the international airport.

Handicrafts and other *artesanía* works are more limited and more expensive in Cancún than in other regions of Mexico because they're not produced here, but they're available. Several **open-air crafts markets** are easily visible on Avenida Tulum in Ciudad Cancún and near the convention center in the Hotel Zone. One of the biggest markets is **Coral Negro,** located at Paseo Kukulkán Km 9.5 (☎/fax **998-883-0758**). It's open daily from 7 a.m. to 11 p.m.

The main venue for shopping in Cancún is the **mall** — not quite as grand as its U.S. counterpart, but close. Cancún's malls are air-conditioned, sleek, and sophisticated, with most located on Paseo Kukulkán between Km 7 and Km 12. You can find everything from fine crystal and silver to designer clothing and decorative objects, along with numerous restaurants and clubs. Stores are generally open daily from 10 a.m. to 10 p.m., with clubs and restaurants remaining open much later. Here's a brief

Cancún Area

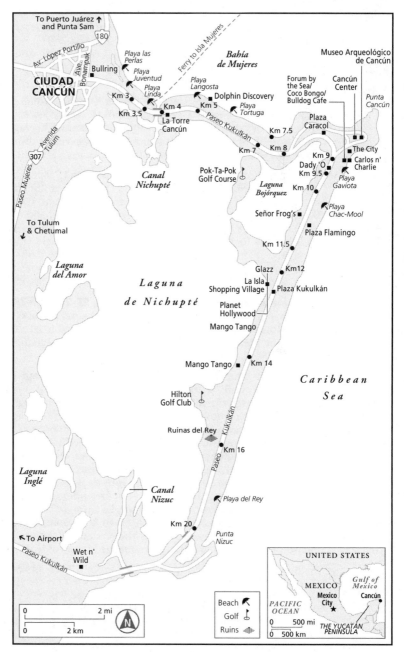

To Puerto Juárez ↑
and Punta Sam

180

Av. López Portillo

Ave. Bonampak

CIUDAD CANCÚN

Bullring ■

Playa las Perlas

Playa Juventud

Playa Linda

Km 3 ●

Km 3.5 ●

Km 4 ■

La Torre Cancún

Ferry to Isla Mujeres

Bahía de Mujeres

Playa Langosta

Dolphin Discovery ■

Km 5 ●

Playa Tortuga

Paseo Kukulkán

Km 7.5 ●

Km 7 ●

Km 8 ●

Forum by the Sea/ Coco Bongo/ Bulldog Cafe

Museo Arqueológico de Cancún ●

Cancún Center ●

Punta Cancún

Plaza Caracol ■

The City ■
Carlos n' Charlie ■

Km 9 ●
Dady 'O ■
Km 9.5 ●

Playa Gaviota

Playa Chac-Mool

Avenida Tulum

307

Paseo Mujeres

To Tulum & Chetumal ↓

Canal Nichupté

Pok-Ta-Pok Golf Course ↑

Laguna Bojórquez

Km 10 ●

Señor Frog's ■

Plaza Flamingo ■

Km 11.5 ●

Laguna del Amor

Laguna de Nichupté

Glazz ■ Km12

La Isla Shopping Village ■ Plaza Kukulkán ■

Planet Hollywood

Mango Tango

Mango Tango ■ Km 14

Caribbean Sea

Hilton Golf Club ↑

Paseo Kukulkán

Ruinas del Rey ◈ Km 16

Laguna Inglé

Canal Nizuc

Playa del Rey

Km 20 ●

Punta Nizuc

↖To Airport

Paseo Kukulkán

Wet n' Wild ■

| 0 | | 2 mi |
| 0 | | 2 km |

N

Beach ☂
Golf ↑
Ruins ◈

UNITED STATES

MEXICO

Mexico City ★

Gulf of Mexico

Cancún ●

PACIFIC OCEAN

| 0 | 500 mi |
| 0 | 500 km |

THE YUCATÁN PENINSULA

rundown on the malls, running from the northern to the southern end of the island — and some of the shops they contain:

- ✔ **Maya Fair Plaza/Centro Comercial Maya Fair,** frequently called "Mayfair" (Paseo Kukulkán Km 8.5; ☎ **998-883-2801**), is Cancún's oldest mall and features a lively, bricked center with open-air restaurants and bars, such as Tequila Sunrise, and several stores selling silver, leather, and crafts.

- ✔ The long-standing **Plaza Caracol** (Paseo Kukulkán Km 8.5; ☎ **998-883-1038;** www.caracolplaza.com) holds Cartier jewelry, Guess, Waterford Crystal, Señor Frog clothing, Samsonite luggage, Gucci, and La Fisheria restaurant. It's just before you reach the convention center as you come from Ciudad Cancún.

- ✔ The entertainment-oriented **Forum by the Sea** (Paseo Kukulkán Km 9; ☎ **998-883-4425;** www.forumbythesea.com.mx) has shops including Tommy Hilfiger, Levi's, Diesel, Swatch, and Harley Davidson, but most people come here for the food and fun. You can choose from Cambalache, Coco Bongo, and Rainforest Cafe, plus an extensive food court. It's open 10 a.m. to midnight (bars remain open later). This mall suffered extensive hurricane damage, so has been in the process of a complete face-lift. Some venues are already open, with the remainder scheduled to reopen by July 2006.

- ✔ **Plaza Flamingo** (Paseo Kukulkán Km 10.5; ☎ **998-883-2945**), has branches of Bancrecer, Subway, and La Casa del Habano (for Cuban cigars) located inside. Following repairs suffered from Hurricane Wilma, the Plaza was renovated and reopened for business in March 2006.

- ✔ The most intriguing mall is the **La Isla Shopping Village** (Paseo Kukulkán Km 12.5; ☎ **998-883-5025;** www.laislacancun.com.mx), an open-air festival mall that looks like a small village, where walkways lined with shops and restaurants crisscross over little canals. The mall also has a "riverwalk" alongside the Nichupté Lagoon and an interactive aquarium and dolphin-swim facility. It suffered extensive hurricane damage but reopened in March 2006. Shops here include Zara clothing, Benetton, Guess, Swatch, Ultra Femme, and much more. Dining choices include Johnny Rockets, The Food Court (not actually a "food court," but an Anderson's restaurant), and the beautiful Mexican restaurant, La Casa de las Margaritas. There's also a first-run movie theater, an Aquarium, a video arcade, and several nightclubs, including Max-O's and Alebrejes. It's located across from the Sheraton, on the lagoon side of the street.

- ✔ Inside **Kukulcan Plaza** (Paseo Kukulkán Km 13; ☎ **998-885-2200;** www.kukulcanplaza.com) is a large selection of more than 300 shops, restaurants, and entertainment venues. There's a branch of Banco Serfin; OK Maguey Cantina Grill; a movie theater with U.S. movies; an Internet-access kiosk; Tikal, a shop with Guatemalan textile clothing; several crafts stores; a liquor store; several bathing-suit specialty stores; record and tape outlets; a leather-goods store (including shoes and sandals); and a store specializing in silver from Taxco. In the food court are a number of U.S. franchise restaurants, including Ruth's Chris Steak House, plus a specialty-coffee shop. For entertainment, the plaza has a bowling alley, the Q-Zar laser game pavilion, and a video game arcade. There's also a large indoor parking garage. The mall is open 10 a.m. to 10 p.m.

Discovering Cancún after Dark

Ready to party? The nightlife in Cancún is as hot as the sun at noon on a cloudless July day, and clubbing is one of the main attractions of this let-loose town. The hot spots are centralized in **Forum by the Sea** and **La Isla Shopping Village,** but finding a party anywhere in town isn't hard. Hotels also compete for your pesos with happy-hour entertainment and special drink prices as they try to entice visitors and guests from other resorts to pay a visit. (Lobby-bar hopping at sunset is one great way to plan next year's vacation.)

Partying at a club

Clubbing in Cancún can go on each night until the sun rises over that incredibly blue sea. Several of the big hotels have nightclubs — some-times still called discos here — and others entertain in their lobby bars with live music. On weekends, expect to stand in long lines for the top clubs, pay a cover charge of $10 to $20 per person, and pay $5 to $8 for a drink. Some of the higher-priced clubs include an open bar or live entertainment.

Check out the "Cancún Area" map on page 163 for various club locations.

 The **Bar Hopper Tour,** offered by the American Express Travel Agency (☎ **998-881-4050;** Fax: 998-884-6942), is a great introduction to the Cancún club scene. It's not as cheesy as it may sound, and it's a great way to check out the top spots without making a major investment in cover charges. For $60, a bus takes you from bar to club to bar to club — generally a range of four to five top choices — where you bypass any lines and spend about an hour at each establishment. Entry to the clubs, one welcome drink at each location, and transportation by air-condi-tioned bus is included in the fee, allowing you to sample the best of Cancún's nightlife.

Most of Cancún's most popular clubs were located at the exact point on the island where the most damage was done, so they've just received a makeover. While many rushed to reopen in time for Spring Break 2006, it's up in the air which will assume the top hot spot, and, as any good clubber knows, popularity can shift like the sands on the beach. So take this list as a starting point — extensive research showed me that these were the current hot spots at press time, listed alphabetically:

✔ **The City** (Bulevar Kukulcán Km 9.5; ☎ **998-848-8380;** www.thecity cancun.com), was Cancún's hottest club, pre-Wilma, and promises to be once again, since reopening in March 2006. It features progressive electronic music spun by some of the world's top DJs. With visiting DJs from New York, L.A., and Mexico City — Moby even played here — the music is sizzling. You actually need never leave, as The City is a day-and-night club. The City Beach Club opens at 8 a.m., and features a pool with a wave machine for surfing and boogie-boarding, a tower-high water slide, food and bar service, plus beach cabañas. The Terrace Bar, overlooking the action on Bulevar Kukulcán, serves food and drinks all day long. For a relaxing evening vibe, the Lounge features comfy couches, chill music, and an extensive menu of martinis, snacks, and deserts. Open at 10 p.m., the 7,600-sq.-m (25,000-sq.-ft.) nightclub has nine bars, stunning light shows, and several VIP areas. Located in front of Coco Bongo, The City also has a second location in Playa del Carmen.

✔ **Coco Bongo** in Forum by the Sea (Paseo Kukulkán Km 9.5; ☎ **998-883-5061;** www.cocobongo.com.mx) continues its reputation as the hottest spot in town. This spot's main appeal is that there's no formal dance floor, so you can dance anywhere you can find the space — that includes on the tables, on the bar, or even on stage with the live band! Coco Bongo can pack in up to 3,000 people — and regularly does. You have to see it to believe it. Despite its capacity, lines are long on weekends and in the high season. The music alternates between Caribbean, salsa, techno, and classics from the 1970s and 1980s. Coco Bongo draws a mixed crowd, but the young and hip dominate. Choose between a $15 cover or $25 for open bar (national drinks).

✔ **Dady'O** (Paseo Kukulkán Km 9.5; ☎ **998-883-3333;** www.dadyo.net) is a highly favored rave with frequent, long lines. It opens nightly at 9:30 p.m. and generally charges a cover of $15. **Dady Rock Bar and Grill** (Paseo Kukulkán Km 9.5; ☎ **998-883-1626**), the offspring of Dady'O, opens early (7 p.m.) and goes as long as any other nightspot, offering a new twist on entertainment with a combination of live bands and DJ-orchestrated music. It also features an open bar, full meals, a buffet, and dancing.

✔ **Glazz,** in the La Isla Shopping Village (Bulevar Kukulcán Km 12.5, Local B-7; ☎ **998-883-1881;** www.glazz.com.mx), is among Cancún's newest nocturnal offerings, combining a restaurant with a sleek lounge and sophisticated nightclub for a complete evening of entertainment. Geared for those over 30, music is mostly lounge and house, and there are live entertainment acts (anything from drummers to sultry dancers) periodically through the evening. The staff is known as being among the top in town. The China Bistro has earned rave reviews, while the Lounge's vast selection of martinis and "tequilitinis" is dangerously tempting. The Club is pure Miami-style, with plenty of neon and a very hot DJ. It's open nightly from 7 p.m. to 5 a.m. Cover is $10, and a dress code prohibits sandals or shorts.

Not into the party scene? The most refined and upscale of all Cancún's nightly gathering spots is the **Lobby Lounge** at the **Ritz-Carlton Hotel** (scheduled to reopen September 5, 2006; ☎ **998-881-0808,** ext. 5310). Live dance music and a list of more than 120 premium tequilas for tasting or sipping are the highlights here.

Hanging out after dinner

Numerous restaurants, such as **Carlos 'n Charlie's, Planet Hollywood, Señor Frog's, T.G.I. Friday's,** and **Iguana Wana,** double as nighttime party spots offering wild-ish fun at much lower prices than the clubs. Check these out:

- **Carlos 'n Charlie's** (Paseo Kukulkán Km 8.5; ☎ **998-883-1862**) is a reliable place to find both good food and fraternity house–type entertainment in the evenings. A dance floor goes along with the live music that starts nightly around 8:30 p.m. A cover charge kicks in if you're not planning to eat. It's open daily 11 a.m. to 2 a.m.

- **Planet Hollywood** (La Isla Shopping Village; ☎ **998-881-8135**; Fax: 998-881-8133; www.planethollywood.com) is the still-popular brainchild (and one of the last-remaining) of Sylvester Stallone, Bruce Willis, and that terminating politician Arnold Schwarzenegger. It's both a restaurant and a nighttime music/dance spot with mega-decibel live music. It's open daily 11 a.m. to 2 a.m. The original branch in Cancún was located at Plaza Flamingos, but at press time, it was uncertain if this locale would reopen.

Enjoying a cultural event

Several hotels host **Mexican fiesta nights,** which include a buffet dinner and a folkloric dance show; the price, including dinner, ranges from $35 to $50.

In the Costa Blanca shopping center, **El Mexicano** restaurant (☎ **998-883-2220**) hosts a tropical dinner show every night and also features live music for dancing. The entertainment alternates each night — *mariachis* entertain off and on from 7 to 11 p.m., and a folkloric show takes place from 8 to 9:30 p.m.

You can also get in the party mood at **Mango Tango** (Paseo Kukulkán Km 14.2; ☎ **998-885-0303;** www.mangotango.com.mx), a lagoon-side restaurant/dinner-show establishment opposite the Ritz-Carlton Cancún. Diners can choose from two seating levels, one nearer the music and the other overlooking the whole production. The music is loud and varied but mainly features reggae or salsa. The one-hour-and-20-minute dinner show begins at 8:30 p.m. nightly and costs $49. If you're not dining and come just for the music and drinks, a $10 cover charge applies.

For entertainment that lets tourists and locals mingle, head for the downtown **Parque de las Palapas** (the main park) for *Noches Caribeños* (Caribbean Nights), where live tropical music is provided at no charge for anyone who wants to listen and dance. Performances begin at 7:30 p.m. on Sundays. Sometimes, performances are scheduled for Fridays and Saturdays, but the calendar varies.

Part IV
Cozumel and the Riviera Maya

The 5th Wave — By Rich Tennant

©RICHTENNANT.COM

"Well, if you're not drinking Tequila with your breakfast burrito, then why is your cereal bowl rimmed in salt?"

In this part . . .

The island of Cozumel and the mainland south of Cancún — called the Riviera Maya — offer a different way of experiencing the transparent blue waters and white-sand beaches of the Mexican Caribbean. Small towns, such as Playa del Carmen and Tulum, and isolated resorts, both small and large, present quite a contrast to Cancún's studded line-up of hotels. Dotting the landscape are nature parks, ruins, and lovely natural features. Life in these parts is slower and holds more local color.

Access by air is easy. Cozumel has its own international airport and the Riviera Maya enjoys easy access to Cancún's airport. As with Cancún, many people speak English, making communication with the locals easy. The two chapters in this part provide the information you need to make your stay in the region relaxing and enjoyable.

Chapter 14

Cozumel

by David Baird

In This Chapter

▶ Adjusting to Cozumel and the lay of the land
▶ Cruising Cozumel for the best accommodations
▶ Finding the best places to dine
▶ Discovering sports and other fun in the sun

Cozumel is a Caribbean island 19km (12 miles) off the Yucatán coast. More relaxed than the booming mainland, Cozumel has the feel of a small island — roads that don't go very far, lots of mopeds, few buses and trucks, and a certain sense of isolation. It's not that small — 45km (28 miles) long and 18km (11 miles) wide — but the vast majority of the land is uninhabited low tropical forest. The island's one small town is San Miguel.

Cozumel is a popular destination for divers and sun-seekers and is a busy port of call for cruise ships. Divers come to Cozumel — the number-one dive destination in the Western Hemisphere — to enjoy the towering reefs lying just off the island's western shore.

For sun-seekers, the island offers the beautiful Caribbean. Except for when a front blows through, the water on the protected side of the island is perfectly calm. It's like having the Caribbean for a swimming pool. And at several beaches you can find all the usual watersports and beach activities. If you're a golfer, you may want to check out a beautiful golf course designed by Jack Nicklaus. If you're not, try out an assortment of tours and other activities. Because the island is a popular cruise-ship port, you find lots of duty-free shops and jewelry stores. Hurricanes Emily and Wilma made a mess of the island in the summer and fall of 2005, but the town has bounced back strong. By the end of the year, the shoreline boulevard, Rafael Melgar, was rebuilt and dressed up with new plantings of palm trees. The stores opened shortly after that, and within a half a year, the restaurants and hotels gradually returned to their pre-hurricane status.

Choosing a Location

The town of San Miguel and almost all of Cozumel's hotels are on the island's protected western shore. Some are north of town, some are south of town, and some are in town. The hotels in town aren't beach hotels, but they're less expensive and offer convenient access to the town's restaurants, nightspots, dive shops, and stores. To go to the beach, you can take a taxi or rent a bike, moped, or car. The hotels in town suffered more from the flooding than from the wind or the storm surge.

If the most you want to do is hang out around the pool with the occasional dip into the Caribbean, select one of the beach hotels either north or south of town. These hotels were forced to close for months to repair hurricane damage. Many took the opportunity to renovate their guest rooms and upgrade amenities. All hotels outside of town have swimming pools and all can provide services for divers and snorkelers. For the most part, the southern coast has better beaches, but many of the southern hotels are far from town, making it more expensive to do some shopping and other activities. Some southern hotels are on the inland side of the road, and some are on the beach side, which makes for a large difference in price. The properties farthest away from town are all-inclusives, which means that the price of your stay includes meals, beverages, tips, taxes, airport transportation, and even some activities, as well as your lodging.

Because Cozumel is a big destination for divers, all the large hotels and many of the smaller ones offer dive packages; I don't mention this in the reviews later in this chapter, but you can ask about them when shopping around for a hotel. All the large waterfront hotels have a dive shop and a pier. If you would rather dive with an operator other than the one at your hotel, that's fine — any dive boat can pull up to any hotel pier to pick up divers.

Evaluating the Top Accommodations

The prices I quote for the hotels are rack rates for two people spending one night in a double room, and they include the 12 percent room tax. Please refer to the Introduction of this book for an explanation of the price categories. See Chapter 7 for tips on avoiding paying rack rates.

The beach hotels in Cozumel, even the smaller ones, work with several vacation packagers for the U.S. and Canadian markets. You can get sizable discounts by booking airfare, ground transfer, and lodging in one package. Working with some tour operators requires flexibility, but the big ones for Cozumel — FunJet and Apple Vacations — offer enough flights to accommodate many people's vacation plans. If you want an all-inclusive hotel, you can get a better deal through a travel agent or packager than by contacting the hotel directly. For more information about working with vacation packagers and travel agents, check out Chapter 6.

Cozumel Island

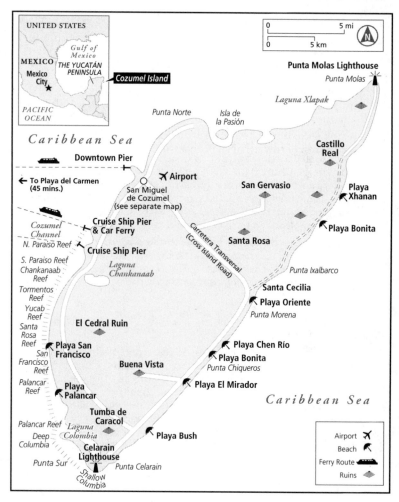

For small groups of friends, a fun alternative to a hotel is to share a villa or condo. Try **Cozumel Vacation Villas and Condos** (Av. 10 Sur no. 124, 77600 Cozumel, Q. Roo; ☎ **800-224-5551** in the U.S., or 987-872-0729 or 872-1375; www.cvvmexico.com), which offers accommodations by the week.

All hotels have air-conditioning unless otherwise indicated.

Allegro Cozumel by Occidental
$$$$$ **South of town**

This all-inclusive has some sister hotels across the way on the mainland, but this one enjoys something those others don't: the placid water of Cozumel's protected coast. There is also a sister hotel next door, the **Grand Cozumel by Occidental**, which is newer and has larger, nicer rooms, but for the money, this hotel works because it has a better beach. Guests at the **Grand** can enjoy the **Allegro**, but not vice versa. Rooms have all been remodeled since the hurricanes and are midsize with standard bathrooms. They are grouped together in two-story Polynesian-style thatched buildings scattered about the resort's grounds. You have a choice of two double beds or one king. There are two large pools (one for activities, one for relaxing) and, of course, the beach, which was made broader by the last hurricane. The hotel gets a mix of families and couples and offers a wide range of activities and water equipment. It's a good choice for families who want only to be on the beach. Taking a taxi to town from here can be expensive; the hotel is at the island's southern end. Three restaurants and a snack bar are available.

Carretera Costera Sur, Km 16.5. ☎ *800-858-2258 in the U.S. or 987-872-9770. Fax: 987-872-9792.* www.occidentalhotels.com. *300 units. Rack rates: High season $330–$375 double; low season $210–$280 double. Rates include food, beverages, and non-motorized watersports equipment. AE, MC, V.*

B&B Caribo
$ **In town**

The Americans who run this B&B are personable, helpful, and have lived on the island for years. Rates are a deal and include breakfast and several little extras. Rooms can be rented by the day, the week, or the month. They come with cool tile floors, painted furniture, and big bottles of purified drinking water. The six apartments come with small kitchens (a minimum stay of one week is required for the apartments). A shared guest kitchen serves the other six rooms. Most rooms have a double bed and a twin bed, but no TVs or phones. A number of common rooms, including a television/computer room and a rooftop terrace, are available. Breakfasts are delicious. To find the Caribo from the central plaza, walk 7 blocks inland on Juárez to Avenida 40.

Av. Juárez No. 799. ☎ *987-872-3195. 12 units. Rack rates: High season $50 double, $60 apartment; low season $35 double, $40 apartment. Rates include breakfast. AE, MC, V.*

El Cid La Ceiba Beach Hotel
$$$$–$$$$$ **South of town**

Located on the beach side of the southbound road, this hotel is great for snorkeling and shore diving — a submerged airplane is just offshore. Most of the hotel is a timeshare, but they still have 30 hotel rooms. It closed down for seven months after the hurricanes, and completely remodeled the rooms and common areas with substantial upgrades. El Cid has

San Miguel de Cozumel

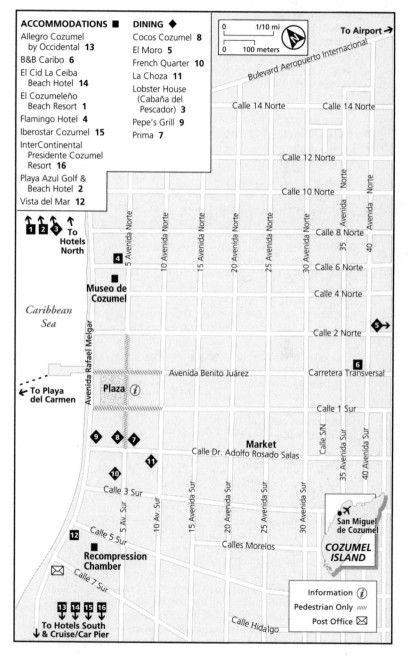

ACCOMMODATIONS ■

Allegro Cozumel
 by Occidental **13**
B&B Caribo **6**
El Cid La Ceiba
 Beach Hotel **14**
El Cozumeleño
 Beach Resort **1**
Flamingo Hotel **4**
Iberostar Cozumel **15**
InterContinental
 Presidente Cozumel
 Resort **16**
Playa Azul Golf &
 Beach Hotel **2**
Vista del Mar **12**

DINING ◆

Cocos Cozumel **8**
El Moro **5**
French Quarter **10**
La Choza **11**
Lobster House
 (Cabaña del
 Pescador) **3**
Pepe's Grill **9**
Prima **7**

To Airport →

0 ⟋ 1/10 mi
0 ⟋ 100 meters

Bulevard Aeropuerto Internacional

Calle 14 Norte   Calle 14 Norte

Calle 12 Norte

Calle 10 Norte

Calle 8 Norte

Calle 6 Norte

Calle 4 Norte

Calle 2 Norte

Carretera Transversal

Avenida Benito Juárez

Calle 1 Sur

Market
Calle Dr. Adolfo Rosado Salas

Calle 3 Sur

Calles Morelos

Calle 5 Sur

Calle 7 Sur

Calle Hidalgo

5 Avenida Norte
10 Avenida Norte
15 Avenida Norte
20 Avenida Norte
25 Avenida Norte
30 Avenida Norte
Norte
Norte
35
40

5 Av. Sur
10 Av. Sur
15 Avenida Sur
20 Avenida Sur
25 Avenida Sur
30 Avenida Sur
35 Avenida Sur
40 Avenida Sur
Calle S/N

1 2 3
To
Hotels
North

4

■
**Museo de
Cozumel**

*Caribbean
Sea*

Avenida Rafael Melgar

← To Playa
del Carmen

Plaza ⓘ

9 8 7

10

11

12

■
**Recompression
Chamber**

✉

13 14 15 16
↓ ↓ ↓ ↓
**To Hotels South
↓ & Cruise/Car Pier**

5

6

✈
**San Miguel
de Cozumel**

**COZUMEL
ISLAND**

Information ⓘ
Pedestrian Only ⫽⫽
Post Office ✉

received plenty of praise from scuba magazines. Diving is available right from the hotel beach. Amenities include two restaurants, a bar, two large pools, a lighted tennis court, a fitness center, a *temazcal* (a Maya-style steam bath), a whirlpool, and watersports-equipment rentals. The resort offers an all-inclusive plan for between $100 and $175 per night per person.

Costera Sur Km 4.5. ☎ *800-525-1925 in the U.S., or 987-872-0844. Fax: 987-872-0065.* www.elcid.com. *30 units. Free limited parking. Rack rates: High season $250–$462 double; low season $135–$240 double. AE, MC, V.*

El Cozumeleño Beach Resort
$$$$$ **North of town**

An all-inclusive resort, El Cozumeleño is for people who want an active vacation with plenty to do, including an extravagant pool and sunning area, and a full array of watersports and equipment rentals. As if that isn't enough to keep you busy, just across the road is the new golf course. Recently, the owners have more than doubled the number of rooms in the hotel and added to the amenities. The rooms in the old part are large, much longer than they are wide; rooms in the new part are also large, and their shape allows for a less awkward arrangement of furniture. All rooms have balconies with a great ocean view, attractive décor, large bathrooms, and either a king bed or two double beds. The hotel has two restaurants and three bars (including a swim-up bar). There are three pools (including a wading pool and a very large pool with a roofed section that provides shade), a large whirlpool, and a tennis court. One drawback is that the beach is small for a resort of this size. Moped rentals, an ample children's program, a game room, and miniature golf are some of the additional highlights.

Carretera Santa Pilar Km 4. ☎ *800-437-3923 in the U.S. and Canada, or 987-872-9530. Fax: 987-872-9544.* www.elcozumeleno.com. *252 units. Rack rates: High season $300 double; low season $210–$260 double; rates are all-inclusive. AE, MC, V.*

Iberostar Cozumel
$$$$$ **South of town**

Just south of the Allegro Cozumel by Occidental (see review earlier in this section), almost at the end of the island, is this all-inclusive hotel laid out much like its neighbors: one- and two-story buildings, each holding between four and eight units, surround a large common area of pools, a snack bar, and the beach. Also, like the Occidental properties, this hotel is operated by a Spanish company that mastered the business of running all-inclusives on the Spanish coast. It has sister properties on the Yucatán mainland, but this is the smallest of the company's Mexican properties. It closed after the hurricanes but reopened in early February 2006. Among the changes are expanded and improved dining areas. Iberostar does a good job with the food and the service, which is why I think it's a step up from most of the other all-inclusives. The tropical foliage that graced the resort's grounds took a hit, but management is working hard to return it to its original condition. The guest rooms have been improved, too. They are medium size and well equipped and come with a terrace or porch equipped with hammocks. The bathrooms are ample, well lit, and come with showers. There was one benefit from these hurricanes: They shifted a lot of sand onto the property's beach, making it larger and more attractive.

Carretera Costera Sur Km 17.75 ☎ **987-872-9900**. *Fax: 987-872-9906.* www. iberostar.com. *306 units. Rack rates: High season $350–$430 double; low season $250–$330 double. Rates include food, beverages, and non-motorized watersports equipment. AE, MC, V.*

InterContinental Presidente Cozumel Resort
$$$$$ South of town

This is Cozumel's finest hotel in terms of location, on-site amenities, and service. Palatial in scale and modern in style, the Presidente spreads across a long stretch of coast with only distant hotels for neighbors. The resort was closed for many months after the hurricanes while undergoing a thorough remodeling. Rooms have been completely redesigned and the amenities modernized. The number of standard rooms was reduced and now come in three categories — pool view, oceanview, and beachfront — distributed among four buildings (two to five stories tall). The pool-view rooms are concentrated around one of the resort's pools and are medium size. The oceanview and beachfront rooms are large with roomy, well-lit bathrooms. Most are located in a long, two-story building facing the water. Beachfronts are at ground level with a large patio and direct access to the beach, and the oceanfronts are on the second floor and come with an ample balcony. A long stretch of sandy beach area dotted with *palapas* and palm trees fronts the entire hotel. This destination features a large pool, plus a wading pool and a watersports-equipment rental booth. You can choose from two restaurants and a bar, plus 24-hour room service. A special in-room dining option with a serenading trio is available for beachfront rooms. Two lighted tennis courts, a fully equipped gym, and a moped-rental service for getting around the island are also on-site. A children's activities center makes this a good choice for families.

Carretera a Chankanaab Km 6.5. ☎ **800-327-0200** *in the U.S., or 987-872-9500. Fax: 987-872-9501.* www.cozumel.intercontinental.com. *220 units. Free parking. Rack rates: High season $390 pool-view double, $440–$525 oceanview/beachfront double, suites from $535; low season $325 pool-view double, $380–$450 ocean-view/beachfront double, suites from $460. Discounts and packages available. AE, DC, MC, V.*

Playa Azul Golf & Beach Hotel
$$$$–$$$$$ North of town

Playa Azul is perhaps the most relaxing of the island's hotels. It's small in comparison with the island's other beach hotels, and the service is attentive and personal. For golfers it's the best choice, as it includes unlimited free golfing (guests pay only for the mandatory cart rental). The hotel's small beach with shade palapas has been restored since the hurricane and is one of the best on this side of the island. It has a great beach bar and a small pool beside it. Almost all the rooms come with balconies and ocean views. The rooms in the original section are all suites — large ones at that, with very large bathrooms. They also come with sleeper sofas in the living room area. The new wing mostly has standard rooms that are comfortable and large. The hotel's restaurant offers the guests complimentary breakfasts.

Carretera San Juan Km 4. ☎ *987-872-0199 or 872-0043. Fax: 987-872-0110.* www. playa-azul.com. *50 units. Free parking. Rack rates: High season $245 double, $300–$350 suite; low season $165 double, $200–$300 suite. AE, MC, V.*

Vista del Mar
$$ In town

This hotel is located on the town's shoreline boulevard. All the rooms in front have ocean views. The balconies are large enough to be enjoyable and are furnished with a couple of chairs. Rooms are a little larger than your standard room, with better lighting than you find in most of the hotels in town. They are simply furnished and decorated, but come with good amenities, including a small fridge, hair dryer, wireless high speed service, and a safe. Bathrooms are medium size or a little smaller and have showers. The rooms in back go for $10 less and have a view of a small pool and large Jacuzzi.

Av. Rafael Melgar 45. ☎ *888-309-9988 in the U.S., or 987-872-0545.* www.hotel vistadelmar.com. *20 units. Rack rates: $85–$100 double. AE, MC, V.*

Settling into Cozumel

You get to the island either by airplane or by ferry from the mainland, which means that you'll arrive at the airport or the municipal pier. In either case, nothing could be more straightforward. Cozumel's airport is small and presents no complications, and the municipal pier is right across from the town's main plaza.

Cozumel's **airport** is immediately inland from downtown. There is only one ground transportation provider: **Transportes Terrestres,** which operates a fleet of air-conditioned Suburbans. Buy your ticket as you exit the terminal. Fares are $5 per person to downtown hotels, $7 for hotels along the north shore, and $10 and up for hotels along the south shore.

More charter flights come to the island than standard commercial flights. You can buy just a plane ticket from one of the travel packagers recommended in Chapter 6. Of course, they would prefer to sell you an entire package, but they'll be happy to fill empty seats on a plane if they have to. Commercial carriers from the United States include **Continental** (☎ 800-525-0280; www.continental.com); **US Airways** (☎ 800-428-4322; www.usairways.com); and **American** (☎ 800-433-7300; www.aa.com). Some of these flights are seasonal. In addition, **Mexicana** (☎ 800-531-7921; www.mexicana.com) flies from Mexico City with several international connecting flights.

If Cozumel is your port of entry, you'll receive a **Mexican tourist permit (FMT)** upon arrival. This document is important, so take good care of it. You're supposed to keep it with you at all times — you may be required to show it if you run into any sort of trouble. You also need to turn it in upon departure.

Passenger ferries travel to and from Playa del Carmen. Of the two companies that service the area — **Barcos México** (☎ 987-872-1508) and **Ultramar** (☎ 987-869-2775) — there is little difference. They operate from the same pier in Cozumel, they charge the same amount for a one-way ticket ($11), and they take the same amount of time (30–45 min.) to make the crossing. Since the hurricanes, the ferry schedules have been in flux, but it's safe to say that you'll find departures every hour in the mornings and, at least, every two or three hours in the afternoon. In Cozumel, both companies dock at the downtown pier, called the **Muelle Fiscal.** Both companies' boats are enclosed and air-conditioned and have comfortable upholstered seats. Short-term luggage storage is available at the Cozumel dock for $2 per day.

The car/passenger ferry to Cozumel from Puerto Calica (11km/7 miles south of Playa del Carmen) takes a little longer, runs less frequently, and costs $80 for a standard car. It's operated by **Marítima Chankanaab** (☎ 987-872-0916), with four departures per day: 7 a.m. and 1, 5, and 9 p.m. Arrive an hour before departure. The schedule is subject to change, so double-check it. The ferry docks in Cozumel are at the **Muelle Internacional** (the **International Pier,** which is just south of town near El Cid La Ceiba Hotel).

Knowing your way around town

San Miguel is logically planned and easy to find your way around. It's laid out on a grid, with *avenidas* (avenues) running north-south, and *calles* (streets) running east-west. The exception is **Avenida Juárez,** which runs east from the passenger-ferry dock directly inland and eventually turns into a road that crosses to the island's eastern shore.

Avenida Juárez divides the town into northern and southern halves. Everything north of Avenida Juárez is labeled *norte,* and everything south is *sur.* What's more, the parallel *calles* to the north of Avenida Juárez have even numbers: 2 Norte, 4 Norte, 6 Norte, and so on, while the ones to the south have odd numbers: 1 Sur, 3 Sur, 5 Sur, and so on. An exception is Calle Adolfo Rosado Salas, running between 1 Sur and 3 Sur.

The *avenida* that runs along the shore is Avenida Rafael Melgar. The *avenidas* running parallel to Melgar are numbered in multiples of five that increase as you move inland: Avenida 5, Avenida 10, Avenida 15, and so on.

The northern extension of Avenida Melgar, called **Carretera Santa Pilar** or **San Juan,** leads to the northern hotels and the golf course. It's only a couple of miles long, but the southward extension of Melgar goes for several miles all the way to the island's tip. It's called **Costera Sur.** The majority of the island's big hotels are along the south road. Also along this road is the **Chankanaab National Park,** encircling the beautiful lagoon of the same name. Beyond Chankanaab are several beach clubs, where you can enjoy the water and find food and beverages. These vary from simple to quite elaborate.

After the Costera Sur reaches the southern tip of the island, it curves to the left and heads up the less-protected eastern shore of the island. Here, the coast is rockier and the surf is harder. Eventually, this road meets up with the road that crosses the island and is the extension of Avenida Juárez, known as the **Carretera Transversal.** This road passes by San Gervasio, the island's most prominent ruins, as well as the airport.

Getting around town

You can walk to most destinations in town. However, getting to outlying hotels and beaches, including the Chankanaab National Park, requires a taxi or rental car.

Car rentals run from $35 to $60 per day for an economy-sized car, depending on the season. All the major rental agencies are present in Cozumel, including **Avis** (☎ 987-872-0219) and **Budget** (☎ 987-872-5177). Usually, you save a little money by renting a car in advance, but if you want to have a car for only a day or two, renting a car through your hotel and having the car-rental company deliver it is easy enough.

Moped rentals are a popular alternative on Cozumel. You can find rental mopeds all over the village for a cost of anywhere from $15 to $30 for 24 hours. If you rent a moped, be careful. Riding a moped made a lot more sense when Cozumel had less traffic; now it's a risky activity — motorists have become pushier.

Moped accidents easily rank as the most common cause of injury in Cozumel. Before renting a moped, give it a careful inspection to see that all the gizmos — horn, light, starter, seat, and mirror — are in good shape and be sure to note all damage to the moped on the rental agreement. If the moped vibrates at cruising speed, it's probably due to an unbalanced wheel, and you should return it. Most importantly, read the fine print on the back of the rental agreement, which states that you aren't insured, that you're responsible for paying for any damage to the bike (or for the entire bike if it's stolen or demolished), and that you must stay on paved roads. It's illegal to ride a moped outside of town without a helmet (subject to a $25 fine).

Taxis remain a good and reasonably priced option unless you plan on doing some major exploring. Scan over these few sample fares for two people (for more than two passengers, you pay an extra charge that varies according to your destination): town to southern hotels, $8 to $15; town to northern hotels, $5 to $7; town to Chankanaab, $8. Call ☎ 987-872-0236 for taxi pickup. Fares on the island are standardized; you won't be able to negotiate.

Fast Facts: Cozumel

American Express

The local representative is Fiesta Cozumel (Calle 11 No. 598; ☎ 987-872-0725).

Area Code

The telephone area code is **987**.

Banks, ATMs, and Currency Exchange

There are several banks and *casas de cambio* (exchange houses) on the island, as well as ATMs. Most places accept dollars, but you usually get a better deal paying in pesos.

Business Hours

Most offices maintain traditional Mexican hours of operation (9 a.m.–2 p.m. and 4–8 p.m. daily), but shops remain open throughout the day. Offices tend to close on Saturday and Sunday, but shops are open on Saturday, at least, and increasingly offer limited hours of operation on Sunday.

Climate

From October to December, strong winds and some rain can prevail all over the Yucatán. In Cozumel, wind conditions in November and December can make diving dangerous. May to September is the rainy season. Temperatures during the day in the summer are 80°F to 90°F (27°C–32°C); in winter 75°F to 80°F (24°C–27°C).

Diving

If you intend to dive, remember to bring proof of your diver's certification. Underwater currents can be very strong here, and many of the reef drops are quite steep, making them excellent sites for experienced divers but too challenging for novice divers.

Hospital and Recompression Chamber

Cozumel has four recompression chambers *(cámaras de recompresión)*. **Buceo Médico,** staffed 24 hours, is on Calle 5 Sur, 1 block off Avenida Rafael Melgar between Melgar and Avenida 5 Sur (☎ 987-872-2387 or 872-1430). Another one is the **Hyperbaric Center of Cozumel** (Calle 4 Norte, between avs. 5 and 10; ☎ 987-872-3070).

Information

The State Tourism Office (☎/fax **987-869-0212**) has information kiosks at the airport and in front of the municipal pier. Hours are from 9 a.m. to 7 p.m. Monday to Friday.

Internet Access

There are a number of cybercafes near the central plaza. One of the most reliable is Modutel (Av. Juárez 15, at the intersection with Av. 10). Hours are 10 a.m. to 8 p.m. The farther you go from the main plaza, the cheaper the rates.

Police

Dial ☎ **060**. Remember that finding an English-speaking operator at the police station is highly unlikely.

Post Office

The post office *(correo),* Avenida Rafael Melgar at Calle 7 Sur, at the southern edge of town (☎ 987-872-0106), is open Monday to Friday 9 a.m. to 6 p.m. and Saturday 9 a.m. to noon.

Taxes

A 15 percent IVA (value-added tax) on goods and services is charged, and it's generally included in the posted price.

Taxis

The government and taxi drivers union fix the fares on the island. Taxis charge extra for more than two passengers. Call ☎ 987-872-0236 for taxi pickup.

Telephone

Avoid the phone booths that have signs in English advising you to call home using a special 800 number — these are absolute rip-offs and can cost as much as $20 per minute. The least expensive way to call is by using a Telmex (LADATEL) prepaid phone card, available at most pharmacies and mini-supers, using the official Telmex (Lada) public phones. Remember, in Mexico you need to dial 001 prior to a number to reach the United States, and you need to preface long distance calls within Mexico by dialing 01.

Time Zone

Cozumel operates on central standard time.

Dining in Cozumel

Like many of Mexico's beach resorts, even Cozumel's finest restaurants are casual when it comes to dress. Men seldom wear jackets, although ladies occasionally wear dressier resort wear. Basically, if you err on the side of casual, you won't go wrong.

For inexpensive alternatives to the restaurants, try one of these suggestions. If you're in the mood for just a little bread or pastry to go with your coffee, try **Zermatt** (☎ 987-872-1384), a terrific little bakery on Avenida 5 at Calle 4 Norte. If you want something really inexpensive and filling, try **Comida Casera Toñita,** on Calle Adolfo Rosado Salas between avenidas 10 and 15 (☎ 987-872-0401). *Comida casera* means home cooking, and this place definitely has the feel of someone's home, in fact, it's Toñita's home, open Monday to Saturday 8 a.m. to 6 p.m.

Please refer to the Introduction of this book for an explanation of the price categories. Remember that tips generally run about 15 percent, and most wait-staff really depend on these gratuities for their income, so be generous if the service warrants. In Mexico it is considered rude to bring the customer the bill before being requested to, and sometimes it takes a while for the cashier to write it up. If you're in a hurry, ask for the bill as soon as you can.

Please see Appendix C for more information on Mexican cuisine.

Cocos Cozumel
$ In town   BREAKFAST

Cocos offers the largest breakfast menu on the island, including all the American and Mexican classics, from *huevos divorciados* (divorced eggs — fried eggs, one in a green sauce, the other in a red sauce) to oatmeal. Tropical fruit smoothies are another great option. Service is fast. The owners are a Mexican/American couple, Terri and Daniel Ocejo, who are helpful sources of information about the island.

Av. 5 Sur 180. ☎ *987-872-0241. Reservations not accepted. Breakfast: $4–$6. No credit cards. Open: Tues–Sun 6 a.m.–noon. Closed Sept–Oct.*

El Moro
$ In town REGIONAL

El Moro consistently offers good food, attentive service, and large portions for moderate prices. What it doesn't offer is stylish surroundings or a convenient location, but a cab ride costs only a couple of bucks. Here you can try some of the best Yucatecan food on the island — anything from *pollo ticuleño,* a specialty from the town of Ticul, which is a layered plate of smooth tomato sauce, mashed potatoes, crispy baked corn tortilla, and batter-fried chicken breast, all topped with shredded cheese and green peas; to *poc chuc,* pork marinated in a tangy sauce and grilled. There are also a number of seafood dishes and Mexican classics on the menu, such as butterfly shrimp, fried fish, or enchiladas. El Moro is 12 blocks inland from Melgar between calles 2 and 4 Norte.

75 BIS Norte No. 124. ☎ *987-872-3029. Reservations not accepted. Main courses: $5–$15. MC, V. Open: Fri–Wed 1–11 p.m.; closed Thurs.*

French Quarter
$–$$ In town LOUISIANA/SOUTHERN

In a pleasant upstairs open-air setting, the French Quarter serves Southern and Creole classics. The jambalaya and étouffée are delicious. The menu also lists such specialties as blackened fish, and the owner goes to great lengths to get the freshest lump crabmeat, which usually appears in one form or another as a daily special. The filet mignon with red-onion marmalade is a real charmer. The French Quarter is on Avenida 5, a block and a half south of the town square.

Av. 5 Sur 18. ☎ *987-872-6321. Reservations recommended during high season. Main courses: $10–$27. AE, MC, V. Open: Daily 4–11 p.m.*

La Choza
$ In town MEXICAN

This is one of the best Mexican restaurants in town. It's also dependable. Platters of poblano chiles stuffed with shrimp, *mole poblano,* and *pollo en relleno negro* (chicken stuffed with a preparation of scorched chiles) are among the specialties. The table sauces and guacamole are great. The Mexican breakfasts are large and satisfying. This is an open-air restaurant with well-spaced tables under a tall thatched roof. From the ferry pier, walk 2 blocks inland on Avenida Juárez, turn right on Avenida 10, and walk 2 more blocks. La Choza is on the corner.

Calle Adolfo Rosado Salas 198 (at Av. 10 Sur). ☎ *987-872-0958. Reservations accepted only for groups of six or more. Main courses: $9–$15; breakfast $4. AE, MC, V. Open: Daily 7:30 a.m.–10 p.m.*

Lobster House (Cabaña del Pescador)
$$–$$$ North of town LOBSTER

The thought that most often occurs to me when I eat a prepared lobster dish is that the cook could have simply boiled the lobster to better effect. This restaurant's owner seems to agree. The only item on the menu is lobster boiled with a hint of spices and served with melted butter accompanied by sides of rice, vegetables, and bread. The price of dinner is determined by the weight of the lobster tail you select, with side dishes provided at no charge. Candles and soft lights illuminate the dining rooms. A rustic, tropical-island feel, gardens, fountains, and a small duck pond make the scene inviting and intimate. The owner, Fernando, welcomes you warmly and sends you next door to his brother's excellent Mexican-food restaurant, El Guacamayo, if you must have something other than lobster.

Carretera Santa Pilar Km 4 (across from Playa Azul Hotel). No phone. Reservations not accepted. Main courses: lobsters sold by weight $20–$30. No credit cards. Open: Daily 6–10:30 p.m.

Pepe's Grill
$$–$$$ In town STEAKS/SEAFOOD

The chefs at Pepe's seem fascinated with fire; what they don't grill in the kitchen, they flambé at your table. The most popular grilled items are the prime rib, filet mignon (good, quality meat), and lobster. For something out of the ordinary, try the shrimp Bahamas, which are flambéed with a little banana and pineapple in a curry sauce with a hint of white wine. Pepe's is a second-story restaurant with a large air-conditioned dining room under a massive beamed ceiling. The lighting is soft, and a guitar trio plays background music. Large windows look out over the town's harbor. The children's menu offers breaded shrimp and broiled chicken. For dessert, Pepe's offers a few more flaming specialties: bananas Foster, crêpes suzette, and café Maya (coffee, vanilla ice cream, and three liquors).

Av. Rafael Melgar at Calle Rosado Salas. ☎ 987-872-0213. Reservations recommended. Main courses: $15–$35; children's menu $6.50. AE, MC, V. Open: Daily 5–11:30 p.m.

Prima
$–$$ In town NORTHERN ITALIAN

Everything is super fresh here — the pastas, vegetables, and the seafood. Owner Albert Domínguez grows most of the vegetables in his local hydroponic garden. The menu changes daily and specializes in northern Italian seafood dishes. It may include shrimp scampi, fettuccine with pesto, or lobster and crab ravioli with cream sauce. The fettuccine Alfredo is wonderful, the salads are crisp, and the steaks are USDA choice. Pizzas are cooked in a wood-burning oven. Desserts include Key lime pie and tiramisu. Dining is upstairs on the breezy terrace.

Calle Rosado Salas No. 109A (corner with Av. 5). ☎ ***987-872-4242.*** *Reservations recommended during high season. Pizzas: $6–$14; pastas: $8–$15; steaks: $15–$20; seafood: $12–$25. AE, MC, V. Open: Daily 5–11 p.m.*

Having Fun on and off the Island

One of the advantages of vacationing in Cozumel is that you can indulge in a true island experience and still be just a short hop from mainland Mexico and its attractions. **Playa del Carmen** is an easy ferry ride away and makes for a relaxing excursion. From there, you can take a bus to one of the large nature parks such as **Xel-Ha** or **Xcaret,** or one of the major ruins, such as **Chichén Itzá** or **Tulum** (see Chapter 13 for more on these attractions).

A trip to Xcaret is the easiest excursion. A visit to Xel-Ha is often combined with a visit to Tulum. The trip to Chichén Itzá, if not done by plane, is by far the longest and most exhausting. Easier still, you can arrange a tour with one of the travel agencies on the island. Try **InterMar Cozumel Viajes** (Calle 2 Norte No. 101-B, between avs. 5 and 10; ☎ **987-872-1098;** Fax: 987-872-0895; `intermar@cozumel.com.mx`).

Cozumel does have its own ruins, which are easy to visit. (But, honestly, they can't compare with the major sites on the mainland.) In pre-Hispanic times, Maya women made a pilgrimage to the island to leave offerings to Ixchel, the goddess of fertility. You can see the remains of about 40 sites on the island today, and archaeologists still uncover the small dolls that were part of the offerings. The most important ruins on the island are at San Gervasio (see the "Seeing the sights" section, later in this chapter).

Travel agencies can schedule activities such as **glass-bottom boat tours, submarine tours, dinner cruises,** or **a romantic supper on the beach.** For **diving and snorkeling,** you can do better by arranging your own trip (see the "Exploring the depths" section, later in this chapter).

 If you schedule a snorkeling or diving trip through a travel agency, you'll most likely end up on a boat full of cruise-ship passengers. Your best bet is to find an operator who uses a small boat.

Combing the beaches

Although most of Cozumel's shoreline is rocky, the island has some nice beaches. And most beaches have what is called a "beach club" on them. A beach club in its simplest form is just a *palapa* (thatched roof) shack on the beach where you can enjoy soft drinks, beer, and fried fish. In a more elaborate form, the beach club may have a full-service restaurant, rent snorkeling gear, and even have a pool. A still larger version offers all kinds of watersports rentals, including banana boats, Jet Skis, and para-sailing equipment. Cozumel has two beach clubs made in this latter mold: **Mr. Sancho's** and **Playa Mía.** Mr. Sancho's has free admission; Playa Mía has entrance fees from $8 to $37 for the all-inclusive rate. Both are on the southern highway Costera Sur, about 13 to 16km (8–10 miles) south of town. A quieter beach club with a pool and full restaurant is **Nachi Cocom** (located almost a mile beyond Mr. Sancho's). It charges $5 for admission.

For beach access without admission, south of Nachi Cocom are **Playa San Francisco, Playa Paraíso,** and **Playa Palancar.** These are good places to enjoy the beach. Beach clubs of the simpler variety include **Paradise Cafe** on the southern tip of the island across from Punta Sur Nature Park and **Playa Bonita, Chen Rio,** and **Punta Morena** on the eastern coast. Except on Sundays when the locals hit the beaches, these places are quiet and uncrowded. Most of the east coast is unsafe for swimming because of the surf.

Chankanaab National Park has a beach, too, and a variety of other activities. Admission is $10. See the "Seeing the sights" section, later in this chapter, for more information.

Exploring the depths

Cozumel is the most popular dive destination in the Western Hemisphere. Don't forget to bring your dive card and dive log. The dive shops on the island rent scuba gear, but they won't take you out on the boat until they see some documentation. If you have a medical condition, bring a letter signed by a doctor stating that you're cleared to dive. A two-tank, morning dive costs around $65; some shops are now offering an additional one-tank, afternoon dive for $15 for folks who took the morning dives. (It's about $30 if you just opt for the one-tank, afternoon dive.) A lot of divers save some money by buying a hotel and dive package with or without air transportation and food. These packages usually include two dives a day.

Diving in San Miguel is different from diving in a lot of places — it's drift diving, which can be a little disconcerting for novice divers. The current that sweeps along Cozumel's reefs pulling nutrients into the reefs and making them as large as they are also dictates how you dive here. The problem: The current pulls at different speeds at different depths and in different places. When it's pulling strong, the current can quickly scatter a dive group. This is why having a dive master experienced with the local conditions is important.

The island has a lot of reefs to choose from. Most of the damage caused by the hurricanes occurred in the shallower parts, above 15m (50 ft.). In deeper areas, the currents produced by the hurricane actually improved matters by clearing some areas of sand, exposing more caverns. Here are just a few recommended sites:

- ✔ **Palancar Reef:** Famous for its caves and canyons, plentiful fish, and a wide variety of sea coral

- ✔ **San Francisco Reef:** Features a shallower drop-off wall than many reefs and fascinating sea life

- ✔ **Santa Rosa Wall:** Monstrous reef famous for its depth, sea life, coral, and sponges

- ✔ **Yucab Reef:** Highlights include beautiful coral

Cozumel has more than 60 dive operators. I can recommend a couple. Bill Horn's **Aqua Safari,** on Avenida Rafael Melgar at Calle 5 Sur (☎ **987-872-0101;** Fax: 987-872-0661; www.aquasafari.com), is a PADI (Professional Association of Diving Instructors) five-star instructor center with full equipment and parts rental and sales. **Liquid Blue Divers** (☎ **987-869-7794;** www.liquidbluedivers.com) offers a real personal service. Owner Roberto Castillo has a small, fast boat and takes a maximum of 12 per dive trip. He's PADI certified, and his wife Michelle handles the reservations through e-mail, responding to any inquiry within 24 hours.

Underwater Yucatán offers a different twist on diving — *cenote* **diving.** On the mainland, the peninsula's underground *cenotes* (seh-*noh*-tehs), or sinkholes, which were sacred to the Maya, lead to a vast system of underground caverns. Here, the gently flowing water is so clear that divers appear to be floating on air through the *cenotes* and caves that look just like those on dry land, complete with stalactites and stalagmites.

The experienced cave divers of **Yucatech Expeditions** (☎/fax 987-872-**5659;** yucatech@cozumel.czm.com.mx) offer a trip five times a week. *Cenotes* are 30 to 45 minutes from Playa del Carmen, and a dive in each *cenote* lasts around 45 minutes (divers usually do two or three). Dives are within the daylight zone, about 39m (130 ft.) into the caverns and no more than 18m (60 ft.) deep. Company owner Germán Yañez Mendoza inspects diving credentials carefully, and divers must meet his list of requirements before cave diving is permitted. For information and prices, call or drop by the office at the corner of Avenida 5 and Calle 3 Sur. There are several other *cenote* dive operators on the mainland who are closer to the *cenotes,* especially in Akumal and near Tulum.

Snorkeling is also an option on Cozumel. The hurricanes did inflict some damage to the shallow reefs visited by snorkelers. It will take a year or two for the fan coral and other delicate structures to grow back. Anyone who can swim can snorkel. Rental of the snorkel (breathing tube), goggles, and flippers should cost only about $5 to $10 for half a day. A number of small boats offer good snorkeling trips because they necessarily take few people for each trip. One person who does a good tour is **Victor Casanova.** He speaks English and takes his time and doesn't rush his customers. You can contact him through e-mail at wildcat cozumel@hotmail.com, or by phone at ☎ **987-872-1028.** Or you can try the **Kuzamil Snorkeling Center** (☎ **987-872-4637**), which offers a trip that goes to several spots and includes lunch for $65 for adults and $50 for children under 12.

Sailing away

Boat trips are a popular pastime on Cozumel. You can choose from evening cruises, cocktail cruises, glass-bottom boats, and other options. You can contract these tours through a local travel agency. One rather novel boat trip is a ride in a submarine, offered by **Atlantis Submarines** (☎ **987-872-5671;** www.atlantisadventures.com). The sub holds 48 people, operates almost 3km (2 miles) south of town in front of the Casa del Mar hotel, and costs $81 per adult and $47 for kids. Call ahead or inquire at one of the travel agents in town. This is a far superior experience to the **Subsee Explorer** offered by **Aquaworld,** which is really a glorified glass-bottom boat.

Catching a big one

The best months for offshore fishing are March through June, when the catch includes blue and white marlin, sailfish, tarpon, swordfish, dorado, wahoo, tuna, and red snapper. You can contact Victor Casanova (☎ **987-872-1028;** wildcatcozumel@hotmail.com), or **Aquarius Travel Fishing** (Calle 3 Sur No. 2, between Av. Rafael Melgar and Av. 5; ☎ **987-872-1092;** www.aquariusflatsfishing.com).

Hitting the links

Cozumel has a lovely 18-hole golf course designed by Jack Nicklaus. It's just north of town in the **Cozumel Country Club** (☎ **987-872-9570**). Greens fees are $165 including taxes and cart rental for morning tee times ($99 for afternoon tee times). A couple of hotels on the island have golf packages. The Playa Azul has the best arrangement, offering free golf to its guests, who have to pay only for the cart rental.

Seeing the sights

Companies offer several kinds of tours of the island, but to be frank, the best part of Cozumel isn't on land; it's what's in the water. But, if you're starting to look like a prune from all the time in the water or you want to try something different, travel agencies can book you on a group tour of the island for around $40. Prices may vary a bit depending on whether the tour includes lunch and a stop for snorkeling and swimming at Chankanaab Park. If you're only interested in Chankanaab, you can go by yourself and save money (keep reading; more info is coming up in this section). Taxi drivers charge $60 for four-hour tours of the island, which most people would consider only mildly amusing depending on the personality of the taxi driver.

A **horseback tour** of the island's interior is fun and inexpensive. A few outfits offer horseback riding, but the best is **Rancho Palmitas** (no phone). This outfit has the best horses and conducts the most interesting tours. It has two locations, both south of town. One is near the

InterContinental Presidente Cozumel Resort and the other is across the road from the Allegro Hotel by Occidental. Both locations are open seven days a week. Tours depart at 8 and 10 a.m., noon, and at 2 and 4 p.m.

Chankanaab National Park is the pride of many of the islanders. It suffered extensive damage from the hurricanes and was closed for repairs until July of 2006. *Chankanaab* means "little sea," which refers to a beautiful, land-locked pool connected to the sea through an underground tunnel — a sort of miniature ocean. Snorkeling in this natural aquarium isn't permitted, but you can snorkel off shore. There is a beach with lounge chairs for sunbathing. Arrive early to stake out a chair and *palapa* before the cruise-ship crowd arrives. The park has bathrooms, lockers, a gift shop, several snack huts, a restaurant, and snorkeling gear available to rent.

Bordering the lagoon is a botanical garden with shady paths. The garden is home to 351 species of tropical and subtropical plants from 22 countries in addition to 451 species of plants from Cozumel. Several Maya structures have been re-created within the gardens to give visitors an idea of Maya life in a jungle setting. A small natural history museum is also on the property. Admission to the park costs $10, and it's open daily 8 a.m. to 5 p.m.

Also at Chankanaab are dolphins. **Dolphin Discovery (☎ 800-293-9698;** www.dolphindiscovery.com) has several programs for sharing a swim with these highly intelligent animals. You need to make reservations in advance, and the surest way is through the Web site. The most intensive dolphin swim program costs $125. There are a couple of more economical programs costing $75 and $99. Dolphin Discovery offers a program only in Cozumel where you can swim with sea lions ($59); reservations also are a must. Finally, a sea lion show costs $5 per adult, $3.50 per kid. Tickets are available through any travel agency in town. The show also includes some scarlet macaws, which, like the sea lions, were rescued from illegal captivity.

 Swimming with dolphins has its critics and supporters. You may want to visit the Whale and Dolphins Conservation Society's Web site at www. wdcs.org. For more information about responsible travel in general, check out these Web sites: Tread Lightly (www.treadlightly.org) and the International Ecotourism Society (www.ecotourism.org).

One of the most popular island excursions is to the ruins of **San Gervasio** (100 B.C.–A.D. 1600). When it comes to Cozumel's Maya ruins, getting there is most of the fun — do it for the mystique and for the trip, not for the size or scale of the ruins. To get to the ruins follow the Carretera Transversal toward the eastern side of the island. The well-marked turnoff is about halfway between town and the eastern coast. Stop at the entrance gate and pay the $1 road-use fee. Head straight over the pothole-infested road for about 3km (2 miles) until you reach the ruins. Pay the $5 fee to enter; camera permits cost $5 for each still or video camera you want to bring in. A small tourist center at the entrance has cold drinks and snacks for sale.

More significant than beautiful, this site was once an important ceremonial center where the Maya gathered. The important deity here was Ixchel, known as the goddess of weaving, fertility, childbirth, the moon, and medicine. You don't see any representations of Ixchel at San Gervasio today, but here's a little history: Bruce Hunter, in his *Guide to Ancient Maya Ruins* (University of Oklahoma Press), writes that priests hid behind a large pottery statue of the goddess and became her voice, speaking to pilgrims and answering their petitions. Ixchel was the wife of Itzamná, the sun god and preeminent deity among all Maya gods.

Tour guides charge $10 for groups of one to six people, but, with a copy of the green booklet *San Gervasio,* sold at local checkout counters and bookstores, you can see the site on your own. Seeing the whole place takes 30 minutes. Taxi drivers offer a tour to the ruins for about $25; the driver waits for you outside the ruins.

In town, check out the small historical museum, **Museo de la Isla de Cozumel,** on Avenida Rafael Melgar between calles 4 and 6 Norte (☎ 987-872-1475). It's more than just a nice place to spend a rainy hour. The museum's first floor has an exhibit displaying endangered species in the area, the island's origin, and its present-day topography and plant and animal life, including an explanation of coral formation. The second-floor galleries feature the town's history, artifacts from the island's pre-Hispanic sites, and colonial-era relics like cannons, swords, and ship paraphernalia. The museum is open daily from 9 a.m. to 6 p.m. Admission is $3; guided tours in English are free. A rooftop restaurant serves breakfast and lunch.

Taking in the shops

If you like shopping for silver jewelry, you can spend a great deal of time examining the wares of all the jewelers along Melgar who cater to cruise-ship shoppers. Numerous duty-free stores sell items such as perfumes and designer wares. If you're interested in Mexican folk art, a number of stores now display a wide variety of interesting pieces. Check out the following shops, all of which are on Melgar within a few blocks of the plaza:

  ✔ **Los Cinco Soles** (☎ 987-872-2040)

  ✔ **Indigo** (☎ 987-872-1076)

  ✔ **Viva Mexico** (☎ 987-872-5466)

Prices for serapes (cotton ponchos), T-shirts, and other tourist-type goods are less expensive on the side streets off Melgar.

While you're shopping in San Miguel, someone will probably approach you to offer a deal in a timeshare apartment. Although investing in time-shares is in many cases a bad idea, weighing financial decisions when you're in vacation mode is a really bad idea. Something about vacationing makes people suspend their critical judgment. Don't mix business with pleasure. Wait until you're back home, where you can do your research, before entering the timeshare market.

Enjoying the nightlife

Cozumel is a town frequented by divers and other active visitors who play hard all day and wind down at night. The nightlife scene is generally low-key and peaks in the early evening. The cruise-ship crowd offers an exception to this rule. On Sunday evenings, the place to be is the main plaza, which usually hosts a free concert and has plenty of people strolling about and visiting with friends. Most of the clubs along Avenida Melgar have been slow to reopen after the hurricane. As of press time the only one to open was **Carlos 'n Charlie's** (☎ **987-869-1646**), in the little Punta Langosta Shopping Center in front of the pier of the same name. Ask at the Tourism information kiosk in front to the municipal pier about other options. If you want to see a movie, the multi-cinema Cinépolis is on the south side of town off Melgar. It shows a lot of first-run Hollywood films, usually in English, with Spanish subtitles.

Chapter 15

Playa del Carmen and the Riviera Maya

by David Baird

In This Chapter

▶ Choosing the right accommodations
▶ Finding your way around the Riviera Maya
▶ Searching for the best grub
▶ Enjoying yourself on and off the beach

The **Riviera Maya** is the area of the Yucatán Peninsula's upper Caribbean coast from just south of Cancún to the town of Tulum, a distance of 132km (82 miles). It's a beautiful place with a mix of small resort communities, nature parks, small beach hotels, and large all-inclusive resorts. A long reef system protects this coast and offers many snorkeling and diving opportunities. Where there are gaps in the reef — Playa del Carmen, Xpu-Ha, and Tulum — you find the best beaches. The action of the surf washes away silt and sea grass and erodes rocks, leaving a sandy bottom. Where the reef is prominent, you can expect good snorkeling just offshore with plenty of fish and other sea life.

Playa del Carmen is the largest town in the Riviera Maya. In the last few years, it has developed a kind of dual personality. Originally it was a hideaway for hippies looking for an undeveloped piece of paradise — a counterculture getaway clothed in native architecture with thatched roofs, rustic clapboard, and adobe walls. Then the developers showed up and built a resort community on the south side of town called Playacar, complete with a golf course, condos, and large all-inclusive hotels. The town continues to attract a lot of young people interested in living the simple life and working only as much as necessary. Playa, as the locals refer to it, is a fun place to stay, with plenty to do or not to do, and a lovely beach for those who choose the latter option. In the evenings, people stroll down the town's Quinta Avenida (Fifth Avenue) shopping, choosing between the many restaurants and bars, or simply enjoying the evening air.

Tulum is another booming town on this coast. It sprung up along the highway near the ruins of the same name. Nearby is a beautiful beach with small hotels and their thatched-roofed (*cabañas* or *palapas*) cabins and small structures. Tulum marks the end of the Riviera Maya. South of here is a large natural preserve called Sian Ka'an and then the lower Caribbean coast, which doesn't have the same quality of beaches as the upper coast.

The Riviera Maya has grown increasingly popular as its lodging and dining options have multiplied. It also holds a wealth of attractions. In fact, many of the day trips offered in Cancún are to places on this coast, such as snorkeling tours; horseback riding; the nature parks of **Xcaret** and **Xel-Ha;** and even the ruins of Tulum. Many Europeans have settled here and set up small hotels and restaurants, lending the area a certain cosmopolitan flavor. But this cosmopolitanism is spread throughout the towns of this coast and not concentrated in an urban center such as Cancún. In the Riviera Maya, you don't find any skyscrapers or broad boulevards. Staying here is a different experience from staying in Cancún, adding to the choices that visitors to the Yucatán have.

In the summer and fall of 2005 the region was hit by two hurricanes. Emily made landfall in the middle of the Riviera Maya, between Playa and Tulum. It damaged hotels in Xpu-Ha, but left Tulum and Playa in fairly good shape. The other was Wilma, which was much stronger and wreaked havoc on Cozumel and Cancún, but didn't make direct landfall on this part of the coast. Most of the damage to the tourism infrastructure occurred north of Playa. Operations have since returned to normal for the entire Riviera Maya.

Deciding Where to Stay

Choosing your lodging depends largely on personal taste and the kind of vacation you have in mind. The Riviera Maya has just about any kind of lodging option:

- ✔ Small, charming hotels in a town where you can interact with the local residents and get a feel for what life is like in this part of the world

- ✔ Villas and condos that rent by the week — a great option for a family vacation or a group of friends

- ✔ Intimate *cabaña* hotels (cabins) on a beach far enough away from the modern world that they have to generate their own electricity or do without

- ✔ Large all-inclusives with all the modern conveniences, including expansive pools, game rooms, and watersports equipment

- ✔ Small, private spa-resorts that pamper their guests

In this chapter, I list some of my favorite hotels in the Riviera Maya, including beach cabañas, inexpensive one-of-a-kind places, and even my favorite secluded spa-resort. For more information about the different towns and locations along this coast, see the "Settling into the Riviera Maya" section, later in this chapter.

If you decide to stay in a hotel in Playa del Carmen, don't hesitate to choose a place that's not on the beach. Town life here is a big part of the fun, and staying on the beach in Playa has its disadvantages — such as higher rates and the noise produced by a couple of the beachside bars. And if you choose accommodations off the beach, you don't have to worry about not being able to find that perfect strip of sand. Beaches are public property in Mexico, and you can lay out your towel anywhere you like without anyone bothering you.

Near the town of Tulum, you can choose from about 30 *cabaña* hotels in a "hotel zone" on the beach. These small hotels generate their own electricity. Only a few offer air-conditioning, and they charge more than the small hotels in the other towns, but you avoid the large-resort feel and the crowds, and you get to enjoy the area's lovely white sand beaches.

For families and groups of friends wishing to rent a condo or villa for a week, the following Web sites are good places to start: **Akumal Vacations** (www.akumalvacations.com), **Caribbean Fantasy** (www.caribbfan.com), or **Loco Gringo** (www.locogringo.com). You can find rentals on many parts of the coast, including an abundance in the town of Akumal, which many families favor because it's quieter and more convenient than some of the booming towns such as Playa or Tulum.

Also popular with families (and couples) are the all-inclusive hotels, of which there are more than 40 on this coast. All-inclusives are large hotels that work with economies of scale to offer lodging, food, and drink all for a single relatively low rate. See Chapter 7 for more details about all-inclusive hotels and resorts.

The best way to get a room at an all-inclusive is by contacting a travel agent who works with vacation packagers. You get a much better deal than by contacting the hotel directly. Even if you have frequent-flier miles to burn, you'll still find it difficult to match the rates of a full package.

All-inclusives tend to look and feel alike, which is why I don't include any in the hotel reviews later in this chapter. Of the many all-inclusives in the Riviera Maya, however, the following are my favorites:

✔ **Aventura Spa Palace** (☎ **984-875-1100;** Fax: 984-875-1101; www.palaceresorts.com) is a hotel in the Palace chain — this one is just for grown-ups. It has a large spa and gym and attractive common areas and guest rooms. There is a large pool but no beach; guests can take a shuttle to the Xpu-Ha property for beach access.

✔ The **Copacabana Beach Resort** in Xpu-Ha (☎ 984-875-1800; Fax: 984-875-1818; www.hotelcopacabana.com) has raised walkways preserving much of the flora and making it visually interesting. And Xpu-Ha is blessed with a stunning beach.

✔ **Freedom Paradise** (☎ 866-548-3995 or 998-887-1101; Fax: 998-887-1102; www.freedomparadise.com) is billed as the first size-friendly vacation resort. The management has worked hard to create an environment that large people will find comfortable. I like it because it doesn't have all the froufrou of so many other resorts — it's friendly and unpretentious.

✔ **Iberostar Quetzal** or **Tucan** (☎ 984-877-2000; Fax: 984-873-0424; www.iberostar.com): Of the several all-inclusives that are in Playa del Carmen/Playacar, I like this one, which has two names for different halves of the same hotel. The food is better than at most all-inclusives, and the central part of the hotel is made of raised walkways and terraces over the natural mangrove habitat. Its neighbor, the **Sandos Gala Playacar**(☎ 984-877-4040; Fax: 984-873-1169; www.sandoshotels.com.mx), is also a good choice.

✔ Also in Xpu-Ha is the **Xpu-Ha Palace** (☎ 984-875-1010; Fax: 984-875-1012; www.palaceresorts.com), which is built on the grounds of a failed nature park. It has some keen features including lagoons and a jungle, and several facilities for kids, including a small crocodile hatchery. The hotel is spread out over a large area and necessarily involves a good bit of walking, but this also makes it feel less crowded.

Evaluating the Top Accommodations

In the following reviews, I note *rack rates* (the maximum that a hotel or resort charges for a room) for two people spending one night in a double room. For Christmas, rates will be higher than the standard high-season rates. Prices quoted here include the 12 percent room tax. Please refer to the Introduction of this book for an explanation of the price categories.

Hotels listed here have both air-conditioning and TVs, unless otherwise indicated, and if the review doesn't say anything to the contrary, you can safely assume that you can walk directly out of your hotel and onto the beach.

Cabañas Ana y José
$$$–$$$$ Tulum

This is a tranquil escape that feels worlds away from the rest of civilization, yet it provides sufficient creature comforts to make for a comfortable stay. The beach in front of the hotel is pure white sand. The rock-walled cabañas closest to the water (called "ocean front") come with two double beds. These are a little more rustic than the rest of the rooms. The second-floor "ocean view" rooms have been completely remodeled with marble countertops and marble tile floors and attractive bathrooms. They also have a terrace or a balcony and one queen or two double beds. The gardenview rooms are much like the "vista al mar" rooms but don't face the sea. There is 24-hour electricity for lights and ceiling fans, and for A/C in the eight gardenview rooms that don't catch the sea breezes. The hotel has a small pool, one of the few on this part of the coast that does. A restaurant takes care of meals. The hotel can have a rental car waiting for you at the Cancún airport.

Carretera Punta Allen Km 7, Punta Allen Peninsula. ☎ **988-887-5470.** *Fax: 988-887-5469.* www.anayjose.com. *22 units. Free parking. Rack rates: $165 gardenview double, $200 pool-view double, $230–$250 beachfront and oceanview double, suites from $245. AE, MC, V.*

Club Akumal Caribe/Hotel Villas Maya Club
$$–$$$ **Akumal**

This hotel's rooms and garden bungalows, set along the pristine and tranquil Akumal Bay, are large and comfortable. The 40 Villas Maya bungalows are simply and comfortably furnished and come with kitchenettes. The 21 rooms in the three-story beachfront hotel are more elaborately furnished. They come with refrigerators and a king bed or two queen beds. Both the bungalows and the rooms have tile floors and good-size bathrooms, but neither have phones or TVs. A large pool on the grounds, a children's activities program (during high season), two restaurants, and a bar round out the facilities. You can also ask about two- and three-bedroom villas for rent.

Carretera Cancún-Tulum (Hwy. 307) Km 104. ☎ **800-351-1622** *in the U.S., 800-343-1440 in Canada, or 984-875-9010.* www.hotelakumalcaribe.com. *70 units. Free parking. Rack rates: High season $115 bungalow, $145 hotel room; low season $90 bungalow, $115 hotel room. AE, MC, V.*

Hotel Jungla Caribe
$$ **Playa del Carmen**

Located right in the heart of the Avenida 5 action, "La Jungla" is an imaginative place, with a highly stylized look that mixes neoclassical with Robinson Crusoe. Its character perfectly keeps with the town's quirkiness. Owner Rolf Albrecht envisioned space and comfort for guests, so all but eight of the standard rooms are large, with gray-and-black marble floors, the occasional Roman column, and large bathrooms. Fifteen of the rooms are suites. Catwalks connect the "tower" section of suites to the hotel. Take a dip in an attractive pool in the courtyard beneath a giant *Ramón* tree. Eight small rooms lack air-conditioning and are priced lower than the rates listed here.

Av. 5 Norte at Calle 8. ☎ /fax **984-873-0650.** www.jungla-caribe.com. *25 units. Rack rates: High season $80 double, $120–$130 suite; low season $50 double, $90–$100 suite. AE, MC, V.*

Playa del Carmen

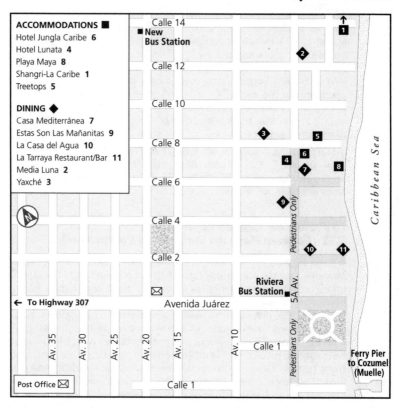

ACCOMMODATIONS ■
Hotel Jungla Caribe **6**
Hotel Lunata **4**
Playa Maya **8**
Shangri-La Caribe **1**
Treetops **5**

DINING ◆
Casa Mediterránea **7**
Estas Son Las Mañanitas **9**
La Casa del Agua **10**
La Tarraya Restaurant/Bar **11**
Media Luna **2**
Yaxché **3**

Caribbean Sea

Calle 14
New Bus Station
Calle 12
Calle 10
Calle 8
Calle 6
Calle 4
Calle 2
Riviera Bus Station
To Highway 307
Avenida Juárez
5A Av.
Av. 35
Av. 30
Av. 25
Av. 20
Av. 15
Av. 10
Calle 1
Pedestrians Only
Ferry Pier to Cozumel (Muelle)
Post Office ⊠
Calle 1

Hotel Lunata
$$ Playa del Carmen

The Lunata offers a combination of location, comfort, and attractiveness that no other hotel in this category can beat. It's built in hacienda style, with cut stone and wrought iron, and is decorated in contemporary Mexican colors. The rooms show a lot of polish, with good air-conditioning and nicely finished bathrooms. They also come with a TV, a small fridge, and a safe. The majority of rooms are deluxe, which are medium to large and come with a king or two doubles. A complimentary continental breakfast is served in the garden, and the third-story terrace makes a nice place to hang out. This hotel is right on Avenida 5; if you like to go to bed early, stay in a room in back.

Av. 5 (between calles 6 and 8). ☎ *984-873-0884.* Fax: 984-873-1240. www.lunata. com. *10 units. Guarded parking $5. Rack rates: $109 standard, $139–$155 deluxe and junior suite. Rates include continental breakfast. AE, MC, V.*

Hotel Ojo de Agua
$ Puerto Morelos

This is a seaside hotel with modern rooms. Two three-story buildings stand on the beach at a right angle to each other. Most rooms have balconies and glass sliding doors. They're simply furnished and clean. Most rooms have two double beds or a double and a twin; those with one double bed go for $10 less. Twenty-four rooms have air-conditioning, and 24 have phones (not the same 24). "Studio" units have kitchenettes. A medium-size pool and a restaurant are available. Service is friendly. You can set up snorkeling and scuba trips with the hotel. Turn left when you get to the town plaza and keep going; look for the sign.

Supermanzana 2, Lote 16. ☎ *998-871-0027 or 871-0507. Fax: 998-871-0202.* www. ojo-de-agua.com. *36 units. Rack rates: High season $60 double, $65–$75 studio or deluxe; low season $50 double, $55–$60 studio or deluxe. Weekly and monthly rates available. AE, MC, V.*

La Posada del Capitán Lafitte
$$$$ Between Playa del Carmen and Puerto Morelos

A large sign on the left side of Highway 307, 13km (8 miles) south of Puerto Morelos, points you in the direction of La Posada del Capitán Lafitte. This lovely seaside retreat sits on a solitary stretch of sandy beach. Here you can enjoy being isolated while still having all the amenities of a relaxing vacation. The one- and two-story white-stucco bungalows, which hold one to four rooms, stretch across a powdery white beach (but the sea floor is a little rocky). They're small but comfortable, with tile floors; small, tiled bathrooms; either two double beds or one king-size bed; and an ocean-front porch. Twenty-nine bungalows have air-conditioning; the rest have fans. The hotel offers transportation to and from the Cancún airport for $50 per person (minimum of two passengers). Your room price includes both breakfast and dinner, plus there's a poolside grill and bar. Amenities include a medium-size pool, watersports equipment, and a TV/game room.

Carretera Cancún-Tulum (Hwy. 307) Km 62. ☎ *800-538-6802 in the U.S. and Canada, or 984-873-0214.* www.mexicoholiday.com. *58 units. Free guarded parking. Rack rates: High season $235 double; low season $170 double. Rates include breakfast and dinner. MC, V.*

Maroma
$$$$$ Near Puerto Morelos

In the area around Puerto Morelos, four spa resorts offer different versions of the hedonistic resort experience. All four pride themselves on their personal service, amenities, and spa and salon treatments. Being in the Yucatán, they like to add the healing practices of the Maya, especially the use of the steam bath known in Mexico as a *temazcal*. Of the four, this resort has been around the longest. It has a gorgeous beach and beautifully manicured grounds. Two- and three-story buildings contain the large guest rooms; most have king beds. The small size makes for personal service and a wonderful sense of escape.

Carretera 307 Km 51. ☎ *866-454-9351 in the U.S., or 998-872-8200. Fax: 998-872-8220.* www.maromahotel.com. *64 units. Free valet parking. Rack rates: $480 gardenview double, $540–$740 premium or deluxe double, from $940 suite. Rates include ground transfer, full breakfast, one snorkeling tour. AE, MC, V.*

Playa Maya
$$–$$$ Playa del Carmen

This is a relaxing beach hotel in the middle of Playa. The only entrance to the hotel is from the beach. Rooms are large with midsize bathrooms. A couple come with private garden terraces with Jacuzzis, others have balconies facing the beach. In-room amenities include a fridge, hair dryer, safe, and high-speed wireless. The pool, Jacuzzi, and the sun deck are in the front of the hotel, facing the sea, and are nicely set apart from the rooms.

Zona FMT between calles 6 and 8 Norte. ☎ *984-803-2022.* www.playa-maya.com. *20 units. Rack rates: High season $125–$165 double; low season $100–$130 double. Rates include a continental breakfast. MC, V.*

Shangri-La Caribe
$$$$ Playa del Carmen

This hotel — a loose grouping of *cabañas* on one of the best beaches in Playa — is hard to beat for sheer fun and leisure. And it's far enough from the center of town to be quiet yet convenient. The older, south side of the hotel (the "Caribe" section) consists of one- and two-story *cabañas*. The north ("Playa") side has a few larger buildings, holding four to six rooms. A preference for one or the other section is a matter of taste; the units in both are similar in amenities, privacy, and price. The real difference in price depends on the proximity to the water — beachfront, oceanview, or gardenview. Many gardenview rooms (mostly in a third section called "Pueblito") have air-conditioning, which adds $6 to the price. All rooms have a patio or porch complete with hammock. Most come with two double beds, but a few have a king bed. Windows are screened, and ceiling fans circulate the breeze. Book well in advance during high season.

Calle 38 and the beach. ☎ *800-538-6802 in the U.S. or Canada, or 984-873-0611. Fax: 984-873-0500.* www.shangrilacaribe.net. *107 units. Free guarded parking. Rack rates: High season $200 gardenview, $230–$300 oceanview or beachfront; low season $155 gardenview, $170–$200 oceanview or beachfront. Rates include breakfast and dinner for two. AE, MC, V.*

Treetops
$$ Playa del Carmen

Treetops not only offers a good price but also a good location — half a block from the beach, and half a block from Avenida 5, which is just enough distance to filter out the noise. The rooms at Treetops encircle a pool, a small *cenote,* and a patch of preserved jungle that shades the hotel and lends the proper tropical feel. Rooms are large and comfortable and have air-conditioning, fans, refrigerators, and either balconies or patios.

Some of the upper rooms, especially the central suite, have the feel of a treehouse. Two other suites are large, with fully loaded kitchenettes, and would work well for groups of four.

Calle 8 s/n. ☎ *984-873-1495. Fax: 984-873-0351.* www.treetopshotel.com. *22 units. Rack rates: High season $94 standard, $105 kitchen studio, $147–$176 suite; low season $85 double, $94 kitchen studio, $116–$145 suite. MC, V.*

Zamas
$$–$$$ Tulum

Zamas is a grouping of stylish beach *cabañas* located out on a rocky point on the coast just south of Tulum. Each *cabaña* comes with a small porch area and hammocks, a thatched roof, a large bathroom, and electricity. Mosquito netting hangs over each bed. What the *cabañas* don't have are ceiling fans, which they generally don't need. In this respect, the hotel's location is enviable in that there's almost always a breeze. Rooms come with a variety of bed combinations and are ranked in three categories: gardenview, oceanview, and beachfront. The gardenview rooms are a good deal. There are two types of beachfront. The small beachfront is exactly that, and that's why it's a little less expensive than the other rooms. The oceanview rooms are extra-large upstairs units, with wonderful terraces. They could easily accommodate four people. Note that the rooms don't have air-conditioning, TV, or phones. The hotel's restaurant has great food. There's a slight increase in rates for the month of August.

Carretera Punta Allen Km 5. ☎ *415-387-9806 in the U.S. or Canada.* www.zamas. com. *20 units. Rack rates: High season $110–$135 gardenview double, $105–$150 beachfront double, $180 oceanview; low season $85–$95 gardenview double, $80–$115 beachfront double, $135 oceanview. No credit cards.*

Settling into the Riviera Maya

For getting through customs and immigration at the Cancún airport, see Chapter 11. The airport is located well south of Cancún, so you don't have to go through the city to get to Playa or the Riviera Maya. If you're **driving,** follow the signs for Puerto Morelos/Playa del Carmen as you exit the airport. Turn right (south) on Highway 307. For more specific directions on entering Playa or going farther south, see "Getting around the area," later in this chapter.

Another option is to take a bus that travels straight from the airport to Playa. After you arrive in Playa, you can catch a bus to any of the major towns along the coast. Turn right after you exit the airport (you walk by a long line of counters with people offering you all kinds of services and info — keep right on walking). Walk to the other side of the airport's main entrance. Look for buses labeled **Autobuses Riviera** in large letters. They offer direct service more than 12 times a day. Cost is $9 one-way.

The Riviera Maya

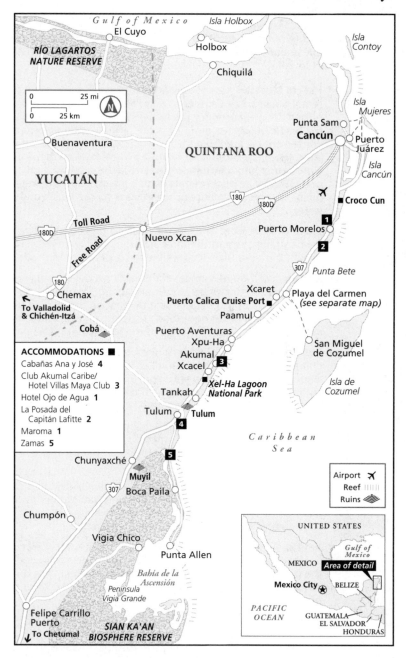

Knowing where to go

If you know where to go, knowing how to get there is easy. The Riviera Maya is a coast with one highway, and anyplace you're heading is going to be either north or south of the place you're coming from. Here's a list of all the major towns and attractions north to south from the Cancún airport to Tulum:

- ✔ **Puerto Morelos:** This sleepy little village has a few small hotels and rental houses. Locals refer to it as "Muerto Morelos" (Dead Morelos) during the off season for the lack of activity. It's a short distance from the bustle of Cancún and Playa del Carmen, and can be considered a convenient escape from the crowds, perfect for a relaxed vacation of lying about the beach and reading a book (with perhaps the occasional foray into a watersport or two). The coast is sandy and well protected by an offshore reef, which means good snorkeling and diving nearby, but plenty of sea grass is on the beach and in the water.

- ✔ **Playa del Carmen:** The largest town on this coast, Playa's got the best restaurants and the most nightlife. It also has a beautiful beach. It's a popular destination, not a place to find solitude.

- ✔ **Xcaret:** Just 7km (4⅓ miles) south of Playa del Carmen is a large nature park. It draws people from Cancún, Cozumel, and all points along this coast. Highlights include floating through an underground river (not for everybody), nightly shows, and loads of seaside activities. Chapter 13 has more details about this park.

- ✔ **Puerto Aventuras:** A modern marina community with tons of condos and a few hotels, I don't care much for staying here, but it's a good place to hook up with sportfishing outfits or to try a swim with dolphins. See the section, "Having Fun on and off the Beach," later in this chapter, for more info.

- ✔ **Xpu-Ha:** This broad beautiful beach with private houses and a few large all-inclusives is a great place to stay for sun worshipers and a good place to go for the day. There's a smattering of beach restaurants and some villas and cabins for rent.

- ✔ **Akumal:** This small, modern, and ecologically oriented community is built on the shores of Akumal Bay and Half-Moon Bay. It's mostly made up of two-story villas, and a few hotels — all on the water. It's a lot quieter than Playa and is good for families.

- ✔ **Xel-Ha:** A large, well-protected lagoon is the centerpiece for this lovely eco-park. It attracts crowds of snorkelers who come to view the fish in the calm, clear waters. The park also offers dolphin swims and a small grouping of ruins. Check out Chapter 13 for more details about this location.

- ✔ **Tulum:** The town of Tulum is on the highway 132km (82 miles) from Cancún, just south of the ruins of the same name. It has a hotel district about 3km (2 miles) away on the coast where about 30 small hotels are lined up along a beautiful beach. Most of these hotels generate their own electricity and can't provide basics such as air-conditioning or phones. Most have small restaurants, and the town itself has at least a dozen more. Construction is booming, both in the town and along the coast. But you can enjoy the beach here in solitude and quiet (unless your hotel is busy building additional rooms). Of course, the downside of peace and quiet is that Tulum doesn't have the variety of restaurants that Playa and Cancún do.

Keeping some cash on hand when traveling this coast is always a good idea. Outside of Playa del Carmen, you don't find many cash machines. In the smaller towns and resorts and at some gas stations, you often can't pay with a credit card. Puerto Morelos has just one ATM in the town and another on the highway at the turnoff junction. After Playa del Carmen, the next cash machines are in Tulum (two). Also, if you're driving, keep some gas in the tank; the coast south of Puerto Aventuras can sometimes experience power failures that last a day, and after the power returns, there can be long lines for gas and cash.

Getting around the area

A single road, Highway 307, runs the length of the Riviera Maya. From the Cancún airport to Playa del Carmen (51km/32 miles), it's a four-lane divided highway with speed limits up to 110kmph (68 mph). There are a couple of traffic lights and several reduced-speed zones around the major turnoffs.

As you approach Playa, two extra lanes are added each way and then divide up. To enter Playa stay in the left lanes so that you can make a left at one of the traffic lights. If you don't stay left, you have to pass through and keep going until you find a turnaround. The main entrances to the town are Avenida Constituyentes, which works for destinations in northern Playa, and Avenida Juárez, leading to the town's main square.

From Playa to Tulum (80km/50 miles), the road becomes a smooth two-lane highway with wide shoulders. Speed limits are a little lower, with more spots that require you to reduce your speed.

Faster traffic on this stretch of road will often move into the middle of the road when passing (as if there were a center lane). Oncoming traffic moves to the right to make room for the passing vehicle. You do the same, but keep a lookout for cyclists on the shoulder. When making a left turn where there is no left-turn lane, move to the shoulder and stop and wait for a gap in the traffic to cross the road. Don't stop in the main lane of the highway! In some places, use the right-hand turnoff that curves around, and then cross the highway at a right angle. Also, all these potential hazards make driving at night especially challenging. (And it gets dark early on this coast.)

You may notice many buses running along this stretch of highway, but I prefer renting a car because many buses stop only in the larger towns or they leave you a half-mile from the beach. Playa has any number of rental agencies. Reserving a car before getting to Mexico is usually cheaper than waiting until after you arrive (see Chapter 9).

Fast Facts: Riviera Maya and Playa del Carmen

Area Code

The telephone area code for most of the Riviera Maya is **984**. The exception is Puerto Morelos and its surroundings, which has the 998 area code.

Banks, ATMs, and Currency Exchange

There are several banks in Playa with ATMs, along with several money-exchange houses. Many of these offices are located close to the pier and along Avenida 5 at Calle 8. There's an ATM in Puerto Morelos and one at the highway turnoff for the town (beside the pharmacy). You can also use the two ATMs and one bank in Tulum.

Business Hours

Most offices maintain traditional Mexican hours of operation (10 a.m.–2 p.m. and 4–8 p.m. daily), but shops remain open throughout the day. Offices tend to close on Saturday and Sunday. Shops are usually open on Saturday but still generally respect the tradition of closing on Sunday. During peak season, many shops remain open until 9 or even 10 p.m.

Internet Access

There are cybercafes and Internet providers in all the major towns, including quite a few in Playa. Prices are cheap.

Medical

For serious medical attention, go to **Hospiten** in Cancún. In Playa, Dr. Jorge Mercado is a capable general practitioner who speaks English. His office is at the corner of avenidas 10 and Constituyentes (☎ **984-873-3908**).

Pharmacy

The Farmacia del Carmen (☎ **984-873-2330**), on Avenida Juárez between avenidas 5 and 10, is open 24 hours.

Post Office

The post office is on Avenida Principal, 3 blocks north of the plaza on the right after the Hotel Playa del Carmen and the launderette.

Taxes

There's a 15 percent IVA (value-added tax) on goods and services, which is generally included in the posted price.

Telephone

Avoid the phone booths that have signs in English advising you to call home using a special 800 number — these are absolute rip-offs and can cost as much as $20 per minute. The least expensive way to call is by using a Telmex (LADATEL) prepaid phone card, available at most pharmacies and mini-supers, using the official Telmex (Lada) public phones. Remember, in Mexico, you need to dial 001 prior to a number to reach the United States, and you need to preface long-distance calls within Mexico by dialing 01.

Time Zone

The Riviera Maya operates on central standard time.

Dining along the Riviera Maya

Every town in the Riviera Maya has at least a few restaurants where you can get good, if not outstanding, food. But Playa del Carmen is the exception; it has an impressive number and variety of restaurants for a town its size. The European influence is quite noticeable, especially with Italian restaurants. With so many options available, this section lists only my favorites in Playa. In most other places, your choices will be so limited, you won't be struggling with any tough decisions.

✔ In Puerto Morelos, the best and most expensive restaurant in town is **John Grey's** (open only for dinner, closed Sun; ☎ 998-871-0449), which is a couple of blocks north of the plaza and a couple inland. The owner is a former chef for the Ritz-Carlton. On the same street as John Grey's is a more economical restaurant that's open for lunch and dinner called **Bodo's** (☎ 998-871-0232) The rest of my suggestions are on or around the main square and include **Los Pelicanos** for overpriced seafood (☎ 998-871-0014); **Hola Asia** for Asian food (☎ 998-871-0679); and **Le Café d'Amancia** for coffee and pastries (☎ 998-850-4110).

✔ Puerto Aventuras has a large open area beside the dolphin pool (see "Swimming with dolphins," later in this chapter) with chairs and tables and a half dozen restaurants where you can get anything from steaks to pizza to pub grub. None is outstanding, but all are passable.

✔ In Akumal, many people rent villas and cook for themselves (there's a convenient grocery store called **Super Chomak** at the entrance to town). There are also a few restaurants: the **Turtle Bay Café and Bakery** (no phone) is my favorite spot for breakfast or a light lunch, **La Buena Vida** for dinner or a drink (☎ 984-875-9061).

✔ Tulum has a few good restaurants with reasonable prices. In the town proper is **Charlie's** (☎ 984-871-2136), my favorite for Mexican food, and **Don Cafeto's** (☎ 984-871-2207), also Mexican. Both places are on the main street. There's a great, authentic Italian restaurant called **Il Giardino di Toni e Simone** (☎ 044-984-804-1316, a cell-phone; closed Wed), 1 block off the highway. Look for a large building-supply store called ROCA — the restaurant is on the opposite side of the road 1 block away. A couple of roadside places grill chicken and serve it with rice and beans for an economical lunch. In the hotel zone, try the food at Zamas.

Please refer to the Introduction of this book for an explanation of the price categories that I use in the following listings. Remember that tips generally run about 15 percent and most waitstaff really depend on gratuities for their income, so be generous if the service warrants.

Please see Appendix C for more information on Mexican cuisine.

Casa Mediterránea
$ Playa del Carmen   NORTHERN ITALIAN

Tucked away on a quiet little patio off Avenida 5, this small, homey restaurant serves excellent food. The owners, Maurizio Gabrielli and Mary Michelon, are usually there to greet customers and make recommendations. They came to Mexico to enjoy the simple life, and this inclination shows in the restaurant's welcoming, unhurried atmosphere. The menu is mostly northern Italian, with several dishes from the rest of the country as well as daily specials. They make their pastas (except penne and spaghetti) in-house, and they aren't precooked. Try fish and shrimp ravioli or penne alla Veneta. You can choose from several wines, mostly Italian. The salads are good and are carefully prepared — dig in without hesitation.

Av. 5 (between calles 6 and 8; look for a sign for Hotel Marieta). ☎ 984-876-3926. Reservations recommended in high season. Main courses: $8–15. No credit cards. Open: Daily 1–11 p.m.

Estas Son Las Mañanitas
$ Playa del Carmen   MEXICAN/ITALIAN

For dependable food in an advantageous spot for people-watching, try this restaurant. It's simple outdoor dining on Avenida 5 — comfortable chairs and tables under *palapa* umbrellas that's not noisy, and the Italian owner is vigilant about maintaining quality and consistency. He offers an excellent *sopa de lima*, a large seafood pasta, grilled shrimp with herbs, and Tex-Mex specialties such as chili and fajitas. The hot sauces are good.

Av. 5 (between calles 4 and 6). ☎ 984-873-0114. Main courses: $8–15. AE, MC, V. Open: Daily 8–11:30 p.m.

La Casa del Agua
$$ Playa del Carmen   EUROPEAN/MEXICAN

This new arrival to Playa offers some of the best of both Old and New Worlds. What I tried was delicious — chicken in a wonderfully scented sauce of fine herbs accompanied by fettuccine, and a well-made tortilla soup listed as *sopa mexicana*. There are a number of cool and light dishes that would be appetizing for lunch or an afternoon meal; for example, an avocado stuffed with shrimp and flavored with a subtle horseradish sauce on a bed of alfalfa sprouts and julienned carrots. For dinner try the grilled seafood platter for two. The dining area is upstairs under a large and airy *palapa* roof.

Av. 5 at Calle 2. ☎ 984-803-0232. Reservations recommended in high season. Main courses: $12–$25. AE, MC, V. Open: Daily 2 p.m.–midnight.

La Tarraya Restaurant/Bar
$ Playa del Carmen   SEAFOOD/BREAKFAST

"The restaurant that was born with the town," proclaims the sign outside this establishment. Locals also recommend this restaurant as the best for seafood. It's right on the beach, and the water practically laps at the foundations. Because the owners are fishermen, the fish is so fresh that it's practically still wiggling. The wood hut doesn't look like much, but you can have your fish prepared in several ways here. If you haven't tried the Yucatecan specialty *tik-n-xic* fish (baked fish in a spicy barbecue-style sauce), this would be a good place to do so. Tarraya is on the beach opposite the basketball court.

Calle 2 Norte at the beach. ☎ *987-873-2040. Main courses: $4–$9; whole fish $8 per kilo. No credit cards. Open: Daily 7 a.m.–9 p.m.*

Media Luna
$ **Playa del Carmen   VEGETARIAN/SEAFOOD**

This restaurant has an outstanding and eclectic menu that favors grilled seafood, sautés, and pasta dishes with inventive combinations of ingredients. Everything I had was quite fresh and prepared beautifully, taking inspiration from various culinary traditions — Italian, Mexican, and Japanese. Keep an eye on the daily specials. The restaurant also makes sandwiches and salads, black-bean quesadillas, and crepes. The restaurant is open-air, and the décor is primitive-tropical chic.

Av. 5 (between calles 12 and 14). ☎ *984-873-0526. Main courses: $8–$15; sandwich with a salad $5–$8; breakfast $4–$7. No credit cards. Open: Daily 8 a.m.–11:30 p.m.*

Yaxché
$–$$ **Playa del Carmen   MAYA/YUCATECAN**

The menu here makes use of many native foods and spices to produce a style of cooking different from what you usually get when ordering Yucatecan food. You find such things as a cream of *chaya* (a native leafy vegetable), or *xcatic* chile (a regional variety of chile pepper) stuffed with savory pit-baked pork called *cochinita pibil.* I also like the classic fruit salad, done Mexican style with lime juice and dried powdered chile. The menu is varied and includes a lot of seafood dishes, and the ones I had were fresh and well prepared.

Calle 8 (between avs. 5 and 10). ☎ *984-873-2502. Reservations recommended in high season. Main courses: $8–$20. AE, MC, V. Open: Daily noon to midnight.*

Having Fun on and off the Beach

The Riviera Maya is an ideal destination for people who like being active and exploring new lands. The region has Maya ruins, caves, crystal-clear underground rivers *(cenotes),* and fascinating flora and fauna to see, plus plenty of options for scuba diving and snorkeling.

Scuba and snorkeling

For scuba diving in Puerto Morelos, contact Victor Reyes, the English-speaking owner of **Mystic Divers** (☎ **998-871-0634**). He knows the local dive spots well and is quite accommodating. His shop is on the main square. You can also arrange a snorkeling tour here, or ask at the Hotel Ojo de Agua. The reef in front of Puerto Morelos has been declared a national park and is protected. It is quite shallow and perfect for snorkeling.

In Playa del Carmen, contact **Tank-Ha Dive Center** (☎ 984-873-0302; www.tankha.com). It's on Playa's Avenida 5 between calles 8 and 10. You can arrange both reef and cavern diving here, plus snorkeling trips.

Akumal has been the main diving center on this coast for quite some time. It was the base of operations of a group known as CEDAM, who became widely known for discovering an old Spanish shipwreck complete with treasure. At least 30 dive sites are offshore near Akumal. The oldest dive operator in town is the **Akumal Dive Shop** (☎ 984-875-9032; www.akumal.com). In addition to the usual certification courses, it offers cavern diving and technical diving instruction.

Cavern diving is big here because the Yucatán has so many underground rivers, especially around the lower Riviera Maya. If you want to try diving or snorkeling in caverns, the easiest and most fun way is to go to **Hidden Worlds Cenotes** (☎ 984-877-8535; www.hiddenworlds.com.mx). It's 2km (1¼ miles) south of Xel-Ha on the right side of the road. You can easily spot the sign. Here, you can rent all the gear including a wet suit (the water is a bit chilly) and tour two caverns. These caverns were filmed for the IMAX production, *Journey into Amazing Caves*. The snorkel tour with gear costs $40 and takes you to two different caverns. The main form of transportation is by truck with a guide who throws in tidbits of information and lore about the jungle plant life that you see. Prepare to do some walking, so take shoes or sandals.

For easy-going snorkeling in warmer water, try the nature parks, especially Xel-Ha, which has scads of fish and rays. For more information on the nature parks, see Chapter 13.

Swimming with dolphins

You can swim with dolphins at two of the nature parks on this coast — Xel-Ha and Xcaret (see Chapter 13) — or you can do so in Puerto Aventuras. An excellent outfit called **Dolphin Discovery** (☎ 998-849-4757; www.dolphindiscovery.com) does a first-rate job of getting people in contact with these marvelous creatures. An hour-long session costs $125. Make your reservations well ahead of time using the Web site.

Swimming with dolphins has its critics and supporters. You may want to visit the Whale and Dolphins Conservation Society's Web site at www.wdcs.org. For more information about responsible travel in general, check out these Web sites: Tread Lightly (www.treadlightly.org) and the International Ecotourism Society (www.ecotourism.org).

Gone fishing

Puerto Aventuras is also the main hangout for fishing. Your best bet for deep-sea fishing is **Capt. Rick's Sportfishing Center** (☎ 984-873-5195 or 984-873-5387; www.fishyucatan.com). The best fishing on this coast is from March to August. The captain can combine a fishing trip with some snorkeling, which makes for a leisurely day.

Getting in touch with nature

The Riviera Maya also provides plenty to do for landlubbers. To start, the ruins of Tulum are easy to get to and interesting to view; for more information, check out Chapter 13.

If you want to see some of the jungle, try out rappelling, or get to know a contemporary Maya community, contact **Alltournative** (☎ 984-873-2036; www.alltournative.com), or book one of its tours through your hotel or a local travel agency. They do small groups and use vans to pick you up at almost any hotel in the Riviera Maya. Most of their tours combine a little adventure with some of the local culture and natural history. The guides are quite professional.

If you want to see more of the region's natural habitat, you can arrange a trip to the **Sian Ka'an Biosphere** to see a great variety of birds and sea life, and with a little luck, some of the rarer forest critters. In Tulum, contact **Sian Ka'an Tours** (☎ 984-871-2362; siankaan_tours@hotmail.com). This company offers two kinds of tours to the preserve. The office is on the town's main street Avenida Tulum at the corner of Calle Beta, next door to El Basilico Italian restaurant.

On the highway between Akumal and Xel-Ha is the turnoff for an interesting large cavern called **Aktun Chen.** You explore the cavern by guided tour ($18 adults, $10 for children 6–12). It takes 45 minutes and involves a good bit of walking. The cavern is well lit and has good footing. On the park's grounds are a number of local species of fauna, including spider monkeys. Chapter 13 has a bit more detail about Aktun Chen.

Several outfits along the road offer horseback riding. The best is 6.4km (4 miles) south of Xcaret. It's called **Rancho Punta Venado.** It's less touristy than other places, and the owner takes good care of his horses. It also offers kayaking and snorkeling. The best way to contact them is through e-mail: gabriela@puntavenado.com. Or you can try the cell-phone: ☎ 044-984-806-4818. The entrance is 2km (1¼ miles) south of the overpass at Puerto Calica.

Teeing off and playing tennis

Your best option for chasing a little white ball and whacking a larger, yellow one is the Playacar Golf Club immediately south of Playa del Carmen. It is owned by the Palace Resorts chain (www.palace-resorts.com). They sell all-inclusive golf packages. The course was designed by

Robert Von Hagge. If you don't sign up for the package, greens fees are $180 in the morning (includes golf cart) and $120 after 2 p.m. Two **tennis** courts are also available at the club at a rate of $10 per hour.

Going shopping

Playa del Carmen offers the most opportunity for **shopping** in the area — along its popular Avenida 5. This pedestrian-only street is lined with dozens of small, trendy shops selling imported batik (Balinese-style) clothing, Guatemalan-fabric clothing, premium tequilas, Cuban cigars, masks, pottery, hammocks, and a few T-shirts. Throw in a couple of tattoo parlors, and you complete the mix. A smattering of interesting shops can be found in some of the smaller towns, and some large jewelry and rug stores line the highway.

Enjoying the nightlife

It seems like everyone in Playa is out on Avenida 5 or on the square until 10 or 11 p.m. Pleasant strolls, meals and drinks at street-side cafes, shops, and bars with live music make up Playa's nightlife. Down by the ferry dock is a **Señor Frog's** (☎ 984-873-0930), with its patented mix of thumping dance music, gelatin shots, and fraternity-house antics; it's on the beach at Calle 4. The real beach bar in Playa is at the **Blue Parrot** (☎ 984-873-0083), and it has quite a following.

I've been hearing a lot of complaints about timeshare salespersons on this stretch of coast lately — more than the usual amount. Some complaints describe tactics that could almost be considered hostage-taking. I've also heard of people being stranded on the highway after they've declined to buy. Don't mix business with pleasure.

Part V
Puerto Vallarta and the Central Pacific Coast

The 5th Wave   By Rich Tennant

Honestly—I thought it was an exotic sea urchin. It never occurred to me that someone would actually snorkel with a toupee on.

In this part . . .

*I*f you're looking to bask in warm hospitality as well as the sun, Puerto Vallarta is an excellent choice that offers exquisite surroundings, friendly people, and tons of things to do and see. As a longtime resident of this picturesque town, Lynne shares an insider's perspective on getting around and exploring the sights.

Puerto Vallarta boasts a wide variety of places to stay and the most delectable array of dining options of any of Mexico's beach resorts. In the upcoming chapters, you find recommendations for the best places to stay in the area, as well as tips on finding the best restaurants — not an easy task considering all the wonderful dining choices Puerto Vallarta offers. Finally, with this part, you can locate the ideal beach along the more than 81km (50 miles) of coastline within Banderas Bay.

Chapter 16

The Lowdown on Puerto Vallarta's Hotel Scene

by Lynne Bairstow

In This Chapter
▶ Getting the scoop on hotel locations
▶ Sizing up Puerto Vallarta's top hotel choices

*P*uerto Vallarta maintains a small-town charm despite offering its visitors a range of sophisticated hotels, great restaurants, a thriving arts community, an active nightlife, and a growing variety of ecotourism attractions. With its traditional Mexican architecture and gold-sand beaches bordered by jungle-covered mountains, Vallarta is currently the second-most visited resort in Mexico (trailing only Cancún).

Most of the luxury hotels and shopping centers have sprung up to the north and south of the original town, allowing Vallarta to grow and become a sizable city of 250,000 without sacrificing its considerable charms. This growth pattern has made it possible for Vallarta to provide visitors with the services and infrastructure of a modern city while retaining the feel of a peaceful Mexican village.

In this chapter, I review the main parts of town, the types of hotel rooms you're likely to find in each place, and the pros and cons of staying in each area. Then I review some of my favorite places to stay in Puerto Vallarta. The selection is so varied that, regardless of your taste or budget, you're sure to find a perfect fit for a satisfying vacation.

Choosing a Location

The part of town you choose to stay in usually impacts your overall vacation experience, although everything is relatively close by and getting around is easy and inexpensive. The term *Vallarta* actually encompasses the entire area that borders **Bahía de Banderas (Banderas Bay)** — an 84km (52-mile) stretch of coastline that extends through two Mexican states. My hotel recommendations extend through this entire area as well.

Nuevo Vallarta and the northern coast

Traveling north from the airport (Gustavo Díaz Ordaz International Airport), you first come to **Nuevo Vallarta.** Many people assume Nuevo Vallarta is a section of Puerto Vallarta, but it's really a stand-alone destination located in the state of **Nayarit.** It's a mega-resort development — complete with marina, two golf courses, and luxury hotels. Most of the hotels here are all-inclusive, located on one of the widest, most attractive beaches on the bay. Two lengthy entrance roads from the highway pass by fields that are great for bird-watching and nearby lagoons that are great for kayaking. The **Paradise Plaza shopping center** (next to the Paradise Village resort) has added a lot to the area in terms of shopping, dining, and services. In addition, there are two golf courses: the **Mayan Palace Golf Club** and the **El Tigre** course of Paradise Village.

Visitors to Nuevo Vallarta usually plan to travel the distance into Puerto Vallarta (about 30 min. and $15 by cab) for anything other than poolside and beach action — options for dining and other diversions outside the Nuevo Vallarta hotels remain limited, but are getting better. Taxis are available 24 hours a day. A regularly scheduled public-bus service runs between 7 a.m. and 11 p.m. daily and costs about $1.50 for a one-way trip.

Bucerías, a small beachfront village of cobblestone streets, villas, and small hotels, is farther north along Bahía de Banderas, 19km (12 miles) beyond the airport. Past Bucerías, following the curved coastline of Bahía de Banderas, is **Punta Mita.** Once a truly rustic village of fishermen and bamboo houses, Punta Mita has developed its own identity as a luxury destination. Three super-exclusive, luxury-boutique resorts, a Chopra Center and Spa, numerous private villas (many available for rent), and two golf courses either exist or are in the works. As of 2006, only the Four Seasons Resort (see review later in this chapter) and its adjacent Jack Nicklaus Signature golf course are open, but the St. Regis Resort, La Solana Resort, Chopra Center, and a second Jack Nicklaus golf course will be completed by 2007. This spot of white-sand beaches and clear waters was once home to an ancient celestial observatory, and you can't imagine a more exquisite setting. Punta Mita is a departure from the other beaches in the area.

Marina Vallarta

If you head south from the airport, the first area you come to is **Marina Vallarta,** a resort city within Puerto Vallarta, located on the immediate right as you come into town from the airport. Guests here feel a world apart from the quaintness of downtown Puerto Vallarta. Marina Vallarta has the most modern luxury hotels of any area in town, plus a huge marina with 450 yacht slips, a golf course, restaurants and bars, and several shopping plazas.

Because the area began life as a swamp and was later filled in for development, the beaches are the least desirable in the area, with darker sand and seasonal inflows of cobblestones washing down from the mountains and rivers and then up on the beaches. However, the exquisite pools at the oceanfront hotels more than make up for this shortcoming.

The **Marina Vallarta Club de Golf** (☎ 322-221-0073), an 18-hole golf course designed by Joe Finger, is within walking distance of most of the hotels. (See Chapter 19 for more information on golf and other activities in Puerto Vallarta.)

Although this isn't the area of choice if you're a true beach aficionado, Marina Vallarta is nice for families and for vacationers looking for lots of centralized activity. The complex is attractive and clean, and the public transportation is good. If you choose to travel by taxi, going from Marina to downtown Puerto Vallarta takes about 20 minutes, which is due to traffic more than distance, and costs about $7.

Hotel Zone

The next area you encounter heading south from the airport toward town is known as the **Hotel Zone** because of all the high-rise hotels located side-by-side along the main roadway. Here, the main street running between the airport and town is called Avenida Francisco Medina Ascencio, but it's sometimes referred to as Avenida de las Palmas for the stately palm trees that line the strip of land that divides the road. The tourism boom that Vallarta enjoyed in the mid-1970s gave birth to the hotels that line this road, and most of them have been exceptionally well maintained. All the hotels offer excellent, wide beachfronts with generally tranquil waters for swimming. This area is home to more casual, less expensive hotels that offer a great beach as a bonus.

The long and wide stretch of golden beach fronting the Hotel Zone has smoother sand and more watersports concessions than either Marina Vallarta or downtown. Although many shopping plazas line the main road in front of the hotels, they mostly service the large residential community to the east. You find the most interesting restaurants and intriguing shops downtown or back in Marina, but from the Hotel Zone, you're only a quick taxi or bus ride away from either of these areas.

El Centro Vallarta

Few beach resorts in Mexico offer what Puerto Vallarta exudes — the feeling that you're actually in Mexico. Staying in the **central downtown** area provides the charm of a traditional village and proximity to a tropical beach. Sophisticated services, all classes and types of restaurants, sizzling nightspots, and enough shops and galleries to tempt even the most jaded consumers are contained within the cobblestone streets and welcoming atmosphere of the central town.

Cool breezes flow down from the mountains along the Río Cuale (Cuale River), which runs through the center of town. The boardwalk, or *malecón,* that borders the main waterfront street boasts fanciful public sculptures, lively restaurants, shops, bars — and timeshare sales booths. The *malecón* is a magnet for both residents and visitors who walk its length while taking in the ocean breeze, a gorgeous sunset, or a perfect, moonlit night.

Accommodations here may be older, but most are inexpensive and generally well kept — plus they have plenty of character. In addition to being able to reach any downtown destination on foot, the neighborhood is as safe as it is charming.

Just south of downtown, the **Playa Los Muertos** area has recently undergone a renaissance. It's now not only a place offering great values in accommodations, dining, and nightlife, but also an added plus for the Los Muertos neighborhood is that it also has funky charm, which you can experience in the sidewalk cafes, great restaurants, and casual nightspots. Economically priced hotels and good-value guesthouses dominate accommodations here. Another bonus for the Los Muertos neighborhood is that most of Vallarta's nightlife activity is now centered in the areas south of the Río Cuale and along Olas Altas.

The southern shore

Hillsides dotted with private villas and a few large hotels border the coastal highway. Immediately south of town lies the exclusive residential and rental district of **Conchas Chinas.** La Jolla de Mismaloya resort lies 10km (6 miles) south of town on **Playa Mismaloya** (where *The Night of the Iguana* was filmed). No roads service the southern shoreline of Bahía de Banderas, but three small coastal villages are popular attractions for visitors to Puerto Vallarta: **Las Animas, Quimixto,** and **Yelapa,** which are all accessible only by boat. Many visitors mistakenly believe that these villages are islands, but they're actually located along the same coast. Yelapa offers some rustic accommodations in addition to making a great destination for an enjoyable day trip (see Chapter 19 for more on things to see and do in Yelapa). Las Animas and Quimixto don't offer any accommodations.

Beyond a varied selection of hotels, Puerto Vallarta has many other types of accommodations. Oceanfront or marina-view condominiums and elegant private villas are also available; both options can offer a better value and more ample space for families or small groups. For more information on short-term rentals, check out the Web site at www. virtualvallarta.com, which lists a selection of rental options. Prices start at $99 a night for non-beachfront condos and go up to $1,000 for penthouse condos or private villas. Susan Wiseman's **Bayside Properties,** Francisca Rodríguez 160, at the corner of Olas Altas (☎ **322-223-4424** or 222-8148; www.baysidepropertiespv.com), rents gay-friendly condos, villas, and hotels for individuals and large groups. She can arrange airport pickup and in-villa cooks. For those travelers looking for luxe accommodations, contact **Punta Mita Properties** (☎ **888-647-0979;** www.puntamitaproperties.com) for rates and availability on private villa rentals, with access to Punta Mita's resort amenities.

Puerto Vallarta's Best Accommodations

For each hotel, I include specific rack rates for two people spending one night in a double room during high season (Christmas to Easter) unless otherwise indicated. *Rack rates* simply mean published rates and tend to be the highest rates paid — you can do better, especially if you're purchasing a package that includes airfare (see Chapter 7 for tips on avoiding paying rack rates). Prices quoted here include the 17 percent room tax. Please refer to the Introduction of this book for an explanation of the price categories.

It's not unusual for many hotels to double their normal rates during Christmas and Easter weeks, but low-season rates can be anywhere from 20 percent to 60 percent below high-season rates. *Note:* Some rates may seem much higher than others, but many of these rates are "all-inclusive" — meaning that your meals and beverages are included in the price of your stay. All-inclusive rates also take into account all tips and taxes and most activities and entertainment.

All hotels listed here have both air-conditioning and TVs, unless otherwise indicated.

Casa Tres Vidas
$$$$$ **South Shore/Conchas Chinas**

Terraced down a hillside to Playa Conchas Chinas, Casa Tres Vidas is actually three individual villas that make a great — and affordable — place to stay for families or groups of friends. Set on a stunning private cove, Tres Vidas provides the experience of having your own private villa — complete with service staff. Under new ownership since 2000, Tres Vidas has been upgraded in furnishings and amenities, and it's an outstanding value for the location (close to town), sweeping panoramic views from every room, and excellent personal service. Each of the three villas has at least two levels, more than 465 sq. m (5,000 sq. ft.) of mostly open-design living area, a private swimming pool, a heated whirlpool, and air-conditioned bedrooms. (Because the layout is so open, the rest of the rooms don't have air-conditioning.) The Villa Alta penthouse villa has three bedrooms, plus a rooftop deck with pool and bar. Vida Sol, the center villa, has a 5.4m-high (18-ft.) domed living room with fireplace, and features graceful arches and columns. Although it has three bedrooms, it can sleep ten — two of the bedrooms have two king-size beds in them. Directly on the ocean, Vida Mar is a four-bedroom villa that can accommodate eight guests. An added bonus: Meals are prepared in your villa twice a day — you only pay for the cost of the food, and you choose the menu. Casa Tres Vidas is owned and managed by the owners of the adjacent Quinta María Cortez (see review later in this chapter).

Calle Sagitario 132, below the Conchas Chinas Mercado (market). ☎ **888-640-8100** *or 801-531-8100 in the U.S., or 322-221-5815. Fax: 322-221-5327.* www.casatresvidas. com. *3 villas. Very limited street parking available. Rack rates: High season $625; low season $450. Prices are per night for complete villa, full services, and two meals prepared. AE, MC, V.*

Dreams Puerto Vallarta
$$$$–$$$$$ South Shore/Conchas Chinas

Formerly the Camino Real, this original luxury hotel in Puerto Vallarta was taken over by AMResorts in 2004 and turned into the premium all-inclusive Dreams Resort. It unquestionably has the nicest beach of any Vallarta hotel — soft, white sand and a private cove. On the beach, numerous shade *palapas* are available, along with a chair, towels, and food and beverage service. Both the nature of the geography and the physical boundaries set it apart from other properties — with a lush mountain backdrop, Dreams retains the exclusivity that made it popular from the beginning — yet it's only a five- to ten-minute ride to town. The hotel consists of two buildings: the 250-room main hotel, which curves gently as it traces the shape of the Playa Las Estacas, and a newer, 11-story tower, also facing the beach and ocean. An ample pool with an in-pool bar fronts the main building and faces the beach. Standard rooms in the main building are large. Some of the rooms have sliding doors that open onto the beach, and others have balconies. The standard rooms in the tower feature balconies with whirlpool tubs. All rooms are decorated in vibrant colors, with marble floors and artwork by locally renowned artist Manuel Lepe. In 2004, all rooms were completely renovated, with additions including two new swimming pools (including an adults-only tranquillity pool), a wedding gazebo, and upgraded health club and spa. For the young travelers, the Explorer's Club for Kids has a program of daily activities, based on science, nature, and exploring, certain to keep them entertained.

Carretera Barra de Navidad Km 3.5, Playa Las Estacas. ☎ **800-722-6466** *in the U.S. and Canada, or 322-226-5000. Fax: 322-221-6000.* www.dreamsresort.com. *337 units. Free secured parking. Rack rates: High season $360 double, $440 junior suite; $520 suite; low season $135–$150 double, $400–$880 suite. AE, DC, MC, V.*

Fiesta Americana Puerto Vallarta
$$$$ Hotel Zone

The Fiesta Americana's towering, three-story, thatched-*palapa* lobby is a landmark in the Hotel Zone, but this hotel is even better known for its excellent beach and friendly service. The nine-story, terra-cotta-colored building embraces a large plaza with a big pool and bar area facing the beach. Marble-trimmed rooms in neutral tones with pastel accents come with carved headboards and comfortable rattan and wicker furniture. All rooms have private balconies with ocean and pool views. In addition to

Puerto Vallarta Hotel Zone Accommodations

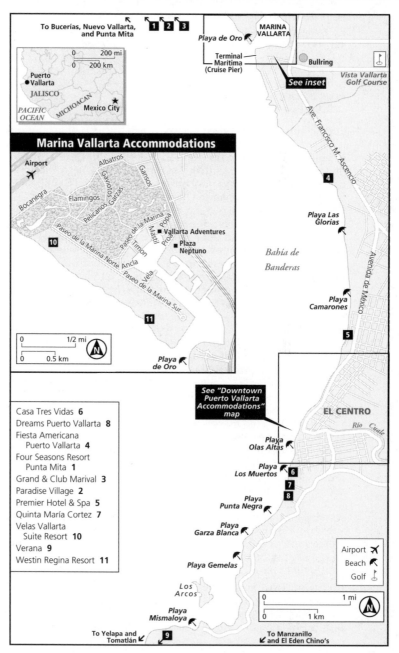

Casa Tres Vidas **6**
Dreams Puerto Vallarta **8**
Fiesta Americana
  Puerto Vallarta **4**
Four Seasons Resort
  Punta Mita **1**
Grand & Club Marival **3**
Paradise Village **2**
Premier Hotel & Spa **5**
Quinta María Cortez **7**
Velas Vallarta
  Suite Resort **10**
Verana **9**
Westin Regina Resort **11**

the three restaurants, the Fiesta Americana has a lobby bar with live music nightly. A children's program and the excellent pool and beach facilities make this hotel a great choice for families.

Av. Francisco Medina Ascencio Km 2.5. ☎ *800-FIESTA-1 in the U.S., or 322-224-2010. Fax: 322-224-2108.* www.fiestaamericana.com. *291 units. Limited free parking. Rack rates: High season $209–$400 double; low season $196 double. AE, DC, MC, V.*

Four Seasons Resort Punta Mita
$$$$$ **Punta Mita**

Located on the undisputed best beach in the area, this boutique hotel artfully combines seclusion and pampered service with a welcoming sense of comfort. The 113 rooms and 27 suites are in three-story *casitas* (little houses), which surround the main building where the lobby, cultural center, restaurants, and pool are located. The stretch of beachfront is the only white-sand beach in the bay, due to a coral reef located just offshore, which also makes the water a dreamy and translucent shade of aquamarine. Every guest room offers an ocean view from a large terrace or balcony. Most suites also offer a private plunge pool, as well as a separate sitting room. Room interiors are plush and spacious with a king or two double beds, a seating area, and an oversized bathroom with a deep soaking tub, a separate glass-enclosed shower, and a dual-vanity sink. This is the place to go to completely get away from it all, but remember that you're at least 45 minutes from Puerto Vallarta's activities. For most guests, this isn't a problem — the Four Seasons is so relaxing and comfortable that thinking of anyplace else is hard. The centerpiece of the resort is the 18-hole (with an optional 19th hole of play on a natural island) Jack Nicklaus Signature golf course. The course has ocean views from every hole, and eight holes border the ocean. A full-service spa, complete tennis center, and watersports center — including guided surf trips and lessons — round out the activities. In addition to the two restaurants, you can enjoy a golf clubhouse, a lobby bar, and 24-hour room service. The heated infinity pool is surrounded by shaded areas and sun chairs, and waiters come by every so often to offer chilled towels or a spritz of water. Newly added in 2006 is a tranquillity pool, surrounded by private *cabañas,* complete with wireless Internet, a minibar, and flat screen TV, which are available for a daily rental fee. A notable attraction is the cultural center — a library-style environment with free Internet access and a menu of entertaining lectures on Mexican culture, including a popular tequila tasting! The Kids for All Seasons activities program is hands-down the best place for children to enjoy their vacation as much as you will. The Four Seasons was the first resort to be located in Punta Mita, an exclusive development north of Vallarta that's all the buzz in luxury travel. In late 2007, the St. Regis Resort, the Chopra Center and Spa, and a second Jack Nicklaus Signature course will join it.

Punta Mita, Bahía de Banderas, Nayarit 63734. ☎ *800-332-3442 or 329-291-6000. Fax: 329-291-6060.* www.fourseasons.com/puntamita. *140 units. Valet parking. Rack rates: High season $691–$796 double, $1,814–$2,048 suite; low season $457–$656 double, $1,170–$1,287 suite. AE, DC, MC, V.*

Downtown Puerto Vallarta Accommodations

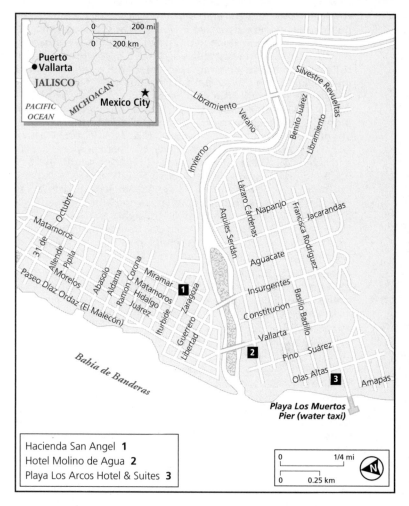

Hacienda San Angel **1**
Hotel Molino de Agua **2**
Playa Los Arcos Hotel & Suites **3**

Hacienda San Angel
$$$$$ Centro

This enchanting boutique hotel may not be on the beach, but you'll hardly miss it, because you'll be so pampered in the stunning suites, or satisfied enjoying the view from the rooftop heated pool or Jacuzzi and sun deck. Once Richard Burton's home in Puerto Vallarta, it's located just behind Puerto Vallarta's famed church — Our Lady of Guadalupe — making it easy walking distance to the downtown restaurants, shopping, and galleries.

The Hacienda is comprised of three villas; the first two are joined to the third villa by a path that winds through a lovely terraced garden filled with tropical plants, flowers, statuary, and a charming fountain. A large, heated pool and deck offer panoramic views of the city and Bahía de Banderas, while a second sun deck with Jacuzzi literally overlooks the church's crown, across to the water beyond. Each of the Hacienda's nine elegant suites is individually decorated, accented with exquisite antiques and original art, and has a private bath, air-conditioning, remote control cable TV, telephone, and bathrobes. Bed linens and coverings are of the finest quality, with touches such as Venetian lace and goose-down pillows. Each morning, you wake up to a continental breakfast served outside your suite at your requested hour, or you can choose a full breakfast (for an additional charge). The Hacienda's private chef also prepares a menu of snacks and light meals during the day, or can prepare a sumptuous private dinner upon request. From Monday through Saturday, guests can attend a cocktail hour and down one of Hacienda's signature drinks (such as the Celestial Sin — a wicked blend of vodka and blue Curacao), accompanied by snacks. With its commitment to highly personalized services, the Hacienda's concierge can arrange excursions, golf games, or on-site spa treatments. Sophisticated style, coupled with casual Vallarta charm, make Hacienda San Angel a true "find" in Mexico for the discriminating traveler.

Miramar 336. ☎ *322-222-2692.* www.haciendasanangel.com. *9 suites. Very limited street parking. Rack rates: High season $475 double; low season $200–$375 double. All rates include daily continental breakfast. Rates for the entire Hacienda or separate villas consisting of three suites each are also available. MC, V.*

Hotel Molino de Agua
$$–$$$ **Centro**

With an unrivaled location adjacent to both the Río Cuale and the ocean, this hotel is a mix of stone and stucco-walled bungalows and small beachfront buildings spread out among winding walkways and lush tropical gardens. If you want a place that's more intimate than a standard hotel, in a location that's more immersed in town activities, this is the best choice. It's located immediately past the Río Cuale — after crossing the southbound bridge, the hotel is on your right. Although the hotel is centrally located on a main street, open spaces, big trees, birds, and lyrical fountains lend tranquillity to the space. The individual bungalows are located in the gardens between the entrance and the ocean; make sure to request one away from the front of the property where street noise can keep you up at night. The bungalows are well maintained, and the simple furnishings include a bed, wooden desk and chair, Mexican tile floors, beamed ceilings, and beautifully tiled bathrooms. Wicker rocking chairs grace their private patios. Rooms and suites in the small, two- and three-story buildings on the beach have double beds and private terraces. There are no TVs or telephones in any of the rooms. In addition to an oceanside pool, a second pool with a whirlpool is adjacent to the Lion's Court restaurant and bar.

Ignacio L. Vallarta 130, just over the southbound bridge on the right side. ☎ *322-222-1957. Fax: 322-222-6056.* www.molinodeagua.com. *58 units. Free secured parking. Rack rates: High season garden bungalows $115 double, oceanfront rooms and suites $135–$155 double; low season bungalows $88 double, rooms and suites $106–$132 double. AE, MC, V.*

Marival Grand & Club Suites
$$$$ Nuevo Vallarta

This all-inclusive hotel, located almost by itself at the northernmost end of Nuevo Vallarta, is a refreshing choice compared to the mega-resorts that tend to dominate all-inclusive options. The broad, sandy beach is one of the real assets here — it stretches more than 450m (1,500 ft.). There's also an extensive activities program, including fun for children. This Mediterranean-style property is relatively small, but it offers a large variety of rooms ranging from standard rooms with no balconies to large master suites with whirlpools. Choose from among six restaurants, plus eight bars, for your dining and drinking desires. The hotel has three pools and a whirlpool for adults, plus two pools for children and four lighted tennis courts. If you're coming from the Puerto Vallarta airport, Club Marival is the first resort to your right on Cocoteros when you enter Nuevo Vallarta from the second entrance.

Paseo de los Cocoteros y Bulevar Nuevo Vallarta s/n. ☎ *322-297-0100. Fax: 322-297-0262.* www.gomarival.com. *646 units. Rack rates: High season $246 double; low season $230 double. Rates are all-inclusive. Ask about seasonal specials. AE, MC, V.*

Paradise Village
$$$–$$$$$ Nuevo Vallarta

This resort truly lives up to its name. It feels more like a self-contained village than a resort and is indeed a paradise bordering one of the most stunning stretches of broad, sandy beach in the bay. Paradise Village offers a full array of guest services, ranging from an on-site disco to a full-service European spa and health club. In 2002, the resort added the 18-hole El Tigre golf course to its roster of guest amenities (see Chapter 19). Styled in a Maya-influenced design, the collection of pyramid-shaped buildings houses all-suite accommodations in studio, one-bedroom, and two-bedroom configurations. All the suites are well designed and feature muted color schemes, sitting areas, and kitchenettes — making them ideal for families or groups of friends. The Maya theme extends to both oceanfront pools with mythical creatures forming water slides and waterfalls. The exceptional spa is reason enough to book a vacation here. Services include treatments, hydrotherapy, massage (including massage on the beach), and fitness and yoga classes. Special spa packages are always available, and they can include a full fitness evaluation if you're up for it. Four tennis courts, a lap pool, a basketball court, beach volleyball courts, and a watersports center complement the spa and fitness center. In addition to the two full-service restaurants, beachfront snack bars and special theme nights add to the dining options. The kid's club and petting zoo are especially popular with families.

Paseo de los Cocoteros 001. ☎ *800-995-5714, or 322-226-6770. Fax: 322-226-6752.* www.paradisevillage.com. *Free covered parking. 490 units. Rack rates: High season $193–$625 double; low season $140–$514 double. AE, DC, MC, V.*

Playa Los Arcos Hotel & Suites
$$–$$$ Centro

An excellent value and always popular, this hotel is a personal favorite of mine. Its stellar location in the heart of Playa Los Muertos is central to the Olas Altas sidewalk-cafe action and close to downtown. The four-story structure is U-shaped, facing the ocean, with a small swimming pool in the courtyard. Rooms with private balconies overlook the pool, and the ten suites have ocean views. Five of the suites have kitchenettes. The standard rooms are small but pleasantly decorated with carved wooden furniture painted pale pink, and they're immaculate. A *palapa* beachside bar with occasional live entertainment, a gourmet coffee shop, and the popular Kaiser Maximilian's gourmet restaurant (see Chapter 18) are on the premises. The hotel is located 7 blocks south of the river.

Olas Altas 380. ☎ *800-648-2403 in the U.S., or 322-222-1583. Fax: 322-226-7104.* www. playalosarcos.com. *175 units. Limited street parking available. Rack rates: High season $105–$145 double, $155–$175 suite; low season $74–$102 double, $112–$130 suite. AE, MC, V.*

Premier Hotel & Spa
$$$–$$$$$ Centro

You couldn't ask for a better location if you want to explore the vibrancy that Vallarta's *centro* has to offer. Located on a wide swath of golden sand beach — and just a few blocks north of the start of the *malecón* — the Premier is easy walking distance or a quick taxi ride to the downtown restaurants, shops, galleries, and clubs. One of the newer hotels in Vallarta (opened in 1999), the architecture is contemporary, but its size gives the hotel an intimate feel. With a first-rate spa and a policy that restricts guests to ages 16 and older, it's a place that caters to relaxation. Four types of rooms are available, and all are decorated in warm colors with tile floors and light wood furnishings. Deluxe rooms have ocean views, with a choice of a king bed or two doubles, a respectable seating area with comfortable chairs, plus a sizable private balcony — request one of several rooms that has an outdoor whirlpool. Premiere suites are larger, and have a separate seating area; seven additional suites have a separate living room plus a dining area with private bar and a spacious terrace. These rooms also have a double whirlpool tub and a separate glass-enclosed shower. The top-of-the-line master suites have all these amenities, plus an outdoor whirlpool on an extra-spacious balcony. Thick terry-cloth robes, slippers, hair dryers, coffeemakers, and a daily restocking of complimentary bottled water are among the notable in-room amenities. The beachfront pool is on the small side, but it's heated in the winter, overlooks the beach, and has attendants to keep you supplied with drinks, snacks, and towels. You have three restaurants to choose from, all which offer spa cuisine dining options, plus 24-hour room service. If you're not tempted by the nearby and accessible dining choices in downtown Vallarta, the Premier offers an all-inclusive option, with all meals and drinks included.

The stunning bi-level spa is the hotel's real attraction. Scented with aromatherapy and glowing with candlelight, it uses top-notch, 100 percent natural products, most based on Mexico's natural treasures such as coconut, aloe, and papaya. The spa has separate men's and women's steam rooms, sauna, locker/dressing rooms, and six private treatment rooms, including hydrotheraphy rooms, for massage and skin care treatments. There's also a salon, and well-equipped fitness room.

San Salvador 117. ☎ *877-886-9176 in the U.S., or 322-226-7001. Fax: 322-226-7043.* www.premiereonline.com.mx. *83 units. Rack rates: High season suite only $135–$430 double, all-inclusive $295–$545 double; low season suite only $135–$370 double, all-inclusive $185–$360 double. AE, MC, V.*

Quinta María Cortez
$$$–$$$$ South Shore/Conchas Chinas

An eclectic, sophisticated, and imaginative B&B on the beach, this is Puerto Vallarta's most original place to stay — and one of Mexico's most memorable inns. Seven large suites, uniquely decorated with antiques, whimsical curios, and original art all feature a private bathroom, and most include a kitchenette and balcony. Sunny terraces, a small pool, and a central gathering area with fireplace and *palapa*-topped dining area (where an excellent full breakfast is served) occupy different levels of this seven-story house. A rooftop terrace offers yet another alternative for taking in the sun and is among the best sunset-watching spots in town. Quinta María is located on a beautiful cove on Playa Conchas Chinas where the rocks sitting just offshore form tranquil tide pools. This B&B wins my highest recommendation, but admittedly, it's not for everyone. Air-conditioned areas are limited due to the open nature of the suites and common areas, but then, the openness is a large part of the allure. Vacationers who love Quinta María find themselves charmed by this remarkable place and its consistently gracious service and return year after year. Not appropriate for children.

Calle Sagitario 126, Playa Conchas Chinas. ☎ *888-640-8100 in the U.S., or 322-221-5317. Fax: 322-221-5327.* www.quinta-maria.com. *7 units. Very limited street parking available. Rack rates: High season $150–$250 double; low season $85–$185 double. Rates include breakfast. AE, MC, V.*

Velas Vallarta Grand Suite Resort
$$$$$ **Marina Vallarta**

The beachfront Velas Vallarta is an excellent choice for families because each suite offers a full-size and fully equipped kitchen, ample living and dining areas, separate bedroom(s), and a large balcony with seating. Following a complete makeover, the suites are decorated in a sophisticated, modern design featuring jewel-tone colors, Huichol art and Mexican textiles, feather beds with goose-down comforters, texturized wall coverings, new 27-inch flat-screen TVs, modern kitchen appliances, and teak wood furniture on balconies and terraces. Special extras include luxury bath amenities and even a pillow menu, from which you can choose the type of pillow you want (based on firmness and stuffing) from a menu of options. This property is actually part hotel and part full-ownership condominium, which means each suite is the size of a true residential unit offering the feeling of a home away from home. The suites all have partial ocean views, and they face onto a central area where three free-form swimming pools, complete with bridges and waterfalls, meander through tropical gardens. A full range of services — including restaurants, mini-market, deli, tennis courts, spa, and boutiques — means you'd never need to leave the place if you didn't want to. The Marina Vallarta Golf Club is across the street, and special packages are available to Velas guests. With a special on-site wedding planner who can arrange every detail in one of a variety of ceremonies, Velas has become a popular place for tying the knot. The resort also offers the Gold Crown All-Inclusive option, with one of the most premium all-inclusive programs in Mexico, offering lobster, finer cuts of beef, and premium liquors, as opposed to the lower-cost food and liquor options provided with most all-inclusives.

Paseo de la Marina 485. ☎ *800-659-8477 in the U.S. and Canada, or 322-221-0091. Fax: 322-221-0751.* www.velasvallarta.com. *361 units. Free indoor parking. Rack rates: Studio $290 double, $420–$720 suite, all-inclusive studio $360 double, all-inclusive suite $720. AE, DC, MC, V.*

Verana
$$$$–$$$$$ **Yelapa**

The magical Verana is among my very favorite places to stay in Mexico. It has an unparalleled ability to inspire immediate relaxation and a deep connection with the natural beauty of the spectacular coast. Although Yelapa is 30 minutes by water taxi from town, even if you're not familiar with the village, I recommend that you consider it. Verana has seven rustic yet sophisticated suites, set into a hillside with sweeping views of the mountains and ocean. Each is a work of art, hand-crafted with care and creativity by owners Heinz Leger, a former film production designer, and prop stylist Veronique Lieve. Each suite has a private terrace and two beds, but you won't find TVs, telephones, stereos, or other distractions. My favorite suite is the Studio; it's the most contemporary, with a wall of floor-to-ceiling windows that perfectly frame the spectacular view. The European-trained chef prepares a nightly dinner of scrumptious creations — global cuisine with a touch of Mexico — at the on-site restaurant, which also serves breakfast and lunch. To wile away your days, soak up some sun at the hilltop pool, raid the small but eclectic library of diverse reading materials, or relax in a sumptuous indoor-outdoor spa. Tours and excursions to nearby — but secluded — beaches are also available, or it's a comfortable walk into Yelapa's town and lively beach. Compare this to the prices of the other rustic-chic resorts along Mexico's Pacific coast, and you find it's a true value. Adventurous travelers shouldn't miss a stay at this unique place. To arrive, management helps arrange transportation to Boca de Tomatlán, where you catch a private boat that takes you to Yelapa; from there, it's a gentle nine-minute hike up to Verana (a mule helps with your bags).

Yelapa, 48300. ☎ *800-530-7176 or 310-360-0155 in the U.S., or 322-222-2360.* www. verana.com. *7 villas. Rack rates: Villa $250–$450 double; 3-bedroom Casa Grande $550 double; five-night minimum stay (seven nights during holiday seasons; shorter stays based on availability). Extra person $60 per night. Mandatory meal plan (breakfast, lunch, and dinner) is $70 per person per day. AE, MC, V.*

Westin Regina Resort
$$$$–$$$$$ Marina Vallarta

The service standard of Westin hotels, combined with the stunning architecture and vibrant colors of this resort, make it a Puerto Vallarta favorite — ideal for almost any traveler or type of vacation. Although the grounds are large — more than 8.4 hectares (21 acres) with 255m (850 ft.) of beachfront — the warm service and gracious hospitality always reminds me of an intimate resort. The central free-form pool with hundreds of tall palms surrounding it is spectacular. You may find hammocks strung between the palms closest to the beach where there are also private beach *cabañas.* Rooms are contemporary in style and brightly colored in textured fabrics. They feature oversized wood furnishings, tile floors, original art, tub/shower-combination bathrooms, and in-room safes. Balconies have panoramic views. Two floors of rooms are designated as the Royal Beach Club and come with special VIP services and private concierge. The fitness center here is one of the most modern, well-equipped facilities of its kind in Vallarta, and three grass tennis courts are available for day or night play, and regularly scheduled classes for spinning, yoga, and Pilates. Guests enjoy play privileges at the Marina Vallarta Golf Club and a kid's club takes care of the activities for younger travelers. **Nikki Beach** (www.nikkibeach.com), a renowned haven for the hip, opened an on-site, beachfront restaurant and club in 2004, complete with big white bed-size lounges for taking in the sun, or enjoying libations anytime from noon until the early morning hours. Their Sunday champagne brunch is especially popular.

Paseo de la Marina Sur 205. ☎ *800-228-3000 in the U.S., or 322-226-1100. Fax: 322-226-1131 or 322-226-1145.* www.westin.com. *280 units. Free parking. Rack rates: High season $255–$599 double, $585–$802 suite; low season $235–$330 double, $480–$600 suite. AE, DC, MC, V.*

Chapter 17

Settling into Puerto Vallarta

by Lynne Bairstow

. . . .

In This Chapter

▶ Knowing what to expect when you arrive

▶ Finding your way around town

▶ Discovering helpful information and resources

. . . .

*F*rom the moment you arrive, you're likely to settle into Puerto Vallarta's welcoming ways. In this chapter, I take you from the plane, through the airport, and to your hotel, helping you quickly get your bearings in this easy-to-navigate town. I also provide tips on everything from taxis to Internet access. You have insider information here — Puerto Vallarta has been my home for the past 15 years!

Arriving in Puerto Vallarta

Puerto Vallarta's airport is easy to get through, so you can segue into sun-soaked days in no time. Recently recognized as the friendliest international city by the travel magazine *Condé Nast Traveler,* Puerto Vallarta is a pleasure. The people here are genuinely welcoming and proud to share their town with visitors. They strive to make your stay as pleasant as possible. Visitors usually get a taste of Puerto Vallarta's hospitality right from the start — you should find both immigration and Customs to be brief, generally easy procedures.

Navigating passport control and Customs

After you deplane, you go through a jetway and wind your way down some stairs into the newly remodeled immigration-clearance area, or a bus may take you directly to immigration from your plane. When you reach immigration, an officer asks you to show your passport and your completed tourist card, the **FMT** (see Chapter 9 for all the FMT details).

 Your FMT is an important document, so take good care of it. You're supposed to keep the FMT with you at all times because you may be required to show it if you run into any sort of trouble. You also need to turn it back in upon departure, or you may be unable to leave without replacing it.

Next up is the baggage claim area. Here, porters stand by to help with your bags, and they're well worth the price of the tip — about a dollar a bag. After you collect your luggage, you pass through another checkpoint. Something that looks like a traffic light awaits you here. You press a button, and if the light turns green, you're free to go. If it turns red, you need to open each of your bags for a quick search. It's Mexico's random search procedure for Customs. If you have an unusually large bag, or an excessive amount of luggage, you may be searched regardless of the traffic-light outcome.

 Just past the traffic light, you pass into an enclosed space with people behind counters — it may look like a tourist information center, but the people behind the counters are actually timeshare sales reps. Unless you want to start your vacation shopping for timeshares with these high-pressure sales pros, keep moving.

Just beyond this entryway you see a bustling crowd of people waiting for fellow passengers, transportation representatives, and taxi drivers promoting their services. If you're part of a package tour that includes ground transportation to your hotel, start looking for your rep here. Generally he or she is carrying a sign with your name or the name of your tour company on it. If you haven't arranged transportation, head for the blue and orange booths marked "Taxi" to purchase set-price tickets to your hotel.

Getting to your hotel

The airport is close to the north end of town near the Marina Vallarta, about 10km (6 miles) from downtown. **Transportes Terrestres** minivans and **Aeromovil** taxis make the trip from the airport to all the hotel areas. Costs for both options are determined by zones — clearly posted at the respective ticket booths. Fares start at $10 for a ride to Marina Vallarta and go up to $30 for a trip to the south-shore hotels. **Airport taxis** (Aeromovil) are federally licensed taxis that operate exclusively to provide transportation from the airport. Their fares are almost three times as high as city (yellow) taxis. A trip from the airport to downtown Puerto Vallarta costs $20, whereas a return trip using a city taxi costs only $6. Yellow cabs are restricted from picking up passengers leaving the airport.

 If you don't have too much baggage, you can walk across the highway via the overpass at the side exit of the airport. Yellow cabs are lined up on the other side of the highway ready to take you anywhere your heart desires for a third of the price of the airport cabs.

Getting Around Puerto Vallarta

Puerto Vallarta is very easy to get around. Essentially, one main road stretches from the airport in both directions around the bay. Puerto Vallarta has followed this central roadway — which changes names a few times along the way — as it has grown along the beach to the north and south. Linking the airport to downtown, the road is called **Avenida Francisco Medina Ascencio** (sometimes still referred to by its previous name, Av. de Las Palmas). Along this main thoroughfare are many luxury hotels (in the area called the **Zona Hotelera,** or **Hotel Zone**), plus several shopping centers with casual restaurants.

As you come into the central downtown area, known as *El Centro,* the main road becomes **Paseo Díaz Ordaz,** which runs north to south through the town. The seaside promenade, called the *malecón,* which borders Paseo Díaz Ordaz, is frequently used as a reference point for giving directions. This section of downtown marked off by the *malecón* is the original town and is sometimes referred to as *Viejo Vallarta* — the cultural and civic heart of Puerto Vallarta. City hall, the waterfront, the open-air Los Arcos Theater, the landmark Our Lady of Guadalupe church, and scores of restaurants, galleries, and shops all call this area home.

From the waterfront, the town stretches back into the hills a half-dozen blocks. The areas bordering the **Río Cuale (Cuale River)** are the oldest parts of town — and home to Gringo Gulch, named for the dozens of U.S. expatriates who made their homes here in the late 1950s.

The area immediately south of the river, called **Olas Altas** after its main street (and sometimes **Los Muertos** after the beach of the same name), is now home to a growing selection of sidewalk cafes, fine restaurants, espresso bars, and hip nightclubs (many with live music).

From the center of town, nearly everything both north and south of the river is within walking distance. **Bridges** on Insurgentes (northbound traffic) and Ignacio L. Vallarta (southbound traffic) link the two sections of town.

Taking a taxi

Taxi travel is the preferred way for getting around Puerto Vallarta. Away from the airport, taxis are plentiful and relatively inexpensive. Most trips from downtown to the northern Zona Hotelera and Marina Vallarta cost between $3.50 and $7; a trip between Marina Vallarta and Playa Mismaloya to the south costs $10. Rates are charged by zone and are generally posted in hotel lobbies. You can also hire taxis by the hour or day for longer trips when you prefer to leave the driving to someone else, a good alternative to renting a car. Rates run between $12 and $15 per hour with discounts available for full-day rates.

Beware of restaurant recommendations offered by taxi drivers — many drivers receive a commission from restaurants where they discharge passengers. Be especially wary if a driver tries to talk you out of a restaurant you've already selected and to one of his own personal "favorites."

Catching a bus

Another option for travel around town — combining cheap, easy transportation with some local color — is Puerto Vallarta's city bus system. Buses run from the airport through the Zona Hotelera along Calle Morelos (1 block inland from the *malecón*), across the Río Cuale, and inland on Vallarta, looping back through the downtown hotel and restaurant districts on Insurgentes and several other downtown streets. To get to the northern Zona Hotelera strip from old Puerto Vallarta, take the Zona Hoteles, Ixtapa, or Las Juntas bus. These buses in the Zona Hotelera follow the same route and may also post the names of hotels they pass such as Krystal, Fiesta Americana, Sheraton, and others. Buses marked "Marina Vallarta" travel inside the Marina Vallarta area and stop at the major hotels there. City buses, which cost about 50¢, can service just about all your transportation needs frequently and inexpensively.

Buses generally run from 6 a.m. to 11 p.m., and waiting more than a few minutes for one is rare. An additional bus route travels south every 10 to 15 minutes to either Playa Mismaloya or Boca de Tomatlán (the last point on the southern shore of the bay that can be reached by land — the destination is indicated in the front window) from Plaza Lázaro Cárdenas, a few blocks south of the river at Cárdenas and Suárez, and along Basilio Badillo, between Pino Suárez and Insurgentes.

Buses in Vallarta tend to be rather aggressive, and some even sport appropriately intimidating names — "Terminator," "Rambo," and "Tornado" are three of my favorites. Don't tempt fate by assuming that these buses stop for pedestrians. Although Vallarta is an extremely low-crime city, bus accidents are frequent — and often fatal.

Renting a car

Rental cars are available at the airport and through travel agencies, but unless you're planning a distant side trip, don't bother. Car rentals are expensive, averaging $66 per day, and parking around town is difficult.

If you see a sign for a $10 Jeep rental or $20 car rental, be aware that it's a lure to get people to attend timeshare presentations. Unless you're interested in a timeshare, stopping to inquire is a waste of your time.

Cruising around

The cruise-ship pier, or *muelle,* also called Terminal Marítima, is where **excursion boats** to Yelapa, Las Animas, Quimixto, and the Marietas Islands depart. The pier is north of town near the airport and just an inexpensive taxi or bus ride away from the Vallarta region. Just take any bus marked "Ixtapa," "Las Juntas," "Pitillal," or "Aurora" and tell the driver to let you off at the Terminal Marítima. ***Note:*** Odd though it may seem, you have to pay a $1.50 fee to access the pier where the tour boats are docked.

Water taxis offering direct transportation to Yelapa, Las Animas, and Quimixto leave at 10:30 and 11 a.m. from the pier at Playa Los Muertos (south of downtown) on Rodolfo Rodríguez next to the Hotel Marsol. Another water taxi departs at 11 a.m. from the beachfront pier at the northern edge of the *malecón*. A round-trip ticket to Yelapa (the farthest point) costs $25. Return trips usually depart between 3 and 4 p.m., but confirm the pickup time with your water-taxi captain. Other water taxis depart from Boca de Tomatlán, located about 30 minutes south of town by public bus. These Boca de Tomatlán water taxis are a better option than those at Playa Los Muertos if you want more flexible departure and return times from the southern beaches. Generally, they leave on the hour for the southern shore destinations, or more frequently if there's heavy traffic. The price is about $12 round-trip with rates clearly posted on a sign on the beach. You can hire a private boat taxi for between $35 and $50 (depending on your destination), which allows you to choose your own return time. The boats take up to eight people for that price, so people often band together at the beach to hire one.

Fast Facts: Puerto Vallarta

American Express

The local office (Morelos 660, at the corner of Abasolo; ☎ 01-800-333-3211 in Mexico, or 322-223-2955) is open Monday to Friday 9 a.m. to 6 p.m. and Saturday 9 a.m. to 1 p.m. This location offers excellent, efficient, travel-agency services in addition to offering currency-exchange and traveler's-checks services.

Area Code

The telephone area code is **322**. The area code for Nuevo Vallarta and the northern areas is **329**.

Baby Sitters

Most of the larger hotels can easily arrange baby sitters, but many sitters speak limited English. Rates range from $5 to $8 per hour.

Banks, ATMs, and Currency Exchange

Banks are located throughout downtown and in the other prime shopping areas of Vallarta. Most banks are open Monday to Friday 9 a.m. to 5 p.m. with partial hours on Saturday. You can find ATMs throughout Vallarta, including the central plaza downtown. They're increasingly becoming the most favorable way to exchange currency because they offer bank rates plus 24-hour, self-service convenience. Money exchange houses *(casas de cambio)* are also located throughout town and offer longer hours than the banks with only slightly lower exchange rates.

Business Hours

Most offices maintain traditional Mexican hours of operation (9 a.m.–2 p.m. and 4–8 p.m., daily), but shops remain open throughout the day. Offices tend to be closed on Saturday and Sunday, but shops are open on Saturday, at least, and increasingly offer limited hours of operation on Sunday. During peak season, many shops and galleries remain open as late as 10 p.m.

Climate

Vallarta is warm all year with tropical temperatures; however, evenings and early mornings in the winter months can turn quite cool. Summers are sunny, but an increase in humidity during the rainy season, between May and October, is the norm. Rains come almost every afternoon in June and July. These usually brief but strong showers are just enough to cool off the air for evening activities. September is the month in which heat and humidity are the least comfortable and rains are the heaviest.

Consular Agents

Both the U.S. and Canadian consulates maintain offices here in the building on the southern border of the central plaza (note the U.S. and Canadian flags). The U.S. Consular Agency office (☎ 322-222-0069; Fax: 322-223-0074; both available 24 hr. a day for emergencies) is open Monday to Friday 10 a.m. to 2 p.m. The Canadian Consulate (☎ 322-293-0099 or 293-0098; 24-hr. emergency line: 01-800-706-2900) is open Monday to Friday 9 a.m. to 3 p.m.

Emergencies

Police emergency (☎ 060); **local police** (☎ 322-290-0513 or 290-0512); **intensive care ambulance** (☎ 322-225-0386; *Note:* English-speaking assistance isn't always available at this number); **Red Cross** (☎ 322-222-1533).

Hospitals

Ameri-Med Urgent Care (☎ 322-221-0023; Fax: 322-221-0026; www.amerimed-hospitals.com) offers healthcare service 24 hours a day that meets U.S. standards and is located at the entrance to Marina Vallarta in the Neptune Plaza. In addition to excellent diagnostic capabilities, it also has emergency facilities and helicopters to evacuate patients to the United States. The excellent San Javier Marina Hospital (☎ 322-226-1010) also offers U.S.-standard healthcare service that's available 24 hours. It's located on the main highway across from the cruise-ship terminal (Terminal Marítima).

Information

The Municipal Tourism Office (Juárez and Independencia; ☎ 322-223-2500, ext. 230, ask for the Tourism Office) is in a corner of the white Presidencia Municipal building (city hall) on the northwest end of the main square. In addition to offering a listing of current events and a collection of promotional brochures for local activities and services, these folks can also assist you with specific questions — an English-speaking person is usually on staff. This is also the office of the tourist police. It's open Monday to Friday 8 a.m. to 4 p.m.

The exceptionally helpful and friendly State Tourism Office (Plaza Marina, Local 144, second floor; ☎ 322-221-2676, -2677, or -2678) also offers promotional brochures and can assist you with specific questions about Puerto Vallarta and other points within the state of Jalisco including Guadalajara, the Costa Alegre, and the town of Tequila. It's open Monday to Friday 9 a.m. to 5 p.m. and Saturday 9 a.m. to 1 p.m.

Internet Access

Puerto Vallarta is probably the best-connected destination in Mexico as far as the Internet goes. Of the numerous cyber-cafes around town, one of the most popular is The Net House (Ignacio L. Vallarta 232, 2 blocks past the southbound bridge; ☎ 322-222-6953; info@vallartacafes.com). It's open daily 8 a.m. to 2 a.m. Rates are $4 per hour, and there are 21 computers with fast connections and English keyboards. Café.com (Olas Altas 250, at the corner of Basilio Badillo; ☎ 322-222-0092) has become a social hub. Rates run $2 for 30 minutes. Complete computer services, a full bar, and food service are also available. It's open daily 8 a.m. to 2 a.m. Some hotels also offer e-mail kiosks in their lobbies, but this is a more expensive option than the Net cafes.

Maps

One of the best around is the free American Express map, usually found at the tourist information offices and the local American Express office. Other free maps of the area are available at the Municipal Tourism Office, on the southeast corner of city hall (the corner nearest to the Our Lady of Guadalupe church).

Newspapers and Magazines

Vallarta Today, a daily English-language newspaper (☎ **322-225-3323** or 224-2829; www.vallartatoday.com), is a good source for local information and upcoming events. The quarterly city magazine, *Vallarta Lifestyles* (☎ **322-221-0106**), is also very popular. It has plenty of helpful information and good colored maps of all the major tourist areas. Both publications are available for sale at area newsstands and hotel gift shops although you can also find them distributed for free at local businesses. The weekly *P.V. Tribune* (☎ **322-223-0585**) is distributed free throughout town and offers an objective local viewpoint.

Pharmacy

CMQ Farmacia (Basilio Badillo 365; ☎ **322-222-1330**) is open 24 hours and can also deliver to your hotel free of charge with a minimum purchase of $20. Farmacia Guadalajara (Emiliano Zapata 232; ☎ **322-224-1811**) is also open 24 hours a day.

Police

The policemen in white, safari-style uniforms with white pith helmets belong to a special corps of English-speaking police established to assist tourists. For the main police department, call ☎ **322-290-0513** or 290-0512.

Post Office

The post office (*correo;* Mina 188; ☎ **322-222-1888**) is open Monday to Friday 9 a.m. to 6:30 p.m. and Saturday 9 a.m. to 1 p.m.

Safety

Puerto Vallarta enjoys a very low crime rate. Public transportation is perfectly safe to use, and tourist police (dressed in white safari uniforms with white hats) are available to answer questions, give directions, and offer assistance. Most crimes or encounters with the police are linked to using or purchasing drugs, so simply don't do it. *Note:* The tourist police are making a more frequent habit of conducting random personal searches for drugs. Although some questions have arisen about their right to do this, the best course of action is to comply if they want to frisk you — objecting may result in a free tour of the local jail. Report any unusual incidents to the local consular office.

Taxes

There's a 15 percent value-added tax (IVA) on goods and services, and it's generally included in the posted price.

Taxis

Taxis are plentiful and relatively inexpensive. Most trips from downtown to the northern Zona Hotelera and Marina Vallarta cost between $3.50 and $7; trips between Marina Vallarta and Mismaloya Beach to the south cost $10. Rates are charged by zone and are generally posted in the lobbies of hotels. You can also hire taxis by the hour or day for longer trips when you prefer to leave the driving to someone else. Rates run between $12 and $15 per hour with discounts available for full-day rates.

Telephone

Avoid the phone booths that have signs in English advising you to call home using a special 800 number — these are absolute rip-offs and can cost as much as $20 per minute. The least expensive way to call is by using a Telmex (LADATEL) prepaid phone card, available at most pharmacies and mini-supers, using the official Telmex (Lada) public phones. In Mexico you need to dial 001 prior to a number to reach the United States, and you need to preface long distance calls within Mexico by dialing 01.

Time Zone

Puerto Vallarta operates on central standard time, but Mexico's observance of daylight saving time varies somewhat from that in the United States.

Chapter 18

Dining in Puerto Vallarta

by Lynne Bairstow

. . . .

In This Chapter

▶ Discovering Puerto Vallarta's best restaurants
▶ Finding a restaurant with true Mexican ambience
▶ Dining on the *malecón* and in the jungle

. . . .

*P*uerto Vallarta has the most exceptional dining scene of any resort town in Mexico. More than 250 restaurants serve cuisines from around the world in addition to fresh seafood and regional dishes. Chefs from France, Switzerland, Germany, Italy, and Argentina have come for visits and then stayed to open their own restaurants. In celebration of the diversity of dining experiences available, Vallarta's culinary community hosts a two-week-long Gourmet Dining Festival each November.

As in many of Mexico's beach resorts, even the finest restaurants in town can be comfortably casual when it comes to dress. Men seldom wear jackets, although ladies frequently don dressy resort wear — basically, everything goes. Remember that dinner tends to take on the dual nature of Puerto Vallarta — many tourists dine at earlier hours, but locals are apt to just be thinking about dinner at 9 p.m., so many restaurants stay open late.

Nonetheless, dining isn't limited to high-end options — you can also find plenty of small, family-owned restaurants, local Mexican kitchens, and vegetarian cafes. Vallarta also has its share of imported, food-and-fun chains: Hard Rock Cafe, Outback Steakhouse, and even Hooters. I don't bother reviewing these restaurants because the consistency and décor are so familiar. Resist the temptation to go with what you know, though. Trust me — the locally owned restaurants offer both the best food and the best value.

Vallarta on the whole is a very child-friendly place, and families are welcome to bring their children almost anywhere. If your young ones are particular to more American tastes, standards such as McDonald's, Burger King, Hard Rock Cafe, Carl's Junior, and KFC — good choices — are here, but you may also want to try one of their Mexican counterparts — Carlos O'Brian's or Papaya 3, both located downtown.

Puerto Vallarta's Best Restaurants

Unless you're visiting during the height of high season, you generally don't need reservations — especially with the number and range of excellent restaurants in Vallarta. I note reservation information for the few exceptions that tend to be very busy.

Contrary to conventional travel wisdom, most of the best restaurants in the Marina Vallarta area are actually located in hotels. Especially notable are **Andrea,** at Velas Vallarta, for fine Italian cuisine, and **Nikki Beach,** on the beachfront of the Westin Regina Resort, for a hip atmosphere with a specialty of seafood and sushi. (See Chapter 16 for more information on these resorts.) You can find other choices along the boardwalk bordering the marina yacht harbor. A notable stop is the **Café Max,** next to the Vallarta Adventures offices in Condominiums Marina Golf, Local 11. It serves excellent coffee and espresso drinks, plus pastries and light snacks and sandwiches, and is open Monday through Saturday from 8 a.m. to 1 p.m., and 4 p.m. to 10:30 p.m. (no credit cards).

The most condensed restaurant area, Zona Romántica, is south of the Río Cuale. The area's street, Basilio Badillo, is even nicknamed "Restaurant Row." A second main dining drag has emerged along Olas Altas, where you can find all varieties of foods and price categories. The wide sidewalks are lined with cafes and espresso bars, which are generally open 7 a.m. to midnight.

All the restaurants I include in the following listings are arranged alphabetically with their location and general price category noted. Please refer to the Introduction of this book for an explanation of the price categories. Remember that tips generally run about 15 percent, and most waitstaff really depend on these for their income, so be generous if the service warrants.

Please see the menu glossary in Appendix C for more information on Mexican cuisine.

Finding inexpensive, vegetarian options

The best inexpensive local spots are downtown. The long-standing favorite spot for light meals and fresh fruit drinks is the tiny **Tutifruti,** Allende 220 (☎ **322-222-1068**), which is open Monday through Saturday 9 a.m. to 4 p.m. An inexpensive, bountiful, and delicious vegetarian buffet is a daily hit at **Planeta Vegetariano,** Iturbide 270, just down the street from the Our Lady of Guadalupe church (☎ **322-222-3073**). The buffet is offered from 11:30 a.m. to 10 p.m. and costs $6.50 (no credit cards). A vegetarian breakfast buffet is also available from 8 until noon for $4.50. Planeta Vegetariano is closed on Sundays.

Agave Grill
$–$$ Centro MEXICAN

Opening its doors in late 2004, Agave Grill took over most of the space at the Casa de Tequila, where it's located in the back, in a beautiful garden setting, within this classic Hacienda-style building in central downtown. The space has been put to excellent use: This cafe serves modern, casual Mexican cuisine and is an ideal spot to stop for a snack or a margarita while shopping. Start with an order of chiles anchos, stuffed with cream cheese and raisins, or the *antojitos mexicanos,* a sampler of Mexican snacks including sopes, quesadillas, a tamale, and guacamole. Favorite main courses include *mole poblano,* or the beef filet in a chile pasilla gravy, served with mashed sweet potatoes and grilled watermelon. For a sweet finish, don't miss their chocolate truffle with coconut foam in a strawberry salsa. All tortillas are handmade, as are the savory salsas. An elegant bar borders the room, serving undoubtedly Vallarta's most original selection of fine tequilas, many from small distilleries. In addition to the tequilas and fresh fruit margaritas, Agave Grill also serves a selection of fine Mexican wines.

Morelos 589. ☎ *322-222-2000. Main courses: $6–$17. MC, V. Open: Mon–Sat noon– 11 p.m.*

Archie's Wok
$–$$ Centro/Zona Romántica ASIAN/SEAFOOD

Since 1986, Archie's has been legendary in Puerto Vallarta for serving original cuisine influenced by the intriguing flavors of Thailand, China, and the Philippines. Archie was Hollywood director John Huston's private chef during the years Huston spent in the area. Today, Archie's wife Cindy continues his legacy. The drinks — including a Thai mai tai and other tropical drinks that are made from only fresh fruit and juices — are a good way to kick off a meal here, as are the Filipino spring rolls, which are consistently crispy and delicious. The popular Singapore fish filet features lightly battered fillet strips in a sweet-and-sour sauce, and the Thai garlic shrimp is prepared with fresh garlic, ginger, cilantro, and black pepper. Vegetarians have plenty of options, including the broccoli, tofu, mushroom, and cashew stir-fry in a black bean and sherry sauce. Finish things off with the signature Spice Islands coffee or a slice of lime cheese pie. Live classical music sets the atmosphere in Archie's Oriental garden Thursday to Saturday from 8 to 11 p.m.

Francisca Rodríguez 130, ½ block from the Los Muertos pier. ☎ *322-222-0411.* awok@ pvnet.com.mx. *Main courses: $6–$21. MC, V. Open: Mon–Sat 2–11 p.m. Closed Sept–Oct.*

Arrayán
$–$$ Centro MEXICAN

The traditional but original Arrayán is the darling of casual, local eateries — and the pot of gold at the end of the rainbow for anyone in search of authentic Mexican cuisine. Owner Carmen Porras enlisted Mexico City

Marina Vallarta Dining

chef Carmen Titita (praised by James Beard for her culinary work) to assist in the design of the kitchen and creation of the restaurant's concise menu, which features the genuine Mexican food of different regions. The open-air (but covered) dining area surrounds a cozy courtyard, while its exposed brick walls and funky-chic décor showcase a modern view of Mexican classics — tin tubs serve as sinks in the bathrooms, while colorful oilcloths cover the tables and Huichol art pieces enliven the dining room. Start with an order of sumptuous plantain empanadas filled with black beans and cheese or an unusual salad of diced nopal cactus paddles with fresh panela cheese. Favorite main courses include their "off the menu special" tacos filled with prime beef filet, or duck *carnitas,* a Mexican style duck confit, served in an *arrayán*-orange sauce. (Arrayán, the namesake of the place, is a small bittersweet fruit, native to the region.) Homemade, fresh-fruit ice creams are an especially tasty finish to your meal. The full bar offers an extensive selection of tequilas and regional liquors, with a creative menu of drink specials — my favorite is their *raicilla* martini — made from a regional distillation, infused with herbs, and their version of the mojito, with vodka and basil, is also quite tasty. Non-alcoholic beverages center around "aqua frescas," blended drinks of fresh fruit and water. You can't miss the pink facade with the large bell at the entry. The excellent service is a plus to this can't-miss dining experience.

Allende 344, just past the intersection with Matamoros, 3 blocks east of the malecón. ☎ *322-222-7195.* www.elarrayan.com.mx. *Main courses: $13–$18. MC, V. Open: Wed–Mon 6–11 p.m., closed Tues.*

Benitto's
$ Marina Vallarta CAFE

Wow! What a sandwich! Benitto's food is reason enough to come, but this tiny yet terrific cafe (located inside the Plaza Neptuno shopping center) also offers an original array of sauces and very personable waitstaff. Popular with locals for light breakfasts, filling lunches, and even fondue and wine in the evenings, Benitto's is the best place in town to find pastrami, corned beef, or other traditional (gringo!) sandwich fare, all served on your choice of gourmet bread. Draft beer and wine are available as are Benitto's specialty infused waters.

Inside Plaza Neptuno, Francisco Medina Ascencio by Marina Vallarta. ☎ *322-209-0287.* benittoscafe@prodigy.net.mx. *Main courses: $5–$7; breakfast $3–$6. No credit cards. Open: Mon–Sat. 8:30 a.m.–9 p.m.*

Café des Artistes/Thierry Blouet Cocina de Autor
$$–$$$$ Centro FRENCH/INTERNATIONAL

If you want one over-the-top dining experience in Puerto Vallarta, Café des Artistes is the hands-down choice. Creative in its menu and innovative in design, this dinner-only location rivals those in any major metropolitan city for its culinary sophistication, and may soon become a reason in itself to visit Vallarta. The award-winning chef and owner, Thierry Blouet, is both a member of the Académie Culinaire de France and a Maître Cuisinier de France. In late 2003, the singular dining experience of the Café des Artistes evolved to complete a trio of special places, adding the upscale Constantini Bar Lounge and the separate but connected Thierry Blouet Cocina de Autor dining area. All are located in a restored house that resembles a castle. The interior of the original Café des Artistes combines murals, lush fabrics, and an array of original artworks, with both an interior dining area as well as a lushly landscaped terraced garden area, open only during the winter and spring. The menu of this section is a changing delight of French gourmet bistro fare, which draws heavily on Chef Blouet's French training, yet uses regional specialty ingredients. A few of the noteworthy entrees include sea bass filet served with polenta, and the renowned roasted duck glazed with honey, soy, ginger, and lime sauce, and served with a pumpkin risotto.

At the Cocina de Autor, the atmosphere is sleek and stylish, and the fixed-price tasting menu (prices depend on the number of plates you select, between three and six, from a long list of starters, entrees, and desserts) offers you a choice of the chef's most innovative and sumptuous creations, with each dish creatively combining ingredients to present one memorable

Downtown Puerto Vallarta Dining

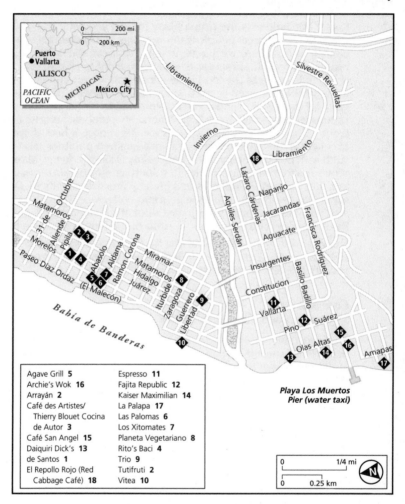

Agave Grill **5**
Archie's Wok **16**
Arrayán **2**
Café des Artistes/
   Thierry Blouet Cocina
   de Autor **3**
Café San Angel **15**
Daiquiri Dick's **13**
de Santos **1**
El Repollo Rojo (Red
   Cabbage Café) **18**

Espresso **11**
Fajita Republic **12**
Kaiser Maximilian **14**
La Palapa **17**
Las Palomas **6**
Los Xitomates **7**
Planeta Vegetariano **8**
Rito's Baci **4**
Trio **9**
Tutifruti **2**
Vitea **10**

*Playa Los Muertos
Pier (water taxi)*

flavor. The Cocina also provides perfect wine pairings, if desired. After your meal, you're invited to the cognac and cigar room, an exquisite blend of old adobe walls, flickering candles, and elegant leather chairs. Or move on to the adjacent Constantini Bar Lounge, with its live jazz music and plush sofas, for a fitting close to a memorable meal. Without a doubt, it's all worth the splurge.

Guadalupe Sanchez 740, at Leona Vicario. ☎ **322-222-3228** *or -3229.* www. cafedesartistes.com. *Reservations required. Main courses: $9–$31; Cocina de Autor tasting menu ranges from $25–$68. AE, MC, V. Open: Daily 6–11:30 p.m.; the lounge stays open until 2 a.m.*

Café Kaiser Maximilian
$–$$ Centro/Zona Romántica   INTERNATIONAL

Kaiser Maximilian is the prime place to go if you want to combine exceptional food with great people-watching. This bistro-style cafe has a casually elegant atmosphere with a genuinely European feel to it. Austrian-born owner Andreas Rupprechter is always on hand to ensure that the service is as impeccable as the food is delicious. Indoor, air-conditioned dining is at cozy tables dressed in crisp white linens; sidewalk tables are larger and great for groups of friends. The cuisine merges old-world European preparations with regional, fresh ingredients. My personal favorite is the filet of trout with watercress and beet sauce, served on a bed of spinach. Also excellent is the mustard chicken with mashed potatoes, and the rack of lamb with polenta, endive, and lima beans is simply divine. Maximilian also offers northern-European classics such as *rahmschnitzel* (sautéed pork loin and homemade noodles in a creamy mushroom sauce). Desserts are especially tempting, as are the gourmet coffees — Maximilian has its own Austrian cafe and pastry shop next door. It's located at the intersection of Basilio Badillo and Olas Altas, in front of the Playa Los Arcos Hotel.

Olas Altas 380, on the sidewalk level of the Playa Los Arcos Hotel. ☎ *322-223-0760.* www.kaisermaximilian.com. *Reservations recommended in high season. Main courses: $16–$26. AE, MC, V. Open: Mon–Sat 6–11 p.m.*

Café San Angel
$ Centro/Zona Romántica   CAFE

A comfortable, classic, sidewalk cafe, Café San Angel is a local gathering place from sunrise to sunset. For breakfast, choose between a burrito stuffed with eggs and chorizo sausage, a three-egg Western omelet, crepes filled with mushrooms, or a tropical fruit plate. Deli sandwiches, crepes, and pastries round out the small but ample menu. The cafe also has exceptional fruit smoothies (such as the Yelapa — a blend of mango, banana, and orange juice) and perfectly made espresso drinks. As much as I love it here, I have to warn you that the service is reliably slow and frequently frustrating, so choose this place if time is on your side, though it does offer the best people-watching in the area to help you endure the slow service. Bar service and Internet access are also available.

Olas Altas 449, corner of Francisca Rodríguez. ☎ *322-223-1273. Main courses: $3.50–$6; breakfast $3.50–$6. No credit cards. Open: Daily 8 a.m.–1 a.m.*

Daiquiri Dick's
$–$$ Centro/Zona Romántica   MODERN AMERICAN

A Vallarta dining institution, Daiquiri Dick's has been around for more than 20 years, evolving its winning combination of décor, service, and scrumptious cuisine. The menu is among Vallarta's most sophisticated, and the genuinely warm staff and open-air location fronting Playa Los Muertos add to the feeling of casual comfort. As lovely as the restaurant is, though, and as notorious as the fresh-fruit daiquiris are, the food is the main attraction, incorporating touches of Tuscan, Thai, and Mexican. Start with grilled asparagus wrapped in prosciutto and topped with shaved asiago cheese, then try an entree such as sesame-crusted tuna, grilled rare and served with wild greens; pistachio chicken served with polenta; or my favorite, simple yet indulgent lobster tacos. Chocolate banana bread pudding makes a perfect finish. Daiquiri Dick's is a great place for groups, as well as for a romantic dinner. It's one of the few places that is equally enjoyable for breakfast, lunch, or dinner.

Olas Altas 314. ☎ **322-222-0566.** www.ddpv.com. *Reservations recommended. Main courses: $6.50–$21. AE, MC, V. Daily 9 a.m.–10:30 p.m. Closed Sept.*

de Santos
$–$$ Centro   MEDITERRANEAN

After it opened a few years ago, de Santos quickly became the hot spot in town for late-night dining and bar action. Although the dining aspect initially didn't live up to the atmosphere and music, it does now. The fare is Mediterranean-inspired; the best bets include lightly breaded calamari, paella Valencia, lobster ravioli, and excellent thin-crust pizzas. Other good choices are the nightly specials — always the most creative offerings on the menu. The cool, refined interior — recently remodeled to expand the dining area — has exposed brick walls, crisp white-clothed tables, and lots of votive candles, and feels more urban than resort. The place boasts the most sophisticated sound system in town — including its own DJ who spins to match the crowd's mood. It probably helps that one of the partners is also a member of Maná, the chart-topping, wildly popular Latin group. Prices are extremely reasonable for the quality and overall experience of an evening here. Start with dinner and then stay on and enjoy the most favored club in town, of the same name, located next door (see Chapter 19).

Morelos 771, between Pipila and Leona Vicario. ☎ **322-223-3052.** www.desantos. com.mx. *Reservations recommended. Main courses: $5–$20; wine and mixed drinks $3–$5. AE, MC, V. Open: Daily 6 p.m.–2 a.m.; bar open until 5 a.m. on weekends.*

El Repollo Rojo (Red Cabbage Cafe)
$–$$ Centro   MEXICAN

This tiny, hard-to-find cafe is worth the effort — a visit here rewards you with exceptional, traditional Mexican cuisine and a whimsical crash course in the contemporary culture of Mexico. The small room is covered wall to wall and table to table with photographs, paintings, movie posters, and news clippings about Mexico's cultural icons. The Mexican painter Frida Kahlo (the same Frida that Salma Hayek portrayed in the film, *Frida*) figures prominently in the décor, and a special menu duplicates dishes that she and husband Diego Rivera prepared for guests. Specialties from all over Mexico are featured, including the divine *chiles en nogada* (poblano chiles stuffed with ground beef, pine nuts, and raisins, topped with a sweet cream sauce and served cold), an intricate chicken *mole* from Puebla, and the hearty *carne en su jugo* (steak in its juice). El Repollo Rojo isn't the place for an intimate conversation, however — the poor acoustics cause everyone's conversations to blend together, although generally what you're hearing from adjacent tables are raves about the food. Also, this is about the only nonsmoking restaurant in town that I'm aware of.

Calle Rivera del Río 204 A, across from the Río Cuale. ☎ *322-223-0411. Main courses: $5–$20. No credit cards. Open: Daily 5–10:30 p.m.*

Espresso
$ **Centro/Zona Romántica   ITALIAN**

This eatery is Vallarta's best late-night dining option, and especially popular with *vallartenses* (locals). The two-level restaurant is on one of the town's busiest streets — across from El Torito's sports bar, and cater-cornered from the lively Señor Frog's — meaning that traffic noise is a factor, though not a deterrent. The food is superb, the service attentive, and the prices more than reasonable. Owned by a partnership of lively Italians, it serves food that is authentic in preparation and flavor, from thin-crust, brick-oven pizzas to savory homemade pastas. My favorite pizza is the Quattro Stagioni, topped with artichokes, black olives, ham, and mushrooms. Excellent calzones and panini (sandwiches) are also options. I prefer the rooftop garden area for dining, but many patrons gravitate to the pool tables in the air-conditioned downstairs, which features major sports and entertainment events on satellite TV. Espresso also has full bar service and draft beer — oh yes, and also espresso.

Ignacio L. Vallarta 279. ☎ *322-222-3272. Main courses: $6.50–$13. MC, V. Open: Daily 9 a.m.–2 a.m.*

Fajita Republic
$–$$ **Centro/Restaurant Row   MEXICAN/SEAFOOD/STEAKS**

Fajita Republic has hit on a winning recipe: delicious food, ample portions, welcoming atmosphere, and low prices. The restaurant is casual, fun, and festive in atmosphere, and situated in a garden of mango and palm trees with a view of the passing action on the bordering street. The specialty is, of course, fajitas, grilled to perfection in every variety: steak, chicken, shrimp, combo, and vegetarian. All come with a generous tray of salsas and toppings. This tropical grill also serves sumptuous BBQ ribs, grilled shrimp, and Mexican *molcajetes* (dishes served in these stone bowls traditionally used in Mexico for grinding and puréeing) with incredibly tender strips of marinated beef filet. Starters include fresh guacamole served in a giant spoon and the ever-popular Maya cheese sticks (cheese, breaded and deep-fried). Try a "Fajita Rita Mango Margarita" — or one of the other spirited temptations — served in oversized mugs or by the pitcher. A new, second location in Nuevo Vallarta, across from the Velas Resort is drawing equal raves, with the same menu and prices.

Pino Suárez 321, corner of Basilio Badillo, 1 block north of Olas Altas. ☎ *322-222-3131. Main courses: $9–$17. MC, V. Open: Daily 5 p.m.–midnight.*

La Palapa
$–$$ Centro/Zona Romántica   SEAFOOD/MEXICAN

This lovely, open-air, *palapa*-roofed (thatched umbrella) restaurant on the beach is a decades-old local favorite, and with each recent visit, I've found that the quality of both the food and service keeps improving. It's an exceptional dining experience, day or night. Enjoy a tropical breakfast by the sea, lunch on the beach, cocktails at sunset, or a romantic dinner — at night the staff sets cloth-covered tables in the sand. For lunch and dinner, seafood is the specialty. Featured dishes include macadamia and coconut shrimp in a litchi-fruit sauce and poached red snapper with fresh cilantro sauce — but note that the menu changes regularly, and that La Palapa also offers daily specials. The fresh catch is listed on a chalkboard and is served in much thicker portions than at most local restaurants — simply sumptuous, and prepared to your preference. La Palapa's location in the heart of Playa Los Muertos makes it an exceptional place to either start or end the day; I favor it for breakfast or, even better, for a late-night dessert and specialty coffee while watching the moon over the bay with the sand at my feet. A particular favorite is the all-you-can-enjoy Sunday brunch, which entitles you to a spot on popular Playa Los Muertos for the day! A plus at lunch is you can enjoy the extra-comfortable beach chairs for post-lunch sunbathing. A classy bar area features acoustic guitars and vocals nightly from 8 to 11 p.m., frequently performed by the very talented owner Alberto himself.

Pulpito 103. ☎ *322-222-5225.* www.lapalapapv.com. *Reservations recommended for dinner in high season. Main courses: $7–$28; salads or sandwiches $5–$12; breakfast $2.50–$12. AE, MC, V. Open: Daily 9 a.m.–11 p.m.*

Las Palomas
$–$$ Centro   MEXICAN

One of Puerto Vallarta's first restaurants, this is the power-breakfast place of choice for local movers and shakers — and a generally popular hangout for everyone else throughout the day. Authentic in atmosphere and menu, Las Palomas is one of Puerto Vallarta's few genuine Mexican restaurants and has the atmosphere of a gracious home. Breakfast is the best value. The staff pours mugs of steaming coffee spiced with cinnamon as soon as you're seated. Try the classic *huevos rancheros* (fried eggs served on a soft fried corn tortilla and topped with red sauce — spicy or mild) or *chilaquiles* (tortilla strips, fried and topped with a red or green spicy sauce, cream cheese, and fried eggs). Lunch and dinner offer other traditional Mexican specialties plus a selection of stuffed crepes. The best place for checking out the *malecón* and watching the sun set while sipping an icy margarita is at the spacious bar or upstairs terrace.

Paseo Díaz Ordaz 594. ☎ *322-222-3675.* www.laspalomaspvr.com. *Main courses: $8.50–$22; breakfast $3.50–$10; lunch $8.50–$20. AE, MC, V. Open: Daily 8 a.m.–11 p.m.*

Vallarta's jungle dining

Want to get wild while you dine? One of the unique attractions of Puerto Vallarta is its group of "jungle restaurants," located to the south of town toward Playa Mismaloya. Each restaurant offers open-air dining in a tropical setting by the sea or beside a mountain river. A stop for swimming and lunch at one of these places is included in many of the "jungle" or "tropical" tours (see Chapter 19 for more about these tours).

If you travel on your own, a taxi is the best transportation because all the jungle restaurants are located quite a distance from the main highway. Taxis are usually waiting for return patrons.

The most recommendable of the jungle restaurants is **El Nogalito** (☎/fax 322-221-5225). Located beside a clear jungle stream, this exceptionally clean, beautifully landscaped ranch serves lunch, beverages, and snacks on a shady terrace in a relaxing atmosphere. Several hiking routes also depart from the grounds. El Nogalito's guides point out the area's native plants, birds, and wildlife. To get to El Nogalito, take a taxi or travel to Punta Negra, just about 8km (5 miles) south of downtown Puerto Vallarta. A well-marked sign points to Calzada del Cedro, a dirt road leading to the ranch. El Nogalito is much closer to town than the other jungle restaurants and is open daily from noon to 5:30 p.m. (no credit cards).

Just past Boca de Tomatlán, at Highway 200 Km 20, is **Chico's Paradise** (☎ 322-223-6005 or -6006), which offers spectacular views of massive rocks and the surrounding jungle and mountains. Natural pools and waterfalls for swimming are located here, plus a small *mercado* (market) selling pricey trinkets. The menu features excellent seafood (the seafood platter for two is excellent — lobster, clams, giant shrimp, crab, and fish fillets) as well as Mexican dishes. The quality is quite good, and the portions are generous, although prices are higher than in town — remember, you're paying for the setting. Chico's is open daily from 10 a.m. to 6 p.m. (no credit cards).

Porto Bello
$–$$ Marina Vallarta   ITALIAN

One of the first restaurants in the marina, Porto Bello remains a favorite. It features authentically flavorful Italian dishes and exceptional service in a casual atmosphere overlooking the marina. For starters, the fried calamari is delicately seasoned, and the grilled vegetable antipasto can easily serve as a full meal. Signature dishes include Fusilli Porto Bello prepared with black olives, artichokes, lemon juice, olive oil, and basil, and veal scaloppine with a creamy white-wine sauce, mushrooms, and shrimp. Most people prefer seating on the gazebo-like patio overlooking the boats in the marina. Indoor dining is air-conditioned, and occasionally, live music fills the air in the evenings.

Marina Sol, Local 7 (Marina Vallarta malecón). ☎ **322-221-0003**. *Main courses: $8–$24. AE, MC, V. Open: Daily noon–11 p.m.*

Rito's Baci
$–$$ Centro   ITALIAN

If the food wasn't a reason to come here (and it definitely is), then Rito himself and his gentle, devoted way of caring for every detail of this cozy *trattoria* would be the draw. His grandfather emigrated from Italy, so the recipes and traditions of Italian food come naturally to him. His passion for food is obvious as he describes the specialties, which include lasagna (vegetarian, *verde,* or meat-filled); ravioli stuffed with spinach and ricotta cheese; spaghetti with garlic, anchovy, and lemon zest; and a side of homemade Italian sausage. Everything, in fact, is made by hand from fresh ingredients. Pizza lovers favor the Piedmonte, with that famous sausage and mushrooms, and the Horacio, a cheeseless pizza with tomatoes, oregano, and basil. Sandwiches come hot or cold and are a two-handed operation. Rito's is located 1½ blocks off the *malecón* on Josefa Ortiz Domínguez next to Galeria A.L.

Domínguez 181, between Morelos and Juárez. ☎ **322-222-6448**. *Pasta $9–$19; salads and sandwiches $4–$7; pizzas $13–$22. No credit cards. Open: Daily 3–11 p.m.*

Trio
$–$$ Centro   INTERNATIONAL

Trio remains the darling of Vallarta restaurants, and is especially popular with Vallarta's local residents. Diners beat a path to this modest but stylish cafe because the chef/owners Bernhard Güth and Ulf Henriksson both share an undeniable passion for food, which is exhibited in each dish. Güth and Henriksson have combined local ingredients with their impressive culinary experience; the result is memorable entrees such as San Blas shrimp in a fennel-tomato vinaigrette served over broiled nopal cactus, herb risotto with toasted sunflower seeds and quail, and pan-roasted sea bass with glazed grapes, mashed potatoes, and sauerkraut in a white pepper sauce — but these dishes may not be on the menu when you arrive because Trio is a constantly changing work of art! Trio is noted for its perfect melding of Mexican and Mediterranean flavors. What's great about this place, besides everything I've already mentioned, is that despite a sophisticated menu, the atmosphere is always comfortable and welcoming — Bernhard and Ulf are regularly seen chatting with guests at the end of an evening. A rooftop bar area makes for a comfortable wait for a table or a great spot to enjoy an after-dinner coffee. A real treat!

Guerrero 264. ☎ **322-222-2196**. www.triopv.com. *Reservations recommended. Main courses: $14–$26. Lunch available in high season only. AE, MC, V. Open: Mon–Sat noon–4 p.m.; daily 6 p.m.–midnight.*

Tapas, anyone?

Certainly, much of modern Mexico's culture draws on the important influence of Spain, so it only makes sense that culinary traditions would be evident as well. Within the last several years, dining on tapas has soared in popularity here. Of the many options, these are my favorites: The long-standing **Barcelona Tapas,** Matamoros and 31 de Octubre streets (☎ 322-222-0510), a large and lovely restaurant on a terrace built high on a hillside, with sweeping views of the bay. They serve tapas and a selection of Spanish entrees, including paella, from 5 p.m. to midnight. **La Taberna de San Pascual,** Corona 176 (☎ 322-223-9371; Wed–Mon 4 p.m.–1 a.m., with bar service extending to 2 a.m.; closed Tues) is a cozy eatery, rich with brick walls and dark wood accents, located on popular Corona Street, in the center of downtown. All ingredients are imported from Spain, and there's a selection of excellent Spanish wines to accompany their flavorful tapas. **La Esquina de los Caprichos,** Miramar 402, corner of Iturbide (☎ 322-222-0911; Mon–Sat 1–10 p.m.) is a tiny tapas place, known as having the most reasonably priced ($2.50–$6) tapas in town, and perhaps the tastiest.

Vitea
$–$$ **Centro   BISTRO**

This beachfront bistro was opened in late 2004 by the chef/owners of Trio, and their recipe for success took hold from day one — the place is already bustling at any hour, and has become the new favorite among local residents. Due to strategically-placed mirrors on the back wall, every seat has a view of the ocean, while the eclectic interior is cheerful and inviting. Seating is at small bistro-style tables, along a banquette that runs the length of the back wall, or at the small but beautiful bar. The long, narrow bistro faces the waterfront between the central plaza and river, which has recently completed a restoration — extending the *malecón* to pass by Vitea. But enough about looks — what counts here is the exceptional fare, which is both classic and original. Starters include a tomato and Roquefort salad with pecans, foie gras with Spanish plum sauce, and an exquisite bistro salad with bacon. Quiche is always on the menu, with changing selections, and main courses include chickpea ravioli with portobello mushrooms, Wiener schintzel with salad, or a traditional steak frites. Lunch offers lighter fare, including heavenly deli sandwiches. You won't be disappointed here, no matter what you order! There's a full bar with an excellent selection of wines, and the service is exceptional.

Malecón #2, at Libertad. ☎ *322-222-8703 or 222-8695. Main courses: $7–$19. MC, V. Open: Daily noon–midnight.*

Xitomates
$–$$ Centro   MEXICAN

Located in the heart of downtown, this creative Mexican restaurant has earned raves for its intimate atmosphere and chef/owner Luis Fitch Gómez's exceptionally creative versions of the country's culinary treasures. It's named for one of Mexico's contributions to gastronomy — the tomato (Xitomatl, in the ancient Aztec language of Náhuatl). The menu mixes Mexican with Caribbean, Asian, and Mediterranean influences, and the presentation is as creative as the preparation. Starters include the signature coconut shrimp in a tangy tamarind sauce, thinly sliced scallops with cucumber and jicama julienne, or mushrooms stuffed with shrimp or *huitlacoche* (itself, a mushroom that grows on corn stalks). Main courses range from grilled salmon filet in a poblano chile sauce, to a tender rib eye steak with mushrooms, delicately flavored with the Mexican herb, *epazote*. The house specialty dessert is a Toluca ice cream cake. The warmly decorated dining room is accented with tin star lamps and flickering candles. An excellent wine list and full bar complement the exquisite dining.

Morelos 570, across from Galeria Uno. ☎ *322-222-1695.* www.losxitomates.com. *Reservations recommended. Main courses: $8–$22. AE, MC, V. Open: Daily 6–midnight.*

Chapter 19

Having Fun on and off the Beach in Puerto Vallarta

by Lynne Bairstow

In This Chapter

▶ Hitting the beaches Puerto Vallarta style
▶ Enjoying Puerto Vallarta's best sports on land and by sea
▶ Sightseeing and shopping like a professional
▶ Heading out beyond Puerto Vallarta
▶ Dancing until dawn, and maybe even later

Decisions, decisions . . . With so many fun-filled options competing for your time, choosing among them may be the biggest problem you encounter on a Vallarta vacation. Besides a bevy of beautiful beaches — some secluded coves, others outrageous in their people-watching potential — dry land also offers intriguing and entertaining possibilities.

In this chapter, I give you an overview of the best beaches tucked into the 42km (26 miles) of coastline surrounding **Bahía de Banderas (Banderas Bay)** and the best ways to get to each. I also reveal the most interesting sights in town and a few cool activities to try.

Vallarta is gaining recognition as a veritable treasure chest for ecotourism. A number of tours permit you to explore the culture or nature of the area — while having a sun-filled good time in the process. I cover these excursions as well.

Hitting the Beaches

For years, beaches were Puerto Vallarta's main attraction. Although visitors today explore more of the surrounding geography, the golden sands and cobalt waters are still a powerful draw. The coast of Bahía de Banderas covers more than 81km (50 miles), with 42km (26 miles) of beaches ranging from action-packed party spots to secluded coves accessible only by boat.

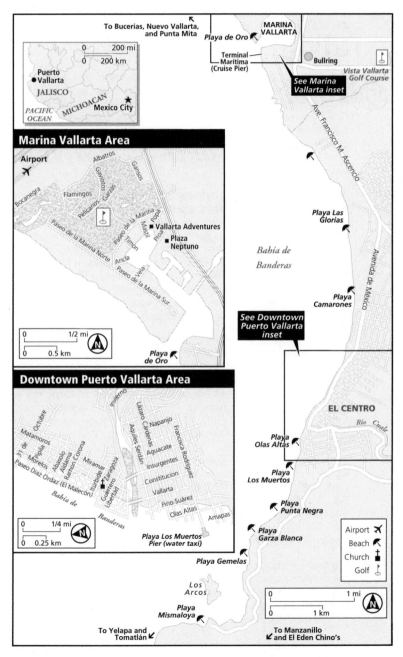

Puerto Vallarta Area

Northern beaches

The entire northern coastline from Punta Mita to Bucerías is a succession of sandy coves alternating with rocky inlets. For years, the beaches to the north, with their long, clean breaks, have been the favored locale for surfers.

Public transportation to any of the north-shore beaches is easy and inexpensive. Buses and minivans marked "Bucerías" or "Punta Mita" stop at the bus stop in front of the airport gas station. You can ask your driver to let you off at any of the beaches listed in this section. Buses generally run every 20 minutes from 6 a.m. to 11 p.m., but check with your hotel concierge for current schedules. For the return trip, simply flag a bus down. The fare is less than $2 each way; that price gets you all the way to Punta Mita.

As you travel south on Highway 200A from Punta Mita, the first public beach you come to is **Playa Anclote** — a broad, sandy beach with protected swimming areas and a few great *palapa* (thatched roof) restaurants. The water is gentle and shallow for quite a distance out, and boats regularly anchor offshore and take dinghies in for a fresh fish lunch. Of the restaurants, El Anclote and El Dorado have been the long-standing favorites, but **Mañana,** by Chef Roger (☎ **329-291-6374**), is raising the culinary bar of this casual dining area. It's open Tuesday through Sunday 10 a.m. to 9 p.m., in summer 1 to 9 p.m. All have beach chairs available for your post-margarita nap in the sun.

You can also hire a *panga* (small motorized boat) at Playa Anclote from the fisherman's cooperative on the beach and have the captain take you to the **Marietas Islands** just offshore. These uninhabited islands are a great place for bird-watching, diving, snorkeling, or just exploring. You can spot blue-footed booby birds (no joke) all along the islands' rocky coast, and giant mantas, sea turtles, and colorful tropical fish swim among the coral cliffs. The islands are honeycombed with caves and hidden beaches — including the stunning Playa del Amor that only appears at low tide. You enter a shallow passageway to access this semi-circular stretch of sand. And a cave 12m (40 ft.) below the surface has an air pocket where divers can dispose of their regulators and have an underwater conversation! Humpback whales congregate around these islands during the winter months, and you can rent a *panga* for a do-it-yourself whale-watching excursion (trips cost about $20 per hour). You can also visit these islands aboard one of the numerous day cruises that depart from the cruise-ship terminal in Puerto Vallarta.

Further south is the rustic, natural setting of **Playa Destiladeras.** It has talc-smooth sand and a couple of thatched-roof restaurants, making for a quick but meaningful getaway from town. **Playa Piedra Blanca** and **Playa Manzanilla** are beaches similar in style and spirit located just before the curve in the bay, past the small town of La Cruz de Huanacaxtle.

The small coastal town of **Bucerías,** with its broad, smooth-sand beaches, has caught on as a great day trip. Come here from Puerto Vallarta to enjoy the long, wide, and uncrowded beach, along with the fresh seafood served at the beachfront restaurants or at one of the great cafes. One of the top choices is **Karen's Place** on the beach at the Costa Dorada, calles Lázaro Cárdenas and Juárez (☎ 322-229-6892). Open Tuesdays through Sundays from 9 a.m. to 9 p.m., it caters to American tastes and has a super Sunday brunch served from 9 a.m. to 3 p.m. Sunday is also street-market day in town, but in keeping with the casual pace of Bucerías, the market doesn't get going until noon or so. The **Coral Reef Surf Shop** (Héroe de Nacozari 114 F; ☎ 329-298-0261) offers a great selection of surfboards and gear for sale. It also features surfboard and boogie-board rentals, surf lessons, ATV tours, and other adventure tours to surrounding areas.

The gold-sand **beaches of Nuevo Vallarta** are the main reason people choose to stay in Nuevo Vallarta hotels. Nuevo Vallarta is south of Bucerías, and technically you could say that it also falls on the northern coastline. If you want to check the beaches out for yourself, spend a day at the **Etc. Beach Club** (Paseo de los Cocoteros 38; ☎ 322-297-0174). This casual beach club has a volleyball net, showers, restroom facilities, and food and drink service on the beach (both day and night). Public transportation is okay to get to Nuevo Vallarta, because it's the most economic way to get there in relative comfort — the buses are fairly new and some even are air-conditioned. Taxis are a bit expensive — $15 one way, but they're a faster, more convenient way to get to Nuevo Vallarta. To get here from Puerto Vallarta, take the second entrance to Nuevo Vallarta and turn right on Paseo de los Cocoteros; it's past the Vista Bahía hotel. The club is open daily from 11 a.m. to 7 p.m. Bring cash for food and drink purchases — credit cards aren't accepted.

Central and town beaches

In Chapter 16, I caution you that the beaches at **Marina Vallarta,** with darker sand and seasonal inflows of stones, are the least desirable in the area. If you're a traveler whose priority is the beauty of the beach, venture to areas other than Marina Vallarta. Though it has its charms, the beaches aren't among them. If you do choose to make it a beach day in Marina Vallarta, Nikki Beach, at the Westin hotel, is the place to go. The oversized lounge beds are great for soaking up the sun, sipping a cool beverage, and enjoying the spot's fusion cuisine and hip tunes. Shade umbrellas are available. It's among the most comfortable ways to enjoy a beach day in the area.

The **Hotel Zone** beach runs for 5km (3 miles) from just beyond the cruise-ship terminal to the north to just south of the *malecón* (boardwalk). The names of the beaches change along the way, from Playa de Oro to Playa Camarones, but most people just refer to the hotel property that the beaches front.

It's a wide, clean, and generally uncrowded stretch of sand, but the shore does drop steeply just offshore. This is the best place to rent watersports equipment, especially Jet Skis and sailboards.

As you reach the central town, you may notice that relatively few people choose to swim along the central stretch of sand running from the start of the *malecón* to the Río Cuale, because it's more of a commercial area, and there are no services for chairs or beverages on the sand, although it's a popular place for parasailing.

Playa Los Muertos (also known as Playa Olas Altas or Playa del Sol) begins just south of the Río Cuale and is hands-down the most popular town beach. The water can be rough here, but the wide beach is home to a large array of *palapa* restaurants with food, beverage, and beach-chair service. The two most popular spots to grab some grub are the adjacent El Dorado and La Palapa (see Chapter 18 for a detailed review of the latter), both of which are located at the end of Calle Pulpito. On the southern end of this beach is a section known as "Blue Chairs" — the most popular gay beach. Vendors stroll the length of Los Muertos, and beach volleyball, parasailing, and Jet Skis are all popular pastimes.

Playa Mismaloya is in a sheltered cove about 10km (6 miles) south of town along Highway 200. The water here is clear and beautiful and ideal for snorkeling off the beach. Entrance to the public beach is just to the left of the **Barceló La Jolla de Mismaloya** (☎ **322-226-0660;** www. lajollademismaloya.com). Colorful *palapa* restaurants dot the small beach, and you can rent beach chairs for sunbathing. You can also stake out a table under a *palapa* for the day. Using a restaurant's table and *palapa* is a reciprocal arrangement — the restaurant provides a comfortable place to hang out, and you buy your drinks, snacks, and lunch there. The 1960s Richard Burton movie, *The Night of the Iguana,* was filmed at Mismaloya. La Jolla de Mismaloya has a restaurant, **The Sets of The Night of the Iguana Restaurant,** on the restored film set that's open daily noon to 11 p.m. The movie runs continuously in **John Huston's Restaurant** (serving drinks and light snacks 11 a.m.–6 p.m.) located below the The Sets of The Night of the Iguana.

About 5km (3 miles) past Mismaloya is **Boca de Tomatlán,** which is similar in setup to Mismaloya but without a large resort looming in the background. Both Mismaloya and Boca de Tomatlán are accessible by public buses that depart from Lázaro Cárdenas Park, at the corner of Basilio Badillo and Insurgentes, every 15 minutes from 5:30 a.m. to 10 p.m. and cost just 50¢. La Boca is the end of the bus line and the point at which the highway turns inland.

South-shore beaches

Boca de Tomatlán is the jumping-off point for the south-shore beaches of **Las Animas, Quimixto,** and **Yelapa,** all of which are accessible only by boat. In addition to having the ambience of a south-seas cove, each location offers intriguing hikes to jungle waterfalls and plays host to restaurants that front a wide beach. Las Animas is my favorite of the three spots. The beach has the most tranquil waters for swimming and two rocky headlands for protection. Quimixto's palm-fringed crescent of sand takes a back seat to hiking and horseback rides to the waterfall. Although the waterfall rages impressively from August to January, as the dry winter season progresses, you're likely to be less than blown away.

Yelapa, located on a beautiful sheltered cove, is the most remote location of these three beaches. Once a haven for those looking to escape the confines of society — or equally likely, the law — it became a popular haven for long-term, expatriate visitors and artists due to its seclusion, natural beauty, and simplicity of life. Yelapa has no cars, has one lone paved (pedestrian-only) road, and got electricity only in the past three years. It offers a few primitive accommodations, plus one stunning six-villa inn, **Verana** (Chapter 16 has a detailed review), as well as beachside restaurants and hikes to one of two jungle waterfalls. Although the mellow attitude still prevails, yoga is rapidly becoming the preferred way to reach an altered state of mind here.

Finding Water Fun for Everyone

You haven't experienced Puerto Vallarta unless you've been to the bay — on a boat, under the water, or playing along the shoreline. Bahía de Banderas is as deep as the surrounding mountains are high, and with the wealth of sea life found here, you're as likely to spot whales or dolphins as you are to see other tour boats. The view of town from the bay is simply stunning. And, when it comes to having fun in the water, your biggest challenge is deciding what to do first.

Cruising Puerto Vallarta

Puerto Vallarta offers a number of different boat trips, including sunset cruises and trips for snorkeling, swimming, and diving. Most of the excursions generally travel one of two routes: to the **Marietas Islands,** which are about a 30- to 45-minute boat ride off the northern shore of Bahía de Banderas, or to **Yelapa, Las Animas,** or **Quimixto** along the southern shore.

All the trips to the southern beaches make a stop at **Los Arcos,** an island rock formation south of Puerto Vallarta, for snorkeling. Don't base your opinion of underwater Puerto Vallarta on this location though. Dozens of tour boats dump large numbers of snorkelers overboard at the same time each day, and the fish have figured out *not* to be there at that time. Los Arcos is, however, an excellent site for night diving.

When comparing all the boat cruises, note that some include lunch and most provide music and an open bar on board. Most boats leave around 9:30 a.m., stop for 45 minutes of snorkeling, arrive at the beach destination around noon for a two-and-a-half-hour stay, and return around 3 p.m. At Quimixto and Yelapa, visitors can take a half-hour hike to a jungle waterfall or rent a horse for the trip. Prices range from $45 for a sunset cruise or a trip (with open bar) to one of the beaches to $85 for an all-day outing with open bar and meals.

Here are some great choices for a boat cruise:

- ✔ One boat, the *Marigalante* (☎ 322-223-0309; www.marigalante.com.mx), an exact replica of Columbus's ship the *Santa María,* was built in honor of the 500-year anniversary of his voyage to the Americas. It offers a daytime "pirate's cruise" complete with picnic barbecue and treasure hunt and a sunset dinner cruise with folkloric dance and fireworks. The day tour is $65 per person, and the sunset dinner cruise is $75 per person.

- ✔ My choice for the best day trip is an excursion to **Caletas,** the cove where John Huston (the director of such movie classics as *The Maltese Falcon, The Treasure of Sierra Madre,* and the Vallarta-filmed *The Night of the Iguana*) made his home for years. **Vallarta Adventures** (☎ 866-256-2739 from the U.S., or 322-297-1212; www.vallarta-adventures.com) holds the exclusive lease on this private cove and has done an excellent job of restoring Huston's former home, adding exceptional day-spa facilities, and landscaping the beach, which is wonderful for snorkeling or diving. The quality facilities, combined with the relative privacy that this day trip offers at $75 per person, has made it one of the most popular excursions. Vallarta Adventures also offers an evening cruise that comes complete with dinner and a spectacular contemporary dance show, "Rhythms of the Night."

- ✔ **Whale-watching tours** are becoming more popular each year because spotting humpback whales is almost a certainty from mid-November (sometimes a few weeks later) through March. For centuries, these majestic whales have migrated to Bahía de Banderas (called Humpback Bay in the 1600s) to reproduce and bear calves. **Open Air Expeditions** (Guerrero 339; ☎ 322-222-3310; www.vallartawhales.com) is the noted, local, whale-watching authority. These folks offer ecologically oriented tours (for up to 12 people) in small, specially designed, soft boats that allow for better observation from a level that is closer to water, and the sound of their engine is less disturbing to the whales than the engines of the larger boats. The twice-daily, $80 tours (8:30 a.m.–2:30 p.m.) last four hours and include a healthful snack.

- ✔ **Vallarta Adventures** (☎ 866-256-2739 from the U.S., or 322-297-1212) offers whale-watching photo excursions in small boats for $70. The trip includes a pre-departure briefing on whale behaviors. This company also features whale-watching on its tours to the Marietas Islands. For $80 you get lunch, time at a private beach, and an ambience that is more festive than educational while traveling aboard the large catamaran boats.

Skiing and surfing

Watersports — including water-skiing, parasailing, and windsurfing — are available at many beaches along the Bahía de Banderas. The best-known spot for watersports-equipment rental is **Club Bananas Water Sports Center,** which is located on the beachfront of the Las Palmas Hotel (Av. Francisco Medina Ascencio Km 2.5, Hotel Zone; ☎ **322-226-1220;** ask for the Water Sports Center). WaveRunners, banana boats, and water-skiing equipment are available for hourly, half-day, or full-day rentals. You can also find rental equipment at Playa Los Muertos in between La Palapa and El Dorado restaurants.

Exploring the deep blue

Although Puerto Vallarta lacks the crystal-clear waters of Cancún and other Caribbean coastal venues, it's still a great dive site. The reefs are much smaller than those in Caribbean destinations; however, the abundance of marine life is spectacular. You can see a great variety of sea life, including giant mantas, sea turtles, dolphins, and tropical fish. During the winter months, you're also apt to hear the beautiful underwater songs of humpback whales as you dive. Underwater enthusiasts from beginners to experts can arrange scuba diving with the following folks:

- ✔ **Vallarta Adventures** (☎ **866-256-2739** from the U.S., or 322-297-1212; www.vallarta-adventures.com) is a five-star PADI dive center that offers instructional programs ranging from the resort-course level to instructor certification. Dives take place at Los Arcos, a company-owned site at Caletas Cove, Quimixto Coves, the Marietas Islands, and the offshore El Morro and Chimo reefs.

- ✔ **Chico's Dive Shop** (Díaz Ordaz 772–5, near Carlos O'Brian's; ☎ **322-222-1895;** www.chicos-diveshop.com) offers similar dive trips and is also a PADI five-star dive center. Chico's is open daily 8 a.m. to 10 p.m. and has branches at the Marriott, Vidafel, Villa del Palmar, Camino Real, Paradise Village, and Playa Los Arcos hotels.

Sailing away

Put some wind in your sails and experience the bay in the most natural of ways:

- ✔ **Sail Vallarta** (Club de Tenis Puesta del Sol, Local 7-B, Marina Vallarta; ☎ **322-221-0096;** sailvallarta@bancomer.com) offers several different sailboats for hire. A group day-sail, including crew, use of snorkeling equipment, beer and sodas, food, and music, costs $65. Most trips include a crew, but you can make arrangements to sail yourself or on a smaller boat. Prices vary for full boat charters depending on the vessel and amount of time you want to spend on the water.

✔ **Vallarta Adventures** (☎ **866-256-2739** from the U.S., or 322-297-1212; www.vallarta-adventures.com) also offers two beautiful sailboats for charter and small group sails (up to 12 people for day or evening sails). Daytime sailing charters are priced at $80 per person, where sunset sails are $60 per person. The service is superb, as is the quality of the food and beverages served on board. And the Vallarta Adventures boats are known for being the sailboats most frequently under sail — many of the other sailing charters prefer to simply motor around the bay.

✔ The newest addition to Vallarta's sailing scene is most impressive — **Coming About** (☎ **322-222-4119**; www.coming-about.com) is a women-only sailing school that provides hands-on sailing instruction for day-sailing excursions, as well as week-long sailing classes at a variety of skill levels. Owned and operated by Pat Henry, who spent eight years sailing around the globe, then wrote about it in her book, *By the Grace of the Sea: A Woman's Solo Odyssey Around the World,* the classes are challenging, inspiring, and entertaining, as Pat shares her adventures with participants. Dubbed "any woman's sailing school," the goal is to take away the fear and the mystery, and make the skill of sailing accessible to everyone. Courses range from a one-day introductory course to a nine-day bareboat charter captain course. Fees for the one-day course are $475 for four people; $2,800 to $3,600 for the nine-day course, including hotel.

Reeling in the big one

You can arrange a fishing trip through travel agencies or through the **Cooperativa de Pescadores** (Fishing Cooperative; ☎ **322-222-1202**) on the *malecón* north of the Río Cuale, next door to the Rosita Hotel. Fishing charters cost $180 (for four hours) to $350 a day for four to eight people; price varies with the boat size. Although the posted price at the fishing cooperative is the same as what you'd find through travel agencies, you may be able to negotiate a lower price at the cooperative. Bring cash — the cooperative doesn't accept credit cards. It's open Monday to Saturday from 7 a.m. to 10 p.m., but make arrangements a day in advance. You can also arrange fishing trips at the Marina Vallarta docks or by calling **Fishing with Carolina** (☎ **322-224-7250** or wireless [044] 322-292-2953; fishingwithcarolina@hotmail.com), which features a 9m (30-ft.) Uniflite Sportsfisher fully equipped with an English-speaking crew. Fishing trips generally include equipment and bait, but drinks, snacks, and lunch are optional, so check to find out what the price includes.

Swimming with dolphins

Ever been kissed by a dolphin? Take advantage of a unique and absolutely memorable opportunity to swim with Pacific bottlenose dolphins in a clear lagoon or oceanarium. **Dolphin Adventure** (☎ **866-256-2739** from the U.S., or 322-297-1212; www.vallarta-adventures.com) operates an interactive dolphin-research facility — considered the finest in Latin America — that allows a limited number of people to swim with the dolphins Monday through Saturday at scheduled times. Cost for the swim is $128, and advance reservations are required — they're generally sold out at least a week in advance.

You may prefer the **Dolphin Encounter** ($60) at the same facility, which allows you to touch and discover more about these dolphins in smaller pools, so you're ensured up-close and personal time with these fascinating creatures — it's also a better choice for children. You can even be a **Trainer for a Day,** a special seven-hour program of working alongside the more experienced trainers and the dolphins, for a cost of $250. The new **Dolphin Kids** program, for children ages 4 to 8, is a gentle introduction to dolphins, featuring the Dolphin Adventure baby dolphins and their mothers interacting with the children participants ($60).

Dolphin Adventures has two facilities — one in the lagoon of Nuevo Vallarta, and a newer, more expansive oceanarium-style facility on Av. Las Palmas No. 39-A., which also serves as the headquarters of Vallarta Adventures. The oceanarium gets my highest recommendation. The experience leaves you with an indescribable sensation, and it's a joy to see these dolphins — they're well cared for, happy, and spirited. After a few swims with these dolphins, I now consider them to be my friends, and they even remember me — that's how it seems to me anyway. The program is about education and interaction, not entertainment or amusement, and I especially recommend it for children 10 and older.

Swimming with dolphins has its critics and supporters. You may want to visit the Whale and Dolphins Conservation Society's Web site at www.wdcs.org. For more information about responsible travel in general, check out these Web sites: Tread Lightly (www.treadlightly.org) and the International Ecotourism Society (www.ecotourism.org).

Enjoying Land Sports

What's great about Puerto Vallarta is that many of the best things to do on land here are free. Vallarta is a town of simple pleasures — walking along the *malécon* at sunset, catching a concert at the open-air theater across from the central plaza, strolling through the impressive Our Lady of Guadalupe church, or wandering into any of the dozens of local art galleries.

In addition to these laid-back diversions, Puerto Vallarta is a virtual playground for activities ranging from mountain biking to golf. Eco-friendly tours can take you into the tropical jungle or to remote mountain villages. I bet that you can find more things to do here than you have days in which to do them.

Teeing off

Puerto Vallarta is rapidly positioning itself to rival Los Cabos as Mexico's golf capital. Five new courses have opened in recent years, and the Vista Vallarta Golf Club was the site of the 2002 World Golf Championships-World Cup.

A set of fairways and greens that has been around for awhile is the Joe Finger–designed course at the **Marina Vallarta Golf Club** (☎ 322-221-0073), an 18-hole, par-74, private course that winds through the Marina Vallarta peninsula and provides great ocean views. It's for members only, but most of the luxury hotels in Puerto Vallarta have memberships that their guests can use. A bar, restaurant, and pro shop are on the premises, and a golf pro is around to offer his services. The greens fees are $121, or $88 after 2 p.m. in high season and $115 during low season. (These rates may vary depending on the type of membership your hotel has.) Fees include golf cart, range balls, and tax. Caddies charge $10. Club rentals, lessons, and special packages are also available.

North of town in the state of Nayarit, about 16km (10 miles) beyond Puerto Vallarta, is the public, 18-hole, par-72 **Los Flamingos Club de Golf** (☎ 329-296-5006; www.flamingosgolf.com.mx), the oldest course in town. It features beautiful jungle vegetation and has just undergone a course renovation and upgrade. The club is open from 6:30 a.m. to 7:00 p.m. daily and has a snack bar (but no restaurant) and full pro shop. The greens fee is $95 and includes the use of a golf cart; a caddy charges $20, and club rentals are $30 to $40. A free shuttle service is available from downtown Puerto Vallarta; call for pickup times and locations.

The breathtaking Jack Nicklaus Signature golf course at the **Four Seasons Punta Mita** (☎ 322-291-6000) is as challenging as it is stunning. It has eight oceanfront holes, but you can see the ocean from every hole on the course. Its hallmark is Hole 3B, the "Tail of the Whale," with a long drive to a green located on a natural island — the only natural-island green in the Americas. It requires an amphibious golf cart to take you to the green when the tide is high, and the management has thoughtfully added an alternative-play hole for times when the ocean or tides aren't accommodating. The course is open only to guests of the Four Seasons resort or to members of other golf clubs with a letter of introduction from their pro. Selected other Vallarta-area hotels also have guest privileges — ask your concierge. Greens fees for guests of the Four Seasons are $170, $230 for non-guests, including cart, with club rentals (Calloway) an extra $60. Golf lessons are also available.

A second Jack Nicklaus course is at the **Vista Vallarta Golf Club** (☎ 322-290-0030; www.vistavallartagolf.com), along with one designed by Tom Weiskopf. These courses were the site of the 2002 World Golf Championships-World Cup. Vista Vallarta is in the foothills of the Sierra Madre, behind the bullring in Puerto Vallarta. A round costs $167 per person, with cart rental fees priced at $43, and club rentals $45 per set/per round.

The Robert von Hagge–designed **El Tigre** course at Paradise Village in Nuevo Vallarta (☎ **322-297-0773;** www.eltigregolf.com) opened in March 2002. The 6,515m (21,717-ft.) course is on a relatively flat piece of land, but the design incorporates challenging bunkers, undulating fairways, and water features on several holes. El Tigre offers lessons and has an expansive clubhouse. Greens fees are $185 a round, or $85 if you play after 2 p.m. and clubs rental $45.

Taking time for tennis

Many hotels in Puerto Vallarta offer excellent **tennis** facilities, several with clay courts, and there's also a full-service public tennis club. The **Canto del Sol Tennis Club** (☎ **322-224-0123;** www.cantodelsol.com), located at the Canto del Sol hotel in the Hotel Zone, offers indoor and outdoor courts (including a clay court), a full pro shop, lessons, clinics, and partner match-ups.

Trailing away

One of the best ways to get some exercise, and see some great local sites in the process, is to take a mountain-bike tour with **Bike Mex** (Calle Guerrero 361; ☎ **322-223-1834;** www.bikemex.com). Bike Mex offers expert **guided biking and hiking tours** up the Río Cuale canyon and to outlying areas. The popular Río Cuale bike trip costs $44 for four hours and includes bike, helmet, gloves, insurance, water, breakfast, lunch, and an English-speaking guide. Trips take off at either 9 a.m. or 2 p.m., but starting times are flexible; make arrangements a day ahead.

And . . . did I say Yelapa is accessible only by boat? For anyone serious about their biking, I've traveled with Bike Mex on its all-day, advanced-level bike trip to this magical cove, and it's great. You and your fellow riders depart at 7:00 a.m. in a van and travel to your starting point in the town of El Tuito. The 53km (33-mile) ride includes 30km (19 miles) of climbs to a peak elevation of a little more than 1,000m (3,600 ft.). The journey covers switchbacks, fire roads, single tracks, awesome climbs, and steep downhills before ending up at a beachfront *palapa* restaurant in Yelapa. You have the option of staying the night in Yelapa or returning that afternoon by small boat. This tour costs $160, takes seven to eight hours, and includes all bike gear, drinks, lunch, boat and land transportation, guide, and *ample* encouragement.

Other bicycle trips are also available. Guided **hiking tours** are available along the same routes. The prices start at $30 and vary depending on the route.

Saddling up

You can arrange guided **horseback rides** through travel agents or directly with one of the local ranches. **Rancho Palma Real** (Carretera Vallarta-Tepic 4766; ☎ **322-222-0501;** Fax: 322-222-8101; ranchopalmareal@ hotmail.com) offers by far the nicest horseback riding tour in the area.

The horses are in excellent health and condition, plus you get an added tour of local farms on your way to the ranch. The office is five minutes north of the airport, and the ranch is in Las Palmas, approximately 40 minutes northeast of Vallarta. The horses are in excellent condition, and you enjoy a tour of local farms on your way to the ranch. Breakfast and lunch are included with the $62 fee.

Rancho El Charro (Av. Francisco Villa 895; ☎ 322-224-0114; www.rancho elcharro.com) and **Rancho Ojo de Agua** (Cerrada de Cardenal 227; ☎/fax 322-224-0607) also offer high-quality tours. Both of these ranches are about a 10-minute taxi ride north of downtown toward the Sierra Madre foothills. The morning and sunset rides last three hours and take you up into the mountains overlooking the ocean and town. The cost is $52. They also have their own comfortable base camp for serious riders who want to stay out overnight.

Enjoying an ecotour

The **Sierra Madre Expedition** is an excellent tour offered by **Vallarta Adventures** (☎ 866-256-2739 from the U.S., or 322-297-1212; www. vallarta-adventures.com). This daily excursion travels in special Mercedes all-terrain vehicles through jungle trails north of Puerto Vallarta, stopping at a small town and in a forest for a brief nature walk. The tour winds up on a pristine secluded beach for lunch and swimming. The $75 outing is worthwhile because it takes tourists on exclusive trails through scenery that would otherwise be off-limits.

In addition to their seasonal whale-watching excursions, **Open Air Expeditions** (☎ 322-222-3310; www.vallartawhales.com) offers other nature-oriented trips, including **bird-watching** outings and **ocean kayaking** sessions in Punta Mita. The tours at **Ecotours de México** (Ignacio L. Vallarta 243; ☎ 322-222-6606; www.ecotoursvallarta.com) include seasonal trips (Aug–Nov) to a **turtle preservation camp** where you can witness baby Olive Ridley turtles hatch.

Tukari Tours travel agency (☎ 322-224-7177; Fax: 322-224-2350; www.tukari.com) specializes in ecological and culturally oriented tours. These folks can arrange bird-watching trips to the fertile birding grounds near **San Blas** (three to four hours north of Puerto Vallarta in the state of Nayarit), shopping trips to **Tlaquepaque** and **Tonalá** (six hours inland near Guadalajara), or a day trip to **Rancho Altamira** (a 20-hectare/50-acre hilltop working ranch) for a barbecue lunch and horseback riding followed by a stroll through **El Tuito**, a small colonial-era village nearby. They can also arrange an unforgettable morning at **Terra Noble Spa Art and Healing Center** (☎ 322-223-3530 or 222-5400; www.terranoble.com), a mountaintop day spa and center for the arts where participants can get a massage or treatment, work in clay and paint, and have lunch in a heavenly setting overlooking the bay.

Vallarta's newest adventure activity is a **canopy tour,** operated by Vallarta Adventures (☎ **866-256-2739** from the U.S., or 322-297-1212; www.vallarta-adventures.com). You glide from treetop to treetop, getting an up-close-and-personal look at a tropical rain forest canopy and the trails far below. Expert guides assist you to the special platforms, and you move from one platform to another using pulleys on horizontal traverse cables, while the guides explain the tropical flora surrounding you. The guides also offer assistance — and moral support! — as you rappel back down to the forest floor. Tours depart from the Vallarta Adventures offices in both Marina Vallarta and Nuevo Vallarta at 8 a.m., returning at 2 p.m. The price ($75 for adults, $50 for children 8–12) includes the tour, unlimited non-alcoholic beverages, and light snacks.

A second option for a canopy tour is available in the southern jungles of Vallarta, over the Orquidias River, with **Canopy Tours de Los Veranos** (☎ **322-223-6060;** www.canopytours-vallarta.com). This tour picks you up at the Canopy office, near the southside Pemex station, to trans-port you to their facilities upriver from Mismaloya. Departures are at 9, 10, and 11 a.m., noon, and 1 and 2 p.m. In addition to the 13 cables — the longest being a full 350m (1,150 ft.) — it also offers climbing walls, water slides, and horseback riding. Price is $80 for adults, or $50 for children ages 6 to 12. Use of the natural-granite climbing wall (helmets and climb-ing shoe use included) is $18; a 90-minute jungle horseback riding tour costs $35.

Sightseeing in Puerto Vallarta

Puerto Vallarta, itself, is a sight to see — cobblestone streets lined with tiny shops, rows of windows edged with curling wrought iron, and vistas of red-tile roofs set against the sea. Start with a walk up and down the *malecón,* the boardwalk that borders the main seaside street.

One of the great pleasures of strolling Puerto Vallarta's *malecón* is taking in the fanciful sculptures that line this seaside promenade. Among the notable works on display is *Nostalgia,* located across from Carlos O'Brian's restaurant. Created by Ramiz Barquet, this sculpture depicts a couple sharing a romantic moment while gazing out on the bay. Farther south is the sculpture group at the *Rotonda del Mar,* locally known as *Fantasy by the Sea.* It's an array of sculpture "chairs" by renowned Mexican artist Alejandro Colunga. This wildly creative series — one chair is topped by a large octopus head, another bench has two giant ears for backrests — seems to always draw a crowd. Closer to the main square is the *Boy on the Seahorse* sculpture, an image that has come to represent this resort town. Photo ops abound — don't miss the fountain across from the main square; its three bronze dolphins seem ready to leap right into the bay.

Across the street from the fountain is the **palacio municipal (city hall)**, located on the main square (next to the tourism office). Besides housing the local government, the building has a large Manuel Lepe mural painted inside its stairwell. Nearby, up Calle Independencia, sits the **Parish of Nuestra Señora de Guadalupe church** (Hidalgo 370; ☎ 322-222-1326), topped with its curious crown held in place by angels — a replica of the one worn by Empress Carlota during her brief time in Mexico as Emperor Maximilian's wife. On the church steps, women sell religious mementos, and across the narrow street, vendors sell native herbs for curing common ailments. Services in English are held Sundays at 10 a.m. (in Jan, there's also a 5 p.m. Mass in English). Regular parish hours are from 7 a.m. until 9:30 or 10 p.m. daily.

Three blocks south of the church, head east on Calle Libertad, lined with small shops and pretty second-story windows, to the **municipal market** by the river. After exploring the market, cross the bridge to the island on the river; sometimes a painter is at work on the island's banks. Walk down the center of the island toward the sea, and you come to the tiny **Museo Río Cuale** (no phone), which has a small but impressive perma- nent exhibit of pre-Columbian figurines. It's open Monday to Saturday 10 a.m. to 5 p.m. Admission is free.

Retrace your steps back to the market and Calle Libertad and follow Calle Miramar to the brightly colored steps up to Calle Zaragoza. There are close to 100 steps, but you walk leisurely to climb them and coming down is a breeze; the idea is to experience the streets of Vallarta and the feel of this place that was built on the side of the mountain. Up Zaragoza a block to the right is the famous **pink arched bridge** that once connected Richard Burton's and Elizabeth Taylor's houses. This area, known as **"Gringo Gulch,"** is where many Americans have houses.

You can also tour the **Taylor-Burton villas** (Casa Kimberley; Calle Zaragoza 445; ☎ 322-222-1336; www.casakimberley.com). Tours of the two houses once owned by Elizabeth Taylor and Richard Burton cost $8. Just ring the bell between 9 a.m. and 6 p.m. Monday to Saturday, and if the manager is available, he'll take you through the house.

A Spectacular Sight

Performances of the **Papantla Flyers (Voladores de Papantla)**, take place every Friday, Saturday, and Sunday night at 6:00 to 6:30, 8:00 to 8:30, and 9:30 to 10:00 p.m., on the *malecón*, adjacent to the "Boy on a Seahorse" statue. In this pre-Columbian religious ritual four men are suspended from the top of a tall pole, circling around it (as if in flight), while another beats a drum and plays a flute while balancing himself at the top. It sig- nifies the four cardinal points, and the mystic "center" of the self, a sacred direction for ancient Mexican cultures.

You can get a peek at some of the other villas in Vallarta every Wednesday and Thursday (late Nov through Easter) on the **International Friendship Club** private-home tours (☎ 322-222-5466). You get to view four private villas in town for a donation of $30 per person with proceeds benefiting local charities. Tour arrangements begin at 10 a.m. at the Hotel Molino de Agua (Av. Ignacio L. Vallarta 130, adjacent to the south-bound bridge over the Río Cuale), where you can buy breakfast while you wait for the group to gather. Arrive early because this tour sells out quickly! The tour departs at 11 a.m. and lasts approximately two and a half hours.

Thanks to a recently completed expansion of the *malecón,* you can now continue strolling the *malecón* from the Los Arcos Amphitheater along the water's edge and over a pedestrian bridge located where the River Cuale meets the sea, directly into the Los Muertos beach zone.

Hotel travel desks and travel agencies can book you on the ever-popular **Tropical Tour** or **Jungle Tour** ($30 each), a basic orientation to the area. These tours are really expanded city tours that include a drive through the workers' village of Pitillal, the affluent neighborhood of Conchas Chinas, the cathedral, the market, the Taylor-Burton houses, and lunch at a jungle restaurant. Any stop for shopping usually means the driver picks up commission for what you buy.

Shopping Puerto Vallarta

What makes shopping in Puerto Vallarta so great is that it's generally concentrated in small, eclectic, and independent shops rather than impersonal malls. You can find excellent-quality **folk art,** original **clothing** designs, and fine **home accessories** at great prices. Vallarta is known for having the most diverse and impressive selection of **contemporary Mexican fine art** available outside Mexico City. If you want the more typical Mexico resort shopping experience, don't worry — you can still find plenty of tacky T-shirts and the ever-present **silver jewelry.**

The best shopping is concentrated in a few key areas: central downtown, the Marina Vallarta *malecón,* the popular *mercados,* and on the beach — where the merchandise comes to you. Some of the more attractive shops are found 1 to 2 blocks in **back of the *malecón.*** Although still home to a few interesting shops, the marina boardwalk *(marina malecón)* is dominated by real estate companies, timeshare vendors, restaurants, and boating services. Start at the intersection of calles Corona and Morelos — you can find interesting shops in all directions from here. **Marina Vallarta** does offer two shopping plazas (Plaza Marina and Plaza Neptuno, both on the main highway coming from the airport into town), but both have a limited selection of shops, with Plaza Neptuno primarily dedicated to items for the home.

Puerto Vallarta's **municipal market** is just north of the Río Cuale where Libertad and A. Rodríguez meet. The *mercado* sells clothes, jewelry, serapes, shawls, leather accessories and suitcases, papier-mâché parrots, stuffed frogs and armadillos, and of course, T-shirts. Be sure to do some comparison-shopping and definitely bargain before buying. The market is open daily 9 a.m. to 7 p.m. Up the *mercado* stairs, a **food market** serves inexpensive Mexican meals — for more adventurous diners, it's probably the best value and most authentic dining experience in Vallarta. You can find an **outdoor market** along Río Cuale Island, between the two bridges. Vendors sell crafts, gifts, folk art, and clothing. New to downtown is the **Small Vallarta** (☎ 322-222-7530) on Paseo Díaz Ordaz 928, on the eastern side, just before the start of the *malecón*. It is a "small mall" featuring tourist-friendly shops and dining options, including Carl Junior's burgers, Häagen-Dazs ice cream, Swatch watch shop, El Mundo de Tequila, and a Diamonds International jewelry store.

Huichol Indian art:
What it is and where to buy it

Puerto Vallarta offers the best selection of Huichol art in Mexico. Descendants of the Aztecs, the Huichol Indians are one of the last remaining indigenous cultures in the world that has remained true to its ancient traditions, customs, language, and habitat. The Huichol live in adobe structures in the mountains north and east of Puerto Vallarta. Due to the decreasing fertility of the land surrounding their villages, they now depend more on the sale of their artwork for sustenance.

Huichol art has always been cloaked in a veil of mysticism — probably one of the reasons this form of *artesanía* (handicrafts) is so sought after by serious collectors. Huichol art is characterized by colorful, symbolic yarn "paintings," inspired by visions experienced during spiritual ceremonies. In these ceremonies, artists ingest peyote, a hallucinogenic cactus, which induces brightly colored visions; these are considered to be messages from their ancestors. The symbolic and mythological imagery seen in these visions is reflected in the art, which encompasses not only yarn paintings but also fascinating masks and bowls decorated with tiny colored beads.

The Huichol may be geographically isolated, but they have business savvy and have adapted their art to meet consumer demand — original Huichol art, therefore, isn't necessarily traditional. Designs depicting iguanas, jaguars, sea turtles, frogs, eclipses, and eggs are a result of popular demand. For more traditional works, look for pieces that depict deer, scorpions, wolves, or snakes.

You may also see Huichol Indians on the streets of Vallarta, dressed in white clothing embroidered with colorful designs. A number of fine galleries that sell Huichol pieces are located in downtown Puerto Vallarta (see "Decorative and folk art" and "Crafts and gifts," later in this chapter). A notable place for finding out more about the Huicholes is **Huichol Collection**, Morelos 490, across from the seahorse statue on the *malecón*

(☎ 322-223-2141). This shop offers an extensive selection of Huichol art in all price ranges, and it has a replica of a Huichol adobe hut, informational displays explaining more about their fascinating way of life and beliefs, and usually a Huichol Indian at work creating art.

Huichol art falls into two main categories: yarn paintings and beaded pieces. All other items you may find in Huichol art galleries are either ceremonial objects or items used in their everyday lives:

✔ **Yarn paintings** are made on a wood base covered with wax that is meticulously overlaid with colored yarn. Designs represent the magical vision of the underworld, and each symbol gives meaning to the piece. Paintings made with wool yarn are more authentic than those made with acrylic; however, acrylic yarn paintings are usually brighter and have more detail because the threads are thinner. Finding empty spaces where the wax base shows is normal. Usually the artist starts with a central motif and works around it, but having several independent motifs that, when combined, take on a different meaning is common. A painting with many small designs tells a more complicated story than one with only one design and fill-work on the background. Look for the story of the piece on the back of the painting. Most Huichol artists write in pencil in Huichol and Spanish.

✔ **Beaded pieces** are made on carved wooden shapes depicting different animals, wooden eggs, or small bowls made from gourds. The artist covers the pieces with wax and applies tiny *chaquira* beads one by one to form different designs. Usually the beaded designs represent animals; plants; the elements of fire, water, or air; and certain symbols that give a special meaning to the whole. Beadwork with many small designs that don't exactly fit into one another is more time consuming and has a more complex symbolic meaning. This kind of work has empty spaces where the wax shows.

Along any public beach, walking **vendors** approach tourists and try to sell merchandise ranging from silver jewelry to rugs, T-shirts to masks. "Almost free!" they call out in seemingly relentless efforts to attract your attention. If you're too relaxed to think of shopping in town, this can be an entertaining alternative for picking up a few souvenirs. (Remember that bargaining is expected.) The most reputable beach vendors are concentrated at Playa Los Muertos in front of the El Dorado and La Palapa restaurants (on the beach near Calle Pulpito).

 You need to be aware that much of the silver sold on the beach is actually alpaca, a lesser-quality silver metal (even though many pieces are still stamped with the designation "9.25," supposedly indicating that it's true silver). The prices for and quality of silver on the beach are much lower than they are elsewhere. If you're looking for a more lasting piece of jewelry, you're better off shopping in a true silver shop.

In most of the better-quality shops and galleries, shipping, packing, and delivery services to Puerto Vallarta hotels are available, and some also ship to your home address.

Clothing

Here are some recommend clothing shops and boutiques:

✔ Vallarta's only true department store is **LANS,** Juárez 867 (☎ 322-226-9100), which also has a second location in the Hotel Zone in front of the Gigante shopping center (☎ 322-2_ _0604). LANS offers a wide selection of name-brand clothing, acc   _   otwear, cosmetics, and home furnishings.

✔ **Laura López Labra Designs,** Basilio Badillo   _2-1 3-0102), just may have the most comfortable cloth_   _orn. LLL is renowned for her trademark, all-white (o_   _esigns in 100 percent cotton or lace. Laura's fine gauze fabrics float through her designs of seductive skirts, romantic dresses, blouses, beachwear, and baby dolls. Men's offerings include cotton drawstring pants and lightweight shirts. It's open Monday to Saturday 10 a.m. to 2 p.m. and 5 to 9 p.m.

✔ **Mar de Sueños,** Leona Vicario 220 (☎ 322-222-2662), is a small but delectable shop that carries stunning swimsuits and exquisite lingerie. Without a doubt, this shop offers the finest women's beachwear, intimate apparel, and evening wear in Vallarta for those special occasions — or just to make you feel extra special. The shop also stocks a selection of fine linen clothing, and it's one of the few places in Mexico that carries the renowned Italian line, La Perla. Other name brands include Gottex, Calvin Klein, and DKNY. Open Monday to Saturday from 10 a.m. to 9 p.m.

✔ Hip and sultry fashions, direct from South America, are the specialties of the **de Santos Boutique,** Morelos 771 (☎ 322-223-5326 or 223-3052; www.desantos.com.mx), found inside of the de Santos restaurant and club. It's open Monday to Saturday 10 a.m. to 2 p.m. and 6 to 10 p.m.

Contemporary art

With one of the stronger art communities in Latin America, Puerto Vallarta has an impressive selection of fine galleries featuring quality, original works of art. Several dozen galleries get together to offer art walks almost every Wednesday between November and April. Here are some that are worth a visit:

✔ **Galería AL (Arte Latinoamericano),** Josefa Ortiz Domínguez 155 (☎/fax 322-222-4406; www.galeriaal.com), showcases contemporary works created by young, primarily Latin-American artists, as well as Vallarta favorite Marta Gilbert. It's open Monday to Saturday 10 a.m. to 9 p.m.

✔ **Galleria Dante,** Basilio Badillo 269 (☎ **322-222-2477;** www.galleria dante.com), showcases contemporary sculptures and classical reproductions of Italian, Greek, and Art Deco bronzes — all set against a backdrop of gardens and fountains in a former private villa. Located on the *"calle de los cafés,"* the gallery is open daily during the winter 10 a.m. to 5 p.m.

✔ **Galería des Artistes,** Leona Vicario 248 (☎ **322-223-0006**), features contemporary painters and sculptors from throughout Mexico, including the renowned original "magiscopes" of Feliciano Bejar. Paintings by Vallarta favorite Evelyn Boren, as well as a small selection of works by Mexican masters, including Diego Rivera and Orozco, are also here, among the exposed brick walls and stylish interior spaces. It's open Monday to Saturday noon to 10 p.m.

✔ Since opening in 1987, **Galería Pacífico,** Aldama 174, second floor, 1½ blocks inland from the fantasy sculptures on the *malecón* (☎ **322-222-1982;** www.galeriapacifico.com), has been considered one of Mexico's finest galleries. The gallery has a wide selection of sculptures and paintings by midrange masters and up-and-comers on display. During high season, it's open Monday to Saturday 10 a.m. to 9 p.m. and Sundays by appointment.

✔ One of Vallarta's first galleries, **Galería Uno,** Morelos 561 at Corona (☎ **322-222-0908**), features an excellent selection of contemporary paintings by Latin American artists, plus a variety of posters and prints. Set in a classic adobe building with an open courtyard, it's also a casual, *salón*-style gathering place for friends of owner Jan Lavender. The gallery is open Monday to Saturday 10 a.m. to 9 p.m.

✔ **T. Fuller Gallery,** Hidalgo 242 (☎ **322-222-8196**), just steps away from Our Lady of Guadalupe church, exhibits a small but stunning collection of contemporary art, paintings, ceramics, and sculptures. Hours are Monday to Saturday 10 a.m. to 2 p.m., and 6 to 9 p.m.

Crafts and gifts

Check out these choices for finding crafts and gifts:

✔ Opened in 1953, **Alfarería Tlaquepaque,** Av. México 1100 (☎ **322-223-2121**), is Vallarta's original source for Mexican ceramics and decorative crafts — all at excellent prices. Talavera pottery and dishware, colored glassware, bird cages, baskets, and wood furniture are just a few of the many items you can find in this warehouse-style store. The hours are Monday to Saturday 9 a.m. to 9 p.m., Sunday 10 a.m. to 3 p.m.

✔ I am enchanted by **La Casa del Feng Shui's** (☎ **322-222-3300**) selection of crystals, candles, talismans, fountains, and wind chimes — along with many more items designed to keep the good energy flowing in your home, office, or personal space. Why not take home something to add more harmony to your life? Open

Monday through Saturday, 9 a.m. to 9 p.m. It's located at Corona 165, around the corner from Morelos street.

✔ Flickering candles glowing from colored-glass holders welcome you into **Safari Accents,** Olas Altas 224, Local 4 (☎ **322-223-2660**), a highly original shop overflowing with creative gifts, one-of-a-kind furnishings, and reproductions of paintings by Frida Kahlo and Botero. It's open 10 a.m. to 11 p.m. daily.

Decorative and folk art

Find some one-of-a-kind pieces at these unique shops:

✔ The **Banderas Bay Trading Company,** Lázaro Cárdenas 263, near Ignacio L. Vallarta (☎ **322-223-4352**), has fine antiques and decorative objects for the home, including unique and contemporary furniture, antique wooden doors, religious-themed items, *retablos* (painted scenes on tin backgrounds depicting the granting of a miracle), original art, beeswax candles in grand sizes, hand-loomed textiles, plus glassware and pewter. Items are hand-picked by one of the most noteworthy interior designers in the area, Peter Bowman. Open Monday to Saturday 9 a.m. to 9 p.m.

✔ **Lucy's CuCu Cabaña and Zoo,** Basilio Badillo 295 (no phone), has one of the most entertaining, eclectic, and memorable collections of Mexican folk art — about 70 percent of which is animal-themed. Each summer they travel Mexico and personally select the hand-made works created by over 100 indigenous artists and artisans. Items include metal sculptures, Oaxacan wooden animals, *retablos,* and fine Talavera ceramics. The shop is open Monday to Saturday 10 a.m. to 10 p.m., but it's closed May 15 to October 15.

✔ **Puerco Azul,** Constitucion 325, just off Basilio Badillo (☎ **322-222-8647**), offers a whimsical and eclectic selection of art and home accessories, much of it created by owner and artist Lee Chapman (a.k.a. Lencho). You can find many animal-themed works in bright colors, including his signature "blue pigs" *(puercos azules).* It's open Monday to Saturday 10 a.m. to 8 p.m.

✔ **Querubines,** Juárez 501 A, at Galeana (☎ **322-223-1727**), is my personal favorite for the finest-quality artisan works from throughout Mexico, including exceptional artistic silver jewelry, embroidered and hand-woven clothing, bolts of loomed fabrics, tin mirrors and lamps, glassware, pewter frames and trays, high-quality wool rugs, straw bags, and Panama hats. It's open Monday to Sunday 10 a.m. to 9 p.m.

Jewelry and accessories

You can find jewelry and other accessories at the following:

✔ **Mosaïqe,** Basilio Badillo 277 (☎ 322-223-3146), is a potpourri of global treasures. The shop features an extensive selection of silk, cotton, and cashmere pareos and shawls, plus resort bags, jewelry, and home decor items. It's open daily 10 a.m. to 7 p.m. There's a second location at Juárez 279 (☎ 322-223-3183). This one is open Monday through Saturday from 10 a.m. to 9 p.m.

✔ At **Viva,** Basilio Badillo 274 (☎ 322-222-4078; www.vivacollection.com), both the shop and jewelry are stunning. You enter through a long corridor lined with displays showcasing exquisite jewelry from 450 international designers. The main room has a large, glass, pyramid-shaped skylight as its roof, and more memorable jewelry displays surround comfy couches. Viva also features the largest selection of authentic French espadrilles and ballet slippers in Latin America, plus a great selection of sunglasses and hats. It's open daily 10 a.m. to 11 p.m.

Tequila and cigars

Looking for quality tequila and cigars? Check out these shops:

✔ **La Casa del Habano,** Aldama 174 (☎ 322-223-2758), is a fine tobacco shop with certified-quality cigars from Cuba, along with humidors, cutters, elegant lighters, and other smoking accessories. It's open Monday to Saturday noon to 9 p.m.

✔ At **La Casa del Tequila,** Morelos 589 (☎ 322-222-2000), you can find an extensive selection of premium tequilas, plus information and tastings to help guide you to an informed selection. The shop has recently been downsized to accommodate the **Agave Grill** (see Chapter 18) in the back, but now you can enjoy tasty Mexican fare and margaritas while you shop! Business hours are Monday to Saturday from noon to 11 p.m.

Embarking on a Side Trip

Anyone for a shot of tequila? I'm talking about taking a picture of the town — although you can also sample the beverage of the same name on this side trip. **Vallarta Adventures** (☎ 866-256-2739 from the U.S., or 322-297-1212; www.vallarta-adventures.com) offers a half-day trip (300km/186 miles) that takes you to the classic town of **Tequila,** where you visit one of the original haciendas and tequila fields. It's just a comfortable 35-minute flight aboard a private, 16-passenger plane to the town of Tequila. This is the only region in the world where this legendary spirit is distilled, much like the exclusive Champagne region in France. The visit centers around Herradura Tequila's impressive 18th-century **Hacienda San José** where you find out about the myth and the tradition of producing tequila from the stately plants that line this town's hillsides — an experience comparable to California's winery tours. The tour departs every Thursday at 1 p.m. from the Aerotron private airport (adjacent to the PV International Airport) and returns to Puerto Vallarta by 8 p.m. The cost is $255, which includes all air and ground transportation, tours, lunch, and beverages.

For other day trip options around Vallarta, worthy choices include San Sebastián, Mascota, Talpa, and Yelapa.

Mining historic San Sebastián

If you haven't heard about **San Sebastián,** it probably won't be long until you do — its remote location (about 160km/100 miles from Vallarta) and historic appeal have made it the media's new darling destination in Mexico. Originally discovered in the late 1500s and settled in 1603, the town peaked as a center of mining operations, swelling to a population of more than 30,000, by the mid-1800s. Today, with roughly 600 year-round residents, San Sebastián retains all the charm of a village locked in time. Highlights include an old church, a coffee plantation, an underground tunnel system — and not a T-shirt shop to be found.

Vallarta Adventure's **Colonial Treasures Air Expedition** (☎ 866-256-2739 from the U.S., or 322-297-1212; www.vallarta-adventures.com) is a great introduction to this town. A 15-minute flight aboard a 13-seat, turbo-prop Cessna Caravan takes you into the heart of the Sierra Madre before settling in San Sebastián. The plane is equipped with raised wings, which allows you to admire — and photograph — the mountain scenery below. The plane arrives on a gravel landing strip in San Sebastián for a half-day tour — it's more like an informal stroll through town and a chance to talk with the more colorful personalities of the area — and each day is different. The package costs $145 and includes the flight, a walking tour of the town (including a stop at the old Hacienda Jalisco, an inn located in a historic building, once used as the headquarters of a silver mining company — a favored getaway of John Huston, Elizabeth Taylor, Richard Burton, and their friends), and brunch in town. For those who prefer to travel by land, they offer another option by bus, at a cost of $75.

This innovative tour company also offers a similar — yet different — air tour to the mountain villages of **Mascota** and **Talpa de Allende,** where you find out about the religious significance of these traditional towns. In Mascota, stroll the cobblestone streets lined with adobe houses and colonial haciendas, stopping at the majestic town church, dedicated to the Virgin de los Dolores (Virgin of Sorrows), which was completed in 1880 and took more than 100 years to construct. You stop for lunch and tour a local *raicilla* distillery to sample this locally popular beverage before traveling on to Talpa. Talpa is known for being home to one of Mexico's most revered icons, the Virgin Rosario de Talpa, believed to grant miracles with her healing powers. Ask for one yourself as you visit the Gothic church that bears her name, or simply wander around this pastoral village, set in a valley that is surrounded by pine-covered mountains. The six-hour adventure includes airfare and lunch, for $140 per person. Departures are Mondays, Thursdays, and Saturdays at 10:30 a.m., from Aerotron (next to Puerto Vallarta's airport).

Pacific Travel (☎ 322-225-2270) offers a **Jeep tour** to San Sebastián for $75 (up to four people per Jeep including a guide). You can choose to drive along steep, narrow, rocky mountain roads or leave that part of the adventure to your guide. This tour departs at 9 a.m. and returns at 5 p.m.

If you want to stay overnight, you have two options. The first is the very basic **El Pabellon de San Sebastián** (☎/fax 322-297-0200), which has nine rooms facing the town square. Don't expect extras here, but the rates run $40 per double or $13 for singles. Reservations are handled through the town's central phone lines — you call and leave a message or send a fax, and hopefully, the hotel receives it. Except on holidays, there's generally room at this inn, but bring cash — credit cards aren't accepted.

A more enjoyable option is the stately **Hacienda Jalisco** (☎ 322-297-2855 or 222-9638), built in 1850 and once the center of mining operations in this old mining town. Located near the airstrip (a 15-min. walk from town), the beautifully landscaped, rambling hacienda has walls that seem to whisper tales of its past. But if proprietor Bud Acord is feeling social, his stories usually outshine any the hacienda has to tell. He's welcomed John Huston, Liz Taylor, Richard Burton, Peter O'Toole, and a cast of local characters as his guests. The extra-clean rooms have wood floors, rustic furnishings and antiques, and working fireplaces; some are decorated with pre-Columbian reproductions. The ample bathrooms are beautifully tiled and have skylights. Hammocks grace the upstairs terrace. A sort-of museum on the lower level attests to the celebrity guests and prior importance the hacienda has enjoyed over the years. Because of its remote location, all meals are included. Rates are $80 per person per night including breakfast and dinner; alcoholic beverages are extra. Group rates are available and discounts may be possible for longer stays. No credit cards are accepted.

Relaxing in Yelapa

Yelapa, the same south-shore beach I discuss earlier in this chapter, is also a great overnight escape. It's a cove straight out of a tropical fantasy and only a 45-minute trip by boat from Puerto Vallarta. Yelapa has no cars, has one lone paved (pedestrian-only) road, and got electricity only in the past four years. (The cove remains accessible only by boat.) Yelapa's tranquillity, natural beauty, and seclusion make it a popular home for hippies, hipsters, artists, writers, and a few expatriates (looking to escape the stress of the rest of the world or, perhaps, the law). Yes, it's a seemingly strange cast of characters, but you're unlikely to ever meet a stranger here — Yelapa remains casual and friendly.

To get to Yelapa, take an excursion boat or an inexpensive water taxi. You can spend an enjoyable day in this wonderful spot, but I recommend a longer stay — it provides a completely different perspective of the place.

When you're in Yelapa, you can lie in the sun, swim, and snorkel; eat fresh, grilled seafood at a beachfront restaurant; or sample the local moonshine, *raicilla*. The beach vendors specialize in the most amazing pies I've ever tasted (coconut, lemon, or chocolate), and the way pie ladies walk the beach while balancing the pie plates on their heads is equally amazing. Vendors sell crocheted swimsuits too. You can also tour this tiny town or hike up a river to see one of two waterfalls. The waterfall closest to town is about a 30-minute walk from the beach.

If you use a local guide for a tour or a hike, agree on a price before you start out. Horseback riding, guided bird-watching excursions, fishing trips, and paragliding are also available.

For overnight accommodations, local residents frequently rent out rooms, or you can check out the rustic **Hotel Lagunita** (☎ **322-209-5055** or 209-5056; www.hotel-lagunita.com). With 32 *cabañas* (all with private bathroom), a saltwater pool, massage services, and an amiable restaurant/ bar, this is the most accommodating place for most visitors — although you may need to bring your own towel because they're known to be in short supply. Also, note that the hotel only has a few hours of power daily. Rates generally run $75 to $110 per night, but they vary depending on the *cabaña* and the time of year. Hotel Lagunita accepts American Express, MasterCard, and Visa with a 10 percent surcharge. This location has become quite popular for yoga students and other groups.

My preferred place to stay is **Verana** (☎ **800-677-7176** or 310-360-0155 in the U.S., or 322-222-2360; www.verana.com). It's a magical six-villa inn located on the mountaintop of the western edge of Yelapa Cove. For details about Verana, check out my review in Chapter 16.

If you stay over on a Wednesday or Saturday night during winter months, don't miss the regular dance at the **Yelapa Yacht Club** (no phone). Typically tongue-in-cheek for Yelapa, the "yacht club" consists of a cement dance floor and a disco ball, but the DJ spins a great range of tunes ranging from Glenn Miller to Black Eyed Peas, attracting all ages and types of musical aficionados to the dance. Dinner is a bonus — the food may be the best anywhere in the bay. The menu changes depending on what's fresh. Ask for directions; it's located in the main village on the beach.

Discovering Puerto Vallarta after Dark

Puerto Vallarta's spirited nightlife reflects the town's dual nature: part resort, part colonial Mexican town. In the past few years, Vallarta's nightlife has seen an expansion of live music, especially in clubs along Calle Ignacio L. Vallarta (the extension of the main southbound road) after it crosses the Río Cuale. A live blues club, a sports bar, live mariachi music, a gay dance club, a steamy-hot live salsa dance club, and the obligatory **Señor Frog's** are along one 3-block stretch of the road. Walk from place to place and take in a bit of it all!

The *malecón,* which used to be lined with restaurants, is now known more for its selection of dance clubs and a few more-relaxed club options, all of which look out over the ocean. You can walk along the broad walkway by the water's edge and check out the action at the various clubs, which extend from the Cuban-themed **La Bodeguita del Medio** on the north end to **Hooters** just off the central plaza.

Marina Vallarta has its own array of clubs with a more upscale, indoor, and air-conditioned atmosphere. South of the Río Cuale, the **Olas Altas zone** literally buzzes with action pouring out of its wide selection of small cafes and martini bars. In this zone, there's also an active gay and lesbian club scene.

Taking in a cultural event

As in most Mexican beach resorts, Vallarta has a limited selection of cultural nightlife beyond the **Mexican fiesta,** but as a growing center for the visual arts in Mexico, Vallarta is more diverse than most. Popular events include the winter season of art-exhibition openings. Puerto Vallarta's gallery community comes together to present almost weekly **art walks** where new exhibits are presented, featured artists are in attendance, and complimentary cocktails are served. These social events alternate between the galleries along the Marina Vallarta *malecón* and the galleries in the central downtown area. Check listings in the daily English-language newspaper, *Vallarta Today,* upon arrival to see what may be on the schedule during your stay.

Celebrating a fiesta

Major hotels in Puerto Vallarta feature frequent fiestas for tourists — an open-bar, a Mexican buffet dinner, and live-entertainment extravaganzas. Some fiestas are fairly authentic and are good introductions for first-time travelers to Mexico; others can be a bit cheesy. Shows are usually held outdoors but move indoors when necessary.

✔ The **NH Krystal Puerto Vallarta** (☎ **322-224-0202;** kvallarta@ krystal.com) hosts one of the best fiestas on Tuesdays at 7 p.m. These things are difficult to quantify, but Krystal's program is probably less tacky than most of its hotel counterparts. The charge is $65, and major credit cards are accepted.

✔ My personal favorite of the nocturnal fiestas is **Rhythms of the Night,** which combines a sunset boat cruise to the cove of Caletas with an evening of dining and entertainment under the stars at John Huston's former home. The smooth, fast Vallarta Adventure catamaran takes you to the site, providing entertainment along the way until you're greeted at the dock by tiki torches and native drummers. There's no electricity here — you dine by the light of the multitude of candles, the stars, and the moon. The buffet dinner is delicious — steak, seafood, and generous vegetarian options, accompanied by wine. Everything is first class. The show, set to the music of native bamboo flutes and guitars, showcases indigenous dances in a contemporary style. The boat departs from the Terminal Marítima at 6 p.m. and returns by 11 p.m. To reserve a spot, contact **Vallarta Adventures** (☎ **866-256-2739** from the U.S., or 322-297-1212; www.vallarta-adventures.com). The cost is $75 and includes the boat cruise, dinner, open bar, and entertainment. Major credit cards are accepted.

Enjoying the club and music scene

You can actually find some of Vallarta's best bets for nightlife in popular restaurants — combining food and fun. Other options are one of the many clubs featuring live music. Whatever your final selection is, one thing is for sure — Vallarta offers something for everyone, and there's rarely a quiet night in town.

Restaurants/bars

The sleek **Bianco,** Insurgentes 109, Col. Emiliano Zapata (☎ **322-222-2748**), is a popular choice for more sophisticated nightlife, with its long, glass-top bar and cozy seating areas where conversation is possible. This is the spot for anyone older than 30 who wants to enjoy an evening out, listening to contemporary music. The air-conditioned lounge also features occasional live music, notably salsa on Thursday and Saturday nights. You can't miss the dramatic entrance. Open daily from 5 p.m. to 4 a.m.

Vallarta's original nightspot is **Carlos O'Brian's,** Paseo Díaz Ordaz 786, along the *malecón* at Pípila (☎ **322-222-1444** or 222-4065), once considered the only place you'd think of going for an evening of revelry. Although the competition is stiffer nowadays, COB's still packs them in — especially the 20-something set. Late at night, the scene resembles a college party. It's open daily noon to 2 a.m.

The newest and most sophisticated lounge in Vallarta is the **Constantini Bar Lounge,** set in the elegant eatery, Cafe des Artistes, Guadalupe Sanchez 740 (☎ **322-222-3228** or 222-3229; www.cafedesartistes. com). Opened in late 2003, it's become a popular option for those looking for a lively yet sophisticated option for after-dinner drinks. The plush sofas are welcoming, and the list of champagnes by the glass, signature martinis, and specialty drinks are suitably tempting. Live jazz and blues in an intimate atmosphere are drawing crowds. An ample appetizer and dessert menu make it appropriate for a late-night dining-and-drinks option. Open from 6 p.m. to 2 a.m.

Kit Kat Club, Pulpito 120, Playas Los Muertos (☎ **322-223-0093**), is swank, sleek, and reminiscent of a New York, high-style club, but don't be fooled — the club also has a terrific sense of humor. In the golden glow of candlelight, you can lounge around in cushy, leopard-patterned chairs or cream-colored, overstuffed chaise lounges listening to swinging tunes while sipping on a martini. The place isn't only hip, but it also serves good food, with especially tasty appetizers that can double as light meals and scrumptious desserts. Michael, the owner, describes his lounge and cafe as cool, crazy, wild, jazzy, and sexy. I agree. Often, in high season, a cross-dressing songstress performs a cabaret-style floor show. The club is open daily 11 a.m. to 2 a.m.

La Bodeguita del Medio, Paseo Díaz Ordaz/*malecón,* at Allende (☎ 322-223-1585), is an authentic Cuban restaurant known for its casual energy, terrific live music, and mojitos — stiff rum-based drinks with fresh mint and lime juice. It's a branch of the original Bodeguita in Havana (reputedly Hemingway's favorite restaurant there), which opened in 1942. If you can't get to that one, the Vallarta version has successfully imported the essence — and it has a small souvenir shop that sells Cuban cigars, rum, and other items. The downstairs has large wooden windows that open to the *malecón* street action, while the upstairs offers terrific views of the bay. Walls throughout are decorated with old photographs and patrons' signatures — if you can, find a spot and add yours! The food is less memorable here than the music and atmosphere, so I suggest drinks and dancing, nothing more. It's open daily from 11:30 a.m. to 2 a.m.

A Mexican classic gone contemporary is **Mi Querencia,** Morelos 709 (☎ 322-222-7701). *Cantinas* are a centuries-old tradition in Mexico, and this one retains the fundamentals while updating the concept to a hip club. Cantinas serve little complimentary plates of food as your table continues to order drinks. The grub is served here from 1 to 5 p.m. and may include *carne con chile* (meat in a chile sauce), soup of the day, or quesadillas. In the evenings, enjoy a romantic, clubby atmosphere with recorded music alternating between sultry boleros and the hottest in Mexican rock at levels that still permit conversation. If you require more stimulation, board games are available to play in one of the brightly colored, smaller rooms or on the larger open-air patio. Mi Querencia is open Sunday to Wednesday noon to 2 a.m. and Thursday to Saturday noon to 4 a.m. No credit cards.

Live music

Currently the most popular live-music club in Vallarta, **Route 66,** Ignacio L. Vallarta 217 (no phone), features a hot house band that plays a mix of reggae, blues, and rock. Live music jams nightly from 10 p.m. to 2 a.m. Route 66 is located south of the river between Madero and Cárdenas, and it's open nightly 6 p.m. to 2 a.m. There's no cover.

El Faro Lighthouse Bar (☎ 322-221-0541 or -0542) is a circular cocktail lounge at the top of the Marina Vallarta lighthouse and is one of Vallarta's most romantic nightspots. Live or recorded jazz plays, and conversation is manageable. Drop by at twilight for the magnificent panoramic views. Open daily 5:30 p.m. to 2 a.m. with no cover.

Mariachi Loco, Lázaro Cárdenas 254, at Ignacio Vallarta (☎ 322-223-2205), is a live and lively mariachi club that also features singers belting out boleros and ranchero classics. The mariachi show begins at 10 p.m. — the mariachis stroll and play as guests join in impromptu singing — and by 10 p.m., things really get going. After midnight, the mariachis play for pay, which is around $10 for each song. The kitchen serves Mexican food until 1 a.m. The club itself is open daily 8 p.m. to 4 a.m.

Dance clubs and discos

A few of Vallarta's clubs or discos charge admission, but generally you just pay for drinks — $4 for a margarita, $3 for a beer, and more for whiskey and mixed drinks. Keep an eye out for the discount passes frequently available in hotels, restaurants, and other tourist spots. Most clubs are open daily 10 p.m. to 4 a.m.:

- ✔ **Collage Club,** Calle Proa s/n, Marina Vallarta (☎ 322-221-0505), is a multilevel monster of nighttime entertainment that features a pool hall, video arcade, bowling alley, and an always-packed disco bar (with frequent live entertainment). Open daily 10 a.m. to 6 a.m., the club is easily visible from the main highway, just past the entrance to Marina Vallarta, and it's very popular with a young and mainly local crowd. Cover charge is $4.

- ✔ **Christine** (☎ 322-224-0202) is a dazzling club that still draws a crowd with an opening laser-light show, pumped-in dry ice and oxygen, flashing lights, and a dozen large-screen video panels. Once a disco — in the true sense of the word — Christine received a face-lift in 2003, and is now a more modern dance club, with techno, house, and hip-hop the primary tunes played. The sound system is truly amazing, and the mix of music can get almost anyone dancing. This spot is open nightly 10 p.m. to 4 a.m.; the light show begins at 11 p.m. No shorts (for men), tennis shoes, or flip-flops are permitted. It's part of the NH Krystal Puerto Vallarta, north of downtown, and is very visible off Avenida Francisco Medina Ascencio. Cover varies from free to $20, depending on the night, and major credit cards are accepted.

- ✔ **de Santos,** Morelos 771 (☎ 322-223-3052 or 223-3053; www.desantos.com.mx), may be among Vallarta's chicest dining spots, but it is really known more for the urban, hip crowd its bar and adjacent club draws. Opened in 2003, this stunning state-of-the-art club quickly became the place for the super-chic to party. The lower level holds an air-conditioned bar and dance floor, where a DJ spins the hottest house and techno. Upstairs, an open-air rooftop bar has chill-out music and acid jazz. Enjoy the tunes and the fresh air while lounging around on one of the several oversize beds. One partner, a member of the super-hot Latin rock group Maná, uses Vallarta as a home base for writing new songs. The restaurant bar is open daily from 5 p.m. to 1 a.m.; the club is open Wednesday through Saturday from 10 p.m. to 6 a.m. On special event nights, there may be a cover charge, but generally admission is free.

- ✔ You'll recognize **Hilo,** Malecón, between Aldama and Abasolo (☎ 322-223-5361), by the giant-sized sculptures that practically reach out the front entrance and pull you into this high-energy club, which has become a favorite with the 20-something set. Music ranges from house and electronic to rock. It seems the later the hour, the more crowded the place becomes. Open daily from 4 p.m. to 6 a.m. Cover charge is $7, weekends and holidays.

✔ The **J&B Salsa Club,** Av. Francisco Medina Ascencio Km 2.5, in the Hotel Zone (☎ **322-224-4616**), is the locally popular place to go for dancing to Latin music — from salsa to samba, the dancing here is hot! The club features live bands on Fridays, Saturdays, and holidays. It's open from 9 p.m. to 6 a.m. with a $10 cover.

✔ **Nikki Beach,** on the beach at the Westin Regina Resort (☎ **322-22-0252** or 226-1150; www.nikkibeach.com), is a haven for the hip, which hails from South Beach, Miami, and St. Tropez, bringing its ultracool vibe to Vallarta. White-draped bed-size lounges scatter the outdoor lounge area, under a canopy of tall palms and umbrellas. Indoor dining and lounge areas are also available. The music is the latest in electronic, house, and chill, with visiting DJs often playing on weekend nights. Sundays feature their signature beach brunch, and Thursday evenings feature "Beautiful People" night. It's a great choice for catching rays during the day while sipping tropical drinks, but its real appeal is the nocturnal action. Open Sunday to Wednesday from 11 a.m. to 1 a.m. (food service stops at 11 p.m.); Thursday to Saturday from 11 a.m. to 3 a.m. (food service stops at 1 a.m.).

✔ At **The Palm Video & Show Bar,** Olas Altas 508 (☎ **322-223-4818**), the big screen above the dance floor plays the most danceable videos in town. At this colorful, lively, and air-conditioned club, the pool table is regularly in play, and you frequently find you're in for a night of great entertainment, as the club regularly books live shows featuring female impersonators. This is a gay-friendly but not exclusively gay club, with a spirited, festive atmosphere. Open daily from 7 p.m. to 2 a.m., a cover charge of about $5 applies on show nights only.

✔ The sheer size of **Señor Frog's,** Ignacio L. Vallarta and Venustiano Carranza (☎ **322-222-5171** or 222-5177), an outpost of the famed Carlos 'n Charlie's chain, may be daunting, but it still fills up with partiers and rocks until the early morning hours. Those cute waiters remain a signature of the chain, and one never knows when they'll assemble on stage and call on a bevy of beauties to join them in a tequila-drinking contest. Occasionally, live bands appear. Although mainly popular with the 20s set, all ages find it fun. There's food service, but the place is better known for its dance-club atmosphere. It's open from noon to 4 a.m., with a cover charge of $11.

✔ A visit to the **Zoo,** Paseo Díaz Ordaz 630, the *malecón* (☎ **322-222-4945;** www.zoobardance.com), gives you a chance to be an animal and get wild in the night — this joint even has cages to dance in if you're feeling really unleashed. The Zoo has a terrific sound system and a great variety of dance music including techno, reggae, and rap. Every hour is a happy hour here with two-for-one drinks. The club is open 11:30 a.m. until the wee hours of the morn, and cover usually ranges from free to $11.

Sports bar

With enough TVs and sports memorabilia to start a mini-museum, **Micky's No Name Café,** Morelos 460 at Mina, the *malecón* (☎ 322-223-2508; www.nonamecafe.net), is a great venue for catching your favorite game, including NBA, NHL, NFL, and MLB games, as well as pay-per-view sporting events. Mickey's also serves great BBQ ribs and imported steaks from the United States. It's open daily 9 a.m. to midnight.

Gay and lesbian clubs

Vallarta has a vibrant gay community and a wide variety of clubs and nightlife options including special bay cruises and evening excursions to nearby ranches. The free *Gay Guide Vallarta* (no phone; www.gayguidevallarta.com) specializes in gay-friendly listings.

- ✔ **Club Paco Paco,** Ignacio L. Vallarta 278 (☎ 322-222-7667; www.clubpacopaco.com), is a combination disco, cantina, and rooftop bar that also hosts a spectacular "Trasvesty" drag show every Friday, Saturday, and Sunday night at 1:30 a.m. The club is open noon to 6 a.m. daily and is air-conditioned. The **Ranch Disco Bar,** around the corner at Venustiano Carranza 239, has nightly specials including Western Night on Tuesdays and Leather Night on Thursdays. A nightly "Ranch Hand's Show" is performed at 1 a.m. and 3 a.m. This club, which can be accessed from Club Paco Paco, is open 9 p.m. to 6 a.m. The cover of $6 applies to both clubs and includes a drink.

- ✔ **Garbo's,** Pulpito 142 (☎ 322-229-7309; www.bargarbo.com), is a small, cozy club that is gay friendly, but not exclusively gay. It features great recorded music and occasional live music on weekends. It's open daily from 6 p.m. to 2 a.m. and is air-conditioned.

- ✔ **Los Balcones,** Juárez 182 (☎ 322-222-4671), one of the original gay clubs in town, is a bi-level space with several dance floors and an excellent sound system. It earned a few chuckles when it was listed as one of the most romantic spots in Vallarta by *Bride's* magazine. This air-conditioned club is open 9 p.m. to 4 a.m. and posts nightly specials including exotic male dancers.

Part VI
Ixtapa and Zihuatanejo

In this part . . .

Think of a vacation here as getting two destinations (and the best of both worlds) for the price of one: The side-by-side beach resorts of Ixtapa and Zihuatanejo may share a common geography, but they couldn't be more different in character. Ixtapa has a modern infrastructure, tons of services, and luxury hotels. Zihuatanejo — or Zihua to the locals — is the quintessential Mexican beach village with one-of-a-kind accommodations.

The only thing that some visitors may find lacking is the nightlife, which is rather subdued in both towns — especially compared to other more developed resorts such as Acapulco, Los Cabos, and Puerto Vallarta. But, if you're looking for laid-back evenings of good conversation and cocktails in the moonlight, the absent party crowd may be a plus.

Chapter 20

The Lowdown on the Ixtapa and Zihuatanejo Hotel Scenes

by Lynne Bairstow

. . . .

In This Chapter

▶ Sizing up the hotel locations
▶ Checking out top hotel choices in Ixtapa and Zihuatanejo

. . . .

*T*hink of a vacation to this slice of Mexico as cashing in a two-for-one coupon and getting the best of both worlds: The side-by-side beach resorts of **Ixtapa** and **Zihuatanejo** may share a common geography, but they couldn't be more different in character. Ixtapa boasts a modern infrastructure, a wide array of services, and luxury hotels. Zihuatanejo — or Zihua to the locals — is the quintessential Mexican beach village and offers lower-priced rooms and one-of-a-kind inns. If you're the type of traveler who prefers comforts reminiscent of home, opt for Ixtapa and take advantage of well-appointed rooms in a setting of tropical beauty. You can easily and quickly make the 6km (4-mile) trip into Zihuatanejo for a sampling of life in this *pueblo* by the sea. But, if you prefer a more rustic retreat with real personality, consider settling in Zihuatanejo. Its funky charm has attracted a community of Swiss and Italian immigrants, adding an air of sophistication to the laid-back village life.

With a backdrop of palm-covered hills and the Pacific Ocean waters serving as a foreground, you can enjoy a full range of activities and diversions here — scuba diving, deep-sea fishing, bay cruises to remote beaches, and golf are among the favorites. The one exception is the nightlife, which is rather subdued in both towns, especially compared to other more-developed resorts such as Acapulco, Los Cabos, and Puerto Vallarta.

As a dual destination, Ixtapa and Zihuatanejo are the ideal choice for the traveler looking for a little bit of everything, from resort-style indulgence to unpretentious good times. Zihua is a relaxed, down-to-earth paradise, and it's also known for its collection of unique hillside boutique hotels, which cater to an international crowd looking for pampered luxury and individualized style. Terrific bargains also exist and still offer character, cleanliness, and safety — if not the full range of amenities. Of all the resorts in Mexico, the Ixtapa/Zihuatanejo region has the best selection of one-of-a-kind places to stay.

 These two resort towns are more welcoming to couples and adults than they are to families. A number of places are off-limits to children under 16 — something of a rarity in Mexico.

Choosing Your Location

Because the ambience is so different between these two sister towns, choosing the right place to stay makes a big difference in your overall vacation experience — though the ride between the two is an easy one.

Ixtapa, as I note earlier in the chapter, is the more modern, made-for-tourism town. Developed by the Mexican government in the 1970s as a complement to Zihua's fetching charms, Ixtapa places a bevy of conveniences at your disposal: shopping centers, sleek eateries, golf courses, and high-rise hotels. Almost everything is accessible by foot or is an inexpensive cab ride away.

Each of the Ixtapa hotels listed in this chapter (with the exception of Las Brisas) lies along the wide, attractive Playa el Palmar and is largely self-contained — with shops, bars, restaurants, and water fun on-site — meaning you never need to leave the resort's property if you don't want to. The main difference between Ixtapa and Zihuatanejo is that while Ixtapa hotels offer every conceivable comfort and convenience, they lack the charm and originality of Zihua accommodations. Also you need to remember that Ixtapa hotels, on the whole, are priced much higher.

If you choose the traditional appeal of **Zihuatanejo,** you still need to narrow down your preference in terms of staying in the central town or on one of Zihua's neighboring beaches. In either case, Zihua is small, friendly, colorful, and full of Mexico's authentic charms.

The places to stay in town — known as *el centro* — are generally small and inexpensive with the exception of Villa Vera Puerto Mio (which isn't technically located downtown anyway, so forget about the whole "exception" thing). Many establishments offer bare-bones accommodations without air-conditioning and are subject to local street noise, but they're clean, priced right, and within easy walking distance of plenty of places to eat and shop. Note that none of the *centro* Zihua hotels are situated directly on the beach, and only Puerto Mio has an ocean view.

Also worth knowing is that the term "bungalow" is loosely defined in Zihuatanejo, just as it is elsewhere in Mexico. Thus, a bungalow may be an individual unit with a kitchen and bedroom, or it may be a mere bedroom. It may also be like a hotel, located in a two-story building with multiple units with or without kitchens. The bungalow may be cozy or rustic, with or without a patio or balcony.

Two lovely beaches and a couple of Mexico's most notable small hotels are just east of *centro* Zihuatanejo. **Playa Madera** and **Playa La Ropa,** separated from each other by only a craggy shoreline, are both accessible by road. Prices here tend to be higher than those in town, but the value is much better, and people tend to find that the beautiful and tranquil setting is worth the extra cost. The area is rich with charm and a stellar selection of sand for anyone who truly treasures a great beach. The only drawback to this area is that dining is limited to *palapa* (thatched roof) beach restaurants or the on-site restaurants at the hotels, and there's essentially no shopping or nightlife to speak of, which means you have to hop in a taxi and go to town for any diversions other than beach-related fun and limited dining. The town is just 5 to 20 minutes away depending on whether you walk or take a taxi, which costs about $2.

Ixtapa's and Zihuatanejo's Best Accommodations

As far as prices go, I note *rack rates* (the maximum that a hotel or resort charges for a room) for two people spending one night in a double room. You can usually do better, especially if you're purchasing a package that includes airfare. Expect to pay more — up to double the rack-rate prices — if you're planning a visit during Christmas or Easter weeks. Prices quoted here include the 17 percent room tax. Please refer to the Introduction of this book for an explanation of the price categories.

As I mention earlier in this chapter, Ixtapa and Zihuatanejo tend to not be very kid friendly, so if you plan on bringing the whole family, including the little ones, please pay special attention to the Kid Friendly icons highlighting the best choices. Unless otherwise indicated, all hotels have air-conditioning.

Apartamentos Amueblados Valle
$–$$ Zihuatanejo Centro

These accommodations are actually apartments, but you can rent them by the day or week, meaning you can enjoy a well-furnished apartment for the price of an inexpensive hotel room. This property is a great choice for friends traveling together on a budget. Five one-bedroom apartments accommodate up to three people; the three two-bedroom apartments can fit four comfortably. Request an apartment that doesn't face the street; they're less noisy. Each apartment is different, but all are clean and airy with ceiling fans, private balconies, and kitchenettes, but no air-conditioning. Maid service is provided daily, and the office offers a paperback-book exchange. Reserve well in advance during high season.

Vincente Guerrero 14, about 2 blocks in from the waterfront between Ejido and N. Bravo. ☎ *755-554-2084. Fax: 755-554-3220. 8 units. Rack rates: High season $60 one-bedroom apartment, $90 two-bedroom apartment; low season $40 one-bedroom apartment, $60 two-bedroom apartment. Ask for special rates during low season and for prolonged stays. No credit cards.*

Barceló Ixtapa
$$$$ Ixtapa

A grand, 12-story resort hotel (formerly the Sheraton), Barceló Ixtapa is one of the best choices in the area for families. A modern, well-equipped resort, Barceló boasts handsomely furnished public areas and tropical gardens surrounding a large pool, which has a swim-up bar and a separate section for children. Most rooms have balconies with ocean or mountain views, and nonsmoking and handicapped-accessible rooms are available. You never need to leave this hotel if you choose not to; the Barceló Ixtapa lacks nothing — four restaurants plus room service, a nightclub, a lobby bar, and the area's most popular Mexican fiesta (held weekly) with a sumptuous buffet and live entertainment outdoors. If you choose to spend all your time here, be sure to take advantage of the optional, all-inclusive pricing rates. Four tennis courts and a fitness room are available for the actively inclined. For all that the Barceló offers on-site, it may be the best value in Ixtapa.

Bulevar Ixtapa s/n, at the southeastern end of Playa el Palmar. ☎ ***800-325-3535*** *in the U.S. and Canada, or 755-553-1858. Fax: 755-553-2438.* www.barcelo.com. *333 units. Free parking. Rack rates: High season $245 double all-inclusive, $180 double with breakfast only; low season $225 double all-inclusive. AE, DC, MC, V.*

Bungalows Ley
$$–$$$$ Zihuatanejo Beaches/Playa Madera

Located on a small complex on Playa Madera, Bungalows Ley is a great option for friends traveling together. If you're traveling with a group, you may want to book the most expensive suite (called Club Madera), which comes with a rooftop terrace, tiled hot tub, outdoor bar and grill, and a spectacular view. No two suites are the same here, but all are immaculate; the simplest layouts are studios with one bed and a kitchen in the same room. All rooms have terraces or balconies just above the beach, and all are decorated in the ice-cream colors reminiscent of Miami South Beach. Bathrooms, however, tend to be small and dark. Clients praise the management and the service. To find the property, follow Calle Eva S. de López Matéos to the right up a slight hill; the hotel is on the left.

Calle Eva S. de López Mateos s/n. ☎ ***755-554-4087***. *Fax: 755-554-1365.* www.zihua. net/bungalosley. *8 units. Rack rates: $103 double with air-conditioning; $162 two-bedroom suite with kitchen for up to four persons or $212 for up to six persons. No credit cards.*

Zihuatanejo and Ixtapa Area Accommodations

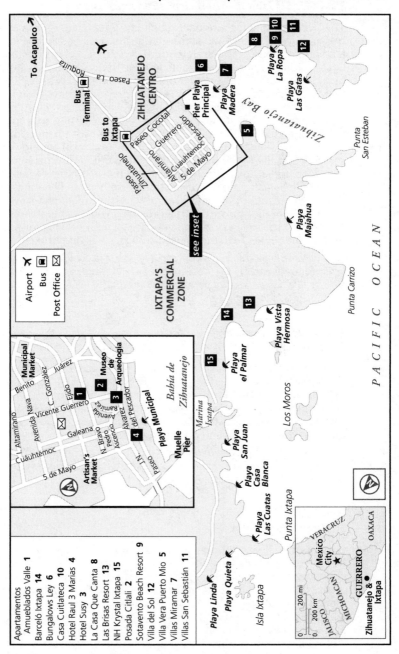

To Acapulco

Paseo La Ropa

Bus Terminal

Bus to Ixtapa

ZIHUATANEJO CENTRO

Paseo Cocotal

Pier Playa Principal

Guerrero

Pescador

Cuauhtémoc

Altamirano

5 de Mayo

Paseo Zihuatanejo

Playa Madera

Playa La Ropa

Playa Las Gatas

Punta San Esteban

Zihuatanejo Bay

see inset

Playa Majahua

IXTAPA'S COMMERCIAL ZONE

Airport ✈
Bus 🚌
Post Office ⊠

Playa Vista Hermosa

Punta Carrizo

PACIFIC OCEAN

Municipal Market

Benito Juárez

C. González

Ejido

Vicente Guerrero

Galeana

Cuauhtémoc

5 de Mayo

Artisan's Market

I. Altamirano

Avenida Nava

Pedro Ascencio

N. Bravo

Álvarez

del Pescador

Museo de Arqueología

Playa Municipal

Muelle Pier

Bahía de Zihuatanejo

Marina Ixtapa

Playa el Palmar

Playa San Juan

Los Moros

Playa Casa Blanca

Playa Las Cuatas

Punta Ixtapa

Playa Linda

Playa Quieta

Isla Ixtapa

Apartamentos
Amueblados Valle **1**
Barceló Ixtapa **14**
Bungalows Ley **6**
Casa Cuitlateca **10**
Hotel Raúl 3 Marías **4**
Hotel Susy **3**
La Casa Que Canta **8**
Las Brisas Resort **13**
NH Krystal Ixtapa **15**
Posada Citlali **2**
Sotavento Beach Resort **9**
Villa del Sol **12**
Villa Vera Puerto Mío **5**
Villas Miramar **7**
Villas San Sebastián **11**

VERACRUZ

Mexico City ★

GUERRERO

MICHOACÁN

JALISCO

OAXACA

Zihuatanejo & Ixtapa ●

0   200 mi
0   200 km

Casa Cuitlateca
$$$$–$$$$$ Zihuatanejo Beaches/Playa La Ropa

The perfect place for a romantic holiday, Casa Cuitlateca is an exclusive bed-and-breakfast and one of the unique inns that has made Playa La Ropa a standout. Done in the architectural style that has made Zihua famous, Casa Cuitlateca has *palapa* roofs and earthy colors and is built into the hillside across from Playa La Ropa, just a short walk away. Three of the four units offer a stunning view. Two smaller rooms have their own private terrace and a small sitting area. There's also a suite with a large terrace, and a second suite with no view but a very nice sitting area and small private garden. Each room is carefully decorated with handicrafts and textiles from all over Mexico. The bar is on the first level behind the pool and serves cocktails to the public from 4:30 to 8 p.m. Guests can help themselves to soft drinks and beers on the honor system when the bar is closed. The small pool, like everything else here, is beautifully designed. On the top level of the two suites, all guests can enjoy a sun deck and a hot tub. From the entrance to the property, you climb a steep staircase of 120 steps. The driveway is also very steep, with parking for six cars. The parking lot connects to the house through a hanging bridge.

Calle Playa La Ropa, a short walk in from La Ropa beach. ☎ *877-541-1234 from the U.S., or 755-554-2448. Fax: 755-554-7394.* www.casacuitlateca.com. *4 units. Rack rates: $340 double, $50 each extra person; low season $220 double. Rates include round-trip transfers to the airport and full breakfast daily. AE, MC, V. No children under 16.*

Hotel Raul 3 Marias
$ Zihuatanejo Centro

Although it's a small, basic hotel with strictly functional rooms, the Raul is very clean and known for its friendly guest services. Nine rooms have a balcony overlooking the street, and the small office offers telephone and fax service to guests. Downstairs is the landmark Zihuatanejo seafood restaurant, Garrobos, which is open for lunch and dinner. The hotel also offers deep-sea fishing and diving charters.

Juan Alvarez 52, between 5 de Mayo and Cuautemoc streets. ☎ *755-554-6706.* garroboscrew@prodigy.net.mx. *17 units. Rack rates: High season $50 double; variable prices in low season. AE, MC, V.*

Hotel Susy
$ Zihuatanejo Centro

Consistently clean with tons of plants along a shaded walkway set back from the street, this two-story hotel offers small rooms with fans (no air-conditioning) and louvered-glass windows with screens. Hotel Susy is a good choice if you're looking for a central location, a cheap price, and a comfortable, simple place to stay. Request an upper-floor room and enjoy a balcony that overlooks the street. To get here, face away from the water at the basketball court on the *malecón* (boardwalk), turn right, and walk 2 blocks; the hotel is on your left at the corner of Guerrero.

Juan Alvarez 3 at Guerrero. ☎ *755-554-2339. 18 units. Rack rates: High season $45 per person, per room; low season $40–$60 double. MC, V.*

La Casa Que Canta
$$$$$ Zihuatanejo Beaches/Playa La Ropa

Another striking inn and another ideal choice for a romantic getaway is "The House that Sings," located on a mountainside overlooking Zihuatanejo Bay. Designed with striking molded-adobe architecture, La Casa Que Canta was the first of a rustic-chic style of architecture now known as Mexican Pacific. All the rooms are individually decorated in unusual, painted, Michoacán furniture; antiques; and stretched-leather *equipales* (a traditional Mexican chair characterized by its round-design and sturdy construction), with hand-loomed fabrics and handsome, natural-tile floors used throughout. All units have large, beautifully furnished terraces with bay views. Hammocks under the thatched-roof terraces, supported by rough-hewn *vigas* (wooden beams), are perfectly placed for watching yachts sail in and out of the harbor. The four categories of rooms (terrace suites, deluxe suites, grand suites, and private-pool suites) are all spacious. Rooms meander up and down the hillside, and although no one staircase is terribly long, you should know that Casa Que Canta doesn't have elevators. Technically, the hotel isn't on Playa La Ropa (or any beach), but on the road leading there. The closest stretch of beach (the very beginning of Playa La Ropa) is down a steep hill. La Casa Que Canta has a small restaurant-bar on a shaded terrace, a small pool on the main terrace, and a second, saltwater pool on the bottom level. A new Well Being Center has been added, offering massage, spa services, and yoga. Little extras such as laundry, room service, and complimentary soft drinks and beer in your minifridge are present to pamper you.

Camino Escénico a Playa La Ropa. ☎ *888-523-5050 in the U.S., or 755-555-7000. Fax: 755-554-7900.* www.lacasaquecanta.com. *21 suites. Rack rates: $420–$690 double. AE, MC, V. No children under 16.*

Las Brisas Resort
$$$$–$$$$$ Ixtapa

Set above the high-rise hotels of Ixtapa on its own rocky promontory, Las Brisas (formerly the Westin Brisas) is clearly the most stunning of Ixtapa's hotels, and the hotel most noted for gracious service. The austere but luxurious public areas, all in stone and stucco, are bathed in sweeping breezes and an air of exclusivity. A minimalist luxury also characterizes the rooms, which have Mexican-tile floors and private, plant-decked patios with hammocks and lounges. All rooms face the hotel's cove and private beach, Vista Hermosa. Although this beach is true to its name (the breezes), it's dangerous for swimming. The six master suites come with private pools, the 16th floor is reserved for nonsmokers, and three rooms on the 18th floor are equipped for travelers with disabilities. Like many of Ixtapa's hotels, Las Brisas is so complete that you may never feel the urge to leave — choose from among five restaurants, room service, and three bars including a lobby bar with live trio music at sunset. Three swimming pools (including one for children) connected to one another by waterfalls, lighted tennis courts (with a pro available on request), and a fitness center with massage services round out the offerings.

Bulevar Ixtapa s/n. ☎ ***888-559-4329*** *in the U.S., or 755-553-2121. Fax: 755-553-1038.* www. brisas.com.mx. *423 units. Free parking. Rack rates: High season $285 deluxe, $490 Royal Beach Club; low season $196 deluxe, $230 Royal Beach Club. AE, DC, MC, V.*

NH Krystal Ixtapa
$$$–$$$$$ Ixtapa

Welcoming, exceptional service is what the Krystal chain of hotels is known for in Mexico, and the Ixtapa version is no exception. In fact, many of the staff members have been with the hotel for all its 20-some years of operation and greet returning guests. The Krystal is probably the area's best hotel for families because it has a playground and a special kid's club activities program. Each spacious and nicely furnished room has a balcony with an ocean view, game table, and tile bathroom. Master suites have large, furnished, triangular-shaped balconies that overlook the spacious grounds and the large pool, which has a special kid's section as well as a waterfall and water slide. A tennis court, racquetball court, and a small gym are also on-site. Note that some rates include a daily breakfast buffet — a great deal if you make the buffet your main meal of the day. Krystal Ixtapa has five restaurants to choose from, including the evenings-only Bogart's, plus room service. Also important to note is that the center of Ixtapa nightlife is found here, at Krystal's famed Christine Disco.

Bulevar Ixtapa s/n, at the northwestern end of Playa el Palmar. ☎ ***800-231-9860*** *in the U.S., or 755-553-0333. Fax: 755-553-0216. 255 units.* www.nh-hotels.com. *Free parking. Rack rates: High season $224 double, $280 suite; low season $110 double, $180 suite. Two children under 12 stay free in parent's room. Ask for special packages. AE, DC, MC, V.*

Posada Citlali
$ Zihuatanejo Centro

A pleasant, three-story hotel, Posada Citlali is a major bargain. Although the rooms are small, they're spotless, and they border a very pleasant plant-filled courtyard decked out with comfortable rockers and chairs. Bottled water is in help-yourself containers on the patio, and fans are found in all rooms (there's no air-conditioning). Although you may hear the children heading for the nearby school in the morning, the location avoids most of the evening noise and traffic sounds, making Posada Citlali a peaceful retreat in *el centro*. The stairway to the top two floors is narrow and steep.

Vicente Guerrero 3, near the corner of Alvarez. ☎ ***755-554-2043.*** citlali@ zihuatanejo.com.mx. *19 units. Rack rates: $45 double. No credit cards.*

Sotavento Beach Resort
$–$$$ Zihuatanejo Beaches/Playa La Ropa

Perched on a hill above the beach, this resort is for people who want to relax near the ocean in a simple, lovely setting without being bothered by televisions or closed up in air-conditioned rooms. A throwback to the style of the 1970s, when Zihua was first being discovered by an international jet set, the Sotavento comprises two multi-story buildings. Quite a variety of rooms are available to choose from — ask to see a few different rooms to find something that suits you, such as the popular doubles on the resort's upper floors, which are about three times the size of a normal double room. The furnishings in all the rooms are simple but comfortable, and all have ocean-view terraces that are half-sheltered and half-open, with chaises for basking in the sun and hammocks for enjoying the shade. Screened windows filter the ocean breezes, and ceiling fans keep the rooms airy even when the breeze is absent (remember — there's no air-conditioning). One curious feature of the Sotavento is that the floors are always slightly slanted in one direction or another — by design of the owner. Two restaurants, a small lobby bar, a pool with whirlpool, and a rooftop yoga studio serve guests. The resort is built into the side of a hill, and isn't for people who dislike climbing stairs. Take the highway south of Zihuatanejo about 2km (1 mile), turn right at the hotel's sign, and follow the road.

Playa La Ropa. ☎ **877-699-6685** *from the U.S., 877-667-3702 from Canada, or 755-554-2032. Fax: 755-554-2975.* www.beachresortsotavento.com. *100 units. Rack rates: High season $60–$105 double, $75–$130 suite; low season $75 double, $85 suite. AE, MC, V.*

Villa del Sol
$$$$$ Zihuatanejo Beaches/Playa La Ropa

Villa del Sol is an exquisite inn known as much for its unequivocal attention to luxurious detail as for its exacting German owner, Helmut Leins, who is almost always present to ensure the quality of his guests' stay. Villa del Sol is a haven of tranquillity that caters to guests looking for complete privacy and serenity. Each room is a harmony of magnificent design. The spacious, split-level suites have one or two bedrooms, plus a living area and a large terrace, some of which have a private mini-pool. King-size beds are draped in white netting, and comfy lounges and hammocks beckon to you at siesta time. Standard rooms are smaller, and they don't have TVs or telephones, but they're still artfully and individually appointed with artistic Mexican details. Nine beachfront suites have recently been added, but I still prefer the original rooms. No two are alike. Suites have CD players and private fax machines, with satellite TVs or DVD players brought to you upon request. No children under 12 are allowed during high season, and a "no children" and "no excess noise" sentiment prevails in general. Travelers who relish a more typically welcoming Mexican ambience may find a stay here less enjoyable. The hotel sits on a private, 180m-long (600-ft.), palm-shaded beach and also has three pools (including one 18m/60-ft. lap pool), two tennis courts, and a massage service. After you work up an appetite, enjoy an outstanding gourmet meal at the open-air, beachfront restaurant-bar or room service in your sumptuous surroundings. The rooms are stocked with deluxe amenities, and the hotel offers every service expected at a five-star resort.

Playa La Ropa. ☎ *888-389-2645, or 755-555-5500. Fax: 755-554-2758.* www.hotel villadelsol.com. *70 units. Rack rates: High season $300–$900 double; low season $250–$750 double. Meal plan, including breakfast and dinner, for $60 per person per day is mandatory during the high season, and is optional, costing $45 during summer season. Three-night minimum stay generally required. AE, MC, V.*

Villas Miramar
$–$$$ Zihuatanejo Beaches/Playa Madera

A lovely hotel with beautiful gardens, Villas Miramar offers a welcoming atmosphere, attention to detail, and superb cleanliness. For the price, you may expect less, but the rooms are colorful and well equipped, and some have kitchenettes. Several of the suites are built around a shady patio that doubles as a restaurant, which serves a basic menu for breakfast, lunch, and dinner. Suites across the street face a swimming pool and have private balconies and sea views. A terrace with a view to Zihuatanejo Bay has a bar that features a daily happy hour from 5 to 7 p.m. Of all the more budget-priced accommodations around, Villas Miramar is the most welcoming to children. To find Villas Miramar, follow the road leading south out of town toward Playa La Ropa, take the first right after the traffic circle, and then hang a left on Adelita.

Calle Adelita, Lote 78. ☎ *755-554-2106 or 554-3350. Fax: 755-554-2149.* www.prodigy web.net.mx/villasmiramar. *18 units. Free enclosed parking. Rack rates: High season $95 suite for one or two or $100 with ocean view, $130 two-bedroom suite; low season $60 suite for one or two or $70 with ocean view, $90 two-bedroom suite. AE, MC, V.*

Villas San Sebastián
$$–$$$ Zihuatanejo Beaches/Playa La Ropa

A nine-villa complex nestled on the mountainside above Playa La Ropa, Villas San Sebastián offers great views of Zihuatanejo's bay and an indulgent sense of seclusion. The villas, all with beautiful ocean views, are surrounded by tropical vegetation and border a central swimming-pool area. Each comes complete with kitchenette and its own spacious, private terrace. The personalized service is one reason these villas come so highly recommended; owner Luis Valle, whose family dates back decades in the community, is always available to help guests with any questions or needs.

Bulevar Escénico, across from the Dolphins Fountain. ☎ *755-554-4154. Fax: 755-554-3220. 9 units. Rack rates: High season $155 one-bedroom, $250 two-bedroom; low season $105 one-bedroom, $155 two-bedroom. No credit cards.*

Villa Vera Puerto Mio
$$$$-$$$$$ **Zihuatanejo Centro**

This idyllic inn is located on 10 hectares (25 acres) of beautifully landscaped grounds apart from the rest of the hotels in Zihuatanejo. Technically not in *el centro,* Villa Vera Puerto Mio is on the farthest end of the bay, almost directly across from Playa Las Gatas. All rooms are decorated with hand-crafted details from around Mexico, and all enjoy beautiful views of either Zihuatanejo's bay or the Pacific Ocean. The rooms are divided into three main areas: Casa de Mar, the cliff-side mansion closer to the main entrance where most of the rooms are located; the Peninsula, located on the tip of the bay; and a more secluded area with two deluxe suites. (These two suites have no TVs to disturb the tranquillity.) Three other suites, located between Casa de Mar and the Peninsula, have recently been added and have private pools. The upper-level suite is the largest in size. One of the hallmarks of Villa Vera Puerto Mio is its seclusion — the location sets the hotel apart, and you can only reach the small private beach below by going through the hotel. The hotel has two restaurants, plus a small marina with a sailboat that's available for charters. Children under 16 are welcome only during the summer.

Paseo del Morro 5. ☎ */fax **755-553-8165**. 23 units. Rack rates: High season $225–$315 double, $425–$475 villa suite; low season prices drop by $25 per room. AE, MC, V.*

Chapter 21

Settling into Ixtapa and Zihuatanejo

by Lynne Bairstow

. . . .

In This Chapter

▶ Knowing what to expect when you arrive
▶ Finding your way around
▶ Discovering helpful information and resources

. . . .

*O*ne of the pleasures of a vacation in Ixtapa and Zihuatanejo is how easy finding your way around really is. The airport is a breeze to navigate, and the towns are just as simple to figure out; both are basically oriented around one main road each.

In this chapter, I cover the basics of getting around the towns, and I provide you with tips on everything from exchanging money to Internet access. Truly, the Ixtapa/Zihuatanejo area is a place for complete relaxation, and it almost seems like the towns have trivialized the everyday details of life to make everything just a little bit easier.

Arriving in Ixtapa and Zihuatanejo

Your first impression at the Ixtapa-Zihuatanejo airport is likely to set the tone for your trip here — arrivals are usually easy, uncomplicated, and hassle-free. But the airport lacks any real source of tourist information or currency exchange, so you're on your own until you reach town.

In recent years, the airport has been in a more-or-less constant state of renovation, but it's a generally simple building to navigate. When you exit the plane, head down the portable stairway to the tarmac and walk to the airport building.

The climate change is likely to be intense upon your arrival, especially if you're heading here during the winter months. Remember to wear layered clothes so that you're not unbearably hot when you get off the plane.

Navigating passport control and Customs

Your task upon entering the airport is to clear immigration. At the immigration booth, an officer will ask you to show your passport (or other proof of citizenship) and your completed tourist card, the **FMT** (see Chapter 9 for all the FMT and entry details).

Your FMT is an important document, so take good care of it. You're supposed to keep the FMT with you at all times because you may be required to show it if you run into any sort of trouble. You also need to turn it back in upon leaving Mexico, or you may be unable to leave without replacing it.

After you pass through immigration, you go through glass doors to the baggage claim area — essentially one carousel, so finding your bags should be simple enough. Here, porters stand by to help with your bags, and they're well worth the price of the tip — about a dollar a bag. After you collect your luggage, you pass through another checkpoint. Something that looks like a traffic light awaits you here. You press a button, and if the light turns green, you're free to go. If it turns red, you need to open each of your bags for a quick search. It's Mexico's random search procedure for Customs. If you have an unusually large bag, or an excessive amount of luggage, you may be searched regardless of the traffic-light outcome.

Finally, you pass through a second set of sliding-glass doors that open to the general airport-arrival area. This is where you find transportation to your hotel. Booths sell tickets for *colectivos* (shared van service) and private taxis. The fares for both are based on distance (see the following "Getting to your hotel" section). Taxis are always around, but *colectivos* gather only for the larger flights. Clear, well-marked signs indicate the way to the taxis.

Getting to your hotel

The **Ixtapa-Zihuatanejo airport** is 11km (7 miles) from Zihuatanejo and 13km (8 miles) from Ixtapa. Taxi fares into town range from $19 to $22.

The least expensive way to make the trip to either town is by using the *colectivos,* operated by **Transportes Terrestres.** For transportation to any of the hotels in Zihuatanejo and Ixtapa, purchase a ticket at the booth located just outside the baggage-claim area. Cost depends on distance, but fares generally run between $6.50 and $8.

Several **car-rental agencies** also have booths in the airport. These companies include **Dollar** (☎ **800-800-4000** in the U.S., or 755-554-2255; www.dollar.com) and **Hertz** (☎ **800-654-3131** in the U.S., or 755-554-2590 or 554-2952; www.hertz.com).

Getting Around Ixtapa and Zihuatanejo

Zihuatanejo is both a fishing village, in the traditional sense of the term, and a resort town. The town spreads out around the beautiful Bay of Zihuatanejo, which is framed by the downtown *(el centro)* to the north and a beautiful, long beach and the Sierra foothills to the east. The heart of Zihuatanejo is the waterfront walkway, **Paseo del Pescador** (also called the *malecón*), bordering the Playa Municipal.

One aspect of Zihua (as the locals call Zihuatanejo) that I enjoy most is that the town centerpiece isn't a plaza, as it is in most Mexican villages, but a **basketball court,** which fronts the beach. It's a useful point of reference for directions. The main thoroughfare for cars is **Juan Alvarez,** a block behind the *malecón.* The town has designated several sections of the main streets as the *zona peatonal* (pedestrian zone blocked off to cars). The *zona peatonal* follows a zigzag pattern, and to me, it seems to block parts of streets haphazardly.

A cement-and-sand walkway, lit at night, runs from the downtown-Zihuatanejo *malecón* along the water to **Playa Madera** making it easy to walk between these two points. Access to **Playa La Ropa** is via the main road, **Camino a Playa La Ropa.** Playa La Ropa and **Playa Las Gatas** are connected only by boat. Playa La Ropa and Playa Madera are connected by car (the rocks between the two beaches are dangerous). Skip to Chapter 23 for a description of these beaches.

Highway 200 connects Zihua to **Ixtapa,** which is located 6km (4 miles) to the northwest. The 18-hole **Ixtapa Golf Club** marks the beginning of the inland side of Ixtapa. Tall hotels line Ixtapa's wide beach, **Playa el Palmar,** against a backdrop of palm groves and mountains. The main street, **Bulevar Ixtapa,** provides access to the beach. A large expanse of small shopping plazas (many of the shops are air-conditioned) and restaurants lie opposite the beach. At the far end of Bulevar Ixtapa, **Marina Ixtapa** has excellent restaurants, private yacht slips, and an 18-hole **golf course.** Condominiums and private homes surround the marina and golf course, with exclusive residential communities in the hillsides past the marina en route to **Playa Quieta** and **Playa Linda.** Ixtapa also has a great paved bicycle track that begins at the marina and continues around the Marina Ixtapa Golf Course and on toward Playa Linda.

Getting around the two resorts is easy — **taxis** are the preferred form of transportation. Rates are reasonable, but from midnight to 5 a.m., they increase by 50 percent. The average fare between Ixtapa and central Zihuatanejo is $4.50; a trip from Playa La Ropa (just east of Zihuatanejo) to downtown Zihuatanejo is about $2.50; and it costs approximately $2.50 to get from one end of the Ixtapa Hotel Zone to the other.

A **mini bus** (35¢) goes back and forth between Zihuatanejo and Ixtapa every 15 or 20 minutes from 5 a.m. to 11 p.m. daily, but it's generally very hot and crowded with commuting workers. In Zihuatanejo, it stops near the corner of Morelos-Paseo Zihuatanejo and Juárez, about 3 blocks north of the market. In Ixtapa, it makes numerous stops along Bulevar Ixtapa.

The highway leading from Zihuatanejo to Ixtapa is now a broad, four-lane highway, which makes driving between the towns easier and faster than ever. Street signs are becoming more common in Zihuatanejo, and good signs now lead you in and out of both towns. However, both locations have an area called the **Zona Hotelera** (Hotel Zone), so if you're trying to reach Ixtapa's Hotel Zone (the area alongside Bulevar Ixtapa), signs in Zihuatanejo pointing to that village's own Hotel Zone (the area alongside Playa Madera and Playa La Ropa) may confuse you.

Fast Facts: Ixtapa and Zihuatanejo

American Express

The main office (☎ 755-544-6242; Fax: 755-544-6242) is located in the Plaza San Rafael, Local 7, on Av. Colegio Heroico Militar 38. It's open Monday to Friday from 9 a.m. to 6 p.m.

Area Code

The telephone area code is **755**.

Baby Sitters

Most of the larger hotels in Ixtapa can arrange baby sitters, but many speak limited English. Rates range from $4 to $10 per hour. Babysitting services may be more difficult to come by in Zihuatanejo because the more upscale places tend to discourage children and the smaller ones simply may not have the resources.

Banks, ATMs, and Currency Exchange

Ixtapa's banks include Bancomer, located in the La Puerta shopping center. The most centrally located Zihuatanejo bank is Banamex, located on Cuauhtémoc 4. Banks change money during normal business hours, which are now generally 9 a.m. to 6 p.m. Monday to Friday and Saturday 9 a.m.

to 1 p.m. ATMs and *casas de cambio* (currency exchange booths) are available during these and other hours, and they generally have the best rates. Most establishments accept U.S. dollars as readily as pesos but at reduced exchange rates, so you're better off using local currency whenever possible. The airport has a currency exchange booth, so upon arrival, exchange just enough to pay for your cab fare and have a bit of cash to move around until you make it to a bank.

Business Hours

Most offices maintain traditional Mexican hours of operation (10 a.m.–2 p.m. and 4–8 p.m. daily), but shops remain open throughout the day. Offices tend to close on Saturday and Sunday, but shops are open on Saturday, at least, and increasingly offer limited hours of operation on Sunday.

Climate

Although the climate is always quite warm, summer is particularly hot and humid, but sea breezes and brief showers temper the heat. September is the peak of the tropical rainy season, and showers are concentrated in the late afternoons.

Consular Agency

A U.S. Consular Agency is located in Zihuatanejo (☎ **755-553-2100**; Fax: 755-557-1106).

Emergencies

Police (☎ **755-554-2040**, 755-554-5370); **fire department** (☎ **755-554-0012**); **Red Cross** (☎ **755-554-2009**).

Hospitals

The larger hotels in Ixtapa have a doctor on premises or on-call. The Hospital de la Marina Ixtapa is at Bulevar Ixtapa s/n, in front of the Hotel Aristos (☎ **755-553-0499**). In Zihuatanejo, try the Clinica Maciel (Calle de la Palma 12; ☎ **755-554-2380**); its staff also includes a reliable dentist.

Information

The State Tourism Office (☎ **888-248-7037** from the U.S., or ☎/fax 755-553-1967 or 553-1968) is in the La Puerta shopping center in Ixtapa across from the Presidente Inter-Continental Hotel. It's open Monday to Friday 8 a.m. to 8:30 p.m. This location is mainly a self-service office where you can collect brochures; the staff is less helpful than in other offices in Mexico.

The Zihuatanejo Tourism Office Module is on the main square by the basketball court at Alvarez. It's open Monday to Friday 9 a.m. to 8 p.m. and serves basic, tourist-information purposes.

Note: According to recent regulations, the very few timeshare sales booths that exist in both towns must be clearly marked with the names of the businesses and can't display signs claiming to be tourist-information centers.

Internet Access

Several cybercafes are located in the Los Patios Shopping Center in Ixtapa. Comunicación Mundial is in Local 105 (☎ **755-553-1177**). Go to the back of the shopping center and take the stairs to the second level; Comunicación Mundial is to your right. You can find many Internet cafes in Ixtapa, and the average fee is $3 per hour.

Maps

One of the best around is the free American Express map, usually found at the tourist information offices and hotel concierge desks.

Pharmacy

Farmacias Coyuca are open 24 hours a day and deliver. The Ixtapa branch doesn't have a phone number; in Zihuatanejo, call ☎ **755-554-5390**.

Post Office

The post office for both towns (☎ **755-554-2192**) is in the SCT building (called Edificio SCT) behind El Cacahuate. It's open Monday to Friday 8 a.m. to 3 p.m. and Saturday 9 a.m. to 1 p.m.

Safety

Generally speaking, both Ixtapa and Zihuatanejo are quite safe, and you should feel very comfortable walking around here — even at night.

The one main safety warning applies to travelers who elect to drive: Motorists planning to follow Highway 200 northwest up the coast from Ixtapa or Zihuatanejo toward Lázaro Cárdenas and Manzanillo should be aware of reports of car and bus hijackings on that route, especially around Playa Azul.

Bus holdups are more common than car holdups. Before heading in that direction, ask locals, the police, or the tourism office about the status of the route. Don't drive at night. According to tourism officials, police and military patrols of the highway have increased recently, and the number of incidents has dropped dramatically.

As is the case anywhere, tourists are vulnerable to thieves, especially so when shopping in a market; lying on the beach; wearing jewelry; or visibly carrying a camera, purse, or bulging wallet.

Taxes

There's a 15 percent value-added tax (IVA) on goods and services, and it's generally included in the posted price.

Taxis

Always establish the price of a ride with the driver before starting out. Taxi rates are reasonable, but from midnight to 5 a.m., rates increase by 50 percent. The average fare between Ixtapa and Zihuatanejo is $4.50.

Telephones

Avoid the phone booths that have signs in English advising you to call home using a special 800 number — these are absolute rip-offs and can cost as much as $20 per minute. The least expensive way to call is by using a Telmex (LADATEL) prepaid phone card, available at most pharmacies and mini-supers, using the official Telmex (Lada) public phones.

In Mexico, you need to dial 001 prior to a number to reach the United States, and you need to preface long distance calls within Mexico by dialing 01.

Time Zone

Ixtapa and Zihuatanejo operate on central standard time, but Mexico's observance of daylight saving time varies somewhat from that in the United States.

Chapter 22

Dining in Ixtapa and Zihuatanejo

by Lynne Bairstow

. . . .

In This Chapter

▶ Uncovering some local institutions and bargains
▶ Discovering the best restaurants in Ixtapa and Zihuatanejo

. . . .

Dining destinations in this area are divided as neatly as the accommodations: You can find more modern, stylized places in Ixtapa, and eateries with more local color (and flavor) tend to be located in neighboring Zihuatanejo (Zihua for short). Although you find the majority of the best-known restaurants in Ixtapa inside the larger hotels, Zihua's top spots are small, mostly family-owned treasures. The restaurants on Zihuatanejo's Playa Madera and Playa La Ropa run the gamut from *palapa*-topped (thatched-roof) seafood shacks to elegant, upscale bistros.

From sunset to dinner, cocktails are the highlight of the nocturnal action here, and although these towns may lack the nightclub action of other resorts, they do offer a varied and excellent selection of restaurants. Seafood is the star, of course, but the preparations vary wildly, and in other cuisines, the influences of the European expatriate community are evident.

Mexico's 15 percent value-added tax (IVA) is added into most restaurant bills, but the tip isn't, and the waitstaff in Mexico depends on tips for the majority of their income — the usual tip here is 15 percent.

Finding Fast and Cheap Eats

Zihuatanejo's **central market,** located on Avenida Benito Juárez (about 5 blocks inland from the waterfront), is a perfect place for cheap and tasty food at breakfast and lunch before the market activity winds down in the afternoon. Look for what's hot and fresh. The market area is one of the best places on this coast for shopping and people-watching.

Ixtapa and Zihuatanejo's Best Restaurants

I list the following restaurants alphabetically with references to price and location. Please refer to the Introduction of this book for an explanation of the price categories.

Because restaurants price shrimp and lobster so much higher than other entrees, I note the price ranges exclusive of these dishes unless they make up the major part of the menu. And, unless otherwise specified, reservations aren't accepted or aren't necessary.

Please see Appendix C for more information on Mexican cuisine.

Beccofino
$–$$ Ixtapa   NORTHERN ITALIAN

Beccofino is a standout not only in Ixtapa but also in all of Mexico. Owner Angelo Rolly Pavia serves up the flavorful northern Italian specialties he grew up enjoying. The breezy location is under a covered slip overlooking the marina's yachts. The menu is strong on pasta. Ravioli, a house specialty, comes stuffed with the freshest seafood, whether swordfish or shrimp. The garlic bread is terrific, and the wine list is extensive with an impressive selection of imported wines to choose from. It's a popular place, and the restaurant tends to be loud when crowded, which is often. Beccofino is increasingly becoming a popular breakfast spot.

Marina Ixtapa, near the lighthouse. ☎ *755-553-1770.* www.ixtapa-mexico.com/beccofino. *Main courses: $14–$30; breakfast $5–$7. AE, MC, V. Open: Daily 9:30 a.m.–midnight.*

Casa Puntarenas
$ Zihuatanejo Centro   MEXICAN/SEAFOOD

A modest spot with a tin roof and nine wooden tables, Puntarenas is one of the best places in town for fried whole fish served with toasted *bolillos* (crusty, white-bread mini-loaves), sliced tomatoes, onions, and avocado. The place is renowned for chile rellenos, served mild and stuffed with plenty of cheese, and the pork chops are divinely inspired. Although it may appear a little too rustic for less experienced travelers to Mexico, Casa Puntarenas is very clean, and the food is known for its freshness. To get to Puntarenas from the pier, turn left on Alvarez and cross the footbridge on your left. Turn right after you cross the bridge; the restaurant is on your left.

Calle Noria s/n. No phone. Main courses: $4.50–$8.50. No credit cards. Open: Daily 6:30–9 p.m.

Coconuts
$–$$$ Zihuatanejo Centro   INTERNATIONAL/SEAFOOD

What a find! Not only is the food innovative and delicious but also the restaurant is housed in a historic building — the oldest in Zihuatanejo.

This popular restaurant set in a tropical garden was the former weigh-in station for Zihua's coconut industry in the late 1800s. Fresh is the operative word on this creative, seafood-heavy menu. Chef Patricia Cummings checks the market daily for the freshest foods and uses only top-quality ingredients to prepare dishes such as seafood pâté and grilled filet of snapper Coconuts. The house specialty is chiles rellenos Luduvina, chile poblanos stuffed with shrimp and potatoes and topped with a tomato coulis. The bananas flambé has earned a loyal following of its own — with good reason. Expect friendly, efficient service here.

Augustín Ramírez 1, at Vicente Guerrero. ☎ *755-554-2518. Fax: 755-554-7980. Main courses: $11–$34. AE, MC, V. Open: Daily 11:30 a.m–4:30 p.m. and 6–11 p.m. during high season. Closed during rainy season.*

Golden Cookie Shop
$ Ixtapa   PASTRIES/INTERNATIONAL

Although the name is misleading — they sell more than cookies here — Golden Cookie's fresh baked goods beg for a detour, and the coffee menu is the most extensive in town — and includes iced-espresso drinks for those sultry Ixtapa days. The prices are high for the area, but the breakfasts are particularly noteworthy, as are the deli sandwiches. Large sandwiches, made with fresh soft bread, come with a choice of sliced deli meats, such as smoked ham. Chicken curry is among the other specialty items, and the Golden Cookie folks serve up a hearty German buffet every Friday evening at 7 p.m. They have recently expanded their menu to include sugar-free options for diabetics and dieters. To get to the shop, walk to the rear of the Los Patios shopping center as you face Mac's Prime Rib; walk up the stairs, turn left, and the restaurant is on the right. An air-conditioned area is reserved for nonsmokers.

Los Patios shopping center. ☎ *755-553-0310. Main courses: $6–$8; breakfast $4–$6; sandwiches $4–$6. MC, V. Open: Daily 8 a.m.–3 p.m.*

Kau-Kan
$–$$ Zihuatanejo Beaches/Playa La Ropa   NUEVA COCINA/SEAFOOD

Open architecture, stunning views of the bay, and refined cuisine are among the hallmarks of this popular restaurant. Head chef Ricardo Rodriguez supervises every detail of this elegantly understated operation from the ultra-smooth background music that invites after-dinner conversation to the spectacular presentation of all the dishes. The baked potato with baby lobster and the mahimahi carpaccio are two of my favorites, but consider the daily specials — Ricardo always gets the freshest seafood available and prepares it with great care. For dessert, the pecan and chocolate cake served with a dark chocolate sauce is simply delicious. During high season, reservations are essential. Located on the road to Playa La Ropa, the restaurant is on the right-hand side of the road past the first curve coming from downtown.

Camino a Playa La Ropa. ☎ *755-554-8446. Reservations recommended during high season. Main courses: $13–$25. AE, MC, V. Open: Daily 5–11:30 p.m.*

Zihuatanejo and Ixtapa Area Dining

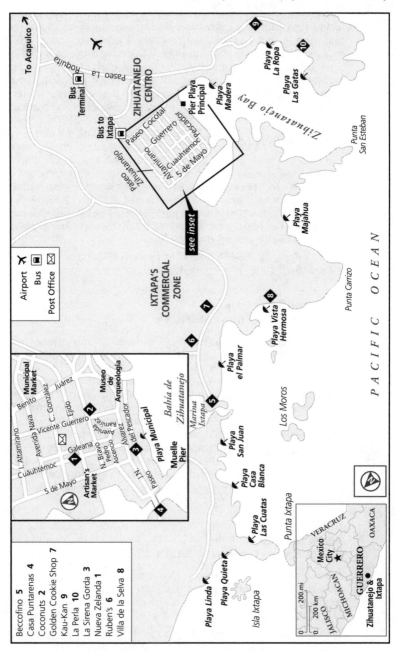

To Acapulco

Bus Terminal

Paseo La Roqueta

ZIHUATANEJO CENTRO

Bus to Ixtapa

Paseo Cocotal

Guerrero

Almirante

Cuauhtémoc

5 de Mayo

Paseo Zihuatanejo

Pier Playa Principal

Pescador

Playa Madera

Playa La Ropa

Playa Las Gatas

Punta San Esteban

Zihuatanejo Bay

Playa Majahua

PACIFIC OCEAN

Punta Carrizo

Playa Vista Hermosa

Punta Cariza

Los Moros

Playa el Palmar

Airport ✈
Bus ▣
Post Office ⊠

IXTAPA'S COMMERCIAL ZONE

see inset

Municipal Market

Benito Juárez

C. González

Vicente Guerrero

Galeana

Cuauhtémoc

5 de Mayo

I. Altamirano

Avenida Nava

Ejido

Avenida Ramírez

N. Bravo

Pedro Ascencio

Álvarez

I.N.

Paseo del Pescador

Museo de Arqueología

Playa Municipal

Muelle Pier

Bahía de Zihuatanejo

Marina Ixtapa

Artisan's Market

Playa San Juan

Playa Casa Blanca

Playa Las Cuatas

Playa Quieta

Playa Linda

Isla Ixtapa

Punta Ixtapa

VERACRUZ

OAXACA

Mexico City ★

GUERRERO

JALISCO

MICHOACÁN

Zihuatanejo & Ixtapa ●

200 mi
200 km

Beccofino **5**
Casa Puntarenas **4**
Coconuts **2**
Golden Cookie Shop **7**
Kau-Kan **9**
La Perla **10**
La Sirena Gorda **3**
Nueva Zelanda **1**
Ruben's **6**
Villa de la Selva **8**

La Perla
$ Playa La Ropa   SEAFOOD

Along Playa La Ropa, you can find any number of casual, *palapa*-style restaurants, but La Perla, with its tables under the trees and a thatched roof, is the most popular. Although it's known more as a tradition than for the food or service, somehow, this long stretch of pale sand and groups of wooden chairs under *palapas* (thatched-roof umbrellas) have made a charming combination. Some diners joke that getting a waiter's attention at La Perla can be so hard that, if you get take-out food from a competitor and bring it here to eat, they won't even notice. Still, La Perla is considered the best spot around for tanning and socializing and serves a whopper of a *gringo* (American) breakfast. Lunches are lighter — ceviche (fresh fish cocktail made with finely cubed raw fish that is marinated with lime, vinegar, and spices) are the specialty. In the evening, casual dinners and cold *cervezas* (beers) are accompanied by satellite-dish-delivered sports. La Perla is located near the southern end of Playa La Ropa. Take the right fork in the road; a sign is in the parking lot. The kitchen doesn't open until 10 a.m. but the restaurant is open at 9 a.m. for customers who arrive early to get the best spots on the beach!

Playa La Ropa. ☎ *755-554-2700. Main courses $6–$11; breakfast $2.50–$5. AE, MC, V. Open: Daily 9 a.m.–10 p.m.; breakfast served 10 a.m.–noon.*

La Sirena Gorda
$ Zihuatanejo Centro   MEXICAN

Head to La Sirena Gorda (the chubby mermaid) for one of the most popular breakfasts in town. Choose from a variety of eggs and omelets, hot cakes with bacon, or fruit with granola and yogurt. The house specialty is seafood tacos — fish in a variety of sauces plus lobster — but I consider these selections overpriced at $4.50 for the fish and $25 for the lobster. To me, a taco is a taco is a taco, but they did earn rave reviews in *Bon Appétit* a few years back. Instead, I recommend something from the short list of daily specials such as blackened red snapper, steak, or fish kebabs. The food is excellent and patrons enjoy the casual sidewalk-cafe atmosphere. To get here from the basketball court, face the water and walk to the right along the *Paseo;* La Sirena Gorda is on your right just before the town pier.

Paseo del Pescador. ☎ *755-554-2687. Main courses: $3–$6; breakfast $2–$4. MC, V. Open: Thurs–Tues 7 a.m.–10 p.m.*

Nueva Zelanda
$ Zihuatanejo Centro   MEXICAN

Rich cappuccinos sprinkled with cinnamon, fresh fruit *licuados* (kind of a smoothie), and pancakes with real maple syrup draw patrons to this open-air snack shop. The mainstays of the menu are tortas and enchiladas, and everything is offered with friendly, efficient service. Dine indoors and watch your food get prepared in the spotless open kitchen, or choose a seat at one of the sidewalk tables for a pleasant people-watching session.

You can easily find Nueva Zelanda by walking 3 blocks inland from the waterfront on Cuauhtémoc; the restaurant is on your right. A second location (☎ 755-553-0838) is located in Ixtapa in the back section of the Los Patios shopping center.

Cuauhtémoc 23 at Ejido. ☎ *755-554-2340. Main courses: Tortas $2.50–$3.50; enchiladas $2.50–$5; fruit-and-milk licuados $2.50; cappuccino $2. No credit cards. Open: Daily 8 a.m.–10 p.m.*

Ruben's
$ Ixtapa   BURGERS/VEGETABLES

If time in Ixtapa also means a vacation from decision making, then check out Ruben's. The choices are easy — you can order a big, juicy burger made from top-sirloin beef grilled over mesquite or a foil-wrapped packet of baked potatoes, chayote, zucchini, or sweet corn. Ice cream, beer, and soda fill out the menu, which is posted on the wall by the kitchen. The place is kind of a do-it-yourself affair: Guests snare a waitress and order, grab their own drinks from the cooler, and tally their own tabs. But because of the ever-present crowds, it can still be a slow process. For years, Ruben's was a popular fixture in the Playa Madera neighborhood, but it moved to two locations in Ixtapa. The food remains as dependable as ever, even if the locale has expanded and spiffed up a bit.

Flamboyant shopping center, next to Bancomer. Also on Bulevar Ixtapa across from the Radisson. ☎ *755-553-0027. Main courses: Burgers $3–$5; vegetables $2; ice cream $1.50. No credit cards. Open: Daily 6–11 p.m. Delivery service also available.*

Villa de la Selva
$$–$$$ Ixtapa   MEXICAN/CONTINENTAL

Once the summer home of one-time Mexican president Luis Echevarria, this exquisite restaurant is set into the edge of a cliff overlooking the sea. Elegant and romantic, it offers diners the most spectacular sea-and-sunset view in Ixtapa. Candlelit tables are arranged on three terraces; try to come early in hopes of getting one of the best vistas — my favorite is the lower terrace. The cuisine is delicious, artfully appointed, and classically rich: *Filet Villa de la Selva* is red snapper topped with shrimp and hollandaise sauce. The cold avocado soup or hot lobster bisque make a good beginning; finish with chocolate mousse or bananas Singapore. The restaurant is just above Las Brisas Resort, overlooking Vista Hermosa beach.

Paseo de la Roca. ☎ *755-553-0362.* www.villadelaselva.com. *Reservations recommended during high season. Main courses: $15–$44. AE, MC, V. Open: Daily 7–11 p.m. Closed in Sept.*

Chapter 23

Having Fun on and off the Beach in Ixtapa and Zihuatanejo

by Lynne Bairstow

- -

In This Chapter

▶ Soaking up the sun
▶ Enjoying the best sports — on land and by sea
▶ Sightseeing and shopping like a licensed professional
▶ Getting *really* away from it all with a side trip to Troncones
▶ Living it up at night

- -

*W*hile you're in Ixtapa and Zihuatanejo, life isn't just a beach; it's a choice of beaches! From rocky coves to smooth stretches of golden sand, this chapter gives you the rundown on all the key beaches in the area and highlights the beaches that are best for watersports and safest for swimming so that you can choose the patch of sand that's perfect for you. If you're looking for adventure beyond the sea, I also have some recommendations for you — along with tips on the best shopping and nightlife.

All beaches in Zihuatanejo are safe for swimming because undertow is rarely a problem, and the municipal beach is protected from the Pacific Ocean's main surge. Beaches in Ixtapa are more dangerous for swimming because of frequent undertow problems, so keep an eye on the safety flags posted in front of the hotel beaches.

Hitting the Beaches

This section contains the skinny on the area's beaches, traveling from the beaches northwest of Ixtapa to those south of Zihuatanejo. Even if you fall in love at first sight with the stretch of sand immediately in front of your hotel, explore a bit to see what other beauties are out there.

Ixtapa and Zihuatanejo Area

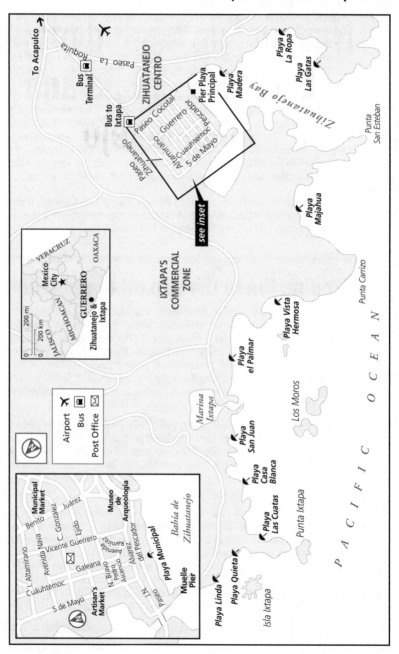

Playa Linda and **Playa Quieta** are about as far out as you're likely to travel to find a beach in this area. Playa Linda, about 13km (8 miles) north of Ixtapa (about 10 min. by taxi), is the departure point for the inexpensive water taxis that ferry passengers to Isla Ixtapa. It's also the primary out-of-town beach, a long stretch of flat sand with watersports equipment and horseback riding. Along with a collection of small stands selling trinkets, the La Palapa restaurant makes a good place to spend the afternoon. Playa Linda faces the open ocean but also lies near a freshwater estuary that's home to birds, iguanas, and the occasional alligator — visible through the safety of a fence. Club Med and Qualton Club have largely claimed neighboring Playa Quieta directly across from Isla Ixtapa. The beach at Playa Quieta is beautiful, but unless you're staying at either of those resorts, you won't find shade, drinks, or any sort of beach club facilities. If you're not staying on Playa Quieta, skip it. The other beaches are just as beautiful and a lot easier to get to.

Around the Punta Ixtapa peninsula lies **Playa Las Cuatas,** a pretty beach and cove a few miles outside of Ixtapa. It has heavy surf and a strong undertow, so I don't recommend it for swimming.

Finding fun in the sun off the mainland

Some notable beaches, along with clear water, snorkeling, and a few nature trails, are out on **Isla Ixtapa.** You can find four small beaches on the island, the busiest of which is **Playa Cuachalatate,** named for a native tree. It's the arrival point for the ferryboats and has a selection of *palapa*-topped restaurants. **Playa Varadero,** with calm clear waters that make it a favorite for snorkeling, is along a paved walkway to the right of Playa Cuachalatate. Group tours here usually include lunch at El Marlin restaurant. El Marlin is one of several restaurants on the island, but it's not appreciably better than the others, so feel confident in making your way on your own.

Continue to the right along the same path past Playa Varadero and you come to **Playa Coral,** which true to name, offers the most varied groupings of underwater coral in the area — it's excellent for snorkeling. The most isolated of the beaches on Isla Ixtapa is **Playa Carey** — to the left of the Playa Cuachalatate dock. It doesn't have any facilities but makes a great spot for a picnic. (Be sure to take your trash with you as you leave — no containers are available here for disposal.)

Boats leave the dock at Playa Linda for Isla Ixtapa every 10 minutes between 11:30 a.m. and 5 p.m., so you can depart and return at your own pace. The round-trip boat ride is $2.50 and takes anywhere from 20 to 35 minutes (depending on the boat and the boat's captain). Along the way, you pass dramatic rock formations, and you can see **Los Moros de Los Pericos islands** in the distance where a great variety of birds nest on its rocky points jutting out into the blue Pacific. When you reach Isla Ixtapa, you can find snorkeling, diving, and other watersports gear available for rent. Be sure to catch the last water taxi back at 5 p.m., but double-check that time upon arrival on the island.

Ixtapa's main beach, **Playa el Palmar,** is a lovely white-sand arc on the edge of the Hotel Zone. Almost 5km (3 miles) long, this beach features dramatic rock formations by the sea. The surf here can be rough; use caution and don't swim when a red flag is posted. Several of the nicest beaches in the area are essentially closed to the public — resort developments rope them off exclusively for their guests. Although by law all Mexican beaches are open to the public, it's a common practice for hotels to create artificial barriers (such as rocks or dunes) to preclude entrance to their beaches.

Next up is lovely **Playa Vista Hermosa,** framed by striking rock formations and bordered by the Las Brisas Resort high on the hill. Although very attractive for sunbathing or a stroll, this patch of sand is also known for its heavy surf and strong undertow, so use extreme caution if swimming or snorkeling here.

Local fishermen still use the Zihuatanejo town beach, **Playa Municipal,** to pull their colorful boats up onto the sand — a fine photo op. The small shops and restaurants lining the waterfront here are great for people-watching and absorbing the flavor of daily village life.

Just east of Playa Municipal lies **Playa Madera,** which is accessible by following a lighted concrete-and-sand walkway that cuts through the rocks for about 90m (300 ft.) from the Paseo del Pescador. The beach itself is open to the Pacific surf but is generally peaceful. A number of attractive budget lodgings overlook this area from the hillside, and beachside restaurants line the shore.

South of Playa Madera is Zihuatanejo's largest and most beautiful beach, **Playa La Ropa,** a long sweep of sand with a great view of the sunset. Some lovely, small hotels and restaurants nestle into the hills; palm groves edge the shoreline. Although it's also open to the Pacific, waves are usually gentle. A taxi from town costs $3. The name "Playa La Ropa," *ropa* means clothing, comes from an old tale of a *galeón* that sunk during a big storm. The silk clothing that the boat was carrying back from the Philippines all washed ashore on this beach — hence the name.

The nicest beach for swimming and the best beach for children is the secluded **Playa Las Gatas.** You can see this delicate ribbon of sand, which is speckled with minute seashells, across the bay from Playa La Ropa and Zihuatanejo. The small coral reef just offshore is a nice spot for snorkeling and diving, and a few small dive shops on the beach rent gear. The waters at Las Gatas are exceptionally clear and there's no undertow or big waves, which is due in large part to a rock wall surrounding the beach that turns the waters into a virtual wading pool. The pre-Hispanic emperor Calzonzin, who chose this beach as his private playground more than 500 years ago, constructed the wall. Open-air seafood restaurants on the beach make it an appealing lunch spot. (Two of the restaurants are now open for dinner as well.) Small, shaded *pangas* (small boats) make the voyage to Las Gatas from the Zihuatanejo town pier, a ten-minute trip. The captains can take you across whenever you want between 8 a.m. and 4 p.m. Evening ferries are less predictable, so check for the current schedule. A round-trip fare generally runs about $3.50.

Finding Water Fun for Everyone

The beaches here are so appealing because the waters are crystal clear and obviously free of pollution and over-fishing. Snorkel, dive, cast a line, or take a dip — it's a slice of heaven. And there are other ways to enjoy splashing around . . . or cruising above the deep blue.

Skiing and surfing

Rental stands with **sailboats, windsurfers,** and other **watersports equipment** are located at numerous points along Playa La Ropa and Playa Las Gatas in Zihuatanejo, Playa el Palmar in Ixtapa, and even on Isla Ixtapa. You can **parasail** (about $20 for a 15-min. ride) at La Ropa and Palmar. **Kayaks** are available for rent at Carlos Scuba (Cuauhtémoc 3; ☎ 755-554-42810 or 554-6003; www.carloscuba.com), hotels in Ixtapa, and some watersports operations on Playa La Ropa. A few places also have **WaveRunners,** which rent for about $30 per half-hour.

Exploring the deep blue

These clear waters, with more than 30 deep-dive sites, just beg to be explored! Water visibility frequently is more than 30m (100 ft.), especially from December through May when the temperature is usually comfortably warm. You're likely to see an abundance of sea life — as well as an old anchor or other artifacts from the days of the Spanish conquistadors.

Arrange your **scuba-diving trip** through **Carlos Scuba** (Cuauhtémoc 3; ☎ 755-554-2810 or 554-6003; www.carloscuba.com). Fees start at around $80 for two dives including all equipment and lunch. Expert, bilingual dive instructors are available for all levels of dive instruction. This group is the most knowledgeable about the area, which has excellent dive sites, including walls and caves, for all experience levels. Certification courses are available, and the dive-guide-to-diver ratio is an outstanding one-to-three.

I suggest that you make advance reservations for dives during Christmas and Easter.

The diving here is great, but you can also enjoy many of the underwater sites without going to such depths. **Snorkeling** is best at Zihuatanejo's Playa Las Gatas, Isla Ixtapa's Playa Varadero, and Playa Vista Hermosa in front of the Las Brisas Resort. Equipment rentals are available at all locations and range from $5 to $15 a day.

Reeling in the big one

Looking for the big one? Billfish — notably blue and black marlin and Pacific sailfish — swim in the waters off Zihuatanejo. And, when you catch the big one, release it. It may sting a bit, but this conservation effort is increasingly popular in Mexico, and I encourage it. You can arrange **fishing trips** with the **boat cooperative** (☎ 755-554-2056) at the Zihuatanejo town pier. Excursions cost $140 to $300 per trip depending on boat size, trip length, and other factors. Most trips last about six hours; no credit cards are accepted. The price includes ten soft drinks and ten beers, bait, and fishing gear. Lunch is on your own.

You pay more for a trip arranged through a local travel agency; the least expensive trips are on small launches called *pangas* — most have shade. Outfits offer both small-game and deep-sea fishing. The fishing here is adequate, but it's not on par with that of Mazatlán or Baja.

You can also arrange trips that combine fishing with a visit to the nearly deserted ocean beaches that extend for miles along the coast north and south of the towns of Zihua and Ixtapa. Sam Lushinsky at **Ixtapa Sportfishing Charters** (19 Depue Lane, Stroudsburg, PA 18360; ☎ 570-688-9466; Fax: 570-688-9554; www.ixtapasportfishing.com) is a noted fishing outfitter. They accept MasterCard and Visa.

Boating and fishing expeditions from the **Marina Ixtapa,** a bit north of the Ixtapa Hotel Zone, can also be arranged. As a rule, everything available in or through the marina is more expensive, in addition to being more "Americanized."

Tipping the captain 10 percent to 15 percent of the total price of your charter is customary, depending on the quality of the service. Give the money to the captain, and he'll split it with the mates.

Cruising Ixtapa and Zihuatanejo

The area's most popular boat trip is probably the voyage to **Isla Ixtapa** for snorkeling and lunch at the El Marlin restaurant or one of several other restaurants on the island. You can book this outing as a tour through any local travel agency or your hotel tour desk, or you can head out on your own from Playa Linda, which allows you to follow your own schedule. (Check out the "Finding fun in the sun off the mainland" sidebar, earlier in this chapter, for more info on getting to Isla Ixtapa from Playa Linda.)

Local travel agencies can also arrange day trips to **Los Moros de Los Pericos** islands for **bird-watching,** though it's less expensive to rent a boat with a guide at Playa Linda. These islands are located offshore from Playa el Palmar; however, you must leave from Playa Linda because no boats depart from Playa el Palmar.

Day cruises and sunset cruises on the *trimaran* (a catamaran with an extra hull) *TriStar* can be arranged through Yates del Sol (☎ 755-554-2694 or 554-8270) or through any travel agent (with no difference in price). Both day and sunset cruises depart from the Zihuatanejo town pier at Puerto Mío.

The day cruise sails to Playa Manzanillo, where you have time for swimming, snorkeling, and shell collecting. On the return trip, the boat anchors off Playa La Ropa. The price of $59 includes lunch, an open bar, and round-trip transportation from your hotel. Snorkeling gear is $5 extra. There's also a day trip to Isla Ixtapa on this very comfortable and rarely crowded yacht that begins at 10 a.m., costs $49, and includes an open bar and lunch. The sunset cruise, generally running from 5 to 7:30 p.m., costs $39 and includes an open bar and snacks. Because schedules and special trips vary, call for current information.

Enjoying Land Sports

Ixtapa and Zihuatanejo offer plenty of popular land sports for vacationers. In this section, I cover golf, tennis, and horseback riding. If you're looking for an activity I don't list here, be sure to consult your hotel or resort concierge for more information.

Teeing off

Ixtapa has two locations where you can tee off. One spot is the Club de Golf Ixtapa Palma Real (☎ 755-553-1062 or 553-1163), located in front of the Barceló Hotel at the entrance to Ixtapa's Hotel Zone as you arrive from Zihuatanejo. Robert Trent Jones, Jr., designed the 18-hole course, and much of the land here is protected as a wildlife preserve, so you may see flamingos or cranes near the lagoon at the 15th hole. Greens fees are $70; caddies cost an additional $20 for 18 holes or $11 for nine holes. Electric carts are $25, and club rentals are $20. Tee times begin at 7 a.m., but the club doesn't take reservations. Another option is the Marina Ixtapa Golf Course (☎ 755-553-1410), which was designed by Robert von Hagge and features 18 challenging holes. It's located at the opposite end of Hotel Zone from the Palma Real — the courses kind of form two bookends. The greens fees are $120; carts, caddies, and club rentals are $20 each. The first foursome tees off at 7 a.m. Call for reservations 24 hours in advance. (Both courses accept American Express, MasterCard, and Visa.)

Taking time for tennis

If you want to work on your tennis game in Ixtapa, both the Club de Golf Ixtapa Palma Real (☎ 755-553-1062 or 553-1163) and the Marina Ixtapa Golf Course (☎ 755-553-1410) have lighted public courts and equipment available for rent. Fees are $10 per hour during the day and $12 per hour at night. In addition, the Dorado Pacífico and most of the better hotels on the Playa el Palmar have courts. Although priority play is given to guests, most hotel courts are also open to the public.

Galloping along

For **horseback riding, Rancho Playa Linda** (no phone) offers guided trail rides from the Playa Linda beach (about 13km/8 miles north of Ixtapa). Guided rides begin at 8:30, 9:45, and 11 a.m. and 3, 4, and 5 p.m. The early morning ride is the coolest, and it's a beautiful way to start a day; the 5 p.m. trip offers a view of the sunset. Groups of three or more riders can arrange their own tour, which is especially nice a little later in the evening around sunset (though you need mosquito repellent). Riders can choose to ride along the beach to the mouth of the river and then follow the river back through coconut plantations, or they can hug the beach for the whole ride (which usually lasts between an hour and an hour and a half). The fee is around $30, cash only. Travel agencies in either town can arrange your trip but do charge a bit more for transportation. During the high season, I suggest that you make reservations. Another good place to go horseback riding is at **Playa Larga.** There's a ranch on the first exit coming from Zihuatanejo on Highway 200 going south (no phone, but you can't miss it — it's the first corral to the right as you drive toward the beach). The horses are in excellent shape, and the fee is $30 for 45 minutes. To arrange riding in advance, call Ignacio Mendiola, at ☎ **755-559-8884** (it's a cellphone, so locally, dial 044 before the number).

Sightseeing in Ixtapa and Zihuatanejo

One of the most enjoyable things to do here doesn't even cost a peso — stroll along Zihuatanejo's **Paseo del Pescador** and take in the local life. Fishing boats bob in the waters, gulls circle overhead, and the basketball court is constantly in use.

The **Museo de Arqueología de la Costa Grande** (no phone), which traces the area's history from Acapulco to Ixtapa and Zihuatanejo from pre-Hispanic times through the colonial era, is at the east end of the Paseo del Pescador near Vicente Guerrero. Most of the museum's pottery and stone artifacts provide evidence of extensive trade between the peoples of this area and far-off cultures and regions, including the Toltec and Teotihuacán cultures near Mexico City, the Olmec culture on both the Pacific and Gulf coasts, and areas along the northern Pacific coast. This museum easily merits the half-hour or less it takes to stroll through; information signs are in Spanish, but an accompanying brochure is available in English. Admission is $1, and it's open Tuesday to Sunday from 10 a.m. to 6 p.m.

Shopping in Ixtapa and Zihuatanejo

Shopping isn't especially memorable in Ixtapa — T-shirts and Mexican crafts make up most of the offerings. Several of the town's numerous plazas have air-conditioned shops that carry resort wear — as well as the requisite T-shirts and silver jewelry. These shops are within the same area on Bulevar Ixtapa, across from the beachside hotels, and most are open 9 a.m. to 2 p.m. and 4 to 9 p.m. including Sunday.

However, the terrific shop **La Fuente** (in the Los Patios shopping center; ☎ 755-553-0812) is worth a stop in Ixtapa. The shop carries gorgeous Talavera pottery, jaguar-shaped wicker tables, hand-blown glassware, masks, tin mirrors and frames, hand-embroidered clothing from Chiapas, and wood and papier-mâché miniatures.

Zihuatanejo, like other resorts in Mexico, also has its quota of T-shirt and souvenir shops, but it's becoming a better place to buy Mexican crafts, folk art, and jewelry. The **artisan's market** on Calle Cinco de Mayo is a good place to start your shopping before moving on to specialty shops. A **municipal market** is located on Avenida Benito Juárez (about 5 blocks inland from the waterfront, sprawling over several blocks), but most of the vendors offer the same things — *huaraches* (Mexican-style sandals made of hard leather), hammocks, and baskets — with little variety. Numerous small shops spread inland from the waterfront some 3 or 4 blocks and are well worth exploring.

Shops are generally open Monday to Saturday 10 a.m. to 2 p.m. and 4 to 8 p.m.; many of the better shops close on Sunday, but some smaller souvenir stands stay open, although the hours vary.

I recommend the following shops:

- ✔ The small **Casa Marina** complex (Paseo del Pescador 9, along the waterfront heading in the direction of Alvarez near Cinco de Mayo; ☎ 755-554-2373) houses four shops, each specializing in hand-crafted wares from all over Mexico including handsome rugs, textiles, masks, colorful woodcarvings, and silver jewelry. Café Marina, the small coffee shop in the complex, has shelves and shelves of used paperback books in several languages for sale.

- ✔ **Coco Cabaña Collectibles** (Guerrero and Alvarez, next to Coconuts Restaurant; ☎ 755-554-2518) is filled with carefully selected crafts and folk art, including fine Oaxacan woodcarvings, from all across the country. Owner Pat Cummings once ran a gallery in New York, and the inventory reveals her discriminating eye.

- ✔ **Viva Zapatos** (Guerrero 33, three doors down from Amueblados Valle; no phone) carries bathing suits to fit every shape and fashion trend, great casual and not-so-casual resort wear, sunglasses, and just about everything else for looking good in and out of the water.

Taking a Side Trip

About 32km (20 miles) northwest of Ixtapa, the tiny fishing hamlet of **Troncones,** with its long beaches, has become a favorite escape for visitors to Ixtapa and Zihuatanejo — when that pace of life becomes too hectic. Troncones is so remote that only a few people have phones. Strolling the empty beach, swimming in the sea, and hiking in the jungle and to nearby caves is about the extent of the action. When you've built up an appetite, satisfy it with fresh seafood at one of the fisherman-shack restaurants.

No public buses serve this area, so you must join a tour or hire a taxi to take you to Troncones. For about $30, the taxi driver can take you to the area and return at the hour you request to bring you back to town. Some travel agencies have day trips here for about $25, which usually include lunch; it's cheaper, but less flexible than a taxi.

If you're only spending the day in Troncones, you can use the restaurant **El Burro Borracho** (☎ 755-553-2834 or 553-2800) as your headquarters and have the taxi return for you there. This casual beachfront establishment isn't your ordinary beach-shack restaurant. Owned by a former chef from San Francisco, it offers fish, shrimp, and lobster as well as steak and grilled meat. Try the shrimp tacos for a uniquely Troncones treat. Wash the tasty grub down with a frosty margarita, an iced cappuccino, a glass of wine, or a cold beer. Remember that El Burro Borracho doesn't accept credit cards, and it's open daily from 8 a.m. to 9 p.m.

Discovering Ixtapa and Zihuatanejo after Dark

With an exception or two, Zihuatanejo nightlife dies down around 11 p.m. or midnight. For a decent selection of clubs, discos, hotel fiestas, and special events, head for Ixtapa. Just keep in mind that shuttle-bus service ends at 11 p.m., and a taxi ride back to Zihuatanejo after midnight costs 50 percent more than the regular price. During low season (after Easter and before Christmas), club hours vary: Some places are open only on weekends, and others are closed completely. In Zihuatanejo, a lively bar with satellite TV sports, is **Bandido's,** at the intersection of Cinco de Mayo and Pedro Ascencio in Zihuatanejo Centro, across from the Artisan's Market (☎ 755-553-8072). It features live music Wednesdays through Saturdays, and is open nightly until 2am, but is closed on Sundays from May to October. A popular hangout for local residents and ex-pats is **Rick's Bar,** Av. Cuatémoc 5, in Zihuatanejo centro (☎ 755-554-2535). On Fridays it's known for its live music jam sessions, open to anyone wanting to share their unique talents. It's open Monday through Saturday from 5 p.m. to 11 p.m.

Many Ixtapa hotels hold Mexican fiestas and other special events that include dinner, drinks, live music, and entertainment for a fixed price (generally $33). The **Barceló Ixtapa** (☎ 755-553-1858) hosts the most popular fiesta, held each Wednesday night. Call for reservations or book your seats through your hotel's travel agency.

Many discos and dance clubs in Zihua and Ixtapa stay open until the last customers leave, so closing hours depend upon the revelers.

Most discos have a ladies night at least once a week — admission and drinks are free for women, making it easy for men to buy them a drink.

The Anderson chain of festive restaurants is a standard in Mexican nightlife, and Ixtapa has two of them. **Carlos 'n Charlie's** (Bulevar Ixtapa, just north of the Best Western Posada Real; ☎ 755-553-0085) runs knee-deep in nostalgia, bric-a-brac, silly sayings, and photos from the Mexican Revolution. This restaurant-nightclub boasts a party ambience and good food. The eclectic menu includes iguana in season (with antacids and aspirin on the house). Out back by the beach is an open-air section (partly shaded) with a raised wooden platform for "pier-dancing" at night. The recorded rock-and-roll mixes with sounds of the ocean surf. The restaurant is open daily from 10 a.m. to midnight; pier dancing is held nightly from 9 p.m. to 3 a.m. The second tried-but-true Mexican nightspot from the Anderson lineup is **Señor Frog's** (Bulevar Ixtapa, in the La Puerta Center; ☎ 755-553-2282), which features several dining sections and a warehouse-like bar with raised dance floors. The rock-and-roll playing from large speakers sometimes prompts even dinner patrons to shimmy by their tables between courses. The restaurant is open daily 6 p.m. to midnight; the bar is open until 3 a.m.

Of all the clubs in Ixtapa, **Christine** (Bulevar Ixtapa, in the Hotel Krystal; ☎ 755-553-0333) is both the best known and the glitziest. A throwback to the days of disco, Christine is famous for its midnight light show, which features classical music played on a mega sound system. A semi-circle of tables arranged in tiers overlooks the dance floor. No tennis shoes, sandals, or shorts are allowed, and reservations are advised during high season. It's open nightly during high season from 10 p.m. to the wee hours of the mornin' (off-season hours vary). Cover varies depending on the day of the week from free to $20, and all major credit cards are accepted.

Ixtapa's most progressive nocturnal option is **Zen** (☎ 755-553-0003 or 553-0293), located on Bulevar Ixtapa, next to the Radisson Hotel. Music includes acid jazz, Drum+Bass, and ambient. With a cover charge ranging from free to $10, a young, hip crowd enjoys Zen.

Part VII
Acapulco

AFTER SAILING AROUND ACAPULCO BAY, RON AND DARLENE HEAD FOR THE INTERESTING GROTTOS OF NOSE CAY.

© RICHTENNANT

In this part . . .

*I*t's a beach resort . . . and it's a big glittering city. The largest and most decadent of Mexico's beach resorts, Acapulco can be daunting at first glance.

With its 24-hour, nonstop action, Acapulco can overwhelm first-time visitors. But have no fear — this part helps you choose your accommodations and serves up insights on the best places to dine — from simply delectable fish-taco stands to cliff-side gourmet restaurants with views of Acapulco Bay's dazzling nightlights. Nightlife? You can't visit Acapulco without sampling this part of the action. The Acapulco club scene remains *the* super-hot attraction of this grand dame of Mexico's beach resorts.

Chapter 24

The Lowdown on Acapulco's Hotel Scene

by Lynne Bairstow

. . . .

In This Chapter

▶ Laying out the hotel locations
▶ Evaluating the *número uno* hotel choices

. . . .

*A*capulco was the first Mexican beach town to attract tourism to its golden sands, warm waters, and sunny days. Since the late 1930s, this beach resort has welcomed visitors from around the world, and at one time, it rivaled Rio de Janeiro as the playground of the elite and famous. Today, Acapulco offers one of the widest ranges of hotel choices among Mexican beach resorts — something for every taste and budget.

Because Acapulco's heyday occurred somewhere between 1950 and 1970, many of the hotels are notably dated; however, others have been kept up admirably, offering a funky, kind of retro charm. To me, the single most striking feature of Acapulco is the view of the twinkling lights of the bay at night — an impressive sight that tends to draw you into its nocturnal energy, tempting you to come out and play. The best views are from the hilltop hotels and from the resorts on the bay's southern border, but any of the high-rise locations along Playa Condesa also offer prime views.

Choosing a Location

During my first encounter with Acapulco, I dismissed it as an outdated resort — a tired and ill-kempt relic most appropriate for those who enjoy a carnival-type atmosphere and sleeping all day to prepare for nights that last until sunrise. But my opinion was colored by where I was staying — in the heart of the rowdiest beach-bar action — which didn't suit my mood at the time. As I grew to know Acapulco and became acquainted with her other sides, it didn't take long for me to succumb to this diva's unique charms. Acapulco's energy is tireless (if occasionally tawdry), and her appeal lies somewhere between that of Las Vegas and Miami. Your decision about where to stay plays a huge role in determining how happy you'll be with your Acapulco vacation.

Although Acapulco is an expansive city of several million residents, most visitors only come in contact with the area directly bordering Acapulco Bay and its beaches, which is easy to navigate and can be divided into three main areas. There's really no need to explore more — and you're not likely to have enough time to take in all the sights, activities, and options for dining and nightlife in these areas during a typical weeklong stay anyway.

Running from north to south, the first principal area is **Old Acapulco,** the historic section with a true downtown and plenty of budget accommodations.

Old Acapulco — the original heart of this grand dame of Mexico's beach resorts — has a great selection of basic, inexpensive hotels, and lots of local color. Travelers familiar with Acapulco — or comfortable with travel in Mexico — tend to prefer this area. Numerous budget hotels dot the streets fanning out from the *zócalo* (Acapulco's official and original central plaza). These accommodations are among the best values in Acapulco but, with the exception of the **Hotel Los Flamingos** — one of my favorite places to stay in Mexico — generally offer only the most basic of comforts.

Next comes the **Costera Hotel Zone.** The mid-range, high-rise hotels — lined up side by side, looking much like Miami Beach — are concentrated along this golden stretch of Playa Condesa. The area offers plenty of options for shopping, dining, and nightlife, and is easy to navigate, so it's the best choice for first-time visitors.

If you're looking to spoil yourself, the hotels in the southern neighborhoods and up in the hillsides overlooking the bay are your best bets. The hillside neighborhood bordering the curve of the southern edge of Acapulco Bay is **Las Brisas,** *the* elegant address in town and home of Acapulco's exclusive villas and lusher hotels. Encompassing the Las Brisas area, south of Acapulco Bay, as you travel toward the airport, are the neighborhoods of Punta Diamante and Revolcadero Beach, which fronts the Pacific Ocean. This is where you find the most expensive and luxurious resorts, complete with golf courses.

Las Brisas is several miles from the heart of Acapulco; anytime you want to travel into the Hotel Zone to enjoy its restaurants, shopping malls, or nightclubs, you're looking at a round-trip taxi fare of anywhere from $12 to $20.

Acapulco's Best Accommodations

Each hotel listing includes specific rack rates for two people spending one night in a double room during high season (Christmas to Easter), unless otherwise indicated. *Rack rates* simply mean published rates and tend to be the highest rate paid — you can do better, especially if you're purchasing a package that includes airfare (see Chapter 7 for tips on how to avoid paying rack rates). Please refer to the Introduction of this book for an explanation of the price categories.

It's not unusual for many hotels to double their normal rates during Christmas and Easter weeks, but low-season rates can be anywhere from 20 percent to 60 percent below high-season rates. Note that some rates may seem much higher than others, until you realize that they're *all inclusive,* meaning that your meals and beverages are included in the price of your stay. These rates also include all tips, taxes, and most activities and entertainment.

All hotels have air-conditioning unless otherwise indicated.

Camino Real Acapulco Diamante
$$$$$ Punta Diamante/Puerto Marqués

I love this hotel — it's an oasis of tranquillity in the middle of Acapulco's nonstop energy. This relaxing, self-contained resort is an ideal choice for families or for travelers who already know Acapulco and don't care to explore much. If swimming in the ocean is a priority, this is your best bet in the area — it's located on the clean and safe-for-swimming Playa Puerto Marqués — but you do miss out on the compelling views of Acapulco Bay. In terms of contemporary décor, services, and amenities, I consider this to be one of Acapulco's finest hotels. The Camino Real is tucked in a secluded, 32-hectare (81-acre) location — part of the enormous Punta Diamante development. From Carretera Escénica, you wind down a handsome brick road to the site of the hotel overlooking Puerto Marqués Bay. The spacious rooms have balconies or terraces, small sitting areas, marble floors, a safe-deposit box in the closet, and comfortable, classic furnishings. A bonus: The Camino Real offers 24-hour room service with a terrific menu at very reasonable prices — competitive with area restaurants after you figure in the cost of a round-trip taxi ride. The property also offers special amenities for children including the kid's "Mischief Club" and a children's pool. For adults, a small health club, spa, and tennis court are on-site.

Carretera Escénica Km 14 and Baja Catita 18. ☎ *744-435-1010. Fax: 744-435-1020.* www.caminoreal.com/acapulco. *146 rooms. Free parking. Rack rates: High season $429 double, $611 master suite (includes American breakfast); low-season and midweek discounts available. AE, MC, V.*

Acapulco Bay Area Accommodations

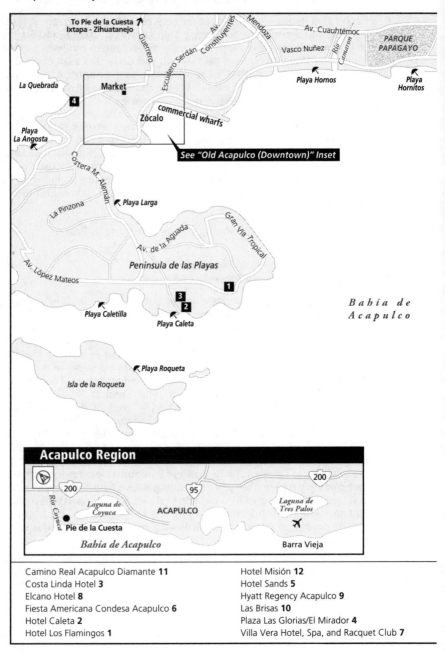

Camino Real Acapulco Diamante **11**
Costa Linda Hotel **3**
Elcano Hotel **8**
Fiesta Americana Condesa Acapulco **6**
Hotel Caleta **2**
Hotel Los Flamingos **1**

Hotel Misión **12**
Hotel Sands **5**
Hyatt Regency Acapulco **9**
Las Brisas **10**
Plaza Las Glorias/El Mirador **4**
Villa Vera Hotel, Spa, and Racquet Club **7**

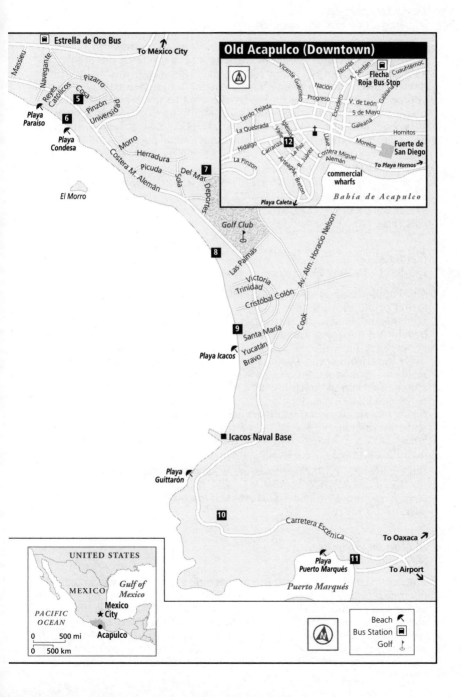

Old Acapulco (Downtown)

Bahía de Acapulco

Costa Linda Hotel
$$ **Playa Caleta/Old Acapulco**

Budget-minded American and Mexican couples are drawn to the clean, sunny, and well-kept rooms of the Costa Linda, one of the area's best values. Playa Caleta is just a 1-block walk from the property. All rooms have a minifridge, and some have a small kitchenette, making it a good choice for longer stays or for those who want to save vacation dollars by preparing a few of their own meals. Although the Costa Linda is cozy, it's situated adjacent to one of the busier streets in Old Acapulco, so traffic noise can be bothersome. Rooms surround a small pool with lounge chairs and tropical plants. Choose an upstairs room for more privacy. A tennis court is also available.

Costera Miguel Alemán 1008, just above the entrance to Caleta Beach pier. ☎ *744-482-5277 or 482-2549. Fax: 744-483-4017. 44 units. Free parking. Rack rates: High season $90 double; low season $35 double. Two children under 8 stay free in parents' room. MC, V.*

Elcano Hotel
$$$–$$$$ **Costera Hotel Zone**

An Acapulco classic and a personal favorite of mine, the Elcano is known for its prime location near the convention center on a broad stretch of golden-sand beach. Its retro-style, turquoise-and-white lobby, and its beachfront pool area are the closest you can get to a South Beach Miami atmosphere in Acapulco, and its popular open-air restaurant adds to the lively waterfront scene. On the whole, the Elcano reminds me of a set from a classic Elvis-in-Acapulco movie — you almost expect to see the King among the tanned beach regulars here. The hotel's reputation is further enhanced by its exceptional service. The continually upgraded rooms, featuring classic navy-and-white accents, are bright and very comfortable, and most offer ample oceanfront balconies. This place is ideal if you attend a convention in Acapulco or want the optimal location between hillside nightlife and the Costera beach zone.

Costera Miguel Alemán 75, just west of the convention center. ☎ *800-972-2162 in the U.S., or 744-435-1500. Fax: 744-484-2230.* http://hotel-elcano.com. *180 units. Rack rates: $176 studio, $208 standard room, $240 junior suite, $299 master suite. AE, DC, MC, V.*

El Mirador Acapulco
$$$ **Old Acapulco**

The best part about staying here is watching those amazing Acapulco cliff divers every day and evening from the comfort of your room. It's an unforgettable sight and a real adrenaline rush. The hotel is built in a horseshoe shape at the apex of La Quebrada, the famous cove where the cliff divers perform. Recently renovated with tropical landscaping and Mexican tile accents, this hotel offers attractively furnished rooms with a choice of double or queen-size beds, kitchenettes with a minifridge and coffeemaker, and large bathrooms with marble counters. Most have a separate living room, some have a whirlpool tub, and all feature colorful, Saltillo-tile accents and other Mexican decorative touches. Be sure to ask for a room with a balcony or ocean view. The restaurant and bar also offer great views of the cliff-diving shows and are popular with tourists from other hotels during the evening performances. The beach here is a steep jump down the cliff, but the resort does offer an alternative in the form of a saltwater pool (though it is occasionally out of service) as well as two freshwater pools. A protected cove with good snorkeling is located nearby.

Quebrada 74. ☎ *800-53-SUITE in the U.S., or 744-483-1221, or 483-1155. Fax: 744-482-4564.* www.hotelelmiradoracapulco.com.mx. *132 units plus 9 junior suites with Jacuzzi. Limited parking on street. Rack rates: High season $185 double, $231 suite with whirlpool; low season $108 double, $135 suite with whirlpool. An extra charge of $20 applies if you use the kitchenette. AE, MC, V.*

Fiesta Americana Condesa Acapulco
$$–$$$$ **Costera Hotel Zone**

The location of this hotel — in the absolute heart of Playa Condesa — is perfect for travelers who don't want to miss a beat and who look to be right in the middle of the casual beach-bar action. The 18-story structure, located just east of and up the hill from the Glorieta Diana (a landmark traffic circle with a statue of Diana the Huntress — which is a duplicate of the one in Mexico City — at its center), towers above Playa Condesa. The unremarkable but comfortable rooms tend to be loud (depending on the crowd) — as music from the pool wafts up into the rooms. All rooms have a private terrace or balcony with an ocean view. In addition to a beach-front pool, an adults-only hilltop swimming pool offers one of the finest views of Acapulco in the city, plus the hotel has a smaller children's pool and a sun deck.

Costera Miguel Alemán 97. ☎ *800-FIESTA-1 in the U.S., or 744-484-2828. Fax: 744-484-1828.* www.fiestamericana.com. *500 units. Free parking. Rack rates: High season $220 double; low season $93–$124 double. Ask about "Fiesta Break" packages, which include meals. AE, DC, MC, V.*

Hotel Caleta
$$ **Playa Caleta/Old Acapulco**

If you prefer the authentic feel of a Mexican holiday with all its boisterous, family-friendly, and spirited charms, then the Hotel Caleta (formerly known as the Grand Meigas Acapulco Resort) is a great choice. It's also a great value. The rooms at this all-inclusive property are simple — stark even — but the hotel itself is usually heavily populated and teeming with activity. This high-quality, nine-floor resort is built into a cliff on the Caleta peninsula and is located adjacent to one of the liveliest beaches in Old Acapulco. Successions of stepped terraces are home to tropical gardens, restaurants, and pools — both saltwater and freshwater. A private beach and boat dock are located down a brief flight of stairs. Rooms surround a central plant-filled courtyard topped by a glass ceiling, and all rooms have large terraces with ocean views, although some layouts lack separation from the neighboring terrace. As is traditional in all-inclusive resorts, meals and drinks are available at almost any hour, and the resort has a changing agenda of theme nights and evening entertainment.

Cerro San Martín 325, just east of Caleta Beach. ☎ **744-483-9940** *or 483-9140. Fax: 744-485-9228.* meigaca@prodigy.net.mx. *255 units. Rack rates: High season $82–$120 per person, all-inclusive; low season $50–$80 per person, all-inclusive. Room-only prices are sometimes available upon request. AE, DC, MC, V.*

Hotel Los Flamingos
$$ Old Acapulco

What a find! You can't help but fall in love with Los Flamingos as soon as you see it — I couldn't! — with its funky charm that transports you back to the days when there was a Hollywood jet set and Acapulco was their playground. Perched on a cliff 150m (500 ft.) above Acapulco Bay, this hotel was frequented by such former Hollywood stars as John Wayne, Cary Grant, Johnny Weissmuller, Fred MacMurray, Errol Flynn, Red Skelton, Roy Rogers, and a host of others. In fact, the stars liked the Flamingos so much that at one point they bought it and converted it into a private club. Though it enjoys a colorful history, it's in excellent shape and is exceptionally clean. Los Flamingos offers visitors a totally different perspective of Acapulco because it maintains all the charm of that grand era gone by. Photos of movie stars grace the lobby, especially those of Wayne, Grant, and Weissmuller — who constructed the large "Tarzan Suite" (also known as the "Round House") as his part-time residence. All rooms have dramatic ocean views with either a large balcony or terrace, but most of them aren't air-conditioned (those that are also have TVs). Still, the constant sea breeze is cool enough. Rooms are colorful with mosaic-tile tables, mirrors, and brightly painted walls. A small pool is the popular gathering point during the day; the large bar is the place to be in the evening. I don't recommend this hotel for small children though — the same dramatic setting that produces such spectacular views can also inspire a constant state of panic for parents. A weekly *pozole* (a special stew made from hominy, served with shredded pork or chicken and an assortment of toppings) party makes Thursdays especially popular. Live music performed by a Mexican band that was probably around in the era of Wayne — note the seashell-pink bass — accompanies the festivities. Even if you don't stay here, plan to come for a margarita at sunset and a walk along the dramatic lookout point — not for the faint of heart!

Av. López Matéos s/n. ☎ **744-482-0690.** *Fax: 744-483-9806. 40 rooms. Rack rates: High season $85 double, $110 with air-conditioning, $130 junior suite; low season $65 double, $88 with air-conditioning, $91 junior suite. AE, MC, V.*

Hotel Misión
$ Old Acapulco (Downtown)

If this courtyard hotel reminds you of an old monastery, it may be because the original structure is more than a century old — truly and authentically

"Old Acapulco!" Rooms are located in the L-shaped building that borders a plant-filled, brick courtyard shaded by two enormous mango trees. The hotel's location, on a narrow street surrounded by tiny shops, lends a distinctly different atmosphere to an Acapulco holiday here. You're in the center of town life just 2 blocks inland from the Costera, fishermen's wharf, *zócalo,* and La Quebrada — the site of the famous cliff divers. Playa Caleta is about a kilometer (half-mile) away. The rooms have colonial touches, such as colorful tile and wrought iron, and come simply furnished with a fan (no air-conditioning here) and one or two beds with good mattresses. Unfortunately, the promised hot water isn't reliable — request a cold-water-only room and receive a discount. Breakfast is served on the patio.

Felipe Valle 12, between La Paz and Hidalgo. ☎ *744-482-3643. Fax: 744-482-2076. 27 units. Rack rates: $56 double. No credit cards.*

Hotel Sands
$ **Costera Hotel Zone**

Comfortable and unpretentious, the Hotel Sands is a great option for budget-minded travelers. The hotel's location on the inland side of the Costera translates to greatly reduced prices, and the fact that it's about a block off the main highway means it's far enough away from all the traffic noise to make your nights peaceful. Still, the Hotel Sands is close enough — walking distance — to the lively Costera Hotel Zone. From the street, you enter the hotel lobby through a stand of umbrella palms and an attractive garden restaurant — one that offers terrific, authentic Mexican food at rock-bottom prices. Rooms are light and airy in the style of a good, modern motel and have basic furnishings, wall-to-wall carpeting, and a terrace or balcony. The bungalow units are located across the street — all have kitchenettes. Two swimming pools (one for adults only), a kid's playground, a volleyball court, and complimentary coffee served in the lobby round out the features.

Costera Miguel Alemán 178, across from the Acapulco Plaza Hotel. ☎ *744-484-2260. Fax: 744-484-1053.* www.sands.com.mx. *93 units. Limited free parking. Rack rates: $62 standard room double, $50 bungalow double (all year except Christmas, Easter, and other major Mexican holidays). AE, MC, V.*

Hyatt Regency Acapulco
$$$$–$$$$$ **Costera Hotel Zone**

The Hyatt is one of the largest and most modern hotels in Acapulco and about as sophisticated as they come here — which is still less sophisticated than most other resorts. It's a good choice for couples looking for a romantic break or for those attending conventions (it's close to the convention center). Two large, free-form pools meander through tropical gardens on the broad, golden-sand beachfront. The sleek lobby has an inviting sitting area and bar that hosts live music every evening and boasts the largest selection of tequilas in Acapulco. All rooms are large with sizable balconies overlooking the pool and ocean. Regency Club guests receive special amenities. (***Note:*** Children aren't allowed in Regency Club rooms.) Kitchenettes are available in some rooms for an extra charge. Three outdoor tennis courts lit for night play and access to a nearby gym are included with your stay, making this hotel a good choice for travelers who prefer their vacations a little on the active side. The Hyatt Acapulco caters to a large Jewish clientele and offers a full-service kosher restaurant, an on-premises synagogue, and a special Sabbath elevator. The hotel recently opened the "Alory Spa" which offers personalized, professional spa and salon services.

Costera Miguel Alemán 1. ☎ *800-633-7313 or 233-1234 in the U.S. and Canada, or 744-469-1234. Fax: 744-484-3087.* www.hyattacapulco.com.mx. *640 units. Rack rates: High season $234 double, $260 Regency Club; low season $208 double, $234 Regency Club. AE, DC, MC, V.*

Las Brisas

$$$$$ Las Brisas

With its hilltop views, terrace pools, and 24-hour, pampering service, the pink-themed Las Brisas hotel is the quintessential Acapulco experience for many Acapulco veterans. A local landmark, Las Brisas is known for its tiered, pink-stucco facade and the 175 pink Jeeps rented exclusively to Las Brisas guests. If you stay here, you better like pink because the color scheme extends to practically everything. Las Brisas is also known for inspiring romance and is best enjoyed by couples indulging in time together — alone. Although the marble-floored rooms with mostly built-in furnishings are simple, they are each like separate villas and offer spectacular panoramic views of Acapulco Bay from the private balconies and terraces. Each room also has a private (or semi-private) swimming pool. (Altogether, Las Brisas boasts 250 swimming pools.) The more spacious Regency Club rooms are located at the apex of the property and offer the best views. You stay at Las Brisas more for the panache and setting than for the amenities. TVs are a recent addition, but they feature volume control so you don't disturb other guests. Early each morning, continental breakfast arrives in a discreet cubbyhole, so your coffee is ready when you are. Although the property isn't located on the beach, Las Brisas offers courtesy shuttle service to its own private beach club located five minutes away on the southwestern tip of Acapulco Bay. Here, freshwater and saltwater pools, plus a large restaurant and bar — though still not much of a real beach — compete for your attention. Five tennis courts, daily activities, and access to a nearby gym round out the action. A mandatory service charge takes care of the shuttle service from the hillside rooms to the lobby and all other service tips. The hotel is located on the southern edge of the bay overlooking the road to the airport and close to the hottest nightclubs in town.

Carretera Escénica 5255. ☎ *800-228-3000 in the U.S., or 744-469-6900. Fax: 744-446-5332. 263 units. Rack rates: High season $330 shared pool, $435 private pool, $540 Royal Beach Club; low season $230 shared pool, $345 private pool, $380 Royal Beach Club. $20 per day service charge extra (in lieu of all tips). Rates include continental breakfast. AE, DC, MC, V.*

Villa Vera Hotel, Spa, and Racquet Club
$$$$–$$$$$ Costera Hotel Zone

Another "address of distinction" in Acapulco is the legendary Villa Vera, which is ideal for a romantic getaway. A smaller inn with a decidedly clubby feel to it, this property started off as a private home with adjacent villas serving as accommodations for houseguests. After a while, it became popular with stars such as Liz Taylor, who married Mike Todd here. Richard M. and Pat Nixon celebrated their 25th wedding anniversary here, and it also served as the set for much of Elvis's film, *Fun in Acapulco*. The hotel is located on a hill above the Costera Hotel Zone and offers the closest experience to Acapulco villa life that you can find on a public property. Several years ago, significant renovations and upgrades in facilities returned Villa Vera to a standard of excellence — in the style of today's more popular boutique-style hotels. Rooms are large, airy, and more sophisticated in décor than most others in Acapulco. Villa Vera offers exceptional spa facilities as well as two clay tennis courts, two lighted racquetball courts, and a small gym. The total of 14 pools includes eight private pools for the six villas and two houses. Most of the other rooms share pools, except for the least expensive standard rooms, which have access to the large public pool located across from the restaurant.

Lomas del Mar 35 (from the Costera, take Av. de los Deportes inland and go left on Av. Prado, which curves right and turns into Av. Lomas del Mar). ☎ **888-554-2361** *from U.S. or Canada, or 744-484-0334 or -0335. Fax: 744-484-7479.* `hotel_villa vera_aca@clubregina.com`. *69 units including suites, villas, and 2 houses. Rack rates: High season $246 studio, $195–$260 double, $340–$405 suite, $481 villa, $1,222 Casa Teddy for four people, $1,261 Casa Julio for six people; low-season rates around 10 percent less than high season. AE, MC, V.*

Chapter 25

Settling into Acapulco

by Lynne Bairstow

In This Chapter

▶ Knowing the scene before you arrive
▶ Finding transportation around town
▶ Reading up on all kinds of useful resources and tips

*A*lthough most beach resorts have "relaxing" written all over them, Acapulco offers visitors nonstop, 24-hour-a-day energy. With so much to do, you won't want to lose a minute figuring out the details, so this chapter guides you through the fundamentals of settling into Acapulco. I help you get your bearings upon arrival at Acapulco's bustling airport, get settled into your hotel, and gain confidence in finding your way around the area. Finally, I give you tips on everything from currency exchanges to Internet access to finding the cheapest — and most entertaining — ways to get around town.

Arriving in Acapulco

No matter the time of year or where you're coming from, the first thing you're likely to notice about Acapulco when you get off the plane is the sizzling climate. You definitely feel the heat, but most travelers quickly adjust. Both immigration and Customs are brief, generally easy procedures. Mexico's second-most important industry is tourism, so the country's aim is to be as welcoming as possible.

Navigating passport control and Customs

The immigration clearance area is generally a lengthy walk from the plane's jetway and then down a flight of stairs. When you reach immigration, an officer asks you to show your passport (or other proof of citizenship) and your completed tourist card, the **FMT** (see Chapter 9 for all the FMT details).

Your FMT is an important document, so take good care of it. You're supposed to keep the FMT with you at all times because you may be required to show it if you run into any sort of trouble. You also need to turn it back in upon departure, or you may be unable to leave without replacing it.

Next up is the baggage claim area. Here, porters stand by to help with your bags, and they're well worth the price of the tip — about a dollar a bag. After you collect your luggage, you pass through another checkpoint. Something that looks like a traffic light awaits you here. You press a button, and if the light turns green, you're free to go. If it turns red, you need to open your bags for a quick search. It's Mexico's random search procedure for Customs. If you have an unusually large bag, or an excessive amount of luggage, you may be searched regardless of the traffic-light outcome.

Getting to your hotel

The airport is 23km (14 miles) southeast of town — over the hills east of Acapulco Bay. Private taxis are the fastest option to get to downtown Acapulco. A taxi ride runs from $15 to $50 depending on your destination.

 The major rental-car agencies all have booths at the airport, but I advise against getting a car unless you determine you really want one, say, for a side trip to Taxco (see Chapter 27) — they tend to be very expensive and generally more troublesome than convenient.

 Transportes Terrestres has desks at the front of the airport (just as you exit the baggage-claim area) where you can buy tickets for *colectivo* (shared minivan) transportation into town for $5 to $10 — rates are preset and based on the distance to your hotel. You must reserve return service to the airport through your hotel. Taxis to the airport tend to be much less expensive (about half the price) than taxis from the airport because the taxis that pick you up at the airport are federally chartered cars with exclusive rights to airport transportation — and the associated steep fares.

Getting Around Acapulco

Acapulco stretches for more than 6km (4 miles) around the huge bay. The most popular tourist areas are divided roughly into three sections: **Acapulco Viejo (Old Acapulco);** the **Costera Hotel Zone,** which follows the main boulevard, Costera Miguel Alemán (or just "the Costera"); and **the southern shore,** whose exclusive neighborhoods border the scenic highway (Carretera Escénica) between the airport and the International Center.

Street names and numbers in Acapulco can be confusing and hard to find — many streets either aren't well marked or change names unexpectedly. Fortunately, you'll seldom have any reason to stray far from the Costera, so getting lost is difficult. But remember that street numbers on the Costera don't follow a logical order; you can't assume that similar numbers are necessarily close together.

Taking a taxi

Taxis, which are more plentiful than tacos in Acapulco (and practically as inexpensive if you're traveling in the downtown area only), are the best way to get around here.

 Significant differences in prices for different types of taxis are common, so always establish the price with the driver before starting out. Hotel taxis may charge three times the rate of a taxi hailed on the street, and nighttime taxi rides cost extra, too. Taxis are also more expensive if you're staying in the Punta Diamante neighborhood, south of Las Brisas, which includes Puerto Marqués — these areas are along the southern highway (Carretera Escénica), between town and the airport. The minimum fare is $2 per ride for a roving VW bug–style taxi in town. The fare from Puerto Marqués costs $8 to the Hotel Zone and $10 into downtown. *Sitio* taxis are nicer cars, but they're also more expensive with a $4 minimum fare.

 Acapulco's taxi fashion demands that drivers decorate their cars with flashy, Las Vegas–style neon lights — the more colorful and pulsating, the better. It almost appears to be a local competition. And there's no extra charge for the added embellishments. These decked-out rides are especially popular in Old Acapulco.

Catching a bus

 Buses are another great option for traveling along the Costera — they're easy to use and inexpensive. Two kinds of buses run along this main drag: pastel, color-coded buses and regular "school buses." The difference is in the price: The newer, air-conditioned, color-coded, tourist buses (Aca Tur Bus) cost 50¢; the older "school buses" cost 35¢. Covered bus stops, with handy maps on the walls showing bus routes to major sights and hotels, are located all along the Costera. If you want to go downtown from the Costera, take the bus marked "Centro" or "Zócalo"; to get to the southeast side (the Punta Diamante area), take a bus marked "Base" (pronounced *bah*-seh). Buses traveling these popular routes come along at least every ten minutes. Buses also head out to more distant destinations such as **Puerto Marqués** to the east (marked "Puerto Marqués-Basa") and **Pie de la Cuesta** to the northwest (marked "Zócalo-Pie de la Cuesta"). Be sure to verify the time and place of the last bus back if you hop on along one of these routes.

Renting a car

Rental cars are available at the airport and at hotel desks along the Costera, but I don't recommend one — they're expensive, and parking is hard to find. Unless you plan on exploring outlying areas, you're better off taking taxis or using the easy and inexpensive public buses. Besides, leaving the driving to someone else is much easier.

Fast Facts: Acapulco

American Express

The main office (Av. Costera Miguel Alemán 121, Hotel Continental Emporio, Local 31; ☎ 744-435-2200) is open Monday to Friday 9 a.m. to 6 p.m. and Saturday 9 a.m. to 1 p.m.

Area Code

The local telephone area code is **744.**

Baby Sitters

Though most of the larger hotels can easily arrange for them, many baby sitters speak limited English. Rates range from $4 to $10 per hour with an additional charge of about $5 for a taxi for the sitter if you stay out past 10 p.m.

Banks, ATMs, and Currency Exchange

Numerous banks are located along the Costera and are open Monday to Friday 9 a.m. to 6 p.m. and Saturday 10 a.m. to 1:30 p.m. Banks, and their ATMs, generally have the best exchange rates. *Casas de cambio* (currency exchange booths) along the street may have better exchange rates than hotels, and they're open late. Most establishments accept U.S. dollars as readily as pesos but at reduced exchange rates, so you're better off using local currency whenever possible.

Climate

Acapulco boasts sunshine 360 days a year and an average daytime temperature of 80°F (27°C). Humidity levels vary. Acapulco receives approximately 59 inches of rain per year — June through October is the rainy season, although July and August are relatively dry. Tropical showers are brief and usually occur at night.

Consular Agents

The U.S. Consular Agency office is at the Hotel Club del Sol on Costera Alemán at Reyes Católicos (☎ 744-469-0556), across from the Hotel Acapulco Plaza. The office is open Monday to Friday 10 a.m. to 2 p.m. The Canadian Consulate (Centro Comercial Marbella, Local 23; ☎ 01-800-706-2900 toll-free emergency number inside Mexico, or 744-484-1305) is open Monday to Friday 9 a.m. to 5 p.m.

Hospitals

Hospital Magallanes (Av. Wilfrido Massieu 2, on the corner with Colón, 1 block from the Costera; ☎ 744-485-6194 or 485-6197) has an English-speaking staff and doctors.

Information

The State of Guerrero Tourism Office (☎/fax 744-484-4583 or 484-4416) operates the Procuraduría del Turista on the street level in front of the International Center, a convention center set back from Costera Miguel Alemán. (It's down a lengthy walkway with fountains.) The office offers maps and information about the city and state as well as police assistance for tourists; it's open daily 9 a.m. to 10 p.m.

Internet Access

A number of small Internet-access services are located along the Costera, but they seem to go out of business quickly. Internet access kiosks are available inside **Wal-Mart**, Costera Miguel Alemán 500 (☎ 744-469-0203), with varying rates depending on usage. Or you can try **Acanet**, Av. Cuatemoc 1632 Centro Commercial Monte Blanco, Local 2, in front of Papagayo Park, across from City Hall (Presidencia; ☎ 744-486-1803 or 486-2343); it's open Monday to Saturday from 10 a.m. to 9 p.m. Internet access costs $1 per hour. This is a computer shop that also offers Internet access and has a very helpful staff.

Maps

One of the best around is the free American Express map, usually found at tourist information offices and hotel concierge desks. Sanborn's or Wal-Mart may also have more detailed maps for sale.

Newspapers and Magazines

The larger Costera hotels generally carry a good selection of English-language newspapers (such as *USA Today*) and magazines in their gift shops, as well as the English-language *Mexico City News.* You can also find English-language paperbacks and magazines at Sanborn's department stores (Costera Miguel Alemán 209, downtown across from the ship docks, ☎ 744-482-6167; Costera Miguel Alemán 1226, in the Estrella Condo Tower, ☎ 744-484-4465; and Costera Miguel Alemán 163, at the Hotel Calinda, ☎ 744-481-2426).

Pharmacy

One of the largest drugstores in town is Farmacia Daisy (☎ 744-481-2635). The Sam's Club and Wal-Mart (open 24 hr.) are both located on the Costera and have pharmacy services and lower prices on medicines.

Police

Policemen in white and light-blue uniforms belong to a special corps of English-speaking police established to assist tourists. For the **main police department**, call ☎ 744-485-0650.

Post Office

The central post office *(correo)* is located next door to Sears (close to the Fideicomiso office). Other branches are located in the Estrella de Oro bus station on Cuauhtémoc, inland from the Acapulco Qualton Hotel, and on the Costera near Playa Caleta.

Safety

Riptides claim a few lives here every year, so pay close attention to warning flags posted on Acapulco beaches. Red or black flags mean stay out of the water, yellow flags signify caution, and white or green flags mean it's safe to swim.

As is the case anywhere, tourists are vulnerable to thieves, which is especially true when shopping in a market; lying on the beach; wearing jewelry; or visibly carrying a camera, purse, or bulging wallet.

Taxes

There's a 15 percent value-added tax (IVA) on goods and services, and it's generally included in the posted price.

Taxis

Always establish the price of a trip with the driver before starting out. Hotel taxis charge more than a taxi hailed on the street, and nighttime taxi rides cost extra, too. The minimum fare is $3 per ride for a roving VW bug–style taxi in town. The fare from Puerto Marqués costs $10 to the Hotel Zone and $12 into downtown. *Sitio* taxis are nicer cars, but they're also more expensive — $4 minimum fare.

Telephone

Phone numbers seem to change frequently in Acapulco — the most reliable source for telephone numbers is the Procuraduría del Turista (☎ **744-484-4583**) where an exceptionally friendly staff can help you locate what you need. Avoid the phone booths that have signs in English advising you to call home using a special 800 number — these are absolute rip-offs and can cost as much as $20 per minute. The least expensive way to call is by using a Telmex (LADATEL) prepaid phone card, available at most pharmacies and mini-supers, using the official Telmex (Lada) public phones.

In Mexico, you need to dial 001 prior to a number to reach the United States, and you need to preface long distance calls within Mexico by dialing 01.

Time Zone

Acapulco operates on central standard time, but Mexico's observance of daylight saving time varies somewhat from that in the United States.

Chapter 26

Dining in Acapulco

by Lynne Bairstow

. . . .

In This Chapter

▶ Discovering Acapulco's best restaurants
▶ Finding the best Mexican cuisine in Acapulco

. . . .

*B*eing the cosmopolitan city that it is, Acapulco offers world-class international cuisine, much of it served in the romantic restaurants located along the southern coast. The quintessential Acapulco dining experience is sitting at a candlelit table with a view of the glittering bay spread out before you. If, however, you're looking for simple, good food or an authentic, local dining experience, you're best off checking out the scene in Old Acapulco. Being a beach town, Acapulco restaurants serve up a ton of fresh seafood. My personal Acapulco favorites include a small place that specializes in fish tacos.

Despite the growing profusion of American-influenced chain restaurants, resist the temptation to go with what you know — trust me, the locally owned restaurants offer the best food and best value.

And, although most of Mexico's beach resorts fall on the casual side when it comes to dress, Acapulco goes against the trend, especially for women. Feel free to go all out with your sexy resort wear when dining here. Also note that dinner tends to be a late affair. Most Acapulco regulars wouldn't think of dining before 10 p.m. so that they can finish up just in time to hit the clubs, which open at midnight.

You can find American standards such as McDonald's, Tony Roma's, Burger King, and Hard Rock Cafe — good choices if you're traveling with kids — but you may also want to try the Mexican alternatives of Carlos 'n Charlie's and 100% Natural, both located along the Costera.

If you're visiting Acapulco on a Thursday, indulge in the local custom of eating *pozole,* a bowl of white hominy and meat in a broth garnished with sliced radishes, shredded lettuce, onions, oregano, and lime. The truly traditional version is served with pork, but a newer chicken version has also become a standard. You can also find green *pozole,* which is made by adding a paste of roasted pumpkin seeds to the traditional *pozole* base, giving the broth its green color. For a uniquely Acapulco experience, enjoy your Thursday *pozole* at the cliff-side restaurant of the Hotel Los Flamingos.

Acapulco's Best Restaurants

All the restaurants included in this chapter are arranged alphabetically with their location and general price category noted. Remember that tips generally run about 15 percent, and most wait-staff really depend on tips for their income, so be generous if the service warrants. See the Introduction of this book for an explanation of the price categories.

Please see Appendix C for more information on Mexican cuisine.

Baikal
$$–$$$$ Las Brisas   FUSION/FRENCH/ASIAN

The exquisite and ultra-hot Baikal is the best place in Acapulco for an over-the-top dining experience. You enter from the street, and then descend a spiral staircase into the stunning bar and restaurant, awash in muted tan and cream colors of luxurious fabrics and natural accents of stone, wood, and water. The restaurant itself is constructed into the cliff, providing sweeping views of Acapulco Bay's glittering lights. The large dining room, with a two-story ceiling, has comfortable seating, including sofas that border the room. The creative menu combines traditional French and Asian fare, and then adds a dash of Mexican flare. Start with the scallops in chipotle vinaigrette, or the black bean soup with duck foie gras. Notable entrees include steamed red snapper with lobster butter sauce, chicken breast rolled and stuffed with asparagus in a white wine reduction, or medallions of New Zealand lamb in a sweet garlic sauce. The service is as impeccable as the presentation. You can also choose from an extensive selection of wines, as well as enjoy live jazz and bossa nova music nightly. Periodically during the evening, large projector screens descend over the floor-to-ceiling glass windows, and show short films of old Acapulco or cavorting whales and dolphins, providing a brief reprise from conversation and dining. A fashionably late dining spot (expect a crowd at midnight), the attire is chic resort wear, because most patrons are headed to the clubs following dinner. Baikal also has wheelchair access, a private VIP dining room, and a wine cellar, as well as an ample bar, ideal for enjoying a sunset cocktail or after-dinner drink. It's located east of town on the scenic highway just before the entrance to the Las Brisas hotel.

Carretera Escénica 16 & 22. ☎ *744-446-6845 or 446-6867.* www.baikal.com.mx. *Reservations required (*reservaciones@baikal.com.mx*). Main courses: $20–$60. AE, MC, V. Open: Daily 7 p.m.–2 a.m. Closed Mon during the summer.*

Acapulco Bay Area Dining

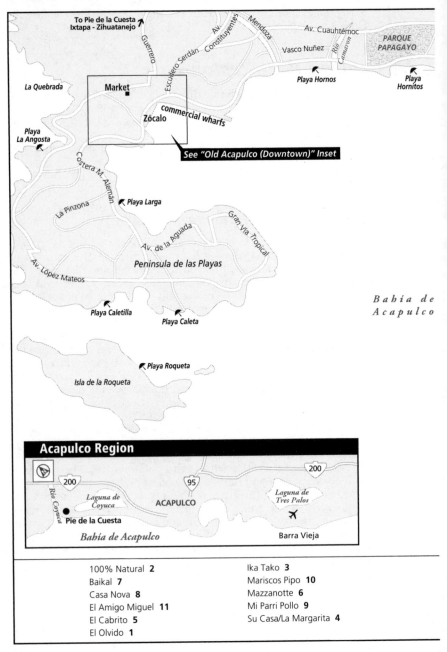

100% Natural **2**

Baikal **7**

Casa Nova **8**

El Amigo Miguel **11**

El Cabrito **5**

El Olvido **1**

Ika Tako **3**

Mariscos Pipo **10**

Mazzanotte **6**

Mi Parri Pollo **9**

Su Casa/La Margarita **4**

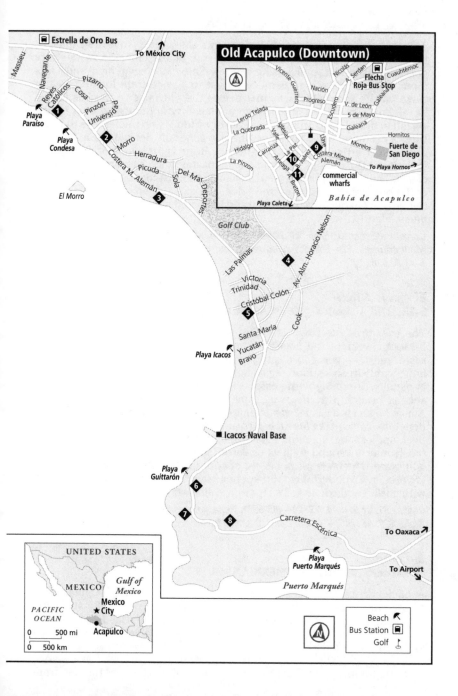

Casa Nova
$$–$$$ Las Brisas   GOURMET ITALIAN

This long-standing favorite of Mexico City's elite is easily one of Acapulco's top spots for a romantic evening, and one of the cliff-side restaurants noted for its food as much as for its view. Enjoy an elegant meal and a fabulous view of glittering Acapulco Bay at this restaurant located east of town on the scenic highway just before the entrance to the Las Brisas hotel. You can dine in one of several elegantly appointed dining rooms awash in marble and stunning murals or outdoors on the terrace that features a dramatic view. The crowd here is generally decked out in fashionable resort attire, and the peak dining hour is 10 p.m. Notable dishes include veal scaloppini and homemade pastas, such as linguini with fresh clams. The service is stellar, and a changing tourist menu offers a sampling of the best selections for a fixed price. You can also enjoy an ample selection of reasonably priced national and imported wines as well as live piano music nightly.

Carretera Escénica 5256. ☎ *744-446-6237, -6238, or -6239. Reservations required. Main courses: $28–$50; $39 fixed-price four-course meal. AE, MC, V. Open: Daily 7–11:30 p.m.*

El Amigo Miguel
$–$$ Old Acapulco   MEXICAN/SEAFOOD

The ever-present crowd of locals is a sure sign that El Amigo Miguel, 3 blocks west of the *zócalo,* is a standout among Acapulco seafood restaurants — you can easily pay more elsewhere and not eat better. Impeccably fresh seafood reigns here, and the large, open-air dining room is usually brimming with seafood lovers. When it overflows, head to a second branch with the exact same menu across the street. Dining at El Amigo Miguel is a casual way to enjoy the best of the bay's bounty. Try the delicious *camarones borrachos* (drunken shrimp) in a sauce made with beer, applesauce, ketchup, mustard, and bits of fresh bacon — the ingredients may not sound great when listed individually, but trust me, this stuff is heaven. The *filete Miguel* is red-snapper filet stuffed with seafood and covered in a wonderful chipotle-pepper sauce. *Mojo de ajo* (grilled shrimp with garlic) and whole red snapper are also served at their classic best.

Juárez 31, at Azueta. ☎ *744-483-6981. Reservations not accepted. Main courses: $2.70–$20. AE, MC, V. Open: Daily 10 a.m.–11 p.m.*

El Cabrito
$ Costera   NORTHERN MEXICAN

A hacienda-inspired facade marks the entrance to this popular joint located in the heart of the Costera. El Cabrito is known for its authentic and well-prepared northern Mexican cuisine. Although the décor appears to shout "tourist trap," this restaurant enjoys a strong reputation among Mexican nationals as well. Among the specialties are *cabrito al pastor* (roasted goat), *charro* beans (a dish made with pinto beans), Oaxaca-style *mole* (a complex sauce that uses a variety of ingredients ranging from chocolate to chiles — there are red, yellow, green, and black moles), and *burritos de machaca.*

Costera Miguel Alemán 1480, on the ocean side of the Costera opposite of Hard Rock Cafe. ☎ 744-484-7711. Reservations not accepted. Main courses: $5–$15. AE, MC, V. Open: Mon–Sat 2 p.m.–1 a.m.; Sun 1–11 p.m.

El Olvido
$–$$$ Costera   MEXICANA

This stylish restaurant tucked in a shopping mall gives you all the glittering bay-view ambience of the posh Las Brisas restaurants without the taxi ride from the Costera hotels. The menu is one of the city's most sophisticated. Each dish is a delight in both presentation and taste — truly some of the finest "new-style" Mexican cuisine in the country. Start with one of the 12 house specialty drinks such as Olvido — made with tequila, rum, Cointreau, tomato juice, and lime juice. Soups include a delicious cold melon and a thick, black bean and sausage. Among the innovative entrees are quail with honey and *pasilla chiles* and thick sea bass with a mild sauce of cilantro and avocado. For dessert, try the chocolate fondue or the *guanabana* (a tropical fruit) mousse in a rich *zapote negro* (black-colored tropical fruit) sauce. El Olvido is in the Plaza Marbella shopping center on Diana Circle. Aca Joe clothing store fronts the plaza. Walk into the passage to the right of Aca Joe and head left; it's in the back.

Plaza Marbella, at the Diana Glorieta (Circle). ☎ 744-481-0203 or 481-0256. Reservations recommended. Main courses: $14–$30. AE, DC, MC, V. Open: Daily 6 p.m.–2 a.m.

Ika Tako
$ Costera   SEAFOOD/TACOS

This is my favorite place to eat in Acapulco, and I never miss it when I'm in town. Perhaps I have simple tastes, but these fresh fish, shrimp, and seafood tacos served in combinations that include grilled pineapple, fresh spinach, grated cheese, garlic, and bacon are addictive. Unlike most inexpensive eateries, the setting here is lovely — a handful of tables overlook tropical trees and the bay below. The lighting may be a bit bright, the atmosphere occasionally hectic, and the service dependably slow, but the tacos are delectable. You can also get beer, wine, soft drinks, and a dessert of the day. This restaurant is located along the Costera, next to Beto's lobster restaurant. A second branch of Ika Tako sits across from the Hyatt Regency hotel, but it lacks the atmosphere of this location.

Costera Miguel Alemán 99. No phone. Reservations not accepted. Main courses: $2.50–$8. No credit cards. Open: Daily 6 p.m.–5 a.m.

Mariscos Pipo
$–$$ Old Acapulco   SEAFOOD

Check out the photographs of Old Acapulco on the walls while relaxing in this airy dining room decorated with hanging nets, fish, glass buoys, and shell lanterns. The English-language menu lists a wide array of seafood, including ceviche, lobster, octopus, crayfish, and baby-shark quesadillas. This local favorite is 2 blocks west of the *zócalo* on Breton, just off the Costera. Another branch (☎ 744-484-0165), open daily 1 to 9:30 p.m., is at Costera Miguel Alemán and Canadá, across from the convention center.

Almirante Breton 3. ☎ *744-482-2237. Reservations not accepted. Main courses: $5.50–$33 (though lobster will be a bit more). AE, MC, V. Open: Daily noon–8 p.m.*

Mezzanotte Acapulco
$$–$$$ Las Brisas   ITALIAN/FRENCH/MEXICAN

Mezzanotte offers a contemporary blending of classic cuisines, but its strongest asset is the view of the bay. This location has changed hands several times; it currently offers a mix of trendy international dishes served in an atmosphere that tries a bit too hard to be upscale and fashionable. Music is loud and hip, so if you're looking for a romantic evening, this is probably not the place. It's a better choice if you want a taste of Mexican urban chic. The view of the bay remains outstanding, though the food still strives for consistency. Dress up a bit for dining here. Mezzanotte is in the La Vista complex near the Las Brisas hotel.

Plaza La Vista, Carretera Escénica a Puerto Márquez 28–2. ☎ *744-446-5727 or -5728. Reservations required. Main courses: $20–$35. AE, MC, V. Open: Daily 6:30pm–midnight. Closed Mon during low season.*

Mi Parri Pollo
$ Old Acapulco   MEXICAN/INTERNATIONAL

Umbrella-covered tables on one of the coolest and shadiest sections of the *zócalo* comprise this tiny and typically Mexican restaurant. It's especially popular for breakfast with specials that include coffee refills and a great fresh-fruit salad with mango, pineapple, and cantaloupe. Other specials include fish burgers, *tortas,* a special rotisserie-grilled chicken, and steak *Milanesa.* Fruit drinks, including fresh mango juice, come in schooner-size glasses. To find the restaurant, enter the *zócalo* from the Costera and walk toward the kiosk. On the right, about midway into the *zócalo,* is a wide, shady passageway that leads onto Avenida Jesús Carranza and to the umbrella-covered tables under the shady tree.

Jesús Carranza 2B, Zócalo. ☎ *744-483-7427. Reservations not accepted. Breakfast: $1.50–$2.50; sandwiches $1–$2; fresh-fruit drinks $1.25; daily specials $2–$4. No credit cards. Open: Daily 7 a.m.–11 p.m.*

100% Natural
$ Costera   MEXICAN/HEALTH FOOD

Healthful versions of Mexican standards are the specialty at this clean, breezy, plant-filled restaurant, located on the second level of the shopping center across from the Acapulco Plaza Hotel. (This chain has five other branches in Acapulco, including another one farther east on the Costera.)

Especially notable are the fruit *licuados,* blended fresh fruit and your choice of purified water or milk. Yogurt shakes, steamed vegetables, and cheese enchiladas are alternatives to their yummy sandwiches served on whole grain breads. If you've over-indulged the night before, get yourself back on track here. It's also a great place for families.

Costera Miguel Alemán 200, across from the Acapulco Plaza Hotel. ☎ **744-485-3982.** *Sandwiches: $4.50–$6; other food items $3–$9. No credit cards. Open: Daily 24 hours.*

Su Casa/La Margarita
$–$$$ Costera Zone (Inland)   INTERNATIONAL

A comfortable setting, terrific food, and moderate prices are what you get at Su Casa. Owners Shelly and Angel Herrera created this pleasant and breezy open-air restaurant on the patio of their hillside home overlooking the city. Both are experts in the kitchen and stay on hand nightly to greet guests on the patio. The menu changes often, so each time you go there's something new to try. But some items are standard — shrimp *a la patrona* in garlic; grilled fish, steak, and chicken; and flaming *fillet al Madrazo,* a delightful brochette marinated in tropical juices. Most entrees come garnished with cooked banana or pineapple. The margaritas are big and delicious. Su Casa is the hot-pink building on the hillside above the convention center.

Av. Anahuac 110, up the hill from the convention center. ☎ **744-484-4350** *or 484-1261.* www.sucasa-acapulco.com. *Reservations recommended. Main courses: $14–$50. MC, V. Open: Daily 6 p.m.–midnight.*

Chapter 27

Having Fun on and off the Beach in Acapulco

by Lynne Bairstow

In This Chapter

▶ Working on that tan at the best beaches
▶ Diving, fishing, golfing, and other fun stuff
▶ Checking out the sights and shops
▶ Visiting Taxco
▶ Partying like you're in Acapulco

*A*capulco's beaches aren't all created equal, and knowing that sun and sand are a key part of any vacation here, I use this chapter to guide you to the areas that are best for watersports and safest for swimming — and I throw in a few out-of-the-way recreational finds.

In and out of the water, Acapulco features a wealth of activities to do and see, so I point out the top attractions. Though the town is lacking in true cultural options, I've found a few hidden gems that I reveal in this chapter.

And then there's the nightlife! Oh, the nightlife! I wrap up this chapter with a guide of the top clubs in town, giving you a rundown of the typical crowd and type of action you're likely to encounter in each location. This info can help you pick a spot that best meets your tastes — without having to cough up a bunch of cover charges just to find the right scene.

Hitting the Beaches

Acapulco Bay is a stunning sight — night or day — that practically cries out in temptation. But, before I dive into the best beaches, I have a few words of wisdom.

Acapulco's golden beaches, cobalt-blue bay, and sun-soaked climate lured so many people here that, by the late 1970s, Acapulco became a victim of its own success. Beaches began to lose their luster as waves of garbage and pollution started coming in with the tides. As the numbers of visitors sharply declined, authorities took notice, and over the past decade, the city has gone to great lengths (and great expense) to clean up the waters of its beautiful bay. Despite the notable success of these efforts, it still pays to be cautious in some areas. (Acapulco is an active, industrial port.) You may also notice the fleet of more than 20 power-sweeper boats that skim the top of the bay each morning to remove any debris or oil film or . . .

The tides in the area can be treacherous, especially in the open ocean north and south of Acapulco Bay. Each year, at least one or two unwary swimmers drown in the area because of the deadly riptides and under-tow, so heed any posted warnings — red or black flags mean stay out of the water altogether, and yellow warns you to exercise caution. The safest swimming is in either Acapulco Bay or Puerto Marqués Bay.

I'm glad I got that off of my chest; now I can tell you about the best places to play. In the old days, the downtown beaches were the focal point of Acapulco, but today, the resort developments stretch along the entire length of the shore. The beaches and coves tucked into Acapulco Bay go by as many as 50 different names, but I just focus on the best and most popular beaches from west to east.

Located 13km (8 miles) west of Acapulco Bay is **Pie de la Cuesta.** Traveling by taxi or car (this is the one time you may want to consider renting a car) is the best way to reach this beach because it's much faster than taking the bus. However, buses run regularly along the Costera, leaving every five or ten minutes. A taxi costs about $22. The water here is too rough for swimming, but it's a great spot for checking out big waves and the spectacular sunset — especially over *coco locos* (drinks served in a fresh coconut with the top whacked off) at one of the rustic beachfront restaurants hung with hammocks. The area is known for excellent bird-watching and the surrounding coconut plantations.

Heading on the road northwest, beyond the bay, along the Pacific coast-line, you come to **Coyuca Lagoon** on your right. *Colectivo* boat tours — or small boats that band together a group of people to comprise a tour — of the lagoon are offered for about $10.

Back toward Acapulco, around the area near La Quebrada (where the cliff divers perform), is **Playa La Angosta,** a small, sheltered, and often-deserted cove. If you're staying in Old Acapulco, this beach is great not only for its location, but also because it's much less crowded than public beaches in Old Acapulco, and much more dramatic in its setting — though generally too rough for swimming.

South of downtown on the Peninsula de las Playas lie **Caleta** and **Caletilla;** the image I hold in my mind of these sister beaches is one of bright colors, and plenty of laughter, kids, and an almost carnival-like atmosphere. A small outcropping of land that contains an aquarium and

Acapulco Bay Area

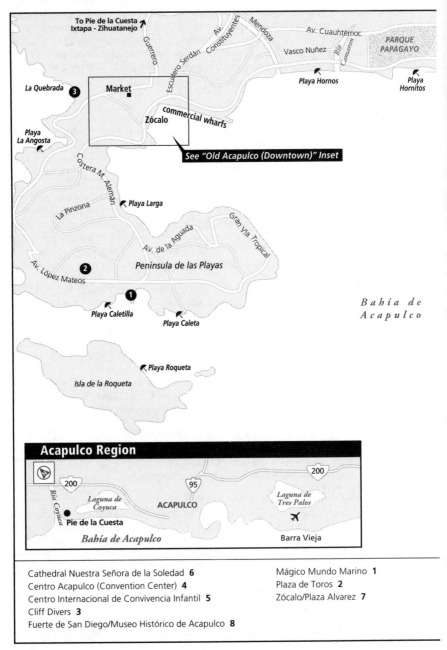

Cathedral Nuestra Señora de la Soledad **6**
Centro Acapulco (Convention Center) **4**
Centro Internacional de Convivencia Infantil **5**
Cliff Divers **3**
Fuerte de San Diego/Museo Histórico de Acapulco **8**

Mágico Mundo Marino **1**
Plaza de Toros **2**
Zócalo/Plaza Alvarez **7**

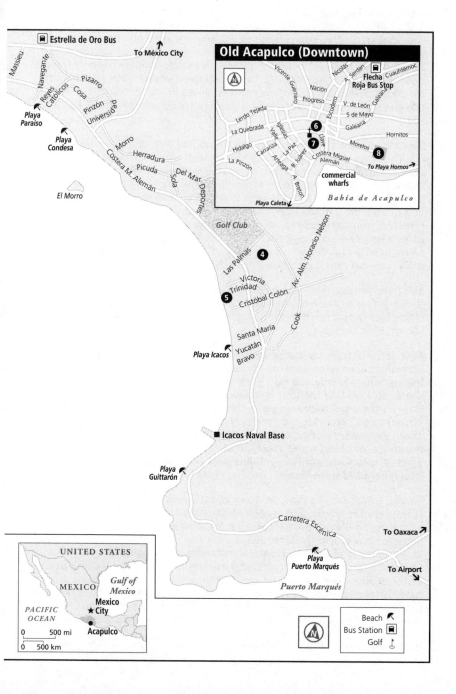

water park, **Mágico Mundo Marino** (open daily 9 a.m.–7 p.m.; ☎ 744-483-1215), separates the two beaches. In this area, you find thatched-roofed restaurants, watersports equipment for rent, and brightly painted boats that ferry passengers to Isla de la Roqueta. You can also rent beach chairs and umbrellas for the day. Mexican families favor these beaches because they're close to several inexpensive hotels. In the late afternoon, fishermen pull their colorful boats up on the sand; you can buy the fresh catch of the day and, occasionally, oysters on the half shell.

Speaking of **Isla de la Roqueta,** this island has two small beaches amidst a hilly, forested terrain. **Playa Marin** is the more deserted of the two. **Playa Roqueta** has thatched-roof restaurants where you can enjoy a snack and a cold beer or rent snorkeling equipment. The island also has a small zoo of exotic animals kept in pitifully small cages — I kindly ask you to boycott it in the hope that these poor creatures will one day be released. You can get here via one of the *panga* boats (small, open-air fishing boats) departing from Playa Caletilla. The boat rides cost about $5 round-trip and depart about every 20 minutes from 10 a.m. to 6 p.m. daily. You can purchase tickets directly from any boat that's loading.

You need to remember the name of **Playa Manzanillo** if you're planning to set out on a pleasure-boat excursion — including chartered fishing trips. This beach is where they dock. It's located just south of the *zócalo* (Acapulco's central plaza).

East of the *zócalo,* the major beaches are **Hornos** (near Papagayo Park and sometimes referred to as Playa Papagayo), **Hornitos, Condesa,** and **Icacos,** which merge one into the other. Icacos is the beach just beyond the Hyatt Hotel. Of the four beaches, it's closest to the naval base (La Base), which is directly opposite the bay from the *zócalo.* All these strips of sand are wide, and the surf is gentle, but I remain cautious about swimming along this interior curve of Acapulco Bay — based on my concerns about water cleanliness. Of these beaches, Condesa is the liveliest with watersports equipment for rent and a regular crowd of beach babes of both sexes.

 As you travel around the bay, down the Costera to the Scenic Highway (Carretera Escénica), and past the legendary Las Brisas hotel, the road continues to **Playa Puerto Marqués,** located in the small, clean, and separate bay of **Puerto Marqués.** It's my top choice for beach swimming in Acapulco, and one key reason for staying at the Camino Real (see Chapter 24). The water is calm, and the bay is sheltered, meaning the water quality here is much better than in Acapulco Bay, and it's a great place for water-skiing — rentals are generally available. A row of *palapa*-topped (thatched-roof), beachfront restaurants draws a sizable crowd every weekend, so arrive early; better yet, come during a weekday.

Past the bay lies **Playa Revolcadero,** a magnificent wide stretch of beach on the open ocean where you can find many of Acapulco's grandest resorts — including the Acapulco Princess, Mayan Palace, and Pierre Marqués. About 6km (4 miles) farther south lies **Barra Vieja,** a lovely, wide beach with firm sand (ideal for running on the beach) — but also strong waves. **Tres Palos Lagoon,** a fascinating freshwater jungle lagoon, is nearby. You can hire a boat for about $15 to take you around these wetlands, which are at the east end of the fishing village that adjoins Barra Vieja.

Finding Water Fun for Everyone

It seems like you can find more ways to have fun in Acapulco in the water than out of it — after all, this resort grew up around the bay. Whether it's plowing through the surf on a Jet Ski or diving below the surface, if you can do it in the water, you can find it in Acapulco!

Skiing and surfing

Acapulco watersports tend to lean toward the motorized variety — the louder the engine, the better the fun. In Acapulco's heyday, images of bronzed, muscled water-skiers were commonplace, and today, this sport remains as popular during the day as dancing is at night. An hour of water-skiing can cost as little as $35 or as much as $65. Boats and rental equipment are available at Playa Caletilla, Puerto Marqués Bay, and Coyuca Lagoon. You can also check out the **Club de Esquís** (Costera Miguel Alemán 100; ☎ 744-482-2034); water-skiing rates run $50 per hour here.

You can find concessions for other watersports equipment on the beaches fronting the Costera hotels — most notably the Qualton Club, Acapulco Plaza, Fiesta Americana, and Hyatt hotels. Banana boats ($5 per person for about 15 min.), parasail rides (about $30 for the longest 10 min. of your life), and Jet Skis ($50 per hour) are usually available. Although these concessions are also available at Playa Caletilla and Coyuca Lagoon near Pie de la Cuesta, the equipment tends to be in better shape along the Costera hotel beaches.

The mother of all motorized watersports in Acapulco is, without a doubt, the **Shotover Jet.** These 12-person, soft-sided boats careen down the otherwise tranquil Laguna Puerto Marqués propelled by 8-liter, V-8 engines. You travel at speeds of 65 to 80kmph (40–50 mph) and make 360-degree turns, so the ride is a thrill. Book these trips directly through the Shotover Jet office (Costera Miguel Alemán 121, in front of the Continental Plaza Hotel; ☎ 744-484-1154; www.shotoverjet-acapulco.com). Tickets cost $44 for adults and $22 for children and include round-trip transportation from this departure point to the lagoon.

The Shotover Jet ride is a four-hour excursion, door-to-door. Be sure to bring a change of dry clothes — you'll get wet on this trip.

Exploring the deep blue

Scuba diving isn't as brilliant in Acapulco as it is in other parts of Mexico (the problems with pollution have resulted in fewer fish and less sea life), so it may disappoint. But, as an avid diver, I always say that there's no such thing as a bad dive. For novice divers, or those needing a refresher course, you can expect to pay $30 for 90 minutes of instruction if you book directly with an instructor on Playa Caleta. One dive operator I recommend is **Divers de México** (☎ 744-482-1398), located at Costera Miguel Alemán 100, near Club de Esquis. Typical prices are about $55 per person for equipment, a dive guide, and a boat for three hours. The best snorkeling sites are off **Isla de la Roqueta.** You can rent gear at a concession on the island, or you can take one of the regularly scheduled snorkeling trips from Playa Caleta to the island, which costs about $20 for two hours, including equipment.

Reeling in the big one

For deep-sea fishing excursions, go to the pale-pink building housing the fishing-boat cooperative **Pesca Deportiva** opposite the *zócalo* or book a day in advance (☎ 744-482-1099). Charter fishing trips run from $150 to $200 for up to four people for six hours, tackle and bait included. Credit cards are accepted, and ice, drinks, lunch, and a fishing license (about $10) are extra. You can usually swing a better deal by paying cash. Generally, boats leave at 8 a.m. and return by 3 p.m. and travel anywhere from 5km to 16km (3–10 miles) offshore. Sailfish, marlin, and tuna are popular catches. If you book through a travel agent or hotel, fishing trips start at around $200 to $280 for four people, and again, fishing license, food, and drinks cost extra.

If you're into planning ahead, consider booking with either of these reliable sportfishing outfitters: **Ixtapa Sportfishing Charters** (19 Depue Lane, Stroudsburg, PA 18360; ☎ 570-688-9466; Fax: 570-688-9554; www.ixtapasportfishing.com/acapulco) and **Fish-R-Us** (Costera Miguel Alemán 100; ☎ 877-3-FISH-R-US in the U.S., or 744-482-8282; www.fish-r-us.com). Their boats range in size from 12m to 14m (40- to 48-ft.) custom cruisers and are priced from $291 to $520 for up to eight people, including crew, tackle, and taxes.

Finding family fun

One of the best options for family fun is the **CICI water park** (Centro Internacional de Convivencia Infantil; Costera Miguel Alemán at Colón; ☎ 744-484-8033). Located just east of the convention center, the park has swimming pools with waves, water slides, water toboggans, and sealife shows. The park is open daily 10 a.m. to 6 p.m. with dolphin shows (in Spanish) taking place at noon, 2:30, and 5 p.m. A dolphin swim program includes 30 minutes of introduction and 30 minutes of swim time, for an additional $95. Swim times are at 10 a.m. and 12:30 and 4 p.m. Reservations are required, with a ten-person maximum per swim for the dolphin swim option. CICI, which recently underwent a $3-million renovation, also has a snack bar and restrooms. General admission is $6 during weekdays, and $8 on weekends; children under 2 are admitted free.

Cruising Acapulco's shores

Although a booze cruise may not technically qualify as a watersport (even though it requires extensive repetitions of the one-arm cocktail curl), I'll go out on a limb: Because the activity takes place on the water, it counts in my book. A booze cruise is one of the most popular ways to spend a day — or evening — in Acapulco, and the options are numerous. Choose from yachts, catamarans, and trimarans (single- and double-deckers) to take in the sun (and a few beverages) and enjoy expansive views of the bay. Cruises run morning, afternoon, and evening, and some offer buffets, open bars, and live music; others just have snacks, selected drinks, and taped music. You notice a difference in prices, too, which can range from $15 to $50. Your hotel's tour desk or any Acapulco travel agency can explain the current options, as well as provide brochures or recommendations.

Enjoying Land Sports

Acapulco has a number of ways to spend the day on land. From golf to tennis to horseback riding, you're sure to find an activity — or two — to suit your interests.

Teeing off

If you aim to hit the links during your stay, the best **golf** is at the courses at Playa Revolcadero. Both the **Acapulco Princess** (☎ 744-469-1000) and **Pierre Marqués** (☎ 744-466-1000) hotels have top-notch courses. The Princess's course is a rather narrow, level, Ted Robinson design. The Marqués course, redesigned by Robert Trent Jones, Sr., in 1972 for the World Cup of Golf tournament, is longer and more challenging. A round of 18 holes at either course costs $125 for guests and $145 for non-guests; American Express, Visa, and MasterCard are accepted. Tee-times begin at 7:35 a.m. Make your reservations a day in advance. Club rental is available, and costs an extra $21. The **Mayan Palace Golf Club** (Geranios 22; ☎ 744-466-2260 and 469-6043), designed by Latin American golf great Pedro Guericia, lies farther east. Greens fees are $115, and caddies are available for an additional $15.

The newest addition to Acapulco's golf scene is the spectacular Robert von Hagge–designed course at the exclusive **Tres Vidas Golf Club,** Carretera a Barra Vieja Km 7 (☎ 744-444-5138). The par-72, 18-hole course, right on the edge of the ocean, is landscaped with nine lakes, dotted with palms, and home to a flock of ducks and other birds. The club is open only to members, guests of members, and guests of certain hotels that have play privileges at the club. Greens fees are $144, including cart; a caddy costs $20. You can also enjoy a clubhouse with a restaurant, open from 7:30 a.m. to 7:30 p.m., as well as a pool and beach club. American Express, Visa, and MasterCard are accepted.

The main public course in town is the **Club de Golf Acapulco** (☎ 744-484-0781), located off the Costera next to the convention center. You can play nine holes for $40 and 18 holes for $60, with equipment renting for $16. There are no carts, but caddies are available for about $14. The course isn't very well maintained.

Taking time for tennis

Tennis is vastly more popular in Acapulco than golf, and getting a game going is a fairly easy process. You can choose from several public tennis clubs — court time averages about $11 an hour. One option is the **Club de Tenis Hyatt** (Costera Miguel Alemán 1; ☎ 744-484-1225), which is open daily 6:30 a.m. to 7 p.m. Outdoor courts cost $15 an hour during the day and $22 per hour at night; the indoor courts cost $25. Rackets rent for $4, and a set of balls will set you back $3.50 Many of the hotels along the Costera have tennis facilities for their guests; the best are at the Acapulco Princess, Pierre Marqués, and Las Brisas hotels.

Galloping along

If you're not entirely comfortable swimming in Acapulco Bay, then try **horseback riding** along the beach. Independent operators stroll the Hotel Zone beachfront offering rides for about $20 to $40 for one to two hours. Horses for riding are also commonly found on the beach in front of the Acapulco Princess Hotel. There's no phone; you have to go directly to one of the beaches to make arrangements.

Experiencing Acapulco's Front Row Attractions

Traditionally called *Fiesta Brava,* **bullfights** are held during Acapulco's winter season at a ring (**Plaza de Toros**) up the hill from Playa Caletilla. Tickets purchased through travel agencies cost around $35 and usually include transportation to and from your hotel. The festivities begin at 5:30 p.m. each Sunday from December to March. Although bullfights in Acapulco tend to feature better matadors than those in other Mexican resort towns, you're still seeing amateur or up-and-coming matadors rather than the real pros who practice this sport in Mexico City.

The must-see spectacle in Acapulco is the renowned **cliff divers.** High divers perform at **La Quebrada** each day at 12:30, 7:15, 8:15, 9:15, and 10:15 p.m. for a $2.50 admission. From a spotlighted ledge on the cliffs, divers (holding torches for the final performance) plunge into the roaring surf 39m (130 ft.) below — after wisely praying at a small shrine nearby. To the applause of the crowd, divers climb up the rocks and accept congratulations and cash tips from onlookers. This is the essential Acapulco experience, and no visit here is complete without watching these death-defying divers — this goes for jaded travelers as well.

The public areas have great views, but arrive early because all performances quickly fill up. Another option is to watch from the lobby bar and restaurant terraces of the **Hotel El Mirador** (☎ **744-483-1155**). At the bar, you have to pay an $18 cover charge, which includes two drinks. Reservations are recommended during the high season. The best way to reach La Quebrada is by taxi. It's located uphill from Avenida López, 3 blocks west of the *zócalo*.

Sightseeing in Acapulco

Acapulco is best known for its beaches and bay, and sadly, few visitors bother to explore its traditional downtown area. But a trip to the shady *zócalo* (also called **Plaza Alvarez**) is an experience that offers a true glimpse of local life and color. Inexpensive cafes and shops border the plaza, and the cathedral **Nuestra Señora de la Soledad** — with its blue, onion-shaped domes and Byzantine towers — is at the north end. Though reminiscent of a Russian Orthodox church, the structure was originally built as a movie set and then later adapted for use as a house of worship. Take a taxi up to the top of the hill from the main plaza and follow the signs leading to **El Mirador** (lookout point) for an unparalleled view of Acapulco.

Of all the exclusive villas and homes in Acapulco, one stands far apart from the others. Though not as elegantly impressive as the villas of Las Brisas, the **home of Dolores Olmedo** in Acapulco's traditional downtown area is a veritable work of art. In 1956, the renowned Mexican artist Diego Rivera covered its outside wall with a mural of colorful mosaic tiles, shells, and stones. The work is unique, and one of the last he created. Rivera, considered one of Mexico's greatest artists, has been credited with being one of the founders of the 20th-century Mexican-muralist movement. The Olmedo mural, which took him 18 months to complete, features Aztec deities such as Quetzalcoatl and Tepezcuincle, the Aztec dog. Rivera and Olmedo were lifelong friends, and Rivera lived in this house for the last two years of his life during which time he also covered the interior with murals. However, because this home isn't a museum, you have to settle for enjoying the exterior masterpiece. The house is located a few blocks behind the Casablanca Hotel, a short cab ride from the central plaza, at Calle Cerro de la Pinzona 6. Have the driver wait while you look around because there's not much traffic and it's a steep climb back to the plaza.

Acapulco wasn't always a beach resort. Originally, it was an important port for the Spanish Empire, and because of the rich trade that took place here, the city was subject to frequent pirate attacks. In 1616, the **Fuerte de San Diego** was constructed to help protect Acapulco. Today,

this fort is home to the **Museo Histórico de Acapulco** (☎ 744-482-3828).
It contains exhibits that tell the story of Acapulco from its roles as a port
in the conquest of the Americas, as a center for local Catholic conversion
campaigns, and as a key site for trade with the Orient. The fort you see
today was rebuilt after a large earthquake damaged the original structure
in 1776, and it benefited from another renovation in 2000. To reach the
fort, follow Costera Miguel Alemán from the Hotel Zone toward Old
Acapulco and the *zócalo;* the fort is on a hill on the right. The museum is
open Tuesday to Sunday from 10 a.m. to 5 p.m. The museum has exceptional bilingual exhibitions, and excellent air-conditioning. The $3.50
admission is waived on Sunday.

Sightseeing on the water isn't limited to the ferryboats that take travelers to Isla de la Roqueta. Old, wooden glass-bottom boats circle the bay,
and you can look down at a few fish and watch a diver or two swim
down to the underwater sanctuary of the **Virgin of Guadalupe,** patron
saint of Mexico. (The statue of the Virgin — created by sculptor
Armando Quesado — was placed at its underwater location in 1958 in
memory of a group of divers who lost their lives at the spot.) You can
purchase tickets (for approximately $5) at any loading boat or from the
information booth on Playa Caletilla at a discount (☎ 744-482-2389).

Shopping in Acapulco

Shopping, like attractions in Acapulco, tends to favor the popular over
the cultural — you're more likely to find a sexy swimsuit than a true
artistic treasure here. Yet, Acapulco does have a few interesting shops.
The best are found at the **Mercado Parazal** (often called the **Mercado
de Artesanías**) on Calle Velázquez de León near Cinco de Mayo in the
downtown *zócalo* area. (When you see Sanborn's, turn right and walk
behind it for several blocks; ask for directions if you need to.) It's a collection of covered stalls selling unique curios from around the country
including silver, embroidered cotton clothing, rugs, pottery, and papier-
mâché. The market is open daily 9 a.m. to 6 p.m.

Markets such as the Mercado Parazal are made for bargaining, and the
shopkeepers here test both your negotiating skills and your patience —
they start with a steep price and then drag it down little by little. The
more time you play their game, the better price you pay. As always,
acting uninterested often brings down prices in a hurry.

What Acapulco does offer in abundance are stores selling resort wear,
casual clothing, and the ever-present T-shirt. The Costera is crowded
with shops and boutiques like these, including some brand-name locations such as Tommy Hilfiger that often have much lower prices than
their stateside counterparts. If you find a sale, you can find incredible
bargains.

For the serious shopper, Acapulco even has a few malls. One of the nicest, air-conditioned shopping centers on the Costera is **Plaza Bahía** (Costera Miguel Alemán 125; ☎ 744-485-6939 or 485-6992), which has four stories of shops, movie theaters, small fast-food restaurants, and a bowling alley. The center is located just west of the Costa Club Hotel. The bowling alley, **Bol Bahía** (☎ 744-485-0970 or 485-7464), is open Monday to Saturday noon to 1:30 a.m. and Sundays 10 a.m. to midnight. Another popular shopping strip is the **Plaza Condesa,** adjacent to the Fiesta Americana Condesa, with shops that include Guess, Izod, and Bronce Swimwear. **Olvido Plaza,** near the restaurant of the same name (see Chapter 26), has Tommy Hilfiger and Aca Joe.

Sanborn's is the hands-down standard in department stores in Mexico and offers an array of staples including cosmetics, drugstore items, electronics, music, clothing, books, and magazines. There are three branches in Acapulco:

- ✔ Downtown at Costera Miguel Alemán 209, across from the boat docks (☎ 744-482-6167)

- ✔ Costera Miguel Alemán 1226 at the Condo Estrella Tower, close to the convention center (☎ 744-484-2025, ext. 24/29)

- ✔ Costera Miguel Alemán 163 at the Hotel Calinda (☎ 744-481-2426 or 484-4465)

Acapulco also has a Sam's Club and a Wal-Mart located on the inland side of the main highway just prior to its ascent to Las Brisas.

Acapulco has a few notable fine-art galleries. My favorite, **Galería Espacio Pal Kepenyes,** Costera Guitarron 140, on the road to the Radisson (☎ 744-446-5619), carries the work of Pal Kepenyes, whose stunning bronzes are among Acapulco's most notable public sculptures. The gallery shows smaller versions, as well as signature pieces of jewelry in brass, copper, and silver, by appointment only.

Works by another notable Mexican artist, Sergio Bustamante, are available at his gallery and shop, **La Colección de Sergio Bustamante,** Costera Miguel Alemán 120-9, at Galerías Picuda (☎ 744-484-4992). You can see his capricious suns, moons, and fantasy figures in a variety of materials.

Taking a Side Trip to Taxco

The nearby colonial town of **Taxco** (*tah*-skoh) is known worldwide for its silver, but when you arrive, you may see that the town's geography and architecture are equally precious. Taxco sits at nearly 1,500m (5,000 ft.) on a hill among hills, and almost any point in the city offers fantastic views.

The center of town is the tiny **Plaza Borda,** shaded by perfectly manicured Indian laurel trees. On one side is the imposing twin-towered, pink-stone **Santa Prisca y San Sebastián Church;** whitewashed, red-tile buildings housing the famous silver shops and a restaurant or two line the other sides. Beside the church, deep in a crevice of the mountain, is the **wholesale silver market** — absolutely the best place to begin your silver shopping, to get an idea of prices for more standard designs. You'll be amazed at the low prices. Buying just one piece is perfectly acceptable, though buying in bulk can lower the per-piece price. One of the beauties of Taxco is that its brick-paved and cobblestone streets are completely asymmetrical, zigzagging up and down the hillsides. The plaza buzzes with vendors of everything from hammocks and cotton candy to bark paintings and balloons.

The tiny, one-man factories that line the cobbled streets all the way up into the hills supply most of Taxco's silverwork. Your success at finding bargains depends somewhat on how much you know about the quality and price of silver, but Taxco's quantity and variety of silver can't be matched anywhere else in the country.

Getting to Taxco

It takes about four hours by bus to travel between Acapulco and Taxco, but the resulting bargains in exquisite silver and jewelry are well worth the trip — you won't be disappointed.

The best way to travel to Taxco from Acapulco is through one of the numerous day-trip charters that you can easily arrange at your hotel's tour desk or a local travel agent. Most excursions leave around 6:30 a.m. and return at 9 p.m. for a cost of about $60. You can also venture on your own — but I strongly recommend taking a bus over renting a car because the bus drivers know the route and much of the trip is along narrow, curvaceous roads through steep mountains.

Exploring Taxco

Shopping for jewelry and other items is the major pastime for tourists. Prices for silver jewelry at the more than 300 shops in Taxco are about the best in the world, and everything is available, from $1 trinkets to artistic pieces costing hundreds of dollars. You can get your fill of silver and an idea of what Taxco is like by spending an afternoon here, but this picturesque town has a lot more to offer than just the Plaza Borda and the shops surrounding it. For example, Taxco is the home of some of Mexico's finest stone sculptors and is also a good place to buy masks. However, beware of so-called "antiques" — there are virtually no real ones for sale.

Stay overnight and give yourself time to wander the steep cobblestone streets and discover the little plazas, fine churches, cultural attractions, and of course, the silversmith shops. If Acapulco is all you've seen during your vacation, a visit here will make you feel that, at last, you're in "Mexico." Take time to visit the following sites:

✔ **Santa Prisca y San Sebastián Church,** Plaza Borda (☎ 762-622-0183 or -0184), is Taxco's centerpiece parish church; completed in 1758 after eight years of labor, it's one of Mexico's most impressive baroque churches. The church is open daily from 10 a.m. to 8 p.m., and admission is free.

✔ Stroll along Ruiz de Alarcón and look for the **Humboldt House/ Museo Virreinal de Taxco,** Calle Juan Ruiz de Alarcón 12 (the street behind the Casa Borda; ☎ 762-622-5501), where the renowned German scientist and explorer Baron Alexander von Humboldt (1769–1859) spent a night in 1803. The museum houses 18th-century memorabilia pertinent to Taxco. Admission is $3 for adults and $1.15 for students and teachers with ID; the museum is open Tuesday to Saturday 9 a.m. to 7 p.m., and Sunday 9 a.m. to 4 p.m.

✔ A plaque in Spanish explains that most of the collection of pre-Columbian art displayed at the **Museo de Taxco Guillermo Spratling,** Calle Porfirio A. Delgado 1 (☎ 762-622-1660), as well as the funds for the museum, came from William Spratling. You'd expect this to be a silver museum, but it's not. This museum's entrance floor and the second floor display a good collection of pre-Columbian statues and implements in clay, stone, and jade. The lower floor has changing exhibits. To find the museum, turn right out of the Santa Prisca Church and right again at the corner; continue down the street, veer right, then immediately left. The museum is facing you. The museum is open Tuesday to Saturday 10 a.m. to 5 p.m., and Sunday 9 a.m. to 3 p.m. Admission is $3.35 for adults and free for children under 13, with free admission for all on Sundays.

Staying a night

Taxco is an overnight visitor's dream: charming and picturesque, with a respectable selection of pleasant, well-kept hotels. Hotel prices tend to rise at holiday times (especially Easter week). The following are some suggestions in case you decide to spend a night or two:

✔ The **Hacienda del Solar,** Paraje del Solar s/n (☎/fax 762-622-0587), comprises several Mexican-style cottages, all on a beautifully land-scaped hilltop with magnificent views of the surrounding valleys and the town. The décor is slightly different in each cottage, but most contain plenty of beautiful handicrafts, red-tile floors, and bathrooms with handmade tiles. Several rooms have vaulted tile ceilings and private terraces with panoramic views. Rates are $130 double and $130 to $150 for a junior or deluxe suite.

✔ **Hotel Los Arcos,** Juan Ruiz de Alarcón 4 (☎ 762-622-1836; Fax: 762-622-7982), with rooms for $39 double, occupies a converted 1620 monastery. The handsome inner patio is bedecked with

Puebla pottery and has a lively restaurant area, all around a central fountain.

✔ Each room at the delightful **Hotel Emilia Castillo,** Juan Ruiz de Alarcón 7 (☎/fax **762-622-1396**), is simply but beautifully appointed with handsome carved doors and furniture; bathrooms have either tubs or showers. Rate is $40 double.

✔ The **Rancho Taxco Victoria,** Carlos J. Nibbi 5 and 7 (☎ **762-622-0004;** Fax: 762-622-0010), clings to the hillside above town, with stunning views from its flower-covered verandas. It exudes the charm of old-fashioned Mexico. The comfortable furnishings, though slightly run-down, evoke the hotel's 1940s heyday. Even if you don't stay here, come for a drink in the comfortable bar and living room, or sit on the terrace to take in the fabulous view. Rooms cost $62 for a standard double, $89 for a deluxe double, and $100 for a junior suite.

✔ The **Santa Prisca,** Cenaobscuras 1 (☎ **762-622-0080** or 622-0980; Fax: 762-622-2938), is one of the town's older and nicer hotels. Rooms are small but comfortable, with standard bathrooms (showers only), tile floors, wood beams, and a colonial atmosphere. A reading area in an upstairs salon overlooks Taxco, as well as a lush patio with fountains. Rooms range from $46 double to $52 superior to $74 suite.

Dining in Taxco

Taxco gets a lot of day-trippers from Mexico City and Acapulco, most of whom choose to dine close to the Plaza Borda. Prices in this area are high for what you get. Just a few streets back, though, you can find some excellent, simple restaurants:

✔ The spectacular view of the city from **La Ventana de Taxco,** in the Hacienda del Solar hotel, Paraje del Solar s/n (☎ **762-622-0587**), makes it one of the best places to dine in Taxco. The food — standard Italian fare — is also quite good, if not predictable. The pasta dishes are the most recommendable. Lasagna is a big favorite, and Sicilian steak is also popular.

✔ An inexpensive alternative is **Restaurante Ethel,** Plazuela San Juan 14 (☎ **762-622-0788**). This family-run place is opposite the Hotel Santa Prisca, a block from the Plaza Borda. It has colorful cloths on the tables and a tidy, homey atmosphere. The hearty *comida corrida* (essentially, a daily special) consists of soup or pasta, meat (perhaps a small steak), dessert, and good coffee.

✔ Another favorite is **Sotavento Restaurant Bar Galería,** Juárez 8, next to City Hall (☎ **762-627-1217**), which offers many Italian specialties — try the deliciously fresh spinach salad and large pepper steak for a hearty meal; or Spaghetti Barbara, with poblano peppers and avocado, for a vegetarian meal. To find this place from the Plaza Borda, walk downhill beside the Hotel Agua Escondida, and then follow the street as it bears left (don't go right on Juan Ruiz de Alarcón) about a block. The restaurant is on the left just after the street bends left.

✔ **Toni's,** in the Hotel Monte Taxco (☎ 762-622-1300), is an intimate, classic restaurant (albeit a tad expensive) enclosed in a huge, cone-shaped *palapa* with a panoramic view of the city. The menu, mainly shrimp or beef, is limited, but the food is superior. Try tender, juicy prime roast beef, which comes with Yorkshire pudding, creamed spinach, and baked potato. Lobster is sometimes available. To reach Toni's, it's best to take a taxi. *Note:* Toni's is only open for dinner.

Discovering Taxco after dark

Paco's (☎ 762-622-0064) is the most popular place overlooking the square for cocktails, conversation, and people-watching, all of which continue until midnight daily. Taxco's version of a disco, **Windows,** is high up the mountain in the **Hotel Monte Taxco** (☎ 762-622-1300). The whole city is on view, and music runs the gamut from the hit parade to hard rock. For a cover of $6.70, you can dance away Saturday night from 10 p.m. to 3 a.m.

Completely different in tone is **Berta's** (Plaza Borda 9; ☎ 762-622-0172), next to the Santa Prisca Church. Opened in 1930 by a lady named Berta, who made her fame on a drink of the same name (tequila, soda, lime, and honey), it's the traditional gathering place of the local gentry and more than a few tourists. Spurs and old swords decorate the walls, and a saddle is casually slung over the banister on the stairs leading to the second-floor room, where tin masks leer from the walls. A Berta (the drink, of course) costs about $2; rum, the same. It's open daily from 11 a.m. to around 10 p.m.

National drinks (not beer) are two-for-one nightly between 6 and 8 p.m. at the terrace bar of the **Hotel Rancho Taxco Victoria** (☎ 762-622-0004), where you can also drink in the fabulous view.

Discovering Acapulco after Dark

If there's anything Acapulco is more famous for than its beaches, it's the nightlife. Even if you feel that your "clubbing" days are behind you — trust me — give it a try. The views from the hillside clubs are among the best in town, and it's an equally fascinating scene inside. As is typical with clubs, the names and crowds change with the seasons, and places don't remain "hot" forever, but the ones I list tend to always be in the upper end of popularity. In addition, here are some general tips:

✔ Every club seems to have a cover charge of around $20 in high season and $10 in low season; drinks can cost anywhere from $3 to $10. Women can count on paying less or entering for free. Don't even think about going out to one of the hillside discos before

11 p.m., and don't expect much action until after midnight. The party goes on until 4 or 5 a.m. — and occasionally until 8 a.m. On weekends, the live dance shows — bordering on performance art — are well worth the lack of sleep.

✔ Many discos periodically waive their cover charge or offer some other promotion to attract customers. Another popular option is to have a higher cover charge but an open bar. Look for promotional materials displayed in hotel reception areas, at travel desks or concierge booths, and in local publications. You may also be hit up with promotions for nightclubs as you take in the sun at the local beaches.

✔ Besides nightclubs, you have other options. The **Gran Noche Mexicana** combines a performance by the Acapulco Ballet Folklórico with one by Los Voladores from Papantla. One of the few options to experience some authentic Mexican culture in town, it's held in the plaza of the convention center every Monday, Wednesday, and Friday at 7 p.m. With dinner and an open bar, the show costs $62; general admission (including three drinks) is $30. Call for reservations (☎ 744-484-7046 or 484-7098) or consult a local travel agency. Many major hotels also host Mexican fiestas and other theme nights that include dinner and entertainment.

✔ If you're brave enough — or inebriated enough — you can try out the **bungee jump** (Costera Miguel Alemán 101; ☎ 744-484-7529) in the midst of the beach bar zone. For $62, you get one jump, plus a T-shirt, diploma, and membership. Additional jumps are $28, and your fourth jump is free. For $67, you can jump as many times as you like from 4 to 11 p.m.

Acapulco has essentially two different club scenes: the strip of beach bars along the Costera Hotel Zone and the glitzier club scene in the hillsides near Las Brisas.

The younger crowd seems to prefer a little fresh air with their nightlife and favor the growing number of open-air, oceanfront dance clubs along Costera Miguel Alemán. These establishments are concentrated between the Fiesta Americana and Continental Plaza hotels; tend to feature techno, house, or alternative rock; and are an earlier and more casual option for nightlife. Faves include the jammin' **DiscoBeach** (☎ 744-484-8230), **El Sombrero** doesn't exist anymore, now it's called **Tacos n'Beer** (☎ 744-484-2549), **Taboo** also closed, and the pirate-themed **Barbaroja** (☎ 744-484-5932). These places generally offer an open bar with cover charge (around $10). Women frequently drink for free or with a lesser charge. (Men may pay more, but then, the young and tanned beach babes are here. So who's complaining?)

Of the more traditional clubs, here's my alphabetical rundown of the current scene including some uniquely entertaining options:

✔ Exterior reflection pools and flaming torches mark the entrance to **Alebrijes** (Costera Miguel Alemán 3308, across the street from the Hyatt Regency Acapulco; ☎ 744-484-5902). Inside, booths and round tables with a seating capacity of 1,200 surround the vast dance floor — the disco doubles as a venue for concerts and live performances by some of Mexico's most notable singers. Usually, you'll join a Mexican crowd in their mid-20s here, but the crowd may vary with featured performers. Alebrijes is open nightly 11 p.m. to 5 a.m. Cover (including open bar) for women is $5 to $25; for men it's $8 to $35. On Mondays, the open bar is for tequila drinks only.

✔ A long-time favorite in Acapulco is **Baby-O's** (Costera Miguel Alemán, across the street from the Hotel Romano Days Inn; ☎ 744-484-7474), which has kept current and maintained its place among the top clubs. This hangout is a great choice for those who shun mammoth clubs in favor of a more intimate setting. The mid- to late-20s crowd dances to everything from swing to hip-hop to rock 'n' roll on the small dance floor surrounded by several tiers of tables and sculpted, cave-like walls. Drinks are more moderately priced than in most Acapulco clubs and cost $3 to $5. Baby-O's is open 10:30 p.m. to 5 a.m. Cover for women is $5 to $17; for men, it's $10 to $35. Both covers include two national drinks.

✔ Venture into the stylish chrome-and-neon extravaganza that is **Mandara** (Carretera Escénica; ☎ 744-446-5712 or 446-5711; www.mandaraacapulco.com.mx) for a true Acapulco-nightlife experience. Perched on the side of the mountain between Los Rancheros Restaurant and La Vista Shopping Center, the club is easy to spot with its neon and laser lights pulsating in the night. The plush, dim interior dazzles patrons with a sunken dance floor and a panoramic view of the lights of Acapulco Bay. The club also has a more intimate piano bar upstairs overlooking the disco, **Siboney,** which draws a more mature and moneyed crowd. Downstairs, the club alternates between pumping in mood smoke and fresh oxygen to keep you dancing. The door attendants wear tuxedos indicating that they encourage a more sophisticated dress — tight and slinky is the norm for ladies; no shorts for gentlemen. The club opens nightly at 10:30 p.m. Fireworks rock the usually full house at 3 a.m., which is when a stylized dance performance takes place on weekends in the style of Euro-clubs. During peak season, call to find out if you need reservations. Cover varies but is around $5 for women and $25 for men, and all major credit cards are accepted.

✔ **Palladium** (Carretera Escénica; ☎ 744-446-5483) is just down the road from Enigma, but it lacks both the style and the classy clientele of the neighboring club. A younger, rowdier crowd enjoys the equally fabulous views and the dancing platforms set in the large glass windows overlooking the bay. Cover is $5 to $15 for women, $8 to $25 for men.

✔ **Pepe's Piano Bar** (Carretera Escénica, Comercial La Vista, Local 5; ☎ **744-446-5736**) has surely been one of the most famous piano bars in the hemisphere, although it appears those days may be numbered. It has inspired patrons of all ages to sing their hearts out for more than 40 years, and it still draws a crowd, though it now caters to karaoke instead of piano — a big mistake, in my opinion. I keep hoping the owners will come to their senses and return to their roots. It's open Wednesday to Sunday from 10 p.m. to 4 a.m.

✔ Billing itself as "the cathedral of salsa," **Salon Q** (Costera Miguel Alemán 3117; ☎ **744-481-0114**) is known as the place to get down to the Latin rhythms when in Acapulco. Frequently, management raises the cover and features impersonators doing their thing as the top Latin American musical acts. Cover runs from $13 to $25.

✔ Across the street from Mandara is **Zucca** (Carretera Escénica 28, in the La Vista Shopping Center; ☎ **744-446-5691** or 446-5690), which offers up yet another fantastic bay view. It claims to cater to a slightly more mature crowd — stating that only those older than 25 are admitted — but seems to bend the rules, especially for younger women. Zucca is particularly popular with the moneyed Mexico City set. Periodically during the evening, the club projects a laser show across the bay. The dress code prohibits shorts, jeans, T-shirts, or sandals. The club is open nightly 10:30 p.m. to 2:30 a.m., but it stays open later (until 4 a.m.) on weekends or when the crowd demands it. The cover charge, which ranges from $10 to $15, is occasionally waived, at least until a sufficient crowd builds.

Part VIII
Huatulco and the Southern Pacific Coast

The 5th Wave   By Rich Tennant

SHELLING ON MEXICO'S SOUTHERN PACIFIC COAST

"Oooo! Back up Robert. There must be a half dozen Lightning Whelks here."

In this part . . .

*T*he southern beach resorts of Huatulco and Puerto Escondido are Mexico's purest ecotourism beach resorts. Unspoiled nature and a laid-back sentiment combine to offer up the uninterrupted experience of Mexico's pure, natural splendor. Puerto Escondido is a little-known paradise of exceptional values and unique, independent accommodations. Neighboring Huatulco puts on a bit of a different face as it combines indulgent hotels and modern facilities with pristine beaches and jungle landscapes.

The following chapters take you through these lesser-known treasures among Mexico's beach resorts and help you uncover their unique and worthwhile charms.

Chapter 28

Bahías de Huatulco

by Lynne Bairstow

. . . .

In This Chapter
▶ Surveying Huatulco's hotel scene
▶ Getting to know Huatulco
▶ Finding great places to dine
▶ Embarking on an adventure

. . . .

*L*ocated in the state of Oaxaca (wah-*hah*-cah), Huatulco's nine bays encompass 36 beaches and countless inlets and coves. The resort as a whole is a staged development project by the Mexican government's tourism development arm (FONATUR) that aims to cover 20,800 hectares (52,000 acres) of land with more than 16,000 hectares (40,000 acres) remaining as ecological preserves. Huatulco hasn't grown as rapidly as Cancún, the previous planned-development resort, so plenty of undeveloped stretches of pure white sand and isolated coves are still around to enjoy.

Huatulco has increasingly become known for its ecotourism attractions — including river rafting, rappelling, and jungle hiking. It's not a destination for travelers who care a lot about shopping, nightlife, or even dining because its options for these pursuits are fewer than other beach resorts in Mexico. However, if you're especially drawn to snorkeling, diving, boat cruises to virgin bays, and simple relaxation, you may quickly find that Huatulco fits the bill perfectly.

The opening of a new cruise-ship dock in Santa Cruz Bay is changing the level of activity in Huatulco, providing the sleepy resort with an important business boost. The new dock handles up to two 3,000-passenger cruise ships at a time (tenders used to ferry passengers to shore).

In this chapter, I describe the layout of Huatulco and review some of the region's best hotels. I also take you from the plane, through the airport, and to your hotel, helping you quickly get your bearings in this easy-to-navigate resort situated along successive bays. I also offer tips on everything from transportation to dining out to enjoying the best of the numerous natural treasures of this pristine part of Mexico.

Choosing a Location

Unspoiled nature can be an idyllic retreat from the stress of daily life —
and for some people, it's even more attractive when viewed from a
luxury-hotel balcony. Huatulco is for vacationers who want to enjoy the
beauty of nature during the day and then retreat to well-appointed comfort by night. Slow-paced and still relatively undiscovered, the hotels
located among the nine bays of Huatulco enjoy the most modern infrastructure of any resort destination along Mexico's Pacific coast.

The area is divided into three principle sections: **Santa Cruz, Crucecita,**
and **Tangolunda Bay.** These locations offer enough variety in accommodations that you're sure to find something to satisfy your vacation
expectations regardless of your taste or budget.

The main differences between locations here can be simply summarized:
Tangolunda Bay hotels are the newest, most deluxe properties in the
area offering full-service pampering. Hotels in Santa Cruz are older, simpler in style, and lower in price. The village of Crucecita by far offers the
best value, but you must take a shuttle to the beach. Although you certainly may find that the part of town you stay in impacts your overall
experience, understand that everything is relatively close by, and getting
around is both easy and inexpensive. **Bahía Chahué** also has some limited accommodations, but is still less prominent for tourism services.

Moderate- and budget-priced hotels in Santa Cruz and Crucecita are generally higher in price compared to similar hotels in other Mexican beach
resorts. But the luxury beach hotels in Tangolunda Bay have rates comparable to similar properties in other destinations, especially when
these hotels are part of a package that includes airfare. The trend is
toward all-inclusive resorts, which in Huatulco are a good option given
the lack of memorable dining and nightlife options around town. Hotels
that aren't oceanfront generally have an arrangement with one of the
beach clubs at Santa Cruz or Chahué Bay and provide shuttle service
to the beach. Low-season rates refer to the months of August through
November only.

Evaluating the Top Accommodations

As far as prices go, I note *rack rates* (the maximum that a hotel or resort
charges for a room) for two people spending one night in a double room
during high season (Christmas to Easter). You can usually do better, especially if you're purchasing a package that includes airfare (read Chapter 7
for tips on avoiding paying rack rates). Prices quoted here include the
17 percent room tax. Note that some rates may seem much higher than
others — until you realize that they're "all inclusive" — your meals and
beverages are included in the price of your stay. These rates also include
all tips, taxes, and most activities and entertainment. Please refer to the
Introduction of this book for an explanation of the price categories.

Bahías de Huatulco

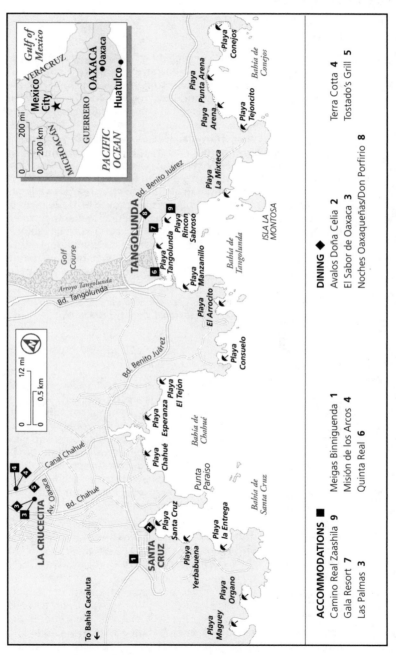

ACCOMMODATIONS ■
Camino Real Zaashila **9**
Gala Resort **7**
Las Palmas **3**
Meigas Binniguenda **1**
Misión de los Arcos **4**
Quinta Real **6**

DINING ◆
Avalos Doña Celia **2**
El Sabor de Oaxaca **3**
Noches Oaxaqueñas/Don Porfirio **8**
Terra Cotta **4**
Tostado's Grill **5**

All hotels have air-conditioning unless otherwise indicated.

Camino Real Zaashila
$$$$$ Tangolunda Bay

One of Tangolunda Bay's original hotels — and my top choice here — the Camino Real is located on a wide stretch of sandy beach secluded from other beaches by small rock outcroppings. With calm water, it's perfect for swimming and snorkeling and ideal for families. The Mediterranean-style white-stucco building is washed in colors on the ocean side, looking a little like a scene from the Greek isles. Rooms on the lower levels — 41 of them — each have their own sizable dipping pools. All rooms are large and have an oceanview balcony or terrace, marble tub/shower-combination bathrooms, wicker furnishings, and décors with bold colors. The main pool is a free-form design that spans 120m (400 ft.) of beach with chaises built into the shallow edges. Well-manicured, tropical gardens surround the pool and the guest rooms. You have your choice of three restaurants here, including Chez Binni, noted for its excellent regional Oaxacan cuisine (featuring pork dishes and moles), plus room service and a lobby bar with live music. A full watersports center is also on its exceptional stretch of beach. Other pluses include a large outdoor whirlpool and a lighted tennis court.

Bulevar Benito Juárez No. 5. ☎ *800-722-6466 in the U.S., or 958-581-0460. Fax: 958-581-0461.* www.caminoreal.com/zaashila, *or* www.camino-zaashila.com. *130 units. Rack rates: High season $300 double, $360 Camino Real Club; low season $165 double, $205 Camino Real Club. AE, DC, MC, V.*

Gala Resort
$$$$$ Tangolunda Bay

With all meals, drinks, entertainment, tips, and a slew of activities included in the price of admission, the Gala is a value-packed experience. It caters to adults of all ages (married and single) who enjoy both activity and relaxation. An excellent kids' activities program probably makes it the best option in the area for families. Rooms have tile floors and Oaxacan wood trim, large tub/shower-combination bathrooms, and ample balconies — all with views of Tangolunda Bay. Three restaurants serve both buffet and a la carte meals, and the Gala has changing theme nights. A large, free-form pool, a complete beachfront watersports center, four lighted tennis courts, and a full gym are on-hand to keep you active.

Bulevar Benito Juárez s/n, located north of the Sheraton, south of Quinta Real. ☎ *958-581-0000. Fax: 958-581-0220.* www.gala-resort-huatulco.com. *290 units. Rack rates: $410 double, $100 per extra adult, $65 per child 7–11, $95 per child 12–15. Children under 7 stay free in parents' room. AE, MC, V.*

Las Palmas
$ Crucecita

The central location and accommodating staff are an added benefit to the clean, bright, but very basic rooms at Las Palmas. Located half a block from the main plaza in the town of Crucecita, the hotel is also connected to the popular El Sabor de Oaxaca restaurant (see the "Dining in Huatulco" section, later in this chapter), which offers room service to guests. Rooms have tile floors, cotton textured bedspreads, tile showers, and cable TV.

Av. Guamúchil 206. ☎ *958-587-0060. Fax: 958-587-0057. 10 units. Free parking. Rack rates: High season $60 double; low season $45 double. AE, MC, V.*

Meigas Binniguenda
$$ Santa Cruz

This property was Huatulco's first hotel, and it retains the Mexican charm and comfort that originally made it memorable. A recent addition more than doubled the hotel's original size. Rooms have Mexican-tile floors, artisan-crafted bedspreads, and colonial-style furniture; French doors open onto tiny wrought-iron balconies overlooking the main street of Juárez or the pool and gardens. The newer rooms have more modern teak furnishings and are generally much nicer — request this section. A nice shady area surrounds the hotel's small pool in back of the lobby. The hotel is away from the marina at the far end of Juárez, only a few blocks from the water. These folks offer free transportation every hour to the beach club at Santa Cruz Bay.

Bulevar Santa Cruz 201. ☎ *958-587-0077 or -0078. Fax: 958-587-0284.* binniguenda@prodigy.net.mx. *165 units. Rack rates: $80–$120 double. Ask about special packages that include breakfast. AE, MC, V.*

Misión de los Arcos
$–$$ Crucecita

This exceptional hotel, just a block from the central plaza, has a similar style to the elegant Quinta Real — at a fraction of the cost. The hotel is mostly white and accented with an abundance of greenery (no flowering plants), which gives it a fresh, clean, and inviting feel. Rooms, washed in white with cream and beige bed coverings and upholstery, have the same ambience. Built-in desks, French windows, and minimal but interesting decorative accents give this budget hotel a true sense of style. A cafe with international magazines and high-speed Internet access (open 8 a.m.–midnight) is at the right side of the entrance level. The adjacent Terra Cotta restaurant serves breakfast, lunch, and dinner, and is equally stylish and budget-friendly. There's also an on-site gym with excellent quality equipment, which is complimentary for guest use, and open to other visitors for a daily fee. Although the hotel has no pool, guests may enjoy the use of the Castillo Beach Club, at Chahué Bay, open from 9 a.m. to 7 p.m. The hotel's central location is ideal for sampling Crucecita's shops and restaurants.

Gardenia 902. ☎ *958-587-0165. Fax: 958-587-1904.* www.misiondelosarcos.com. *13 rooms. Rack rates: High season $70, suites $75–$95; low season $35, suites $40–$60. AE, MC, V.*

Quinta Real
$$$$$ **Tangolunda Bay**

The most romantic of Huatulco's hotels, the Quinta Real is known for its understated elegance and efficient service. Double Moorish domes mark this relaxed hotel that has a richly appointed cream-and-white décor. The Quinta Real cascades down a hillside — from the welcoming reception area to the luxurious beach club below. The small groupings of suites are built into the sloping hill down to Tangolunda Bay and offer spectacular views of the ocean and golf course. (Rooms on the eastern edge of the resort sit above the highway and have some traffic noise.) Interiors are elegant and comfortable with stylish Mexican furniture, wood-beamed ceilings, marble tub/shower-combination bathrooms with whirlpool tubs, and original artwork. Telescopes grace many of the suites. Balconies have overstuffed seating areas and floors of stone inlay. Selected suites have private pools of their own. One restaurant serves breakfast and dinner, and the beach club poolside-casual restaurant is open for lunch. The beach club has two pools — one for children — as well as showers and *palapas* on the beach with chair and towel service. The elegant, library-style bar offers up a stunning view and makes a great place for a drink even if you're not staying here. The Quinta Real is perfect for weddings, honeymoons, or small corporate retreats.

Bulevar Benito Juárez No. 2. ☎ *866-621-9288 in the U.S., or 958-581-0428. Fax: 958-581-0429.* www.quintareal.com. *28 units. Rack rates: High season $390 Master Suite, $430 Grand Class Suite, $490 with private pool; low season $295 Master Suite, $351 Grand Class Suite, $395 with private pool. AE, DC, MC, V.*

Settling into Huatulco

In Huatulco, getting into the swing of things is easy. From the small airport, the ride into town along well-paved roads is quick. You're likely to encounter exceptional graciousness and a truly warm welcome from everyone from taxi drivers to bellhops.

Arriving in Huatulco by air

Huatulco's international airport (☎ 958-581-9004 or 581-9005), is located about 19km (12 miles) northwest of the Bahías de Huatulco. As you deplane, you go down some stairs onto the tarmac and take a brief walk into the terminal — important to know if you're carrying on any heavy luggage. After you're inside the small terminal, you reach the immigration clearance area. At the immigration booth, an officer asks you to show your passport (or other proof of citizenship) and your completed tourist card, the **FMT** (see Chapter 9 for all the FMT details).

Your FMT is an important document, so take good care of it. You're supposed to keep the FMT with you at all times because you may be required to show it if you run into any sort of trouble. You also need to turn it back in upon departure, or you may be unable to leave without replacing it.

Next, grab your baggage from the baggage-claims carousel. If needed, porters are available to help with your bags for a tip of about a dollar a bag. After you collect your luggage, you pass through another check-point. Something that looks like a traffic light awaits you here. You press a button, and if the light turns green, you're free to go. If it turns red, you need to open each of your bags for a quick search. It's Mexico's random search procedure for Customs. If you have an unusually large bag, or an excessive amount of luggage, you may be searched regardless of the traffic-light outcome.

With your bags, exit the terminal where taxis and other transportation services are waiting.

Getting from the airport to your hotel

From the airport, private **taxis** charge $40 to Crucecita, $42 to Santa Cruz Bay, and $48 to Tangolunda Bay. **Transportes Terrestres** (☎ 958-581-9014) a *colectivo* (shared) minibus fares range from $8 to $10 per person.

When returning to the airport, make sure to specifically ask for a taxi unless you have a lot of luggage. Taxis to the airport run $20, but unless you request one, companies send a van, which costs $40 for the same trip.

Because this beach destination is so spread out and has excellent roads, you may want to consider a rental car (at least for a day or two for a bit of exploring). The bays are spread out, and having a car allows you to see more of them, and explore a bit on your own on the modern and well-paved roads. If you opt for a rental, consider timing it so that you either pick up your car upon arrival or return it as you depart, saving an extra trip to the airport. **Budget** (☎ 800-322-9976 in U.S., or 958-587-0010 or 581-9000) has an office at the airport, which is open when flights arrive. Daily rates run around $56 for a Volkswagen sedan, $79 for a Nissan Sentra or Geo Tracker, and $100 for a Jeep Wrangler.

Knowing your way around town

Bahías de Huatulco include all nine bays of this resort area. The town of Santa María de Huatulco, the original settlement in this area, is 27km (17 miles) inland. **Santa Cruz Bay,** usually just called Santa Cruz, was the first area on the coast to be developed. It has a central plaza with a bandstand kiosk that has been converted into a cafe serving regionally grown coffee. Santa Cruz also has an artisan's market on the edge of the plaza that borders the main road, a few hotels and restaurants, and a marina from which bay tours and fishing trips set sail, as well as the cruise ships. **Juárez** is Santa Cruz's main street. It's about 4 blocks long in all and anchored at one end by the Hotel Castillo Huatulco and at the other by the Meigas Binniguenda hotel. Opposite the Hotel Castillo is the marina, and beyond the marina are restaurants housed in new, colonial-style buildings facing the beach. The area's banks are on Juárez. Getting lost is impossible; you can take in almost everything at a glance.

About 2.5km (1½ miles) inland from Santa Cruz is **Crucecita,** a planned city that sprang up in 1985 centered on a lovely grassy plaza edged with flowering hedges. Crucecita is the residential area for the resorts. Neighborhoods of new stucco homes are mixed with small apartment complexes. The town has evolved into a lovely, traditional town where you can find the area's best — and most reasonably priced — restaurants, plus some shopping and several clean, less-expensive hotels.

Tangolunda Bay, 5km (3 miles) east of Crucecita, is the focal point of bay development. Over time, half of the bays should have resorts. But for now, Tangolunda has the lion's share, with an 18-hole golf course; the elegant Las Brisas Resort; and the Quinta Real, Barceló Huatulco, Gala Resort, Casa del Mar, and Camino Real Zaashila hotels, among others. Small strip centers with a few restaurants occupy each end of Tangolunda Bay. **Chahué Bay,** between Tangolunda and Santa Cruz, is a small bay with a beach club, along with houses and some small restaurants.

Walking between any of the three destinations (Crucecita, Santa Cruz, and Tangolunda) is too far, but **taxis** are inexpensive and readily available. The fare between Santa Cruz and Tangolunda is roughly $2.50; between Santa Cruz and Crucecita, $2; and between Crucecita and Tangolunda, $3.

Minibus service between towns costs 50¢. In Santa Cruz, catch the bus across the street from Castillo Huatulco; in Tangolunda, it stops in front of the Grand Pacific; and in Crucecita, the bus stop is cater-corner from the Hotel Grifer.

Fast Facts: Huatulco

Area Code

The telephone area code is **958.**

Baby Sitters

Most of the larger hotels can easily arrange baby sitters, but many sitters speak limited English. Rates range from $4 to $10 per hour.

Banks, ATMs, and Currency Exchange

All three areas have banks, including the main Mexican banks Banamex and Bancomer, with ATMs. Banks change money during business hours, which are 9 a.m. to 5 p.m. Monday to Friday and 9 a.m. to 1 p.m. on Saturdays. Banks are located along Calle Juárez in Santa Cruz and surround the central plaza in Crucecita.

Business Hours

Most offices maintain traditional Mexican hours of operation (10 a.m.–2 p.m. and 4–8 p.m., daily), but shops remain open throughout the day. Offices tend to be closed on Saturday and Sunday, but shops are open on Saturday, at least, and increasingly offer limited hours of operation on Sunday.

Emergencies

Police emergency (☎ 060); **local police** (☎ 958-587-0815); **transit police** (☎ 958-587-0186); and **Red Cross** (Bulevar Chahué 110; ☎ 958-587-1188).

Information

The State Tourism Office (Oficina del Turismo; ☎ **958-581-0176** or -0177; sedetur6@oaxaca.gob.mx) has an information module in Tangolunda Bay near the Grand Pacific hotel, and another inside the Gala Resort.

Internet Access

Several Internet cafes are located in Crucecita. One is at the cafe in the Misión de los Arcos (Av. Gardenia 902; ☎ **958-587-0165**), which in addition to paid service is also a free wireless hot spot; another is on the ground-floor level of the Hotel Plaza Conejo (Av. Guamúchil 208, across from the main plaza; ☎ **958-587-0054** or 587-0009; conejo3@mexico.com).

Maps

One of the best around is the free American Express map, usually found at the tourist information offices.

Medical Care

Dr. Ricardo Carrillo (☎ **958-587-0687** or 587-0600) speaks English.

Pharmacy

Farmacia del Carmen (☎ **958-587-0878**), one of the largest drugstores in Crucecita, is located just off the central plaza. Farmacia La Clinica (☎ **958-587-0591**) is located at Sabalí 1602 in Crucecita and offers both 24-hour service and home/hotel delivery.

Post Office

The post office at Bulevar Chahué 100, Sector R (☎ **958-587-0551**), is open Monday to Friday 9 a.m. to 3 p.m. and Saturdays 9 a.m. to 1 p.m.

Safety

Huatulco enjoys a very low crime rate. Most crime or encounters with the police are linked to pickpocket thefts, so use common sense and never leave your belongings unattended at the beach.

Taxes

A 15 percent IVA (value-added tax) on goods and services is charged, and it's generally included in the posted price.

Taxis

In Crucecita, a taxi stand is opposite the Hotel Grifer and another is on the Plaza Principal. Taxis are readily available in Santa Cruz and Tangolunda through your hotel. The fare between Santa Cruz and Tangolunda is roughly $2.50; between Santa Cruz and Crucecita, $2; and between Crucecita and Tangolunda, $3. You can also rent taxis by the hour (about $15 per hour) or for the day if you want to explore the area.

Telephone

Avoid the phone booths that have signs in English advising you to call home using a special 800 number — these are absolute rip-offs and can cost as much as $20 per minute. The least expensive way to call is by using a Telmex (LADATEL) prepaid phone card, available at most pharmacies and mini-supers, using the official Telmex (Lada) public phones. Remember, in Mexico you need to dial 001 prior to a number to reach the United States, and you need to preface long distance calls within Mexico by dialing 01.

Time Zone

Huatulco operates on central standard time, but Mexico's observance of daylight saving time varies somewhat from that in the United States.

Dining in Huatulco

Contrary to conventional travel wisdom, many of the better restaurants in the Tangolunda Bay area — or from a practical standpoint, most of the restaurants, period — are located in the hotels. Outside the hotels, the best choices are in Crucecita and on the beach in Santa Cruz.

Like many of Mexico's beach resorts, even the finest restaurants in town can be comfortably casual when it comes to dress. Men seldom wear jackets, although ladies frequently wear dressy resort garb — basically, everything goes.

I list the following restaurants alphabetically and note their location and general price category. Remember that tips generally run about 15 percent, and most wait-staff really depend on these for their income, so be generous if the service warrants. Please refer to the Introduction of this book for an explanation of the price categories.

Please see Appendix C for more information on Mexican cuisine.

Avalos Doña Celia
$–$$ **Santa Cruz Bay   SEAFOOD**

For years, Doña Celia, an original Huatulco resident, chose to stay in business in the same area where she started her little thatch-roofed restaurant. Now, she's in a new building at the end of Santa Cruz's beach serving the same good eats. Among her specialties are *filete empapelado,* a foil-wrapped fish baked with tomato, onion, and cilantro, and *filete almendrado,* a fish filet covered with hot-cake batter, beer, and almonds. The ceviche is terrific (one order is plenty for two), as is the *platillo a la huatulqueño* (shrimp and young octopus fried in olive oil with chile and onion and served over white rice). The ambience is basic, but the food is the reason for its popularity. If you dine here during the day, beach chairs and shade are available, so you can make your own "beach club" away from your hotel in this more traditional and accessible part of Huatulco.

Santa Cruz Bay, at the end of Playa Santa Cruz. ☎ *958-587-0128. Seafood prices: $4–$25; breakfast $3.50–$6. MC, V. Open: Daily 8:30 a.m.–11 p.m.*

El Sabor de Oaxaca
$–$$ **Crucecita   OAXACAN**

El Sabor de Oaxaca is the best place in the area to enjoy authentic and richly flavorful Oaxacan food, which is among the best of traditional Mexican cuisine. This restaurant is a local favorite that also meets the quality standards of tourists. The mixed grill for two — with chorizo (a zesty Mexican sausage), Oaxacan beef filet, tender pork tenderloin, and pork ribs — is among the most popular items, and the Oaxacan special for two — a generous sampling of the best of the menu with tamales, Oaxacan cheese, pork mole, and more — is a can't-miss selection. Generous breakfasts are just

$3.90 and include eggs, bacon, ham, beans, toast, and fresh orange juice. The colorful décor and lively music create a nice ambience, and special group events are happily arranged.

Av. Guamúchil 206. ☎ *958-587-0060. Main courses: $5–$20. AE, MC, V. Open: Daily 7 a.m.–11 p.m.*

Noches Oaxaqueñas/Don Porfirio
$$$ Tangolunda Bay SEAFOOD/OAXACAN

At this restaurant with a dinner show, local dancers perform the colorful, traditional folkloric dances of Oaxaca in an open-air courtyard reminiscent of an old hacienda despite being located in a modern strip mall. For dinner, I recommend the *plato oaxaqueño,* a generous, flavorful sampling of traditional Oaxacan fare including a tamale, *sope,* Oaxacan cheese, a grilled filet, a pork enchilada, and a chile relleno for $15. Other house specialties include shrimp with mezcal and spaghetti marinara with seafood. Meat lovers can enjoy American-style cuts of beef or a juicy *arrachera* (skirt steak).

Bulevar Benito Juárez s/n, across from Gala Resort. ☎ *958-581-0001. Reservations recommended. Show: $15; dinner and drinks available a la carte. Main courses: $15–$20. AE, MC, V. Open: Fri–Sun 12:30–10 p.m.; Tues and Thurs 8:30–10:00 p.m.*

Terra-Cotta
$–$$ Crucecita INTERNATIONAL/MEXICAN

This stylish yet casual restaurant is fast becoming Huatulco's best bet for dining, whether for breakfast, lunch, or dinner. Start the day in this sleek, attractive setting for gourmet coffee, fruit salad, or an array of morning favorites, or unusual specials such as their French toast stuffed with cream cheese and orange marmalade. Lunch and dinner shares the same menu, which offers standards such as fajitas, baby back ribs, and gourmet tacos, with a specialty being the Terra-Mar, a combination of shrimp and tenderloin, served over a creamy chipotle chile sauce. Scrumptious desserts such as peach Melba or tiramisu, offer a sweet finish.

Gardenia 902, at the Hotel Misión de los Arcos, in front of La Crucecita's central plaza. ☎ *958-587-0165. Breakfast: $1.50–$6. Lunch and dinner main courses: $4–$13. AE, MC, V. Open: Daily 8 a.m.–10 p.m.*

Tostado's Grill
$–$$ Crucecita MEXICAN

This traditional family-oriented Mexican restaurant serves typical Mexican fare in a casual, friendly atmosphere. It's the place to dine if you're looking for a dose of local color with your meal and want something authentically Mexican. Especially delectable is the Aztec soup (tortilla soup), and the beef is known for its tenderness. It's one of the few restaurants in La Crucecita that is open late during low season.

Flamboyan 306, in front of La Crucecita's central plaza. ☎ *958-587-1697. Reservations not accepted. Main courses: $3–$30. AE, MC, V. Open: Daily 7 a.m.–midnight.*

Having Fun on and off the Beach

Attractions around Huatulco concentrate on the nine bays in the area and their related watersports. Huatulco is truly a nature-lover's paradise offering the more adventurous travelers activities from rafting to rappelling.

Hitting Huatulco's best beaches

Huatulco's major attraction is its coastline — that magnificent stretch of pristine bays bordered by an odd blend of cactus and jungle vegetation that runs right to the water's edge. The only way to really grasp its beauty is by taking a cruise of the bays, stopping at **Organo Bay** or **Maguey Bay** for a dip in the crystal-clear water and a fish lunch at one of the *palapa* restaurants on the beach.

As far as the more accessible, local beaches go, a section of the beach at **Santa Cruz** (away from the small boats), is the location of the beach clubs that guests of non-oceanfront hotels use. Several restaurants are also on this beach, and you can find *palapa* umbrellas down to the water's edge.

For about $15 one way, *pangas* (small boats) from the marina in Santa Cruz ferry passengers to **Playa La Entrega,** also in Santa Cruz Bay. A row of *palapa* restaurants, all with beach chairs out front, greet you at La Entrega. Find an empty *palapa,* call it home for the day, and in return, use that restaurant for your refreshment needs. A snorkel-equipment-rental booth is about midway down the beach, and there's some fairly good snorkeling on the end away from where the boats arrive.

Between Santa Cruz and Tangolunda bays is **Chahué Bay.** A beach club here has *palapas,* beach volleyball, and refreshments for an entrance fee of about $4. However, a strong undertow makes this a dangerous place for swimming.

Playa Tangolunda, fronting the best hotels, is wide and beautiful. Theoretically, all beaches in Mexico are public; however, if you're not a guest at a Tangolunda Bay hotel, you may have difficulty entering a hotel to get to the beach.

Cruising Huatulco

The most popular way to tour Huatulco's bays is to jump on a boat, such as the *Tequila,* and join one of the organized day-long bay cruises complete with guide, drinks, and on-board entertainment. You can call direct (☎ 958-587-0856), or any travel agency can easily arrange these tours, which cost about $25 per person with an extra charge of $4 for snorkeling equipment rental and lunch. Another, more romantic option is the *Luna Azul,* a 13m (44-ft.) sailboat that offers bay tours and sunset sails. Call ☎ **958-587-0945** or 587-1145 (at the Hotel Chahué) for reservations.

If you prefer to venture out on your own, arrange your own bay tour by going to the **boat-owners' cooperative** (☎ 958-587-0081) in the red-and-yellow tin shack at the entrance to the marina in Santa Cruz. Prices are posted there, and you can buy tickets for sightseeing, snorkeling, or fishing. Besides Playa la Entrega, other more distant beaches are noted for good offshore snorkeling, plus they also have *palapa* restaurants and other facilities. These strips of sand include **Playa Maguey** and **Playa San Agustín.** Just remember that several of these beaches are completely undeveloped and pristine, so you need to bring your own provisions. Boatmen at the cooperative can arrange return pick-up at an appointed time. Prices run about $15 for one to ten people to La Entrega and $35 for a trip to Maguey and Organo bays. The most distant bay is **San Agustín,** and that all-day trip runs $80 in a private *panga* (small boat).

Taking time for tennis or golf

For the more traditional sports aficionados, the 18-hole, par-72 **Tangolunda Golf Course** (☎ 958-581-0037) is adjacent to Tangolunda Bay and has tennis courts as well. The greens fee is $73 with an extra charge for carts. Tennis courts are also available at the **Barceló** hotel (☎ 958-581-0055).

Sightseeing and shopping

A day in Crucecita can be enjoyable. Just off the central plaza is the **Iglesía de Guadalupe** with its large mural of Mexico's patron saint gracing the entire ceiling of this church's chapel. The image of the Virgin is set against a deep-blue, night sky, which includes 52 stars — a modern interpretation of the original cloak of Juan Diego.

Considering that **shopping** in Huatulco is generally limited, and unmemorable, the bays' best choices are in Crucecita — in the shops that surround the central plaza. The stores tend to stay open late and offer a good selection of regional goods and typical, tourist take-homes including *artesanías* (local crafts), silver jewelry, Cuban cigars, and tequila. Plus, you can **dine** in Crucecita for a fraction of the price of dining in Tangolunda Bay and get the added benefit of some local color.

You can also check out the **Crucecita Market** (open 10 a.m.–8 p.m.) on Guamúchil, half a block from the plaza in Crucecita, and the Plaza Oaxaca, adjacent to the central plaza. This small shopping center has several clothing shops including **Poco Loco Club/Coconut's Boutique** (☎ 958-587-0279) for casual sportswear; **Mic Mac** (☎ 958-587-0565), featuring beachwear and souvenirs; and **Sideout** (☎ 958-587-0254) for active wear. **Coconuts** (☎ 958-587-0057) has English-language magazines, books, and music. A small, free trolley is available to take visitors on a short tour of the town. Hop on at the central plaza.

The other main option for shopping is the **Santa Cruz Market** (open 10 a.m.–8 p.m.), located by the marina in Santa Cruz. Among all the typical souvenirs, you may want to search out regional specialties that

Brewing up some fun

Mexico's Huatulco region is known for its rich *pluma* coffee, grown in the region's mountainous areas. Centuries-old plantations, most of which continue to use traditional methods, grow and harvest coffee beans. The majority of the plantations are located around the mouth of the Río Copalita in small towns, including Pluma Hidalgo, Santa María de Huatulco, and Xanica, located roughly an hour to an hour and a half from Tangolunda Bay. Both day tours and overnight stays from Huatulco are available to select coffee plantations.

Café Huatulco (☎ 958-587-0339) is a unique project developed by the area's coffee producers' association to bring awareness to the region's coffee and to offer an unusual excursion for tourists. Café Huatulco, located in a kiosk in the central plaza of Santa Cruz, sells whole-bean, regional coffee and serves coffee and espresso beverages. The association can arrange coffee tastings for groups of six or more and overnight stays at the coffee plantations for travelers who are really serious about their coffee.

Paraíso Tours (☎ 958-581-1218; pariasohuatulco@prodigy.net.mx) also offers an eight-hour **Coffee Plantation Tour,** traveling by bus to the coffee plantations to learn first hand about the cultivation of the local coffee.

include Oaxacan embroidered blouses and dresses and *barro negro,* a pottery made from a dark clay found exclusively in the Oaxaca region. Several shopping centers in Tangolunda Bay offer a selection of crafts and Oaxacan goods but are pricier than the markets.

The most worthwhile sightseeing excursion in the area is the daylong trip to **Oaxaca City** and **Monte Albán.** The tour includes round-trip airfare on Aerocaribe, lunch, admission to the archaeological sight of Monte Albán, and a tour of the architectural highlights of Oaxaca City — all for $100. Contact any travel agency or the **Aerocaribe** office (☎ 958-587-1220) for more information.

Enjoying the nightlife

Only a very limited selection of dance clubs is available around Huatulco — so everyone goes to these places. Note that these seem to change ownership and names almost annually, but the locations should be accurate. **El DexkiteLitros** (☎ 958-587-0971) has open-air dancing on the Santa Cruz beachfront. Located next to the Marina Hotel on the beach, it spins techno and rock from 10 p.m. until 5 a.m. For live music, try **Magic Tropic,** Paseo Mitla 304, Santa Cruz (no phone). In Crucecita, one block has a collection of party places, including the popular **Bar La Crema** (Gardenia and Guanacaste) with a lounge style atmosphere and a mix of tunes; **La Peña,** and **Cafe Dublín,** on Carrizal, 1 block east, and ½ block south from the southeastern corner of the *zócalo.*

Chapter 29

Puerto Escondido

by Lynne Bairstow

. . . .

In This Chapter

▶ Finding a place to stay
▶ Getting the lay of the land in Puerto Escondido
▶ Dining in Puerto Escondido
▶ Hitting the beach and checking out turtles

. . . .

*A*lthough it may be best known as Mexico's top surf break, Puerto Escondido has a much broader appeal — it simply offers the very best all-around value of any beach resort in Mexico. What's the attraction? Consider this: stellar beaches; friendly locals; and terrific and inexpensive dining, places to stay, and nightlife — plus an abundance of English-language speakers and a notable absence of beach vendors and timeshare salespeople. But if you're traveling with children, Puerto Escondido may not be the perfect fit — it's really a better choice for young adults or more adventurous travelers.

In this chapter, I cover the best of Puerto Escondido — where to stay and dine and where to find the best adventures. I also offer tips on everything from transportation to where to find the best nightlife.

Evaluating the Top Accommodations

The town of Puerto Escondido is very small — all the hotels are in or bordering the town. The main pedestrians-only zone is known locally as the *Adoquín* after the hexagonal-shaped, interlocking bricks used in its paving. The hotels along Playa Zicatela really cater to surfers.

As far as prices go, I note *rack rates* (the maximum that a hotel or resort charges for a room) for two people spending one night in a double room during high season (Christmas to Easter). You can usually do better, especially if you're purchasing a package that includes airfare (read Chapter 7 for tips on avoiding paying rack rates). Prices quoted here include the 17 percent room tax. Please refer to the Introduction of this book for an explanation of the price categories.

The hotels that I list here have both air-conditioning and TVs, unless otherwise indicated; and if the review doesn't say anything to the contrary, you can safely assume that you can walk directly out of your hotel and onto the beach.

Arcoíris Hotel
$–$$ Playa Zicatela

This hotel offers a winning combination of Zicatela's laid-back charms, together with more amenities and services than the nearby bare-bones surfer hotels, making it a good choice for families. Rooms are located on three levels in this Mexican colonial-style inn, and all have large balconies or terraces that face either Playa Zicatela or an interior garden. You can string a hammock up on the balcony — a common sight, with no air-conditioning in the rooms — and relax away the afternoon. Ground-floor rooms are sans TV, while upper-level rooms have satellite TV. About half of the rooms have a small kitchenette. Hotel amenities include a smallish swimming pool, game room with satellite TV, bookstore, and pharmacy, as well as a restaurant and popular rooftop bar — one of Playa Zicatela's favorite spots for sunset-watching and happy hour. The attentive staff is a plus.

Calle del Morro s/n. ☎ 954-582-0432 or 582-1494. 33 units. Rack rates: First-floor rooms $52, upper-level rooms: $80. MC, V.

Best Western Posada Real
$$$ Playa Bacocho

Set on top of a cliff overlooking Playa Bacocho just west of town, this property is the area's best choice for family travelers. The clean but smallish standard rooms are less enticing than the hotel grounds, which include an expansive, manicured lawn that is one of the most popular places in town for a sunset cocktail. A big plus here is the hotel's Coco's Beach Club — a .8km (½-mile) stretch of soft-sand beach, a large swimming pool, a kid's playground, and a bar with swing-style chairs and occasional live music. A shuttle service (or a lengthy walk down a set of stairs) takes you to the beach club, which is also open to the public ($2.50 cover for non-guests). The hotel is located only five minutes from the airport and about the same distance from Puerto Escondido's Tourist Zone — you must take a taxi to get to town. In addition to Coco's, the hotel has two restaurants and a lobby bar plus two swimming pools — one is a wading pool for children — tennis courts, and a putting green. It's the most traditional (hotel-chain style) hotel I recommend in Puerto Escondido.

Av. Benito Juárez 11. ☎ 800-528-1234 in the U.S., or 954-582-0133 or 582-0237. Fax: 954-582-0192. www.bestwestern.com. *100 rooms. Rack rates: High season $140 double; low season $110 double. AE, DC, MC, V.*

Puerto Escondido

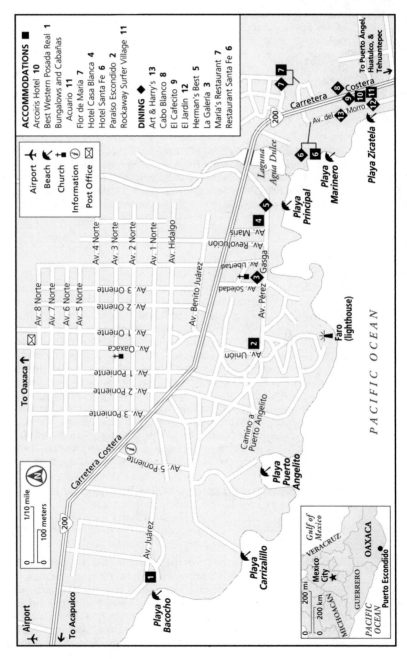

Bungalows and Cabañas Acuario
$–$$ Playa Zicatela

Facing Playa Zicatela, this surfer's sanctuary offers clean, cheap accommodations plus an on-site gym, surf shop, vegetarian restaurant, and Internet cafe. The two-story hotel and the bungalows surround a pool shaded by great palms. Rooms are small and basic, but bungalows offer fundamental kitchen facilities. The *cabañas* are more open and have hammocks. Parking, public telephones, money-exchange facilities, a pharmacy, and the vegetarian restaurant (Mango's) are located in the adjoining commercial area. The well-equipped gym costs an extra $1 per day or $15 per month.

Calle del Morro s/n. ☎ **954-582-0357** *or 582-1026.* www.oaxaca-mio.com/ bunacuario.htm. *40 units. Rack rates: High season $66 double without air-conditioning, $80 double with air-conditioning, $120 bungalow (no air-conditioning); low season $25 double without air-conditioning, $34 double with air-conditioning, $45 bungalow (but you can often negotiate a better deal after you're there). No credit cards.*

Flor de María
$ Playa Marinero

Though not right on the beach, this hotel is a real find and very popular with older travelers. Canadians María and Lino Francato own this cheery, three-story hotel facing the ocean, which you can see from the rooftop. The structure is built around a garden courtyard, and each room is colorfully decorated with beautiful, realistic still lifes and landscapes painted by Lino. Two rooms have windows with a view; the rest face into the courtyard. All have double beds with orthopedic mattresses and small safes. The roof, in addition to the great view, has a small pool, a shaded hammock terrace, and an open-air bar (open 5–9 p.m. during high season) with a TV that receives U.S. channels. All in all, the roof is a great sunset spot. I highly recommend the first-floor María's Restaurant (see the "Dining in Puerto Escondido" section, later in this chapter). Ask about off-season discounts for long-term stays. The hotel is just steps from the center of town and up a sandy road from Playa Marinero on an unnamed street at the eastern end of the beach.

Playa Marinero. ☎*/fax* **954-582-0536.** *24 units. Rack rates: $50 and $60 double. MC, V.*

Hotel Casa Blanca
$ Tourist Zone

If you want to be in the heart of the *Adoquín,* this hotel is your best bet for excellent value and clean, ample accommodations; plus it's just a block from the main beach. The courtyard pool and adjacent *palapa* (thatched roof) restaurant is a great place to hide away and enjoy a margarita or a book from the hotel's exchange rack. The bright, clean, and simply furnished rooms offer a choice of bed combinations, but all have at least two beds and a fan. Some rooms have air-conditioning and a minifridge. The best rooms have a balcony overlooking the action in the street below. If you're a light sleeper, consider a room in the back. Some rooms can sleep up to five ($60), an excellent and economical choice for families.

Av. Pérez Gasga 905. ☎ *954-582-0168. 21 units. Rack rates: $40 double without air-conditioning, $80 double with air-conditioning. MC, V.*

Hotel Santa Fe
$$$ Playa Zicatela

If Puerto Escondido is Mexico's best beach value, then the Santa Fe is without a doubt one of the best hotel values — and a personal, all-around favorite of mine. It has a winning combination of unique Spanish-colonial style, a welcoming staff, and clean, comfortable rooms. The hotel has grown up over the years alongside the surfers who came to Puerto in the 1960s and 1970s — and nostalgically return today. It's located about 1km (⅗ mile) southeast of the town center off Highway 200, at the curve in the road where playas Marinero and Zicatela join — a prime sunset-watching spot. The three-story, hacienda-style buildings have clay-tiled stairs, archways, and blooming vines surrounding the two courtyard swimming pools. The ample but simply stylish rooms feature large tile bathrooms, colonial furnishings, handwoven fabrics, Guerrero pottery lamps, and TVs with local channels only. Most rooms have a balcony or terrace — ocean views on upper floors. Bungalows are next to the hotel, and each has a living room, kitchen, and bedroom with two double beds. The Restaurant Santa Fe is one of the best on the southern Pacific coast (see the "Dining in Puerto Escondido" section, later in this chapter).

Calle del Morro s/n. ☎ *954-582-0170 or 582-0266. Fax: 954-582-0260.* www.hotel santafe.com.mx. *69 units. Free parking. Rack rates: High season $150 double, $165 junior suite, $245 suite, $160 bungalow; low season $105 double, $140 junior suite, $245 suite, $115 bungalow. AE, MC, V.*

Paraíso Escondido
$$ Tourist Zone

The curious collection of Mexican folk art, masks, religious art, and paintings on the walls make this eclectic inn an exercise in Mexican magic realism in addition to a tranquil place to stay. An inviting pool, surrounded by gardens, Adirondack chairs, a restaurant, and a fountain, has a commanding view of the bay — but it's several blocks to the main public beach in town. Each room has one double and one twin bed, a built-in desk, and a cozy balcony or terrace with French doors. Each has a slightly different decorative accent, and all are very clean. The suites have a much more deluxe décor than the rooms and feature recessed lighting, desks set into bay windows with French-paned windows, living areas, and large private balconies. The penthouse suite has its own whirlpool tub and kitchenette plus a tile chessboard inlaid in the floor and murals adorning the walls — it's the owners' former apartment. Limited free parking is available in front of the hotel.

Calle Union 10. ☎ *954-582-0444. 25 units. Rack rates: $75 double, $150 suite. No credit cards.*

Rockaway Surfer Village
$ **Playa Zicatela**

Facing Playa Zicatela, this surfer's sanctuary offers very clean — and very cheap — accommodations geared for surfers. Every *cabaña* is equipped with a private bath, as well as ceiling fans and mosquito nets. In the central courtyard, there's a good-size swimming pool, *palapa* bar, and a 24-hour soft-drink fridge. They recently added a section of new rooms with air-conditioning, hot water, and cable TV.

Calle del Morro s/n. ☎ **954-582-0668.** *Fax: 954-582-2420. 14 units. Rack rates: High season $40–$55 double, new rooms $60 double; low season $18 double, new rooms $30 double. No credit cards.*

Settling into Puerto Escondido

Puerto Escondido's very small **airport** is about 4km (2½ miles) north of the center of town near Playa Bacocho. A trip on the collective **minibus** to your hotel is $2.25 per person. **Transportes Terrestres** sells *colectivo* tickets to the airport through **Turismo Dimar Travel Agency** (☎/fax **954-582-1551**) on Avenida Pérez Gasga (the pedestrian-only zone) next to Hotel Casa Blanca. The minibus can pick you up at your hotel.

TIP 🎯 Flying directly into Puerto Escondido can be a challenge. I find it generally easier (and less expensive) to fly into the Huatulco airport via scheduled or charter flights. An airport taxi costs $85 between Huatulco and Puerto Escondido. If you can find a local taxi, rather than the government-chartered cabs, you can reduce this fare by about 50 percent, including the payment of a $5 mandatory airport exit tax. Frequent bus service also travels between the two destinations. **Budget Car Rental** has cars available for one-way travel to Puerto Escondido with an added drop charge of about $10. In Puerto Escondido, Budget is located at the entrance to Playa Bacocho (☎ **954-582-0312**). By car, the trip from Huatulco to Puerto Escondido takes just under two hours. Because the roads are unlit and frequently curvy through a mountainous zone, plan on traveling only during daylight hours.

Knowing your way around town

Looking out on the Bahía Principal and its beach, to your left is the eastern end of the bay consisting of a small beach, **Playa Marinero,** followed by rocks jutting into the sea. Beyond this is **Playa Zicatela,** unmistakably the main surfing beach. Playa Zicatela has really come into its own as the most popular area for visitors with restaurants, bungalows, surf shops, and hotels located well back from the shoreline. The western side of the bay, to your right, is about 1.6km (1 mile) long with a lighthouse and low green hills descending to meet a long stretch of fine sand. Beaches on this end aren't quite as accessible by land as those to the east, but hotels are overcoming this difficulty by constructing beach clubs accessed by steep private roads and Jeep shuttles.

The town of Puerto Escondido has roughly an east-west orientation with the long Playa Zicatela turning sharply southeast. Residential areas behind (east of) Playa Zicatela tend to have unpaved streets; the older town (with paved streets) is north of the Carretera Costera (Hwy. 200). The streets are numbered — Avenida Oaxaca serves as the dividing line between east *(este)* and west *(oeste),* and Avenida Hidalgo acts as the divider between north *(norte)* and south *(sur).*

North of Zicatela is the old town, through which Avenida Pérez Gasga makes a loop. Part of this loop is a paved, pedestrian-only zone, known as the ***Adoquín.*** Hotels, shops, restaurants, bars, travel agencies, and other services are all conveniently located here. In the morning, taxis, delivery trucks, and private vehicles are allowed to drive here, but at noon it's closed off to all but foot traffic.

Avenida Pérez Gasga angles down from the highway at the east end of the *Adoquín;* on the west, where the *Adoquín* terminates, it climbs in a wide northward curve to cross the highway, after which it becomes Avenida Oaxaca.

The beaches — Playa Principal in the center of town and Marinero and Zicatela southeast of the town center — are interconnected. Walking from one to the other crossing behind the separating rocks is easy. Puerto Angelito, Carrizalillo, and Bacocho beaches are west of town, and you can reach them by road or water. Playa Bacocho hosts the few more-expensive hotels located in Puerto Escondido.

Getting around Puerto Escondido

Almost everything is within walking distance of the *Adoquín.* **Taxis** are inexpensive when traveling around town; call ☎ **954-582-0990** or 582-0955 for service.

Hiring a boat is easy, but you can walk beside the sea from Playa Principal to the tiny beach of Puerto Angelito, though it's a bit of a hike.

Fast Facts: Puerto Escondido

Area Code

The telephone area code is **954**.

Banks, ATMs, and Currency Exchange

Banamex, Bancomer, Bancrear, and Banco Bital all have branches in town, and all exchange money during business hours; each bank's hours vary, but you can generally find one of them open Monday to Saturday 8 a.m. to 7 p.m. ATMs and currency-exchange offices are also located throughout town.

Business Hours

Most offices maintain traditional Mexican hours of operation (10 a.m.–2 p.m. and from 4–8 p.m. daily). During high season, businesses and shops are generally open all day, but during low season, they close between 2 and 5 p.m. Offices tend to close on Saturday and Sunday. Shops are usually open on Saturday but still generally respect the tradition of closing on Sunday.

Hospitals

Try Unidad Médico-Quirúrgica del Sur (Av. Oaxaca 113; ☎ 954-582-1288), which offers 24-hour emergency services and has an English-speaking staff and doctors.

Information

The State Tourist Office, SEDETUR (☎ 954-582-0175), is about 1km (⅔ mile) from the airport at the corner of Carretera Costera and Bulevar Benito Juárez. It's open Monday to Friday 9 a.m. to 7 p.m. and Saturday 10 a.m. to 2 p.m. A kiosk at the airport is open for incoming flights during high season, and another, near the west end of the paved Tourist Zone, is open Monday to Saturday 9 a.m. to 2 p.m.

Internet Access

Cyber-café is a small, extremely busy Internet service at the entrance to the Bungalows and Cabañas Acuario (Calle de Morro s/n; ☎ 954-582-0357, ask for the cybercafe). It's open daily 8 a.m. until 9 p.m. The rate to get online is $1.50 for 15 minutes, $3 for a half-hour, or $5 per hour. Graficom (Av. Pérez Gasga 210; ☎ 954-582-1853 or 582-1313; graficom@ptoescondido. com.mx). offers public e-mail and Internet service, fax, telephone, snacks, and is air-conditioned.

Pharmacy

Farmacia de Mas Ahorro, on Primera Norte corner and Segunda Poniente (☎ 954-582-1911), is open 24 hours a day.

Post Office

The post office is on Avenida Oaxaca at the corner of Avenida 7 Norte (☎ 954-582-0959). It's open Monday to Friday 8 a.m. to 3 p.m.

Safety

Depending on whom you talk to, you need to be wary of potential beach muggings, primarily at night. However, the hope is that the new public lighting at Playa Principal and Playa Zicatela goes a long way in preventing these incidents. Local residents say most incidents happen after tourists overindulge and then go for a midnight stroll along the beach. Puerto Escondido is so casual that letting your guard down is easy, but don't carry valuables, and use common sense and normal precautions. Also, respect the power of the magnificent waves here. Drownings occur all too frequently.

Taxes

A 15 percent value added tax (IVA) is charged on goods and services, and it's generally included in the posted price.

Taxis

Taxis are easy to find around town. They're also inexpensive, generally costing $1 to $3 for various parts of town; call ☎ 954-582-0990 or 582-0955 for service.

Telephone

Numerous businesses offer long-distance telephone service. Many of these establishments are along the *Adoquín,* and several accept credit cards.

Avoid the phone booths that have signs in English advising you to call home using a special 800 number — these are absolute rip-offs and can cost as much as $20 per minute. The least expensive way to call is by using a Telmex (LADATEL) prepaid phone card, available at most pharmacies and mini-supers, using the official Telmex (Lada) public phones. Remember, in Mexico, you need to dial 001 prior to a number to reach the United States, and you need to preface long-distance calls within Mexico by dialing 01.

Time Zone

Puerto Escondido operates on central standard time, although Mexico's observance of daylight saving time varies somewhat from that in the United States.

Dining in Puerto Escondido

I find dining in Puerto Escondido an absolute pleasure. The food is excellent — generous portions display innovative flavorings at some of the lowest prices I've ever seen anywhere. The atmosphere is exceedingly casual — but don't let that throw you. I've enjoyed some very memorable meals in these funky settings, starting with the mango éclairs at **El Cafecito.** In fact, Puerto Escondido is even more casual than Mexico's other beach resorts — no need to even think about bringing dressy attire or jackets. Personally, I think that Playa Zicatela has the highest concentration of great eats.

All the restaurants I include in the listings are arranged alphabetically with their location and general price category noted. Remember that tips generally run about 15 percent, and most waitstaff really depend on these for their income, so be generous if the service warrants.

In addition to the places I list in this section, the *palapa* restaurants on Playa Zicatela are a Puerto Escondido tradition for early-morning surfer breakfasts or casual dining and drinks by the sea at night. One of the most popular *palapa* restaurants is **Los Tíos,** offering very economical prices and surfer-sized portions. After dinner, enjoy homemade Italian ice cream from **Gelateria Giardino.** It has two locations, on Calle del Morro at Zicatela Beach, and Pérez Gasga 609, on the *Adoquín* (☎ 954-582-2243).

Art & Harry's
$ **Playa Zicatela   SEAFOOD/STEAKS**

About 1.2km (¾ mile) southeast of the Hotel Santa Fe, on the road fronting Zicatela Beach, this robust watering hole is great for taking in the sunset, especially if you're having a giant hamburger or grilled shrimp dinner. Late afternoon and early evening here affords the best portrait of Puerto Escondido. Watch surfers, tourists, and the resident cat all slip into lazy silhouette as the sun dips into the ocean.

Av. Morro s/n. No phone. Main courses $4.50–$15. No credit cards. Open: Daily 10 a.m.–10 p.m.

Cabo Blanco
$–$$$ Playa Zicatela   INTERNATIONAL

"Where Legends Are Born" is the logo at this beachfront restaurant, and the local crowd craves chef Gary's special sauces that top his grilled fish, shrimp, steaks, and ribs. Favorites include his dill-Dijon mustard, wine-fennel, and Thai-curry sauces. But you can't count on these sauces always being on the menu because Gary buys what's fresh and then goes from there. An added bonus is that Cabo Blanco turns into a hot bar on Playa Zicatela with special parties on Mondays featuring all-you-can-eat plus dancing, and a Friday night reggae dance. Gary's wife Roxana and a top-notch team of bartenders keep the crowd well served and well behaved.

Calle del Morro s/n. ☎ *954-582-0337.* www.geocities.com/oaxiki/cabo_ blanco_pe.html. *Reservations not accepted. Main courses: $7–$45. V. Open: Daily 6 p.m.–2 a.m.*

El Cafecito
$ Playa Zicatela   FRENCH PASTRY/SEAFOOD/VEGETARIAN/COFFEE

With a motto of "Big waves, strong coffee!" this cafe opened several years ago on Playa Zicatela as an offshoot of a locally popular bakery named for its amiable proprietor, Carmen. El Cafecito features an array of unforgettable pastries to start your day, and is also open for lunch and dinner. This restaurant actually spans two facing corners; the northern corner is set up more for coffee or a light snack with oceanfront bistro-style seating. The southern corner offers a more relaxed setting with wicker chairs and Oaxacan cloth-topped tables set under a *palapa* roof. Giant shrimp dinners are priced under $5, and the creative, daily specials are always a sure bet. An oversized mug of cappuccino is $1, a fresh and filling fruit smoothie goes for $1.50, and Carmen's mango éclairs — I'd pay any price — are a steal at $1.

Calle del Morro s/n. ☎ *954-582-0516. Reservations not accepted. Main courses: $2.10–$5.70; pastries 50¢–$1.25. No credit cards. Open: Wed–Mon 6 a.m.–10 p.m.*

El Jardín
$ Playa Zicatela   SEAFOOD/VEGETARIAN/COFFEE

This popular vegetarian restaurant, located just in front of the Bungalows Acuario, is generally packed — it's known for healthy food, ample portions, and low prices. Under a *palapa* roof and facing Playa Zicatela, Gota de Vida offers an extensive menu that includes fruit smoothies, espresso drinks, herbal teas, and a complete juice bar. These folks make their own tempeh, tofu, pasta, and whole grain bread. Creative vegetarian offerings are based on Mexican favorites like chiles rellenos, cheese enchiladas, and bean tostadas. Fresh seafood is also featured.

Calle del Morro s/n. No phone. Reservations not accepted. Main courses: $1.80–$5.40. No credit cards. Open: Daily 10 a.m.–11 p.m.

Herman's Best
$ Adoquín   MEXICAN/SEAFOOD

This small restaurant's atmosphere is about as basic as it comes, but clearly Herman's is putting all its attention into the kitchen — offering simply delicious, home-style cooking. The menu changes daily, but generally includes a fresh fish filet, rotisserie chicken, and Mexican staples like enchiladas — all served with beans, rice, and homemade tortillas. Herman's Best is just outside the pedestrian-only zone at the eastern end of the *Adoquín*.

Av. Pérez Gasga s/n. No phone. Main courses: $1.80–$4.20. No credit cards. Open: Mon–Sat 5–10 p.m.

La Galería
$ Adoquín   ITALIAN

By far the best Italian restaurant in town, La Galería combines great food in an atmosphere of art, available for sale by local and regional artists. Open for breakfast, lunch, and dinner, the eatery is known for its brick-oven pizzas, homemade with fresh ingredients. La Galería also has a full selection of pastas, including exceptional lasagna. One of the *Adoquín*'s long-standing restaurants, La Galería recently opened a second location in Playa Zicatela (next to Casa Babylon and Arcoíris Hotel). Beautifully decorated with tiny mosaic tiles on the bar and in the bathrooms, the second Galería serves up the same great fare in a beautiful garden setting.

Av. Pérez Gasga s/n. ☎ 954-582-2039. Reservations not accepted. Breakfast: $3–$5; main courses: $4–$9. No credit cards. Open: Daily 8 a.m.–11 p.m.

María's Restaurant
$ Playa Marinero   INTERNATIONAL

This first-floor, open-air, hotel dining room near the beach is popular with the locals. The menu changes daily and features specials such as María Francato's fresh homemade pasta dishes. María's is in the Hotel Flor de María, just steps from the center of town and up a sandy road from Playa Marinero on an unnamed street at the eastern end of the beach.

Playa Marinero. ☎ 954-582-0536. Main courses: $5–$14; breakfast $2–$3.50. MC, V. Open: Daily 8–11:30 a.m., noon to 2 p.m., and 6–10 p.m. Closed May–July and Sept.

Restaurant Santa Fe
$–$$ Playa Zicatela   INTERNATIONAL

The atmosphere here (in the Hotel Santa Fe) is classic and casual with great views of the sunset and Playa Zicatela. Big pots of palms are scattered around, and fresh flowers grace the tables — all beneath a lofty *palapa* roof. The shrimp dishes are a bargain relative to the rest of the world, but at $15, they're a little higher-priced than in the rest of the town's

eateries. Perfectly grilled tuna, served with homemade french-fried potatoes and whole-grain bread, is an incredible meal deal for under $10. A
nopal (cactus leaf) salad on the side ($2.50) is a perfect complement.
Vegetarian dishes are reasonably priced and creatively adapted from traditional Mexican and Italian dishes. A favorite is the house specialty, chiles
rellenos. The bar offers an excellent selection of tequilas.

Calle del Morro s/n. ☎ *954-582-0170. Reservations recommended during high season.
Main courses: $5–$15; breakfast $4.50–$6. AE, MC, V. Open: Daily 7 a.m.–11 p.m.*

Having Fun on and off the Beach

Playa Principal is the main beach in town where small boats are available for fishing and tour services. Playa Principal and the adjacent **Playa
Marinero** are the best swimming beaches. Beach chairs and sun shades
rent for about $2, a charge that may be waived if you order food or
drinks from the restaurants that offer them.

Playa Zicatela, a world-class surf spot, adjoins Playa Marinero about
2.5km (1½ miles) from Puerto Escondido's town center and extends to
the southeast for several miles. Due to the size and strength of the
waves here, it's not a swimming beach, and only experienced surfers
should attempt to ride Zicatela's powerful waves. A surfing competition
is held each August, and Fiesta Puerto Escondido, held for at least three
days each November, also celebrates Puerto Escondido's renowned
waves. (The tourism office can supply exact dates and details; call
☎ 954-582-0175.) Beginning surfers often start out at Playa Marinero
before graduating to Zicatela's awesome waves.

New, stadium-style lighting has recently been installed in both of
these beach areas in an attempt to crack down on nocturnal beach
muggings. The lights have diminished the appeal of the Playa Principal
restaurants — you look into bright lights rather than at the nighttime
sea now. Lifeguard service has recently been added to Playa Zicatela.

Barter with one of the fishermen on the main beach for a ride to **Playa
Manzanillo** and **Puerto Angelito,** two beaches separated by a rocky outcropping (the best way to get here is by boat). Here, and at other small
coves just west of town, swimming is safe and the overall atmosphere is
calmer than it is in town. You can also find *palapas,* hammock rentals,
and snorkeling equipment — the clear blue water is perfect for snorkeling. Enjoy fresh fish, tamales, and other Mexican dishes cooked right at
the beach by local entrepreneurs. Puerto Angelito is also accessible by
a dirt road that's a short distance from town, so it tends to be busier.

Playa Bacocho is on a shallow cove farther to the northwest and is best
reached by taxi or boat rather than walking. It's also the location of
Coco's Beach Club at the Best Western Posada Real. It's open to the
public for a cover charge of $2.50, which gains you access to the pools,
food and beverage service, and facilities.

An unusual spa experience

For terrific massage services — the ideal answer to a day spent in pounding surf — **Espacio Meditativo Temazcalli** (Calle Temazcalli, corner of Av. Infraganti; ☎ 954-582-1023; www.temazcalli.com) is the place to go. A variety of therapeutic massages range in price from $15 to $32. Body Beauty treatments (priced $27–$33) and facials ($27) are designed to minimize the effects of too much sun. Bioenergetic Balance Techniques and the indigenous Mexican Temazcal steam bath (both individual and group) are treatments designed to purify body and soul. The center is a tranquil haven, lushly landscaped, with the sound of the nearby ocean prevalent in the treatment areas. On full moon nights, the spa has a special group Temazcal ceremony, a truly fascinating experience!

Embarking on an excursion

Ana's Eco Tours (Calle Futuro 214, Costa Chica; ☎ 954-582-2001; ana@anasecotours.com) is an exceptional provider of ecologically oriented tour services. "Ana" Marquez was born in the small, nearby, mountain village of Jamiltepec and has an intimate knowledge of the area's customs, people, flora, and fauna. She and her expert guides lead small groups on both eco-adventures and cultural explorations. Tours into the surrounding mountains include a five-hour horseback excursion up to the jungle region of the Chatino **healing hot springs** and a trip to **Nopala,** a Chatino mountain village, and a neighboring coffee plantation. An all-day trip to **Jamiltepec** (a small, traditional regional Indian community called a Mixtex village) offers the opportunity to experience day-to-day life in an authentic village. The visit includes stops at a market, the church, the cemetery, and the homes of local artisans.

For local information and guided walking tours, visit the **Oaxaca Tourist Bureau** booth (☎ 954-582-0276; GinaInPuerto@Yahoo.com). It's found just west of the pedestrian mall. Ask for "Gina" who calls herself "the information goddess." She offers up information with a smile, and many say she knows more about Puerto Escondido than any other person. On her days off, Gina offers walking tours to the market and to little-known nearby ruins. Filled with history and information on native vegetation, a day with Gina promises fun, adventure, and insight into local culture.

Turismo Dimar Travel Agency (☎ 954-582-0737 or 582-2305; viajes dimar@hotmail.com), on the landward side of the *Adoquín,* is an excellent source of information and can arrange all types of tours and travel. It's open daily 8 a.m. to 10 p.m. Manager Gaudencio Díaz speaks English and can arrange individualized tours or more standard ones such as **Michael Malone's Hidden Voyages Ecotours.** Malone, a Canadian ornithologist, takes you on a dawn or sunset trip to **Manialtepec Lagoon,** a bird-filled mangrove lagoon about 19km (12 miles) northwest of Puerto Escondido. The cost is $32 and includes a stop on a secluded beach for a swim.

Another reputable agency is **Cantera Tours** (Av. Pérez Gazga at Andador Gloria; ☎ **954-582-1926** or 582-1927; Fax: 954-582-1926).

One of the most popular all-day tours offered by both companies is a trip to **Chacahua Lagoon National Park,** about 68km (42 miles) west of Puerto, at a cost of $38 with Dimar or $25 with Ana's. These excursions are true ecotours — small groups treading lightly. You visit a beautiful sandy spit of beach and the lagoon, which has an incredible array of birds and flowers including black orchids. Locals provide fresh barbecued fish on the beach. If you know Spanish and get information from the tourism office, staying overnight under a small *palapa* is possible, but bring plenty of insect repellent.

An interesting and slightly out-of-the-ordinary excursion is **Aventura Submarina** (Av. Pérez Gasga 601A, in front of the tourism office; ☎ **954-582-2353**). Jorge, who speaks fluent English and is a certified scuba instructor, guides individuals and small groups of qualified divers along the Coco trench just offshore. The price is $55 for a two-tank dive. This outfit offers a refresher scuba course at no extra charge. Jorge also arranges surface activities such as deep-sea fishing, surfing, and trips to lesser-known yet nearby swimming beaches.

Fishermen keep their colorful *pangas* (small boats) on the beach beside the *Adoquín.* A **fisherman's tour** around the coastline in a *panga* costs about $35, but a ride to Playa Zicatela or Puerto Angelito is only $10. Most hotels offer or gladly arrange tours to meet your needs.

A Mixtec Ceremonial Center was discovered in early 2000 just east of Puerto Escondido and is considered a major discovery. The site covers many acres with about 10 pyramids and a ball court, with the pyramids appearing as hills covered in vegetation. A number of large carved stones have been found. Situated on a hilltop, it commands a spectacular view of Puerto Escondido and the Pacific coast. The large archaeological site spans several privately-owned plots of land, and is not open to the public, although Gina, "the information goddess" (see information, above), has been known to offer a guided walking tour to it.

Planning a side trip to Puerto Angel and Playa Zipolite

About 80km (50 miles) southeast of Puerto Escondido and 48km (30 miles) northwest of the Bahías de Huatulco is the tiny fishing port of **Puerto Angel** (not to be confused with Puerto Angelito, which is a beach in Puerto Escondido). Puerto Angel, with its beautiful beaches, unpaved streets, and budget hotels, is popular with the international backpacking set and travelers seeking an inexpensive and restful vacation. Its small bay and several inlets offer peaceful swimming and good snorkeling. The village follows a slow and simple way of life: Fishermen leave very early in the morning and return with their catch shortly before noon.

The golden sands and peaceful village life of Puerto Angel are the reasons to visit. **Playa Principal,** the main beach, lies between the Mexican navy base and the pier that's home to the local fishing fleet. Near the pier, fishermen pull their colorful boats on the beach and unload their catch in the late morning while trucks wait to haul it off to processing plants in Veracruz. The rest of the beach seems light years away from the world of work and purpose. Except on Mexican holidays, it's relatively deserted.

The beaches around Puerto Escondido and Puerto Angel (located between Huatulco and Puerto Escondido) are important **turtle nesting grounds** for the endangered Ridley sea turtle. During the summer months, tourists can sometimes see the turtles laying eggs or observe the hatchlings trekking to the sea. **Playa Escobilla,** near Puerto Escondido, and **Playa Barra de la Cruz,** near Puerto Angel, seem to be the favored nesting grounds of this species.

In 1991, the Mexican government established the Centro Mexicano la Tortuga, known locally as the **Turtle Museum,** for the study and life enhancement of the turtle. Examples of all species of marine turtles living in Mexico are on view, plus six species of freshwater turtles and two species of land turtles. The center is located on **Playa Mazunte** near the town of the same name. Hours are 10 a.m. to 4:30 p.m. Tuesday to Saturday and Sunday 10 a.m. to 2 p.m.; entry is $2.50.

Mazunte is also home to a unique shop that sells naturally produced shampoos, bath oils, and other personal-care products. The local community women make and package all the products as part of a project to replace the income lost from turtle poaching. The products are excellent in quality, and purchasing them goes a long way in ensuring the cessation of turtle poaching in the community. Buses go to Mazunte from Puerto Angel about every half-hour, and a taxi ride is around $5.50. You can fit this trip in with a visit to Playa Zipolite, the next one closer to Puerto Angel.

Playa Panteón is the main swimming and snorkeling beach. "Cemetery Beach," ominous as that sounds, is about a 15-minute walk from the center of town. Just walk straight through town on the main street that skirts the beach. The *panteón* (cemetery), which is also worth a visit with its brightly colored tombstones backed by equally brilliant blooming vines, is on the right.

In Playa Panteón, some of the *palapa* restaurants and a few of the hotels rent snorkeling and scuba gear and can arrange boat trips, but they all tend to be rather expensive. Check the quality and the condition of the gear — particularly scuba gear — that you rent.

Playa Zipolite and its village are 6km (4 miles) down a paved road from Puerto Angel. Taxis charge around $1 to $1.50 (taxis are relatively inexpensive here), or you can catch a *colectivo* on the main street in the town center and share the cost.

Zipolite is well known as a good surf break and nude beach. Although public nudity (including topless sunbathing) is technically against the law throughout Mexico, it's allowed here — one of only a handful of beaches in Mexico to allow it. This sort of open-mindedness has attracted an increasing number of young European travelers. Most sunbathers concentrate beyond a large rock outcropping at the far end of the beach. Police occasionally patrol the area, but they're much more intent on searching for drug users than harassing au natural sunbathers. Spots to tie up a hammock and a few *palapa* restaurants where you can grab a light lunch and a cold beer dot the beach.

In Zipolite, as in the rest of Mexico, the purchase, sale, or use of drugs is definitely against the law, no matter what the local custom may be (and their use is relatively customary here). Because the ocean currents are quite strong (that's why the surf is so good!), a number of drownings have occurred over the years — so, know your limits.

If you're traveling here by car, you arrive via Highway 200 from the north or south. Take coastal Highway 175 inland to Puerto Angel. The road is well marked with signs leading to Puerto Angel. From either Huatulco or Puerto Escondido, the trip takes about an hour.

Taxis are a readily available to take you to Puerto Angel, Playa Zipolite, the Huatulco airport, or Puerto Escondido for a reasonable price.

Shopping in Puerto Escondido

The *Adoquín* sports a row of tourist shops selling straw hats, postcards, and Puerto Escondido T-shirts, and a few excellent shops feature Guatemalan, Oaxacan, and Balinese clothing and art. You can also get a tattoo or rent surfboards and bodyboards here. Pharmacies and mini-markets for basic necessities are interspersed among the shops, hotels, restaurants, and bars.

The largest of these mini-marts is **Oh! Mar** (Av. Pérez Gasga 502; ☎ 954-582-3056), which not only sells anything you'd need for a day at the beach but also sells phone (LADATEL) cards, stamps, and Cuban cigars. Plus, the store has a mail drop box and arranges fishing tours.

During high season, businesses and shops are generally open all day, but during low season, they close between 2 and 5 p.m. Some highlights along the *Adoquín* include:

- ✔ **Bazaar Santa Fe** (in the Hotel Santa Fe lobby, on Playa Zicatela, Calle del Morro s/n; ☎ 954-582-0170), which sells antiques including vintage Oaxacan embroidered clothing, jewelry, and religious artifacts.

- ✔ **Central Surf** shops are located on the *Adoquín* (☎ 954-582-0568) and on Playa Zicatela (Calle Morro s/n; ☎ 954-582-2285). The stores rent and sell surfboards and related gear and offer surf lessons.

✔ **Bikini Brazil** (Calle de Morro s/n, Zicatela Beach; no phone), where you'll find super-hot bikinis imported from Brazil, land of the *tanga*. Shops are located on the *Adoquín* (☎ **954-582-0568**) and on Playa Zicatela (Calle Morro s/n; ☎ **954-582-2285**). The stores rent and sell surfboards and related gear and offer surf lessons.

✔ **360 Surf Shop** sells everything for your out-of-town surf needs, as well as sells, trades, and rents boards. Board rentals start at $10 per day, with lessons available for $20. They don't have a phone number, but you can contact them by e-mailing 360@puerto connection.com.

✔ Just in front of the Rockaway Resort on Playa Zicatela, a 24-hour **mini-super** (no phone) sells the basic necessities: beer, suntan lotion, and basic food supplies.

Enjoying the nightlife

As hot as the daytime surf action is in Puerto Escondido, the nocturnal offerings offer some stiff competition that can make catching those first morning waves somewhat of a challenge.

Sunset-watching is a ritual to plan your day around, and good lookout points abound here. Watch the surfers at Zicatela and catch up on local gossip at **La Galería** (Calle del Morro s/n; ☎ **958-582-0432**), upstairs on the third floor of the Arcoíris hotel. La Galería has a nightly happy hour (with live music during high season) from 5 to 7 p.m. For other great sunset spots, head to the **Hotel Santa Fe** at the junction of playas Zicatela and Marinero or the rooftop bar of **Hotel Flor de María.** For a more tranquil, romantic setting, take a cab or walk half an hour or so west to the **Best Western Posada Real.** The hotel's cliff-top lawn is a perfect sunset perch. You can also climb down the cliff (or take the Posada Real's shuttle bus) to Coco's on the beach below.

When it comes to bars and clubs, Puerto has a nightlife that satisfies anyone dedicated to late nights and good music. Along the *Adoquín,* here are some spots that may lure you in:

✔ **Bar Fly, The Blue Iguana,** and **Rayos X** cater to a younger surf crowd with DJs spinning alternative, house, and techno tunes.

✔ Located across the street, **Wipeout** is a multilevel club that packs in the crowds until 4 a.m.

✔ The **Bucanero Bar and Grill** has a good-sized bar and outdoor patio fronting Playa Principal.

✔ **Montezuma's Revenge** has live bands usually playing contemporary Latin American music.

✔ **Son y la Rumba** is home to live jazz featuring its house band with Andria Garcia playing each night 8 to 11 p.m. with a $1 cover. Wednesdays through Saturdays, it switches over to DJs playing house music after 11 p.m. This club is located beneath the Un Tigre Azul, on the western end of the *Adoquín*.

✔ **El Tubo** is an open-air, beachside disco just west of Restaurant Alicia on the *Adoquín*.

Also downtown is **Tequila Sunrise,** a spacious two-story disco overlooking the beach. It plays Latino, reggae, *cumbia,* tropical, and salsa. It's a half-block from the *Adoquín* on Avenida Marina Nacional. A small cover charge ($1.20–$2.40) generally applies.

Out on Zicatela, don't miss **Cabo Blanco's** (see the "Dining in Puerto Escondido" section, earlier in this chapter) Monday night dine and dance party (all you can eat), or their Friday reggae night. **Split Coco,** just a few doors down, has live music on Tuesdays and Fridays and TV sports on other nights. It has one of the most popular happy hours on the beach and serves barbecue as well.

There's a new movie theater on Playa Zicatela — **PJ's Book Bodega and Music Shop.** It's a pretty simple setup consisting of a large screen and some beach chairs, and it serves up popcorn and movies nightly.

Most nightspots are open until 3 a.m. or until the customers leave.

Part IX
Los Cabos and Southern Baja

"Since we lost the dolphins, business hasn't been quite the same.

In this part . . .

Cabo San Lucas, San José del Cabo, and the stretch of coastline (the Corridor) that connects them are collectively known as Los Cabos (The Capes). They're located at the tip of Mexico's Baja Peninsula. "The end of the line," "the last resort," and "no man's land" are all terms used in the past to describe Mexico's remote but diverse Baja Sur, an exquisite setting that artfully blends desert landscapes with vibrant seascapes. With seven championship golf courses open for play, golf has overtaken sportfishing as the main draw here. Other activities you can find in Cabos to keep you busy are sea kayaking, whale-watching, diving, surfing, and hiking.

In the next four chapters, you discover the differences between the three distinct parts of Los Cabos and their unique attractions. And you get clued in on the best places to stay and dine, great things to do, and the craziest spots for nighttime diversion.

Chapter 30

The Lowdown on the Hotel Scene in Los Cabos

by Lynne Bairstow

- -

In This Chapter

▶ Laying out the hotel locations
▶ Reviewing the top hotel choices in Los Cabos

- -

*P*art of the attraction of the towns of Los Cabos — on the tip of the Baja Peninsula — seems to be the feeling that they're an extension of Southern California's brand of American style — luxury accommodations, golf courses, shopping, franchise restaurants, and a spirited nightlife. **Cabo San Lucas** has retained its boisterous, party-town traditions, and **San José del Cabo** still has the appearance and ambience of a quaint Mexican town, though in recent years, it is becoming more and more gentrified.

Nearly 30km (18 miles) of smooth highway, known as **the Corridor,** lie between the two Cabos. Along this stretch of pavement, major new resorts, including some of the world's finest golf courses and residential communities, have developed. And the area's signature natural beauty continues to beckon: Dozens of pristine coves and inlets with a wealth of marine life just offshore greet visitors.

The Los Cabos area has earned a deserved reputation for being much higher priced than other Mexican resorts. Although a boom in new hotel construction has occurred, these new properties have all been luxury resorts — solidifying Los Cabos' higher average room prices, not adjusting prices downward with the added supply of rooms. The other factor driving up prices here is that compared to mainland Mexico, little agricultural activity takes place in Baja; most foodstuffs (and other daily required items) must be shipped into the area. U.S. dollars are the preferred currency here, and seeing price listings in dollars rather than pesos isn't uncommon.

In this chapter, I review the two main towns, the Corridor between them, and the types of hotel rooms you're likely to find in each as well as the pros and cons of staying in each area. Then, I run down a selection of my favorite places to stay in Los Cabos. The accommodation options are so varied here that no matter your taste or budget, you're sure to find the perfect fit for a satisfying vacation.

Choosing a Location

Los Cabos is actually three destinations in one — the traditional town of San José, the rowdy party town of Cabo San Lucas, and the luxury-lined corridor between the two. Where you stay impacts your overall experience, although you can move around from one location to another — for a price. My hotel recommendations extend through this entire area.

 San José del Cabo, located closest to the airport, has pastel cottages and flowering trees lining its narrow streets, retaining the air of a provincial Mexican town. Originally founded in 1730 by Jesuit missionaries, it's the seat of the Los Cabos government and the center of the region's business community. The main square, adorned with a wrought-iron bandstand and shaded benches, faces the cathedral, which was built on the site of an early mission.

San José is becoming increasingly sophisticated. A collection of noteworthy cafes, art galleries, and intriguing small inns adds a newly refined flavor to the central downtown area. Still, San José is the best choice for travelers who want to travel to this paradoxical Mexican landscape but still be aware that they're in Mexico. Most of the hotels I list here are found in the town — that is, away from the beaches of San José, but not so far away that it's an inconvenience.

The Corridor between the towns of San José del Cabo and Cabo San Lucas contains some of Mexico's most lavish resorts designed as self-contained dream getaways. Most growth in this area is occurring along the Corridor, which has already become a major international locale for championship golf. The three major resort areas are Palmilla, Cabo Real, and Cabo del Sol. Each location is a self-enclosed community with golf courses, elegant hotels, and million-dollar homes.

 If you plan to explore the region while staying at a Corridor hotel, consider renting a car for at least a day or two for easier access; cars are available at the hotels. Even if you're not staying here, the beaches and dining options are worth a visit. All the hotels along the Corridor qualify as "very expensive" selections. Golf and fishing packages are available at most resorts.

The hundreds of luxury hotel rooms along the Corridor to the north of Cabo San Lucas have transformed the very essence of this formerly rustic and rowdy outpost. Although it still retains a boisterous nightlife that runs counter to the pampered services that surround it, Cabo San Lucas is no longer the simple town John Steinbeck wrote about and enjoyed. Once legendary for the big-game fish that lurk beneath the deep blue sea, Cabo San Lucas now draws more people for its nearby fairways and greens — and the world-class golf played on them. Today, it caters to a traveler getting away for a long weekend or indulgent stay of sport and relaxation. Cabo San Lucas has become Mexico's most elite resort destination.

Travelers here enjoy a growing roster of adventure-oriented activities, and playtime doesn't end when the sun goes down. The nightlife here is as hot as the desert in July and oddly casual, having grown up away from the higher-end hotels. It remains the raucous, playful party scene that helped put Cabo on the map. A collection of popular restaurants and bars, spread along Cabo's main street, stay open and active until the morning's first fishing charters head out to sea. Despite the growth in diversions, Cabo remains more or less a "one-stoplight" town with most everything located along the main strip within easy walking distance.

Budget accommodations are scarce in Cabo San Lucas, but a number of small inns and B&Bs, with several notable ones, fit the bill nicely. Because most of the larger hotels are well maintained, and packages are available through travel agents, I focus on the smaller, more unique accommodations available in Cabo San Lucas.

Best Accommodations in Los Cabos

There's more demand than supply for hotel rooms in the Corridor, so prices tend to be higher than equivalent accommodations in other parts of Mexico. San José has only a handful of budget hotels, so call ahead for reservations if you want economical accommodations. In the town of San José, you'll find smaller inns, or B&Bs, offering stylish accommodations. The beachfront Hotel Zone in San José often offers package deals that bring room rates down to the moderate range, especially during summer months. Shop around or check with your travel agent.

For each hotel, I include specific rack rates for two people spending one night in a double room during high season (Christmas to Easter), unless otherwise indicated. Keep in mind that summer rates are about 20 percent less. *Rack rates* simply mean published rates, and tend to be the highest rate paid — you can do better, especially if you're purchasing a package that includes airfare (read Chapter 7 for tips on avoiding paying rack rates). Please refer to the Introduction of this book for an explanation of the price categories.

 Many hotels double their normal rates during Christmas and Easter weeks. Note that some rates may seem much higher than others — until you realize that they're "all-inclusive" — meaning that your meals and beverages are included in the price of your stay. This rate also includes all tips and taxes and most activities and entertainment.

All hotels I list here have both air-conditioning and TVs, unless otherwise indicated; if the review doesn't say anything to the contrary, you can safely assume that you can walk directly out of your hotel and onto the beach.

The Bungalows
$$ Cabo San Lucas

The Bungalows is one of the most special places to stay in Los Cabos. Each "bungalow" is a charming retreat decorated with authentic Mexican furnishings. Terra-cotta tiles, hand-painted sinks, wooden chests, blown glass, and other creative touches make you feel as if you're a guest at a friend's home rather than in a hotel. Each room has a kitchenette, a private bath, purified water, a TV with VCR, and designer bedding. The varied bungalows, which include eight one-bedrooms, two deluxe one-bedrooms, and six two-bedrooms, surround a lovely heated pool with cushioned lounges and tropical gardens — but the nearest beach is a few miles away. You can enjoy fountains and flowers throughout the grounds, and a brick-paved breakfast nook serves a complete gourmet breakfast daily including fresh-ground coffee and fresh juices. The breakfast nook is also where guests become friends and share travel tips and experiences. Under the warm and welcoming management, this is Cabo's most spacious and comfortable full-service inn with exceptionally helpful service. A 100-percent smoke-free environment, the property is located 5 blocks from downtown Cabo.

Miguel A. Herrera s/n, in front of Lienzo Charro. ☎ ***888-424-CABO*** *from the U.S., 624-143-5035, or 624-143-0585.* www.cabobungalows.com. *16 units. Street parking available. Rack rates: High season $115 double, $125–$145 suites; low season $99 double, $105–$115 suites. Rates include complimentary full gourmet breakfast. AE, V.*

Cabo Inn
$–$$ Cabo San Lucas

This three-story hotel on a quiet street is a real find, and it keeps getting better. The Cabo Inn is a rare combination of low rates, extra-friendly management, and great, funky style — not to mention extra clean — but you're about a mile to the nearest public beach. Rooms are basic and very small — this inn was a bordello in a prior life. All rooms have recently upgraded furnishings and new air-conditioning (2005) and those on the lower level also have a minifridge. Muted desert colors add a spark of personality, and rooms come with either two twin beds or one queen bed. The rooms surround a courtyard where you can enjoy satellite TV, a barbecue grill, and free coffee. The third floor has a rooftop terrace with *palapa* (thatched roof) and a small swimming pool. Also on this floor is Juan's Love Palace, also known as the honeymoon suite. It's a colorful, *palapa*-topped, open-air room with hanging *tapetes* (woven palm mats) for additional privacy. The hotel is just 2 blocks from downtown and the marina. A lively restaurant next door can deliver pitchers of margaritas and dinner to your room.

20 de Noviembre and Leona Vicario. ☎/fax *624-143-0819.* www.caboinnhotel. com. *20 units. Street parking available. Rack rates: $58–$120 double. Weekly rates are available. No credit cards.*

San José del Cabo Accommodations

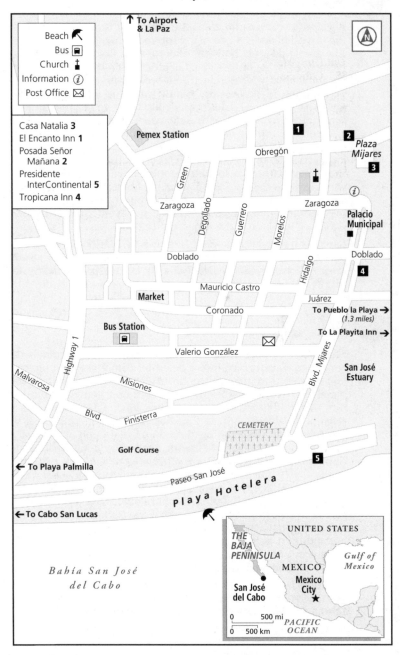

Beach ⌐
Bus ▣
Church ⚎
Information ⓘ
Post Office ✉

Casa Natalia **3**
El Encanto Inn **1**
Posada Señor
   Mañana **2**
Presidente
   InterContinental **5**
Tropicana Inn **4**

To Airport
& La Paz

Pemex Station

1

2 Plaza
   Mijares

Obregón

3

Green

Degollado

Guerrero

Morelos

Zaragoza

Zaragoza

ⓘ

Palacio
Municipal

Doblado

Hidalgo

Doblado

4

Mauricio Castro

Market

Coronado

Juárez

To Pueblo la Playa →
(1.3 miles)

Bus Station
▣

Valerio González

✉

To La Playita Inn →

Blvd. Mijares

San José
Estuary

Highway 1

Malvarosa

Misiones

Blvd. Finisterra

CEMETERY

Golf Course

← To Playa Palmilla

Paseo San José

Playa Hotelera

← To Cabo San Lucas

⌐

Bahía San José
del Cabo

UNITED STATES

THE
BAJA
PENINSULA

Gulf of
Mexico

MEXICO

San José
del Cabo

Mexico
City
★

0   500 mi
0   500 km

PACIFIC
OCEAN

Casa del Mar Golf Resort & Spa
$$$$$ **Corridor**

A little-known treasure, this intimate resort is one of the best values along the Corridor, and it's one of my top recommendations for honeymooners. The hacienda-style building offers guests luxury accommodations complemented by an on-site spa. Located within the Cabo Real development, it's conveniently located by the 18-hole championship Cabo Real, a Robert Trent Jones, Jr., golf course. Gentle waterfalls lead to the adults-only pool area with hot tub, and a flowered path takes you farther along to the wide, sandy stretch of beach with a clear surf break. The Casa del Mar even has a "quiet area" on the lawn for those looking for a siesta. Guest rooms have a clean, bright feel to them with white marble floors, light wicker furnishings, separate sitting areas, and large hot tubs, plus separate showers on the raised bathroom level. Balconies have oversized chairs and ocean views beyond the pool. It's a romantic hotel known for its welcoming, personalized service. In addition to golf, four lighted AstroTurf tennis courts, one paddle tennis court, the full-service Avanti Spa, and a small but well-equipped workout room round out the offerings.

Carretera Transpeninsular (Hwy. 1) Km 19.5. ☎ **888-227-9621** *in the U.S., or 624-144-0030 or 145-7700. Fax: 624-144-0034.* www.casadelmarmexico.com. *56 units. Rack rates: High season $470 double, $500 suite; low season $290 double, $340 suite. AE, MC, V.*

Casa Natalia
$$$$$ **San José**

This property may be Mexico's most exquisite boutique hotel, a former residence transformed into a beautiful combination of palms, waterfalls, and flowers that mirrors the beauty of the land. The inn itself is a completely renovated historic home, which now combines modern architecture with traditional Mexican touches. Each of the rooms has a name that reflects the décor such as Conchas (seashells), Azul (blue), or Talavera (ceramics); all have sliding glass doors that open onto small private terraces with hammocks and chairs, shaded by bougainvillea and bamboo. The two spa suites each have a private terrace with a hot tub and hammock. Thirty-nine tall California palms surround a small courtyard pool; the terraces face this view. The inn, however, is several miles from the nearest public beach, but does offer its guests a daily shuttle to a beach club along the corridor. In its favor, Casa Natalia offers its guests privacy, style, and romance, and it welcomes children 13 and older only. One of the highlights of being here is being so close to the exceptional gourmet restaurant, Mi Cocina (see Chapter 32). It's in the heart of the Bulevar Mijares action, just off of the central plaza.

Bulevar Mijares 4. ☎ **888-277-3814** *in the U.S., or 624-142-5100. Fax: 624-142-5110.* www.casanatalia.com. *20 units including 2 spa suites. Rack rates: High season $295 double, $475 spa suite; low season $220 double, $350 spa suite. AE, MC, V.*

Cabo San Lucas Accommodations

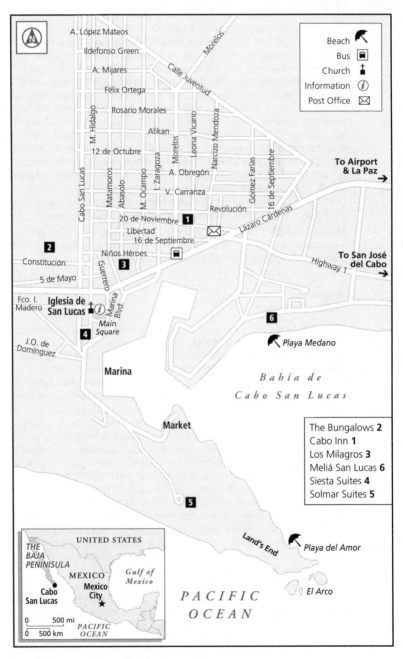

The Bungalows **2**
Cabo Inn **1**
Los Milagros **3**
Meliá San Lucas **6**
Siesta Suites **4**
Solmar Suites **5**

El Encanto Inn
$$–$$$ San José

Located on a quiet street in the historic downtown district, this charming, small inn borders a grassy courtyard with a fountain and small pool, offering a very relaxing alternative to busy beachfront hotels. Rooms are all attractively — and uniquely — decorated with rustic wood and contemporary iron furniture. The nice-sized bathrooms have colorful tile accents. Rooms have two double beds, and suites have king-size beds and an added sitting room. A pool area with *palapa* bar and 14 poolside suites were recently added. These new suites have minibars and other extras, while all rooms offer satellite TV. El Encanto's welcoming owners, Cliff and Blanca, can also help arrange fishing packages, as well as golf and diving outings. Blanca is a lifelong resident of San José, so she's a great resource for information and dining tips. This inn is best for couples or singles looking for a peaceful place from which to explore historic San José. Continental breakfast is included with room rates. It's located between Obregón and Comonfort, half a block from the church.

Morelos 133. ☎ *210-858-6649 in the U.S., or 624-142-0388. Fax: 624-142-4620.* www. elencantoinn.com. *26 units. Limited street parking available. Rack rates: $75 double, $99–$169 suites. Breakfast included. AE, MC, V.*

Esperanza
$$$$$ Corridor

Although this luxury resort along Cabo's over-the-top Corridor sits on a bluff overlooking two small, rocky coves, the absence of a real beach doesn't seem to matter much to its guests — the hotel more than makes up for it in terms of pampering services and stylish details. Created by the famed Auberge Resorts group, this hotel's architecture is dramatic, elegant, and comfortable. The casitas and villas are spread across 6.8 hectares (17 acres), designed to resemble a Mexican village, and are connected to the resort facilities by stone footpaths. The top-floor suites have handmade *palapa* ceilings and a private outdoor whirlpool spa. All rooms are exceptionally spacious, with woven wicker and tropical wood furnishings, original art, rugs and fabrics in muted colors with jeweled-tone color accents, and Frette linens gracing the extra-comfortable feather beds. Terraces are large, extending the living area to the outdoors, and all have hammocks and views of the Sea of Cortez. In-room amenities include fully stocked honor bars; plush bathrobes; high-speed Internet access; and entertainment centers with plasma televisions, stereos, and DVDs. The oversize bathrooms have a separate tub and shower with dual shower-heads. You can also enjoy an acclaimed oceanfront restaurant, fitness center, full-service spa, gourmet market, infinity swimming pool, and the private beach.

Carretera Transpeninsular (Hwy. 1) Km 7, at Punta Ballena. ☎ *866-311-2226 in the U.S., or 624-145-6400. Fax: 624-145-6403.* www.esperanzaresort.com. *50 suites and 6 villas. Valet parking. Rack rates: High season $575–$1,050 double, $4,000–$5,500 villas; low season $375–$775 double, $2,500–$3,500 villas. AE, MC, V.*

The Corridor Accommodations

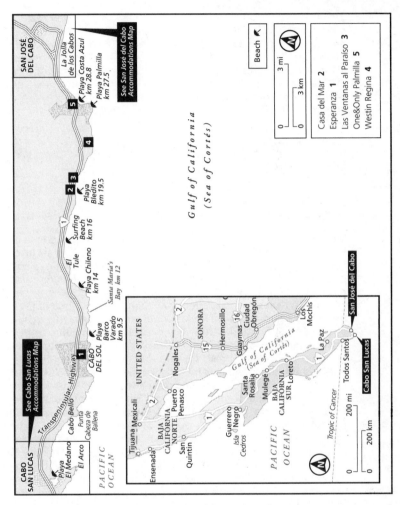

La Playita Inn
$ San José

Removed from even the slow pace of San José, this older yet impeccably clean and friendly courtyard hotel is ideal for fishermen and those looking for something removed from a traditional hotel vacation. It's the only hotel on San José's only beach that's safe for swimming. Steps from the water and the lineup of fishing *pangas* (small boats), the two stories of sunlit rooms frame a patio with a pool just large enough to allow you to swim laps. Each room is spacious, with high ceilings, high-quality if basic furnishings, screened windows, and nicely tiled bathrooms, plus cable TV. Two large suites on the second floor have small refrigerators. If you catch a big one, there's a fish freezer for storage. Services include coffee every morning and golf-cart shuttle to the beach. Next door, the hotel's La Playita Restaurant is open daily from 11 a.m. to 10 p.m. and serves a great mix of seafood and standard favorites, plus occasional live jazz or tropical music. To the north of La Playita, the new Puerto Las Cabos mega-development is under construction, which will be changing this stretch of beach in coming years. Rates include continental breakfast.

Pueblo la Playa s/n. (From Bulevar Mijares, follow the sign pointing to PUEBLO LA PLAYA, *taking a dirt road for about 3.2km/2 miles to the beach. The hotel is on the left, facing the water at the edge of the tiny village of Pueblo la Playa.)* ☎/fax **624-142-4166**. *26 units. Free parking. Rack rates: $60–$75 double. MC, V.*

Las Ventanas al Paraíso
$$$$$ Corridor

Mexico's most renowned luxury hotel, Las Ventanas consistently offers luxury accommodations and attention to detail. The architecture, with adobe structures and rough-hewn wood accents, provides a soothing complement to the desert landscape. The only burst of color comes from the dazzling *ventanas* (windows) of pebbled rainbow glass — handmade by regional artisans — that reflect the changing positions of the sun. Richly furnished, Mediterranean-style rooms are large (starting at 93 sq. m/1,000 sq. ft.) and appointed with every conceivable amenity, from wood-burning fireplaces to computerized telescopes for stargazing or whale-watching from your room. Fresh flowers and glasses of tequila welcome each guest, and room standards include satellite TVs with VCRs and DVD players, stereos with CD players, and dual-line phones. Larger suites offer pampering extras such as rooftop terraces, sunken hot tubs on a private patio, or personal pools. Note that Las Ventanas is also booking the surrounding Las Ventanas condominiums as part of its room inventory, so be certain to verify where you'll be placed, if this is not your preference. Although spacious and boasting a full kitchen, the condominiums lack the views of the resort rooms and suites. The Spa is among the best in Mexico — particularly notable is its Sea and Stars nighttime massage for two, a relaxing aromatherapy massage with two therapists that takes place on the rooftop terrace of your private suite. With a staff that outnumbers guests by four to one, this is the place for travelers who want (and can afford) to be seriously spoiled. The oceanview gourmet restaurant has an impressive wine cellar and an adjoining terrace bar with live classical music. A seaside casual-dining grill and a fresh-juice bar are also on the property. Guests enjoy access to the adjoining championship Cabo Real golf course. And Las Ventanas has its own sportfishing boats and luxury yachts for charter.

Carretera Transpeninsular (Hwy. 1) Km 19.5. ☎ **888-767-3966** *in the U.S., or 624-144-2800. Fax: 624-144-2801.* www.lasventanas.com. *61 suites. Complimentary valet parking. Rack rates: $800 double with partial ocean view, $975 double with full ocean view, $1,200 split-level suite with rooftop terrace. Special spa and golf packages available, as are inclusive meal plans and summer rates. AE, DC, MC, V.*

Los Milagros
$$ Cabo San Lucas

The elegant, white, two-level buildings that contain the 11 suites and rooms of Los Milagros (The Miracles) border either a grassy garden area or small pool. All rooms are different, but they're all decorated with contemporary iron beds with straw headboards, buff-colored tile floors, and artistic details — but no TVs. Some units have kitchenettes, and the master suite has a sunken tub. E-mail, fax, and telephone services are available only through the office, and morning coffee service takes place on the patio. In the evenings, candles light the garden, and classical music plays. Request a room in one of the back buildings because conversational noise is less intrusive. Los Milagros is located just 1½ blocks from the Giggling Marlin and Cabo Wabo nightclubs and a couple of miles from Cabo's main public beach.

Matamoros 116. ☎ *624-143-4566. Fax: 624-143-5004.* www.losmilagros.com.mx. *11 units. Limited street parking. Rack rates: $84 double; ask for summer discounts, group rates, and long-term discounts. No credit cards.*

Meliá San Lucas
$$$$ Cabo San Lucas

If you've come to Cabo to party, this is your place. The recently renovated Meliá San Lucas has been converted into Cabo's hot spot, with the upgrade of its rooms, and the addition of the hip Nikki Beach on its beachfront. It's location on Medano Beach is central to any other action you may want to seek out, but you'll find plenty right here. Rooms are awash in blues and white, with a sleek, contemporary décor. All suites have ocean views and private terraces looking across to the famed El Arco. Master suites have a separate living room area. Guests gather by the beachfront pool where the Nikki Beach trademark oversized day beds perfectly accommodate this lounge atmosphere. There are also VIP tepees, and the live DJ music keeps the party here going day and night. In addition to Nikki Beach, several dining options are at the hotel, including a Saturday night Mexican Fiesta.

Playa El Medano s/n. ☎ *624-145-7800. Fax: 624-143-0420.* www.meliasanlucas. solmelia.com. *150 units. Parking lot. Rack Rates: $181–$238 double, $394 junior suite, $441 master suite. AE, MC, V.*

One&Only Palmilla
$$$$$ Corridor

One of the most comfortably luxurious hotels in Mexico, the One&Only Palmilla is the grande dame of Los Cabos resorts, and its last renovation made it among the most spectacular resort hotels anywhere. Perched on a cliff top above the sea (with beach access), the resort is a series of white buildings with red-tile roofs, towering palms, and flowering bougainvillea. The feeling here remains one of classic resort-style comfort, but the new sophisticated details bring it up-to-date with the most modern of resorts. The décor features muted desert colors and luxury fabrics, with special extras such as flat-screen TVs, DVD/CD players, and Bose surround-sound systems. Bathrooms feature inlaid stone rain-showers and sculpted tubs. Ample, private balconies or terraces have extra-comfortable, overstuffed chairs, and each room also has a separate sitting area. Guests receive twice-daily maid service, a personal butler, and an aromatherapy menu — to ensure you leave completely relaxed or rejuvenated. Their signature restaurant — simply named C — is under the direction of the renowned Chicago Chef Charlie Trotter, and offers 24-hour in-room dining. A second, more casual dining choice is the *palapa*-topped Agua restaurant, with so-called Mexiterranean cuisine. The Palmilla has become renowned as a location for destination weddings and anniversary celebrations with a renewal of vows; ceremonies take place in its small, signature chapel that graces a sloped hillside. Across the highway, the resort's own championship golf course, designed by Jack Nicklaus, is available for guests, and the Palmilla also has two lighted tennis courts, a 186-sq.-m (2,000-sq.-ft.) state-of-the-art fitness center, and a yoga garden. Also among the new additions is an exceptional spa, with 13 private treatment villas for one or two people.

Carretera Transpeninsular (Hwy. 1) Km 27.5. ☎ **866-829-2977** *in the U.S., or 624-146-7000. Fax: 624-146-7001.* www.oneandonlypalmilla.com. *172 units. Rack rates: High season $550–$775 double, $850 and up for suites and villas; low season $375–$575 double, $650 and up for suites and villas. AE, MC, V.*

Posada Señor Mañana
$ **San José**

This comfortable two-story guesthouse, set in a grove of tropical fruit trees, offers basic rooms with tile floors and funky furniture and an abundance of hammocks strewn about the property. Younger travelers, surfers, and the backpack set are the mainstays here. Guests have cooking privileges in a large, fully equipped community kitchen set beside two *palapas.* Ask about discounts and weekly rates. It's next to the Casa de la Cultura, behind the main square in San José. A small swimming pool is on-site, but you're about 5km (3 miles) from the beach here.

Obregón 1. ☎ **624-142-0462.** *Fax: 624-142-1199.* www.srmanana.com. *8 units. Rack rates: $35–$67 double. MC, V.*

Presidente InterContinental
$$$$$ **San José**

The Presidente, set on a long stretch of beach next to the San José Estuary, is San José's most upscale all-inclusive property and an ideal choice for vacationers wanting to simply stay put on a lovely stretch of beach and have their every need attended to. Low-rise, Mediterranean-style buildings frame the beach and San José's largest swimming pool, which has a swim-up bar. If possible, select a ground-floor oceanfront room because the lower level offers spacious terraces as an alternative to a tiny balcony on upper-level units. The rooms have satellite TVs and large bathrooms; suites include a separate sitting area. The resort's all-inclusive nature makes it a good choice for families. In addition to the three restaurants and a garden cafe, theme-night buffet dinners take place a few nights per week. The roster of activities and facilities includes golf clinics, tennis, yoga, a small gym, bicycle rentals, and horseback riding. For a fee, the hotel also offers a twice-daily shuttle to Cabo San Lucas.

Bulevar Mijares s/n, at the very end of the road abutting the estuary. ☎ *800-327-0200 in the U.S., or 624-142-0211. Fax: 624-142-0232.* www.loscabos.interconti.com. *395 units. Rack rates: $316 double standard room, $364 double oceanfront room. Rates include all meals, beverages, and many sports. AE, DC, MC, V.*

Siesta Suites
$ Cabo San Lucas

Reservations are a must at this immaculate, small inn popular with return visitors to Cabo. (It's especially popular with fishermen.) The very basic rooms have white-tile floors and white walls, kitchenettes with seating areas, TVs, refrigerators, and sinks. The mattresses are firm, and the bathrooms are large and sparkling clean. Rooms on the fourth floor have two queen beds each. The accommodating proprietors offer free movies and VCRs, a barbecue pit and outdoor patio table on the second floor, and a comfortable lobby with TV. They can also arrange fishing trips. Weekly and monthly rates are available. The hotel is 1½ blocks from the marina, where parking is available.

Zapata at Hidalgo. ☎ *866-271-0952 from the U.S., or 624-143-2773.* www.cabosiesta suites.com. *20 suites (15 with kitchenette). Rack rates: $59–$69 double. Weekly and monthly rates are available. AE, MC, V.*

Solmar Suites
$$$$–$$$$$ Cabo San Lucas

Set against sandstone cliffs at the very tip of the Baja Peninsula, the Solmar is beloved by travelers seeking seclusion, comfort, and easy access to Cabo's diversions. The beach here is spectacular, though not for swimming. Suites are located in two-story, white-stucco buildings along the edge of the broad beachfront and have either a king bed or two double beds, satellite TVs, separate seating areas, and private balconies or patios on the sand. Guests gather by the pool and on the beach at sunset and all day long during the winter whale migration. With one of the best sportfishing fleets in Los Cabos, including the deluxe *Solmar V* that is used for long-range diving, fishing, and whale-watching expeditions, the Solmar is especially popular with fishing enthusiasts. Every Saturday, Solmar hosts a popular Mexican fiesta; advance reservations are necessary almost year-round. A small timeshare complex adjoins the Solmar; some units are available for nightly stays. Rates include the hotel's mandatory 10 percent service charge.

Av. Solmar 1, past the marina. ☎ **800-344-3349** *in the U.S., or 624-143-3535. Fax: 624-143-0410.* www.solmar.com. *194 units. Rack rates: $190–$330 double, $433 suite. AE, MC, V.*

Tropicana Inn
$$ **San José**

This small, colonial-style inn has been a long-standing favorite in San José and welcomes many repeat visitors. The Tropicana is considered "gringo central" in San José and caters to American tastes in a very traditional Mexican setting. Set just behind (and adjacent to) the Tropicana Bar and Grill (see review in Chapter 32), it frames a plant-filled courtyard with a graceful arcade bordering the rooms and inviting swimming pool. Each nicely furnished, medium-size room in the L-shaped building (which has both a two- and three-story wing) comes with tile floors, two double beds, a window looking out on the courtyard, a brightly tiled bathroom with shower, and a coffee pot. Each morning, the staff sets out freshly brewed coffee, delicious sweet rolls, and fresh fruit for hotel guests. You can order room service until 11 p.m. from the Tropicana Bar and Grill (owned by the hotel). The inn is a block south of the town square, and about 2.5km (1½ miles) from the nearest beach.

Bulevar Mijares 30. ☎ **624-142-0907** *or 142-1580. Fax: 624-142-1590.* www.tropicana cabo.com. *38 units. Free limited parking in back. Rack rates: High season $100 double; low season $89 double. AE, MC, V.*

Westin Resort and Spa Los Cabos
$$$$$ **Corridor**

Architecturally dramatic, the Westin Resort & Spa Los Cabos sits at the end of a long, paved road atop a seaside cliff. Vivid terra-cotta, yellow, and pink walls rise against a landscape of sandstone, cacti, and palms with fountains and gardens lining the long pathways from the lobby to the rooms. Electric carts carry guests and their luggage through the vast property. The rooms are gorgeous and feature air-conditioning and ceiling fans, private balconies, satellite TVs, and walk-in showers separate from the bathtubs. This property is probably the best choice among my selections for families vacationing along the Corridor because of the wealth of activities available for children (plus babysitting). With six restaurants and two bars, you may never need to leave the resort. For golfers, both the Palmilla and Cabo Real golf courses are nearby, and the Westin also has two tennis courts, seven pools, two children's pools, a beach club, and complete fitness center with spa and massage services.

Carretera Transpeninsular (Hwy. 1) Km 22.5. ☎ **800-228-3000** *in the U.S., or 624-142-9000. Fax: 624-142-9050.* www.westin.com. *243 units. Rack rates: $415 double with partial ocean view, $579 double with full ocean view. Rates drop 20 percent in low season. AE, DC, MC, V.*

Chapter 31

Settling into Los Cabos

by Lynne Bairstow

- -

In This Chapter

▶ Knowing what to expect when you arrive
▶ Getting the lowdown on the layout
▶ Discovering helpful information and resources

- -

*E*ven though Los Cabos may feel like an extension of Southern California in spirit, it's still a foreign country, so a few things are important to know and keep in mind. Still, if you're a first-time traveler to Mexico, you'll immediately feel comfortable — English appears to be more accepted than Spanish in terms of languages, and U.S. dollars are the widely accepted currency.

In this chapter, I take you from the plane, through the airport and to your hotel, helping you quickly get your bearings in this easy-to-navigate area. I continue with tips on everything from where to find Internet access to how to save a buck or two on transportation.

Arriving in Los Cabos by Air

Los Cabos International Airport is small and easy to navigate. It's located closest to San José del Cabo. From this town, continue down a long, well-paved stretch of highway known as the Corridor until you reach the proverbial "end of the line" — Cabo San Lucas and its rowdy charms. From the very beginning of your Cabo experience, everything should be smooth sailing — you can find both immigration and Customs to be brief, generally easy procedures.

Navigating passport control and Customs

When you arrive, you walk right from your plane straight into the immigration clearance area. Here, an officer asks you to show your passport (or other proof of citizenship) and your completed tourist card, the **FMT** (see Chapter 9 for all the FMT details).

Your FMT is an important document, so take good care of it. You're supposed to keep the FMT with you at all times because you may be required to show it if you run into any sort of trouble. You also need to turn it back in upon departure, or you may be unable to leave without replacing it.

Next up is the baggage claim area. Here, porters stand by to help with your bags, and they're well worth the price of the tip — about a dollar a bag. After you collect your luggage, you pass through another check-point. Something that looks like a traffic light awaits you here. You press a button, and if the light turns green, you're free to go. If it turns red, you need to open each of your bags for a quick search. It's Mexico's random search procedure for Customs. If you have an unusually large bag, or an excessive amount of luggage, you may be searched regardless of the traffic-light outcome.

Inside the baggage claim are the rental-car booths, geared for people who haven't reserved a car in advance. If you do have a reservation, agents can advise you where to go to pick up your car. After you're outside the baggage claim area and past the timeshare booths, you find an area with more rental-car information as well as taxi info and other transportation options. If you're part of a package tour that includes ground transportation to your hotel, this is where you look for your representative — generally carrying a sign with your name or the name of your tour company on it.

After you collect your bags, you may notice a corral-like area that you pass through, decorated with stunning photos of Los Cabos, and populated by lots of people waving you over. You may think this is a perfect place for tourism information, what with such exceptionally friendly locals; but you'd be wrong. These are timeshare salespeople — hot to offer you a deal on a rental car, transportation to your hotel, or some other ploy in exchange for a generally aggressive sales pitch. Trust me — settle into the area first and then decide if a timeshare presentation is something you want to include in your vacation agenda.

Getting to your hotel

The one airport that serves both Cabos and the connecting Corridor is 12km (7½ miles) northwest of San José del Cabo and 35km (22 miles) northeast of Cabo San Lucas. Public transportation here is minimal — but improving — and taxis are expensive. This is one Mexican beach resort where I find having a rental car for even part of your stay is not only practical but also economical if you plan on exploring the area even a little bit. The main road connecting the two Cabos is a modern, well-paved stretch of road, and driving here is easy — getting lost is hard, and parking, though a challenge in the heart of the two towns, isn't impossible.

Renting a car

Advance reservations aren't always necessary, and don't be afraid of requesting a better price than the first one a representative quotes — bargaining sometimes works. You can, however, generally get a much better rate by booking your car in advance through a company's U.S. toll-free number or Web site. Before signing your name, be sure you understand the total price after insurance and taxes are added. Rates can run between $40 and $75 per day with insurance costing an extra $15 per day.

National Car Rental is my favorite here; its "all inclusive" rate includes the insurance and taxes. I find this to be much clearer and preferable to trying to figure out the various options that other companies offer — that is, you don't have any surprises. The major car-rental agencies all have counters open at the airport during hours of flight arrivals. Major car-rental services include:

- ✔ **Avis** (☎ **800-331-1212** in the U.S., or 624-146-0201; www.avis.com; Open: 7 a.m.–9 p.m.)
- ✔ **Budget** (☎ **800-527-0700** in the U.S., or 624-143-4190; www.budget.com; Open: 8 a.m.–7 p.m.)
- ✔ **Hertz** (☎ **800-654-3131** in the U.S., or 624-146-1803 or 146-1821; www.hertz.com; Open: 7 a.m.–9 p.m.)
- ✔ **National** (☎ **800-328-4567** in the U.S., or 624-142-2424; www.nationalcar.com; Open: 7 a.m.–8 p.m.)

Of the local car-rental agencies, I find the most economical to be **Advantage Rent-A-Car** (Lázaro Cárdenas, between Leona Vicario and Morelos, downtown Cabo San Lucas; ☎ **800-777-5500** in the U.S., or 624-143-0909; Fax: 624-143-1060; www.arac.com). Volkswagen sedan convertibles rent for $58 per day, and weekly rates include one free day. The collision damage waiver adds $14 per day to the rental price. If you pick up the car downtown, you can return it to the airport at no extra charge.

If you decide to rent a car, picking it up at the airport may be a good idea because doing so saves you the airport-to-hotel transportation expense. You don't have to drive to the airport to return it either — most of the car companies have pick-up service at your hotel or local offices within both towns. On the other hand, if you prefer to settle in first, plan your car rental for the last part of your vacation. The agency can deliver the car to your hotel, and then you can return it to the airport prior to departing (but allow as much as an extra 30 min. for checking it in).

Hiring transportation

If you do opt to let someone else do the driving, buy a ticket inside the airport for a *colectivo* (shared minivan) or a taxi. *Colectivo* fares run about $12 to San José, about $15 to hotels along the Corridor, and $20 to Cabo for up to eight passengers, and they're only available from the airport. A private taxi can be shared by up to four people and costs about $25 to San José and about $85 to Cabo San Lucas.

If you prefer private transportation, but don't want to pay the high rates of a taxi, book through **Gray Line** (☎ **624-146-9410;** Fax: 624-146-9412; www.graylineloscabos.com), a company offering full tour services in Los Cabos. Rates from the airport to hotels range from $27 to $35 per person for shared rides, and include a bilingual driver who meets you with a sign bearing your name, luggage assistance, and bottled water. Private transportation ranges from $65 to $116, and includes all the previously mentioned items, plus extras such as a welcome kit of information. You can book in advance and prepay online (Visa and MasterCard are accepted).

Getting Around Los Cabos

You exit the airport onto Highway 1, also known as Carretera Transpeninsular. The first main town you come to is San José del Cabo. The highway continues west to the shore and then curves and heads south for about the next 32km (20 miles), where you reach Cabo San Lucas. In the center of Cabo, Highway 1 turns into Lázaro Cárdenas.

If you're staying in San José del Cabo, turn off Highway 1 on Zaragoza, the main street leading from the highway into town; Paseo San José runs parallel to the beach and is the principal boulevard of this hotel zone. The mile-long boulevard is the main street in San José with restaurants, shops, banks, and other services. San José has two principal zones: downtown, where sophisticated inns as well as traditional budget hotels are located, and the hotel zone along the beach. Note that no local bus service runs between downtown San José and the beach; a taxi is the only means of getting between the two places.

The road that connects San José del Cabo to Cabo San Lucas is the centerpiece of resort growth. Known as the Corridor, this stretch of four well-paved lanes offers cliff-top vistas but still has no nighttime lighting. You find the area's most deluxe resorts and renowned golf here, along with a collection of dramatic beaches and coves.

 A toll-road expressway was recently added to bypass the traffic around San José, connecting the Corridor directly to the airport. The toll is $2.50 along this stunning — and mostly empty — stretch of road, and can be a faster way to reach the airport, or get to your destination, if you're in a hurry.

The small town of Cabo San Lucas, edged by foothills and desert mountains to the west and south, grew up around the harbor of Cabo San Lucas Bay and spreads out to the north and west. The main street leading into town from the airport and San José del Cabo is Lázaro Cárdenas.

As Cárdenas nears the harbor, Marina Boulevard branches off from it and becomes the main artery that curves around the waterfront. Lázaro Cárdenas, the main street into town from Highway 1, splits off to the right and then loops back around a shady plaza, turning into Marina Boulevard, which runs along the waterfront. Most of the shops, restaurants, and nightlife in Cabo are all located within this loop.

Touring around town

Many of the Corridor hotels offer some sort of shuttle service into the two towns, usually for a $15 charge, but the hotels have to disguise it as a "tour" due to the strength of the taxi union.

Taking a taxi

Finding taxis may be easy, but comparing them to the high cost of everything else, they're expensive within Cabo. Expect to pay about $25 for a taxi between Cabo and the Corridor hotels, and about $35 if you're going all the way to San José.

 Whenever you take a taxi, establish the price before setting out, because different taxis seem to have different charges. Your hotel should have the rates to various places posted in the lobby, enabling you to easily find out the average rates to and from different areas.

Considering a car rental

Because more than 32km (20 miles) separate the two Cabos — with numerous attractions in between — consider renting a car, even if it's only for a day. Transportation by taxi is expensive here, and if you're at all interested in exploring, a rental car is your most economical option. Each of the two towns has its own distinctive character and attractions, so make the most of this two-for-one resort.

See "Renting a car," earlier in this chapter, for car-rental information.

Fast Facts: Los Cabos

American Express

The representative for the area is located in San José, at Plaza La Misión, Local 1-b, Bulevar Mijares/Paseo Finisterra (☎ 624-142-1336 or 624-1343).

Area Code

The local telephone prefix is **624**. Calls between Cabo San Lucas, San José del Cabo, and northern Corridor hotels are toll calls, so you must use the area code.

Baby Sitters

Most of the larger hotels can easily arrange for baby sitters, but many sitters speak limited English. Rates range from $4 to $10 per hour.

Banks, ATMs, and Currency Exchange

Banks exchange currency during normal business hours, generally Monday through Friday from 9 a.m. to 6 p.m. and Saturday from 10 a.m. to 2 p.m. Currency-exchange booths, found all along Cabo's main tourist areas, aren't as competitive, but they're more convenient. ATMs are widely available, and even more convenient, and they dispense pesos — and in some cases dollars — at bank-exchange rates.

Beach Safety

Before swimming in the open water here, check whether the conditions are safe. Undertows and large waves are common. In Cabo, Playa Medano (close to the marina and town) is the principal beach that's safe for swimming. It has several lively beachfront restaurant-bars. It's also easy to find watersports equipment for rent here. The Hotel Meliá San Lucas, on Playa Medano, has a roped-off swimming area to protect swimmers from Jet Skis and boats. *Note:* Colored flags signaling the safety of swimming conditions aren't generally used in Cabo, and neither are lifeguards.

Business Hours

Most offices maintain traditional Mexican hours of operation (10 a.m.–2 p.m. and 4–8 p.m. daily), but shops remain open throughout the day. Offices tend to be closed on Saturday and Sunday, but shops are open on Saturday, at least, and increasingly offer limited hours of operation on Sunday.

Climate

It's warm all year; however, evenings and early mornings in the winter months can turn quite cool. Summers can be very hot, but tropical rainstorms may cool the afternoons.

Emergencies

You can try **060**, but generally, no one answers. The local city-hall number is ☎ **624-142-0361**.

Hospitals

In Cabo, Baja Medico (Camino de la Plaza s/n, on the corner with Pedegral; ☎ **624-143-0127** or 143-0175) has a 24-hour walk-in clinic. Most of the larger hotels have a doctor on-call.

Information

In San José, the city tourist information office (☎ **624-142-3310** or 142-0465) is in the old post-office building on Zaragoza at Mijares. It offers maps, free local publications, and other basic information about the area. It's open Monday through Friday from 8 a.m. to 2 p.m.

The Secretary of Tourism functions as the information office in Cabo. It's on Madero between Hidalgo and Guerrero (☎ **624-146-9628** or 142-0446).

Prior to arrival, contact the Los Cabos Tourism Board at ☎ **866-567-2226**, toll-free from the U.S.

Note: The many visitor-information booths along the street are actually timeshare sales booths, and their staffs aim to pitch a visit to their resort in exchange for discounted tours, rental cars, or other giveaways.

Internet Access

In San José, Trazzo Internet, on the corner of Zaragoza and Morelos (☎ **624-142-0303**), 1 block from the central plaza, is open Monday to Friday from 8 a.m. to 9 p.m. and Saturday from 9 a.m. to 7 p.m. and charges $2.50 for 30 minutes or less for high-speed access.

Access in Cabo San Lucas is available at Onda Net Café & Bar (Lázaro Cárdenas 7, Edificio Posada, across from the Pemex gas station; ☎ **624-143-5390**). Access costs $5 for 15 minutes, $7 for 30 minutes, or $8 for an hour. It's open 8 a.m. to 6 p.m. Monday to Saturday.

Maps

One of the best around is the free American Express map, usually found at the tourist information offices and the hotel concierge desks.

Newspapers and Magazines

Most hotels and shops distribute the English-language _Los Cabos Guide, Los Cabos News, Cabo Life, Baja Sun,_ and the irreverent and extremely entertaining _Gringo Gazette_ (www.gringogazette. com). These publications have up-to-date information on new restaurants and clubs.

Books, Books, in Cabo San Lucas (☎ 624-143-3172 or -3173), sells a good selection of English- and Spanish-language reading material, with a specialty of regional guides and publications. It's located on Bulevar Marina, Plaza de la Danza, Local 7, next to Tanga Tanga, and is open daily from 9 a.m. to 10 p.m. A second location is in San José at Bulevar Mijares 41 near the Tropicana Inn (☎ 624-142-4433), open daily 9 a.m. to 9 p.m.

English-language books and magazines are also generally available for sale in hotel gift shops.

Pharmacy

In San José, Farmacia ISSTE (Carretera Transpeninsular Km 34, Plaza California; ☎ 624-142-2645) is the major pharmacy in the area. It's open from 8 a.m. to 8 p.m.

A long-standing drugstore in Cabo San Lucas, with a wide selection of toiletries as well as medicines, is Farmacia Aramburo (Lázaro Cárdenas at Zaragoza, Plaza Aramburo; ☎ 624-143-1489). It's open daily from 7 a.m. to 9 p.m.

Police

In San José, call ☎ 624-142-0361; in Cabo San Lucas, the number is ☎ 624-143-3977.

Post Office (_Correo_)

In San José, the _correo_ on Bulevar Mijares 1924 at Valerio González (☎ 624-142-0911) is open Monday through Friday 8 a.m. to 6 p.m. and Saturday 9 a.m. to noon.

The _correo_ (☎ 624-143-0048) in Cabo San Lucas is at Lázaro Cárdenas and Francisco Villa on the highway to San José del Cabo, east of the El Squid Roe bar. It's open Monday through Friday 8 a.m. to 6 p.m. and Saturday from 9 a.m. to noon.

Special Events

The feast of the patron saint of San José del Cabo is celebrated on March 19 with a fair, music, dancing, feasts, horse races, and cockfights. October 12 is the festival of the patron saint of Todos Santos, a town about 105km (65 miles) north. October 18 is the feast of the patron saint of Cabo San Lucas, celebrated with a fair, feasts, music, dancing, and other special events.

Taxes

There's a 15 percent value-added tax (IVA) on goods and services, and it's generally included in the posted price.

Taxis

Taxis are plentiful but relatively expensive. Trips between the two towns average $35; trips between hotels along the Corridor average $20. Rides within San José cost around $5, but rides within Cabo cost between $8 and $12.

Telephone

Avoid the phone booths that have signs in English advising you to call home using a special 800 number — these are absolute rip-offs and can cost as much as $20 per minute. The least expensive way to call is by using a Telmex (LADATEL) prepaid phone card, available at most pharmacies and mini-supers, using the official Telmex (Lada) public phones. In Mexico you need to dial 001 prior to a number to reach the United States, and you need to preface long distance calls within Mexico by dialing 01.

Time Zone

Los Cabos operates on mountain standard time, but Mexico's observance of daylight saving time varies somewhat from that in the United States.

Chapter 32

Dining in Los Cabos

by Lynne Bairstow

● ●

In This Chapter

▶ Discovering the best of Los Cabos
▶ Dining with the locals

● ●

*P*aying a lot for mediocre food isn't uncommon in Los Cabos, so try to get a couple of unbiased recommendations before settling in for a meal. If people are only drinking and not dining, take that as a clue because many seemingly popular places are long on party atmosphere but short on food quality. Prices decrease the farther you walk inland from the waterfront.

With several exceptional choices and culinary offerings more representative of Mexico, San José is becoming known as the preferred dining town. Prices also tend to be more reasonable. If you're staying along the Corridor, remember to figure in transportation costs when calculating the price of your meal — you may just decide to dine at your hotel, which is likely to have a top-notch chef anyway. Cabo has the most restaurant offerings, but sad to say, few are truly spectacular.

Cabo is a very casual town, and shorts and jeans are accepted everywhere except the most upscale resort restaurants, but dressier resort wear is still acceptable, too. Despite the relaxed atmosphere, prices here are generally higher than you find in comparable restaurants in the United States or other parts of Mexico. This situation is due to the necessity of importing many ingredients from the mainland. Cabo has also imported some customs of "upper" California — it's becoming more common to have segregated nonsmoking areas in restaurants here due to the demand by visitors.

Besides the restaurants mentioned in this chapter, dozens of good, clean taco stands and taco restaurants dot the downtown area. To find additional good restaurants, explore Hidalgo and Cárdenas and the Marina at the Plaza Bonita. North-of-the-border tastes have heavily influenced Cabo's dining scene. The usual suspects (U.S. franchise chains such as KFC, Subway, Pizza Hut, and a host of others) are everywhere downtown. Note that many restaurants here automatically add the tip to the bill.

When it comes to welcoming young ones at restaurants, Los Cabos is more like the United States than Mexico — less than enthusiastic, except at the more traditional establishments and casual hotel restaurants. If your children are particular to American tastes, you can go with the standards such as McDonald's, Burger King, and Hard Rock Cafe — all good choices. But you may also want to try the Mexican alternatives of Carlos O'Brian's or Squid Roe, which seem to be fun at any age — and if you dine early, the atmosphere is less raucous.

The Best Restaurants in Los Cabos

I arrange the following restaurants alphabetically, noting their location and general price category. Remember that tips generally run about 15 percent, and most wait-staff really depend on these for their income, so be generous if the service warrants. Please refer to the Introduction of this book for an explanation of the price categories.

Please see the menu glossary in Appendix C for more information on Mexican cuisine.

Baan Thai
$$ San José PAN-ASIAN

Pan-Asian cuisine seems to be in the spotlight worldwide these days, and Baan Thai does an impressive job of combining Thai flavors with a hint of those of Mexico in this exceptional restaurant, under the direction of Chef/owner Carl Marts. Move beyond traditional starters like spring rolls or satay to one of Baan Thai's more unique offerings, such as blue crab stir-fried with chile, garlic, and tomatoes, or mild chilies stuffed with smoked marlin and served with a soy-ginger dipping sauce. From there, move on to entrees such as wok tossed Chilean salmon, with chiles and basil; steamed Baja mussels in a coconut herb broth; or seared steak tossed with mangoes, green apples, and chiles. An impressive wine list and full bar service are available to complement your meal. For more than a decade prior to opening Baan Thai, Chef Marts presided over the kitchen at the Corridor's Twin Dolphin resort. Air-conditioned indoor dining, as well as outdoor dining, in an exotic garden patio, is available.

Morelos s/n, 1 block behind the church and plaza. ☎ *624-142-3344.* www.baja baanthai.com. *Main courses: $8–$21. MC, V. Open: Mon–Sat noon–10:30 p.m.*

C
$$$$ Corridor GOURMET

Under the direction of renowned Chicago chef Charlie Trotter (this is his first restaurant outside the U.S.), a table for dinner at C is the most coveted reservation in Cabo. Baja's influence on Trotter's culinary innovation is obvious in the menu selections, which change daily, but emphasize seafood and indigenous ingredients, although selections of meat and game are also available. To experience the restaurant's best, order the signature

Cabo San Lucas Dining

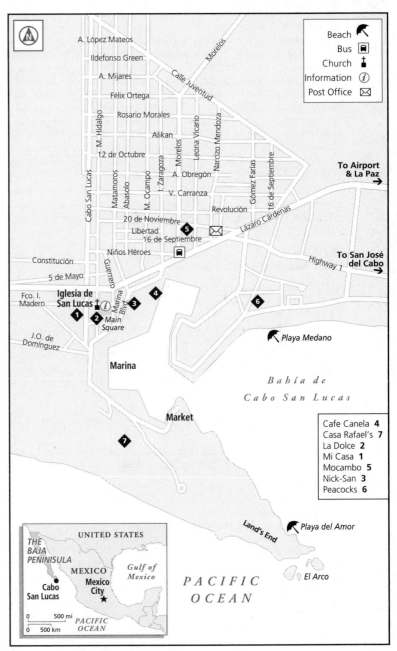

Beach 🏄
Bus 🚌
Church ✝
Information ⓘ
Post Office ✉

To Airport & La Paz →

To San José del Cabo →

Bahía de Cabo San Lucas

Playa Medano

Marina

Market

Cafe Canela	**4**
Casa Rafael's	**7**
La Dolce	**2**
Mi Casa	**1**
Mocambo	**5**
Nick-San	**3**
Peacocks	**6**

Land's End

Playa del Amor

El Arco

UNITED STATES

THE BAJA PENINSULA

MEXICO

Gulf of Mexico

Cabo San Lucas

Mexico City ★

PACIFIC OCEAN

0   500 mi
0   500 km

PACIFIC OCEAN

Damiana
$$$ **San José** **SEAFOOD/MEXICAN**

For one of the area's finest Mexican meals, this casually elegant restaurant in an 18th-century hacienda is a great bet. The 150-year-old colonial home is decorated in the colors of a Mexican sunset: walls painted a deep orange, and tables and chairs clad in bright rose, lavender, and orange cloth. Mariachis play nightly from 8 to 9 p.m. (mid-Dec through Mar) in the tropical courtyard where candles flicker under the trees and flowering vines. For an appetizer, try the mushrooms diablo — a moderately zesty dish of mushrooms with garlic and guajillo chiles. For a main course, the ranchero shrimp in cactus sauce or grilled lobster tail are flavorful choices. You can also enjoy brunch almost until the dinner hour. The interior dining room is nice, but the courtyard is the most romantic dining spot in San José. It's located on the east side of the town plaza.

San José town plaza. ☎ *624-142-0499 or 142-2899. Reservations recommended during Christmas and Easter holidays. Main courses: $30–$42; lunch $7.50–$20. AE, MC, V. Open: Daily 11 a.m.–10:30 p.m.*

El Chilar
$–$$ **San José** **MEXICAN**

In this rustically casual restaurant, you may feel like you're dining at a friend's home, as welcoming as chef Armando Montano is. His passion for Mexican cuisine is evident, as he blends the traditional flavors of this country — including an array of chiles — into imaginative and heavenly offerings. Among the most popular dinner options are shrimp in a roasted garlic and guajillo chile sauce, or the creative grilled tortilla and salmon Napoleon accompanied by a mango *pico de gallo* (lime juice with a salty chile powder). These choices may not be offered when you arrive, however, as chef Armando is known to frequently change his menu. At night, candlelight adds a sparkle of romance to the setting. El Chilar also offers a full bar and an ample selection of wines, with suggestions for pairings with your meal. Air-conditioned indoor dining is available.

Benito Juárez 1490, corner with Morelos, near the Telmex tower. ☎ *624-142-2544 or 146-9798. Reservations suggested. Main courses: $5–$29. No credit cards. Open: Mon–Sat 3–10 p.m.*

French Riviera
$–$$ **San José** **FRENCH/PASTRIES/COFFEE**

What a great place to start the day — or end it! This casual restaurant, located in a classic historic building in San José, not only serves tempting French fare but also absolutely irresistible sweets! Its on-site bakery, with an exhibition window for watching the pastry chefs at work, results in smells so delectable I dare you to leave without a sweet something. Start the day with a croissant and cappuccino, or any number of coffee and pastry choices, or end it with a full meal of delicious French fare. A second

The Corridor Dining

Beach ◂

Pitahayas **1**
The Restaurant **2**
Zipper's **3**

SAN JOSÉ DEL CABO

La Jolla de los Cabos

Playa Costa Azul km 28.8
Playa Palmilla km 27.5

See San José del Cabo Dining Map

Gulf of California (Sea of Cortés)

Playa Bledito km 19.5

Surfing Beach km 16

El Tule
Playa Chileno km 14

Sansa María's Bay km 12

Playa Barco Varado km 9.5

CABO DEL SOL

See Cabo San Lucas Dining Map

Transpeninsular Highway

Cabo Bello

Punta Cabeza de Ballena

El Arco

El Medano

Playa El Medano

CABO SAN LUCAS

PACIFIC OCEAN

UNITED STATES

SONORA

Hermosillo

Guaymas

Ciudad Obregón

Los Mochis

Nogales

BAJA CALIFORNIA NORTE

Puerto Penasco

San Quintin

Tijuana Mexicali

Ensenada

Isla Negro Cedros

Guerrero

Santa Rosalia

Mulegé

Loreto

BAJA CALIFORNIA SUR

La Paz

Todos Santos

San Jose del Cabo

Cabo San Lucas

Gulf of California (Sea of Cortés)

Tropic of Cancer

PACIFIC OCEAN

location in Cabo San Lucas (☎ **624-104-3125**) offers a traditional restaurant setting and menu, with a great selection of wines, and a lovely view overlooking Los Arcos in the distance. You can find it in Plaza del Rey, next to the Misiones del Cabo entrance on the highway Km 6; it's open from noon until 11 p.m.

Corner of Hidalgo and Manuel Doblado s/n. ☎ *624-142-3350.* www.french rivieraloscabos.com. *Breakfast: $4–$12; dinner: $7–$23. MC, V. Open: Daily 7:30 a.m.–11 p.m.*

La Dolce
$–$$ Cabo San Lucas   ITALIAN

This Cabo restaurant, with authentic Italian thin-crust, brick-oven pizzas and other specialties, is the offspring of Puerto Vallarta's La Dolce Vita. The food is some of the best in the Baja Peninsula, and the fact that 80 percent of La Dolce's business is from local customers underscores the point. It's known for its reasonable prices and attentive and welcoming service. The simple menu also features sumptuous pastas and calzones, beef or fish carpaccio, plus great salads. Due to its popularity, a second location (☎ 624-142-6621) has opened in one of San José's historical buildings, right on the main Plaza Jardin Mijares. With a true bistro atmosphere, this La Dolce is open Tuesday through Sunday, from 2 p.m. to 11 p.m.

Corner of M. Hidalgo and Zapata. ☎ *624-143-4122. Reservations not accepted. Main courses: $8–$19. MC, V. Open: Mon–Sat 6 p.m.–midnight. Closed Sept.*

Mi Casa
$$ Cabo San Lucas   MEXICAN/NOUVELLE MEXICAN

The building's vivid, cobalt-blue facade is your first clue that this place celebrates Mexico; the menu confirms that impression. Mi Casa is one of Cabo's most renowned gourmet Mexican restaurants, although it's equally noted for its inconsistency. Traditional specialties, such as *manchamanteles* (literally interpreted as "tablecloth stainers," it's a stew of meat and vegetables), *cochinita pibil* (a local pork dish), and *chiles en nogada* (chile peppers stuffed with a mixture of meat, nuts, and fruit) are everyday menu staples. Fresh fish is prepared with delicious seasonings from recipes found throughout Mexico. Especially pleasant at night, the restaurant's tables, scattered around a large patio, are set with colorful cloths, traditional pottery, and glassware. It's across from the main plaza.

Calle Cabo San Lucas at Madero. ☎ *624-143-1933. Reservations recommended. Main courses: $4–$25. MC, V. Open: Mon–Sat noon–3 p.m. and 5:30–10:30 p.m.*

Mi Cocina
$$ San José   NOUVELLE MEXICAN/EURO CUISINE

Without a doubt, Mi Cocina is currently the best dining choice in the entire Los Cabos area. From the setting to the service, a dinner here is sure to be unforgettable. The plant-filled courtyard, with its towering palms, dramatic lighting, and art-filled exposed brick walls, accommodates alfresco dining on several different levels. But it's not just the romantic setting that makes this restaurant special — the food is creative and consistently superb. Notable starters include steamed baby clams topped with a light creamy cilantro sauce and served with garlic croutons, or a healthy slice of Camembert cheese, fried and served with homemade toast and grapes. Among the favorite main courses are the baked baby rack of lamb served with grilled vegetables, and the Provençal-style shrimp served with risotto, roasted tomato, basil, and cilantro-fish consommé. Save room for dessert; choices include the famous chocolate-chocolate cake and a perfect crème brûlée. The full-service *palapa* bar offers an excellent selection of wines, premium tequilas, and single-malt scotches. Be adventurous and try one of the special martinis, such as the Flor de Mexico, an adaptation of the Cosmo, using hibiscus flower infusion rather than cranberry juice.

Bulevar Mijares 4, inside Casa Natalia. ☎ *624-142-5100. Reservations recommended. Main courses: $15–$30. AE, MC, V. Open: Daily 7 a.m.–4 p.m. to hotel guests only and 6:30–10:30 p.m. to the public.*

Mocambo
$–$$ Cabo San Lucas   SEAFOOD

The location of this long-standing Cabo favorite isn't very inspirational — it's basically a large cement building — but somebody obviously likes the food. The place is always packed, generally with local diners tired of high prices and small portions. Ocean-fresh seafood is the order of the day here, and the specialty platter can easily satisfy the healthy appetites of four people. The restaurant is 1½ blocks inland from Lázaro Cárdenas.

Leona Vicario and 20 de Noviembre. ☎ *624-143-6070. Reservations not accepted. Main courses: $5–$30. MC, V. Open: Daily 11 a.m.–11 p.m.*

Nick-San
$–$$$ Cabo San Lucas   JAPANESE/SUSHI

Exceptional Japanese cuisine and sushi are the specialties in this air-conditioned restaurant with a clean, minimalist décor. A rosewood sushi bar with royal blue-tiled accents invites diners to watch the master sushi chef at work. An exhibition kitchen behind the sushi chef demonstrates why this place has been honored with a special award for cleanliness. It's a personal favorite of mine — as well as of many local residents.

Bulevar Marina, Plaza de la Danza. ☎ *624-143-4484. Reservations recommended. Main courses: $9–$30; sushi $3.50 and up. MC, V. Open: Tues–Sun 11:30 a.m.– 10:30 p.m.*

Peacocks
$$–$$$ Cabo San Lucas   INTERNATIONAL

One of Cabo's most exclusive patio-dining establishments, Peacocks emphasizes creatively prepared fresh seafood. Start off with the house pâté or a salad of feta cheese with cucumber, tomato, and onion. For the main course, try one of the pastas — linguini with grilled chicken and sun-dried tomatoes is one of my favorites. Heartier entrees include steaks, shrimp, and lamb, all prepared several ways.

Paseo del Pescador s/n, corner of Meliá Hotel. ☎ *624-143-1858. Reservations recommended. Main courses: $15–$35. AE, MC, V. Open: Daily 6–10:30 p.m.*

The Restaurant (Las Ventanas al Paraíso)
$$$–$$$$ Corridor INTERNATIONAL

It may just be called "The Restaurant," but that's where simplicity ends and the extraordinary begins. Where Los Cabos is known for its pricey dining, this is one restaurant that is worth the price. Start off with a cocktail before dinner in The Lounge, the casually elegant bar area bordering Las Ventanas' stunning pool, lit from above with a constellation of tin stars illuminated by candles. When you move into the dining area, you get a sense of the Las Ventanas signature service — such as, if you're wearing black, your server gives you a black napkin. As remarkable as the service is, the dining itself is even better. First courses may include Ensenada steamed mussels served in coconut milk with a hint of chile arbol and a dash of tequila, or a stone crab salad with baby watercress, mango, phyllo, and sweet mustard sauce. The constantly changing menu of main courses generally includes an ample selection of seafood, including lobster, done in creative presentations, but the grilled rack of lamb with garlic potatoes is as good as anywhere. Especially recommendable are the chef's gourmet variations on traditional Mexican cuisine — such as the suckling pig enchilada in chile ancho sauce, a grilled New York steak in a tequila-infused red wine sauce served with spicy cactus paddle *(nopal),* or the chocolate tamale with *guanábana* sorbet, for an intriguing finish. A stellar selection of premium wines is served, and dress is resort attire. You have your choice of alfresco dining on the patio, or in indoor, air-conditioned comfort. Reserve at least a day prior, because dinner at The Restaurant is quite popular in Cabo at any time during the year.

Las Ventanas al Paraíso, Hwy. 1 Km 19.5. ☎ *624-144-2800.* www.lasventanas. com. *Reservations required. Main courses: $38–$60. AE, MC, V. Open: Daily 5–11 p.m.*

Tequila
$–$$$$ San José MEXICAN/ASIAN

The contemporary Mexican cuisine with a light and flavorful touch is the star attraction here, although the garden setting, with rustic leather and twine furniture and lanterns scattered among palms and giant mango trees, is also lovely. Start with a heavenly version of the traditional *chiles en nogada* stuffed with couscous, raisins, and papaya and seasoned with cinnamon. Grilled tuna with cilantro ginger sauce arrives perfectly seared; the whole-grain bread is fresh and hot. Seriously consider trying one of the specialties: shrimp in tequila sauce or the ribs in tamarind sauce. Attentive service complements the fine meal. An added touch: Cuban cigars and an excellent selection of tequilas are available, as is an extensive wine list emphasizing California vintages.

M. Doblado s/n, near Hidalgo. ☎ *624-142-1155 or 142-3742.* www.tequila restaurant.com. *Reservations recommended. Main courses: $10–$45. AE. Open: Daily 5:30–10:30 p.m.*

Tropicana Bar and Grill
$–$$ San José   SEAFOOD/MEAT

The Tropicana remains a popular mainstay, especially for tourists. The recently remodeled restaurant and bar retains its steady clientele day and night, as well as its offerings of live music and special sporting events on satellite TV. The main dining area is in a garden (candlelit in the evening) with a tiled mural at one end. A new interior area, done in a rustic-chic décor, adds about 100 new seats to the restaurant. Cafe-style sidewalk dining is also available. The menu is too extensive to lay claim to any specialty; it aims to please everyone. All meats and cheeses are imported, and dinners include thick steaks and shrimp fajitas. Paella is the Sunday special. The restaurant is a block south of the Plaza Mijares.

Bulevar Mijares 30. ☎ *624-142-1580. Reservations recommended. Main courses: $10–$25; breakfast: $4–$6. AE, MC, V. Open: Daily 8 a.m.–midnight.*

Zipper's
$–$$ Corridor   BURGERS/MEXICAN/SEAFOOD

Enjoy a hearty, American-style lunch served seaside at this popular, casual hangout. Sitting at the far south end of the beach heading toward Cabo San Lucas and fronting the best surfing waters, Zipper's has become popular with gringos in search of American food and TV sports. Burgers have that back-home flavor — you can even order one with a side of spicy curly fries. Steaks, lobster, beer-batter shrimp, deli sandwiches, and Mexican combination plates round out the menu, which is printed with prices in U.S. dollars.

Playa Costa Azul, just south of San José. No phone. Main courses: $7–$18; burgers and sandwiches: $7–$10. No credit cards. Open: Daily 8a.m.–10 p.m.

Chapter 33

Having Fun on and off the Beach in Los Cabos

by Lynne Bairstow

. . . .

In This Chapter

▶ Checking out the beach scene
▶ Landing the big one and shooting a low score
▶ Venturing into the wild — and shopping, too
▶ Visiting La Paz and Todos Santos
▶ Saddling up to the bar

. . . .

*G*eographically, Baja California is set apart from mainland Mexico, which greatly contributes to its unique culture and personality, as well as to its many attractions and diversions. Volcanic activity created the craggy desertscape populated mainly by forests of cardón cactus, spiky Joshua trees, and spindly ocotillo bushes that you see today. Hard to believe such a formidable landscape could become home to a vacation haven, but it has. Today, Los Cabos offers visitors a bevy of options for fun in the sun — ecotours, golfing, sportfishing, diving, and whale-watching, to name a few — amidst beautiful settings and posh resorts.

In this chapter, I give you an overview of the best beaches tucked into the miles of coastline between the two Cabos (and in the neighboring areas). I point out the most interesting sights in these twin towns, and I also offer a rundown of the best ways to spend an active day — or night — here.

Hitting the Beaches

The beaches of Los Cabos are stunning — cobalt-blue waters set against a backdrop of rugged desert terrain. The countless inlets and small coves in the Sea of Cortez have made Los Cabos a popular destination for ocean kayaking, and the abundant sea life attracts both divers and sport fishermen. And as for the beaches here (see the "Los Cabos" map, in this section), you can choose from dozens of tranquil coves or opt to

Los Cabos

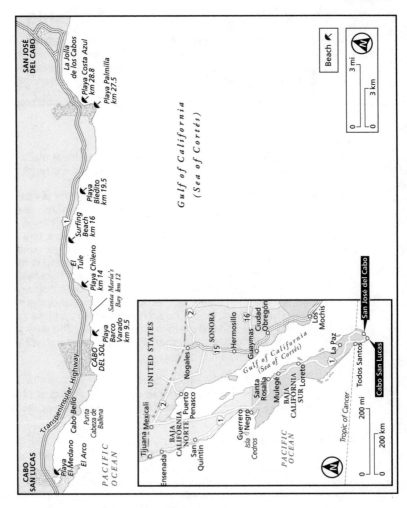

take on the long stretches of challenging surf breaks. One after another, these beautiful patches of sand hug the shoreline between the two Cabos (San José del Cabo and Cabo San Lucas).

If you're a beach aficionado who wants to explore the beautiful coves and beaches along the 35km (22-mile) coast between the two Cabos, consider renting a car for a day or so. Rental cars cost $40 to $75 per day and up. (Check out Chapter 31 for all the details on renting a car in Cabo.) Frequent bus service between San José del Cabo and Cabo San Lucas also makes it possible to take in the pleasures of both towns.

Watching your feathered friends

Between Pueblo la Playa and San José's Presidente InterContinental Hotel lies the **Estero San José**, an estuary and protected ecological reserve with at least 270 species of birds. Across from the entrance to the InterContinental, a footpath leads you into the estuary for one heck of a bird-watching experience.

Cabo's northern beaches

The relaxed pace of San José del Cabo makes it an ideal place to unwind and absorb authentic Mexican flavor while enjoying a stretch of sand.

The nearest beach to San José that's safe for swimming is **Pueblo la Playa** (also called La Playita), located about 3km (2 miles) east of town. From Bulevar Mijares, turn east at the small "Pueblo la Playa" sign and follow the dusty, dirt road through cane fields and palms to a small village and beautiful beach where local fishermen pull their *pangas* (skiffs) ashore. This whole area is likely to be significantly changed by press time, as the new Puerto Los Cabos marina and resort is rapidly developing just to the north. It will include, in addition to the marina, a golf course, hotels, and real estate, so certainly, additional options will be popping up. But for now, enjoy the La Playita Resort and its adjacent restaurant (☎ **624-142-4166**), which currently offer the only formal sustenance on the beach. Also note that the beach has no shade *palapas* (thatched roofs).

The beach that forms the southern border of San José is a broad stretch of sand, but because hotels front most of it, hotel guests are the primary beachgoers here — it can be a hassle for non-guests to access the beach.

Corridor beaches

Traveling from San José to Cabo San Lucas along Highway 1, the first beach along the Corridor is **Playa Costa Azul** (Km 29) where Zipper's restaurant is located (see Chapter 32). It's a long stretch of sand next to the Mykonos and La Jolla condo developments. Most of the year, Costa Azul has a gentle, but regular, surf break; however, from late summer to early fall, a southwest swell brings consistent wave action with some truly exceptional surf conditions.

Playa Palmilla (Km 27.5), with its beautiful rock formations, is the nearest swimming beach after you've set off down the Corridor. It's located just west of Playa Costa Azul near the One&Only Palmilla — an elegant place to stay or dine. To reach Playa Palmilla, take a taxi to the road that leads to the One&Only Palmilla grounds. Then take the left fork in the road (without entering the hotel grounds) and follow the road to the beach.

Playa Chileno (Km 14) is the largest and most popular of the public beaches along the corridor, and it has both public restrooms and showers — a rarity in Mexico. A watersports-equipment rental facility located at the southern end of the beach can come in handy — the rocky headlands at both ends of this small bay offer some good snorkeling. Nearby **Playa Santa María** (Km 12) has less in the way of facilities and shade, but it's better for snorkeling and diving. Both of these beaches are noted for their abundance of marine life.

The remains of the Japanese tuna boat *Inari Maru* make **Playa Barco Varado** (Km 9–10) noteworthy and provide the beach with its name — Shipwreck Beach. The boat became stranded on the rocky shoals in 1966. It's now one of the main dive sites in the area. The hull and other wreckage lie 2 to 26m (6½–85 ft.) underwater.

Although a few travel agencies run snorkeling tours to some of these beaches, no public transportation is available. If you want to explore these beaches on your own, your only option is to rent a car. To find these beaches, follow the blue-and-white signs along Highway 1. The signs are sometimes labeled ACCESO A PLAYA, but more often, they simply bear the international symbol for a swimmer or a snorkeler.

 In addition to Playa Palmilla, the beaches of Chileno and Santa María are generally safe for swimming — but always be careful. The other beaches along the Corridor aren't safe. Experienced snorkelers may want to check them out, but other visitors should go for the view only. Always check at a hotel or travel agency for directions and swimming conditions.

Cabo's southern beaches

The main beach in Cabo San Lucas is a curving sweep of sand known as **Playa El Medano,** located on the east side of the bay. The swimming conditions here are generally safe. You can also rent snorkeling gear, boats, WaveRunners, kayaks, pedal boats, and windsurf boards and score some windsurfing lessons. The people-watching at El Medano is as hot as the action — take your pick from the many outdoor restaurants along the shore and settle in for a cold one.

Finding Water Fun for Everyone

It began with John Steinbeck's stories and continued with the tall tales of the early sport fishermen who came here in the 1940s and 1950s. With more than 3,000 estimated species of fish in the waters offshore Baja California and the title of undisputed bill-fishing capital of the world, Los Cabos enjoyed early fame among visitors who wanted to tackle these larger species, such as tuna, marlin, and swordfish (see "Reeling in the big one," later in this chapter). In the years that followed, travelers to Los Cabos have discovered an even greater number of ways to revel in the treasures of this deep, blue sea.

Cruising Los Cabos

Whether by day or in the fading light of the sunset, numerous cruises are available to take you around Land's End — the famed tip of Baja California — to enjoy this truly stunning sight. Boats depart from Cabo San Lucas. The cruise prices and offerings vary but usually include music, an open bar, and snacks for between $30 and $45 per person. Variables include the type of boat, duration of the cruise, and amenities.

The sunset cruise on the 13m (42-ft.) catamaran *Pez Gato* (☎ 624-143-3797 or 143-5297; www.pezgatocabo) is always a favorite. The excursion departs from the Muelle Principal dock at 5 p.m. This two-hour cruise costs $35 and includes margaritas, beer, and sodas. Similar boats also leave from the Plaza las Glorias Hotel dock and from the marina. Almost any travel agency or hotel tour desk can make the arrangements for you, or you can call **Gray Line Los Cabos** (☎ 624-146-9410; www.grayline loscabos.com). Gray Line works with all the tour providers in the area and can give you the unbiased lowdown on which one will meet your individual needs.

Another great way to see the aquatic sights is aboard a **glass-bottom boat.** These boats leave from the Cabo San Lucas marina every 45 minutes between 9 a.m. and 4 p.m. daily. The cost is about $10 for an hour-long tour past sea lions and pelicans to the famous El Arco (Rock Arch, or simply "The Arch") at Land's End where the Pacific Ocean and the Sea of Cortez meet. Most boats make a brief stop at Playa del Amor or drop you off if you ask; you can use your ticket to catch a later boat back. (Be sure to find out what time the last boat departs.)

You don't want to miss the **whale-watching cruises** when the gray whales migrate to the Los Cabos area between January and March. In San José, fishermen at Pueblo la Playa take small groups out to see the whales; a four-hour trip runs about $45 per person.

Sportfishing boats, glass-bottom boats, and cruise catamarans also offer whale-watching trips at prices ranging from $35 to $60 for a half-day trip. You can also spot the whales from shore; good whale-watching spots include the beach by the Solmar Suites hotel on the Pacific (see review in Chapter 30) and the beaches and cliffs along the Corridor.

The ultimate whale excursion is an all-day trip to Magdalena Bay, a one-hour plane ride away. In a small skiff, you get close enough to touch the whales. The cost for the trip, including air transportation, is $380, available through most local travel agents. If you want to spend more time with the whales, **Sea Kayak Adventures** (☎ 800-616-1942; www.sea kayakadventures.com) offers an eight-day trip to Magdalena Bay, with kayaking among whales for four to five hours per day, hiking, and camping in remote coves. Prices start at $1,280 per person.

Preferring a paddleboat

Fully guided, ecologically oriented **sea-kayaking tours** are available through **Baja's Moto Rent** (☎ 624-143-2050), **Cabo Expeditions** (☎ 624-143-2700), and **Aqua Deportes** (☎ 624-143-0117). Most ocean kayaking tours depart from Cabo San Lucas.

The tours generally run from 8:30 to 11:30 a.m. and include breakfast and beverages for a price of about $70. No previous experience is necessary — guides provide complete instructions at the start of the tour. Kayaks are the most popular and practical way to explore the pristine coves that dot this shoreline.

Another excellent source for kayak tours is **BajaWild Expeditions** (☎ 624-142-5300; www.bajawild.com), specialists in adventure tours in the Cabos area. They offer a variety of kayaking and snorkeling tours to venues that include Cabo Pulmo, the Arch and Lover's Rock, and excursions within the estuary. Prices range from $50 to $95.

Catching a wave

When summer hurricanes spin off the southern end of the peninsula, they send huge surf northward to beaches such as **Zippers, Punta Gorda,** and **Old Man's.** People have compared Zippers (near the Brisa del Mar Trailer Park and the Costa Azul surf shop outside San José del Cabo) with places such as Pipeline on the North Shore of Oahu. That may be a bit of an exaggeration, but this area does feature great waves nonetheless.

Playa Costa Azul (Hwy. 1 Km 29, just south of San José) is the most popular surfing beach in the area. A few bungalows are available for rent here, and surfers can camp on the beach. You can rent surfboards and surf racks for your rental car by the day here. Spectators can watch the action from the highway lookout point at the top of the hill south of Costa Azul.

You can find good surfing from March through November all along the beaches west of Cabo, and **Playa Chileno,** near the Cabo San Lucas Hotel east of town, has a famous right break. Other good surfing beaches along the corridor are **Acapulquito, El Tule,** and **La Bocana.**

The Pacific coast has yet to face the onslaught of development that has rapidly changed the landscape to the east. An hour-long drive up the coast to the little towns of Pescadero and Todos Santos can be a great surf journey, with a couple of good point breaks near here. You can reach **Playa San Pedrito** via the dirt road that begins about 7km (4½ miles) south of the Todos Santos town limits. Follow the "San Pedrito Campground" signs. The point is very rocky and sharp, but it's a wonderful wave at the right swell direction and tide (north-west swell, rising tide). Farther down the road is **Playa los Cerritos,** located 13km (8 miles) south of Todos Santos. Cerritos is a lovely beach with a surfable point break off a big headland.

New to surfing? **Baja Wild** (☎ 624-142-5300; www.bajawild.com) offers surf lessons as well as surf tours, so you can get right to the best waves in the briefest amount of time. Trips take you to any of 15 breaks within the Sea of Cortez or to the big breaks on the Pacific Ocean. You can even combine surfing and kayaking.

Exploring the deep blue

Diving in Los Cabos is so special because of the abundance of marine life, which includes giant mantas, sea turtles, dolphins, and tropical fish. You can choose between diving the coral reefs at the southern tip of the cape region or one of the shipwrecks in the area. April through November is the best time to dive, but diving is most crowded from October to mid-January. Making reservations in advance is important if you're planning to dive then. During the winter months, you're also likely to hear the moving, tonal songs of the humpback whales as you dive. Note that during the winter months, the water here can be quite cold, so a wet suit is necessary — even for most snorkelers.

Several companies offer snorkeling; a two-hour cruise to sites around El Arco costs $30, and a four-hour trip to Santa María costs $55. Both prices include gear rental. Certain beaches, such as Playa del Amor, Santa María, Chileno, and Barco Varado, have snorkeling gear for rent at the beach; it's generally priced between $10 and $15.

For scuba diving, contact **Amigos del Mar** (☎ 800-344-3349 in the U.S., or 624-143-0505; Fax: 310-454-1686 in the U.S., or 624-143-0887; www.amigosdelmar.com), located at the marina in Cabo San Lucas. Diving specialist Ricardo Sevilla has all the answers to your Cabo diving questions. Dives are made along the wall of a canyon in San Lucas Bay where you can see the "sandfalls" that even Jacques Cousteau couldn't figure out — no one knows their source or cause. Amigos del Mar also has scuba trips to Playa Santa María and places farther away including the Gordo Banks and Cabo Pulmo. Dive prices start at $40 for a one-tank dive and $70 for two tanks. Trips to the coral outcropping at Cabo Pulmo start at $130. Located two hours from Cabo San Lucas, Cabo Pulmo is rated for beginners and up. Gordo Banks, for advanced divers, is an underwater mountain about 5 miles offshore with a black-coral bottom and schools of game fish and manta rays at a rate of $125 for a two-tank dive. Resort courses cost $100 per person and open-water certification costs around $450.

In addition to Amigos del Mar in Cabo San Lucas, snorkeling and scuba trips can also be arranged through **Gray Line** (☎ 624-146-9410; www.graylineloscabos.com), in San José.

Reeling in the big one

Superb sportfishing put Cabo San Lucas on the map, and many travelers still come here with the dream of dropping a line and waiting for the big one. The fishing really lives up to its reputation — bringing in a 100-pound marlin is considered routine. Angling is good all year, though the catch varies with the season. Here's the fishing lineup by time of year and the most prevalent fish:

January to April: Yellowtail

May to December: Yellowfin tuna

June to November: Sailfish and wahoo

July to December: Black and blue marlin

All year: Striped marlin

For most cruises and excursions, try to make fishing reservations at least a day in advance, keeping in mind that some trips require a minimum number of people. You can arrange your fishing trip through a travel agency or directly at one of the fishing-fleet offices at the marina's far south end in Cabo San Lucas.

The marina is located on the south side of the harbor. You can easily find fleet operators with offices near the docks. To choose a boat, take a stroll around the marina and talk with the captains — you may arrive at an economical deal. Try **ABY Charters** (☎ 624-144-4203; Fax: 624-143-0874; www.abycharters.com) or **Picante/Bluewater Sportfishing** (☎ 624-143-2474; Fax: 624-143-5969; www.picantesportfishing.com). Both companies have booths located at the sportfishing dock at the marina's far south end.

The going rate for a day on a fully equipped cruiser with captain and guide (many of the larger hotels, such as the Solmar, have their own fleets) starts at around $700 for up to four people. For deluxe trips with everything included aboard a 12m (40-ft.) boat, budget $1,300.

The *panga* fleets offer the best deals. Pair up with another angler and charter a *panga*, a 6.6m (22-ft.) skiff used by local fishermen, at Playa la Puebla near San José. Several *panga* fleets offer up to six-hour sportfishing trips, usually from 6 a.m. to noon, for $25 per hour (with a three-hour minimum). You can split the cost with one or two other people. For information, contact the fisherman's cooperative in Pueblo la Playa, or you can call **Palmilla Bay Sportfishing** (☎ 624-146-9681; Fax: 624-130-7786) at the Hotel Posada Real. Palmilla Bay's also has its own fishing fleet with both *pangas* ($190 for six hours) and cruisers ($380–$495). Outfitters supply the boat and tackle, and the client buys the bait, drinks, and snacks.

You need daily fishing permits in Cabos, but your captain can take care of the details. Daily permits range from $4 to $10, and annual permits are also available. Check with your outfitter when you make your reservation to determine how he handles permits.

Catch and release is strongly encouraged in Los Cabos. Anglers reel in their fish, which are tagged and released unharmed into the sea. Anglers get a certificate that documents the catch, and they leave Los Cabos with the knowledge that plenty of billfish will still be in the sea when they return.

Enjoying Land Sports

The rugged terrain of Baja and the cape region once kept people out of the area. Now it seems to be a main lure, attracting travelers in search of an active vacation and true interaction with nature. If you prefer your nature somewhat on the tame side, you may find your game on one of Cabo's many famed golf courses. In fact, golf has overtaken sportfishing in popularity in Cabo.

Teeing off

Los Cabos has become Mexico's golf mecca. The master plan for golf in Los Cabos calls for 207 total holes in the future. The fees I list in this section are for 18 holes of play during high season, including golf cart, water, club service, and tax. Summer rates are about 25 percent lower, and many hotels offer special golf packages. I list the courses in geographical order, starting in San José, heading down along the Corridor, and ending in Cabo San Lucas (for specifics on the playability of the various courses, see the "Lowdown on golfing in Cabo" sidebar in this chapter):

✔ As with many things in Los Cabos, visitors find that the most economical way to enjoy this sport is to play in San José. Greens fees at the nine-hole **Mayan Resort Golf Los Cabos** (previously the Club Campo de Golf San José; Paseo Finisterra, across from the Howard Johnson Hotel; ☎ 624-142-0900 or 142-0905) are just $99 for nine holes or $119 for 18 holes. They offer discounted rates if you bring your own equipment, and also for tee times between 2 and 6 p.m. The course is open daily from 6:30 a.m. to 6 p.m., and club guests can also use the swimming pool.

✔ The newest course to open in Los Cabos is **Querencia** (Bulevar Querencia 1; ☎ 624-145-6670), a Tom Fazio–designed course, which includes an 18-hole championship course along with a nine-hole Fazio short course and practice facility. It's billed as a strictly private club with play limited to property owners and golf club members, however, you may find there are provisions for guests of the resort hotels along the Corridor.

✔ The 27-hole course at the **Palmilla Golf Club** (One&Only Palmilla resort, the Corridor; ☎ 800-386-2465 in the U.S., or 624-144-5250; www.palmillaresort.com) was the first Jack Nicklaus Signature layout in Mexico. The course was built in 1992 on 900 acres of dramatic oceanfront and desert. The 27-hole course offers you a choice between two back-nine options. High-season greens fees are $220 (lower after 1 p.m.), and low-season greens fees are between $120 and $210. Although Palmilla is currently a semiprivate club, most Corridor hotels have membership benefits.

✔ Just a few miles down the road from the Palmilla is another Jack Nicklaus Signature course, the 18-hole **Ocean Course at Cabo del Sol** (Cabo del Sol resort, the Corridor; ☎ **866-231-4677** in the U.S., or 624-145-8200; www.cabodelsol.com). The 7,100-yard course is known for its challenging final three holes. Tom Weiskopf designed the new 18-hole Desert Course, also at Cabo del Sol. Greens fees are $220 to $295.

✔ Robert Trent Jones, Jr., designed this 18-hole, 6,945-yard course at **Cabo Real** (Meliá Cabo Real resort, the Corridor; ☎ **800-543-2044** in the U.S., or 624-144-0232; www.caboreal.com), which features holes that sit high on mesas overlooking the Sea of Cortez. Fees run $260 for 18 holes, $180 after 3 p.m.

✔ The **El Dorado Golf Course** (Meliá Cabo Real resort, next to the Westin Regina hotel, the Corridor; ☎ **877-795-8727** in the U.S., or 624-144-5451) is a Jack Nicklaus Signature course. The course is open daily from 7 a.m. until dusk. Eighteen holes are $260. After 2 p.m., a twilight special offers a round for $168. Carts are included; caddies are available for $80.

✔ Located in Cabo San Lucas, the **Raven Club** (Palo Blanco 501; ☎ **888-328-8501** in the U.S., or 624-143-4653; Fax: 624-143-5809) features an 18-hole course designed by two members of the Dye family, so the front and back nines play like two different courses. The entire course overlooks the juncture of the Pacific Ocean and Sea of Cortez, including the famous Land's End rocks. The layout includes the 607-yard, par-five seventh hole — the longest hole in Mexico. Greens fees are $176 for morning tee times, $160 for the noon rate (noon–2:30 p.m.), and $127 after 2:30 p.m.

Several specialty tour operators offer golf packages to Los Cabos, which include accommodations, greens fees, and other amenities. Among the best is **Sportours** (☎ **888-GOLF-MEX** from the U.S., no phone in Mexico; www.sportours.com).

Making time for tennis

You can play tennis at the two courts of the **Mayan Resort Golf Los Cabos** (Paseo Finisterra 1; ☎ **624-142-0905**) for $13 an hour during the day or $22 an hour at night. (Club guests can also use the swimming pool.) Tennis is also available at the **One&Only Palmilla** (two lighted courts) classes $70 an hour and regular playing free of charge, guests only and the **Presidente InterContinental** (two lighted courts) $10 an hour.

Lowdown on golfing in Cabo

Golf isn't always how you play the course, but how the course plays you. Los Cabos is now considered one of the world's finest golf destinations, which means some of the courses can be pretty challenging. Picking a course that matches your abilities is important so that a challenge doesn't become a frustration. Los Cabos has an ample and intriguing variety of courses for golfers of all levels.

Beyond the selection, quality, and beauty of the courses in Los Cabos, a key reason so many golfers choose to play here is the very reliable weather. The courses highlighted in this chapter compare to the great ones in Palm Springs and Scottsdale with the added beauty of the ocean views, as well as the wider variety of desert cacti and flowering plants.

Course fees are high in Cabo — generally over $200 per round. But these are world-class courses, worth the world-class price. Courses generally offer 20 percent to 30 percent off rates if you play after 2 or 2:30 p.m. This is actually a great time to play, because the temperature is cooler and play is generally faster. The golf offerings in Los Cabos will only continue to expand; four courses are in various phases of construction. At **Puerto Los Cabos,** a new mega-development northeast of San José del Cabo, construction has started on the first of two 18-hole courses, with nine holes designed by Jack Nicklaus, and the other nine by Greg Norman. It's scheduled to be playable by June 2006. At the other end of the peninsula near Cabo San Lucas on the Pacific side, the **Cabo Pacífica** development will soon be launching two more championship courses. Below are a Cabo's best courses:

✔ **Cabo del Sol:** The Ocean Course was the second Jack Nicklaus course constructed in Los Cabos. It is much more difficult than the Palmilla course, with less room for error.

Don't be fooled by the wide, welcoming first hole. This is challenging target golf, with numerous forced carries — even from the red tees. Seven holes are along the water. At the par-three signature 17th hole, the golfer is faced with a 178-yard shot over sandy beach and rocky outcroppings to a tiny green framed by bunkers on one side and a drop to the ocean on the other. The finishing hole, guarded by desert and cactus on the right and rock cliffs leading to the sea on the left, is modeled after the 18th at Pebble Beach.

Cabo del Sol offers another option, the Desert Course, which is Tom Weiskopf's first course design in Mexico. Spread over 56 hectares (140 acres) of gently rolling desert terrain, it provides sweeping ocean views. The course's large landing areas ensure a pleasant game for players at all levels.

✔ **Cabo Real:** This Robert Trent Jones, Jr., design is known for its holes along the Sea of Cortez; exceptional among these is the frequently photographed 12th hole, which sits high on a mesa facing the sea. Jones designed the course to test low handicappers, but multiple tees make it enjoyable for average players as well. While the first six holes are in mountainous terrain, others skirt the shore. Rolling greens and strategically placed bunkers on narrow terrain work their way up to the sixth tee, 138m (460 ft.) above sea level. The par-72 layout is 6,945 yards long and was designed with professional tournament play in mind. The most celebrated hole, the 15th, sits right on the beach between the Meliá Cabo Real Golf & Beach Resort and Las Ventanas al Paraíso.

✔ **El Dorado Golf Course:** Another Jack Nicklaus Signature course located at Meliá Cabo Real, El Dorado is a links-style course in the Scottish tradition. The layout is challenging — seven holes border the Sea of Cortez and 12 are carved out of two pristine canyons. The ocean isn't the only water you see on this course — man-made lakes are also a part of the scenery. El Dorado bills itself as the "Pebble Beach of Baja" — but then again, so does Cabo del Sol — you decide. Note that this course was recently purchased and is in the process of being redesigned; it was closed at press time, but scheduled reopen sometime in 2006.

✔ **The Raven Club** (formerly known as the Cabo San Lucas Country Club): Different Dye family members designed the front and back nine here, so the course plays like two different courses. It has deep waste bunkers, subtle terracing up hillsides, and holes built into the natural desert terrain. The most challenging hole is the extremely long, 607-yard, par-five seventh around a lake; it's the longest hole in Mexico. The Dye family redid the whole course in 2002. Although the layout is essentially the same, some greens have moved slightly and some holes are a little shorter than before, but all the bunkers and hazards have remained, and the course is now considered better than before. From the greens on higher ground, you'll enjoy views overlooking the famous El Arco, the Sea of Cortez, the town of Cabo San Lucas, and the Pacific Ocean.

✔ **Palmilla Golf Club:** The original Cabo course is now a 27-hole layout. You must play the Arroyo (the original front nine) for your first nine holes, and then you choose between Mountain (the name given to the original back nine) and Ocean Nine (the new holes — although these newer holes lie closer to the water, only one of them has a true ocean view) for your back nine. If you play this course only once, choose the Mountain back nine — it offers better ocean views. The views at the mountaintop clubhouse are also pretty spectacular. The eventual plan is for this course to be exclusive to One&Only Palmilla guests and residents of the adjacent real estate development. It's beautiful, playable, and well maintained, and views of desert mountains and the cobalt ocean without any interfering construction are featured throughout. It's one of a handful of places in the world where a golfer can play by water, mountain, and desert views surrounded by flowering vegetation. Bermuda short-cut grass makes putting fast, and the signature hole is the Mountain five hole; you hit over a canyon and then down to the greens below over a forced carry. This is target golf, and as a Jack Nicklaus course, the layout was constructed with strategy in mind. A mountaintop clubhouse provides spectacular views. Although it is currently a semiprivate club, most Corridor hotels have membership benefits. The eventual plan is for guests of the One&Only Palmilla and residents of the adjacent real estate development to have exclusive use of this course.

Taking Adventure and Nature Tours

Expeditions on all-terrain vehicles (ATVs) to the Cabo Falso lighthouse and La Candelaria (an Indian pueblo in the mountains) are among the most popular of the adventure tours available in Los Cabos. These excursions are a great way to explore the land, and they're available through most travel agencies.

- ✔ The three-hour tour to **Cabo Falso** includes a stop at the beach, a look at some sea-turtle nests (without disturbing them) and the remains of a 1912 shipwreck, a ride over 150m (500-ft.) sand dunes, and a visit to the lighthouse. Guided tours cost around $45 per person on a single vehicle or $60 for two people riding on one ATV. You can also rent ATVs for $35 for three hours. Ask your hotel concierge for more information.

- ✔ **La Candelaria** is an isolated Indian village in the mountains 40km (25 miles) north of Cabo San Lucas. As described in *National Geographic,* the old pueblo is known for the white and black witch-craft still practiced here. An underground river that emerges at the pueblo provides water for the lush landscape of palms, mango trees, and bamboo. The tour's return trip travels down a steep canyon, along a beach (giving you time to swim), and past giant sea-turtle nesting grounds. Departing at 9 a.m., the La Candelaria tour costs around $80 per person or $100 for two on the same ATV.

Driving Tours

A uniquely "Cabo" experience is offered by **Outback Baja** (☎ 624-142-9200; Fax: 624-142-3166; www.bajaoutback.com) via their caravan style **Hummer Adventures.** You drive these luxury Hummer H2s, going off-road to cruise desert and beachfront terrain in style while learning about the surrounding area by expert guides. Communication links the up to ten vehicles in the caravan, allowing you to listen to the narrations of the guide. There's a choice of four routes, which include treks to Todos Santos, the East Cape, Santiago and Cañon de la Zorra, and Rancho la Verdad. Tours depart at 9 a.m. and return at 3 p.m., with prices ranging from $165 to $220, depending upon the route, and include lunch. Visa, MasterCard, and American Express are accepted, and you must bring your valid driver's license. Special group rates are also available.

If that sounds too tame, **Wide Open Baja Racing Experience** (☎ 888-788-2252 or 949-340-1155 in the U.S., or 624-143-4170; office located in Plaza Nautica; www.wideopencabo.com) gives you the chance to drive actual Chenowth Magnum race cars at their 600-hectare (1,500-acre) racing ranch on the Pacific Coast. There's a varied terrain to drive, with twists, turns, sand-washes, and plenty of bumps for thrillseekers. Session times for the **Test Drive** are at 10 a.m. and 1:30 p.m. The price of $250 includes shuttle transportation from downtown Cabo to the ranch, driver orientation, and safety equipment. Private group rates are also available. Wide Open Baja also offers multi-day tours driving race vehicles through Cabo, Ensenada, and the entire Baja peninsula.

A variety of land- and water-based adventure and nature tours are available through **Tio Sports** (☎ 624-143-3399; www.tiosports.com), including the popular ATV tours to Cabo Falso and Candelaria and parasailing at $50 single or $70 tandem. **Gray Line Tours** (☎ 624-146-9410) is a great contact for a complete rundown of what's available. They offer all the tours from all the local companies rather than working with only a select few.

For horseback riding, here are a couple of good options for the Los Cabos area:

✔ I highly recommend **Cuadra San Francisco Equestrian Center,** Km 19.5 along the Corridor, in front of the Casa del Mar resort (☎ 624-144-0160). Master horseman Francisco Barrena, with more than 30 years of experience in training horses and operating equestrian schools, can assist any level rider in selecting and fitting a horse to his or her skill level. Your choice of English or Western saddles are available on well-trained, exceptional horses. A two-hour canyon ride in and around Arroyo San Carlos or Venado Blanco costs $80; a one-hour ride to the beach or desert is $35.

✔ **Rancho Collins** (☎ 624-143-3652) also has horses available for rent for $25 per hour, with guide. Rides include trotting along the beach and sunset tours. They also take you to the Pacific for sunset-riding on the beach for a cost of $35 per person per hour. It's open daily from 8 a.m. to noon and 2 to 5 p.m. They're located in front of the Hotel Club Cascadas de Baja.

Sightseeing in Los Cabos

Sports and partying are Cabo's main attractions, but you can find a few — very few is a better description — cultural and historical points of interest. In San José, the Spanish missionary Nicolás Tamaral established the stone **Iglesia de San Lucas** (Church of San Lucas; Calle Cabo San Lucas, close to the main plaza; no phone) in 1730. According to local lore, the Pericúe Indians reportedly resisted Tamaral's demands that they practice monogamy and eventually killed the missionary. Buildings on the streets facing the main plaza in San José are being renovated to house restaurants and shops, and the picturesque neighborhood promises to have the strongest Mexican ambience of any place in town.

Shopping in Los Cabos

San José has the better shopping of the two towns when it comes to higher quality items, but if you're after a beer-themed T-shirt, Cabo San Lucas can't be topped. In San José, a growing selection of unique shops, hip boutiques, and collections of fine Mexican *artesanía* (handicrafts) is clustered around Bulevar Mijares and Zaragoza, the main street. The municipal market on Mauricio Castro and Green has edibles and utilitarian wares.

In Cabo San Lucas, the most notable shops are now concentrated in the **Puerto Paraíso Entertainment Plaza.** Opened in 2002, this is now the focal point for shopping for tourists, complete with parking, a food court, movie theatres, and a video arcade. With more than 50,000 sq. m (538,195 sq. ft.) of air-conditioned space on three levels, it's too bad that the shops don't live up to the promise of this attractive mall. Although it bills itself as having an array of designer shops, this claim is a bit misleading; you may find only one or two name-brand items within any store, and many of the locales are vacant. It *is* a good place to shop for swimwear or resort wear, and there are plenty of gift items to choose from, but don't expect the equivalent of a U.S. shopping mall experience. However, Puerto Paraíso does have some choice dining options, the best being the local branch of **Ruth's Chris Steak House** (adjacent to the marina; ☎ 624-144-3232). The plaza is located marina-side between the Plaza Bonita Mall and Marina Fiesta Resort — you couldn't miss it if you tried. Most other shops in Cabo are on or within a block or two of Bulevar Marina and the plaza.

Clothing

Escape (Plaza Florentine, Zaragoza 20, across from the cathedral in San José; ☎ 624-142-2799) features designer and casual sportswear and accessories including designer jeans, leather bags, belts, and a trendy selection of sunglasses. An interior-décor shop by the same name next door has a small cafe and espresso bar in the connecting courtyard.

H2O has a tempting selection of women's swimwear, casual wear, dresses and evening wear, as well as casual resortwear for men (Vicente Guerrero and Madero; ☎ 624-143-1219). The gallery is open Monday to Saturday 9 a.m. to 8 p.m.; Sunday 11 a.m. to 5 p.m. They accept MasterCard and Visa.

Contemporary art

San José has a growing number of art galleries — mainly artist studios open to the public — and the town's creative ambience is blossoming. The most notable gallery is **Galería Wentworth Porter** (Av. Obregón 20; ☎/fax 624-142-3141), which features a selection of original fine art along with prints and art cards by local artists. As the name implies, the work of locally popular artist Dennis Wentworth Porter figures prominently. The gallery is open Monday through Saturday 10 a.m. to 5 p.m.

The area's longest-standing art gallery, in Cabo San Lucas, is the **Golden Cactus Studio-Gallery** (Vicente Guerrero and Madero; ☎ 614-143-6399; www.goldencactusgallery.com), which shows original art by regional artists, including Chris MacClure, as well as reproductions and posters of popular Mexican works. It's open Monday to Saturday from 10 a.m. to 2 p.m. and 4 to 7 p.m.

Also in Cabo San Lucas, in the Medano Beach area, the handsome **Galería Gattamelata** (Hacienda Rd.; ☎ **624-143-1166**) specializes in antiques and colonial-style furniture. It's open daily from 10 a.m. to 8 p.m.

Crafts, gifts, and jewelry

Copal (in San José at Plaza Mijares; ☎ **624-142-3070**) features traditional and contemporary Mexican *artesanía* and silver jewelry in a former residence tastefully converted into a contemporary shop. You can shop here daily from 8:30 a.m. to 9:30 p.m.

Cuca's Blanket Factory (in Cabo San Lucas at Cárdenas and Matamoros; ☎ **624-143-4575**) is an open-air stand that sells standard, Mexican, cotton and woolen blankets with an added attraction — you can design your own blanket and have it ready the next day. The stand is open daily from 9 a.m. to 9 p.m.

For unusual and well-priced jewelry, visit **SAX** (Mijares 2 in San José; ☎ **624-142-4696;** www.saxstyle.com), where two local designers create one-of-a-kind pieces using silver, coral, and semi-precious stones. They can even create a special request design for you, ready in 24 hours. Located next to Casa Natalia, SAX is open from 10 a.m. to 9 p.m., closed Sundays.

Decorative and folk art

Arte, Diseño y Decoración (**ADD;** Zaragoza at Hidalgo, San José; ☎ **624-142-2777**) sells creative home accessories and furnishings, mostly made of rustic wood, pewter, and Talavera ceramics, and offers shipping services back home for travelers who shop too much and can't carry it all.

Other stores

The Plaza Bonita Shopping Center (Bulevar Marina at Cárdenas) is an older shopping center that is still worth a visit. This large terra-cotta-colored plaza on the edge of the Cabo San Lucas marina has been around since 1990, and it finally has a group of successful businesses. A branch of **Dos Lunas** (☎ **624-143-1969**) sells colorful casual sportswear. **Cartes** (☎ **624-143-1770**) offers hand-painted ceramic vases and dishes, pewter frames, carved furniture, and hand-woven textiles. Most shops in the plaza are open daily from 9 a.m. to 9 p.m.

Ultrafemme is Mexico's largest duty-free shop, with an excellent selection of fine jewelry and watches, including Rolex, Cartier, Omega, TAG Heuer, and Tissot; perfumes (Lancôme, Chanel, Armani, Carolina Herrera); and other gift items, all at duty free prices. It's located in Plaza Ultrafemme (Bulevar Marina, across from Carlos & Charlies; ☎ **624-145-6090** or 145-6099; www.ultrafemme.com.mx), and is open daily, 10 a.m. to 10 p.m. American Express, MasterCard, and Visa are accepted.

One of the spiffiest (but commercial) shops in Los Cabos is **Mamma Eli's** (Calle Cabo San Lucas, west of the plaza at Madero; ☎ 624-143-1616), a three-level store packed with folk art, crafts, clothing, and furniture. It's open Monday through Sunday from 9 a.m. to 2 p.m. and 4 to 7 p.m.

Books, Books, in Cabo San Lucas (Bulevar Marina 7n, Plaza de la Danza next to Dairy Queen; ☎ 624-143-3172 or 143-3173), sells a good selection of English- and Spanish-language books, magazines, and newspapers, as well as a fine collection of regional guides and publications. This location is open daily from 9 a.m. to 10 p.m. A second location in San José, at Bulevar Mijares 41 near the Tropicana Inn (☎ 624-142-4433), is open daily 9 a.m. to 9 p.m.

For fine Cuban cigars and cigarettes, as well as Veracruz cigars, a visit to **Los Amigos Smokeshop and Cigar Bar** (☎ 624-142-1138) in San José is a must. Here you can buy not only high-quality cigars but also a whole range of smoking accessories, including humidors and cutters, with friendly assistance from a knowledgeable staff. In a new, expanded location (Hidalgo 11, across from the French Riviera bakery), they offer private lockers, a bar with an excellent selection of single malts and California wines, Wednesday evening cigar tastings, and a VIP club for frequent visitors. Los Amigos is open Monday to Wednesday 9 a.m. to 8 p.m. and Thursday to Saturday from 9 a.m. to 10 p.m.

For smokes in Cabo, visit **J & J Habanos** Cabo's largest cigar shop, selling premium Cuban and fine Mexican cigars — it even has a walk-in humidor. It's found on Madero between Bulevar Marina and Guerrero (☎ 624-143-6160 or 143-3839) and is open Monday to Saturday 9 a.m. to 10 p.m.; Sunday 9 a.m. to 9 p.m., and accepts American Express, MasterCard, and Visa.

A large selection of fine tequilas and other liquors, as well as cigars, is available at **Tequila's House.** There are two locations: Bulevar Marina 624, in front of Caliente (☎ 624-143-5666), and Morelos at Lázaro Cárdenas (☎ 624-143-9070). Both are open Monday to Saturday 8 a.m. to 11 p.m.; they accept MasterCard and Visa.

Embarking on a Side Trip

You can book a day trip to the city of **La Paz** through a travel agency for around $55, which includes beverages and a tour of the countryside along the way. The tours usually stop at the weaving shop of Fortunato Silva, who spins his own cotton and weaves it into wonderfully textured rugs and textiles. Day trips are also available to **Todos Santos** for $95, including a guided walking tour of the Cathedral Mission, a museum, the Hotel California, and various artists' homes.

A few years back, Todos Santos became known as "Bohemian Baja." It found its way on the travel agendas of folks looking for the latest, the trendiest, and the hippest of artist outposts — and in the plans of travelers who were simply weary of the L.A.-ization of Cabo San Lucas. In no time, Todos Santos blossomed as a true gem of a place that seems to foster the creative spirit while retaining its pervasive beauty and lovely heritage that held the original attraction.

The art and artistry created here now — from the culinary plate to the canvas — cares less about commercial appeal than quality, and in doing so, it becomes more of a draw. Don't overlook the attendant arts of agriculture, masonry, and weavings that some of the town's original residents created. From the superb meals at **Café Santa Fe** to an afternoon spent browsing the numerous shops and galleries, Todos Santos is intriguing to its core. Following is a sampling of what the town has to offer:

- ✔ For me — and I suspect for many others — a meal at the **Café Santa Fe** (Calle Centenario 4; ☎ 612-145-0340) is reason enough to visit Todos Santos. Much of the attention the town has received in recent years can be directly attributed to this outstanding cafe, which opened 15 years ago; it continues to live up to its lofty reputation. Owners Ezio and Paula Colombo refurbished a large stucco house across from the plaza, creating an exhibition kitchen, several dining rooms, and a lovely courtyard adjacent to a garden of hibiscus, bougainvillea, papaya trees, and herbs.

  The excellent Northern Italian cuisine emphasizes local produce and seafood. Try the homemade ravioli stuffed with spinach and ricotta in a Gorgonzola sauce or the ravioli with lobster and shrimp accompanied by one of their organic salads. In high season, the wait for a table at lunch can last quite a while. Everything is prepared fresh when ordered, and reservations are recommended. Main courses run between $35 and $40. The restaurant is open Wednesday through Monday from noon to 9 p.m., but it's closed September 1 to October 30.

- ✔ A more casual option, and a magical place to kick off a day in Todos Santos, is the garden setting of the **Caffé Todos Santos** (Calle Centenario 33, across from the Todos Santos Inn; ☎ 612-145-0300). Try the bowl-sized cafe latte with a freshly baked croissant or one of the cafe's signature cinnamon buns. Lunch or a light meal may include a frittata or a fish filet wrapped in banana leaves with coconut milk. Main courses average $6 to $20, and the cafe is open Tuesday through Sunday from 7 a.m. to 9 p.m. and Monday from 7 a.m. to 2 p.m.

- ✔ A new and notable addition is the **La Coronela** restaurant/bar (Calle Benito Juárez and Morelos; ☎ 612-145-0525), at the recently remodeled **Hotel California** (allegedly the inspiration for The Eagles' popular song of the same name). With its high-style design (think Philipe Stark meets Baja), the Belgian chef creates a changing menu to accompany the ever-present and very popular margaritas.

- ✔ At least a half dozen galleries are in town including the noted **Galería de Todos Santos** (Topete and Legaspi; ☎ 612-145-0500), which features a changing collection of works by regional artists.

> ✔ **El Tecolote Libros** (Hidalgo and Juárez; ☎ 612-145-0295), though tiny, gets my vote for the best bookstore in Mexico due to its exceptional selection of Latin American literature, poetry, children's books, and reference books centering on Mexico. You can purchase English- and Spanish-language books, both new and used, along with maps, magazines, cards, and art supplies. Adjacent to El Tecolote (you enter through the bookshop) is the whimsical **Traditions** shop that sells fun folk art and Mexican kitsch at its best. It's a great place for finding that perfect, creative, and inexpensive something to bring home.

Casual visitors can easily explore Todos Santos in a day, but a few tranquil inns welcome charmed guests who want to stay a little longer. You can arrange a day's visit through tour companies in Los Cabos or venture on your own with a rental car.

Discovering Los Cabos after Dark

San José's nightlife is nonexistent outside of the restaurant and hotel bars. The bars at Casa Natalia and Tropicana — the former catering to sophisticated romantics and the latter to those in search of rowdier good times — are particularly notable. On some weekends, Tropicana even brings in a live Cuban band for dancing. Several of the larger hotels along the beach have Mexican fiestas and other weekly theme nights that include a buffet (usually all-you-can-eat), drinks, live music, and entertainment for $25 to $35 per person. A large disco on Bulevar Mijares seems to be under different ownership each year — it was closed at press time but had a "re-opening soon" sign on the door. If you're looking for real nightlife, look to Cabo San Lucas, because even the restaurants in San José close between 9 and 10 p.m.

In fact, Cabo San Lucas is the undisputed nightlife capital of Baja and a contender for the title among all of Mexico's resorts. After-dark fun is centered around the party ambience and camaraderie found in the casual bars and restaurants on Bulevar Marina and those facing the marina, rather than around a flashy disco scene. You can easily find a happy hour with live music and a place to dance or a Mexican fiesta with mariachis.

To enjoy live music in a more sedate setting, check out the **Sancho Panza Wine Bar and Bistro** (☎ 624-143-3212; see "Hanging out and happy hours," later in this chapter). It offers classic jazz in a club-style atmosphere that accommodates conversations.

Enjoying a theme night

Some of the larger hotels have weekly fiesta nights, Italian nights, and other buffet-plus-entertainment theme nights that can be fun and a good buy. Check with travel agencies and the following hotels: the **Solmar** (☎ 624-143-3535), the **Finisterra** (☎ 624-143-3333), and the **Meliá San**

Lucas (☎ **624-145-7800**). Prices generally range from $25 (drinks, tax, and tips are extra) to $50 (everything is covered including an open bar with national drinks).

Watching a sunset

At twilight, check out Land's End — where the Sea of Cortez meets the Pacific Ocean — and watch the sun sink into the Pacific. The **Whale Watcher's Bar** (Hotel Finisterra; ☎ **624-143-3333**) is considered Los Cabos' premier place for sunset-watching. Its location at Land's End offers a truly world-class view of the setting sun. The high terrace offers vistas of both sea and beach as well as magical glimpses of whales from January to March. "Whale margaritas" cost $6, and beers set you back $3. The bar is open daily from 10 a.m. to 11 p.m.

Hanging out and happy hours

If you shop around, you can usually find an *hora alegre* (happy hour) somewhere in town between noon and 7 p.m. On my last visit, the most popular places to drink and carouse until all hours were the Giggling Marlin and El Squid Roe. Here are the best nightlife options:

✔ **El Squid Roe** (Bulevar Marina, opposite Plaza Bonita; ☎ **624-143-0655**; www.elsquidroe.com) is one of the late Carlos Anderson's inspirations, and it still attracts wild, fun-loving crowds of all ages. This two-story bar features nostalgic décor and eclectic food that's far better than you'd expect from such a party place. As fashionable as blue jeans, El Squid Roe is a place to see and see what can be seen — women's tops are known to be discarded with regularity here as the tabletop dancing moves into high gear. A patio out back serves as a place to dance when the tables, chairs, and bar spots have all been taken. It's open daily from noon to 4 a.m.

✔ Live music alternates with recorded tunes at the **Giggling Marlin** (Cárdenas at Zaragoza, across from the marina; ☎ **624-143-0606**; www.gigglingmarlin.com) to get the happy patrons dancing — and occasionally jumping up to dance on the tables and bar. A contraption of winches, ropes, and pulleys above a mattress provides entertainment as couples literally string each other up by the heels — just like a captured marlin. The food is only fair here; stick with nachos and drinks. It's open daily 9 a.m. to 2 a.m. Drinks are half-price during happy "hour," which in the tradition of excess that Cabo adores, lasts for four hours — 2 to 6 p.m.

✔ **Latitude 22+ Roadhouse** (Hwy. 1 Km 4.5, next to Costco; ☎ **624-143-1516**; www.lat22nobaddays.com) is a semi-seedy restaurant/bar. License plates, signs, sports caps, and a 959-pound blue marlin are the backdrop for U.S. sports events that play on six TVs scattered among pool tables, dart boards, and assorted games. The kitchen offers dishes from hamburgers to chicken-fried steak, or you can have breakfast any time. Latitude 22+ is a block north of the town's only traffic light. It's open from Wednesday to Monday 8 a.m. to 11 p.m., and is closed on Tuesdays.

✔ **Mambo Café** is a recent addition to the Cabo nightlife scene, part of a chain of bars around Mexico. It features a Caribbean concept club with a marine tropical ambience, playing contemporary Latin music. Live music is also featured. It's open Tuesday through Sunday from 9 p.m. to 5 a.m. It's located at Marina Local 9 and 10, next to the Costa Real Cabo Resort (☎ 624-143-1484; www.mambo cafe.com.mx). Cover charge, if any, varies with the night and the entertainment.

✔ **Nikki Beach,** a haven of the hip that hails from South Beach, Miami and St. Tropez, brought its ultra-cool vibe to the Meliá San Lucas resort beachfront in March 2005. White-draped bed-size lounges scatter the outdoor lounge area, under a canopy of umbrellas, surrounding a pool and overlooking Cabo's best swimming beach. A teak deck offers covered dining. The music is the latest in electronic, house, and chill, with visiting DJs often playing on weekend nights. Sundays feature their signature beach brunch. It's a great choice for catching rays during the day while sipping tropical drinks, but its real appeal is the nocturnal action. It's open Sunday through Wednesday from 11 a.m. to 1 a.m. (food service stops at 11 p.m.); Thursday through Saturday from 11 a.m. to 3 a.m. (food service stops at 1 a.m.), and is located on the beach at the Meliá San Lucas, on Medano Beach (☎ 624-145-7800; www.nikkibeach.com).

✔ Finally, an alternative to beer bars! **Sancho Panza Wine Bar and Bistro** (Plaza Las Glorias boardwalk, next to the lighthouse; ☎ 624-143-3212; www.sanchopanza.com) combines a gourmet-food market with a wine bar that features live jazz music plus an intriguing menu of nuevo-Latino cuisine. The place has a cozy neighborhood feeling. Tourists and locals take advantage of the selection of more than 150 wines, plus espresso drinks. During high season, you need reservations. It's open daily, 4 p.m. until the last guest leaves (the kitchen remains open until 11 p.m.).

✔ The **Tropicana Bar and Grill** (Mijares 30, San José; ☎ 624-142-0907) is definitely the most popular place in San José. This long-standing bar was undergoing extensive renovations during my last visit, but promises to have a more elegant ambience — rather than its previous "rustic chic." Don't worry though, the Tropicana will still feature all types of American sports events — on plasma TV screens — and a new area to segregate drinkers from diners. Live mariachi music plays nightly from 6 to 9 p.m., with live Mexican and Cuban dance music playing from 9:30 p.m. until about 1 a.m. Truly, this is your sole nightlife option in tranquil San José. The Tropicana is open daily from 7 a.m. to 1 a.m.

Going dancing

Owned by Sammy Hagar (formerly of Van Halen) and his Mexican and American partners, the **Cabo Wabo Cantina** (Vicente Guerrero at

Cárdenas; ☎ 624-143-1188; www.cabowabo.com) packs in youthful crowds — especially when rumors fly that a surprise appearance by a vacationing musician is imminent. Rock bands from the United States, Mexico, Europe, and Australia frequently perform live on the well-equipped stage. When live music is absent, a disco-type sound system plays mostly rock but some alternative and techno music as well. Overstuffed furniture frames the dance floor. For snacks, the Taco-Wabo, just outside the club's entrance, stays up late too. The cantina is open from 11 a.m. to 4 a.m.

Mens' clubs

What do the guys do after they're finished with golf? Often, they end the evening at one of the many strip clubs in Cabo. There's a changing selection of them to choose from, but the mainstays include **Mermaid's** (corner of Lázaro Cárdenas and Vicente Guerrero; ☎ 624-143-5370; www.loscabosnights.com/mermaids.htm), which offers its patrons their choice of topless stage shows or private dances. Admission is $5 for the general show, or $20 for the private dances. It's open nightly from 7 p.m. to 3 a.m. Another popular option is **Twenty/20 Showgirls** (Lázaro Cárdenas at Francisco Villa; ☎ 624-143-5380; www.loscabosnights.com/exoticclubs/twenty20.htm), also with a bevy of beauties to entertain you with their dancing skills on any one of the numerous stages. It's the largest of these clubs in Cabo. In addition to a topless cabaret show, they offer topless lap dances, as well as televised sports, pool tables and food service. It's open from 8:30 p.m. to 3 a.m., closed Tuesdays.

The best Web sites for Los Cabos and Baja

All About Cabo (www.allaboutcabo.com) features a weekly fishing report, live golf cam, and information on hotels, restaurants, golf courses, and more.

Baja Travel Guide (www.bajatravel.com) provides a good overview of activities and how to get around, but its extensive Yellow Pages are the most useful part of the site. The site can help you with tours, ground transportation, and outdoor excursions before you go.

Visit Cabo (www.visitcabo.com and www.visitloscabos.org) are official sites of the Los Cabos Tourism Board. Both have plenty of details about activities to do, current news, and a lodging and dining guide. You can also book your reservations online for select hotels.

Los Cabos Guide (www.loscabosguide.com) is a site presented by one of the most popular publications in town, and although commercial in nature, it offers a wide array of links and information.

Part X
The Part of Tens

The 5th Wave   By Rich Tennant

"All I know is what the swim-up bartender told me. Wearing these should improve our game by 25 percent."

In this part . . .

We give you the ten most common myths and misconceptions about Mexico. For instance, if you think all Mexican food is fiery hot, keep reading. And, speaking of Mexican food, you also find ten picks for the most delicious Mexican dishes. We also pass along ten quintessential Mexican moments — those places and experiences that you can only find in this magical, charismatic culture. Just a few *Dummies*-friendly lists that can help ensure your trip is a breeze.

Chapter 34

Ten Top Mexican Moments

In This Chapter

▶ Enjoying an authentic Mexican fiesta
▶ Watching for whales along Mexico's beaches
▶ Experiencing a singularly Mexican moment

*W*ant to watch the sun sink into the horizon from the deck of a sailboat while balmy breezes swirl around you? Care to be amazed by watching men leap into a narrow, rocky passage of surging ocean from a ledge 39m (130 ft.) above the water's surface?

Along with all of the classic, beach-going fun you can have at a Mexico beach resort, several singular experiences exist that you can only have here in grand old Mexico. These events become the unforgettable moments that make traveling to another country and another land a unique experience.

Enjoying a Mexican Fiesta

Mexican fiestas, colorful celebrations of Mexican food, dance, and fun, are mainstays among the entertainment options at Mexican beach resorts. Though the varieties of a *fiesta mexicana* can range from the cheesy to the sublime, a fiesta is generally a party that begins with a shot of tequila and an ample buffet, goes on to take you through presentations of different regional dances, and ends in a display of fireworks. ¡Viva Mexico!

Setting Sail at Sunset

Virtually every Mexican beach resort offers some variation of the sunset sail, which is just about the very best way to experience a Mexican beach resort. In Acapulco, Ixtapa, Huatulco, and Puerto Vallarta, these trips tend to be romantic bay cruises — with plenty of libations. In Cancún, try a replica pirate cruise with a lobster dinner; in Los Cabos, make that sail at sunset around the famous *El Arco* (The Arch) at the end of the Baja Peninsula past Lovers Beach. No matter where you set sail from, an excursion at sunset provides memories that can make a vacation.

Mixing It Up with Mariachi Music

From the first impressive note of the trombone, to the last strum of the guitar, mariachi music is synonymous with Mexico. Strolling musicians, often dressed to the nines in charro outfits and sombreros, play mariachi music on the streets and in restaurants.

Sipping on Margaritas at Sunset

Actually, feel free to pick your poison, but a cocktail at sunset is the quintessential Mexican beach vacation experience. This plan works best when you're on the Pacific coast so that you can watch the sun sink below the horizon; however, sipping at sunset on the East Coast doesn't seem to dampen the spirits either!

Strolling the Malecón

Call it a cheap thrill, but in most of Mexico's beach resorts, one of the best experiences is absolutely free — just stroll along the seaside walkway *(malecón)* in Puerto Vallarta or Zihuatanejo or sit in the plaza in San José de Los Cabos or Acapulco. You're certain to be both charmed and entertained by the parade of local life. And while you're at it, splurge on classic fare sold by vendors — we're talking corn on the cob and a colorful swirl of cotton candy.

Feasting on Fresh Fish under a Palapa

Eating fresh fish — or, more specifically, grilled fresh fish on a plate served under a *palapa* (a thatched umbrella) by the ocean's edge and accompanied by a cold *cerveza* (beer) and a balmy sea breeze — is an experience. We promise — you've never tasted anything more delicious.

Looking for Whales in Baja or Puerto Vallarta

Watching the majestic — and enormous — whales leap out of the water, splash their tail, or corral in their young is a thrill. Each winter, whales migrate to Mexico's Pacific shores. You can find the greatest concentration of whales in Baja California and in Banderas Bay, just offshore Puerto Vallarta. Ecologically sensitive whale-watching tours are becoming a favored Mexico-vacation experience.

Watching Cliff Divers in Acapulco

The only place in the world to see this sight is in Acapulco — bikini brief–clad men dive from a rocky cliff into the roaring surf of a narrow crevice 39m (130 ft.) below. Why? Because they can . . . and because you keep watching them do it! Don't miss this sight when in Acapulco.

Visiting Tulum

Although Tulum isn't the largest or most important Maya ruin, it's the only one by the sea, which makes it the most visually impressive. Ancient Tulum is a stunning site — and our personal favorite of all the ruins — poised on a rocky hill overlooking the transparent, turquoise Caribbean Sea. You can't visually sum up Mexico's combination of exquisite beaches and a centuries-old culture more aptly.

Shopping — While Sunbathing

Call it Mexican multitasking, but you can make the most of your precious vacation time by doing a little shopping while soaking up the sun. Along Mexico's public beaches, being approached by strolling vendors, peddling everything from silver jewelry to Spiderman parachute dolls, is quite common. Woven baskets, colorful ceramics, and even woven rugs are also common finds. And the shopping isn't limited to tangibles — services are available as well! Have your hair braided, your portrait sketched, or even get a temporary tattoo, all from the comfort of your beach chair. Where else but Mexico?

Chapter 35

Ten Myths and Misconceptions about Mexico

In This Chapter

▶ Getting the geography straight

▶ Dissecting the stereotypical preconceptions

▶ Steering clear of illegal activities

▶ Solving food and drink misconceptions

▶ Respecting the country and its residents

*I*f you've never visited Mexico, you may have some preconceptions about what you're likely to find here. Perhaps you think that the geography — apart from the beaches — is an arid landscape with a uniformly hot climate. Or you may think that you should only drink tequila as a shot — doused with lime and salt.

This chapter explains some of the most common misconceptions about this vast country and its rich culture. Read on — and the next time someone starts talking about how you shouldn't drink the water in Mexico, you can set them straight!

Mexico Is a Desert, and It's Hot Everywhere

Not true: Mexico's geography includes pine forests, and occasional snowfalls hit some of the country's higher elevations. Most of the beach resorts in this book, however, do enjoy sultry climates, but bringing along a sweater or light jacket for cool evenings, especially during winter months, is always wise.

Mexico Is the Land of Sombreros and Siestas

The common image of a Mexican napping under his sombrero exists in some minds, but this stereotype is mostly made of myth. Today, Mexico is a mix of contemporary business professionals and traditional agrarian populations. The afternoon break — between 2 and 4 p.m. — is still a wonderful tradition, but rather than being a time for *siesta,* it's the time when families come together for the day's main meal.

Mexico Has No Drinking or Drug Laws

Because of the welcoming and casual nature of Mexico, many visitors believe that the sale of alcoholic beverages — or illegal drugs — is unregulated. This belief simply isn't true. The legal drinking age in Mexico is 18, and technically, you're not allowed to drink openly in public. However, if you're not acting intoxicated, you can generally enjoy a beer or even a cocktail while you stroll around town. As with most things in Mexico, it's not what you do but how you do it. Although you can drink on public beaches, you can't be inebriated in public.

With regard to drugs, we want to get straight to the point: They're illegal, and carrying even a small amount of marijuana can earn you a very unpleasant trip to jail. Remember that Mexican law states that you're guilty until proven innocent.

If in Trouble, Pay a Mordida

Although the idea of paying a *mordida,* or "bite," may have been rooted in truth for a long time, in Mexico's new political era, an active campaign is underway to keep dishonesty to a minimum and to clean house of corrupt public servants. Many old-school traffic cops still take a bribe when offered; however, officers belonging to the new generation of federal policemen are tested for honesty, and the penalties for corrupt behavior are severe — as are the penalties for those civilians inducing corruption by offering bribes to police officers. Our suggestion is don't offer a "tip" to ease your way out of trouble; the best course of action is to just act politely and find out what the problem is.

All Mexican Food Is Spicy

Not all Mexican food is spicy — although Mexican food does include some of the most intriguingly flavored foods we've ever enjoyed. Although spicy sauces may likely be in the vicinity of the food you're served, the truth is that many delicious Mexican dishes don't include chile peppers among their ingredients.

Don't Drink the Water

In the past, visitors often returned home from Mexico with stomach illnesses, but this type of vacation souvenir is a rarity today. Massive investments in an improved infrastructure and a general increase in standards of cleanliness and hygiene have practically wiped out the problem. However, play it safe and drink bottled water. Ice served in tourist establishments is purified.

Tequila Is Best with a Pinch of Salt and Lime

Tequila is a drink to be appreciated and sipped — not slammed down in a shot, its flavor masked by salt and lime. If you need to do that, you're drinking the wrong tequila. Insist on only 100-percent blue agave tequila — the mark of a pure, quality tequila — and then discover how to appreciate the subtleties and nuances of this tasteful beverage.

A Jeep Rental Is Really $10 a Day

One of the most common lures a timeshare salesperson uses is the "Rent a Jeep for $10 per day" enticement. Sure, it's true that the Jeep is only $10, but only after you spend up to half a day listening to an often high-pressured sales pitch. You decide — what's your vacation time really worth? And always remember: *If it looks too good to be true . . .*

Going Anywhere in Just Your Swimsuit Is Okay

Although you may be at a seaside resort, keep in mind that it's also a home and place of business for many Mexicans. Wearing swim trunks or a pareo skirt wrapped around your bikini is okay while you're on your way to the beach, but we recommend that you put on a shirt or a sundress when you plan to explore the town. You can still go casual, but Mexicans frown upon tourists who can't tell the difference between beach and town attire — especially true when it comes to going into any church wearing inappropriate clothing.

Mexicans Who Don't Speak English Are Hard of Hearing

Or at least it appears that many tourists buy into this statement. Some travelers seem to believe that a native Spanish-speaker will somehow get over his or her inability to understand English if the English-speaking individual talks really loudly into the Spanish-speaker's face. The truth is that many Mexicans understand at least some English, especially in popular tourist areas. Try this: Instead of panicking and starting to yell in order to get your point across, ask nicely for help, and an English-speaking local will come to assist you.

Chapter 36

Ten Most Deliciously Mexican Dishes

In This Chapter

▶ Knowing your Mexican meals and sauces

▶ Indulging in uniquely Mexican beverages

Some like it hot . . . and then there's Mexican food! But true Mexican cuisine is noted more for its unique way of combining flavors — chocolate and chiles, sweet and hot — than for its fire appeal.

This chapter explains some of the most flavorful and traditional Mexican dishes that you're likely to find on a menu here — go ahead and be adventurous! Let your taste buds have a vacation from the foods you know — explore the favored flavors of Mexico.

Café de Olla

The popularity and tradition of drinking coffee is nothing new to Mexico, so to experience a taste of the past, try the traditional Mexican version called *café de olla*. The espresso-strength coffee is prepared in an earthenware pot. It's spiced with cinnamon, cloves, and raw brown sugar. It's certain to wake you up!

Ceviche

Ceviche is one of Mexico's more traditional ways to enjoy fish and seafood. Ceviche is usually made of fish, but it may also be made from seafood including shrimp, octopus, crab, and even conch. The fresh fish — or seafood — is marinated in lime and vinegar and mixed with chopped tomatoes, onions, and, depending on the region, cucumbers and carrots.

Chilaquiles

One of the most traditional and satisfying breakfast dishes in Mexico is *chilaquiles,* fried tortilla strips cooked in a mild or spicy red or green sauce. They're usually served with a fried egg or shredded chicken and topped with fresh cream, chopped onions, and shredded white cheese.

Licuados

Not quite a meal, yet much more than a beverage, *licuados* are essentially smoothies, blended drinks of fresh fruit, ice, and either water or milk. Popular flavors include mango, banana, pineapple, or watermelon. You can also make up your own combination of tropical fruit flavors!

Mole

Mole is a rich sauce that's often considered Mexico's most important culinary contribution. A thick, deeply colored sauce, mole comes in hues of green, red, yellow, and even black. Mole blends the flavors of fresh and dried peppers, nuts, and — depending on the area — fruits or chocolate. Mole is traditionally served with chicken but is sometimes found accompanying fish and pork. It truly reflects the spirit of Mexico — the ingredients are a combination of both European and pre-Hispanic elements. The final taste varies according to the individual chef. If we had to compare it with something, curry would be the closest association.

Pescadillas

Pescadillas, flour tortillas filled with melted cheese and fresh grilled fish, are truly succulent. Most places serve them with a mild tomato sauce.

Pescado Sarandeado or Pescado en Talla

You're at a Mexican beach resort, so you're almost certain to indulge in the fresh fish *(pescado).* One of the most traditional and tasty ways to prepare fish is *sarandeado* (the term used along the beaches of Puerto Vallarta) or *en talla* (as they refer to this dish in Acapulco and Huatulco). The fish is prepared by marinating it in a sauce of Worcestershire, lime, mild red-pepper paste, and other seasonings that vary slightly depending on the region. The fish is then cooked slowly over a wood fire. The Mexican-Caribbean variation of this fish is called *tikik-chik* or *tikin-chik,* and it includes a regional *achiote* (annatto seed) paste in the marinade.

Pozole

A traditional dish from the coastal states of Jalisco, Colima, and Guerrero, *pozole* represents the blending of the pre-Hispanic Mexican culture and European influences. It's a souplike dish made with hominy and pork, but nowadays many places make it with chicken. You can find red, green, and white versions of *pozole,* depending on the area, and garnishes include shredded lettuce, radish slices, or cabbage.

Tacos al Pastor

When ordered from a street vendor, *tacos al pastor* are only for the more adventurous travelers, but they're truly a Mexican specialty. *Tacos al pastor* are made from shanks of marinated pork, which are skewered and slowly cooked on a vertical charcoal grill. The traditional ones are served with a chunk of fresh pineapple, diced onion, and cilantro. You may have heard about the dangers of eating tacos on the street; however, the common sense that you apply to purchasing food from any street vendor also applies here. If you want to be really safe, though, we recommend you enjoy them at a small taco restaurant rather than from a street stall.

Tamales

Tamales in Mexico are quite different from the ones you typically find in the United States, which tend to be compact and greasy. In Mexico, these tasty bundles of corn dough are fluffy and come with a variety of fillings ranging from spicy to sweet. One popular variety is *rajas con queso,* a filling of poblano pepper strips and cheese. Other possibilities are *rojos* (red) or *verdes* (green) tamales filled with shredded chicken or pork — the names refer to the type of sauce included. Sweet tamales may come filled with cinnamon and raisins, stewed mangoes, or pineapple. On the southern-Pacific coast, tamales come wrapped in banana leaves and have a heavier consistency. Traditional *Oaxaqueño* (from Oaxaca) tamales are filled with mole and chicken and wrapped in palm leaves.

Part XI

Appendixes

The 5th Wave

By Rich Tennant

"Of all the stuff we came back from Mexico with, I think these adobe bathrobes were the least well thought out."

In this part . . .

*L*ooking for a quick phone number or Web site to help you finalize the details of your Mexican beach resort vacation? Want to bone up on a few common Spanish words and phrases? Or simply hoping to get your hunger pangs going for some authentic Mexican cuisine? You can search this part for that kind of information and more, including contact information for some reputable resort tourist associations and a helpful glossary of common Mexican dishes and ingredients.

Appendix A

Quick Concierge

• •

Fast Facts

Abbreviations

Common address abbreviations include *Apdo.* (post office box), *Av.* or *Ave.* (*avenida;* avenue), *Blv.* (*bulevar;* boulevard), *c/* (*calle;* street), *Calz.* (*calzada;* boulevard), *Dept.* (apartments), and *s/n* (*sin número;* without a number).

The c on faucets stands for *caliente* (hot), and F stands for *fría* (cold). PB *(planta baja)* means ground floor, and most buildings count the next floor up as the first floor (1).

American Express

All major resort destinations have local American Express representatives. For a detailed list of all representatives, visit the AmEx Web site at `http://travel.americanexpress.com/travel/personal/resources/tso`. For credit card and traveler's check information, call ☎ 800-528-2122 toll-free inside Mexico. The local offices in the beach resorts covered in this guide are Acapulco (Av. Costera Miguel Alemán 121, Hotel Continental Emporio Local 31; ☎ 744-435-2200), Cabo San Lucas (Plaza Bonita Mall, Local 48e/49e; ☎ 624-143-5766), Cancún (Av. Tulum 208; ☎ 998-881-4025), Ixtapa and Zihuatanejo (Av. Heróico Colegio Militar 38, Plaza San Rafael Local 7, Col. Centro; ☎ 755-544-6242), Puerto Vallarta (Morelos 660; ☎ 322-223-2955), and San José del Cabo (Plaza La Misión, Local 1-b, Bulevar Mijares/Paseo Finisterra; ☎ 624-142-1306).

ATMs

Automated teller machines are widely available in all major resort towns, with fewer to be found in the smaller destinations. They're a great option to get cash at an excellent exchange rate. To find the closest ATM, visit the Web sites for the most popular networks: Plus (`www.visa.com/pd/atm`) and Cirrus (`www.mastercard.com/atmlocator`). (See Chapter 5 for further details.)

Business Hours

In general, businesses in resort destinations are open daily between 9 a.m. and 8 p.m.; although many close between 2 and 4 p.m. Smaller businesses also tend to close on Sundays. The larger resort destinations have extended business hours — many shops stay open until 10 p.m. Bank hours are Monday to Friday 8:30 or 9 a.m. to anywhere between 3 and 7 p.m. Increasingly, banks are offering Saturday hours in at least one branch for at least a half-day, usually from 10 a.m. until 2 p.m.

Credit Cards

Most stores, restaurants, and hotels accept credit cards. However, smaller destinations such as Puerto Escondido, where telephone lines aren't always available to process the authorization for the charge, may not be so credit-card friendly. The same goes for smaller, family-run shops and restaurants. You can withdraw cash from your credit card at most ATMs, but make sure that you know your PIN and you've cleared the card for foreign withdrawals with your bank. For credit-card emergencies, call the following numbers: American Express ☎ 001-800-528-2122, MasterCard ☎ 001-800-MC-ASSIST, and Visa ☎ 001-800-847-2911. These numbers connect you to the U.S. toll-free numbers to report lost or stolen credit cards; however, the call isn't toll-free from Mexico.

Currency

The currency in Mexico is the Mexican peso. Paper currency comes in denominations of 20, 50, 100, 200, 500, and 1,000 pesos. Coins come in denominations of 1, 2, 5, 10, 20, and 50 centavos (100 centavos equal 1 peso). The currency-exchange rate is about 11 pesos to US$1.

Customs

All travelers to Mexico are required to present proof of citizenship, such as an original birth certificate with a raised seal, a valid passport, or naturalization papers, and need to have a Mexican tourist card (FMT), which is free of charge and can be attained through travel agencies and airlines and at all border-crossing points going into Mexico. For more information, see Chapter 9.

Doctors and Dentists

Every embassy and consulate can recommend local doctors and dentists with good training and modern equipment; some of the doctors and dentists also speak English. See the list of embassies and consulates under the "Embassies & Consulates," section later in this appendix. Hotels with a large foreign clientele can often recommend English-speaking doctors as well. Most first-class hotels in Mexico's resort areas have a doctor on call.

Drug Laws

To be blunt, don't use or possess illegal drugs in Mexico. Mexican officials have no tolerance for drug users, and jail is their solution. If you go to jail, you have little hope of getting out until you complete the sentence (usually a long one) or pay heavy fines. Remember, in Mexico, the legal system assumes that you're guilty until proven innocent. (*Note:* It isn't uncommon to be befriended by a fellow user, only to be turned in by that "friend," who's collected a bounty.) Bring prescription drugs in their original containers. If possible, pack a copy of the original prescription with the generic name of the drug.

U.S. Customs officials are also on the lookout for diet drugs that are sold in Mexico but illegal in the United States. Possession of these could land you in a U.S. jail. If you buy antibiotics over the counter (which you can do in Mexico) — say, for a sinus infection — and still have some left, you probably won't be hassled by U.S. Customs.

Electricity

The electrical system in Mexico is 110 volts AC (60 cycles), as it is in the United States and Canada. But in reality, it may cycle more slowly and overheat your appliances. To compensate, select a medium or low speed for hair dryers. Many older hotels still have electrical outlets for flat, two-prong plugs; you'll need an adapter for any modern electrical apparatus that has three prongs or an enlarged end on one of the two prongs. Many first-class and deluxe hotels have the three-holed outlets (*trifásicos* in Spanish). Hotels that don't have modern outlets may have adapters to loan, but to be sure, carry your own.

Embassies and Consulates

Embassies and consulates can provide valuable lists of doctors and lawyers, as well as regulations concerning marriages in Mexico. Contrary to popular belief, your embassy can't get you out of a Mexican jail, provide postal or banking services, or fly you home when you run out of money. However, consular officers can provide you with advice on most matters and problems. Most countries have a representative embassy in Mexico City, and many have consular offices or representatives in the provinces.

The embassy of the United States is in Mexico City (Paseo de la Reforma 305; ☎ 555-080-2000; Fax: 555-525-5040). Its hours are Monday to Friday 8:30 a.m. to 5:30 p.m. You can visit the embassy's Web site at www.usembassy-mexico.gov for a list of street addresses for the U.S. consulates inside Mexico. U.S. consular agencies are located in Acapulco (☎ 744-469-0556 or 484-0300), Cabo San Lucas (☎ 624-143-3566), Cancún (☎ 998-883-0272), Cozumel (☎ 987-872-4574 or 987-872-4485), Ixtapa (☎ 755-553-2100), and Puerto Vallarta (☎ 322-222-0069).

The embassy of Australia is in Mexico City at Rubén Darío 55, Polanco (☎ 551-101-2200; Fax: 551-101-2201). It's open Monday to Friday 9 a.m. to 1 p.m. (www.mexico.embassy.gov.au).

The embassy of Canada is also in Mexico City (Schiller 529, in Polanco; ☎ 555-724-7900). It's open Monday through Friday 9 a.m. to 1 p.m. and 2 to 5 p.m. (At other times, the name of a duty officer is posted on the embassy door.) Visit the Web site at www.canada.org.mx for a complete list of the addresses of the consular agencies in Mexico. Canadian consulates are located in Acapulco (Centro Comercial Marbella, Local 23, Prolongación Farallón s/n; ☎ 744-484-1305; acapulco@canada.org.mx), Cancún (Plaza Caracol 11, Bulevar Kukulkán; ☎ 998-883-3360; cancun@canada.org.mx), Puerto Vallarta (Edificio Obelisco, Local 108,

Av. Francisco Medina Ascencio 1951; ☎ 322-293-0098 or 293-0099; vallarta@canada.org.mx), and San José del Cabo (Plaza José Green, Local 9, Bulevar Mijares s/n; ☎ 624-142-4333; loscabos@canada.org.mx).

The embassy of New Zealand in Mexico City is at Jaime Balmes 8, fourth floor, Col. Los Morales Polanco (☎ 555-283-9460; Fax: 555-283-9480; kiwimexico@compuserve.com.mx).

The embassy of the United Kingdom is in Mexico City at Río Lerma 71, Col. Cuauhtémoc (☎ 555-242-8500). The embassy's Web site, which you can visit at www.embajadabritanica.com.mx, has an updated list of honorary consuls in Mexico. There are honorary British consuls in Acapulco (☎ 744-484-1735), Cancún (☎ 998-881-0100), and Huatulco (☎ 958-587-2373 or 587-2372 — leave a message).

The embassy of Ireland is located in Mexico City on Bulevar Cerrada Avila Camacho 76, third floor Forum Building, Col. Lomas de Chapultepec (☎ 555-520-5803; Fax: 555-520-5892; embajada@irlanda.org.mx).

The embassy of South Africa is also in Mexico City at Andres Bello 10, ninth floor, Col. Polanco (☎ 555-282-9260; www.sre.gob.mx/acreditadas/sud.htm).

Emergencies

In case of emergency, always contact your embassy or consulate. For police emergencies, you must dial ☎ 060 — this number connects you to the local police department. Remember that in most cases the person answering the phone doesn't speak English. The 24-hour tourist help line from Mexico City (INFOTUR) is ☎ 800-987-8224 or 555-089-7500. A tourist legal assistance office *(Procuraduría del Turista)* is located in Mexico City (☎ 555-625-8153) or dial 078. Although the phones are frequently busy, they do offer 24-hour service, and an English-speaking person is always available.

Health

No special immunizations are required. As is often true when traveling anywhere in the world, intestinal problems are the most common afflictions experienced by travelers. Drink only bottled water and stay away from uncooked foods, especially fruits and vegetables. Antibiotics and anti-diarrheal medications are readily available in all drugstores. Contact your embassy or consulate for a list of accredited doctors in the area.

Hot Lines

While in Mexico, contact the 24-hour tourist help line, INFOTUR (☎ 800-987-8224), for information regarding hotels, restaurants, tourist attractions, hospitals with English-speaking staff, and so on.

Information

The best source of information is the tourist help line INFOTUR (☎ 800-987-8224); however, having a general idea of the information you're requesting — the approximate name of the hotel or restaurant, the name or subject matter of the museum, and so on — is important. You can also find telephone-number information inside Mexico by dialing ☎ 040; however, it's very common to find that the telephone numbers aren't listed under the known name of the establishment. A reminder: Very few information operators speak English.

Internet Access

In large cities and resort areas, most five-star hotels offer business centers with Internet access. You also find cybercafes in destinations that are popular with expatriates and business travelers. Even in remote spots, Internet access is very common — it's often their best way of communicating with the outside world. Note that many Internet service providers automatically cut off your Internet connection after a specified period of time (say, 10 min.) because telephone lines are at a premium. Some Telmex offices also have free-access Internet kiosks in their reception areas. If you plan to check your e-mail while in Mexico, register for a Web-based e-mail address, such as those from Hotmail or Yahoo!

Language

The official language in Mexico is Spanish, but you find that a fair number of Mexicans who live and work in resort areas speak some English. Mexicans are very patient when it comes to foreigners trying to speak Spanish. See Appendix B for commonly used terms in Spanish.

Legal Aid

International Legal Defense Counsel (111 S. 15th St., 24th floor, Packard Building, Philadelphia, PA 19102; ☎ 215-977-9982) is a law firm specializing in legal difficulties of Americans abroad. Also, see the "Embassies & Consulates" and "Emergencies" sections, earlier in this appendix.

Liquor Laws

The legal drinking age in Mexico is 18; however, it's extremely rare that anyone is asked for identification or denied purchase. Grocery stores sell everything from beer and wine to national and imported liquors. You can buy liquor 24 hours a day, but during major elections and a few official holidays, dry laws often are enacted as long as 24 hours beforehand. The laws apply to foreign tourists as well as local residents, even though it's not uncommon to find a few hotels and nightclubs that manage to obtain special permits to sell alcohol. Mexico doesn't have any "open container" laws for transporting alcohol in cars, but authorities are beginning to target drunk drivers more aggressively. Driving defensively is a good idea.

Drinking in the street isn't legal, but many tourists do it. Use your better judgment and try to avoid carrying on while sporting beer bottles and cans — you're not only exposing yourself to the eyes of the authorities, but most Mexicans consider public intoxication to be tacky behavior. If you're getting too drunk, don't drink in the street because the police will most likely stop you. As is the custom in Mexico, it's not so much what you do, but how you do it.

Mail

Postage for a postcard or letter is 1 peso, and the item may arrive at its destination anywhere between one to six weeks after you send it. A registered letter costs $1.90. Sending a package can be quite expensive — the Mexican postal service charges $8 per kilo (2.2 lb.) — and is unreliable — it takes between two and six weeks, if it arrives at all. Packages are frequently lost within the Mexican postal system, although the situation has improved in recent years. Federal Express, DHL, UPS, or any other reputable, international-mail service is the recommended option for a package or important letter.

Newspapers and Magazines

Newspaper kiosks in larger Mexican cities carry a selection of English-language magazines. Most resort towns have their own local publications in English, which provide helpful hints and fun reading tailored to tourists and foreigners who have made their homes in the different resort destinations around Mexico. In Puerto Vallarta, the *Vallarta Today* and *PV Tribune* are two

of these newspapers — the former is a daily publication, and the latter is published weekly. In Los Cabos, you can find a wealth of information in the *Los Cabos Guide, Los Cabos News, Cabo Life, Baja Sun,* and the irreverent and extremely entertaining *Gringo Gazette.*

Pets

Taking a pet into Mexico is easy but requires a little pre-planning. For travelers coming from the United States and Canada, your pet's health needs to be checked within 30 days before arrival in Mexico. Most veterinarians in major cities have the appropriate paperwork — an official health certificate, to be presented to Mexican Customs officials, which ensures the pet is up-to-date on its vaccinations. When you and your pet return from Mexico, U.S. Customs officials will require the same type of paperwork. If your stay extends beyond the 30-day time frame of your U.S.-issued certificate, you need to get an updated certificate of health issued by a veterinarian in Mexico that also states the condition of your pet and the status of its vaccinations. To find out about any last-minute changes in requirements, consult a Mexican-government tourist office.

Pharmacies

Farmacias sell you just about anything you want, with or without a prescription. Most pharmacies are open Monday to Saturday 8 a.m. to 8 p.m. Generally, one or two 24-hour pharmacies are located in the major resort areas. Pharmacies take turns staying open during off-hours, so if you're in a smaller town and you need to buy medicine after normal hours, ask for the *farmacia de turno* (pharmacy on duty).

Police

It's quite common to find that the majority of police forces in tourist areas are very protective of international visitors. Several cities, including Cancún, Puerto Vallarta, and Acapulco, have gone so far as to set up a special corps of English-speaking tourist police to assist with directions, guidance, and more. In case of a police emergency, dial ☎ **060** to contact the local police department, keeping in mind that, unless you're dealing with tourist police, the force is very unlikely to speak English.

Restrooms

Public restrooms are usually more of an adventure than a service — you can never tell whether they'll be clean or toilet paper will be available. You can usually resort to using the restroom in a restaurant.

Safety

Most resort areas in Mexico are very safe; however, it's better to be prepared than sorry. A few points to keep in mind: Before you leave home, prepare for the theft or loss of your travel documents by making two photocopies of them. Keep each copy and the original documents in separate places. Lock your passport and valuables in the hotel safety-deposit box. Keep credit-card company phone numbers and the numbers of traveler's checks somewhere other than your purse or wallet. Don't dress or behave in a conspicuous manner. When visiting crowded places, be aware of your wallet or purse at all times. Leave your best jewelry at home — who wants jewelry tan lines anyway?

Taxes

Most of Mexico has a 15 percent value-added tax (IVA) on goods and services, and it's supposed to be included in the posted price. This tax is 10 percent in Cancún, Cozumel, and Los Cabos. Mexico charges all visitors an entry tax of $24, which is usually included in the price of your plane ticket. Mexico also imposes an exit tax of around $24 on every foreigner leaving the country, which again, is usually included in the price of airline tickets.

Telephone and Fax

In November 2001, telephone area codes were changed. Now, all telephone numbers in Mexico are seven digits plus a three-digit area code, except for Mexico City, Guadalajara, and Monterrey where local calls require that you dial the last eight digits of the published phone number. Many fax numbers are also regular telephone numbers — you have to ask whoever answers your call for the fax tone *("Me da tono de fax, por favor.")*. Wireless phones are very popular for small businesses in resort areas and smaller communities. To dial a wireless number inside the same area code, dial 044 and then the number — depending on the area, you may need to dial the last seven digits or the seven digits plus the three-digit area code. To dial the cellular phone from anywhere else in Mexico, first dial 01, and then the ten-digit number, including the area code. To dial any number inside Mexico from the United States, just dial 011-52 plus the ten-digit number.

The country code for Mexico is 52. To call home from Mexico, dial 00 plus the country code you're calling and then the area code and phone number. To call the United States and Canada, you need to dial 001 plus the area code and the number. The country code for the United Kingdom is 44, the country code for New Zealand is 64, and the country code for Australia is 61.

To call operator assistance for calls inside Mexico, dial 020; for operator assistance for international calls, dial 090. Both numbers provide assistance for person-to-person and collect calls.

Time Zone

Central standard time prevails throughout most of Mexico. The west-coast states of Sonora, Sinaloa, and parts of Nayarit are on mountain standard time. The state of Baja California Norte is on pacific time, but Baja California Sur is on mountain time. Most of Mexico observes daylight saving time, but the time change lasts for a shorter period of time than it does in the rest of the world. Mexico doesn't spring forward until June, and the country falls back in early October. This time-change pattern has created a lot of political arguments, and the guidelines may change again.

Tipping

Most service employees in Mexico count on tips for the majority of their income — especially true for bellboys and waiters. Bellboys should receive the equivalent of 50¢ to $1 per bag; waiters generally receive 10 percent to 20 percent, depending on the level of service. In Mexico, tipping taxi drivers isn't customary, unless you hire them by the hour, or they provide guide or other special services. Don't use U.S. coins to tip.

Water

Most hotels have decanters or bottles of purified water in the rooms, and the better hotels have purified water from regular taps or special taps marked AGUA PURIFICADA. Some hotels charge for in-room bottled water. Virtually any hotel, restaurant, or bar brings you purified water if you specifically request it, but they usually charge you for it. Bottled, purified water is sold widely at drugstores and grocery stores. Some popular brands are Santa María, Ciel, and Bonafont. Evian and other imported brands are also widely available.

Toll-Free Numbers and Web Sites

Airlines serving select Mexican destinations

Aeroméxico
☎ 800-237-6639
www.aeromexico.com
Acapulco, Cancún, Huatulco, Los Cabos, Ixtapa-Zihuatanejo, Puerto Vallarta

Air Canada
☎ 888-247-2262
www.aircanada.ca
Cancún, Cozumel, Puerto Vallarta

Alaska Airlines
☎ 800-252-7522
www.alaskaair.com
Cancún, Ixtapa-Zihuatanejo, Los Cabos, Puerto Vallarta

American Airlines
☎ 800-223-5436
www.aa.com
Acapulco, Cancún, Cozumel, Ixtapa-Zihuatanejo, Los Cabos, Puerto Vallarta

America West Airlines
☎ 800-327-7810
www.americawest.com
Acapulco, Cancún, Ixtapa-Zihuatanejo, Los Cabos, Puerto Vallarta

ATA Airlines
☎ 800-435-9282
www.ata.com
Cancún, Ixtapa-Zihuatanejo, Puerto Vallarta

British Airways
☎ 800-247-9297
www.britishairways.com
Flights from London to Cancún

Continental Airlines
☎ 800-537-9222
www.continental.com
Acapulco, Cancún, Cozumel, Ixtapa-Zihuatanejo, Los Cabos, Puerto Vallarta

Delta Air Lines
☎ 800-221-1212
www.delta.com
Cancún, Los Cabos, Puerto Vallarta

Frontier Airlines
☎ 800-432-1359
www.frontierairlines.com
Cancún, Ixtapa-Zihuatanejo, Los Cabos, Puerto Vallarta

United Airlines
☎ 800-538-2929

www.united.com
Cancún, Los Cabos

Serviced through Aeroméxico

Mexicana
☎ 800-531-7921
www.mexicana.com
Acapulco, Cancún, Cozumel, Huatulco, Ixtapa-Zihuatanejo, Los Cabos, Puerto Vallarta

Northwest Airlines
☎ 800-225-2525
www.nwa.com
Seasonal flights to Acapulco, Cancún, Cozumel, Los Cabos, Puerto Vallarta

US Airways
☎ 800-428-4322
www.usairways.com
Cancún, Cozumel

Major car-rental agencies

Advantage
☎ 800-777-5500
www.advantagerentacar.com
Cancún, Huatulco, Los Cabos, Puerto Vallarta

Alamo
☎ 800-GO-ALAMO
www.goalamo.com
Acapulco, Cancún, Cozumel, Huatulco, Ixtapa-Zihuatanejo, Los Cabos, Puerto Escondido

Avis
☎ 800-331-1212 in the continental U.S.
☎ 800-TRY-AVIS in Canada
www.avis.com
Acapulco, Cancún, Cozumel, Los Cabos, Puerto Vallarta

Budget
☎ 800-527-0700
www.budgetrentacar.com
Acapulco, Cancún, Cozumel, Huatulco, Ixtapa-Zihuatanejo, Los Cabos, Puerto Escondido, Puerto Vallarta

Dollar
☎ 800-800-4000
www.dollar.com
Cancún, Huatulco, Ixtapa-Zihuatanejo, Los Cabos, Puerto Vallarta

Hertz
☎ 800-654-3131
www.hertz.com
Acapulco, Cancún, Cozumel, Ixtapa-Zihuatanejo, Los Cabos, Puerto Vallarta

National
☎ 800-CAR-RENT
www.nationalcar.com
Cancún, Cozumel, Ixtapa-Zihuatanejo, Los Cabos, Puerto Vallarta

Payless
☎ 800-PAY-LESS

www.paylesscarrental.com
Los Cabos

Thrifty
☎ 800-THRIFTY
www.thrifty.com
Cancún, Ixtapa-Zihuatanejo, Los Cabos, Puerto Vallarta

Major and select local hotel and motel chains

Best Western
☎ 800-780-7234
www.bestwestern.com
Acapulco, Cancún, Cozumel, Huatulco, Ixtapa-Zihuatanejo, Los Cabos, Puerto Escondido, Puerto Vallarta

Camino Real
☎ 800-722-6466
www.caminoreal.com
Acapulco, Cancún, Huatulco

Days Inn
☎ 800-DAYS-INN
www.daysinn.com
Cozumel

Fiesta Americana
☎ 877-CAESAR-2
www.fiestaamericana.com
or www.posadas.com
Acapulco, Cancún, Cozumel, Los Cabos, Puerto Vallarta

Hilton Hotels
☎ 800-HILTONS
www.hilton.com
Cancún, Los Cabos

Holiday Inn
☎ 800-HOLIDAY or 800-262-9168
www.ichotelsgroup.com
Cancún, Puerto Vallarta

Hyatt Hotels and Resorts
☎ 888-96-HYATT

www.hyatt.com
Acapulco, Cancún

Inter-Continental Hotels and Resorts
☎ 800-000-6633
www.ichotelsgroup.com
or www.intercontinental.com
Cancún, Cozumel, Los Cabos, Puerto Vallarta

Le Méridien Hotel
☎ 866-559-3821
www.lemeridien.com
Cancún

Marriott Hotels
☎ 800-932-2198
www.marriott.com
Cancún, Puerto Vallarta

Quinta Real
☎ 866-621-9288
www.quintareal.com
Acapulco, Huatulco

Radisson Hotels International
☎ 888-201-1718
www.radisson.com
Acapulco, Cancún, Ixtapa-Zihuatanejo

Ritz-Carlton Hotel
☎ 800-241-3333
www.ritzcarlton.com
Cancún

Sheraton Hotels and Resorts
☎ 800-625-5144
www.sheraton.com
or www.starwoodhotels.com/
sheraton/reservations/index.
html
Cancún, Los Cabos, Puerto Vallarta

Westin Hotels and Resorts
☎ 888-625-5144
www.westin.com
or www.starwoodhotels.com/
westin/reservations/index.
html
Cancún, Los Cabos, Puerto Vallarta

Where to Get More Information

The following **tourist boards** and **embassies** provide valuable information regarding traveling in Mexico, including information on entry requirements and Customs allowances:

✔ **Mexico Tourism Board:** There are several offices in major North American cities, in addition to the main office in Mexico City (☎ 555-278-4200; www.visitmexico.com). The toll-free information number is ☎ **800-44-MEXICO.**

Locations in the United States: Chicago (300 N. Michigan, fourth floor, Chicago, IL 60601; ☎ 312-228-0517; Fax: 312-606-9252); Houston (4507 San Jacinto, Suite 308, Houston, TX 77074; ☎ 713-772-2581 ext. 105); Los Angeles (2401 W. 6th St., Los Angeles, CA 90057; ☎ 310-282-9112); Miami (5975 Sunset Dr., Suite 305, Miami, FL 33143; ☎ 305-381-6996); New York (21 E. 63rd St., third Floor, New York, NY 10021; ☎ 212-821-0314; Fax: 212-821-0367); and the Mexican Embassy Tourism Delegate in Washington D.C. (1911 Pennsylvania Ave., Washington, DC 20006; ☎ 202-728-1750 and 728-1650).

Locations in Canada: Montreal (1 Place Ville-Marie, Suite 1931, Montreal, PQ H3B 2C3; ☎ 514-871-1052; Fax: 514-871-3825); Toronto (2 Bloor St. W., Suite 1502, Toronto, ON M4W 3E2; ☎ 416-925-0704 and 925-2753; Fax: 416-925-6061); Vancouver (999 W. Hastings, Suite 1110, Vancouver, BC V6C 2W2; ☎ 604-669-2845; Fax: 604-669-3498); and the embassy office in Ottawa (Suite 1500, 45 O'Connor St., Ottawa, ON K1P 1A4; ☎ 613-233-8988; Fax: 613-235-9123).

✔ **U.S. State Department:** Travel information from the U.S. State Department and the Overseas Citizens Services division (☎ 202-501-4444; www.travel.state.gov) offers a consular information sheet on Mexico that contains a compilation of safety, medical, driving, and general travel information gleaned from reports by official U.S. State Department offices in Mexico. In addition to calling, you can request the consular information sheet by fax at ☎ 201-647-1488. The State Department is also on the Internet: Check out http://travel.state.gov/mexico.html for the consular information sheet on Mexico; http://travel.state.gov/travel_warnings.html for other consular information sheets and travel warnings; and http://travel.state.gov/tips_mexico.html for the State Department's *Tips for Travelers to Mexico*.

✔ **INFOTUR (24-hour tourist help line):** Dial ☎ 01-800-987-8224 toll-free inside Mexico, and you can get information from English-speaking operators as to where to go for medical assistance and other types of assistance. It's also a great source for general tourism information. You can always find helpful operators who will try to get the information that you need. To call this office from the United States, dial ☎ 800-482-9832.

✔ **Centers for Disease Control (CDC):** A source for medical information for travelers to Mexico and elsewhere, the Centers for Disease Control (☎ 800-311-3435 or 404-639-3534; www.cdc.gov/travel) provides detailed information on health issues for specific countries. For travelers to Mexico and Central America, the number with recorded messages about specific health issues related to this region is ☎ 877-FYI-TRIP. The toll-free fax number for requesting information is ☎ 888-407-4747.

Local **tourist information offices** offer all kinds of information to travelers, including brochures, maps, and destination-specific magazines and posters. If you want them to mail information to you, allow four to six weeks for the mail to reach you.

✔ **Acapulco's State of Guerrero Tourism Office** (Costera Miguel Aleman 4455, Centro Internacional Acapulco, Acapulco, Guerrero, located on the Costera side of the convention center; ☎ 744-484-4416; Fax: 744-484-4583; www.acapulco.gob.mx). Note that the Web site is currently available in Spanish only.

✔ **Cancún Convention and Visitors Bureau** (Kukulkán Km 9, "Cancún Center," first floor, Hotel Zone-Cancún, Quintana Roo, México 77500; ☎ 998-881-2745 or 881-2774; www.cancun.info).

✔ **Huatulco Hotels Association** (Bulevar Benito Juárez 8, Local 1, Interior Hotel Crown Pacific, Bahía de Tangolunda, Bahías de Huatulco, Oaxaca, 70989; ☎ 866-416-0555 from the U.S. or 958-581-0486; Fax: 958-581-0487; www.hoteleshuatulco.com.mx; www.hotels.baysofhuatulco.com.mx).

✔ **Huatulco State Tourism Office** (Bulevar Benito Juárez s/n, Bahía de Tangolunda, Bahías de Huatulco, Oaxaca, 70989; ☎ 958-581-0176 or 581-0177; www.oaxaca.gob.mx/sedetur). The Web site offers information about the whole state of Oaxaca, including some information on Huatulco; however, the information is in Spanish and not very consumer-oriented.

✔ **Isla Mujeres Tourism Office** (Av. Rueda Medina 130, Isla Mujeres, Quintana Roo, Mexico, 77400, across from the main pier between Immigration and Customs; ☎ 998-877-0767; www.isla-mujeres.com.mx).

✔ **Ixtapa Tourism Office** or Subsecretaría de Fomento Turístico (Centro Comercial La Puerta, Locales 2, 3, 8, and 9, Ixtapa, Guerrero, 408880; ☎ 755-553-1967; Fax: 755-553-1968).

- **Los Cabos Tourism Office** (Bulevar Mauricio Castro, Plaza San José, Locales 3 and 4, Col. 1° de Mayo, Cabo San Lucas, BCS; ☎ 624-146-9628; www.visitcabo.com or www.loscabos.gob.mx). You can try to call the office for information, and who knows, someone may even be there to answer the phone; however, you're better off visiting the Web site.

- **Puerto Escondido State Tourism Office** (SEDETUR, Bulevar Benito Juárez s/n, Fraccionamiento Bacocho, Puerto Escondido, Oaxaca, 71980; ☎ 954-582-0175; www.oaxaca.gob.mx/sedetur).

- **Puerto Vallarta Tourism Board and Convention and Visitors Bureau** (Local 18, Planta Baja, Zona Comercial Hotel Canto del Sol, Zona Hotelera Las Glorias, Puerto Vallarta, Jalisco, 48310; ☎ 888-384-6822 from the U.S., and 01-800-719-3276 from Mexico or 322-224-1175; Fax: 322-224-0915; www.visitpuertovallarta.com).

- **State of Jalisco Tourism Office in Puerto Vallarta** (Centro Comercial Plaza Marina, Locales 144 and 146, Marina Vallarta, Puerto Vallarta, Jalisco, 48321; ☎ 322-221-2676 or 221-2677; Fax: 322-221-2678).

- **Zihuatanejo Tourism Office or Dirección de Turismo Municipal** (in the city-hall building in Zihuatanejo; ☎ 755-554-2001, ask for the tourism office; presidencia@ixtapa-zihuatanejo.com).

Following is a list of several Web sites where you can find updated information about Mexico and traveling to the most popular beach resorts; however, keep in mind that most of the companies that these Web sites recommend received this lofty status by paying some sort of advertising fee:

- The **Mexico Ministry of Tourism's** official Web site (www.mexico-travel.com) offers ample information (15,000 pages worth) about Mexico. However, the pages are slow to load and the information is a little outdated.

- The **Mexico Tourism Board** developed another official site (www.visitmexico.com) with more current information on the different destinations in Mexico. Again, the pages are slow to load, but the navigation is a lot easier. The site features sections for travelers divided by region; a good search engine usually takes you to the information you're looking for.

- For low-impact travel planning, visit the **Eco Travels in Mexico** section of the award-winning Web site **Planeta.com** (www.planeta.com/mexico.html). You can find up-to-date information on reliable ecotour operators in Mexico. This site also offers an excellent source to find banks and telephone services. Planeta.com is one of the best sources for current information because it's updatedmonthly.

- The electronic version of *Mexico Connect* magazine (www.mexconnect.com) offers a wealth of information and is the ideal site to begin a more in-depth, online exploration about when and where to visit Mexico. The site offers a great index where you can find everything from out-of-the-way adventures to Mexico's history to recommended accommodations.

✔ **Cancun South** (www.cancunsouth.com) is a great site for independent travelers looking to explore the Riviera Maya. The site is easy to navigate and offers a wealth of information specific to the area.

✔ **Cozumel.net** (www.cozumel.net) provides detailed information about the island's life. In our opinion, this site has the most reliable information about Cozumel and it even lists ferry schedules in the "About Cozumel" section.

✔ Two good sites feature information on Los Cabos: **Baja Travel Guide** (www.bajatravel.com) and **All About Cabo** (www.allaboutcabo.com). We prefer the factual and less flashy presentation of the Baja Travel Guide site; however, if you want to find out a bit more about activities such as golf and fishing and get an up-to-date beach forecast, All About Cabo is the site to visit.

Following is a selection of Web sites that can help you with all the important stuff related to your Mexican beach resort vacation, such as figuring out where to get cash, how to ask for a cold beer, where to go to send an e-mail to your friends back home, how to find really great deals, and so on:

✔ **Cybercafes** (www.cybercafes.com): Search this interactive database to find Internet and cybercafes worldwide, though given the fluctuating state of these businesses, locations change frequently. For Mexican cybercafes, you have to search by state, rather than city or resort.

✔ **Foreign Languages for Travelers** (www.travlang.com): Find out what basic terms mean in more than 70 languages and click on any underlined phrase to hear what it sounds like. *Note:* Free audio software and speakers are required.

✔ **Intellicast** (www.intellicast.com): Get weather forecasts for all 50 United States and cities around the world. *Note:* Temperatures are in Celsius for many international destinations.

✔ **Mapquest** (www.mapquest.com): Choose a specific address or destination, and in seconds, get a map and detailed directions.

✔ **Travel Secrets** (www.travelsecrets.com): This site is one of the best compilations around. The site offers advice and tips on how to find the lowest prices for airlines, hotels, and cruises, and it also provides a listing of links for airfare deals, airlines, booking engines, discount travel, resources, hotels, and travel magazines.

✔ **Universal Currency Converter** (www.xe.net/ucc): See what your dollar or pound is worth in more than 100 other countries.

✔ **Visa ATM Locator** (www.visa.com/pd/atm) or **MasterCard ATM Locator** (www.mastercard.com/atmlocator): Find ATMs in hundreds of cities in the United States and around the world.

Appendix B

Glossary of Spanish Words and Phrases

● ●

*M*ost Mexicans are very patient with foreigners who try to speak their language. And your trip can be much easier and more enjoyable if you know a few basic Spanish phrases.

In this glossary, we include a few lists of simple words and phrases for expressing basic needs.

English-Spanish Phrases

English	Spanish	Pronunciation
Good day (Good morning)	**Buenos días**	*bweh*-nohs *dee*-ahs
Good evening/afternoon	**Buenas tardes**	*beh*-nahs *tar*-dehs
Good night	**Buenas noches**	*bweh*-nahs *noh*-chehs
How are you?	**¿Cómo está?**	*koh*-moh eh-*stah*
Very well	**Muy bien**	mwee byehn
Thank you	**Gracias**	*grah*-syahs
You're welcome	**De nada**	deh *nah*-dah
Good-bye	**Adiós**	ah-*dyohs*
Please	**Por favor**	pohr fah-*bohr*
Yes	**Sí**	see
No	**No**	noh
Excuse me	**Disculpe**	dee-*skool*-peh
Give me	**Déme** or **Dame**	*deh*-meh or *dah*-meh
Where is . . .?	**¿Dónde está . . .?**	*dohn*-deh eh-*stah*
the station	**la estación**	lah eh-stah-*syohn*

English	Spanish	Pronunciation
a hotel	un hotel	oon oh-*tehl*
a gas station	una gasolinera	*oo*-nah gah-so-lee-*neh*-rah
a restaurant	un restaurante	oon reh-stow-*rahn*-teh
the toilet	el baño	el *bah*-nyoh
a good doctor	un buen médico	oon bwehn *meh*-dee-coh
the road to . . .	el camino a . . .	el cah-*mee*-noh ah
To the right	A la derecha	ah lah deh-*reh*-chah
To the left	A la izquierda	ah lah ee-*skyehr*-dah
Straight ahead	Derecho	deh-*reh*-choh
I would like	Quisiera	kee-*syeh*-rah
I want	Quiero	*kyeh*-roh
to eat	comer	koh-*mehr*
a room	una habitación	*oo*-nah ha-bee-tah-*syohn*
Do you have . . . ?	¿Tiene usted . . . ?	*tyeh*-neh oo-*sted*
a book	un libro	oon *lee*-broh
a dictionary	un diccionario	oon deek-syoh-*nah*-ryoh
How much is it?	¿Cuánto cuesta?	*kwahn*-toh *kweh*-stah
When?	¿Cuándo?	*kwahn*-doh
What?	¿Cómo?	*koh*-moh
There is (Is there . . .?)	(¿)Hay(?)	eye
What is there?	¿Qué hay?	keh eye
Yesterday	Ayer	ah-*yehr*
Today	Hoy	oy
Tomorrow	Mañana	mah-*nyah*-nah
Good	Bueno	*bweh*-noh
Bad	Malo	*mah*-loh
Better (best)	Mejor	meh-*hohr*

(continued)

English-Spanish Phrases *(continued)*

English	Spanish	Pronunciation
More	**Más**	mahs
Less	**Menos**	*meh*-nohs
No smoking *mahr*	**Se prohibe fumar**	seh proh-*ee*-beh foo-
Postcard	**Tarjeta postal**	tar-*heh*-tah poh-*stahl*
Insect repellent	**Repelente contra insectos**	reh-peh-*lehn*-teh *cohn*-trah een-*sehk*-tohs

More Useful Phrases

English	Spanish	Pronunciation
Do you speak English?	**¿Habla usted inglés?**	*ah*-blah oo-*sted* een-*glehs*
Is there anyone here who speaks English?	**¿Hay alguien aquí que hable inglés?**	eye *ahl*-gyehn ah-*kee* keh *ah*-bleh een-*glehs*
I speak a little Spanish.	**Hablo un poco de español.**	*ah*-bloh oon *poh*-koh deh eh-spah-*nyohl*
I don't understand Spanish very well.	**No entiendo español muy bien.**	noh ehn-*tyehn*-doh eh-spah-*nyohl* mwee byehn
The meal is good.	**Me gusta la comida.**	meh *goo*-stah lah koh-*mee*-dah
What time is it?	**¿Qué hora es?**	keh *oh*-rah ehs
May I see your menu?	**¿Puedo ver el menú?**	*pweh*-doh behr el meh-*noo*
The check, please.	**La cuenta, por favor.**	lah *kwehn*-tah pohr fah-*bohr*
What do I owe you?	**¿Cuánto le debo?**	*kwahn*-toh leh *deh*-boh
What did you say?	**¿Mande?** (formal)	*mahn*-deh
	¿Cómo dijo? (informal)	*koh*-moh *dee*-hoh
I want (to see)	**Quiero (ver)**	*kyeh*-roh behr
a room	**un cuarto** or **una habitación**	oon *kwahr*-toh; *oo*-nah ah-bee-tah-*syohn*

English	Spanish	Pronunciation
for two persons	**para dos personas**	*pah*-rah dohs pehr-*soh*-nahs
with (without) bathroom	**con (sin) baño**	kohn (seen) *bah*-nyoh
We are staying here only	**Nos quedamos aquí solamente**	nohs keh-*dah*-mohs ah-*kee* soh-lah-*mehn*-teh
one night	**una noche**	*oo*-nah *noh*-cheh
one week	**una semana**	*oo*-nah seh-*mah*-nah
We are leaving	**Partimos** or **Salimos**	pahr-*tee*-mohs; sah-*lee*-mohs
Do you accept . . .?	**¿Acepta usted . . .?**	ah-*sehp*-tah oo-*sted*
traveler's checks?	**. . . los cheques de viajero?**	lohs *cheh*-kehs deh byah-*heh*-roh
credit cards	**. . . las tarjetas de crédito**	lahs tar-*heh*-tahs deh *kreh*-dee-toh
Is there a laundromat (or laundry)?	**¿Hay una lavandería?**	eye *oo*-nah lah-*bahn*-deh-*ree*-ah
Is . . . near here?	**. . . esta cerca de aquí?**	eh-*stah sehr*-kah deh ah-*kee*
Please send these clothes to the laundry.	**Hágame el favor de mandar esta ropa a la lavandería.**	*ah*-ga-meh el fah-*bohr* deh mahn-*dahr* eh-stah *roh*-pah a lah lah-*bahn*-deh-*ree*-ah

Numbers

1	**uno** (*ooh*-noh)	9	**nueve** (*nweh*-beh)
2	**dos** (dohs)	10	**diez** (dyess)
3	**tres** (trehs)	11	**once** (*ohn*-seh)
4	**cuatro** (*kwah*-troh)	12	**doce** (*doh*-seh)
5	**cinco** (*seen*-koh)	13	**trece** (*treh*-seh)
6	**seis** (sayss)	14	**catorce** (kah-*tohr*-seh)
7	**siete** (*syeh*-teh)	15	**quince** (*keen*-seh)
8	**ocho** (*oh*-choh)	16	**dieciseis** (dyeh-see-*sayss*)

(continued)

Numbers *(continued)*

17	**diecisiete** (dyeh-see-*syeh*-teh)	60	**sesenta** (seh-*sehn*-tah)
18	**dieciocho** (dyeh-*syoh*-choh)	70	**setenta** (seh-*tehn*-tah)
19	**diecinueve** (dyeh-see-*nweh*-beh)	80	**ochenta** (oh-*chehn*-tah)
20	**veinte** (*bayn*-teh)	90	**noventa** (noh-*behn*-tah)
21	**veintiuno** (bayn-*tyooh*-noh)	100	**cien** (syehn)
30	**treinta** (*trayn*-tah)	200	**doscientos** (doh-*syehn*-tohs)
40	**cuarenta** (kwah-*rehn*-tah)	500	**quinientos** (kee-*nyehn*-tohs)
50	**cincuenta** (seen-*kwehn*-tah)	1,000	**mil** (meel)

Transportation Terms

English	Spanish	Pronunciation
Airport	**Aeropuerto**	ah-eh-roh-*pwer*-toh
Arrival gates	**Llegadas**	yeh-*gah*-dahs
Departure gate	**Puerta de embarque**	*pwer*-tah deh ehm-*bahr*- keh
Baggage	**Equipajes**	eh-kee-*pah*-hehs
Baggage-claim area	**Recibo de equipajes** or **reclamo de equipajes**	reh-*see*-boh deh eh-kee-*pah*-hehs; reh-*klah*-moh deh eh-kee-*pah*-hays
First class	**Primera clase**	pree-*meh*-rah *klah*-seh
Second class	**Segunda clase**	seh-*goon*-dah *klah*-seh
Flight	**Vuelo**	*bweh*-loh
Nonstop	**Directo** or **sin escala**	dee-*rehk*-toh; seen eh-*skah*-lah
Rental car	**Coche de alquiler**	coh-*cheh* deh ahl-*kee*-lehr
Bus	**Autobús**	ow-toh-*boos*
Bus or truck	**Camión**	ka-*myohn*
Intercity	**Foraneo**	foh-rah-*neh*-oh
Lane	**Carril**	kah-*reel*
Luggage storage area	**Guarda equipaje**	*gwar*-dah eh-kee-*pah*-heh

English	Spanish	Pronunciation
Originates at this station	**Local**	loh-*kahl*
Originates elsewhere	**De paso**	deh *pah*-soh
Stops if seats available	**Para, si hay lugares**	*pah*-rah see eye loo-*gah*-rehs
Waiting room	**Sala de espera**	*sah*-lah deh eh-*speh*-rah
Ticket window	**Taquilla**	tah-*kee*-yah
Toilets	**Baños**	*bah*-nyohs

Appendix C

Authentic Mexican Cuisine

● ●

*A*uthentic Mexican food differs quite dramatically from what is frequently served up in the United States under that name. For many travelers, Mexico is new and exciting culinary territory. Even grizzled veterans are pleasantly surprised by the wide variation in specialties and traditions offered from region to region.

Despite regional differences, you can make some generalizations. In fact, Mexican food usually isn't pepper-hot when it arrives at the table (though many dishes must have a certain amount of spiciness, and some home cooking can be very spicy, depending on a family's or chef's tastes). The piquant flavor is added with chiles and sauces after the food is served; you never see a table in Mexico without one or both of these condiments. Mexicans don't drown their cooking in cheese and sour cream (which is the case in many Tex-Mex restaurants), and they use a great variety of ingredients. But the basis of Mexican food is simple — tortillas, beans, chiles, squash, and tomatoes — the same as it was centuries ago, before the Europeans arrived.

Knowing the Basic Dishes

Traditional **tortillas** are made from corn that has been cooked in water and lime, and then ground into *masa* (a grainy dough), patted and pressed into thin cakes, and cooked on a hot griddle known as a *comal.* In many households, tortillas take the place of fork and spoon; Mexicans merely tear the tortillas into wedge-shaped pieces, which they use to scoop up their food. Restaurants often serve bread rather than tortillas because it's easier to prepare, but you can always ask for tortillas. A more recent invention from northern Mexico is the flour tortilla, which you don't see as frequently in the rest of Mexico. If asked, choose corn over flour tortillas for a more authentic Mexico dining experience.

Dishes made with tortillas

The tortilla is the basis of several Mexican dishes, and the most famous dish is the **enchilada.** The original name for this dish was *tortilla enchilada,* which simply means a tortilla dipped in a chile sauce. In a similar manner, there's the *entomatada* (tortilla dipped in a tomato sauce) and the *enfrijolada* (tortilla dipped in a bean sauce). The enchilada begins as a very simple dish: A tortilla is dipped in chile sauce (usually with ancho chile) and then into very hot oil, and then is quickly folded or rolled on a plate and sprinkled with chopped onions and a little *queso cotija* (crumbly white cheese) and served with a few fried potatoes and carrots. You can get this basic enchilada in food stands across the country. If you come across them in your travels, give them a try. In restaurants, you get the more elaborate enchilada, with different fillings of cheese, chicken, pork, or even seafood, and sometimes in a casserole.

A **taco** is anything folded or rolled into a tortilla, and sometimes a double tortilla. The tortilla can be served either soft or fried. *Flautas* and *quesadillas* are offshoots of tacos. For Mexicans, the taco is the quintessential fast food, and the taco stand *(taquería)* — a ubiquitous sight — is a great place to get a filling meal. See the section, "Eating Out: Restaurants, Taquerías, and Tipping," later in this appendix for information on *taquerías*.

All about beans

An invisible "bean line" divides Mexico: It starts at the Gulf Coast in the southern part of the state of Tamaulipas and moves inland through the eastern quarter of San Luis Potosí and most of the state of Hidalgo, and then goes straight through Mexico City and Morelos and into Guerrero, where it curves slightly westward to the Pacific. (Check out the map of Mexico on the inside back cover of this book to gain a little perspective about this bean line.) To the north and west of this line, the pink bean known as the *flor de mayo* is the staple food; to the south and east, the standard is the black bean.

In private households, beans are served at least once a day and, among the working class and peasantry, with every meal, if the family can afford it. Mexicans almost always prepare beans with a minimum of condiments — usually just a little onion and garlic and perhaps a pinch of herbs. Beans are a contrast to the heavily spiced dishes. Sometimes they're served at the end of a meal with a little Mexican-style sour cream, which is basically just cream.

Mexicans often fry leftover beans and serve them on the side as *frijoles refritos*. *Refritos* is usually translated as refried, but this translation is a misnomer — the beans are fried only once. The prefix *re* actually means *well* (as in thoroughly), and what Mexicans actually mean is the beans are well fried.

Getting to know tamales

You make a *tamal* by mixing corn *masa* with a little lard, adding one of several fillings — such as meats flavored with chiles (or no filling at all) — and then wrapping it in a corn husk or in the leaf of a banana or other plant, and finally steaming it. Every region in Mexico has its own traditional way of making *tamales*. In some places, a single *tamal* can be big enough to feed a family, although in other places, they're barely 3 inches long and an inch thick.

Understanding the chile pepper

Many kinds of chile peppers exist, and Mexicans call each of them by one name when they're fresh and another when they're dried. Some are blazing hot with only a mild flavor; some are mild but have a rich, complex flavor. They can be pickled, smoked, stuffed, stewed, chopped, and used in an endless variety of dishes.

Eating Out: Restaurants, Taquerías, and Tipping

First of all, we feel compelled to debunk the prevailing myth that the cheapest place to eat in Mexico is in the market. Actually, this is almost never the case. You can usually find better food at a better price without going more than 2 blocks out of your way. Why? Food stalls in the marketplace pay high rents, they have a near-captive clientele of market vendors and truckers, and they get plenty of business from many Mexicans for whom eating in the market is a traditional way of confirming their culture.

On the other side of the spectrum, avoid eating at those inviting sidewalk restaurants that you see beneath the stone archways that border the main plazas. These places usually cater to tourists — so authenticity may be suspect — and they don't need to count on getting any return business. But they're great for getting a coffee or beer.

During your trip, you're going to see many *taquerías* (taco stands). These are generally small places with a counter or a few tables set around the cooking area; you get to see exactly how they make their tacos before deciding whether to order. Most tacos come with a little chopped onion and cilantro, but not tomato and lettuce. Find one that seems popular with the locals and where the cook performs with *brio* (a good sign of pride in the product). Sometimes you see a woman making the tortillas right there (or working the *masa* into *gorditas, sopes,* or *panuchos* if the *taquería* serves them). You'll never see men making tortillas — this is perhaps the strictest gender division in Mexican society. Men do all other cooking and kitchen tasks, and work with already-made tortillas, but they never work with *masa.*

For the main meal of the day, many restaurants offer a multicourse blue-plate special called **comida corrida** or **menú del día.** This dish is the most inexpensive way to get a full dinner. In Mexico, you need to ask for your check; Mexican culture generally considers presenting a check to someone who hasn't requested it as inhospitable. If you're in a hurry to get somewhere, ask for the check when your food arrives.

Tips are about the same as in the United States. You sometimes find a 15 percent **value-added tax** on restaurant meals, which shows up on the bill as "IVA." If you're an arithmetically challenged tipper, you may be (slightly) thankful for this tax, saving you from the undue exertion of trying to calculate a 15 percent tip in your head.

To summon the waiter, wave or raise your hand, but don't motion with your index finger, which is a demeaning gesture that may even cause the waiter to ignore you. Or if you want your check, you can motion to the waiter from across the room using the universal pretend-like-you're-writing gesture.

Most restaurants don't have **nonsmoking sections;** when they do, we mention it in the restaurant reviews throughout this book. But Mexico's wonderful climate allows for many open-air restaurants, usually set inside a colonial house's courtyard, or in rooms with tall ceilings and plenty of open windows.

Drinking in Mexico

All over Mexico you find shops selling *jugos* (**juices**) and *licuados* (**smoothies**) made from several kinds of tropical fruit. They're excellent and refreshing; while in Mexico, take full advantage of them. You also come across *aguas frescas* — water flavored with hibiscus, melon, tamarind, or lime. Soft drinks come in more flavors than in any other country we know. Pepsi and Coca-Cola taste the way they did in the United States years ago, before the makers started adding corn syrup. The coffee is generally good, and **hot chocolate** is a traditional drink, as is *atole,* a hot, corn-based beverage that can be sweet or bitter.

Of course, Mexico has a proud and lucrative **beer**-brewing tradition. A lesser-known brewed beverage is *pulque,* a pre-Hispanic drink: the fermented juice of a few species of maguey or agave. Mostly you find it for sale in *pulquerías* in central Mexico. It's an acquired taste, and not every gringo acquires it. **Mezcal** and **tequila** also come from the agave. Tequila is a variety of mezcal produced from the *A. tequilana* species of agave in and around the area of Tequila, in the state of Jalisco. Mezcal comes from various parts of Mexico and from different varieties of agave. The distilling process is usually much less sophisticated than that of tequila, and, with its stronger smell and taste, mezcal is much more easily detected on the drinker's breath. In some places such as Oaxaca, it comes with a worm in the bottle; you're supposed to eat the worm after polishing off the mezcal. But for those teetotalers who are interested in just the worm, we have good news — you can find these worms for sale in Mexican markets when in season.

Glossary of Spanish Menu Terms

The following is a list of common menu items and a description for each to take some of the guesswork out of ordering meals on your vacation.

Achiote: Small, red seed of the *annatto* tree.

Agua fresca: Fruit-flavored water, usually watermelon or cantaloupe where ingredients such as lemon and hibiscus flower are added.

Antojitos: Typical Mexican supper foods, usually made with *masa* or tortillas and containing a filling or topping such as sausage, cheese, beans, and onions; includes such items as *tacos, tostadas, sopes,* and *garnachas* (thick tortillas).

Atole: A thick, lightly sweet, hot drink made with finely ground corn and usually flavored with vanilla, pecan, or chocolate.

Botana: An appetizer.

Buñuelos: Round, thin, deep-fried, crispy fritters dipped in sugar.

Carnitas: Pork that's been deep-cooked (not fried) in lard, then simmered, and then served with corn tortillas for tacos.

Ceviche: Fresh, raw seafood marinated in fresh lime juice, garnished with chopped tomatoes, onions, chiles, and sometimes cilantro, and served with crispy, fried, whole-corn tortillas or crackers.

Chayote: A type of spiny pear-shaped squash boiled and served as an accompaniment to meat dishes.

Chiles en nogada: Poblano peppers stuffed with a mixture of ground pork and chicken, spices, fruits, raisins, and almonds, fried in a light batter, and covered in a walnut-and-cream sauce.

Chile relleno: Usually a poblano pepper stuffed with cheese or spicy ground meat with raisins, rolled in a batter, and fried.

Churro: Tube-shaped, bread-like fritter, dipped in sugar and sometimes filled with *cajeta* (caramel) or chocolate.

Enchilada: A tortilla dipped in a sauce and usually filled with chicken or white cheese; sometimes topped with mole sauce (*enchiladas rojas* or *de mole*), tomato sauce and sour cream (*enchiladas suizas,* or Swiss enchiladas), a green sauce (*enchiladas verdes*), or onions, sour cream, and guacamole (*enchiladas potosinas*).

Escabeche: A lightly pickled sauce used in Yucatecan chicken stew.

Frijoles charros: Beans flavored with beer; a northern Mexican specialty.

Frijoles refritos: Pinto beans mashed and cooked with lard.

Gorditas: Thickish fried-corn tortillas, slit and stuffed with choice of cheese, beans, beef, or chicken; served with or without lettuce, tomato, and onion garnish.

Gusanos de maguey: Maguey worms, considered a delicacy; delicious when deep-fried to a crisp and served with corn tortillas or tacos.

Horchata: Lightly sweetened, refreshing drink made of ground rice or melon seeds, and ground almonds. Also known as *agua de arroz* in certain destinations on the Pacific coast, such as Puerto Vallarta and Ixtapa.

Huevos mexicanos: Scrambled eggs with chopped onions, hot peppers, and tomatoes.

Huevos rancheros: Fried eggs on top of a fried corn tortilla covered in a spicy or mild tomato sauce.

Huitlacoche: Sometimes spelled "cuitlacoche." A mushroom-flavored black fungus that appears on corn in the rainy season; considered a delicacy.

Machaca: Shredded, dried beef scrambled with eggs, onion, and a mild red sauce; a specialty of northern Mexico.

Masa: Ground corn soaked in lime used as the basis for tamales, corn tortillas, and soups.

Menudo: Stew made with the lining of the cow's stomach. It can be served in a red or white broth. A traditional hangover cure.

Pan dulce: Lightly sweetened bread in many configurations, usually served at breakfast or bought in any bakery.

Pibil: Pit-baked pork or chicken in a sauce of tomato, onion, mild red pepper, cilantro, and vinegar.

Pipián: A sauce made with ground pumpkin seeds, nuts, and mild peppers.

Poc chuc: Slices of pork with onion marinated in a tangy, sour, orange sauce and charcoal-broiled; a Yucatecan specialty.

Pozole: Pork or chicken broth with hominy and shredded pork or chicken. The traditional recipe calls for the pig's head, but now it's commonly prepared with chicken or pork loin. Pozole is served red in Jalisco and white in Guerrero. Thursdays are the traditional day to eat pozole in Acapulco and Ixtapa.

Quesadilla: Corn or flour tortillas stuffed with melted white cheese and lightly fried.

Queso relleno: "Stuffed cheese"; a mild yellow cheese stuffed with minced meat and spices; a Yucatecan specialty.

Rompope: Delicious Mexican eggnog, invented in Puebla, made with eggs, vanilla, sugar, and rum.

Salsa verde: A cooked sauce using the green tomatillo puréed with spicy or mild hot peppers, onions, garlic, and cilantro; on tables countrywide.

Sopa de lima: A tangy soup made with chicken broth and accented with fresh lime; popular in the Yucatán.

Sopa de tortilla: A traditional chicken broth–based soup, seasoned with chilies, tomatoes, beans, onion, and garlic, with crispy fried strips of corn tortillas.

Sope: Pronounced "*soh*-pay;" an *antojito* similar to a *garnacha* (a thick tortilla), except spread with refried beans and topped with crumbled cheese and onions.

Tacos al pastor: Thin slices of flavored pork roasted on a revolving cylinder dripping with onion slices and the juice of fresh pineapple slices. Served in small corn tortillas, topped with chopped onion and cilantro.

Tamal: Incorrectly called a "tamale" in English (*tamal,* singular; *tamales,* plural). A meat or sweet filling rolled with fresh *masa,* wrapped in a corn husk or banana leaf, and then steamed; many varieties and sizes throughout the country.

Torta: A sandwich, usually on *bolillo* bread, typically comprising sliced avocado, onions, and tomatoes with a choice of meat and often cheese.

Tostadas: Crispy, fried corn tortillas topped with meat, onions, lettuce, tomatoes, cheese, avocados, and sometimes sour cream.

Index

• *Numerics* •

100% Natural
  Acapulco, 342–343
  Cancún, 140
360 Surf Shop, 395

• *A* •

AARP, 82
abbreviations, 469
Above and Beyond Tours, 85
ABY Charters, 439
Acapulco
  area map, 346–347
  arriving in, 330–331
  attractions, 352–353
  beaches, 344–349
  choosing location to stay in, 319–320
  description of, 42–43, 319
  dining, 19, 336–337, 340–343
  dining map, 338–339
  Fast Facts, 333–335
  getting around, 331–333
  land sports, 351–352
  lodging, 16, 321, 324–329
  lodging map, 322–323
  nightlife, 21, 359–362
  pozole, 19
  shopping, 354–355
  side trips from, 355–359
  sightseeing, 353–354
  telephone area code, 333
  water activities, 349–351
Acapulco Princess golf course, 351
Acapulco's State of Guerrero Tourism
  Office, 479
Acapulquito beach (Los Cabos), 437
Access-Able Travel Source, 83
accessibility issues, 84–85
Accessible Journeys, 83
accommodations
  Acapulco, 321–329
  all-inclusive, 3, 58, 75, 194–195
  best good-value, 16
  best luxury, 15–16
  bungalow, 285
  Cancún, 111–112, 114, 116–123
  Ciudad Cancún, 115
  condo, apartment, or villa, 75
  cost of, 3, 56, 76
  Cozumel, 172–178
  cutting cost of, 60
  finding deals on, 77–79
  hotel and motel chains, 477–478
  hotels, 74–75
  Huatulco, 366, 368–370
  Isla Cancún, 113
  Ixtapa and Zihuatanejo, 285–293
  Los Cabos, 401–412
  options for, 74–75
  Puerto Escondido, 379–380, 382–384
  Puerto Vallarta, 217–227
  rack rate, 76–77
  reserving best room, 79
  resort, 74
  Riviera Maya, 195–200
  Taxco, 357–358
  unique places, 17
achiote, 465, 492
active vacations, best, 17–18
Adoquín (Puerto Escondido), 379, 385
Advantage Rent-A-Car, 415
Aerocaribe, 378
agave, 491
Agave Grill (Puerto Vallarta), 238
aguas frescas, 33, 491, 492
AIM (Adventures in Mexico)
  newsletter, 82
Aioli (Cancún), 119, 133
Air-Evac, 95

airlines
  contact information, 67, 475–476
  flying to Mexico, 66–69
  security measures, 103–104
airports
  Acapulco, 330–331
  Cancún, 124
  Cozumel, 178
  Huatulco, 370
  Ixtapa-Zihuatanejo, 294
  Los Cabos, 413–414
  Mexico City, 66
  Puerto Escondido, 384
  Puerto Vallarta, 228
Aktun Chen, 158, 209
Akumal
  description of, 202
  dining, 205
Akumal Dive Shop, 208
Akumal Vacations, 194
Alebrijes (Acapulco), 361
Alfarería Tlaquepaque, 269
All About Cabo (Web site), 453, 481
All About Cancún (Web site), 126
All Hotels on the Web (Web site), 78
Allegro Cozumel by Occidental, 174
all-inclusive
  booking room at, 194
  definition of, 3, 58, 75
  Riviera Maya, 194–195
Alltournative, 209
American Express
  contact information, 469
  traveler's check, 63
American Foundation for the Blind, 84
Amigos del Mar, 438
Ana's Eco Tours, 391
Ancient Kingdoms of Mexico
  (Davies), 33
Andrea (Puerto Vallarta), 237
Antillano (Cancún), 112
antojitos, 33, 492
Apartamentos Amueblados Valle
  (Zihuatanejo), 285–286
apartment, renting, 75, 111
Apple Vacations, 72
applying for passport, 91–92

Aqua Deportes, 437
Aqua Safari, 187
Aquaworld, 146–147, 188
Arau, Alfonso (director), 34
archaeological sites
  Cancún area, 29, 50, 51, 154–157, 459
  Cozumel, 185, 189–190
Archie's Wok (Puerto Vallarta), 238
architecture, 29–30
Arco Iris travel agency, 86
Arcoíris Hotel (Puerto Escondido), 380
Arrayán (Puerto Vallarta), 19, 238–240
art
  contemporary, shopping for in Los
    Cabos, 446–447
  contemporary, shopping for in Puerto
    Vallarta, 268–269
  decorative and folk, shopping for in
    Puerto Vallarta, 270
  Huichol, 19, 266–267
Art & Harry's (Puerto Escondido), 387
art walks in Puerto Vallarta, 275
Arte, Diseño y Decoración, 447
Atlantis Submarine, 153, 188
ATM, 62–63, 203, 469, 481
atole, 33, 491, 492
ATV tours
  of jungle in Cancún, 151
  in Los Cabos, 444
Autobuses Riviera, 200
Avalos Doña Celia (Santa Cruz), 374
Avenida Francisco Medina Ascencio
  (Puerto Vallarta), 230
Avenida Juárez (San Miguel de
  Cozumel), 179
Avenida Melgar (San Miguel de
  Cozumel), 179–180
Avenida Tulum (Cancún), 127
Aventura Spa Palace (Riviera Maya),
  194
Aventura Submarina, 392
Aztecs, 23, 25, 26

● **B** ●

Baan Thai (Los Cabos), 422
Baby-O's (Acapulco), 361

Bahía Chahué, 366, 372, 376
Bahía de Banderas, 214, 250
Bahía de Huatulco, 18. *See also* Huatulco
Bahía de Mujeres, 14, 144
Baikal (Acapulco), 337
Baja Peninsula, 432, 457. *See also* Los Cabos
Baja Travel Guide (Web site), 453, 481
Baja Wild Expeditions, 437, 438
Baja's Moto Rent, 437
Banderas Bay, 11, 18
Banderas Bay Trading Company, 270
Bandido's (Zihuatanejo), 315
banks, 62
Bar Fly (Puerto Escondido), 395
Bar Hopper Tour, 165
Bar La Crema (Crucecita), 378
Barceló Ixtapa, 286, 315
Barceló La Jolla de Mismaloya, 254
Barcelona Tapas (Puerto Vallarta), 248
Barcos México, 179
Barquet, Ramiz (*Nostalgia*), 263
Barra Vieja beach (Acapulco), 349
Barrena, Francisco (horseman), 445
barro negro, 378
Bayless, Rick (*Mexico, One Plate at a Time*), 34
Bays of Huatulco, 18. *See also* Huatulco
Bayside Properties, 85, 216–217
Bazaar Santa Fe, 394
B&B Caribo (Cozumel), 174
beach resorts, ratings of, 47
beaches
  Acapulco, 344–349
  best, 11, 14
  Cancún, 144, 146
  choosing between, 35–36
  Cozumel, 185–186
  Huatulco, 376
  Hurricane Wilma, 110
  Ixtapa and Zihuatanejo, 306–310
  Los Cabos, 418, 432–435
  Puerto Escondido, 386, 390
  Puerto Vallarta, 250, 252–255
  riptides, 334, 345

vendors on, 267, 274, 459
water-safety pennant system, 144
beaded pieces, 267
bean dishes, 489
Beccofino (Ixtapa), 301
beer, 58, 491
Bennito's (Puerto Vallarta), 240
Bernstein, Michelle (chef), 116
Berta's (Taxco), 359
Best Western Posada Real (Puerto Escondido), 380, 395
Better Business Bureau, 71
Bianco (Puerto Vallarta), 276
BiddingforTravel (Web site), 78
Bike Mex, 261
biking tour in Puerto Vallarta, 261
Bikini Brazil, 395
bird sanctuary
  Cancún, 153
  Los Cabos, 434
bird-watching tour
  Ixtapa and Zihuatanejo, 311
  Puerto Vallarta, 262
birth certificate, 89–90
Blouet, Thierry (chef), 240
Blue Bay Getaway & Spa Cancún, 112
The Blue Iguana (Puerto Escondido), 395
Blue Parrot (Playa del Carmen), 210
boating. *See also* panga
  Acapulco booze cruise, 351
  Cozumel, 188
  glass-bottom boat, 436
  Huatulco, 365, 376–377
  Ixtapa and Zihuatanejo, 311–312
  Lobster Dinner Cruise, 139
  Los Cabos, 436
  Puerto Escondido, 385
  Puerto Vallarta, 231–232, 252, 255–256, 257–258
  renting boat, 377
  sunset sail, 457
Boca de Tomatlán (Puerto Vallarta), 254
Bodo's (Puerto Morales), 205
Boingo, 102

Bol Bahía, 355
booking
  accommodations, 74–79
  in advance, 69
  trip online, 69–70
Books, Books, 448
books, recommended, 33–34
booze cruise, 351
botana, 492
bottled water, 61, 95, 462, 475
Boy on the Seahorse (sculpture), 263
Breakfast plan, 57
bribe, paying, 461
Bucanero Bar and Grill (Puerto
  Escondido), 395
Bucerías, 214, 253
bucket shop, 68
budget, planning
  cutting costs, 59–61
  dining cost, 3, 57–58
  hotel cost, 3, 56, 76
  Los Cabos, 399
  nightlife, 59
  overview of, 55–56
  shopping, 59
  sightseeing, 58–59
  tipping, 58
  transportation cost, 56–57, 60
bullfighting
  Acapulco, 352
  Cancún, 161–162
bungalow, 285
Bungalows and Cabañas Acuario
  (Puerto Escondido), 382
Bungalows Ley (Zihuatanejo), 286
The Bungalows (Los Cabos), 402
bungee jumping, 360
buñuelo, 492
Burton, Richard (actor), 264, 273
bus service
  Acapulco, 332
  Cancún, 128–129
  Huatulco, 372
  Ixtapa and Zihuatanejo, 297
  Los Cabos, 433
  to Playa del Carmen, 200

Puerto Vallarta, 231
  safety issues, 299
business hours, 469
Bustamante, Sergio (artist), 355
*By the Grace of the Sea: A Woman's
  Solo Odyssey Around the World*
  (Henry), 258

• **C** •

C (Los Cabos), 410, 422, 424
cab service
  Acapulco, 332
  Cancún, 125–126, 128
  Cozumel, 180
  Huatulco, 371, 372
  Ixtapa and Zihuatanejo, 296
  Los Cabos, 417
  Puerto Escondido, 385
  Puerto Vallarta, 230
Cabaña del Pescador, 19
cabaña hotels, 193, 194
Cabañas Ana y José (Tulum), 195–196
Cabo Blanco (Puerto Escondido),
  388, 396
Cabo del Sol golf course
  Desert Course, 442
  Ocean Course, 441, 442
Cabo Expeditions, 437
Cabo Falso, 444
Cabo Inn (Los Cabos), 16, 402
Cabo Pacífica, 442
Cabo Real golf course, 441, 442–443
Cabo San Lucas
  beaches, 435
  description of, 45–46, 399, 400–401
  dining, 421, 424, 428, 429
  dining map, 425
  getting around, 416–417
  lodging, 16, 402, 409, 411
  lodging map, 405
  nightlife, 21, 450–453
  shopping, 446
  sportfishing, 18
Cabo Wabo Cantina (Los Cabos),
  452–453

Cafe Canela (Los Cabos), 424
café de olla, 464
Café des Artistes (Puerto Vallarta), 240
Cafe Dublín (Crucecita), 378
Café Huatulco, 378
Café Kaiser Maximilian (Puerto Vallarta), 242
Café Max (Puerto Vallarta), 237
Café San Angel (Puerto Vallarta), 242
Café Santa Fe (Todos Santos), 449
Caffé Todos Santos (Todos Santos), 449
calendar of events, 49–52
Caleta beach (Acapulco), 345, 348
Caletas, excursion to, 256
Caletilla beach (Acapulco), 345, 348
calling code
  Acapulco, 333
  Cancún, 129
  Cozumel, 181
  dialing, 474
  Huatulco, 372
  Ixtapa and Zihuatanejo, 297
  Los Cabos, 417
  Nuevo Vallarta, 232
  Puerto Escondido, 385
  Puerto Morelos, 204
  Puerto Vallarta, 232
  Riviera Maya and Playa del Carmen, 204
Camino Real Acapulco Diamante, 321
Camino Real Zaashila (Tangolunda Bay), 368
Cancún
  area map, 145, 163
  arriving in, 124–127
  beaches, 14, 144, 146
  choosing location to stay in, 110–111
  Ciudad Cancún accommodations, 115
  development of, 109
  dining, 19, 132–142
  Fast Facts, 129–131
  getting around, 127–129
  Hurricane Wilma, 14, 36, 37, 109, 110
  Isla Cancún accommodations, 113
  land sports, 149–151
  lodging, 15, 16, 111–112, 114, 116–123
  nightlife, 21, 165–168
  overview of, 36–38
  shopping, 20, 162–165
  sightseeing, 161–162
  telephone area code, 129
  travelers with disabilities, 84
  water activities, 146–149
Cancún Convention and Visitors Bureau, 126, 479
Cancún Hideaways, 111
Cancún Mermaid, 148, 151
Cancún South (Web site), 481
Cancún Travel Guide (Web site), 126
Cancún.com (Web site), 126
canopy tour in Puerto Vallarta, 263
Canopy Tours de Los Veranos, 263
Cantera Tours, 392
Canto del Sol Tennis Club, 261
Capt. Rick's Sportfishing Center, 209
Captain's Cove (Cancún), 133
car, driving
  Riviera Maya, 203
  rules of road, 99
  safety issues, 298–299
car rental agencies, 415, 476–477
car, renting
  Acapulco, 333
  Cancún, 126–127
  Cozumel, 180
  Huatulco, 371
  Ixtapa-Zihuatanejo, 295
  Los Cabos, 400, 414–415, 417
  overview of, 57, 97–99
  Puerto Escondido, 384
  Puerto Vallarta, 231
  Riviera Maya, 203–204
car seat, 81
Cárdenas, Lázaro, 28
Caribbean Fantasy, 194
Carlos 'n Charlie's
  Cancún, 167
  Cozumel, 191
  Ixtapa, 316
Carlos O'Brian's
  Los Cabos, 422
  Puerto Vallarta, 276

Carlos Scuba, 310
Carnaval, 50
carnitas, 492
Carretera Transversal (Cozumel), 180
carry-on luggage, 105
Cartes, 447
Casa Cuitlateca (Zihuatanejo), 288
casa de cambio (house of
    exchange), 62
Casa de las Margaritas (Cancún), 134
Casa del Mar Golf Resort & Spa (Los
    Cabos), 404
Casa Marina shopping complex, 314
Casa Mediterránea (Playa del
    Carmen), 206
Casa Natalia (Los Cabos), 17, 404
Casa Nova (Acapulco), 340
Casa Puntarenas (Zihuatanejo), 301
Casa Rafael's (Los Cabos), 424
Casa Rolandi (Cancún), 142
Casa Tres Vidas (Puerto Vallarta),
    217–218
CasaMagna Marriott (Cancún), 112, 114
Casanova, Victor (tour operator), 187
cash advance on credit card, 63
cash, traveling with, 62–63, 203
castas, 27
Cave of the Sleeping Sharks, 147
cavern diving, 208
cellphone, 100–101
cenote diving, 18, 187
Centers for Disease Control and
    Prevention, 95, 479
Central Surf, 394
Centro Mexicano la Tortuga, 393
ceviche, 464, 492
Chaac (Maya rain god), 32
Chacahua Lagoon National Park, 392
Chahué Bay, 372, 376
change, getting, 61
Chankanaab National Park, 180, 186, 189
Charlie's (Tulum), 205
chayote, 492
Chen Rio beach club, 186
Chichén Itzá
    area map, 157
    description of, 29
    fall equinox, 51

    spring equinox, 50
    visiting, 156
Chico's Dive Shop, 257
Chico's Paradise (Puerto Vallarta), 246
chilaquiles, 245, 465
children
    Acapulco, 43
    dining in Los Cabos with, 422
    entertaining, 81
    hotel costs for, 56
    Ixtapa, Zihuatanejo, 41, 284
    keeping healthy, 96–97
    Puerto Escondido, 45
    Puerto Vallarta, 236
    travel documents for, 90
    traveling with, 80–81
chile pepper, 31–32, 490
chile relleno, 492
chiles en nogada, 428, 492
Christine
    Ixtapa, 316
    Puerto Vallarta, 278
Christmas, 49
Christmas Posadas, 52
churches
    dress code for, 105
    Iglesia de Guadalupe, 377
    Iglesia de San Lucas, 445
    Nuestra Señora de la Soledad, 353
    parish, 30
    Parish of Nuestra Señora de
        Guadalupe, 264
    Santa Prisca y San Sebastián, 357
Churrigueresque, 30
churro, 492
CICI water park, 350–351
cigars, 271, 448
Cinco de Mayo, 51
Cirrus ATM network, 62
citizenship, proof of, 89–90
The City (Cancún), 166
city tour of Puerto Vallarta, 265
Ciudad Cancún
    description of, 37
    dining map, 137
    lodging, 111
    lodging map, 115
    restaurants, 127, 132

Classic Custom Vacations, 72
cliff divers, 352–353, 458–459
climate, 460
clothing
  in Acapulco, 336
  in church, 105
  packing, 104–106
  for restaurant dining, 132, 182, 236
  shopping for in Los Cabos, 446
  shopping for in Puerto Vallarta, 268
  in town, 462
Club Akumal Caribe/Hotel Villas Maya
  Club (Akumal), 196
Club Bananas Water Sports, 257
Club de Esquís, 349
Club de Golf Acapulco, 352
Club de Golf Cancún, 150
Club de Golf Ixtapa Palma Real, 312
Club de Tenis Hyatt, 352
The Club Grill (Cancún), 122, 134
Club Paco Paco (Puerto Vallarta), 280
clubs. *See also* dance clubs and discos
  Acapulco, 359–360
  Cancún, 165–166
  gay and lesbian in Puerto
    Vallarta, 280
  mens', in Los Cabos, 453
cochinita pibil, 428
cocktail at sunset, 458
Coco Bongo (Cancún), 166
Coco Cabaña Collectibles, 314
Coconuts (Zihuatanejo), 301–302
Cocos Cozumel, 182–183
Coe, Michael D.
  The Maya, 33
  *Mexico: From the Olmecs to
    the Aztecs*, 33
coffee, 378
colectivo
  Cancún, 125
  Ixtapa and Zihuatanejo, 295
  Los Cabos, 415–416
Collage Club (Puerto Vallarta), 278
Colunga, Alejandro, sculpture by, 263
comal, 488
Comida Casera Toñita (Cozumel), 182
comida corrida, 490

Coming About, 258
communication, 462–463
Conchas Chinas, 216
Condesa beach (Acapulco), 348
condo, renting
  Cancún, 111
  Cozumel, 173
  Los Cabos, 408
  overview of, 75
  Puerto Vallarta, 216–217
  Riviera Maya, 194
connection kit, 102–103
consolidator, 68
Constantini Bar Lounge (Puerto
  Vallarta), 241, 276
consulate, 470–471
Continental plan, 57
convents, 30
Cooperativa de Pescadores, 258
Copacabana Beach Resort
  (Xpu-Ha), 195
Copal, 447
Coral Reef Surf Shop, 253
the Corridor (Los Cabos)
  beaches, 434–435
  description of, 45, 46, 399, 400, 416
  dining, 422, 424, 430, 431
  dining map, 427
  lodging, 404, 406, 408, 409–410, 412
  lodging map, 407
Cortez, Hernán (explorer), 26
cost cutting tips, 59–61
Costa Linda Hotel (Acapulco), 324
Costera Sur (Cozumel), 180
costs
  cutting, 59–61
  dining, 3, 57–58
  hotel, 3, 56, 76
  Los Cabos, 399
  nightlife, 59
  overview of, 55–56
  shopping, 59
  sightseeing, 58–59
  tipping, 58
  transportation, 56–57, 60
country code, 474
Coyuca Lagoon, 345

Cozumel
 activities, 185–190
 area map, 173
 choosing location to stay in, 172
 description of, 38–39, 171
 dining, 19, 182–185
 diving, 18
 Fast Facts, 181–182
 getting around, 179–180
 nightlife, 191
 shopping, 190–191
 telephone area code, 181
Cozumel Country Club, 188
Cozumel Vacation Villas and
  Condos, 173
Cozumel.net (Web site), 481
crafts, shopping for
 Cancún, 162
 Los Cabos, 447
 Puerto Vallarta, 269–270
credit card, 63, 64–65, 469–470
credit-reporting bureau, 65
criollos, 27
Crucecita, 366, 372
Crucecita Market, 377
cruising. *See also* panga
 Acapulco booze cruise, 351
 Cozumel, 188
 glass-bottom boat, 436
 Huatulco, 365, 376–377
 Ixtapa and Zihuatanejo, 311–312
 Lobster Dinner Cruise, 139
 Los Cabos, 436
 Puerto Escondido, 385
 Puerto Vallarta, 231–232, 252,
  255–256, 257–258
 renting boat, 377
 sunset sail, 457
Cuadra San Francisco Equestrian
  Center, 445
Cuca's Blanket Factory, 447
cuisine
 basic dishes, 488–490
 best dishes, 464–466
 eating out, 490–491
 overview of, 31–33, 488
 spiciness of, 461
 Viva Mexico icon, 58

Cummings, Patricia (chef), 302
curandero section of market, 30–31
currency, 61–62, 470
currency conversion, 61, 62, 481
currency sign, universal, 62
customs
 Acapulco, 330–331
 Cancún, 124–125
 description of, 92, 470
 Huatulco, 371
 Ixtapa-Zihuatanejo, 295
 Los Cabos, 413–414
 Puerto Vallarta, 228–229
cutting costs, 59–61
cybercafe, finding, 101
Cybercafes (Web site), 481

• D •

Dady Rock Bar and Grill (Cancún), 166
Dady'O (Cancún), 166
Daiquiri Dick's (Puerto Vallarta),
  242–243
Damiana (Los Cabos), 426
dance clubs and discos
 Acapulco, 359–362
 Los Cabos, 452–453
 Puerto Vallarta, 278–279
Davies, Nigel (*Ancient Kingdoms
  of Mexico*), 33
day trips
 from Acapulco, 355–359
 from Huatulco, 378
 from Ixtapa and Zihuatanejo, 314–315
 in Los Cabos, 448–450
 from Puerto Escondido, 392–394
 from Puerto Vallarta, 271–274
de Santos Boutique (Puerto
  Vallarta), 268
de Santos (Puerto Vallarta), 243, 278
deep-sea fishing
 Acapulco, 350
 Cancún, 148–149
 Cozumel, 188
 Los Cabos, 438–440
 Puerto Aventuras, 209
 Puerto Vallarta, 258
 Zihuatanejo, 311

dehydration, 96–97
dentist, finding, 470
destination wedding, 87–88
Día de Independencia, 51
Día de la Candelaria, 50
Día de la Constitución, 50
Día de los Muertos, 51
Día de Nuestra Señora de
  Guadalupe, 52
Día de Revolución, 52
Día de Reyes, 50
diarrhea, avoiding, 95–96
Díaz, Porfirio (general), 27–28
dining. *See also* cuisine
  Acapulco, 336–343
  best, 19
  breakfast buffets, 58
  Cancún, 132–142
  choosing place to eat, 490
  cost of, 3, 57–58
  Cozumel, 182–185
  cutting cost of, 61
  Huatulco, 374–375
  Isla Cancún, 135
  Ixtapa and Zihuatanejo, 300–305
  Los Cabos, 421–431
  Puerto Escondido, 387–390
  Puerto Vallarta, 236–249
  Riviera Maya, 205–207
  taquería, 489, 490
  Taxco, 358–359
  tipping, 490–491
  waiter, summoning, 491
dinner show, 375. *See also* Mexican
  fiesta night
disability, traveler with, 83–85
discount rates, 60
Distant Neighbors (Riding), 34
Divers de México, 350
diving
  Acapulco, 350
  best, 18
  Cancún, 147
  cavern, 208
  cenote, 18, 187
  Cozumel, 172, 186–187
  drift, 186

Ixtapa and Zihuatanejo, 310
Los Cabos, 438
Puerto Escondido, 392
Puerto Vallarta, 252, 255–256, 257
Riviera Maya, 207–208
doctor, finding, 470
Dolphin Adventure, 258–259
Dolphin Discovery
  Cancún, 149
  Cozumel, 189
  Puerto Aventuras, 208
dolphins, swimming with
  Cancún, 149
  Chankanaab National Park, 189
  Puerto Vallarta, 258–259
  Riviera Maya, 208
Don Cafeto's (Tulum), 205
Dorado Pacífico, 312–313
Dos Lunas, 447
Dreams Cancún Resort & Spa, 114
Dreams Puerto Vallarta, 218
dress code
  in Acapulco, 336
  in church, 105
  for restaurant dining, 132, 182, 236
  in town, 462
drift diving, 186
drift snorkeling, 148
drinking. *See also* tequila
  beer, 58, 491
  bottled water, 61, 95, 462, 475
  legal age for, 461
  liquor laws, 472–473
  options for, 491
driving car
  Riviera Maya, 203
  rules of road, 99
  safety issues, 298–299
driving tour, 444–445
drug laws, 470
drug use, illegal, 97, 234, 394, 461
dry season, 48
duty-free shopping
  bringing goods home, 92
  description of, 20
  Los Cabos, 447
Dzibanché, 29

• E •

Easter, 49
Eco Travels in Mexico, 480
eco-theme parks, 157–161
ecotourism. *See* Huatulco
ecotours
    Puerto Escondido, 391
    Puerto Vallarta, 262–263
Ecotours de México, 262
Ehécatl (wind god), 32
Eisenstein, Sergei (filmmaker), 34
El Amigo Miguel (Acapulco), 340
El Anclote (Puerto Vallarta), 252
El Arco (The Arch), 457
El Burro Borracho (Troncones), 315
El Cabrito (Acapulco), 340–341
El Cafecito (Puerto Escondido),
    19, 387, 388
El Chilar (Los Cabos), 426
El Cid La Ceiba Beach Hotel (Cozumel),
    174, 176
El Cozumeleño Beach Resort, 176
El DexkiteLitros (Santa Cruz), 378
El Dorado Golf Course, 441, 443
El Dorado (Puerto Vallarta), 252
El Encanto Inn (Los Cabos), 406
El Faro Lighthouse Bar (Puerto
    Vallarta), 277
El Garrafón National Underwater Park
    drift diving, 147
    entrance fee, 153
    getting to, 151
    snorkeling, 148
El Jardin (Puerto Escondido), 388
El Mexicano (Cancún), 167
El Mirador Acapulco (hotel), 324–325
El Mirador (Acapulco, restaurant), 19
El Moro (Cozumel), 183
El Nogalito (Puerto Vallarta), 246
El Olvido (Acapulco), 341
El Pabellon de San Sebastián, 273
El Repollo Rojo (Puerto Vallarta),
    243–244
El Sabor de Oaxaca (Crucecita),
    374–375

El Squid Roe (Los Cabos), 451
El Tecolote Libros, 450
El Tigre golf course, 214, 261
El Tubo (Puerto Escondido), 396
El Tuito, 262
El Tule beach (Los Cabos), 437
Elcano Hotel (Acapulco), 324
Elderhostel, 82–83
ElderTreks, 83
electricity, 470
embassy, 470–471
emergency, dealing with, 471–472
enchilada, 488–489, 492
enfrijolada, 488
English-Spanish phrases, 482–487
entering Mexico, 89
escabeche, 492
Escape, 446
escorted tour, 70
Espacio Meditative Temazcalli, 391
Esperanza (Los Cabos), 406
Espresso (Puerto Vallarta), 244
Esquivel, Laura (author), 34
Estas Son Las Mañanitas (Playa del
    Carmen), 206
Estero San José, 434
Etc. Beach Club, 253
European plan, 58
events calendar, 49–52
exchange rate, 61, 62
exit tax, 64
Expedia online travel agency, 69, 77

• F •

Fajita Republic (Puerto Vallarta), 244
fall equinox, 51
Family Travel Files (Web site), 81
Family Travel Network (Web site), 81
family, traveling with
    Acapulco, 43
    dining in Los Cabos with, 422
    entertaining, 81
    hotel costs for, 56
    Ixtapa, Zihuatanejo, 41, 284
    keeping healthy, 96–97

Puerto Escondido, 45
Puerto Vallarta, 236
travel documents for, 90
traveling with, 80–81
fare, getting lowest, 68–69
Fast Facts
  Acapulco, 333–335
  Cancún, 129–131
  Cozumel, 181–182
  description of, 4
  Huatulco, 372–373
  Ixtapa and Zihuatanejo, 297–299
  Los Cabos, 417–420
  Puerto Escondido, 385–387
  Puerto Vallarta, 232–235
  Riviera Maya and Playa del
    Carmen, 204
fax, 474
ferry
  from Cozumel, 179
  to Isla Mujeres, 153
Fiesta Americana Condesa
  Acapulco, 325
Fiesta Americana Grand Aqua
  (Cancún), 15, 114, 116
Fiesta Americana Grand Coral Beach
  (Cancún), 116–117
Fiesta Americana Puerto Vallarta,
  218, 220
fiesta mexicana (Mexican fiesta) night
  Cancún, 167–168
  description of, 457
  Ixtapa, 315
  Los Cabos, 450–451
  Puerto Vallarta, 275–276
filete almendrado, 374
filete empapelado, 374
fish, fresh, feasting on, 458
fishing
  Acapulco, 350
  Cancún, 148–149
  Cozumel, 188
  Los Cabos, 438–440
  Puerto Aventuras, 209
  Puerto Vallarta, 258
  Zihuatanejo, 311

Fishing with Carolina, 258
Fish-R-Us, 350
Flamingo Cancún, 117
flauta, 489
Flor de Maria (Puerto Escondido), 382
flor de mayo, 489
flying to Mexico, 66–69
Flying Wheels Travel, 83
FMT (Mexican tourist permit), 90
folk art, shopping for
  Los Cabos, 447
  Puerto Vallarta, 270
folklore, 30–31
FONATUR destinations, 44, 365
Foreign Languages for Travelers
  (Web site), 481
Forum by the Sea, 164, 165
Four Seasons Resort Punta Mita,
  15, 220, 260
Fox, Vicente (president), 28
Francato, María (chef), 389
Freedom Paradise (Riviera Maya), 195
French Quarter (Cozumel), 183
French Riviera (Los Cabos), 426–427
Frida (movie), 34
frijoles charros, 492
frijoles refritos, 489, 492
Fuerte de San Diego, 353–354
Full American plan, 57
full fare, 68
Funjet Vacations, 72

• G •

Gala Resort (Tangolunda Bay), 368
Galería AL, 268
Galería de Todos Santos, 449
Galería des Artistes, 269
Galería Espacio Pal Kepenyes, 355
Galería Gattamelata, 447
Galería Pacífico, 269
Galería Uno, 269
Galería Wentworth Porter, 446
Galleria Dante, 269
Garbo's (Puerto Vallarta), 280

Garrafón National Park (El Garrafón
National Underwater Park)
drift diving, 147
entrance fee, 153
getting to, 151
snorkeling, 148
Garrafón Reefs, 153
gay and lesbian clubs, 280
gay or lesbian traveler, 85–86
Gelateria Giardino (Puerto
Escondido), 387
gemstones, 20
gifts, shopping for
Los Cabos, 447
Puerto Vallarta, 269–270
Giggling Marlin (Los Cabos), 451
Gilbert, Marta (artist), 268
glass-bottom boat, 436
Glazz (Cancún), 134, 166–167
Global System for Mobiles (GSM), 100
gods and goddesses, 24–26, 32, 50
GOGO Worldwide Vacations, 72
Golden Cactus Studio-Gallery, 446–447
Golden Cookie Shop (Ixtapa), 302
golf
Acapulco, 351–352
best, 17
Cancún, 150
Cozumel, 188
Huatulco, 377
Ixtapa, 296, 312
Los Cabos, 46, 440–441, 442–443
Puerto Vallarta, 260–261
Riviera Maya, 209–210
gorditas, 492
GoToMyPC (Web site), 101
Gran Arrecife Maya (Great Mesoamer-
ican Reef), 147, 148
Gran Meliá Cancún, 150
Gran Noche Mexicana, 360
Grand Cozumel by Occidental, 174
Grant, Cary (actor), 326
Gray Line, 416, 436, 438, 445
Gringo Gulch, 264
GSM (Global System for Mobiles), 100
Guerrero, State of. *See* Acapulco

guide, using book as, 2
gusanos de maguey, 492
Güth, Bernhard (chef), 247

• H •

Hacienda Cancún, 117
Hacienda del Solar (Taxco), 357
Hacienda Jalisco (San Sebastián), 273
Hacienda San Angel (Puerto Vallarta),
221–222
Hacienda San José, 271–272
Hagar, Sammy (rock singer), 452
Hayek, Salma (actress), 34
health insurance, 94
health issues, 94–97, 472
Henriksson, Ulf (chef), 247
Henry, Pat (*By the Grace of the Sea:
A Woman's Solo Odyssey
Around the World*), 258
Herman's Best (Puerto Escondido), 389
Herrera, Shelly and Angel (chefs), 343
Hidalgo, Miguel (priest), 27
Hidden Worlds Cenotes, 208
hieroglyphs, 29
high season, 49
hiking tour of Puerto Vallarta, 261
Hilo (Puerto Vallarta), 278
Hilton Cancún Beach & Golf Resort,
117–118, 150
Hola Asia (Puerto Morales), 205
Honeymoon Vacations For Dummies
(Wiley Publishing, Inc.), 88
Hooters (Puerto Vallarta), 275
horchata, 492
Hornitos beach (Acapulco), 348
Hornos beach (Acapulco), 348
horseback riding
Acapulco, 352
Cancún, 150
Cozumel, 188–189
Ixtapa, 313
Los Cabos, 445
Puerto Vallarta, 261–262
Riviera Maya, 209
hot chocolate, 33, 491

hot line, 472
Hotel Caleta (Acapulco), 325–326
Hotel Casa Blanca (Puerto Escondido), 382–383
Hotel Emilia Castillo (Taxco), 358
Hotel Flor de María (Puerto Escondido), 395
Hotel Jungla Caribe (Playa del Carmen), 17, 196
Hotel Lagunita (Yelapa), 274
Hotel Los Arcos (Taxco), 357–358
Hotel Los Flamingos (Acapulco), 16, 320, 326
Hotel Lunata (Playa del Carmen), 197
Hotel Margaritas (Cancún), 118
Hotel Misión (Acapulco), 326–327
Hotel Molino de Agua (Puerto Vallarta), 222–223
Hotel Ojo de Aqua (Puerto Morales), 198
Hotel Rancho Taxco Victoria (Taxco), 359
Hotel Raul 3 Marias (Zihuatanejo), 288
Hotel Sands (Acapulco), 327
Hotel Santa Fe (Puerto Escondido), 383, 395
Hotel Susy (Zihuatanejo), 288–289
Hotel Zone
  Acapulco, 320
  Ixtapa and Zihuatanejo, 297
  Puerto Vallarta, 215, 219, 230, 253–254
hoteldiscount!com (Web site), 78
hotels, 74–75. *See also* lodging
Hotels.com (Web site), 77
Hotwire (Web site), 70, 78
H2O, 446
Huatulco
  activities, 376–377
  area map, 367
  arriving in, 370–371
  beaches, 376
  choosing location to stay in, 366
  day trip from, 378
  description of, 43–44, 365, 371–372
  dining, 374–375
  Fast Facts, 372–373

  getting around, 371
  lodging, 16, 366, 368–370
  nightlife, 378
  shopping, 20, 377–378
  telephone area code, 372
Huatulco Hotels Association, 479
Huatulco State Tourism Office, 479
huevos mexicanos, 492
huevos rancheros, 245, 492
Huichol art, 19, 266–267
Huichol Collection, 266–267
huitlacoche, 493
Humboldt House/Museo Virreinal de Taxco, 357
Hummer Adventures (Outback Baja), 444
Hurricane Emily, 193
hurricane season, 48
Hurricane Wilma
  Cancún, 14, 36, 37, 109, 110
  Cozumel, 38
  reef damage by, 186
Huston, John (director), 256, 273
Hyatt Regency Acapulco, 327–328

• *I* •

Iberostar Cozumel, 176–177
Iberostar Quetzal (Riviera Maya), 195
Icacos beach (Acapulco), 348
identification, lost or stolen, 65
identity theft or fraud, 65
Iglesía de Guadalupe, 377
Iglesia de San Lucas, 445
Ika Tako (Acapulco), 341
Il Giardino di Toni e Simone (Tulum), 205
Inari Maru (ship), 435
Incidents of Travel in the Yucatan, Vol. I and II (Stephens), 34
INFOTUR help line, 472, 479
InnSite (Web site), 78
insurance
  rental car, 98–99
  travel, 93–94
Intellicast (Web site), 481

Interactive Aquarium, 149
InterContinental Presidente Cozumel
    Resort, 177
InterMar Cozumel Viajes, 185
International Association for Medical
    Assistance to Travelers, 95
International Friendship Club home
    tours, 265
International Gay and Lesbian Travel
    Association, 85
Internet access, 101–103, 472
Internet Service Provider (ISP), 102
intomatada, 488
InTouch USA (Web site), 100–101
INTRAV tours, 83
iPass network, 102
Isla Cancún
    description of, 37
    dining map, 135
    lodging, 127
    lodging map, 113
    restaurants, 132, 135
Isla Contoy, 148, 153
Isla de la Roqueta beaches, 348, 350
Isla Ixtapa, 308, 311
Isla Mujeres, 20, 151–153
Isla Mujeres Tourism Office, 479
ISP (Internet Service Provider), 102
Itzamná (Maya god above all), 32
IVA (value-added tax), 64, 474, 490–491
Ixchel (Maya goddess of water), 32
Ixtapa
    area map, 307
    arriving in, 294–295
    beaches, 14, 306–310
    choosing location to stay in, 284
    description of, 41–42, 283–284
    dining, 300–305
    dining map, 303
    Fast Facts, 297–299
    getting around, 295–296
    land sports, 312–313
    lodging, 285–293
    lodging map, 287
    nightlife, 315–316
    shopping, 313–314
    side trips from, 314–315
    sightseeing, 313
    telephone area code, 297
    water activities, 310–312
Ixtapa Golf Club, 296
Ixtapa Sportfishing Charters, 311, 350
Ixtapa Tourism Office, 479

• *J* •

J & J Habanos, 448
Jalisco, State of. *See* Puerto Vallarta
Jamiltepec, 391
J&B Salsa Club (Puerto Vallarta), 279
jeep rental, 462
jeep tour, 273
jewelry, shopping for
    Los Cabos, 447
    Puerto Vallarta, 270–271
John Grey's (Puerto Morales), 205
John Huston's Restaurant (Puerto
    Vallarta), 254
Journey into Amazing Caves
    (IMAX film), 208
Juárez, Benito, 27, 50
Juárez (street), 371
jugos, 33, 491
jungle cruise, 146–147
jungle restaurants (Puerto
    Vallarta), 246
JW Marriott Cancún, 114

• *K* •

Karen's Place (Bucerías), 253
Kau-Kan (Zihuatanejo), 302
kayaking
    best, 18
    Los Cabos, 437
    Puerto Vallarta, 262
Kid Friendly icon, 81
Kinich Ahau (Maya sun god), 32
Kit Kat Club (Puerto Vallarta), 276–277
Kukulcan Plaza, 164–165
Kukulkán (serpent god), 25, 32, 50
Kuzamil Snorkeling Center, 187–188

• L •

La Bocana beach (Los Cabos), 437
La Bodeguita del Medio (Puerto Vallarta), 275, 277
La Buena Vida (Akumal), 205
La Candelaria, 444
La Casa del Agua (Playa del Carmen), 206
La Casa del Feng Shui, 269–270
La Casa del Habano, 271
La Casa del Tequila, 271
La Casa Que Canta (Zihuatanejo), 17, 289
La Choza (Cozumel), 183
La Colección de Sergio Bustamante, 355
La Coronela (Todos Santos), 449
La Destileria (Cancún), 136
La Dolce (Los Cabos), 428
La Dolce Vita (Cancún), 136, 138
La Esquina de los Caprichos (Puerto Vallarta), 248
La Fisheria (Cancún), 138
La Fuente, 314
La Galería (Puerto Escondido), 389, 395
La Habichuela (Cancún), 138–139
La Isla Shopping Village, 164, 165
La Palapa (Puerto Vallarta), 245
La Paz, 448
La Peña (Crucecita), 378
La Perla (Playa La Ropa), 304
La Playita Inn (Los Cabos), 407–408
La Playita (Los Cabos), 434
La Posada del Capitán Lafitte (Riviera Maya), 198
La Sirena Gorda (Zihuatanejo), 304
La Taberna de San Pascual (Puerto Vallarta), 248
La Tarraya Restaurant/Bar (Playa del Carmen), 206–207
La Torre Cancún, 162
La Ventana de Taxco (Taxco), 358
Labná (Cancún), 19, 136
Labor Day, 51
The Labyrinth of Solitude (Paz), 34

Ladatel phone card, 60
Laguna Grill (Cancún), 138
Laguna Nichupté, 127
language
  English-Spanish phrases, 482–485
  menu terms, 491–493
  numbers, 485–486
  speaking, 462–463, 472
  transportation terms, 486–487
LANS department store, 268
Las Animas (Puerto Vallarta), 216, 254–255
Las Brisas (Acapulco), 328
Las Brisas area of Acapulco, 320
Las Brisas Resort (Ixtapa), 289–290
Las Palmas (Crucecita), 368–369
Las Palomas (Puerto Vallarta), 245
Las Ventanas al Paraíso (Los Cabos), 15, 408, 430
last-minute deal, finding, 69–70
Latitude 22+ Roadhouse (Los Cabos), 451–452
Laura López Labra Designs, 268
law, Mexican
  drug use, 97, 234, 394, 461, 470
  liquor, 472–473
Le Café d'Amancia (Puerto Morales), 205
Le Méridien Cancún Resort & Spa, 15, 118–119
legal aid, 472
Legorreta, Ricardo (architect), 123
Liberty Travel (Web site), 71
licuados, 33, 465, 491
Like Water for Chocolate (movie), 34
Liquid Blue Divers, 187
liquor laws, 461, 472–473, 491
Lobby Lounge (Cancún), 122, 167
Lobster Dinner Cruise, 139
Lobster House (Cozumel), 184
locking luggage, 104
Loco Gringo, 194
lodging
  Acapulco, 321–329
  all-inclusive, 3, 58, 75, 194–195
  best good-value, 16

best luxury, 15–16
bungalow, 285
Cancún, 111–112, 114, 116–123
Ciudad Cancún, 115
condo, apartment, or villa, 75
cost of, 3, 56, 76
Cozumel, 172–174, 176–178
cutting cost of, 60
finding deals on, 77–79
hotel, 74–75
hotel and motel chains, 477–478
Huatulco, 366, 368–370
Isla Cancún, 113
Ixtapa and Zihuatanejo, 285–293
Los Cabos, 401–412
options for, 74–75
Puerto Escondido, 379–380, 382–384
Puerto Vallarta, 217–227
rack rate, 76–77
reserving best room, 79
resort, 74
Riviera Maya, 195–200
Taxco, 357–358
unique places, 17
Lorenzillo's (Cancún), 139
Los Amigos Smokeshop and
    Cigar Bar, 448
Los Arcos, 255
Los Balcones (Puerto Vallarta), 280
Los Cabos
  area map, 433
  arriving in, 413–414
  beaches, 14, 418, 432–435
  choosing location to stay in, 400–401
  costs in, 399
  description of, 45–46, 399
  dining, 421–431
  Fast Facts, 417–420
  getting around, 414–417
  golf, 17
  land sports, 440–443
  lodging, 15, 401–412
  nightlife, 450–453
  shopping, 20, 445–448
  side trips, 448–450
  sightseeing, 445
  telephone area code, 417
  tours, 444–445
  water activities, 435–440
Los Cabos Guide (Web site), 453
Los Cabos Tourism Office, 480
Los Flamingos Club de Golf, 260
Los Milagros (Los Cabos), 409
Los Moros de Los Pericos islands,
    308, 311
Los Pelicanos (Puerto Morales), 205
Los Tíos (Puerto Escondido), 387
lost luggage insurance, 94
lost wallet, 64–65
The Lounge (Los Cabos), 430
low season, 49
Lucy's CuCu Cabaña and Zoo, 270
luggage
  carry-on, 105
  insurance, 94
  locking, 104
Luna Azul (sailboat), 376
lunch, as main meal, 61

• *M* •

machaca, 493
MacClure, Chris (artist), 446
Madero, Francisco (president), 28
magazines, 473
Magdalena Bay, 436
Magic Tropic (Santa Cruz), 378
Mágico Mundo Marina (water
    park), 348
Maguey Bay, 376
mail, 473
mail2web service, 101
malecón
  Puerto Vallarta, 216, 230,
      263, 265, 275, 458
  Zihuatanejo, 296, 458
mall, shopping
  Acapulco, 355
  Cancún, 162, 164–165
Mambo Café (Los Cabos), 452
Mamma Eli's, 448

Mañana (Puerto Vallarta), 252
manchamanteles, 428
Mandara (Acapulco), 361
Mango Tango (Cancún), 140, 167–168
Manialtepec Lagoon, 391
Many Mexicos (Simpson), 34
Mapquest (Web site), 481
maps
  Acapulco Bay, 346–347
  Acapulco Bay accommodations,
    322–323
  Acapulco Bay dining, 338–339
  Cabo San Lucas accommodations, 405
  Cabo San Lucas dining, 425
  Cancún and environs, 145, 163
  Chichén Itzá, 157
  Ciudad Cancún accommodations, 115
  Ciudad Cancún dining, 137
  the Corridor accommodations, 407
  the Corridor dining, 427
  Cozumel Island, 173
  Huatulco Bahías, 367
  Isla Cancún accommodations, 113
  Isla Cancún dining, 135
  Isla Mujeres, 152
  Ixtapa and Zihuatanejo, 307
  Ixtapa and Zihuatanejo
    accommodations, 287
  Ixtapa and Zihuatanejo dining, 303
  Los Cabos, 433
  Marina Vallarta dining, 239
  Mexico, 12–13
  Playa del Carmen, 197
  Puerto Escondido, 381
  Puerto Vallarta, 251
  Puerto Vallarta accommodations,
    219, 221
  Puerto Vallarta dining, 241
  Riviera Maya, 201
  San José del Cabo accommodations,
    403
  San José del Cabo dining, 423
  San Miguel de Cozumel, 175
  Tulum, 155
Mar de Sueños, 268
Mariachi Loco (Puerto Vallarta), 277

mariachi music, 458
María's Restaurant (Puerto
  Escondido), 389
Marietas Islands, 252
Marigalante tour boat, 256
Marina Ixtapa, 296, 311
Marina Ixtapa Golf Course, 312
Marina Vallarta
  area map, 251
  beaches of, 253
  description of, 214–215
  dining, 239
  lodging, 219
  nightlife, 275
  shopping, 265
Marina Vallarta Club de Golf, 215, 260
Mariscos Pipo (Acapulco), 341–342
Marítima Chankanaab, 179
Marival Grand & Club Suites (Puerto
  Vallarta), 223
market
  curandero section of, 30–31
  food stalls in, 490
  Puerto Vallarta, 264, 266
  Taxco, 356
  Zihuatanejo, 300, 314
Maroma (Puerto Morales), 16, 198–199
Marts, Carl (chef), 422
masa, 31, 488, 493
Mascota tour, 272–273
MasterCard
  ATM Locator, 481
  traveler's check, 64
Mature Outlook, 83
Maya. *See also* archaeological sites
  architecture of, 29
  cenotes, 18
  development of civilization of, 24
  ruins of, 23
Maya Art and Architecture (Miller), 34
The Maya (Coe), 33
Maya Fair Plaza/Centro Comerical
  Maya Fair, 164
Mayan Palace Golf Club, 214, 351
Mayan Resort Golf Los Cabos, 440, 441
MB (Cancún), 116

McHenry, J. Patrick (*A Short History of Mexico*), 33
meal system, 32–33
MEDEX Assistance, 93
Media Luna (Playa del Carmen), 19, 207
medical insurance, 93–94
MedicAlert identification tag, 94–95
Meigas Binniguenda (Santa Cruz), 369
Meliá (Cancún), 118
Meliá San Lucas (Los Cabos), 409
mens' clubs, 453
menú del día, 490
menudo, 493
Mercado Parazal, 354
Mermaid's (Los Cabos), 453
Mexican fiesta night
    Cancún, 167–168
    description of, 457
    Ixtapa, 315
    Los Cabos, 450–451
    Puerto Vallarta, 275–276
Mexican tourist permit (FMT), 90
Mexico
    architecture, 29–30
    books on, 33–34
    colonial period, 27
    conquest of, 26
    cuisine, 31–33
    geography of, 26, 460
    independence of, 27
    introduction to, 22–23
    map of, 12–13
    modern, 28
    movies about, 34
    Porfiriato and revolution, 27–28
    pre-Hispanic civilizations, 23–26
    religion, myth, and folklore, 30–31, 32
    retirement in, 82
Mexico Boutique Hotels (Web site), 79
Mexico City airport, 66
Mexico Connect online magazine, 480–481
Mexico: From the Olmecs to the Aztecs (Coe), 33
Mexico Ministry of Tourism, 480

Mexico, One Plate at a Time (Bayless), 34
Mexico Tourism Board, 87–88, 478, 480
mezcal, 33, 491
Mezzanotte Acapulco (Acapulco), 342
Mi Casa (Los Cabos), 428
Mi Cocina (Los Cabos), 428–429
Mi Parri Pollo (Acapulco), 342
Mi Querencia (Puerto Vallarta), 277
Michael Malone's Hidden Voyages Ecotours, 391
Micky's No Name Café (Puerto Vallarta), 280
Miller, Mary Ellen (*Maya Art and Architecture*), 34
Misión de los Arcos (Crucecita), 16, 369
missions, 30
Mitla, 25
Mixtec Ceremonial Center, 392
Mobility International USA, 84
Mocambo (Los Cabos), 429
Moctezuma II (ruler), 26
Modified American plan, 57
molcajetes, 244
mole (sauce), 465
Molina, Alfred (actor), 34
monasteries, 30
Montano, Armando (chef), 426
Monte Albán, 25, 378
Montezuma's Revenge (Puerto Escondido), 395
Moon Palace Golf Resort, 150
moped rental
    Cancún, 129
    Cozumel, 180
mordida, 461
Mosaïqe, 271
MossRehab, 83
Mr. Sancho's beach club, 186
Muelle Fiscal, 179
Muelle Internacional, 179
murals, 29
Museo Arqueológico de Cancún, 161
Museo de Arqueología de la Costa Grande, 313

Museo de la Isla de Cozumel, 190
Museo de Taxco Guillermo
    Spratling, 357
Museo Histórico de Acapulco, 354
Museo Río Cuale, 264
music. *See also* Mexican fiesta night
    mariachi, 458
    in Puerto Vallarta, 276–277
Mystic Divers, 207–208
mythology, 31, 32

• N •

Nachi Cocom beach club, 186
National Car Rental, 415
Neuva Zelanda, 304–305
New Spain, 26
newspapers, 473
NH Krystal Ixtapa, 290
NH Krystal Puerto Vallarta, 275
Nick-San (Los Cabos), 429
The Night of the Iguana (movie),
    254, 256
nightlife
    Acapulco, 359–362
    best, 21
    Cabo San Lucas, 401
    Cancún, 165–168
    cost of, 59
    Cozumel, 191
    Huatulco, 378
    Ixtapa and Zihuatanejo, 315–316
    Los Cabos, 450–453
    Playa del Carmen, 210
    Puerto Escondido, 395–396
    Puerto Vallarta, 274–280
    Taxco, 359
Nikki Beach
    Los Cabos, 452
    Puerto Vallarta, 227, 237, 279
Noches Oaxaqueñas/Don Porfirio
    (Tangolunda Bay), 375
non-smoking room, 75
Nopala, 391
Nostalgia (Barquet), 263
November, 49

Now, Voyager, 85
nude beaches, 112, 394
Nuestra Señora de la Soledad
    cathedral, 353
Nuevo Vallarta, 214, 253
numbers, in Spanish, 485–486

• O •

Oasis Cancún, 119
Oaxaca. *See* Huatulco
Oaxaca City, 378
Oaxaca Tourist Bureau, 391
Oaxacan textiles, 20
Oaxaqueño tamale, 466
ocean (sea) kayaking
    best, 18
    Los Cabos, 437
    Puerto Vallarta, 262
off-peak travel, 59–60, 69
Oh! Mar mini-mart, 394
Old Acapulco, 320, 323
Olivia Cruises & Resorts, 85
Olmec, 24
Olmedo, Dolores, home of, 353
Olvido Plaza, 355
Ometeotl (god/goddess), 32
100% Natural
    Acapulco, 342–343
    Cancún, 140
One&Only Palmilla (Los Cabos),
    15, 409–410, 441
online, researching and booking trip,
    69–70
Open Air Expeditions, 256, 262
Orbitz online travel agency, 69
Organo Bay, 376
Outback Baja, 444
outdoor activities
    Acapulco, 349–352
    Cancún, 146–151
    cost of, 58–59
    Ixtapa and Zihuatanejo, 310–313
    Los Cabos, 435–443
    Puerto Vallarta, 255–263
    Riviera Maya, 207–210

• *P* •

Pacific Travel, 273
package tour
 Cancún, 110
 Cozumel, 172
 for cutting costs, 60
 description of, 70–71
 finding, 71–73
 for honeymooners, 56
 insurance, 93
 Playacar Golf Club, 209–210
 transportation, 57
packing, 104–106
Paco's (Taxco), 359
palacia municipal (Puerto
 Vallarta), 264
Palancar Reef, 187
palapa, 185
Palladium (Acapulco), 361
The Palm Video & Show Bar (Puerto
 Vallarta), 279
Palmilla Bay Sportfishing, 439
Palmilla Golf Club, 440–441, 443
Paloma Bonita (Cancún), 140–141
pan dulce, 493
panga
 Los Cabos, 439
 Puerto Escondido, 392
 Puerto Vallarta, 252
Papantla Flyers, 264
Paradise Cafe beach club, 186
Paradise Plaza shopping center, 214
Paradise Village (Puerto Vallarta),
 223–224
Parador (Cancún), 120
Paraíso Escondido (Puerto Escondido),
 16, 383
Paraíso Tours, 378
Parish of Nuestra Señora de Guadalupe
 church, 264
Parque de las Palapas, 168
Partido Revolucionario Institucional
 (PRI), 28
Paseo del Pescador, 296, 313
Paseo Díaz Ordaz (Puerto Vallarta), 230

passport, 90–92
Paz, Octavio (*The Labyrinth of
 Solitude*), 34
Peacocks (Los Cabos), 429
Pepe's Grill (Cozumel), 184
Pepe's Piano Bar (Acapulco), 362
Pepto-Bismol, 96
Périco's (Cancún), 141
Pesca Deportiva, 350
Pescadero, 437
pescadillas, 465
pescado en talla, 465
pescado sarandeado, 465
peso, 61–62, 470
pets, 473
Pez Gato (catamaran), 436
pharmacy, finding, 473
phone call, 60
pibil, 493
Picante/Bluewater Sportfishing, 439
pico de gallo, 426
Pie de la Cuesta beach (Acapulco), 345
Pierre Marqués golf course, 351
pipián, 493
PJ's Book Bodega and Music Shop
 (Puerto Escondido), 396
Places to Stay (Web site), 78–79
Planet Hollywood (Cancún), 167
Planeta Vegetariano (Puerto
 Vallarta), 237
Planeta.com (Web site), 480
planning trip. *See also* budget,
 planning
 flying to Mexico, 66–69
 package tours, 70–71
 packing, 104–106
 researching and booking online,
 69–70
 wedding in Mexico, 87–88
platillo a la huatulqueño, 374
Playa Anclote (Puerto Vallarta), 252
Playa Azul Golf & Beach Resort
 (Cozumel), 177–178
Playa Bacocho (Puerto
 Escondido), 390
Playa Barco Varado (Los Cabos),
 435, 438

Playa Barra de la Cruz, 393
Playa Bonita beach club, 186
Playa Caracol (Cancún), 146
Playa Carey (Isla Ixtapa), 308
Playa Chac-Mool (Cancún), 146
Playa Chileno (Los Cabos),
    435, 437, 438
Playa Coral (Isla Ixtapa), 308
Playa Costa Azul (Los Cabos), 434, 437
Playa Cuachalatate (Isla Ixtapa), 308
Playa del Amor (Los Cabos), 14, 438
Playa del Carmen
  area map, 197
  beaches, 14
  choosing location to stay in, 194
  description of, 39, 192, 202
  dining, 19, 205, 206–207
  Fast Facts, 204
  lodging, 16, 17, 196–200
  nightlife, 210
  Quinta Avenida, 14, 20, 21
  shopping, 20, 210
  telephone area code, 204
Playa del Rey (Cancún), 146
Playa Destiladeras (Puerto
    Vallarta), 252
Playa El Medano (Los Cabos), 435
Playa el Palmar (Ixtapa), 296, 309
Playa Escobilla (Puerto
    Escondido), 393
Playa La Angosta (Acapulco), 345
Playa La Entrega (Huatulco), 376
Playa La Ropa (Zihuatanejo),
    14, 285, 296, 304, 309
Playa Langosta (Cancún), 144
Playa Las Cuatas (Ixtapa), 308
Playa Las Gatas (Zihuatanejo),
    14, 309–310
Playa Linda
  Cancún, 144
  Ixtapa, 308
Playa Los Arcos Hotel & Suites (Puerto
    Vallarta), 224
Playa los Cerritos (Los Cabos), 437
Playa Los Muertos (Puerto Vallarta),
    11, 216, 254

Playa Madera (Zihuatanejo),
    285, 296, 309
Playa Maguey (Huatulco), 377
Playa Manzanillo
  Acapulco, 348
  Puerto Escondido, 390
  Puerto Vallarta, 252
Playa Marin (Isla de la Roqueta), 348
Playa Marinero (Puerto
    Escondido), 384
Playa Maya (Playa del Carmen), 199
Playa Mazunte, 393
Playa Medano (Los Cabos), 418
Playa Mía beach club, 186
Playa Mismaloya (Puerto Vallarta),
    216, 254
Playa Municipal (Zihuatanejo), 309
Playa Norte (Isla Mujeres), 151
Playa Palancar (Cozumel), 186
Playa Palmar, 14
Playa Palmilla (Los Cabos), 434
Playa Panteón (Puerto Angel), 393
Playa Paraíso (Cozumel), 186
Playa Piedra Blanca (Puerto
    Vallarta), 252
Playa Principal
  Puerto Angel, 393
  Puerto Escondido, 390
Playa Puerto Marqués (Acapulco), 348
Playa Quieta (Ixtapa), 308
Playa Revolcadero (Acapulco), 348–349
Playa Roqueta (Isla de la Roqueta), 348
Playa San Agustín (Huatulco), 377
Playa San Francisco (Cozumel), 186
Playa San Pedrito (Los Cabos), 437
Playa Santa María (Los Cabos),
    435, 438
Playa Tangolunda (Huatulco), 376
Playa Tortuga (Cancún), 146
Playa Varadero (Isla Ixtapa), 308
Playa Vista Hermosa (Ixtapa), 309
Playa Zicatela (Puerto Escondido)
  description of, 14, 384, 390
  palapa restaurants on, 387
Playa Zipolite (Puerto Angel), 393–394
Playacar, 192

Playacar Golf Club, 209–210
Plaza Bahía, 355
Plaza Bonita Shopping Center, 447
Plaza Caracol, 164
Plaza Condesa, 355
Plaza Flamingo, 164
Pleasant Mexico Holidays, 73
pluma coffee, 378
Plus ATM network, 62
poc chuc, 493
police, 473–474
Porto Bello (Puerto Vallarta), 246–247
Posada Citlali (Zihuatanejo), 290
Posada Señor Mañana (Los Cabos), 410
pottery
  Huatulco, 378
  of Maya, 29
pozole, 19, 336–337, 466, 493
Premier Hotel & Spa (Puerto Vallarta),
  224–225
Presidente InterContinental
  Cancún, 120
  Los Cabos, 410–411, 441
PRI (Partido Revolucionario
  Institucional), 28
Priceline (Web site), 70, 78
Prima (Cozumel), 184–185
proof of citizenship, 89–90
publications
  books, recommended, 33–34
  gay and lesbian travelers, 85–86
  senior travel, 83
  travelers with disabilities, 84
Pueblo la Playa (Los Cabos), 14, 434
Puerco Azul, 270
Puerto Angel, 392
Puerto Angelito, 390
Puerto Aventuras
  description of, 202
  dining, 205
Puerto Escondido
  area map, 381
  arriving in, 384
  beaches, 14, 390
  description of, 44–45, 379, 384–385
  dining, 19, 387–390
  Fast Facts, 385–387

getting around, 385
lodging, 16, 379–380, 382–384
nightlife, 395–396
shopping, 394–395
side trips from, 392–394
spa, 391
surfing, 18
telephone area code, 385
tours, 391–392
Puerto Escondido State Tourism
  Office, 480
Puerto Los Cabos, 442
Puerto Madero (Cancún), 141
Puerto Marqués bay, 348
Puerto Morales
  description of, 202
  dining, 205
  lodging, 198–199
  telephone area code, 204
Puerto Paraíso Entertainment
  Plaza, 446
Puerto Vallarta
  area map, 251
  arriving in, 228–229
  beaches, 11, 14, 250, 252–255
  choosing location to stay in, 213–217
  description of, 40–41, 213
  dining, 19, 236–249
  dining map, 241
  downtown/el centro, 215–216,
    221, 251
  Fast Facts, 232–235
  for gay and lesbian travelers, 85
  golf, 17
  land sports, 259–263
  lodging, 15, 17, 217–227
  lodging map, 219, 221
  malecón, 216, 230, 263, 265, 275, 458
  nightlife, 21, 274–280
  shopping, 20, 265–271
  side trips from, 271–274
  sightseeing, 263–265
  southern shore, 216–217
  telephone area code, 232
  for travelers with disabilities, 85
  water activities, 255–259
  whale-watching, 18

Puerto Vallarta Tourism Board
and Convention and Visitors
Bureau, 480
pulque, 491
Punta Mita, 14, 214
Punta Mita Properties, 217
Punta Morena beach club, 186
Puuc style architecture, 25
pyramids, 29, 50

• *Q* •

Que Viva México (movie), 34
Querencia golf course, 440
Querubines, 270
quesadilla, 489, 493
queso cotija, 489
queso relleno, 493
Quetzalcoatl (serpent god), 24–26, 32
Quickbook.com (Web site), 77
Quimixto (Puerto Vallarta),
216, 254, 255
Quinta María Cortez (Puerto Vallarta),
17, 225
Quinta Real (Tangolunda Bay), 370
Quintana, Patricia (chef), 116

• *R* •

rack rate, 76–77
Radisson Hacienda (Cancún), 120–121
rainy season, 48
rajas con queso, 466
Ranch Disco Bar (Puerto Vallarta), 280
Rancho Altamira, 262
Rancho Collins, 445
Rancho El Charro, 262
Rancho Loma Bonita, 150
Rancho Ojo de Agua, 262
Rancho Palma Real, 261–262
Rancho Palmitas, 188–189
Rancho Playa Linda, 313
Rancho Punta Venado, 209
Rancho Taxco Victoria (Taxco), 358
rate of exchange, 61, 62
ratings of beach resorts, 47
Raven Club golf course, 441, 443

Rayos X (Puerto Escondido), 395
reentering United States, 90
Refugio del Pirata Morgan
(Cancún), 121
religion, 30–31. *See also* churches
renting. *See also* condo, renting
boat, 377, 385
cellphone, 100
moped, 129, 180
panga, 252, 392, 439
watersports equipment, 254, 310, 349
renting car
Acapulco, 333
Cancún, 126–127
Cozumel, 180
Huatulco, 371
Ixtapa-Zihuatanejo, 295
Los Cabos, 400, 414–415, 417
overview of, 57, 97–99
Puerto Escondido, 384
Puerto Vallarta, 231
Riviera Maya, 203–204
researching trip on line, 69–70
reserving best room, 79
resort
best luxury, 15–16
description of, 74
resort wear, 20
The Restaurant (Los Cabos), 430
Restaurant Santa Fe (Puerto
Escondido), 389–390
Restaurante Ethel (Taxco), 358
restaurants. *See also* cuisine
Acapulco, 336–343
best, 19
breakfast buffets, 58
Cancún, 132–142
choosing place to eat, 490
cost of, 3, 57–58
Cozumel, 182–185
cutting cost of, 61
Huatulco, 374–375
Isla Cancún, 135
Ixtapa and Zihuatanejo, 300–305
Los Cabos, 421–431
Puerto Escondido, 387–390
Puerto Vallarta, 236–249

Riviera Maya, 205–207
taquería, 489, 490
Taxco, 358–359
tipping, 490–491
waiter, summoning, 491
restroom, public, 474
retirement in Mexico, 82
Rey del Caribe Hotel (Cancún), 16, 121
Reyes, Victor (owner), 207–208
Rhythms of the Night, 275–276
Rick's Bar (Zihuatanejo), 315
Riding, Alan (*Distant Neighbors*), 34
riptides, 334, 345
Rito's Baci (Puerto Vallarta), 247
Ritz-Carlton Cancún, 122
Riu Palace Las Americas, 122
Rivera, Diego (artist), 353
Riviera Maya. *See also* Playa del
     Carmen; Tulum
  activities, 207–210
  area map, 201
  choosing location to stay in, 193–194
  description of, 39–40, 192–193
  dining, 205–207
  Fast Facts, 204
  lodging, 16, 195–200
  telephone area code, 204
RoadPost (Web site), 100
Rockaway Surfer Village (Puerto
     Escondido), 384
Rodriguez, Ricardo (chef), 302
Rolandi's Pizza (Cancún), 142
rompope, 493
Roots (Cancún), 142
Route 66 (Puerto Vallarta), 277
Ruben's (Ixtapa), 305
Ruinas del Rey, 156
Ruth's Chris Steak House
     (Los Cabos), 446

• S •

Safari Accents, 270
safety issues
  Acapulco, 334
  airline security, 103–104

at ATM, 63
bus travel, 299
Cancún, 127, 131
driving, 99, 298–299
for female traveling alone, 86–87
HIV/AIDS rate, 97
Huatulco, 373
lost or stolen wallet, 64–65
moped accident, 180
overview of, 2, 474
Playa Zipolite, 394
Puerto Escondido, 386
Puerto Vallarta, 231, 234
riptides, 334, 345
water-safety pennant system, 144
Sail Vallarta, 257
sailing in Puerto Vallarta, 257–258
Salon Q (Acapulco), 362
salsa verde, 493
San Agustín Bay, 377
San Blas, 262
San Francisco Reef, 187
San Gervasio ruins, 189–190
San José del Cabo
  beaches, 434
  description of, 45–46, 399, 400
  dining, 421, 422, 426–431
  dining map, 423
  getting around, 416
  golf, 440
  lodging, 17, 401, 404, 406–408,
     410–412
  lodging map, 403
  nightlife, 450
  shopping, 445–446
San Miguel de Cozumel, 172,
     175, 179–180
San Sebastián, 272
Sanborn Tours, 82
Sanborn's department store, 355
Sancho Panza Wine Bar and Bistro
     (Los Cabos), 450, 452
Sandos Gala Playacar (Riviera
     Maya), 195
Santa Cruz, 366, 376
Santa Cruz Bay, 365, 371
Santa Cruz Market, 377–378

Santa María de Huatulco, 371
Santa Prisca (Taxco), 358
Santa Prisca y San Sebastián
   church, 357
Santa Rosa Wall, 187
SATH (Society for Accessible Travel
   and Hospitality), 83–84
SAX (jewelry), 447
scorecard, 47
Scuba Cancún, 147
scuba diving
   Acapulco, 350
   best, 18
   Cancún, 147
   cavern, 208
   cenote, 18, 187
   Cozumel, 172, 186–187
   drift, 186
   Ixtapa and Zihuatanejo, 310
   Los Cabos, 438
   Puerto Escondido, 392
   Puerto Vallarta, 252, 255–256, 257
   Riviera Maya, 207–208
Sea Kayak Adventures, 436
sea kayaking
   best, 18
   Los Cabos, 437
   Puerto Vallarta, 262
Sea of Cortez, 18
sea turtle, 393, 444
seasons, 49, 295
Semana Santa, 51
senior traveler, 82–83
Señor Frog's
   Ixtapa, 316
   Playa del Carmen, 210
   Puerto Vallarta, 274, 279
The Sets of The Night of the Iguana
   Restaurant (Puerto Vallarta), 254
Shangri-La Caribe (Playa del
   Carmen), 199
shopping. See also duty-free shopping;
   market
   Acapulco, 354–355
   best, 20
   Cancún, 162–165
   cost of, 59

Cozumel, 190–191
Huatulco, 377–378
Ixtapa and Zihuatanejo, 313–314
Los Cabos, 445–448
Playa del Carmen, 210
Playa Mazunte, 393
Puerto Escondido, 394–395
Puerto Vallarta, 265–271
Taxco, 356
vendors on beaches, 267, 274, 459
A Short History of Mexico
   (McHenry), 33
Shotover Jet, 349
shuttle service in Los Cabos, 417
Sian Ka'an Biosphere, 209
Siboney (Acapulco), 361
side trips
   from Acapulco, 355–359
   from Huatulco, 378
   from Ixtapa and Zihuatanejo, 314–315
   in Los Cabos, 448–450
   from Puerto Escondido, 392–394
   from Puerto Vallarta, 271–274
SideStep online travel agency, 69
Sierra Madre Expedition (Vallarta
   Adventures), 262
siesta, 461
Siesta Suites (Los Cabos), 411
SIETE (Cancún), 116
sightseeing. See also side trips
   Acapulco, 352, 353–354
   Cancún, 161–162
   cost of, 58–59
   Cozumel, 188
   Huatulco, 377, 378
   Ixtapa and Zihuatanejo, 313
   Los Cabos, 445
   Puerto Vallarta, 263–265
   Taxco, 357
   silver, 267, 356
Simpson, Lesley Byrd (Many
   Mexicos), 34
single traveler, 86–87
Small Vallarta, 266
Smarter Travel (Web site), 69, 70
smoking, 75, 491

snorkeling
  Acapulco, 350
  Cancún, 148
  Cozumel, 187–188
  drift, 148
  Ixtapa and Zihuatanejo, 310
  Los Cabos, 435, 438
  Puerto Vallarta, 255–256
  Riviera Maya, 208
snuba, 161
Society for Accessible Travel and
    Hospitality (SATH), 83–84
soft drinks, 491
Solmar Suites (Los Cabos), 411–412
sombrero, 461
Son y la Rumba (Puerto Escondido),
    395–396
sopa de lima, 493
sopa de tortilla, 493
sope, 493
Sotavento Beach Resort
    (Zihuatanejo), 291
Sotavento Restaurant Bar Galería
    (Taxco), 358–359
souvenirs, 60
Spa del Mar, 119
Spanish conquest and colonization of
    Mexico, 26–27
Spanish language
  English-Spanish phrases, 482–485
  menu terms, 491–493
  numbers, 485–486
  speaking, 462–463, 472
  transportation terms, 486–487
spas
  Cancún, 119
  Los Cabos, 404, 408, 410, 412
  Puerto Escondido, 391
special events, 49–52
Split Coco (Puerto Escondido), 396
sportfishing
  Acapulco, 350
  best, 18
  Cancún, 148–149

Cozumel, 188
  Los Cabos, 438–440
  Puerto Aventuras, 209
  Puerto Vallarta, 258
  Zihuatanejo, 311
sports. *See also* diving; golf; horseback
    riding; tennis
  Cancún, 149–151
  Los Cabos, 440–443
sports bar, 280
spring break, 49
spring equinox, 50
Squid Roe (Los Cabos), 422
State of Jalisco Tourism Office in
    Puerto Vallarta, 480
stelae, 29
Stephens, John L. (*Incidents of Travel in
    the Yucatan, Vol. I and II*), 34
stolen wallet, 64–65
street stall, buying food from, 466
Su Casa (Acapulco), 343
Subsee Explorer, 147–148, 188
sunburn, 96
sunset-watching, 451, 457, 458
Super Chomak, 205
surfing
  best, 18
  Los Cabos, 437–438
swimming
  riptides, 334, 345
  water-safety pennant system, 144
swimming with dolphins
  Cancún, 149
  Chankanaab National Park, 189
  Puerto Vallarta, 258–259
  Riviera Maya, 208

• *T* •

T. Fuller Gallery, 269
taco, 31, 489
tacos al pastor, 466, 493
Tales of Retirement in Paradise
    (Vicars), 82

Talpa de Allende tour, 272–273
tamal, 466, 489, 493
Tamaral, Nicolás (missionary), 445
Tangolunda Bay, 366, 372
Tangolunda Golf Course, 377
Tank-Ha Dive Center, 208
tapas (Puerto Vallarta), 248
taquería, 489, 490
Taxco
    description of, 355–356
    dining, 358–359
    getting to, 356
    lodging, 357–358
    nightlife, 359
    sightseeing, 356–357
Taxco silver, 20, 356
taxes, 64, 474
taxi service
    Acapulco, 332
    Cancún, 125–126, 128
    Cozumel, 180
    Huatulco, 371, 372
    Ixtapa and Zihuatanejo, 296
    Los Cabos, 417
    Puerto Escondido, 385
    Puerto Vallarta, 230
Taylor, Elizabeth (actress), 264, 273
telephone area code
    Acapulco, 333
    Cancún, 129
    Cozumel, 181
    dialing, 474
    Huatulco, 372
    Ixtapa and Zihuatanejo, 297
    Los Cabos, 417
    Nuevo Vallarta, 232
    Puerto Escondido, 385
    Puerto Morelos, 204
    Puerto Vallarta, 232
    Riviera Maya and Playa del
        Carmen, 204
telephone call, 60, 474

tennis
    Acapulco, 352
    Cancún, 150
    Huatulco, 377
    Ixtapa, 312–313
    Los Cabos, 441
    Puerto Vallarta, 261
Teotihuacán, people of, 24–25
tequila
    description of, 33, 491
    drinking, 462
    Los Cabos, 448
    Puerto Vallarta, 271
Tequila (boat), 376
Tequila (Los Cabos), 430
Tequila Sunrise (Puerto
    Escondido), 396
Tequila (town), 271–272
Tequila's House, 448
Terra Cotta (Crucecita), 369, 375
Terra Noble Spa Art and Healing
    Center, 262
Tezcatlipoca (god, "smoking
    mirror"), 25
Thai Lounge (Cancún), 142
theme night, 450–451
Thierry Blouet Cocina de Autor, 240
360 Surf Shop, 395
tikik-chik/tikin-chik, 465
tik-n-xic, 207
time zone, 475
timeshare sales
    Cozumel, 190–191
    jeep rental, 462
    Los Cabos, 414
    Puerto Vallarta, 229
    Riviera Maya, 210
Tio Sports, 445
tipping
    fishing charter captain, 311
    at restaurants, 490–491
    standards for, 58, 475
Titita, Carmen (chef), 239

Tlaloc (Aztec rain god), 32
Tlaquepaque, 262
T-Mobile Hotspot, 102
Todos Santos, 437, 448–450
Toltec, 24–25
Tonalá, 262
Toni's (Taxco), 359
torta, 493
tortilla, 31, 488–489
tostada, 493
Tostado's Grill (Crucecita), 375
tourist information, 472, 478–481
tours. *See also* ecotours; package tour
    ATV, 151, 444
    biking, 261
    bird-watching, 262, 311
    canopy, 26
    driving, 444–445
    golf packages, 441
    hiking, 261
    jeep, 273
    Los Cabos, 444–445
    Puerto Escondido, 391–392
Traditions, 450
transportation
    Acapulco, 331–333
    Cancún, 125–126, 127–129
    cost of, 56–57, 60
    Cozumel, 178–179
    flying to Mexico, 66–69
    Huatulco, 371
    to Isla Mujeres, 151, 153
    Ixtapa, 295–296
    Los Cabos, 414–416
    Puerto Escondido, 385
    Puerto Vallarta, 229–232, 252
    to Riviera Maya, 200–201
    Spanish phrases, 486–487
    to Taxco, 356
    Zihuatanejo, 295–296
Transportation Security Administration
    (Web site), 104
Transportes Terrestres
    Acapulco, 331
    Cozumel, 178
    Huatulco, 371
    Ixtapa and Zihuatanejo, 295
    Puerto Escondido, 384

travel agencies, online, 69, 71, 77
Travel Assistance International, 94
Travel Companion Exchange, 86
travel documents
    for children, 90
    entering and departing Mexico, 89–90
    passport, 90–92
Travel Guard Alerts, 93
travel insurance, 93–94
travel seasons, 49
Travel Secrets (Web site), 481
Travel Sentry luggage lock, 104
TravelAxe (Web site), 77
traveler's check, 63–64, 65
Traveling Internationally with Your
    Kids (Web site), 81
Travelocity online travel agency, 69, 77
Travelweb (Web site), 77–78, 79
Treetops (Playa del Carmen),
    16, 199–200
Tres Palos Lagoon, 349
Tres Rios, 158–159
Tres Vidas Golf Club, 351–352
Trio (Puerto Vallarta), 247
trip planner, using book as, 2
trip-cancellation insurance, 93
TriStar catamaran cruise, 312
Troncones, 314–315
Tropicana Bar and Grill (Los Cabos),
    431, 452
Tropicana Inn (Los Cabos), 412
Trotter, Charlie (chef), 410, 422
Tucan (Riviera Maya), 195
Tukari Tours, 262
Tulum
    archaeological area, 154–156, 459
    city, 193, 202–203
    dining, 205
    lodging, 194, 195–196, 200
    map of ruins, 155
Turismo Dimar Travel Agency, 384, 391
turista, avoiding, 95–96
Turtle Bay Café and Bakery
    (Akumal), 205
Turtle Museum, 393
Tutifruti (Puerto Vallarta), 237
Twenty/20 Showgirls (Los Cabos), 453

• U •

ultrabaroque, 30
UltraFemme
  Cancún, 162
  Los Cabos, 447
Ultramar, 179
Universal Currency Converter
  (Web site), 481
U.S. Customs & Border Protection
  (Web site), 92
U.S. State Department, 478
Uxmal, 29

• V •

Vacation Hot Line, 72
Vallarta Adventures
  Caletas, trip to, 256
  canopy tours, 263
  Colonial Treasures Air Expedition,
    272
  diving tours, 257
  Rhythms of the Night, 275–276
  sailing charters, 258
  Sierra Madre Expedition, 262
  Tequila, trips to, 271–272
  whale-watching tours, 256
value-added tax (IVA), 64, 474, 490–491
vegetarian restaurants in Puerto
  Vallarta, 237
Velas Vallarta Grand Suite Resort
  (Puerto Vallarta), 226
vendors on beaches, 267, 274, 459
Verana (Yelapa), 17, 226–227, 255, 274
Vicars, Polly (*Tales of Retirement in
  Paradise*), 82
Villa de la Selva (Ixtapa), 305
Villa del Sol (Zihuatanejo), 15, 291–292
villa, renting
  Cancún, 111
  Cozumel, 173
  overview of, 75
  Puerto Vallarta, 216–217
  Riviera Maya, 194
Villa Vera Hotel, Spa, and Racquet Club
  (Acapulco), 329

Villa Vera Puerto Mio (Zihuatanejo),
  293
Villas Miramar (Zihuatanejo), 292
Villas San Sebastián (Zihuatanejo), 292
Virgin of Guadalupe underwater
  sanctuary, 354
Visa
  ATM Locator (Web site), 481
  traveler's check, 63–64
Visit Cabo (Web site), 453
Vista del Mar (Cozumel), 178
Vista Vallarta Golf Club, 260
Vitea (Puerto Vallarta), 248
Viva, 271
Viva Zapatos, 314

• W •

waiter, summoning, 491
wallet, lost or stolen, 64–65
water
  bottled, 61, 95, 462
  purified, 475
water activities
  Acapulco, 349–351
  Cancún, 144, 146–149
  Ixtapa and Zihuatanejo, 310–312
  Los Cabos, 435–440
  Puerto Vallarta, 255–259
water park, 348, 350–351
water taxi in Puerto Vallarta, 232
water-safety pennant system, 144
water-skiing, 349
Wayne, John (actor), 326
Wayport, 102
weather, 48, 295
Web sites
  airlines, 475–476
  Cancún, 126
  car rental agencies, 98, 476–477
  cybercafe, 101, 481
  family travel advice, 81
  female traveling alone, 87
  hotel and motel chains, 477–478
  lodging, 77–79
  Los Cabos and Baja, 453
  package tours, 71, 72–73

responsible travel, 149
senior travel, 82–83
tourist information, 478–481
Transportation Security
    Administration, 104
Travel Guard Alerts, 93
travel insurance, 94
travel planning, 69–70
Travel Sentry, 104
for traveler with disability, 83–84
U.S. Customs & Border Protection, 92
U.S. State Department Bureau of
    Consular Affairs, 90
Wi-Fi service, 102
wireless rental companies, 100–101
wedding, planning, 87–88
Weissmuller, Johnny (actor), 326
Wentworth Porter, Dennis (artist), 446
Western Union, 65
Westin Regina Resort (Puerto
    Vallarta), 227
Westin Resort & Spa Cancún, 123
Westin Resort and Spa Los Cabos, 412
Wet n'Wild, 149
whale-watching
    best, 18
    description of, 458
    Los Cabos, 436
    Puerto Vallarta, 252, 256
Wide Open Baja Racing Experience,
    444–445
Wi-Fi access, 102
Wiley Publishing, Inc. (*Honeymoon
    Vacations For Dummies*), 88
Windows (Taxco), 359
Wipeout (Puerto Escondido), 395

• X •

Xcaret, 159–160, 202
Xel-Ha, 160, 202
Xitomates (Puerto Vallarta), 249
Xpu-Ha, 202
Xpu-Ha Palace (Riviera Maya), 195

• Y •

Yahoo! Mail, 101
yarn paintings, 267
Yates del Sol, 312
Yaxché (Playa del Carmen), 207
Yelapa
    beaches, 254–255
    description of, 216
    lodging, 17, 226–227
    visiting, 273–274
Yelapa Yacht Club, 274
Yucab Reef, 187
Yucatán Caribbean coast, diving
    along, 18
Yucatech Expeditions, 187

• Z •

Zamas (Tulum), 200
Zapotec, 24, 25
Zen (Ixtapa), 316
Zermatt (Cozumel), 182
Zicatela Beach (Puerto Escondido), 18
Zihuatanejo
    area map, 307
    arriving in, 294–295
    beaches, 14, 306–310
    choosing location to stay in, 284–285
    description of, 41–42, 283–284
    dining, 300–305
    Fast Facts, 297–299
    getting around, 295–296
    land sports, 312–313
    lodging, 15, 17, 285–293
    nightlife, 315–316
    shopping, 313–314
    side trips from, 314–315
    sightseeing, 313
    water activities, 310–312
Zihuatanejo Tourism Office, 480
Zippers beach (Los Cabos), 437
Zipper's (Los Cabos), 431
zócalo (Acapulco), 353
Zoo (Puerto Vallarta), 279
Zucca (Acapulco), 362

Notes

BUSINESS, CAREERS & PERSONAL FINANCE

0-7645-5307-0   0-7645-5331-3 *†

Also available:

✓Accounting For Dummies †
0-7645-5314-3
✓Business Plans Kit For Dummies †
0-7645-5365-8
✓Cover Letters For Dummies
0-7645-5224-4
✓Frugal Living For Dummies
0-7645-5403-4
✓Leadership For Dummies
0-7645-5176-0
✓Managing For Dummies
0-7645-1771-6

✓Marketing For Dummies
0-7645-5600-2
✓Personal Finance For Dummies *
0-7645-2590-5
✓Project Management
For Dummies
0-7645-5283-X
✓Resumes For Dummies †
0-7645-5471-9
✓Selling For Dummies
0-7645-5363-1
✓Small Business Kit For Dummies *†
0-7645-5093-4

HOME & BUSINESS COMPUTER BASICS

0-7645-4074-2   0-7645-3758-X

Also available:

✓ACT! 6 For Dummies
0-7645-2645-6
✓iLife '04 All-in-One Desk Reference
For Dummies
0-7645-7347-0
✓iPAQ For Dummies
0-7645-6769-1
✓Mac OS X Panther Timesaving
Techniques For Dummies
0-7645-5812-9
✓Macs For Dummies
0-7645-5656-8
✓Microsoft Money 2004 For Dummies
0-7645-4195-1

✓Office 2003 All-in-One Desk
Reference For Dummies
0-7645-3883-7
✓Outlook 2003 For Dummies
0-7645-3759-8
✓PCs For Dummies
0-7645-4074-2
✓TiVo For Dummies
0-7645-6923-6
✓Upgrading and Fixing PCs
For Dummies
0-7645-1665-5
✓Windows XP Timesaving
Techniques For Dummies
0-7645-3748-2

FOOD, HOME, GARDEN, HOBBIES, MUSIC & PETS

0-7645-5295-3   0-7645-5232-5

Also available:

✓Bass Guitar For Dummies
0-7645-2487-9
✓Diabetes Cookbook For Dummies
0-7645-5230-9
✓Gardening For Dummies *
0-7645-5130-2
✓Guitar For Dummies
0-7645-5106-X
✓Holiday Decorating For Dummies
0-7645-2570-0
✓Home Improvement All-in-One
For Dummies
0-7645-5680-0

✓Knitting For Dummies
0-7645-5395-X
✓Piano For Dummies
0-7645-5105-1
✓Puppies For Dummies
0-7645-5255-4
✓Scrapbooking For Dummies
0-7645-7208-3
✓Senior Dogs For Dummies
0-7645-5818-8
✓Singing For Dummies
0-7645-2475-5
✓30-Minute Meals For Dummies
0-7645-2589-1

INTERNET & DIGITAL MEDIA

0-7645-1664-7   0-7645-6924-4

Also available:

✓2005 Online Shopping Directory
For Dummies
0-7645-7495-7
✓CD & DVD Recording For Dummies
0-7645-5956-7
✓eBay For Dummies
0-7645-5654-1
✓Fighting Spam For Dummies
0-7645-5965-6
✓Genealogy Online For Dummies
0-7645-5964-8
✓Google For Dummies
0-7645-4420-9

✓Home Recording For Musicians
For Dummies
0-7645-1634-5
✓The Internet For Dummies
0-7645-4173-0
✓iPod & iTunes For Dummies
0-7645-7772-7
✓Preventing Identity Theft
For Dummies
0-7645-7336-5
✓Pro Tools All-in-One Desk
Reference For Dummies
0-7645-5714-9
✓Roxio Easy Media Creator
For Dummies
0-7645-7131-1

* Separate Canadian edition also available
† Separate U.K. edition also available
Available wherever books are sold. For more information or to order direct: U.S. customers
visit www.dummies.com or call 1-877-762-2974.
U.K. customers visit www.wileyeurope.com or call 0800 243407. Canadian customers visit
www.wiley.ca or call 1-800-567-4797.

SPORTS, FITNESS, PARENTING, RELIGION & SPIRITUALITY

0-7645-5146-9   0-7645-5418-2

Also available:

✔Adoption For Dummies
0-7645-5488-3
✔Basketball For Dummies
0-7645-5248-1
✔The Bible For Dummies
0-7645-5296-1
✔Buddhism For Dummies
0-7645-5359-3
✔Catholicism For Dummies
0-7645-5391-7
✔Hockey For Dummies
0-7645-5228-7

✔Judaism For Dummies
0-7645-5299-6
✔Martial Arts For Dummies
0-7645-5358-5
✔Pilates For Dummies
0-7645-5397-6
✔Religion For Dummies
0-7645-5264-3
✔Teaching Kids to Read
For Dummies
0-7645-4043-2
✔Weight Training For Dummies
0-7645-5168-X
✔Yoga For Dummies
0-7645-5117-5

TRAVEL

0-7645-5438-7   0-7645-5453-0

Also available:

✔Alaska For Dummies
0-7645-1761-9
✔Arizona For Dummies
0-7645-6938-4
✔Cancún and the Yucatán
For Dummies
0-7645-2437-2
✔Cruise Vacations For Dummies
0-7645-6941-4
✔Europe For Dummies
0-7645-5456-5
✔Ireland For Dummies
0-7645-5455-7

✔Las Vegas For Dummies
0-7645-5448-4
✔London For Dummies
0-7645-4277-X
✔New York City For Dummies
0-7645-6945-7
✔Paris For Dummies
0-7645-5494-8
✔RV Vacations For Dummies
0-7645-5443-3
✔Walt Disney World & Orlando
For Dummies
0-7645-6943-0

GRAPHICS, DESIGN & WEB DEVELOPMENT

0-7645-4345-8   0-7645-5589-8

Also available:

✔Adobe Acrobat 6 PDF
For Dummies
0-7645-3760-1
✔Building a Web Site For Dummies
0-7645-7144-3
✔Dreamweaver MX 2004
For Dummies
0-7645-4342-3
✔FrontPage 2003 For Dummies
0-7645-3882-9
✔HTML 4 For Dummies
0-7645-1995-6
✔Illustrator CS For Dummies
0-7645-4084-X

✔Macromedia Flash MX 2004
For Dummies
0-7645-4358-X
✔Photoshop 7 All-in-One Desk
Reference For Dummies
0-7645-1667-1
✔Photoshop CS Timesaving
Techniques For Dummies
0-7645-6782-9
✔PHP 5 For Dummies
0-7645-4166-8
✔PowerPoint 2003 For Dummies
0-7645-3908-6
✔QuarkXPress 6 For Dummies
0-7645-2593-X

NETWORKING, SECURITY, PROGRAMMING & DATABASES

0-7645-6852-3   0-7645-5784-X

Also available:

✔A+ Certification For Dummies
0-7645-4187-0
✔Access 2003 All-in-One Desk
Reference For Dummies
0-7645-3988-4
✔Beginning Programming
For Dummies
0-7645-4997-9
✔C For Dummies
0-7645-7068-4
✔Firewalls For Dummies
0-7645-4048-3
✔Home Networking For Dummies
0-7645-42796

✔Network Security For Dummies
0-7645-1679-5
✔Networking For Dummies
0-7645-1677-9
✔TCP/IP For Dummies
0-7645-1760-0
✔VBA For Dummies
0-7645-3989-2
✔Wireless All In-One Desk Reference
For Dummies
0-7645-7496-5
✔Wireless Home Networking
For Dummies
0-7645-3910-8

HEALTH & SELF-HELP

0-7645-6820-5 *†   0-7645-2566-2

Also available:
- ✔Alzheimer's For Dummies
  0-7645-3899-3
- ✔Asthma For Dummies
  0-7645-4233-8
- ✔Controlling Cholesterol For Dummies
  0-7645-5440-9
- ✔Depression For Dummies
  0-7645-3900-0
- ✔Dieting For Dummies
  0-7645-4149-8
- ✔Fertility For Dummies
  0-7645-2549-2

- ✔Fibromyalgia For Dummies
  0-7645-5441-7
- ✔Improving Your Memory For Dummies
  0-7645-5435-2
- ✔Pregnancy For Dummies †
  0-7645-4483-7
- ✔Quitting Smoking For Dummies
  0-7645-2629-4
- ✔Relationships For Dummies
  0-7645-5384-4
- ✔Thyroid For Dummies
  0-7645-5385-2

EDUCATION, HISTORY, REFERENCE & TEST PREPARATION

0-7645-5194-9   0-7645-4186-2

Also available:
- ✔Algebra For Dummies
  0-7645-5325-9
- ✔British History For Dummies
  0-7645-7021-8
- ✔Calculus For Dummies
  0-7645-2498-4
- ✔English Grammar For Dummies
  0-7645-5322-4
- ✔Forensics For Dummies
  0-7645-5580-4
- ✔The GMAT For Dummies
  0-7645-5251-1
- ✔Inglés Para Dummies
  0-7645-5427-1

- ✔Italian For Dummies
  0-7645-5196-5
- ✔Latin For Dummies
  0-7645-5431-X
- ✔Lewis & Clark For Dummies
  0-7645-2545-X
- ✔Research Papers For Dummies
  0-7645-5426-3
- ✔The SAT I For Dummies
  0-7645-7193-1
- ✔Science Fair Projects For Dummies
  0-7645-5460-3
- ✔U.S. History For Dummies
  0-7645-5249-X

Get smart @ dummies.com®

- **Find a full list of Dummies titles**
- **Look into loads of FREE on-site articles**
- **Sign up for FREE eTips e-mailed to you weekly**
- **See what other products carry the Dummies name**
- **Shop directly from the Dummies bookstore**
- **Enter to win new prizes every month!**